Robert Maxwell is one of the most remarkable men of our time. Much admired, sometimes feared, always respected, he remains an unknown figure behind a well-known face. In writing his biography, Joe Haines has had access to Maxwell's archives, family and friends, without conditions as to the use he would make of his sources or the judgements he would come to. The result is the only authentic portrait of the man who started twice with nothing and fought his way to the pinnacle of global recognition and success against all the odds.

JOE HAINES

A *Futura* Book

First published in Great Britain in 1988
by Macdonald & Co (Publishers) Ltd
London & Sydney
This Futura edition published in 1988

ISBN 0 7088 4303 4

Printed and bound in Great Britain by
Hazell Watson & Viney Limited
Member of BPCC plc
Aylesbury, Bucks, England

Futura Publications
A Division of
Macdonald & Co (Publishers) Ltd
Greater London House
Hampstead Road
London NW1 7QX
A member of Maxwell Pergamon Publishing Corporation plc

For Betty Maxwell

Contents

Illustrations

Captain Maxwell pictured with Barry, the dog that came from Hitler's personal kennels.

Maxwell tries on civilian clothes, with Betty in Berlin in December 1945.

In Berlin with Fritz Neuman, head of the SDP, Berlin, and Arno Scholz, Editor of the German newspaper *Der Telegraf* in 1945.

Brigadier General Carthew-Yorstoun, Major Christopher Rhodes, Major Nick Huysmans and others at Michael's christening, Berlin, 1947.

The twins Christine and Isabel at two weeks, 1950.

In France, 1957, Betty with Ian, Isabel, Christine, Philip, Anne and Michael.

Section 2 between pp.176-177

A letter from Eisenhower, November 21, 1949.

Celebrating Ferdinand Springer's 70th birthday at Heidelberg.

With Tonjes Lange at Heidelberg, 1950.

Maxwell mountain climbing with Sir Robert and Lady Robinson on the Swiss side of the Matterhorn.

With Sir Robert Robinson for the launch of *Tetrahedron*.

The picture taken for Maxwell's political campaign posters.

Welcoming Hugh and Dora Gaitskell at the Bletchley Labour Party hall in 1962.

At the Kremlin with Nikita Kruschev, Anastas Mikoyan, Ambassador Frank Roberts and Reginald Maudling.

Laughter with Margot Fonteyn.

Doctor Kervran, the French doctor whose advice saved Robert Maxwell's life during his illness in 1955.

With Galina Ulanova, 1956.

With David Frost at Headington Hill Hall in the early sixties.

With Betty at the Worshipful Company of Gardeners' banquet, 1960.

Victory march after winning Buckingham in 1964.

Bob and Betty after winning Buckingham in 1966.

Maxwell arrives at the Commons as MP for Buckingham.

With Edward Heath and Horace King.

With George Brown on the terrace of the Commons in 1964.

With Professor Theodore von Karman, the father of rocketry.

Meeting Valentina Tereshkova, the first woman in space, 1964.

With Harold Wilson and the Mayor of Bletchley in 1965.

Maxwell presenting Leonid Brezhnev with a copy of his book, Moscow, 1978.

With King Faisal of Saudi Arabia, 1967.

With Indira Gandhi, Prime Minister of India, 1967.

Robert Maxwell with Lord Mountbatten in 1978.

Betty with Michael, Anne, Philip, Christine, Isabel, Ian and Kevin, 1959.

Karine.

Section 3 between pp.336–337

Fireworks at Headington Hill Hall for Maxwell's 60th birthday celebrations.

Celebrating Betty's D.Phil. degree at Oxford in 1981.

President Ronald Reagan greets Maxwell at the White House, 1987.

Australian Treasurer, Paul Keating, meeting with Maxwell at the *Mirror*.

Informal talks: Maxwell with Shimon Peres, President of Israel.

Mutual applause: with Deng Xiaoping in 1986.

President Jimmy Carter and Ryoichi Sasakawa shake hands with Maxwell.

Talking politics with Michael Foot.

Global discussions with Henry Kissinger in Tokyo.

Maxwell and team, about to leave Ulan Bator in his private jet.

Familiar sight over the *Mirror*'s London HQ - the private helicopter.

Robert Maxwell and President Arap Moi of Kenya.

Laughing press barons Rupert Murdoch, Yosaji Kobayashi and Maxwell.

In Moscow visiting Mr A.N. Yakovlev, Secretary of the Central Committee of the C.P.S.U.

With Terry Wogan.

Cordial greetings to the Aga Khan.

Fraternal greetings to Neil Kinnock, Leader of the Labour Party.

An informal presentation for the Princess of Wales.

Lady Ghislaine, Maxwell's ocean-going yacht.

Discussions with Mr Batmunkh, President and General Secretary of the Central Committee, in Ulan Bator, Outer Mongolia.

New *Daily Mirror* newsroom in 1988, equipped with the very latest in newspaper technology.

With Her Majesty the Queen at the Edinburgh Commonwealth Games.

Talks with Dr Silva, Prime Minister of Portugal, in 1987.

A private word with President Mitterrand in Paris in 1988.

With Juan Carlos of Spain in 1987.

Hand signals: from President Soares of Portugal in 1987.

The Publisher with his Editors.

Red Square, 1987, with son Kevin.

Family fun: Bob and Betty with son Kevin and daughters Anne and Isabel.

Daughter Christine Maxwell at work in America.

Section 4 between pp.432–433

With Sir Robert Robinson and Giulio Natta, Nobel Prize winner, Stockholm, 1963.

With Professor Hodgkin, Nobel Prize winner.

With Maria Mayer, Nobel Prize winner and her husband.

Maxwell canvassing in Buckingham in 1974.

Ghislaine, director of Oxford United, and team.

Philip speaking at Maxwell's 60th birthday celebration.

Ian speaking in Tokyo at the Pergamon BPCC launch.

At Downing Street with the Duke of Westminster receiving £500,000 from Ryoichi Sasakawa for the NSPCC.

With Edgar Faure and Prime Minister Chirac, Paris, 1987.

Robert Maxwell with Mr Zhivkov, President of Bulgaria.

With James Callaghan, Lord King and Jack Jones.

With Lord Kearton unveiling BPC's survival plan.

Speaking to workers about the BPC survival plan.

Maxwell's team winning the Milk Cup, 1986.

Doctor of Science at Moscow University, 1983.

Doctor of Science at the Polytechnic Institute of New York, 1985.

Having a drink with Elton John.

A friendly moment with Prime Minister Margaret Thatcher.

Betty with Elizabeth Taylor at an AIDS fund-raising function.

Headington Hill Hall in the snow.

Greeting Mr Gorbachov in London, 1984.

Fly Past: Publisher, Prince Charles and William watch the Red Devils.

Jak cartoon commenting on the rumour that Maxwell might buy *The Observer*.

Mac's observation on Maxwell buying the *Mirror*.

Comment on the union attitudes to Maxwell taking over the *Mirror*.

Mac again, with another view of Maxwell.

The author's acknowledgements are due to the *Illustrated London News*; the *North Bucks Times*; *Home Counties Newspapers Ltd*; *Layton Photo Graphic*; *Central Press*; *United Press*; the *Daily Mail*; the *Free Media Digest*; the *Evening Standard*.

The vast majority of the illustrations in this book come from Maxwell family records or are photographs taken by Mike Maloney, F.R.P.S., Bill Rowntree and Kent Gavin of Mirror Group Newspapers.

The author expresses his gratitude for the help and assistance received from all those involved with the pictorial content of this work.

Preface

My first book in 1976 took three months to write and six months to publish. This book took me six months to write and three weeks to publish. Whatever else may be said about Bob Maxwell, he is a publisher extraordinary.

From the start I have been greatly assisted by his wife Betty, who has, since their marriage, been his archivist and has lovingly compiled a record of his life, business and personal, which must make it among the best-documented in existence. I have been given access to all these papers; those I have selected to use are at best a snapshot; any omissions of episodes in Maxwell's career are my responsibility. There are 47,000 letters on file for Pergamon Press between 1956 and 1968 alone and an exhaustive investigation of them would have delayed publication of this volume beyond my expected working life and even his.

For his 60th birthday in 1983 Mrs Maxwell gathered together tributes to him from 248 friends, colleagues and members of the family. Far and away the greatest number came from the sciences, the encouragement of which has been much the larger part of Maxwell's life work and the least known to the general public. The list of contributors is distinguished. It includes 38 professors, two Academicians, one President (Ceausescu of Romania), one Duke, one Duchess, two ambassadors, six knights, one US senator, two peers and 14 holders of doctorates. Each of his seven surviving children - Anne, Philip, Christine, Isabel, Ian, Kevin and Ghislaine - wrote of their love for their father and their words went beyond filial duty.

This is not a book I - or my colleagues at the *Daily Mirror* - ever expected I would write. When Maxwell was bidding to take over the Mirror Group I was his most open adversary. That we established a close working relationship is still a source of surprise to me and of suspicion by others. I think the reason lies in the fact that though we are both men with a tendency to issue ultimatums, neither has yet done so to the other.

I began this book on September 1, 1987. Fortunately, I have never learned to write slowly, otherwise it would not have been printed well in advance of his 65th birthday. But I could never have managed it without the willing help of many people. I owe especial thanks, first, to my wife, who patiently suffered my impatience while I was writing and who restored my spirits after the hurricane of October 1987 devastated large parts of southern England and destroyed between 30 and 40 trees, which was nearly all of them, in my garden. My secretary, Gloria Sharp, similarly bore with fortitude the pressures of completing this work. She travelled a great many miles, worked every day it was necessary, which was most days, and every hour required, which were a great many. She put in order the sometimes erratic output of my word processor as I wrestled with its newfangled technology. The help of four of my other *Mirror* colleagues was also invaluable. Bob Head, the paper's City Editor, guided me through some of the financial intricacies. Alan Law, its industrial correspondent, who reported the Park Royal dispute at the time, provided a readable and simple digest of events there. Anton Antonowicz took on the chore of tracking down and interviewing a number of scientists who had worked with and for Maxwell. Peter Donnelly, an author of more books than I expect to write, "gutted" the long and tedious reports from the Inspectors of the Department of Trade. I am also grateful to Lord Silkin, the former Attorney-General, for his account of the trial of Maxwell's action against the Inspectors before Mr Justice Wien, and to Jean Baddeley, who brought 25 years of experience working for a demanding employer to organising the speediest production of a book I have ever encountered. Mike Molloy, editor-in-chief of Mirror Group Newspapers, and Lord Donoughue gave me great encouragement after reading the early chapters, and Molloy was also responsible for choosing, with Mrs Maxwell, the photographs with which this volume is liberally supplied.

But the person to whom I owe the greatest thanks is my researcher, Dr Wendy Whitworth. She worked even longer hours than I did; she knows more about the Maxwell family than most of its members; and she was an infallible source of information. Never once did she concede defeat to any request I made, nor did she ever complain. It is absolutely true that without her this book could not and would not have been written. She is the most disciplined worker I have ever met.

I accepted a fixed fee for writing this biography. All royalties and income above that sum, from book sales, book clubs, serialisation, syndication, overseas publication rights, paperback rights and those for film and television rights, will go to the Maxwell Foundation whose purposes are outlined in Chapter 1.

February 12, 1988

1

Contrasts and Paradoxes

Ambition's debt is paid
Julius Caesar

Ian Robert Maxwell of Headington Hill Hall, Oxford, England, multi-millionaire, began life as Ludvik Hoch, eldest son of a Ruthenian labourer and his wife who had no money at all. Half a century ago, in the small village of Solotvino in the Carpathians of Eastern Czechoslovakia, his dream was to own a field and a cow and he never made it. Today his ambition is to create an international printing, publishing and communications empire which will be among the first ten in the world, and he is well on the way to achieving it. As a child he shared a bed with the several other children of his family. As a man, if he stays at a hotel and wakes during the night, he moves to another bed because he likes cool sheets. In the 1930s he and his cousin Michael Tabak, without a penny between them, had to walk nearly four hundred miles to Bratislava to experience the big city and, maybe, find the path from poverty to prosperity. In the 1980s he has a private yacht, a private jet, a private helicopter, a couple of Rolls Royces and a Bentley he won in a charity raffle (he also won the second prize, £500, and gave back four times as much to the charity).

The story of his life is, in part, the distance which his ambitions have travelled. Throughout it his targets have changed. Most of them have been achieved, but those that have not have either been abandoned, without apparent regret, or put into suspense until such time as they come within reach. But the existence of ambition itself has remained constant. His French wife Elisabeth (Betty) vividly recalls Maxwell's promises to her when he proposed marriage in December 1944. He said:

> I shall win an MC. I shall recreate a family. I shall make my fortune. I shall be Prime Minister of England. And I shall make you happy until the end of my days.

She says today that "only one of those promises remains unfulfilled". That one was audacious enough by any standard, even though it was romantically made in wartime Paris by a young army officer barely 21. At the time he was not even a citizen of the country he aspired to lead. But the Military Cross was won within six weeks of the promise being made, and pinned on his chest by Field Marshal Sir Bernard Montgomery five weeks after that.

The family of his parents was largely destroyed by the Nazis - two of his eight brothers and sisters died in infancy, but his mother and father, three sisters, a brother and his grandfather perished in Auschwitz. He has, as he said he would, created his own in its place, though two of his nine children, one of them his first-born son, Michael, have died. He made his fortune early, lost it in middle age and then made it again, many times over. He has undoubtedly made Betty Maxwell happy. She is his most loving and loyal admirer and the skilful and dedicated archivist of his life story. But Prime Minister of England was a dream too much and one which was discarded long ago.

Maxwell has been accused of trying to hide the fact that he is a Jew. But he told the *Jewish Chronicle* in 1986:

> My family were observant Jews and I was given a traditional Jewish education. I ceased to be a practising Jew just before the war when I left home. I still believe in God and Judaism's moral education which teaches the difference between right and wrong.... I don't believe in any church, just God. I certainly do consider myself Jewish. I was born Jewish and I shall die Jewish.

But his Britishness seems to matter more. He repeatedly stresses that he is British because he chose to be, and compares his change of nationality to that of the religious convert who became more Catholic than the Pope. His ambition to head one of the largest media empires in the world is inhibited by the American laws which prevent foreigners from owning United States' television stations; he is not prepared to change his nationality for any prize or at any price. He admires the British for their concern for the underdog[1]:

> Ordinary people may not understand the meaning of democracy but they've a passionate regard for fair play.

What he hates is:

> The old school tie type who takes advantage of his position, who says, "You don't need to learn a foreign language", who doesn't recognise we can learn from Germans, Japanese and Italians.

When he left Czechoslovakia in 1939 it was for good and he

probably suspected as much at the time. He abandoned Solotvino without any regret or wish to return to it. The only time he went back he was disappointed by what he found. The town was changing and every Maxwell relative had either died or emigrated.

Whatever the views about him - and there appear to be only two, for and against, with some employees, friends and business acquaintances managing to hold both at once - there is no doubt that he is a remarkable, and often irresistible, man. A nurse, Benita de Roemer, now Benita Moxon, who met him when he was a teenaged recruit in the Pioneer Corps, recalled more than 40 years later:

> No-one who knew him could ever forget him and no-one was indifferent. He inspired either love or hate - no grey shades.

Two former employees, Geoffrey Goodman, long-time industrial editor of the *Daily Mirror* and left-wing socialist with a Czechoslovakian wife, and Janet Hewlett-Davies, Maxwell's Director of Public Relations between 1986 and 1987, succinctly summarised the reluctant admiration he compels from those with no obvious cause to praise him. Goodman told me shortly before he left the *Mirror:*

> You know, I find it increasingly difficult to dislike Bob Maxwell.

Mrs Hewlett-Davies was my deputy in the 10 Downing Street press office for many years. Though she worked for three Prime Ministers and several other cabinet ministers, she lasted less than a year with Maxwell, but could still say:

> He is an attractive monster with a touch of genius.

Lord Kearton, former chairman of the Industrial Reorganisation Corporation and non-executive chairman of the British Printing Corporation before Maxwell rescued it from the brink of bankruptcy, told me:

> If we had had another ten men like Robert Maxwell, Britain would not have suffered from the economic problems which have plagued it since the war.

But two Board of Trade inspectors were to accuse him in 1971 of being unfit to hold the stewardship of a public company, a judgement which is revived by journalists and opponents on every possible occasion and one which has left him with a lasting feeling of injustice and bitterness.

An unpublished book, privately compiled by Betty Maxwell to mark her husband's 60th birthday, contains tributes to him from

nearly 250 people - from relatives to rivals - who have known or
befriended him over the years from his earliest days in Solotvino.
Inevitably, given the nature of the volume, some of the tributes are
especially flattering; nevertheless, the messages, especially from the
scientific community, are a testimony to the regard in which the
contributors hold him. Of course, it would be easy to gather
together a different volume of contrary opinions, especially from
printing trade unionists who fought and lost many wounding battles
with him, inside and outside the High Court, during the 1980s. But
that is the nature of the man. It is what Mrs Moxon was talking
about.

Maxwell has been written about so extensively that almost every
description has become a cliché. He is, it is said, flamboyant,
controversial, vulgar, insufferable, ruthless, brazen, fiery,
humourless, impatient, intolerant, rude, rampant and even Rambo.
His ego and his ambition are said to rival Everest and Kilimanjaro in
their majesty. He is accused of wanting power over the press,
television and the English Football League. On the other hand,
there are as many who would say he is cool, calm and collected,
industrious, generous, amusing, jovial, kind, thoughtful, brave,
charming, caring and attractive, a publisher and printer without
peer, with no interest in power for himself, only in the uses he can
put it to for the general good; a superdog who champions the
underdog. He is called the Bouncing Czech, but instead of resenting
it he revels in it.

There are more questions about him than there are answers, and
more questioners. At a charity reception attended by royalty,
Maxwell was talking to the Prince of Wales and then broke off to
greet another member of the family. The Prince grabbed the arm of
one of the Mirror Group's editors and asked in a whisper:

Tell me - what is he really like to work for?

There are several responses to that question. One of them was
discovered some years ago when Maxwell was told that 10 of his
senior managers all needed their company cars replaced because
their existing cars were no longer economic to run. Instead of
authorising the purchase of the cars, Maxwell asked whether all the
managers were necessary, found out that they were not and
abolished the jobs of six of them. He says that over the next year
there was a 90 per cent fall in the requests from senior managers for
new company cars.

Some say Maxwell is thin-skinned; others maintain that he has the hide of a rhinoceros because he never seems to be embarrassed by anything. The truth might be hidden in a letter which he sent to Betty in the winter of 1944:

I have constructed during my years of exile a glittering surface as a kind of protection.

Professor Guy Ourisson of Strasbourg says he is

a personality ... feared, admired, envied, hated and adulated ... a skilful and perspicacious tycoon ... transparent in his actions, naïve in his motivation, limpid in his mysteries ... a friend who skims immoderation but who remains human.

Professor Ourisson was right about his naïvety. For a suspicious man he is sometimes too unquestioning. He invests faith in subordinates, colleagues and partners which is not always justified. Jack Straton-Ferrier, chairman of Maxwell's first company, wrote to him in 1952:

I don't think you are an awfully good chooser [of men].

Maxwell himself told Lynda Lee-Potter of the *Daily Mail*[2]:

I probably have been made to look a fool but I'm not a man with phobias and complexes. I'm not a man who needs sleeping pills. I don't care what you think about me. I don't care if you're wrong about me but I like to be wanted. Ask me for help and I'll always say Yes. I'm not ashamed of anything I've done. I'm sorry about certain things. Life has taught me I'm not a very good judge of character. My weakness is, I think, that I start off by believing in people. I have a certain amount of naïveté.

He also told Mrs Lee-Potter:

The only thing I've become very successful at hiding is how much one is hurt or upset. That sort of control of emotion I've become very good at. I've developed a very thick skin. I'll never give in, never run away. I believe in what I'm doing. Convince me that I'm wrong and I'll quickly apologise and change my ways.

Benita Moxon described the young Hoch she knew as "mercurial, mostly exuberant but sometimes deeply melancholy". He is a creature of mood, switching from laughter to anger in a second. He can be both ruthless and soft-hearted, swift to make up his mind and even swifter to change it if he decides he has made a mistake. If he is vain it does not extend to a fear of losing face. He exasperates and he soothes, terrifies and reassures. He has sacked men and then reprieved them when they deserved to stay sacked; or he has sacked them publicly and so compensated them privately that they were only too glad to be fired. He hates poor quality, whether in men or

materials. On a Qantas airline flight he ordered a cigar and a
brandy. When they came, he found they were both Australian. He
stubbed out the first in the second and said to the stewardess that
they deserved each other. She broke down and cried.

What most people concede to him is his courage, even if at times
it is difficult to distinguish it from recklessness or foolhardiness. The
merchant banker Jacob Rothschild once said of him:

> I have shot that man 17 times and he still will not lie down.

After one of the many *Sunday Times* attacks upon him, which
have returned, malarial-like, over the years, a former wartime
comrade[3] wrote:

> I feel compelled to write ... to assure you that there are still people
> who remember with gratitude and admiration the bold and devoted
> way in which you put your life at risk in the service of your adopted
> country.

Minutes before the action for which he insistently volunteered,
and in which he won the Military Cross, his battalion commander
told him that if he survived he would probably be court-martialled.
He did and he wasn't. He not only has the nerve which is called
courage but the nerve which is called cheek or insubordination,
though there is no one to whom he can be insubordinate today.

On a flight from Mexico City to Acapulco a Mexican official -
bribed, according to Maxwell, by travellers anxious to get on an
overbooked aircraft - told him and his companion that they would
have to give up their seats. The companion was Michael
Richardson, then a partner in the stockbrokers Panmure Gordon,
and today managing director of Rothschild's. He recalled what
happened next:

> Bob marched past protesting officials, across the tarmac and up the
> steps to the plane. At the top a Mexican police lieutenant whipped
> out his revolver and pointed it at Bob's stomach, saying, "You're not
> going another step." Bob said, "I'm not moving." The Mexican said,
> "Then I'm going to shoot you." Bob said, "You try to get this plane
> off the ground without me." He stood his ground for over half an
> hour facing the cocked revolver. Then officials removed two other
> passengers from the plane and off we went. It was a great test of
> Bob's steel.

As with most men of power, every libel about Maxwell contains a
grain of truth. There is an element in him of all of the qualities for
which he is lauded or of which he is accused, some in much larger
measure than others. Unpredictability is the only thing which is

certain about him. He enjoys provoking waves and then calming them. He deliberately creates storms and then quietens them. He pours oil on troubled waters which were smooth before he arrived. He incites anecdotes about himself.

This is, in part, a matter of style and temperament, but it is also part of his negotiating technique. He forces issues to a crisis so that they may be speedily resolved, implementation of the political theory that to alleviate is to perpetuate and therefore to be avoided. The result, frequently, is to leave opponents confused about exactly what they might have conceded and his own staff uncertain about what he has achieved, knowing only that he has not done what they had expected him to do. He can be persuaded but not bullied. Several printing union negotiators have failed to recognise the distinction and their members have suffered in consequence. One chapel official at the *Daily Mirror* was having some success with his argument until he allowed his rhetoric to get the better of him; he accused Maxwell of putting his members "on the train to Auschwitz". He could not have chosen a worse simile and his chances of winning concessions ended before his mouth had closed. But normally Maxwell can be generous once he has won a negotiation and will freely allow those whom he has defeated to save face. That is the politician in him. Equally, defeat for him is never final. If he wants something badly enough he will not be content until he succeeds. He cannot bear to lose.

The apparent contradictions and seeming paradoxes abound. He is rich, but cares nothing for personal possessions. He doesn't collect butterflies or postage stamps, but he wouldn't be averse to buying the company which prints them. He is a democrat by conviction and a dictator in practice; authoritarian in many things, a libertarian in others. He supports the traditional pillars of the establishment - the monarchy, Parliament, the City of London and the law - but is deeply anti-establishment, once offering the toast "To the devil with the diplomats" at a dinner where the guests included the wife of a former ambassador to the USSR. He is a socialist who is a capitalist. He believes that the tenants of local authorities should have the right to buy their own homes, yet he does not own Headington Hill Hall where he lives. Instead, he rents it on a 99-year lease from Oxford City Council, boasts that it is the finest council house in Britain and has a viscount as his head gardener. He is devoted to his large family, as they all are to him, but he is opposed on principle to inherited wealth and has told his children since birth he will leave them nothing when he dies. "The passing on of too much wealth", he says, "can stifle initiative in a later generation." He is against privilege, but all but one of his children work for him or have done so; he explains that he is in favour of nepotism provided those who benefit from it have the ability to do the job. As six of his seven surviving offspring are Oxford graduates and the other graduated from an American university, all seem to meet his criterion. He is an indulgent but stern parent. Though he would provide his children with cars, the gift would be taken back from any whom he found smoking cigarettes and he sacked his son, Ian, for preferring the company of a girl to an appointment with him.

He moves freely within the communist world, has accepted the highest Bulgarian honour, the Order of Stara Planina, First Class, the Order of Merit with Star from Poland, and a doctorate from Moscow University, and he has published the speeches and writings of most of the leaders of the communist countries; yet he detests communism. (The awards are not exclusively from the Eastern bloc: he is an honorary Doctor of Science at the Polytechnic Institute of New York, and holds the Swedish Order of the Polar Star and a medal from the Nobel Foundation and various other honours. Aberdeen University proposes to award him an honorary doctorate in 1988.) He is repelled by homosexuality, but has devoted a considerable amount of time and a substantial sum of his money towards helping to find a cure for AIDS. He has little time for conferences and board meetings, but is a believer in workers' co-operatives. He is almost certainly the richest supporter the British Labour party has ever had, but says[4]:

> I don't see why I should give up my ideals and abandon my class origins because I have made a few shillings.

He threw himself into the fight to defeat Margaret Thatcher's Government during the British general election of 1987 with a zeal which confounded those on the far left of the Labour party who had clung to the belief that he was a closet Thatcherite who would sell out. Yet his business affairs, and especially those of his several newspapers, could not have prospered so well but for his implementation of the laws introduced by Mrs Thatcher which emasculated the powers of the trade unions to initiate industrial action.

He insists that his newspapers must pay their way, yet he refused £300,000-worth of advertising from the Conservative party during that general election when its advisers panicked as the Labour party appeared to be closing the opinion poll gap. The Tories wanted to blanket the Mirror Group Newspapers with three full pages of advertising a day for the last five days of the campaign. Maxwell said they could have one page, no more. The policies which the papers were advocating should not be overwhelmed, he said, by the power of Conservative money.

It is in keeping with the paradoxes that a good number of left-wing trade unionists are among his friends or well-disposed towards him. They include Ray Buckton who was, until his retirement in 1987, the militant general secretary of the train drivers' union ASLEF; Clive Jenkins, the 1987-88 chairman of the Trades Union Congress and general secretary of the scientific, managerial and technical staff union ASTMS - Maxwell's own union; and Mark Young, general secretary of the British Airline Pilots' Association. It is not surprising, given his contradictions, that Lord King, the right-wing chairman of British Airways, who sits on the other side of the negotiating table from Young, is also a friend, as are innumerable other City, financial and business tycoons. Strangers still find Maxwell's friendship with Buckton surprising, though both in their time have been near the top of the league of most-vilified men. But it goes back a long way. They first met during the Buckingham election campaign of 1959 when Buckton worked hard in the attempt to get Maxwell elected. He says today:

> My wife Barbara and I were treated just like family by Bob and Betty. He was a loyal friend and you could always rely upon him in a crisis.

Maxwell is as rich as any man could ever want to be, but says that the greatest benefit he has gained from his wealth is that he no longer has to worry about parking his car. He will spend millions of pounds within seconds if he judges it to be necessary, but will haggle for minutes over a few hundreds until he is convinced that the expenditure is desirable or unavoidable. Yet he can be amazingly generous with employees in trouble. Ann Robertson, a secretary who was with him for eight years in the 1950s, was told by her doctor that she had to live at altitude for six months. Maxwell paid for her to do so - in India. Christina Foyle, of the world's most famous bookshop, tells the story of how she wanted to recruit an Afrikaaner, Dr Cornelius Pama, to run Foyle's bookshop in Cape Town. Dr Pama explained that he was employed by Robert Maxwell and was worried about a loan which Maxwell had made to him so that he might buy his house. Miss Foyle says:

> Robert Maxwell just replied, "Where is this mortgage you speak of?"

Dr Pama had it in his pocket and handed it to him. Without further ado, Maxwell tore it up and threw it into the wastepaper basket, saying "That's that, Dr Pama, and the end of your troubles. The very best of luck."

He can also be generous in salaries if they buy the talents he wants, but he is reluctant to authorise even a few pounds to be spent on overtime unless there is absolutely no other way to cope with an emergency. Time is money to him, yet he rarely wears a watch; indeed, frequently and literally he doesn't know what day it is. His appointments book is meticulously kept, invariably crowded, and rarely adhered to. He admires punctuality in others but has none himself. He is remorselessly late for almost every engagement. Schedules are disrupted by an ever-open door which leads to unscheduled meetings and by a compulsive answering of every telephone call which makes coherent discussion almost impossible. He bought a private plane not for its luxury but because it freed him from the tyranny of airline timetables.

To an outsider the biggest paradox of all is in his marriage. He is the storm; his wife is the rock. When he rages, she stays serene. Where he is impatient, she is patient; when he is intolerable, she tolerates it. He rushes; she is unhurried. Where there are the two distinct opinions about him, there is only one about her. I have not met anyone who doesn't like Betty Maxwell. She has an independent spirit, but even so it was a daring step for the daughter of an upper-class French family of Protestants to entrust her life to the care of an exiled, near-penniless Czechoslovakian Jewish sergeant in the British army who spoke no French and didn't have a home to return to when the war was over. When she agreed to marry him his prospects lay only in his personality, because he had no possessions at all. He was demanding from the start; she was acquiescent. She recalls[5]:

> One of the first things he ever said to me was that I'd have to realise that he would not live in France. If ever anything was to happen out of our romance it would happen in England.

The only time she appeared to hesitate was at the civil ceremony for her marriage. When the mayor asked her whether she was prepared to accept her husband's nationality, the thought flashed through her mind that as Maxwell was Czechoslovakian and Czechoslovakia was occupied by Germany saying "Oui" would make her German. "Non", she cried. "Non, non, non." The English guests at the wedding whose French was imperfect thought she was jilting Maxwell at the last moment.

When he wanted to be a Member of Parliament she canvassed every home in his Buckingham constituency. When he lost control of Pergamon Press she never doubted that he would win it back. When she was told he would shortly die of inoperable cancer she rarely left his side.

Publicity is an essential tool of his business and he exploits it ruthlessly; yet he is a secretive man. Knowledge is power and he keeps it to himself; but he will talk indiscreetly about his most confidential affairs if someone he trusts is in the room. He appoints press officers to do an impossible job and sacks them when they eventually fail him, as any mortal must. Snowdrops in summer last longer than most press officers hired to work for him at his headquarters in the Mirror Group Newspapers building. Because he keeps every detail of his affairs locked in his own mind, he deals directly with journalists, leaving bemused press officers trying to catch up, often by asking a reporter "What did he say?"

Communication is his business and his passion, but his handwriting is so appalling that he is often unable to read it himself. A wartime friend, Australian-born Mrs Eileen Straton-Ferrier, wife of Jack and hostess at the Overseas League Club for foreign servicemen at St James's, London, remembers receiving a letter from him, "a somewhat crumpled piece of paper" which looked "as if a drunken spider had crawled over it". (Fortunately, she was able to decipher a single sentence because it said: "I am sending my wife to you.")

This dreadful script is a legacy of being born left-handed and being forced by a teacher for three years to write with the right hand by the simple expedient of tying the left one behind his back. He now writes notes with whichever hand is closest to pen and paper; it makes little difference to the end result, which is universally bad. A prescription written by a family doctor while tumbling over Niagara in a barrel in total darkness could hardly be more illegible. It was a cruel medieval superstition which regarded those born left-handed to be the offspring of the devil.

Inevitably, the first impression of Bob Maxwell is a physical one. His sheer size intimidates, and to many a nervous newcomer he appears to fill a room, whatever its proportions. He stands over six feet tall and weighs around 250lb, the exact poundage depending on whether he is slimming or not. He moves fast and not ungracefully for a large man lacking part of one lung and in his seventh decade. In addition, he has the gift, which seems reserved for politicians and tycoons who do no exercise, of an apparently inexhaustible stamina which disregards the calls upon it until the task in hand is completed. The equivalent for those who do exercise is the marathon runner who can do the course twice, or the heavyweight champion who can go fifteen rounds when the challenger can't manage more than twelve. He says he gave up exercise when his wife bought him a self-winding watch.

Size and stamina alone don't explain the power and presence with which he can strike a stranger or scare and often overwhelm a subordinate, though they help. He has an air of certainty about him, of knowing where he is going even when he doesn't, of finality even when the outcome is obscured, which gives him a negotiating advantage with businessmen and trade union leaders alike. Those who deal with him too frequently equate his size with brute strength and forget that he is a skilful chess player and good enough at poker to have relieved Rupert Murdoch of considerable sums on more than one occasion. Michael Richardson recalled how he and Maxwell negotiated with Murdoch in Australia over the purchase of some magazines:

> I'll never forget that trip. We worked and negotiated for three days, starting at 7 am and usually going on non-stop to 2 am the next morning. Bob finally pulled off the deal after midnight. Then Rupert said: "How would you like a game of poker?" Murdoch and some Australian pals then turned up at 1 am. Bob was dealt five cards and cried "Well, I never did! What a hand!" When asked how many more cards he wanted, he said "I don't want any - these will do." The Australians thought he was bluffing. The opening bid of $A100 was quickly raised to 1,000. Bob raised it to 5,000. An Australian said "See you for 5,000" and Bob scooped the pool with a high straight.... He walked off with a lot of money that night.

> Next day I met a pretty fair-haired girl at a party in Sydney. She said, "I'm not happy with you Englishmen." I asked her why not and she replied, "Well, I was nicely tucked up in bed with my husband last night when the phone rang. It was Rupert calling to say come over and play poker - 'We've got a couple of Poms ready for fleecing.' I was upset but my husband said I could have half his winnings. At breakfast this morning I asked my husband, 'How much have I won?' and he said, 'You owe me thirty thousand dollars.' "

Maxwell's bargaining techniques are drawn from both his leisure pastimes. He knows when to concede a draw or resign a game, which explains why he has so often begun a takeover bid and then abandoned it when the price has become too high; he is not inclined to pay over the odds for anything. He also bluffs and raises stakes with what looks like spendthrift recklessness; but he operates on the principle that if you want to win you must be ready to lose. He knows his last ditch and he won't go beyond it. The trick for opponents is to know where that ditch is, whether he has gone as far as he will go or whether there is still some mileage left.

Those who miscalculate usually end up the poorer in the literal sense of the word. A young American, about to be made a dollar millionaire by Maxwell's purchase of his business, found himself at the end of a day's negotiations without an extra dime. His lawyer and his accountant hadn't believed Maxwell when he said the final deadline was 6 pm. But it was and the deal was abandoned by him. The young American hadn't been able to settle a dispute between the two about the terms of the deal and, in the view of the American lawyer Ellis J. Freedman, who represented Maxwell in the negotiations, he didn't want to buy a business whose chief executive was unable to impose his will upon his employees.

In the autumn of 1987 I went with him to the Soviet Union to negotiate the printing of an English edition of *Pravda* or a daily or weekly digest of the Russian press or any other kind of publication which would give the USSR a voice in the West. Maxwell promised to provide the technology (while telling *Pravda* it should get rid of its old-fashioned hot metal form of production) but asked the Russians to provide the necessary translators. "No", said the Russians. "We cannot do that. You must do it." "No", replied Maxwell. "You will do it. You must resolve this matter before it can proceed." The Soviets immediately backed down.

Maxwell has always had a presence even when he was without power. More than 40 years ago Eileen Straton-Ferrier was writing to her son John about the "devastating young Czech" she had met. He had, she said, "a sort of aura of suppressed fury" about him. It is a description which those who have known him since would instantly recognise. Another of Mrs Straton-Ferrier's sons, Brian, has recalled his first meeting with Maxwell, who at that time was known as Ivan du Maurier, a surname he had taken from a cigarette popular in wartime and the only kind he smoked. In a 60th birthday tribute to him, Mr Straton-Ferrier wrote:

> You didn't forget Ivan du Maurier once you met him. A mere private in rough battle-dress he may have been; one of London's thousands of displaced and anonymous Europeans he was; only a month or two out of his teens, and a bit brash and immature he may have seemed; but this was a striking, memorable man, even at first brush.
>
> He was extremely good-looking, with his thick shock of dark hair, heavily arched eyebrows, expressive, sensuous mouth, strong chin

and alert, observing eyes. He seemed a big man, although he was quite thin.

There was an overwhelming impression of masculinity, perhaps reinforced by the deep resonant speaking voice that so much impressed my mother, coming from deep down in the diaphragm, confident, self-assured, not at all the hesitant voice of a boy shattered by the appalling experiences one soon knew he had been through.

Benita Moxon recalled the days in 1940 when Maxwell was Ludvik Hoch and a private in the Pioneers, virtually a non-combatant unit to which most foreigners who arrived in Britain to carry on the struggle against Hitler's Germany were sent, whatever their fighting experience. (The young Hoch's previous units had been the French Foreign Legion and the Czech army in France.) Reaching Britain after the fall of France, he was sent to the Palace Convalescent Home at Ely in Cambridgeshire to recover from appendicitis. His secretive nature, which still creates a disconcerting sense of mystery, was evident even then. So was much else which is still part of him today. Mrs Moxon, a nurse at the home, describes an "extraordinary young foreigner" who "enchanted, fascinated, infuriated and, above all, baffled the lot of us":

One of the most baffling things about him was the way he seemed able to move around as, when and how he pleased. Even the higher ranks in the army were subjected to stringent restrictions in wartime and leave was very limited.

Ludvik, supposedly a humble private, seemed exempt from all this. He came and went, appeared and disappeared.... There were many things about him that were inexplicable and nothing seemed impossible. One thing was for sure, he literally and absolutely did not give a damn what anyone thought of him, and that made him enemies.

Another remarkable trait was that he would attempt absolutely anything, regardless of previous knowledge or experience, or lack of it! One day the resident corporal could not be found to meet a new nurse arriving at the station. Ludvik volunteered for the job and I went with him as a welcoming committee. It was a hair-raising experience. He was 17 and I don't believe he had ever driven a car in his life. After a bit of jiggling around of the gears, we suddenly shot out of the garage backwards, across the main road. We then proceeded to the station in a series of swoops and jolts and life was preserved due to the fact that the little traffic there was, after alarmed glances, gave us a very wide berth indeed.

Even today those who share a car with Maxwell, whether he is driving it or, more alarmingly, giving instructions as to how it should be driven, understand what Mrs Moxon was talking about.

The illuminating aspect of these stories of his early life is that they demonstrate how little his character has changed in the last 40 or 50 years. That self-confidence which the English respect as effortless superiority in their own public schoolboys but call arrogance in foreigners has not been sapped by the years of experience. Indeed, they have fortified it to the point where it seems unassailable and the most unlikely stories about it prove to be true, such as his sale of £100-worth of expensive medical textbooks to a doctor who was examining him, after a "technical medical discussion" between them.

The "resonant" voice which so impressed Mrs Straton-Ferrier is still there, but it will today sink into a growl which matches his physique and, in alliance with it, enhance the sense of alarm which he creates. The hair is still thick and black, like the brows beneath it. He doesn't stare so much as fix a gaze upon those to whom he is speaking or upon those to whom, less commonly, he is listening. Though he professes surprise when he is told so, he can terrify people, especially those who have known him previously only by repute. Even his laughter, which is frequent, and his courtesy, which can be elaborate, fail to put apprehensive visitors at their ease. There is a well-attested story of a timid businessman whom Maxwell was anxious should feel comfortable. "Coffee?" he inquired genially of his guest. "N-no thanks", stammered the visitor. "Black or white?" asked Maxwell.

But there is substance to his fearsome reputation. Robert Worcester, the chairman of the opinion polling organisation MORI, physically trembled as Maxwell berated him for producing for the *Daily Mirror* a poll on the Brecon by-election in 1985 which was hopelessly inaccurate. Maxwell informed him that he would be reducing his fee by two-thirds, that he was lucky to be treated so generously and that if he wasn't prepared to accept the amended bill he could sue for the full amount. Worcester took the money and fled. On the other hand, Maxwell is not as ruthless as his victims believe or make out. Often those who have denounced him as a bully have first meekly surrendered themselves to be bullied. Stoats wouldn't be stoats if there weren't any rabbits.

One who allowed the Maxwell reputation to overcome him was a promising young journalist interviewed by me for the post of political editor of the *Daily Mirror*. First he said Yes, then he said Maybe, then he said he would and then he said he wouldn't, giving Maxwell's "interference" with his political journalists as his reason. He was so scared of the *Mirror* publisher's reputation, even before he met him, that he was unsuitable for the post anyway.

Public concentration upon the flamboyant, even violent, side of his personality is inevitable. Maxwell has used publicity to further his ends, whether as a businessman or as chairman of a First Division Football League Club, as saviour of the Commonwealth Games in 1986 or as the purchaser of a chain of national newspapers. He lives by and thrives upon communication in all its forms, though he is adept at saying only what he wants to say and concealing what others, especially inquisitive journalists employed by rival proprietors, want to know. But there is a price to pay for this and it is paid by his reputation. The common denominator of journalists is insecurity, and Maxwell has played his full part in adding to it, and not only by dismissing some of them. When Maxwell had a bad press over his intention to buy Watford Football Club from Elton John, not the least reason for it was that football reporters and commentators were fed up with reading exclusive stories about Watford, Derby County (of which he was chairman) and Oxford United (of which his son, Kevin, was chairman) in Maxwell's daily and Sunday newspapers. Journalists who miss a story usually miss a night's sleep as well. They fashion the fame they help to create to fit their prejudices as well as their perceptions. Only a Keith Waterhouse could dub him, with some affection, Cap'n Bob, and regard him accordingly as the master of the ship on which he was travelling at the time and not the arbiter of his fate.

Maxwell's lasting public achievement, without doubt, will not prove to be in the fields of popular newspapers, politics, football or big business, for which the public knows him best, but as the originator, initiator and publisher of scientific journals and reference and textbooks, for which the public knows him least. In this, he is without parallel. He has contributed more to the advancement of late-twentieth-century science than any layman alive, which is the opinion of scientists, not another layman. Through Pergamon Press he expanded the dissemination of scientific information to a degree never thought possible by the scientists themselves and usually against the opposition of the learned societies to which they belonged. At the darkest time of his business life it was the scientific community, in the United States as well as Britain and Europe, which came to his rescue. They restored him to the control of Pergamon Press after he had been ousted by Leasco and its allies in the City of London and deposited into what seemed lasting disgrace by the damning report of the two Board of Trade inspectors.

Mrs Maxwell has written that her husband seems to lose interest in the past as soon as he has achieved his goal or accomplished the task in hand. The Leasco affair, which is dealt with at length in a later chapter of this book, is, in my experience, the one exception to that rule. He still burns with what he sees as the injustice of the inspectors. In a conversation with me during the summer of 1987, after he had pulled out of the negotiations to buy the *Today* newspaper on discovering that "Tiny" Rowland, the paper's owner, was secretly discussing a more profitable deal with Rupert Murdoch, he unconsciously referred to Rowland's company Lonrho, as "Leasco", the name of the company which had usurped his position at Pergamon in 1969. The sense of betrayal by Rowland prompted him to think of Leasco. If the loss of Pergamon Press and all that followed was his personal slough of despair, its recovery, with the aid of professors whose concern with the world, especially the commercial world outside their own speciality, was notoriously non-existent, was his proudest moment. They fulfilled the same role for him as Blucher did for Wellington at Waterloo.

He is, of course, master of his own fate, insofar as that determination is given to any of us. His successes and his failures, his inspirations and his mistakes, are largely his own. But what Lady Falkender has called his "steely resolve" has been there from almost the beginning. The danger of such a resolve, however, is that those who ought to caution him against a reckless action will often buckle before it. It is an abiding defect of power.

Detlev Raymond, a former member of the Hitler Youth, who was appointed in the spring of 1946 to be trainee-editor of *Der Berliner*, the British military government newspaper for the British sector of Berlin, says that Maxwell's bark is worse than his bite. He might readily be regarded as an expert, having frequently been threatened with being shot by a Maxwell who brutally "confided" to him that he had won his Military Cross for conquering and shooting a number of Germans just like him. Maxwell, at the age of 22 and with the rank of captain in the British army, was the press officer - effectively the censor - of Berlin's post-war democratic press. He was thus in charge of *Der Berliner*.

After being bellowed at by Maxwell on his first day in charge for taking an "illegal" hot bath - such luxuries being reserved for British officers - Raymond recounts:

> On the second day of this experience - that's what I called it at the time - he bellowed again in my direction "Stuelpnagel, I want you to sell 20,000 cigarettes on the black market, and sell them to the

Russians - they pay better. So you will proceed to Leipzig in the Soviet zone of occupation...." At which point I was already fresh enough to interrupt him to say: "Sir, my name is D.J. Raymond and I have been hired by this paper to learn the finer points of putting together a democratically-oriented newspaper, and nowhere does it say in my book that I should sell black market cigarettes to the Russians or go to Leipzig." "Now, you shut up and listen to what I have to tell you", he retorted. "Number one, this here is a democratic institution where I make all the rules and, number two, Leipzig has the only factory intact able to provide us with photographic emulsion to publish this goddamn newspaper. Now you go to Leipzig."

This, said Raymond, was his introduction to a practising democracy, but somehow it made Maxwellian sense and saved the paper. And far from being on the wrong end of a firing squad devised by Maxwell, Raymond was later employed by him in Britain and the United States until he was encouraged by Maxwell to start up his own business.

But before he did so he was involved with him in an incredibly boyish act of mischief in New York in the mid-1950s. Raymond said that Maxwell was not popular in some of the best hostelries in Manhattan because of his habits of choking the switchboard with incoming overseas telephone calls, regularly returning sandwiches he had ordered on the grounds that they were made of cardboard, throwing business correspondence out of the window and scattering newspapers in the corridors. So when Maxwell failed to get a suite in one of his regular hotels he asked Raymond to book him into the Winslow on 55th Street and Madison. Raymond takes up the story:

I said to him "Bob, the Winslow isn't really your type of place. They haven't fixed the rooms in years, the plumbing leaks and, most important, they have switchboard service only until midnight" ... to which he replied "Never mind, when will you learn to do what you are told and not always start arguing like a Jewish grandmother?"

The next morning Raymond was denounced by Maxwell for booking him into a flea-pit and told he would be fired (which he wasn't). Maxwell said to him:

I would not have wished on Hitler to have stayed here. Let's put our heads together and think up a good solid lesson we can teach them.

The "good solid lesson" was implemented after Maxwell visited the National Institute of Health where a strain of large fleas was being bred. He acquired a small box full of them - several thousand in all - arranged to check out of the hotel and then released the fleas into the lift shaft. In the early hours of the morning, it is said, the other guests in the Winslow had to be evacuated.

* * * * *

Maxwell is best known today for being a multi-millionaire, a financier and businessman who employs thousands and spends billions, who is here today, in Tokyo tomorrow and yesterday was between Paris and Minnesota. Whenever there is a takeover bid his is the first name thought of by city and financial editors.

At his office at Holborn Circus he sits behind a large desk or at a large round table. On each squats a flat, high-tech switchboard, as there is in every room, at home or at work, which he uses. A computer gives him changes in Stock Market prices all over the world at a touch. Next door at Strand House, his alternative office which has a helicopter pad on the roof, he has established a 24-hour, 21st-century office where he can hold video conferences with his staff in Asia, America, Australia and Europe all at the same time. (Time differences mean that some members of the staff will be expected to be in discussion in the middle of the night, but Maxwell works when he is awake and he assumes that every executive has the same flexible approach to corporate affairs as he has.) It all creates an atmosphere of power which is itself intimidating. But employees who visibly wilt before it are told that "confidence is like virginity - it can only be lost once". Timidity has no place in his values.

There is a restlessness about him which is unsettling, apart from his insatiable appetite for answering the telephone. Shirt-sleeved informality doesn't modify the impatience which explodes when instant decisions are not instantly complied with. It is always swifter to declare war than to' wage it, a fact which he seems reluctant to accept. The nervousness which this attitude creates is no doubt an advantage in business affairs.

If a man is measured by the anecdotes he generates then Maxwell is very big indeed. His astonishing felicity with foreign languages doesn't infallibly extend to his grasp of English aphorisms and metaphors. The list of his Maxwellpropisms is forever being added to, the most cherished being:

> He has made his apple pie bed and he must lie in it.
>
> Jerusalem wasn't built in a day.
>
> You are running around like chickens without necks.

Other sayings which conscientious employees have noted include:

> You've made it about as difficult or impossible as a one-legged Chinaman trying to skate across the Atlantic on his left ear.

> I'd need a left-legged canary and a German shepherd dog to find my way around it.

> That's about as useful as last year's snow.

> Giving you something to do is like making love to an elephant. You might get a twitch if you are lucky, but it will still be 13 months before you actually produce something.

> Never pick a quarrel with a man who buys ink by the barrel.

> I couldn't trust you with a burnt-out box of matches.

> What's between your ears apart from fresh air?

> Who let me sign that cheque?

Not all of these are calculated to instil that confidence which he seeks in his employees.

When he signed the agreement to print *China Daily* in London, his then press secretary, Janet Hewlett-Davies, conscientiously provided an expensive gold pen given to her by the former Prime Minister, Harold Wilson, when she worked for him at 10 Downing Street. The editor-in-chief of *China Daily*, Feng Xiliang, admired it greatly. "It's yours", said Maxwell generously. Another member of the staff quietly pointed out to the Chinese that splendid though the gift was, it wasn't Mr Maxwell's to make. But Feng wouldn't let it go. It would occupy an honoured place, he said, in a museum in Beijing. Mrs Hewlett-Davies let him take it, not least because there was no way in which she could reclaim her pen without an unfriendly incident. When it was subsequently explained to Maxwell what he had done he was horrified. Later that week he called Mrs Hewlett-Davies to his sitting room at Holborn Circus. With him was Lord Wilson, holding an identical pen to the one he had given her 10 years before. The old statesman then formally presented it to her. Maxwell had so liked the pen that he bought one for himself too.

Another much-told story concerned Maxwell's senior secretary Debbie Dines, a tough, Junoesque New Zealander. She is not normally given to tears, but one day she gave way to them, borne down by the weight of work thrust upon her by her employer and the brusque, to put it mildly, manner in which it had been done. While she was crying, Maxwell emerged from his office and looked at her aghast. "Who's done that to you?" he demanded angrily. "I'll sack him!"

Since his acquisition of the Mirror Group, Maxwell's activities have spread in all directions. He is now a global businessman, a book, magazine and newspaper publisher, a television and cable TV operator in Britain and abroad, a compact disc manufacturer, the owner of a fleet of helicopters serving the North Sea oilfields and of a fast-expanding engineering company. He has turned the loss on the *Mirror* newspapers into a profit of over £30 million a year. A rival proprietor, Lord Stevens of United Newspapers, owner of the Express Group, said:

> Murdoch claims the credit [for tackling the problems of Fleet Street] but Maxwell did it first.

* * * * *

Even after the world-wide Stock Exchanges crash of October 1987, the market capitalisation of Maxwell Communication Corporation was over $2 billion, and he is still on course for his empire to produce sales of between $3 billion and $5 billion by 1990.

One of the great pleasures of life is to have absolutely nothing to do. It is not one that he would enjoy or understand. Outside his business life he also finds time to be chairman of the Sasakawa Foundation to improve relations between Britain and Japan and to be chairman of Derby County. He was the originating force behind the AIDS Foundation, to which he gave £500,000. He is intolerant of bureaucrats; he talks to ministers, prime ministers and presidents about buying into their nations' TV and radio networks, not officials if he can help it. The demon in him that makes him work seems to grow with age. Within a few months he visited the USSR, Bulgaria, Japan (twice), Mongolia, China, Macao, Hong Kong, the USA (several times), Canada (frequently - he has become junior partner in a new English-language newspaper the *Montreal Daily News*), Paris (constantly), Spain, Portugal, Kenya, Germany and Israel. He has met Deng Xiaoping, Chou En Lai, President Reagan, Mikhail Gorbachov, President Mitterrand and Prime Minister Jacques Chirac, Margaret Thatcher, the King of Spain, the President of Portugal, Mario Soares, and many other world and national leaders. In 1987 he accepted an invitation from the American administration to join its newly-established International Council of Advisers, charged with improving the United States Government's image abroad.

Among the simpler pleasures of the incessant excursions abroad
was a headline in a Portuguese newspaper, after he had concluded a
deal which won him participation in Portugal's TV and newspaper
development, which read:

Maxwell wins. Murdoch loses.

His companies now have offices in 26 countries. He employs some
27,000 people, of whom 20,000 are in Britain and 5,000 in the USA
and Canada. He publishes the second biggest newspaper in Britain
and the largest, by far, in Scotland. He has three Sunday
newspapers and the one in Scotland, again, has achieved a record
circulation. He owns *Sporting Life*, Britain's oldest and leading
sporting newspaper, which is a must with the Royal Family. He is
the biggest printer and publisher in Europe and the second-largest
printer in the United States. He is chairman of Première, the
leading cable TV movie channel in the United Kingdom, and
chairman of Rediffusion Cable, Britain's largest cable TV interest -
and is extending his cable network into Europe - chairman of MTV,
a European "pop" music channel and will, in 1989, unless the
unexpected intervenes, become publisher of the first European
daily newspaper, which will be based in Paris.

This is partly due to the fact that he is a passionate Francophile.
His wife and all his children have dual nationality, British and
French. His son Ian runs his expanding businesses in France, and
Pergamon is the second largest shareholder in the company chosen
in 1987 to hold 50 per cent of TF1, the main French TV channel,
when it was privatised. TF1 reaches 95 per cent of the population
and the choice of the Bouygues consortium, which includes
Pergamon, was a surprise. It was commonly expected that
Hachette, the major French newspapers' distributors and
publishers, would secure the contract. When Maxwell appeared
before the Commission examining applicants for TF1 he impressed
by speaking in fluent French. He began:

My name is Robert Maxwell. I am married to a French lady. We have
seven children, each of whom was born at Maisons Laffitte....

That may not have been decisive - his knowledge of and
involvement in television mattered more - but it helped.

His company, Pergamon Press, is also publishing in 1989 on
microfiche an archive of 1,150,000 pages of original documents on
the French revolution, to coincide with the bicentennial
celebrations. The *French Revolution Research Collection*, as it is
called, was first conceived by Maxwell in 1983. It is the most

ambitious project of its kind ever attempted, and even though it is non-profit-making, it will cost subscribers £33,600 before the publication date and £42,000 thereafter. President Mitterrand attended the launch of it; it was his first engagement in the celebrations. Maxwell is the only foreigner to have been elected a vice-chairman of the French Government's Bicentennial Commission.

In Japan a Maxwell subsidiary is marketing a revolutionary new portable language trainer, developed by Toshiba, which is no bigger than a Sony Walkman, and in China another subsidiary is working on a TV series about the latest trends in science and technology. Maxwell Communication Corporation is developing in Spain, Portugal and Macao; Pergamon has offices in Frankfurt, Sydney, Tokyo and Beijing as well as Oxford, London, Paris and New York. In the second half of the 1980s hardly a month has passed without a new acquisition, project or development overseas. In Canada MCC has a 56 per cent interest in Donohue of Quebec, acquired from the Quebec Government through a joint venture with Quebecor, a major Canadian publisher. But inevitably the biggest expansion abroad has been in the United States.

In 1988 Maxwell Communication Corporation expected sales approaching a billion dollars in the United States. By the beginning of the year Maxwell had bought five printing firms there - the Webb Co. of Minnesota; Providence Gravure of Rhode Island; The Diversified Printing Corporation of Pennsylvania; and Alco Gravure and Pub/Data Inc., both of Illinois - and publishes through Pergamon and its subsidiaries its scientific, academic, computer, foreign policy and defence books. Yet another subsidiary was established to send newspaper advertising by satellite to over 100 United States newspapers with a combined circulation of 27 million. Maxwell looked for new businesses all the time.

But one business he didn't succeed in buying was Harcourt Brace Jovanovich, a publishing company which fiercely - and in the event suicidally - resisted his blandishments. HBJ is one of the world's largest publishing houses, diversified into the ownership and management of parks and insurance companies. But it was the publishing business - school textbooks, scientific and medical books and journals, general fiction and non-fiction and children's books, etc. - which Maxwell particularly wanted. He was willing to pay $44 a share ($1.94 billion, or £1.16 billion) and was hoping for an agreed takeover. But a courteous and friendly letter to the chairman of HBJ, William Jovanovich, received a discourteous and hostile reply.

Maxwell's bid, he said, was "preposterous both as to intent and value", which in takeover circles is not normally to be considered a flat No. But Jovanovich did mean No, and he delved deep into the dregs to fight off the English invader. The fact that he was the son of a Serbian immigrant did not prevent him from saying[6]:

> Mr Maxwell's dealings since he emerged from the mists of Ruthenia after World War II haven't always favoured shareholders.

He added, for bad measure[7]:

> Mr Maxwell has money, but not enough. He has ambition, but no standing. He ought to be sent packing to Liechtenstein.

Jovanovich's first line of defence was clearly to be a personal attack on Maxwell, and he used every weapon, real or imaginary, he could lay his hands upon, including the "fact" that Maxwell's sympathies lay with Moscow, as evidenced by his accepting an honorary doctorate from Moscow University. The second was to become known as "the poison pill". In brief, Jovanovich embarked on a recapitalisation plan which meant that shareholders would get a bonus of $40 a share, paid for by huge borrowings of $3 billion, which tripled the company's debt. If Maxwell had pursued his bid he would have been faced with repaying the debt immediately and he announced he was withdrawing it. Attempts by him in the United States' courts to prevent HBJ proceeding with its recapitalisation failed and he ceased to pursue, at least for the time being, his ambitions to capture the United States' publishers. His bid to buy HBJ had been expensive, but at the end of it he was able to show a net profit of £5 million on the shares he had bought and then sold. But by the early months of 1988 the value of the HBJ shares had slumped from a peak of over $53 to only $6. The poison and the Stock Exchanges' crash of October 1987 had had their effect.

Jovanovich could never have seen the crash coming, but Maxwell fortunately did. On September 4, six weeks beforehand, he advised the four main pension funds of the Mirror Group and of Maxwell Communication Corporation to sell up to 25 per cent of the shares they owned and to put the cash into British Government securities. The manager of the funds, Trevor Cook, wrote that same evening to the eight City investment managers who handled them conveying Maxwell's advice. Seven accepted it and one did not. After the crash, Maxwell relieved that one of its responsibilities.

After the devastation of the equity market, it was Maxwell's support for the Eurotunnel share offer which was decisive in its success. Alastair Morton, co-chairman of the project, said:

Confidence in our share issue was rudely shattered. But Maxwell was extremely positive. He said he would be in for £37 million, about a tenth of the British underwriting. It made our day. It enabled our bankers to take a confident line with waverers.

Which is more than the *Daily Mirror* did. Its City editor, Bob Head, advised his readers not to buy shares in the Tunnel. Head is proud of the fact that Maxwell did not interfere in the guidance the paper gave to its readers and nor has he ever attempted to do so. Maxwell says he would probably go to jail if he tried to.

*   *   *   *   *

The general belief among journalists - and through them millions of their readers - is that Maxwell is power and publicity mad and wants to control everything he can lay his hands on, from television stations to football clubs and from communications to the Commonwealth Games. The truth is that when Maxwell is asked to help, especially in a public cause, he finds it impossible to refuse the challenge. As those who worked with him at the *Mirror* know, he needed the burden of saving the Commonwealth Games in Edinburgh in 1986 from bankruptcy like he needed a piano on his foot. The Games had proved too much for the organising committee of Edinburgh worthies and others who were in charge. There was a deficit of several million pounds in the sum needed to put them on and the committee was in danger of trading illegally. The Secretary of State for Scotland, Malcolm Rifkind, approached Maxwell and asked for his help at a time when the Games were within a few days of being cancelled. A statement from the committee on June 19 announcing that Maxwell had agreed declared[8]:

The response at short notice has been magnificent and has had the simple purpose of averting the national embarrassment of a failure or even cancellation of the Games through financial difficulties.

But *The Scotsman*'s headline announced baldly and typically:

Maxwell takes over the Games.

However, the *New Statesman* grudgingly admitted[9]:

There is, it must be said, no evidence of Maxwell having sought to foist his leadership qualities on the Commonwealth Games. He became involved because, as the hours ticked away to the opening ceremony, the directors of Commonwealth Games Scotland 1986 Ltd were in a state of panic.

Had he refused to step in and the news had leaked - which was certain - he would have been excoriated as the millionaire too mean or too busy to lend a hand. As it was, the publicity could hardly have been worse. The Scottish press demanded to know how much Maxwell was putting into the Games personally. He refused to commit himself for the simple reason that had he said he was bailing out the Games no one else would have bothered to raise the finance. It was a simple point the newspapers seemed unable to grasp. Scottish-based newspapers, whose proprietors could easily have afforded to put all the money necessary into saving the Games, hardly stopped carping at Maxwell's "intervention". But the real disaster for the Games came when a carefully-prepared ambush by the African Commonwealth countries broke into the open. They announced a boycott of the Games as a protest against the British Government's tenderness towards the apartheid policies of South Africa. In carefully staggered announcements, Nigeria, Ghana, Kenya, Uganda, India, Malaysia, Zambia, Zimbabwe and 20 others pulled out. The Games went on, nevertheless, because the non-boycotters, which included all the athletically powerful white nations, outnumbered those who stayed away. But they were undoubtedly marred. The result was that the Games, which were non-political, suffered from a political action. The Commonwealth Conference, which followed immediately afterwards, illogically was not boycotted. Neither the sporting demonstration nor the political discussions had the slightest effect on Margaret Thatcher's policies.

The speculation about the financing of the Games went on long after their ending. The final accounts showed that the deficit was some £4.3 million on a gross cost of £35 million. For more than 18 months there was acrimony and threats of legal action from creditors, but eventually all debts were settled. Between them, Maxwell and his friend Ryoichi Sasakawa, a wealthy Japanese philanthropist whom Maxwell asked to give financial help, contributed £2 million to the final accounting. If he had said No at the beginning he would have saved his money and Scotland would have been forced to abandon the Games.

But in the sporting field Maxwell is best known for the Football League clubs with which he is linked. When Elton John approached Maxwell and asked him to buy Watford FC, the First Division club which he owned and which he was finding it difficult to continue to afford, Maxwell agreed that his company, BPCC, a major employer in Watford, would acquire John's shares for £2 million but stipulated it had to have the agreement of the Football League

Management Committee. There was an outcry because he already owned Derby County and his son, Kevin, was chairman of Oxford United - both First Division clubs. The furore mainly originated on the sports pages of rival newspapers, but was taken up by the management committee - which Maxwell promptly dubbed the Mismanagement Committee - because, according to the League's loosely-drafted constitution, no individual was permitted to control more than one club.

Maxwell's proposed association with yet another club was to the sportswriters "proof" that he was power hungry. Visions were conjured up of his dictating the professional game in Britain; behind them all lurked, though no one dared say it publicly, the suggestion that matches between the Maxwell clubs might be "fixed". The simple point, which hardly a single commentator was prepared to recognise, was that once again Maxwell had been approached to save a sporting organisation. Had he wanted to become a power in the land of football he could easily have afforded to buy the biggest clubs. Why waste his time and money on a struggling one?

The Watford story was a repeat of the Derby story, which was itself a repeat of the Oxford story. In 1982 Oxford United, whose ground is less than a mile from the Maxwell home, was within days of going into liquidation. Directors who had mortgaged their homes to try to keep the club solvent were faced with losing them. Maxwell took the club over, paid its immediate creditors and threw himself into making it a success. As a result Oxford won the Third Division championship, the Second Division championship and the second most important knockout competition, the Milk Cup. (When Oxford won promotion to the Second Division Maxwell placed several bets that they would either win that division or be promoted. His winnings totalled some £223,000, which he gave to the club.)

In 1984 Derby County, once one of the biggest names in English football - which Oxford never were - were languishing in the Third Division and on the edge of bankruptcy and liquidation. Again, Maxwell was asked to perform a rescue, by the then chairman of the Management Committee, Jack Dunnett. Again he agreed and put his son Ian in as chairman. Again, the club's fortunes were restored. It followed the Oxford pattern, winning promotion to the Second and then to the First Division. When Ian's work meant that he had to spend most of his time in France, Maxwell took over the chair at Derby and Kevin became chairman of Oxford.

As a result of agreeing to save yet another club drifting towards the rocks there was a public row which went on for weeks. An agreement which Maxwell reached with the latest chairman of the Management Committee, Philip Carter, under which BPCC could buy Watford provided Maxwell sold either Derby or Oxford, was repudiated by other members of it, though one of those who voted against Maxwell then went to him privately and advised him to ignore what the committee was saying. Maxwell, for his part, threatened to pull out of football altogether.

The truth is that Maxwell's whole energies are devoted to building up his global media empire. Besides that, football is of no importance. He has neither the time nor the inclination to "take over" the game; Oxford, Derby and Watford were further examples of how impossible he finds it to refuse help when it is asked. Had he turned aside when approached, the sport would have lost two of its clubs, and the football supporters of Derby and Oxford would have lost the teams which mean so much to them.

* * * * *

When he is abroad Maxwell works when he is awake, whatever time it is in the country where he has momentarily landed or the country which he is telephoning. His senior staff expect and get calls at any time of the day or night and I have heard him rebuke an executive for not calling him at 2 am to deal with a printing problem because it was feared he would be asleep. He has a facsimile machine wherever he goes, plus secretaries to operate it and the telephones and a butler to ensure that all are properly fed. When he is at the office in London or at home in Oxford the pace never slackens. He barely recognises, except with irritation, week-ends or bank holidays. The first time he went on holiday after acquiring the Mirror Group he announced he would be away for three weeks and was back after three days. There are working breakfasts (ideally, he would start at 7.30, a time which is usually likely to encounter dismayed resistance), working lunches and working dinners. There are also working teas and working coffees in between. In truth, Mirror Group Newspapers are only a small part of his business activities, but he enjoys and relaxes in the company of journalists, though he professes himself shocked by their cynicism and scandalous conversation. But even relaxation embraces work. He likes to gossip, but there is no such thing in his repertoire as idle gossip. Gossip, like everything else, has its merits - it is a source of information. It sounds boring but isn't; there are no awkward pauses and no subject has a long life.

It is his pride to try to master every subject with which he has to deal, whether in newspapers, printing or the City of London, which means that the advertising director might be instructed on some new development in his field or the chief printer in his. Michael Richardson recalled when he first met Maxwell in 1964 to discuss the floating of Pergamon as a public company:

> I suddenly realised at that meeting that this astonishing man knew more about floating a company than some merchant bankers did. He knew more about accounting than his accountant. He knew more about company law than the solicitors. But he knew very little about the stock market at that time. Within three weeks he knew more about it than I did - he picked it up that fast.

Like most busy men he prefers his staff to bring him solutions not problems, though he will rarely leave a solution without his mark being placed upon it. He also likes to try to improve what a journalist has written because he is a compulsive sub-editor. Persuading him that adjectives are more likely to weaken a sentence than strengthen it can be an arduous task.

He eats little but often and rarely between meals, at which he also works. Two lunch engagements a day on the same floor at Holborn or in adjoining dining rooms at Headington Hill Hall are not uncommon. He is even reputed to have held three dinners at the same time one working week-night at the *Mirror*. He will eat the first course at one table and a later course at another, or just take coffee. There is always time for an anecdote but not for a long-winded report. The telephone is by the dining table as well; calls are rarely refused. This not only makes mealtime discussions as disjointed as any other but, when telephone conversations are in French, German or Russian, it makes it difficult for his guests to understand what is going on. There are few situations more frustrating than to be an uncomprehending eavesdropper.

One evening, with the pride of a man who had discovered perpetual motion, he explained to me what he was doing at that moment. The Chase Manhattan Bank was in one room in the corridor which begins with his own office; Brenda Dean and her colleagues from the print union, Sogat '82, were in another; a team of financial solicitors was in a third; the executives of one of his out-of-London companies was housed in a fourth; and the National Graphical Society was in a fifth. He was negotiating with them all. He was also discussing the next day's *Daily Mirror* leader with me which, in the circumstances, did not take long.

The need to be busy is compulsive. He is impatient enough when he has a mountain of work to clear. He is worse when he hasn't. He gathers power to himself, but he doesn't seek to use it where influence matters most, which is in government. He works to fulfil his ambition of becoming head of one of the top ten media empires in the world which, in its train, will give him control of billions, yet the possession of money means little to him. Ask him why he does it and he will reply that he wants to be of service.

* * * * *

Journalists and others have portrayed him as a man of mystery and he has enjoyed enhancing that reputation, not because of any romantic aura it creates, but because he is a mischievous man. The effect has not done his reputation any good. In particular, he allowed a belief to grow up that he had "something to hide" in Liechtenstein, the Alpine principality used by some as a tax haven. It was a tactic continuously exploited by Kleinwort Benson's in its "defence" against his takeover bid for Waddington's, the printing firm which makes Monopoly, one of the world's most successful table games. In 1984 Waddington's board fiercely resisted Maxwell's takeover offer of £5 a share, though financial editors were advising the company's shareholders that it ought to be accepted.

Waddington's and its merchant bank advisers, Kleinwort Benson, decided to play the "Liechtenstein card", a game in which xenophobia, innuendo and irrelevance were deployed to mislead and confuse; it was a tactic which Kleinwort's was to use again later, despite the fact that it knew there was nothing to hide. The chairman of Waddington's, Victor Watson, told his shareholders that it was of "fundamental importance to know who ultimately controls BPCC", which was making the takeover bid. He did not explain what the importance was, nor did Kleinwort's. The trailing of a hint of a suggestion of a smear had the desired effect. It was newsworthy. John Junor in the *Sunday Express* asked in his usual style[10]:

> Why Liechtenstein?
> Such an upstanding chap who lectures us all on our civic responsibilities couldn't possibly be avoiding tax, could he?

The answer was No, as any knowledge of Liechtenstein law would have shown, but it was exactly the kind of question which

Waddington's and Kleinwort's were hoping would be asked. They hadn't suggested tax avoidance, but there was no sign of tears on their part that someone else had. The *Mail on Sunday* sent a reporter to Vaduz, capital of Liechtenstein. He found nothing sinister, but commented[11]:

> With adviser Kleinwort Benson the Waddington board successfully made the issue of who owns Maxwell's business interests a key factor of its defence.

It quoted Watson as saying:

> We may have to take the Pergamon Holding Foundation [the ultimate holder of the "Maxwell companies"] to court to find out who is really behind it.

The *Financial Times* said the City had been surprised by the defence tactics and that Watson was eager to deny that there was any kind of personal vendetta against Maxwell. The paper's reporter, Duncan Campbell-Smith, said[12]:

> Perhaps, when BPCC's struggle to win control of Waddington's shares is long finished and forgotten, this aspect of the current battle will turn out to be a lasting reminder of Kleinwort's unusual defence.

The Times commented[13]:

> Pergamon was subject to the usual inquiries by National Westminster Bank when the bank was arranging for Mr Maxwell to rescue BPC in 1981. National Westminster is also Waddington's bank, and has been unable or unwilling to sustain Mr Watson's innuendoes, despite his requests. This has been an ill-judged campaign by Waddington, particularly in view of the fact that its own results speak more than any slur.

Maxwell had explained to Watson and the Waddington board more than the law required it to know about the ownership of BPCC. In addition, Dr Walter Keicher, director of the Foundation, authorised Maxwell's bankers Henry Ansbacher and Co. Ltd. to say categorically that, as was already well-known, the beneficiaries of the Foundation comprised "a number of charities and relatives of the respective grandparents of Mr and Mrs Robert Maxwell not resident in the United Kingdom". Maxwell said[14]:

> Every public statement I have ever made has made it clear that neither I, nor my wife, nor my family, will inherit one penny of all the wealth that I have managed to create.

Remarkably similar stories appeared in several newspapers to the effect that Waddington's might refuse to pay any dividends on

Maxwell's stake in the company until "the mystery" was solved.

Maxwell said it was all "an irrelevant smokescreen", but he should have known that most people believe the adage that there is no smoke without fire. The issue continued to smoulder even after Maxwell withdrew his offer for Waddington's following the sale by Norwich Union - which had previously underwritten BPCC's offer - of 5% of Waddington's shares to the company's stockbrokers to ensure that Maxwell would lose. The *Mail on Sunday* returned to it two days before Christmas 1984, announcing that Lord Matthews, chairman of Fleet Holdings in which Pergamon was a substantial shareholder, was to challenge Maxwell in the courts about the "ultimate ownership" of his empire. Lord Matthews denied it on the same day.

On January 2, 1985 Maxwell wrote to Watson quoting newspaper stories suggesting that he had dropped his bid for the company because of the Liechtenstein factor and that Watson had "reluctantly had to drop his strenuous efforts to find out the truth about PHF after Maxwell sold his stake in the company". He went on:

> As you must know, Waddington has been provided with all information required by law, and more, not by me but by Liechtenstein lawyers of the highest repute after the most careful consideration by leading company counsel and merchant bankers.... We have also been advised that notwithstanding the disposal of our shares ... your company retains the right to pursue its rights and remedies through the courts. I cannot understand why therefore you say that you have been deprived of your rights by our sale ... or seek to imply that we have run away to prevent you going to the courts. That is manifestly untrue. Your decision not to pursue the matter through the courts demonstrates that you realise that Waddington already have all information to which they are entitled by law.

To a subsequent letter from Watson, Maxwell replied:

> I suggest that you know that the answers were perfectly satisfactory, and that is why you have refused to proceed further....

* * * * *

The Liechtenstein card was played yet again in the spring of 1987 when Maxwell told the chairman of Extel that he was going to mount a bid for the group. Once more Kleinwort's was advising the defending company and one of its directors Philip Boothman, himself a barrister, took part in a conference with a leading QC

Mary Arden, which had been arranged by William Underhill of the Solicitors Slaughter & May. Philip Arkless, company secretary of Extel, was also there. In its instructions to Miss Arden Slaughter & May said:

> The company is determined to resist a possible takeover by Mr Maxwell and his interests. One method by which it hopes to do this is by establishing or at least threatening to be able to established the ultimate control of the Maxwell companies.

Miss Arden asked for

> any evidence of Maxwell's embarrassment as to public disclosure of the ultimate ownership of Pergamon Holding Foundation.

It would be "useful" she said. She also asked whether the Foundation was in the nature of a trust (it is not, it is a foundation) and for further information regarding the charitable nature of the Maxwell Charitable Trust. The note goes on:

> Counsel indicated that to support an application to the court it would be necessary to show that absence of information about the ultimate ownership [of] PHF would give an advantage to Maxwell in a bid for Extel…. Counsel asked whether Kleinwort Benson had formally advised Extel that it should know the identity of the offeror. Phillip Boothman indicated that no such formal advice had been given but that it was implicit and could be made express if necessary.

In its instructions Slaughter & May further asked:

> Do the disclosures made by the Maxwell side support a claim that the Pergamon Holding Foundation has failed to make a proper disclosure?

Miss Arden's reply to that was "No." She further advised:

> The standard of proof was proof on the balance of probabilities. It would be necessary to obtain Liechtenstein advice, if possible, so as to indicate that *of necessity* some other person had to be interested in shares in which PHF was interested. For example, if PHF constitutes a trust and the trustees have failed to notify, that would be grounds for the restrictions being imposed. Albeit that evidence would only be circumstantial, it was worth seeking out whatever was available. It would be helpful to have a dossier of public information about Maxwell's past history regarding 212 [Section 212 of the Companies' Act] disclosure (Kleinwort Benson's experience with Waddington could be helpful).

The participation of Kleinwort's in this kind of conference was despite the fact that it knew that there was nothing more which needed to be found out and that in its "experience with

Waddington" nothing improper was discovered. That it repeated its previous behaviour demonstrated its belief in the power of innuendo to frustrate a bona fide bid.

This tactic was also employed by HBJ when Maxwell proposed making a bid for the US company later in 1987. Kleinwort's smear, inevitably, had travelled the Atlantic, and the merchant bank was hired by HBJ for a fat fee to assist the American publishers in its defence.

Robert Pirie, President and Chief Executive of Rothschild's, New York, told me that he advised Maxwell and the Foundation that if the bid for HBJ (which was likely to be hostile because of Jovanovich's attitude) proceeded then the Foundation would have to disclose to the courts its ultimate ownership and control of BPCC and the Pergamon Group. He added:

> Bob said "We have no problem", and as a result our lawyers went to Liechtenstein and Zürich and there was an absolute understanding and commitment that everything would be disclosed in respect of the Foundation. We were absolutely willing and able to do that and the director of the Foundation was ready to make any deposition or any court appearance.

When I agreed to write this book I told Maxwell that I would like to know all about "the mystery of Liechtenstein" and he replied:

> Certainly. That is easy. There *is* no mystery.

I said:

> And I would need to know all about the money.

"That's easy, too", he replied. "All that I have helped to create belongs to the Pergamon Foundation which is going to give it all away."

The association of the Maxwell family with Liechtenstein began in 1953 when his sister, Brana, former inmate of Buchenwald, was concerned about the safety of the small capital she possessed - a couple of thousand pounds - during the breakup of her marriage. A solicitor advised her to set up a trust in Liechtenstein. Why she did it Maxwell doesn't know, but the insecurity which prompted it can be guessed at.

Today the Pergamon-Maxwell group of companies is owned and controlled by the Maxwell Foundation, known until recently as the Pergamon Foundation and before that as the Pergamon Holding Foundation, which is located in Vaduz. It was originally established in 1970 as the Swico Foundation by Dr Ludwig Gutstein, a leading

Swiss lawyer and an old friend of the Maxwells. After the Leasco débâcle he was concerned about Mr and Mrs Maxwell and all the family interests being defendants in a $22 million Leasco law suit. Gutstein set up and funded a foundation which he thought would provide some safety from the depredations of Leasco's lawyers. He put 20,000 Swiss francs into it, then worth about £1,500. In 1987 Gutstein appointed another Swiss lawyer, his former colleague and friend, Dr Werner Rechsteiner, to take over in his place. Its director, appointed by Dr Gutstein, was from its inception until 1986 Dr Walter Keicher. It is now his son Werner. The Foundation was never set up for commercial objects or for tax purposes. As Slaughter & May advised Extel:

> A [Liechtenstein] foundation cannot freely be formed to pursue commercial objects.

It had no income before 1986 other than small amounts needed for legal expenses. The first dividends were received in 1986. Coopers and Lybrand are the Foundation's auditors. Its first public annual report was being prepared as this book was being printed.

* * * * *

By 1974 Maxwell and his family had virtually no money. Pergamon, the keystone to their fortune, had been regained but was heavily in debt. Its shares were bought back by a loan from a New York bank. Today [February 1988] the Maxwell Communication Corporation has a London Stock Exchange valuation of over £1.5 billion. The Foundation now owns, among many other investments, the majority of Maxwell Communication Corporation, Mirror Group Newspapers, Hollis plc (the growing engineering group which Pergamon bought when it was near bankruptcy), Pergamon Holdings, Pergamon Group plc, and the Pergamon Media Trust who are the second largest shareholders in *TF1*, the most successful television channel in France. The annual income from those holdings, currently estimated to be over £25 million, will be available for distribution to further five main charitable causes:

> 1. The support of primary scientific and medical research in the areas of cancer, heart disease, the brain and the nervous system, and AIDS. A World AIDS Research Centre, with facilities in the United States and Europe and with funding of US$50 million, is under active consideration.

2. The provision of financial assistance to the people of Israel, Jews and Arabs, in order to contribute to establishing a lasting peace in that area.

3. The encouragement and assistance with cash grants to capable young entrepreneurs throughout the world wishing to set up their own businesses in the fields of the media, communications and information. The Foundation will also finance world young entrepreneurs' forums and prize-giving symposia.

4. The improvement of education, the avoidance of conflicts between nations and the elimination of racial hatred throughout the world.

5. The support of charitable institutions in Liechtenstein.

The grants from the Foundation will be made by a Board of "Collators", or "Kollatoren", a German word used in Liechtenstein law for individuals with the power to select beneficiaries and to determine grants.

The Maxwell Foundation will be one of the richest of its kind in the world. There are no racial or national barriers to those who qualify for its assistance. Some of its first donations include £500,000 to the British National AIDS Trust; £250,000 towards the restoration of Westminster Abbey; FF5 million for the International Foundation for Human Rights and the Humanities being set up in Paris under the chairmanship of Edgar Faure to celebrate the bi-centenary of the French Revolution; FF1,800,000 to the French Academy of Sciences to support a number of annual scholarships which will be awarded to european scientists, particularly in chemistry; and DM500,000 for the Beethoven Appeal in West Germany.

It means that the poor boy from Solotvino, whose daily bread often depended upon the charity of others, is now returning the wealth he has helped to create to the professions who supported him; to help find peace in the country which is the Jewish national home; to the young who need the chance he had to make for himself; and to promoting for others the education which he never had.

2

Escape from Poverty

The youth, who daily farther from the East,
Must travel, still is Nature's priest.

Wordsworth

Solotvino nestles among the hills and mountains, the woods and forests, of Ruthenia, which at various times has straddled the border areas of Hungary, Romania, Poland, Czechoslovakia and the Soviet Union. It is a town whose history is barely worth recording and whose architecture is not worth remembering. It is said to be the very centre of the continent; if so, it was the only distinction which, in pre-war Europe, set it apart from thousands of other small towns, villages and hamlets in that part of the world. For those who lived there, life was inevitably hard. The winters were as bitterly cold as the summers were swelteringly hot. The mountainous regions of East Carpathia are infertile, and less than a fifth of the land in the region is fit for ploughing and tilling.

For nearly 1,000 years, Ruthenia, a county of less than 5,000 square miles, was ruled by the kingdom of Hungary and the Austro-Hungarian empire. When that empire vanished at the end of the First World War, Ruthenia was annexed by the fledgling republic of Czechoslovakia under the terms of the Treaty of Trianon. Its sojourn in the republic was brief. Within 20 years it was back in the hands of Hungary, a tit-bit tossed to it for helping the big beast to have his feast; the reward for supporting Hitler first in intimidating and then in dismembering Czechoslovakia. Each time its rulers changed, so did its name. It has been called Carpatho-Ruthenia, Hungarian Ruthenia, Carpathian Russia, Transcarpathia and Sub-Carpathian Russia. In the autumn of 1944 it was liberated - or, less euphemistically, occupied - by the troops of the Soviet Union and is now known as Karpatska-Ukraina. It has remained firmly in the Soviet grasp ever since that time and looks likely to remain so for any foreseeable future.

But though its name has changed, the economic plight of those who live in Ruthenia has only marginally improved. Half of the province is dense forest, rarely seen by humans except those who hunted the bear and the boar or sought sight of the wolf. The mountain areas are sparsely populated by peasants struggling to make a living on inhospitable slopes. It is one of the quirks of history that lonely lands of harsh and remorseless poverty can attract so many covetous eyes.

For centuries that poverty was the dominating, ever-present fact of life for the peasants of Ruthenia, especially those of the Jewish faith. It aged the men, debilitated the women and provided a diet for the children which barely fitted them for the struggle for survival.

Solotvino (which has also in living memory been called Solotvina, Slatinské Doly, Selo Slatina, Szlatina, Slatina and Slotfina, depending upon who was occupying it at the time) lay in the Ruthenian county of Maramures, about which an old Jewish proverb said[1]:

> Ten measures of poverty were given to the world; nine of them were taken by Maramures.

It was one of those regions which concern had passed by. In the 1920s and 1930s the Czechoslovak Government made a few half-hearted attempts to develop its mountains, lakes and forests as some kind of tourist attraction. A travel book of the period tried to make the best of a difficult job. The area where Solotvino was located, it said, "was entirely surrounded by mountains"; naturally, "the very best thing here is fresh air". The faces of the Jews, it added, were "in great contrast to the rather unintelligent Ruthenians whose expression is almost blank-stare as they sit in the market-place, side by side, gazing at the distance, seldom speaking a word or moving a muscle"[2].

That was a disguised admission that the Ruthenians were a surly people who did not offer a welcome to strangers.

Since the war, the Soviet Union has developed the sawmilling and timber-working industries of the region and there are factories in the larger towns making furniture and prefabricated houses. Now, in Solotvino, modern steel and concrete buildings rise above unpaved streets and spacious villas within ample gardens stand beside the old wooden homes in which the peasants live. In the rural areas traditional crops are raised - corn, wheat, oats and potatoes, even some tobacco - and pig rearing is intensive. There are vineyards in the foothills of the mountains and orchards in the valley of the Tisza river, but it is still one of the backwaters of Europe.

The only feature of the area to strike awe in a stranger is the salt mines, which have been worked for thousands of years. Roman coins and artefacts and Bronze Age relics have been found there. The mines have changed little since 1938 when an American visitor recorded his impressions[3]:

> If the Great Salt Lake were poured into Jackson's Hole, Wyoming, evaporated and slid under the next county; if a shaft with a fast elevator were sunk through solid salt; and if, since 1777, men had carved crystal columns, vaulted roofs, nave, transept, chapels, and cloister garth, the breathless grandeur of that subterranean cathedral would be the prospect of the excavated slopes of the salt mine at Slatinské Doly.

> On a little wooden catwalk anchored to the roof, I stood with the chief engineer. Below us yawned a gulf so profound that workers loading salt blocks looked as small as mice.... Crystalline walls reflected twinkling lights. Around us, like the roar of a far-off waterfall, rumbled the echoes of pneumatic chisels, cutting this titanic temple vaster still.

This grandeur was unlikely to have made the same impact upon those whose job it was to mine the salt.

In the years when Robert Maxwell - Ludvik Hoch - was growing up there, Solotvino had a town hall, a main street, a Friday market, a few shops, a communal bath for the menfolk and another, the Mikvah, for Jewish women, a cinema, a railway station to serve the only kind of public transport which existed, four synagogues and a bar. Bicycles were common, though the Hochs could never afford one, and the town also boasted, according to the recollection of a former inhabitant now living in the United States, a grand total of five cars, one of which was a taxi and another of which was owned by a Romanian priest whose pride and joy it was. Maxwell described it many years later as "a very primitive village - a sort of Fiddler on the Roof type".

But, above all, Solotvino had poverty, penury and privation, an endemic, chronic misery from which there was no escape. Maxwell's abiding, "haunting" memory of those days is that he was perpetually hungry. "I have not come across any greater poverty anywhere in the world", he says, and he is a much-travelled man. One of his cousins recalls a recurring dream of childhood - that of filling his stomach with food and not having to get up in the morning. It seemed then to be an impossible dream; daytime's reality was not far from starvation.

The population of the town was mixed, consisting largely of Jews and Gentiles of Hungarian, Romanian, Polish, Ukrainian and Slovak origin. Its mayor was a Hungarian, but there was little or no discrimination in its governance and the "town council" included several elders of the different communities, regardless of nationality. The town crier was a Jew and there were Jews working in the tax office. The police were Czechoslovakian; the fire brigade was a multi-racial group of volunteers. Children of the various nationalities played together and acts of anti-semitism were isolated, though Jewish girls rarely went with Gentile boys and Gentile girls were even less likely to go with Jewish boys.

The Solotvino of Maxwell's childhood was a straggling town, built on the lower slopes of a mountainside, and three of its streets ran, undulating and roughly parallel, down to the Tisza, a tributary of the Danube which flooded the poorer homes near its banks when the mountain snows melted in the spring. The crudest houses in the town - that is, the majority of them - were wooden; others were built with a mixture of wood and an inferior brick, made by the gipsies from yellow clay and straw. In Upper Solotvino, the posher part of the town known as the Kolonie and reserved for the middle classes - mainly teachers and the Czech management of the nearby salt mines - the houses were made entirely of brick. The streets were haphazardly lined with trees and most of the homes, however mean, had a small garden. All the trees in them were fruit-bearing - walnut, cherry, apple or plum - if only because ornamental trees were a luxury.

Across the river, reached by a long and narrow bridge of wood and iron, was Sziget (also known as Sighet and Maramuressziget), one of the principal towns of Maramures, both larger and better off than - or, at least, not as badly off as - Solotvino. A modern author has described it as "squalid". Until 1918 Sziget's economic superiority over its neighbours was marked and those who could afford to shop there crossed the bridge (the one which Maxwell knew was destroyed in the spring floods of 1940). Only the most basic goods were available in Solotvino itself: there was a tailor's and a textile shop and stores selling grain and sweets for the children, a baker's, a barber's, a shoe shop and one selling china. Solotvino did not even have a rabbi for the Jews, mainly of Hungarian origin, who made up a good third of the town's population. Those who needed the services of one, other than on a Tuesday when the rabbi crossed the bridge himself, had to go to Sziget.

But after the post-war annexation, the gap narrowed, though poverty was still the enduring lot of both towns. The territorial spoils of war meant that Solotvino was now divided from Sziget, which was placed beyond the border with Romania. This change was beneficial to both communities, but especially to Solotvinians, who profitably engaged in smuggling textiles, haberdashery, clothing and footwear into Romania, where they were dearer, and bringing back food and alcohol from there, where it was considerably cheaper. At night the more adventurous citizens would smuggle spirits from Sziget. They ran the risk of being intercepted by patrol boats and fired upon and there are highly-coloured recollections of the river smelling of alcohol after the failure of one of these contraband runs. It seems an unlikely story, given that it was a fast and wide waterway. More legally, shops were opened in Solotvino to sell shoes and clothing and most of these were owned by Jews.

In 1930 38 per cent of the population of Sziget were Jews. Elie Wiesel, the Nobel Peace Prize winner and a distant relative of Maxwell's who survived Auschwitz and Buchenwald, was born in Sziget and grew up in the town. He has since recalled its special Jewish atmosphere[4]:

> You went out on the street on Saturday and felt Shabbat (Sabbath) in the air. Stores were closed, business centres at a standstill, municipal offices deserted. For the Jews, as well as their Christian neighbours, it was a day of total rest. The old men gathered in the synagogues and houses of study to listen to itinerant preachers, the young went strolling in the park, through the woods, along the river bank. Your concerns, anxieties and troubles could wait; Shabbat was your refuge.

Concerns, anxieties and troubles there certainly were and in abundance, especially across the Tisza from Sziget.

Emigration from Solotvino to the United States and Argentina began before the First World War when a few dozen Jews left the town to escape the poverty; in the late 1920s Maxwell's Uncle Nathan went to America and the flight to a better land accelerated in the early 1930s when the economic plight of the Jews became more desperate. But the emigrants never forgot those whom they had left behind. Twice a year - before the High Holidays and before Passover - donations were sent from the United States to the heads of the community who distributed them to the poor. Apart from this assistance from abroad, the Jewish community itself helped those whose need was greatest and collections were organised, for example, for brides from penniless families and the synagogues distributed food to the poorest, among whom were included the Hochs.

One of the few repatriates was Joseph Shimonovitch, who emigrated to become wealthy in the United States and later returned to open a wholesale general store. But his business was a victim of the latent anti-semitism which was spreading in the rural areas and which could sometimes erupt into violence. One of his employees, a money collector named Gershon, was killed by non-Jews while on his rounds in a neighbouring village. The horse and carriage returned with Gershon's body inside it.

Apart from the salt mines, which employed close on a thousand labourers and clerks, there was little or no industry of any consequence in Solotvino. When the mines were owned by Hungarians, they did not recruit Jewish labour. Although discrimination was officially ended with the coming of the new Czechoslovak state, between the two world wars no more than half a dozen Jews ever found employment in them. Today any question of discrimination or anti-semitism is academic. Fifty years ago there were some 3,000 Jews living in Solotvino. Now there is none. There were still two until a few years ago, but Kalman Slomowitz, first cousin of Maxwell's mother (son of her father's brother), emigrated to Israel in 1973 when he was 68 and the other stayed to die of old age.

The common tongue of the Jews of Solotvino was Yiddish but, in fact, because of the mixed nature of the town's population, almost every Jew spoke at least three or four languages, usually Hungarian, regarded as the language of the intellectuals - learned by Maxwell from his mother and later polished when he was in jail in Budapest - Czech and Romanian.

Jewish families were large - most of them had anything between six and 14 children - and their diet was mean and repetitious: beans one day and potatoes or maize the next. Meat was eaten only on the Sabbath and one chicken was expected to be shared by up to 16 people. Few had more than one set of clothes and many, adults and children alike, went barefoot in the summer.

Because work in the mines was effectively reserved for Czechs and Hungarians, the Jews followed their traditional crafts of shoe-mending, shoe-making, tailoring and carpentry or eked out a living by casual labouring or sheer ingenuity. But indirectly, their community benefited from the salt mines because they were needed to supply the goods and skills required by those who worked in them. The biggest Jewish employer was one Moses Shlomovitch, who owned a salt mill and a sawmill which provided work for some 50 souls.

To supplement their families' daily diet, Jewish men would fish in the Tisza. This "fishing" consisted of either poisoning the fish with a paste made from red pepper - the effect of which was to cause them to swell up and float to the surface - or, for more speedy results, killing them by exploding a crude kind of petrol "bomb", a forerunner of the Molotov cocktail, or with dynamite stolen, probably, from the salt mines. The medium-sized fish would be eaten at once and the larger ones dried for storage for the days when the river was frozen or in flood. This method of fishing was a help also on festive occasions. To celebrate Maxwell's circumcision, eight days after his birth, his parents were required to offer food to their guests. His father was so successful with his explosive angling that half the village, so it is said, came to enjoy the feast.

* * * * *

If the poverty in the towns of Maramures was almost indescribable, the rural poverty was worse. In the 1920s the Ruthenian peasant and the average Jew both had to struggle to maintain an existence.

When the depression years came in the 1930s, the relationship between Ruthenian and Jew deteriorated, following a pattern common throughout Central and Eastern Europe. In the countryside the Jews were accused of exploiting the peasants by supplying them with alcohol and loans at exorbitant rates, while in the towns they were charged with being "aliens" who ruined their Gentile competitors by driving down prices. It is part of the history of the Jews to be made the scapegoat for depressed economies and the Jews of Maramures were no exception. A Jewish member of the Czechoslovakian Parliament, Dr Kugel, told the assembly in 1935 about the worsening conditions in Sub-Carpathian Ruthenia[5]:

> Today, it is completely impossible adequately to describe the poverty in this area. The Jews who number one-seventh of the total population of the region are affected equally with the rest.
>
> Particularly in the rural areas, their fate is in no way better than that of non-Jews. I strongly wish to protest against any attempt to blame the poverty of Sub-Carpathian Ruthenian peasantry on the Jews.

Such accusations are malicious gossip; were the fabricators to visit the Jewish houses in the villages ... they would see for themselves how many Jews have been forced to sell their last possessions to stay alive. The fact that a few Jews receive concessions for the sale of alcohol does not mean that the masses of their fellow-Jews are benefited by it, and if some obtain these licences by means of bribes, one must recall that this was the accepted practice under the old Hungarian régime.... The economic crisis, which was heightened in the Carpathians by the collapse of the lumber industry and its associated occupations, has had its inevitable effects on the region's Jews, who were already living in great poverty and hardship. Hundreds of Jewish labourers, wagoners and hired hands remain without jobs. Due to the flight of industry, hundreds of skilled Jewish workers have been deprived of their livelihood.

But conditions continued to grow worse and the Ruthenians pressed their claims for the autonomy which the Czech Government had once promised them, an ambition which they were fleetingly to achieve in 1939 before it was brutally and finally extinguished by Hungarian troops. But all that was in the future and part of the horrors yet to come.

* * * * *

As in many other communities which were remote from the outside world, superstition was widespread and strong in Solotvino. If a button was being sewn back on a garment, a piece of thread had to be chewed at the same time in order to prevent the brain from being sewn up too, a belief probably deriving from the sewing of a shroud. If a baby were seriously ill, it was taken to a synagogue and its name changed - usually to Haim, because it means Life - so that when the Angel of Death came, the child it was looking for would not be there. And the foot of a bed never faced the door because that was the way corpses left a room - feet first.

Not surprisingly, education for Jewish children was limited. There was a religious elementary school, the Heder, for the teaching of Judaïsm, but most of the pupils were from poor families and the supervision was weak.

The children of better-off parents, or from homes prepared to make sacrifices, studied with private tutors, whose quality of instruction was far higher than at the Heder. The Jewish community did not establish a school for general education and Jewish pupils (including the young Maxwell) attended the Government school where the language of instruction was Czechoslovakian. Maxwell began his schooling in the Heder when he was seven and attended the Government school in the following year, 1931. He was generally regarded as being very bright. He himself says he was very good at "calculations" or mental arithmetic. The one subject at which he was inept was drawing, which, given the attempts to stop him using his left hand, was probably inevitable. It was at the Government school he suffered the misery experienced by most schoolboys - unrequited first love. He reminisced a few years ago[6]:

> I fell in love with a girl at school, three years my senior. I was eleven years of age. I remember being very unhappy ... she would not take any notice of me and treated me as a little child.

The Heder was held in the house of the Schacter family, which let out a room for the purpose of bringing in a little extra money. Some pupils would rise as early as 5.30 and study the Torah until 7.30, then attend the Czech school from 8 am until 1 pm and return to the Heder at 2 pm. Once Maxwell started at the Czech school, he went there in the morning and to the Heder in the late afternoon. The Heder was for boys only and the régime was strict. The cane was used with painful regularity and the punishment for being late for classes could be severe - children might, for example, be required to kneel on pebbles for up to 10 minutes to atone for their transgression.

But life for the youth of Solotvino was not always grim nor one of unremitting and everlasting study. The young Maxwell and other boys in the town played football with a rag ball on the sandy banks of the Tisza, just as children learned to play 2,000 miles away on the streets of Glasgow and London. Their games were the games of boys throughout the world: they threw stones aimlessly into the river, played hide and seek and, more dangerously, swam in the Tisza or balanced themselves on the timber which was floated down from the forests upriver. They made wooden skis for themselves for their winter sport and in summer picked mushrooms, blackberries and strawberries in woods less than a mile from town. Jewish children were not allowed to gather fruit with their fingers on the Sabbath, a restriction which they circumvented by climbing on each other's shoulders and biting the berries off straight into the mouth.

Gyorgy Bernat, a Budapest publisher and in later life a friend of Maxwell's, wrote of life in the Carpathians when both of them were young in his birthday tribute:

> The foothills we grew up on were a beautiful sight but the land was not open-handed. Trees were all that really grew; the summers were

short, and had to be made the most of. Very young we learned never
to put off until the following day whatever could be done that very
moment. We had to, in order to survive, regardless what trade one
was in: working on the land or in a tiny general store or making
deliveries with a one-horse carriage. It became a habit that has stayed
with Bob throughout his life. He keeps no working hours, for he sees
to everything as the need arises, no matter how much longer a
working day becomes....

* * * * *

In the second half of the eighteenth century a new popular
religious movement, Hasidism, began among the Jews living in the
extreme south-east of Poland and Lithuania. Its distinguishing
characteristics were described by the *Encyclopaedia Judaïca* as
"ecstasy, mass enthusiasm, close-knit group cohesion and
charismatic leadership" which led to a new outlook in social and
religious behaviour. That behaviour included a belief in mysticism,
magic, the seeing of visions and the working of miracles. Prayer was
loud as well as ecstatic, and involved song, body movements,
shaking and clapping. A melancholy mind is anathema to Hasidism
because it creates a barrier between man and God. Hasidic Jews
believed that a man should not grieve too much over his sins
because he might thus be brought into a state of melancholy, and
melancholy was a hindrance to God's service; a doctrine of comfort
to the troubled and, no doubt, convenient to the less high-minded.
The sorry condition of the Jews in the lands where Hasidism began
was, says the *Encyclopaedia*, "keenly felt by the hasidic masters who
considered it a duty of the highest order to alleviate their sufferings.
In the hasidic court, the wealthy were instructed to help their poorer
brethren; they learned not to look down upon their untutored
fellows."

The pattern of life for the early hasidic Jews was mostly ascetic;
many of them spent their days in seclusion, fasting and undergoing
self-mortification. The reaction of the established Jewish sects to its
coming was hostile: they denounced the miracles as delusions and
the faith in the ability of the leaders of Hasidism, the zaddikim,
to perform miraculous acts was proclaimed to be idolatrous.
Nevertheless, the new movement began to spread its appeal and
attracted more and more Jews to its ranks, especially in Belo-
Russia, Galicia and central Poland and, later, in Hungary after
Galicia was incorporated into the Austro-Hungarian empire. By the
1830s Hasidism had ceased to be a persecuted sect and had become

the way of life for the majority of Jews in those areas of Eastern Europe.

During the First World War the regions where Hasidism was strongest became battlegrounds and many of its leaders fled to the big cities, never to return once the fighting was over. The most devastating blow to the movement was to be cut off from its Russian branch with the coming of the Soviet régime. But between the wars the Hasidim were, at times, the only section of the Jewish population of Eastern Europe carefully to maintain the traditions of dress, language and education. During the Holocaust all the hasidic centres in Eastern Europe were destroyed and most of their leaders murdered.

* * * * *

It was to the orthodox Hasidim, Mehel and Chanca Hoch, that Maxwell was born on June 10, 1923, the third child and the first son of a family which lived in the front room of the house of Grandfather Yankel's on Synagogue Street in the centre of Solotvino. The first of their children had been Gisl. She was born in 1919 but died within two years. The next child, another girl, Brana, was born in 1920. Tall and athletic, she was one of the three children to survive the war, even though she was imprisoned in the concentration camps, first at Mauthausen and then in Buchenwald. After reaching Britain in 1946 she settled in America, married an engineer, David Atkin, and had two children of her own, Helene and Michael. She died in 1972 from heart disease, a legacy of the camps.

A second son, Chamhersch, was born in 1925, two years after Maxwell, but in 1927 he succumbed to diphtheria, then commonly a fatal illness. Maxwell also contracted diphtheria when he was six years old; though he was desperately ill, he survived after his mother gave her only pillow in payment for the sleigh to take him to hospital in the middle of a winter's night.

The next daughter, Shenya, was born in 1926 and was, by all accounts, the glamour girl of the family, tall, like most of her family, dark and good-looking.

Sylvia, who also survived the Holocaust, was born in 1929. She, with Brana, was brought to Britain by her brother after the war and married Dennis Rosen, a biophysicist.

The last three children were two daughters, Zissel (born 1931) and Tzipporah (1933), and the youngest son, Itzak, born in 1940 after Maxwell had made his escape to the West.

The father of this large family, Mehel, was born in 1887, a casual labourer known, because of his extraordinary height - he was 6ft 5in - as Mehel der Lange, or Mehel the Tall. He was an industrious man when there was work to be done, but that was not often.

He scoured the surrounding countryside looking for employment, buying cattle for local butchers and receiving the skins in payment (never the meat - it wasn't kosher) for selling on to leather merchants. Mehel was thin, blue-eyed and handsome, but for a perpetually troubled face. He was known in Solotvino for his honesty and integrity, not universal attributes in a town in which up to 80 per cent of the population was engaged in cross-border smuggling.

Mehel had a brother, Lipman, a butcher in a nearby village, who fell out with his religious community and set up his own synagogue. For him, Mehel broke into the existing synagogue and removed the Torah so that Lipman's synagogue would became the official one, the first being unable to hold its services without the Jewish Book of Law. Despite this escapade, which Christians would regard as sacrilegious, Mehel was an upright man, morally as well as physically. But the family's driving force and dominant spirit was undoubtedly his wife, Chanca, six years his junior.

Chanca is remembered by those of her children and relatives who survived the Holocaust as an "intelligent, brainy and modern woman, shrewd and well-read and never without a book or a newspaper in her hand". She was also intensely interested in politics and current affairs, attending and intervening - a rare occurrence then for a woman - in community matters to such an extent that anyone in Solotvino, where everyone knew everyone else, who became excited over political issues was described as being "like Chanca". She was a member of the Czechoslovakian Social Democratic Party from its inception and her influence upon the son she and Mehel had named Lev (Ludvik in the Czechoslovakian translation) but addressed as Laiby - it was a Jewish tradition to call a child after a deceased relative and Maxwell was named after his grandfather, Abraham Leib - was as great as it is obvious. For her part, she never had any doubts about the future which awaited him. She told Lilly Goldstein, a relative in Solotvino who now lives in the United States:

My son Laiby will be famous some day. I just feel it and I know it.

She certainly did all she could for him, teaching him to read and
write when he was only four-and-a-half. Her first hope was that her
son would become a great rabbi, and shortly before his Barmitzvah
he was sent on the recommendation of Rabbi Teitelbaum to a
Yeshiva, a Jewish traditional academy devoted to the study of
rabbinic literature, in Sziget. There he lived in his Aunt Myriam's
house for a year until moving on in 1936 to a larger Yeshiva in
Bratislava, 380 miles from Solotvino. He remembers vividly today
that he was self-conscious about his patched clothing. He had no
money. Each day he went to a different house to be fed, in
accordance with Jewish tradition, an experience which may in part
account for the fact that he is a generous and open-handed host to
any casual visitor.

Patrick Leigh Fermor, who set out in December 1933 to walk
from Rotterdam to Constantinople, has described the Bratislava of
those days[7]:

> It was the outpost of a whole congeries of towns where far-wanderers
> had come to a halt, and the Jews, the most ancient and famous of
> them, were numerous enough to give a pronounced character to the
> town ... very early on, I singled out one of the many Jewish coffee
> houses.... There were rabbis in the café now and then, easily singled
> out by their long beards and beaver hats and by black overcoats down
> to their heels. Occasionally they were accompanied by Talmudic
> students ... who wore small skullcaps or black low-crowned hats with
> the wide brims turned up, and queer elf-locks trained into corkscrews
> which hung besides their ears....

Had Leigh Fermor arrived in Bratislava a couple of years later,
among the students with "elf-locks" might well have been the young
Maxwell.

After Slovakia became a "protectorate" of the Third Reich in
March 1939 he was compelled to leave Bratislava. But he had given
up his study in the previous summer, irked by the restrictions of the
school. It was clear that the rabbinate was not for him. In later life
he was to say that he was born a Jew, that he lived as a Jew and that
he would die as a Jew, but it was as a free-thinking, unideological
Jew that he started to feel his way in the world and became, while in
Bratislava, a youthful salesman of cheap jewellery.

Sylvia, one of Maxwell's two sisters to survive the war, wrote to
him in her tribute to his 60th birthday, saying:

> I have some early recollections of you when you returned home for
> visits from the Yeshiva in Bratislava. I remember your arrival home,
> probably only a few months after your first departure. We were still

living in grandfather's house. I suppose you were about 13 or 14 years old. This incident stuck in my memory because you came with the pockets of your overcoat stuffed with bead jewellery and trinkets which were, I think, your stock as a part-time travelling salesman. You were selling these things to make a little cash - perhaps the money which paid your fare home. Anyway, I remember this very clearly because you allowed me to choose one of the necklaces from your collection as a present for myself. In our impoverished family presents were unknown; the best I had experienced before then was a new dress or a pair of new shoes for important religious festivals. Your generosity made an impression upon me which has lasted nearly half a century.

The second incident I can remember is your arrival home on a subsequent visit from Bratislava some years later. We had by then moved into our own house in Nagyhely Utca [a quarter of Solotvino largely populated by Hungarians and Romanians]. Brana and I went to meet you at the station. When you got off the train we could barely recognise you; instead of the shy Yeshivabucher we expected, we saw in front of us a flashy young chap, the pre-war central European equivalent of a teddy boy.... No paiyes (sidelocks) but a stylish head of hair with all traces of the orthodox young scholar gone. We were amazed and worried about the effect your changed appearance would have on mother. All hopes of her favourite son becoming a great Rabbi would be shattered. We both advised you to call at a barber's on the way home to have your head shaved.... You asked us to calm down and leave to you the problem of meeting mother and explaining your changed personality. You were quite confident she would understand. I am afraid I do not remember the reunion between you and mother, but I assume you were forgiven because she continued to adore you.

In truth, his mother does appear to have been upset by the loss of his side-curls and his discarding of the kaftan. But Maxwell was shaking off Solotvino. He had seen the world outside and wanted to be more modern, a desire he shared with others boys in the town who had also travelled beyond its religious and geographical confines.

Sylvia, whose obedience to parental wishes was itself intermittent - she was, apparently, a tomboy who gave a lot of trouble, getting into fights and playing truant - records another incident concerning her brother. Though she would have been too young to have remembered it personally, it was recounted to her by other members of the family:

You decided to join in the then fashionable sport of jumping from the formidable Slatina-Sziget bridge into the rushing Tisza river. This was considered to be a very dangerous feat for first-class swimmers. It

remains a mystery how you escaped with your life because you could
not swim.

It was, she said, "a narrow escape from drowning". That was
barely surprising, seeing that Maxwell was only five at the time. He
recalls:

> I was watching the older boys jumping into the river and decided to
> emulate them and jump in myself, not knowing how to swim. I found
> myself being carried down the fast flowing river and I remember the
> thought coming into my mind that I was going to die. The next thing I
> knew I woke up. I had been fished out.

I asked Maxwell if he could remember why he had done such a
foolish thing. He shrugged and replied, "A dare, I suppose."

His mother, as ever, was forgiving. His father was not and gave
him a severe beating. It was probably no less than Maxwell himself
would have done to one of his own children; he draws a line
between love and indulgence.

* * * * *

Grandfather Yankel's house was similar to those of the peasants
of Northern Russia, wooden with a verandah and looking out on to
a courtyard containing a well - an enviable amenity in a small town
where most people drew their water from a pump in the street.

Yankel was a proud man, like his son-in-law an occasional cattle
dealer but, unlike Mehel, a busybody who enjoyed contradicting
others and short-tempered with passers-by who dared take a
short-cut across the grass in front of his home. On the other hand,
he was also a good and generous man who fed beggars and allowed
them to sleep in his house after his daughter and her family moved
out in 1937; he always brought someone home to dinner on a
Friday.

He was also very religious, rising at 4 am to go to the synagogue.
His eldest grandchild, Martin Tabak, son of Chanca's sister, recalls
staying with him one winter and both sleeping in a bedroom where
the windows were broken. He woke one morning to find his
grandfather's beard encrusted with frost and ice and thought,
mistakenly, that Yankel was dead. Later, the Hochs' eldest
daughter, Brana, moved in with her grandfather to look after him.
If he had more money than the Hochs it was probably because he
was engaged, like so many other Solotvinians, in the smuggling
trade and his home was sometimes used as a hiding place for

contraband alcohol, a practice which was to lead to an unhappy experience for the young Maxwell. He says:

> The smugglers had an arrangement to store the alcohol in tins behind a cupboard in our one room. Part of the "fee" was paid in alcohol to my grandfather. Unusually, I found myself alone in the room and picked up a mug which was half-full of alcohol and I drank some of it. I was later found in the gutter by the gendarmerie and brought home at 3 am, sick as a puppy, and beaten within an inch of my life by my father. From that day until I found myself facing a Tiger tank in the Orne bridgehead in 1944 I could not smell alcohol without feeling sick.

The floor of the Hoch family's room was earthen and Chanca cooked on a black, wood-burning stove whose flue went straight up and out through the roof. There was no oven - bread was baked at the communal bakery and then only for the Sabbath. The Hochs all ate, slept and washed in the same room, though there was a communal bath nearby for the use of men and boys and the Mikvah, which Jewish women were obliged to use to purify themselves after menstruation. Like other families in Solotvino, their staple diet consisted of maize purées and potatoes and, rarely, and only on religious days, a chicken. Once a year a goose would be killed and no part of it was ever wasted: the skin would be roasted, the fat would be stored and the meat not immediately eaten would be preserved in the fat. Mehel and Chanca could not afford to buy "full" milk and drank only skimmed, or milk watered down. Clothes were rarely, if ever, bought; the growing number of Hoch children were dressed in hand-me-downs, respectable, but patched. There were other, more pressing, difficulties in the regular arrival of a new baby Hoch. The family's room contained only two beds - one for the parents and one for the children. The older children would sleep up to five in a bed and the babies would lie in cots suspended from the ceiling. In a shack at the back of the house was the lavatory, typical of its time and era - i.e. a hole in planks of wood spanning a pit. Gipsies would call every year to empty the pit and spread the manure on the gardens, not a practice which would be recommended by modern horticulturists.

Because of their poverty, the Hochs were unable to follow the practice of some other Jewish families of employing a Gentile to do domestic work on the Sabbath. Their Sabbath occupations were confined to walking and going to the synagogue. Those at the synagogue were well aware of the family's plight and Sylvia Rosen recalls that they would be given beans, flour and sugar for the High religious holidays.

In 1936 things began to look up for the Hochs. Uncle Nathan, Chanca's brother, returned from the United States, where he had successfully started a laundry business, to visit his relatives in Solotvino. He was so moved and distressed at the plight and poverty of his sister's family that he gave her five hundred dollars so that they could buy their own home. This they did in the next year, moving into a two-roomed house with a garden-cum-orchard on a hillside at the back of it, which they extensively planted with potatoes, beans, onions, cabbages and maize. The Hochs were even able to keep a few geese, though it was not until after Maxwell left home that they reached the level of affluence which enabled them to own a goat. They were never well off enough to buy a cow. Chanca and Mehel Hoch thought they had found paradise.

Chanca still had to cook on a black wood-burning stove, but now she had an oven and the floor was made of wood. There was even a second oven for baking bread. The only inconvenience was the lack of a nearby well; water had to be drawn from a pump some way down the street. Lighting was by paraffin lamp but, according to Jewish custom, at least two candles were lighted for the Sabbath day. One Maxwell cousin said that Friday was the "nicest" day of the week, the day when the mother of the family would start baking bread at 4 am and setting the table with a candle for each child when it could be afforded.

Sylvia remembers the new house well, but by the time the Hochs moved in Maxwell had started on his travels to Bratislava and then to Budapest and today he has only the barest recollection of it.

Physically, he is remembered as being powerfully built, even chubby, despite the chronically poor diet. He is also described in phrases which strike a chord of authenticity today - "lively", "mischievous" and "well able to look after himself" as well as "quick to learn". His football was characterised as "aggressive". Those who can recall playing with him said he liked to play at centre-forward. He says he was a left-winger, which suggests his political leanings have conquered his sporting memory. His build is not that of an outside left and nor is it his inclination to be out of the thick of things.

The accounts of Maxwell's early life all dwell on his voracious appetite for reading and for politics. His cousin, Michael Tabak, who went with him to Budapest in 1939, says that one day Maxwell cannoned into him in the streets, unseeing, his nose buried in a book. Having gone to the Hungarian capital to find work, he seems to have spent most of his time in public reading rooms. Another recollection is of his visiting a further cousin during a bitter Czechoslovakian winter and finding her reading a book. He took it from her - a peremptory manner was evident even then - and read it outside the house, even though the snow was lying waist-high.

Politically, he was intervening in Zionist meetings in Solotvino when he was only 12. He joined the Betar, a religious movement but also a para-military organisation which went on training exercises and made preparations for going to Israel. War, military training, coups, new political movements, anti-semitism and territorial ambition were part of the fabric of pre-war Europe. That another Great War was inevitable was felt deep in the bones of countless millions of ordinary people throughout the continent, even if so many of their national leaders remained insensitive or impervious to the threat up to the moment when the guns started to fire.

* * * * *

Maxwell was still three months off his 16th birthday when the dismemberment of the Czechoslovak republic was completed and with it Europe set irrevocably upon the path to war. The betrayal of that nation, first at Munich in September 1938 and finally in March 1939, was to condemn a continent and then a world to war and to see, through a policy of genocide, the destruction of a substantial part of the Jewish race, including the majority of it which lived in Europe. No Jew who escaped the Holocaust - and Maxwell was one of the few who not only escaped but prospered - can ever forget what happened to the less fortunate. In Maxwell's family, both his parents, his grandfather, three sisters and a brother, as well as numerous aunts, uncles, cousins and boyhood friends, were to die either by the bullet or in the gas chamber. The scars left are permanent and deep and no account of his life would be complete without at least a brief rehearsal of the political and military events which unfolded during the crises and ended the existence of free, democratic Czechoslovakia.

The seeds of war and the Holocaust were sown when the Hungarian state was virtually dismantled by the victorious Allies under the 1920 Treaty of Trianon. It had to cede Transylvania to Romania, part of Croatia to Yugoslavia, border areas of Galicia and Slovakia to Poland and 61,000 square kilometres of its territory in Slovakia and Sub-Carpathian Ruthenia to Czechoslovakia. In addition, further small areas of land were transferred to Austria and to Italy. The consequence was that the boundaries of Hungary were reduced by two-thirds and its population cut from 20,886,000 in 1910 to 7,615,000 in 1920. The size of Hungary's armed forces was reduced to 35,000 and they were restricted to duties on the frontier and internal order.

Like the Treaty of Versailles, the principal treaty to reshape Europe following the 1914-18 war, the Treaty of Trianon was to nurture the grievances, grudges and territorial ambitions which produced the conditions for a further, even more horrific, conflict within less than a generation. Every Hungarian administration from 1920 onwards regarded the peace settlement as intolerably hard and unjust. It totally dislocated Hungary's economy and caused extreme hardship; even in the climate of victory, the Allies were unfair: a million Magyars were among the people placed under the rule of Czechoslovakia. When the time came, the increasingly fascist-minded Hungarian régime of Admiral Miklos Horthy, its Regent, was to be a willing and enthusiastic tool of Hitler's demolition of Czechoslovak independence. Most of all, it wanted to recover the land in Ruthenia which it had lost and Hitler was to give it to them. Ruthenia was a sprat to catch a jackal.

After recovering the Rhineland and swallowing Austria, Hitler actively began to seek the subjugation of Czechoslovakia throughout the spring and summer of 1938. By a carefully calculated and cynical raising of international tension, he created a crisis over the Sudeten German minority in Czechoslovakia. Incidents of "brutality" against them were manufactured until the moment was ripe for the Fuehrer to proclaim that his patience was exhausted. On September 15, 1938 Neville Chamberlain, the British Prime Minister, flew to Berchtesgarden to confer with the German Chancellor to see whether the gathering storm could be abated. From Britain, Chamberlain's journey was seen as a mission to preserve peace. From Berlin, it was seen as an appeasing gift from a nation which had lost its nerve. Chamberlain agreed that the Sudetenland should be ceded to the Third Reich, a generosity with another nation's sovereignty which was not immediately welcomed or appreciated by the Czechoslovak Government.

On September 19 joint Anglo-French proposals for concessions by Czechoslovakia were put to Prague and firmly rejected the next day by the Government of President Edvard Beneš, which was, however, willing to accept arbitration. The British and French, who had been so anxious to placate a powerful country which was their potential enemy, reacted toughly to the spirited stand of a small one which was their ally and friend. The Czech Government was told that same evening that unless it complied with the Allied request, Britain and France would abandon Czechoslovakia - to whom the French, at least, were bound by treaty obligations, while Britain was bound similarly to France with all the consequences that implied - and leave it to its fate.

Beneš was ready to defy the aggressor, but in the event he capitulated to his protectors and accepted the Anglo-French proposals.

On September 22 Chamberlain flew to see Hitler once more, this time at the Hotel Dresden at Bad Godesberg, on the Rhine near Bonn. He told Hitler that the British, French and Czech Governments were now ready to cede the Sudetenland to Germany without a plebiscite. "I am sorry", said Hitler, "but after the events of the past few days, this plan is no longer of any use"[8].

The crisis deepened. Chamberlain returned to England and Europe prepared for war. Then, at the apparent instigation of the Italian fascist dictator, Mussolini, a last-gasp conference was held at Munich on September 29 between Hitler, Mussolini, Chamberlain and the French premier, Edouard Daladier.

The Czechs were not even allowed to be present in the conference room while the fate of their country was decided. It was left to the four powers to agree that German troops should begin the occupation of the Sudetenland on October 1. Czech property there would be sequestrated without compensation. All the main fortifications against a possible German attack were within the 11,000 square miles of territory which the Czechs were to be forced to give up, leaving them defenceless should the Germans come again. Czechoslovakia lost two-thirds of its coal, 86 per cent of its chemicals, 70 per cent of its iron and steel and electric power and 40 per cent of its timber. It was effectively crippled economically and militarily. Mr Chamberlain returned home to announce, amid acclamation, "peace in our time" and Winston Churchill said, with little support, the Allies had sustained "a total and unmitigated defeat". Even he, however, could not have fully comprehended what was to follow for the peoples of Europe, especially the Jews.

Hitler had told Chamberlain that he wanted "no Czechs at all" and that, after the Sudetenland issue had been resolved, Germany had no "territorial ambitions in Europe". To prove it, the Munich Agreement said that the four big European powers would guarantee the international frontiers of Czechoslovakia, as amended. (The victim of the Agreement was now officially renamed Czecho-Slovakia, the hyphen indicating that Slovakia, whose leaders were admirers of Hitler, had been granted substantial autonomy.) There was, however, one crucial condition to the promise of guarantees by Germany and Italy. It would only operate, according to Article 1, "when the question of the Polish minorities and the Hungarian minorities in Czechoslovakia has been settled". Poland had, in fact, taken the opportunity of the crisis to seize the district of Teschen, a small area of some 625 square kilometres in which 230,000 people, most of them of Polish origin, lived. That seemingly left only Hungary's claims outstanding as an obstacle to what Chamberlain prophesied would be "an era of peace".

The Czechoslovakian Foreign Minister, Frantisek Chvalkovsky, and his Hungarian counterpart, Kalman Kanya, quickly began talks and negotiated fruitlessly for four days before agreeing to put their cases before the "independent" arbitration of Joachim von Ribbentrop, the German Foreign Minister, and Count Galeazzo Ciano, Italy's Foreign Minister and Mussolini's son-in-law, meeting in Vienna. Their decision, after Ciano had at least made an effort to be fair to the Czechs - not being aware of what Hitler really intended - was "to allot to Hungary those territorial zones which otherwise could well have become the objects of numerous bitter disputes"[9]. The "arbitration" gave Hungary everything it wanted, except Sub-Carpathian Ruthenia, which it wanted most of all. The districts ceded covered an area of 7,500 square miles and contained a population of 775,000. It left Czecho-Slovakia with only one city on the Danube and that the semi-autonomous Slovakian capital, Bratislava. The Hungarians were furious and, reputedly, Hitler and Mussolini were hard put to prevent them from seizing Ruthenia by force, though it is difficult to believe that a nation whose leader a short while before had been afraid of Britain and France taking action to defend Czechoslovakia would have had the temerity to defy Hitler.

In fact, throughout all the Czechoslovakian crises, Admiral Horthy was a willing Hungarian puppet on the German string. On August 23, while the situation was still simmering, Hitler had entertained Horthy and members of his government during naval exercises at Kiel. He told his guests that if they wanted to join in the division of Czechoslovakia they had better act quickly. "He who wants to sit at the table", he told them, "must at least help in the kitchen."[10] The Hungarians were only too willing; their only concern was that the Allies would intervene with force against them.

Once it was apparent they had nothing to fear from that quarter, they were Hitler's enthusiastic helpmates.

On September 20, five days after he had first seen Chamberlain, Hitler had received the Hungarian Prime Minister, Bela Imredy, and his Foreign Minister. A German Foreign Office memorandum at the time recorded that "the Fuehrer reproached the Hungarian gentlemen for the undecided attitude of Hungary"[11], which hardly suggests that those gentlemen would have to be forcibly restrained from being foolhardy barely two months later. He assured them that "neither England nor France would intervene" and, he told them, in the words of the memorandum:

> It was Hungary's last opportunity to join in. If she did not, he would not be in a position to put in a word for Hungarian interests. In his opinion, the best thing would be to destroy Czechoslovakia.

The Czechs had been unable to do anything but accept the arbitration of Vienna, but they did ask that now the new frontiers had been decided the Munich guarantees against future changes in them should be put into effect by Germany and Italy. No, said Berlin, not until the new frontiers have been delineated by a commission appointed to the task. That process was completed by late November and the Czechs renewed their request. There was no response. In December the French Ambassador to Berlin asked on behalf of his Government that the guarantees so solemnly promised at Munich should now come into force. All he met was evasion.

What neither he nor his Government, nor the British Government, were aware of - though even they might have begun to suspect the truth of the matter - was that on October 21, 1938 Hitler had ordered the Wehrmacht, in an official Directive, to prepare for the final liquidation "of the remainder of Czechoslovakia". Indeed, only two days after the Munich Agreement, Hitler had asked General (later Field-Marshal) Keitel of the OKW, the German High Command, how much time and how much military strength he estimated would be needed to subdue the rest of Czechoslovakia. Keitel replied, succinctly, that it wouldn't take much time or much effort.

By January Hitler had renewed his intimidation of Czechoslovakia, demanding that its army be reduced to 10,000 or 20,000 men. By March the rebellious Slovakians had become too much for the Czech President, the ageing Dr Emil Hacha, who had succeeded Dr Beneš in the previous October. Hacha bravely dismissed the pro-German Prime Minister, Jozef Tiso, and two of his Ministers and occupied Bratislava with Government troops.

But though it was courageous, it gave Hitler a pretext for his final demolition of Czechoslovakia. There is no doubt, however, that he would have acted without one if it had not been forthcoming. Germany had a growing disdain for the need internationally to justify its actions. On March 10 the Fuehrer sent an ultimatum to Prague; on March 13 he summoned Tiso and told him that the situation had become "intolerable" and that he intended to settle it "once and for all". It was no longer a question of days, he added, but of hours. Ribbentrop intervened to tell Tiso that the German Government had information that Hungary was moving troops up to the Slovakian border. What he did not say was that the troops were not aimed against Slovakia but against Ruthenia and that the operation had been instigated and organised from Berlin. The proposal that Hungary should start its army on the march had been put to Horthy only that morning and it had been received by him "with enthusiasm", though he had wanted to delay the action for a week because his troops were not ready. But when he was told a delay did not suit Hitler's plan, Horthy gave the orders to his army.

On March 14 the Slovakian parliament in Bratislava, fearful of the Hungarian invasion about which Ribbentrop had hinted, declared that Slovakia was an independent state and asked for Hitler's "protection", a request to which he graciously acceded, seeing that it cost him nothing as the threat was a fiction. On the same day Sub-Carpathian Ruthenia, under a new president, Mr Volosin, followed Bratislava's example and declared its independence; it, too, asked for Hitler's "protection". But in this instance there was a brusque refusal and Berlin told Mr Volosin to forget any ideas he might have of resistance.

Meanwhile, Hitler was in Berlin meeting, at their request, President Hacha and Foreign Minister Chvalkovsky, who were making one last desperate attempt to salvage something from the wreck of their country. Hitler told them he now wanted nothing less than the complete surrender of Czech sovereignty. "This is no time for negotiations", he said. "It is time to take note of the irrevocable decisions of the German Government."

At 1.30 am on March 15 - the Ides of March - he told Hacha that the Wehrmacht had orders to begin the occupation of Bohemia and Moravia at 6.30 am. If there were any resistance, Prague would be destroyed by 800 German bombers. Hacha was 70 and suffering from severe heart trouble. Indeed, several times during the night and early hours he collapsed. Shortly before 4 pm he lost consciousness altogether, causing the Germans their one moment of panic - they feared that if Hacha died they would be accused of murdering him, which would have been ironic, for it was the one crime of which they would have been innocent. However, Hitler's doctor, Theodor Morell, successfully revived Hacha to a sufficient state of health for him to sign the agreement which effectively ended his nation.

Germany marched that morning and met no resistance. Hungary's army moved into Ruthenia almost at the same time and formally annexed it on the 16th, the day on which Horthy originally intended to stage a frontier incident which would justify an invasion. It wasn't necessary. The Czechoslovakia born in 1920 was dead. The death of most of its Jews was to follow. Munich had made that inevitable.

* * * * *

Robert Maxwell was in Bratislava in March 1939 with his cousin, Martin, still trying to earn a living as a salesman of trinkets. They both had to leave. Maxwell went first to Solotvino and then in the summer, as he reached his 16th birthday, walked the 275 miles to Budapest, seeking work, and living as a vagrant on the way. In the Hungarian capital he was befriended by a member of the banned youth group, SOKOL; thus began the bizarre series of events which were to lead to his arrival in England a year later.

Maxwell was taken by his new acquaintance to a meeting in the cellar of the French consulate in Budapest where, in effect, he was recruited into the underground movement which was helping volunteers for a free Czech Army to escape to the West. His first task was to go to the main Budapest railway station and buy tickets to various towns in Hungary. He then had to return to the cellar and give the tickets to a man - whose name he cannot now remember - from whom he had received the money. After a month the man told Maxwell he would accompany him on a train to the border with Yugoslavia. The younger man had to purchase food and drink at the stations on the route and his companion would then pass it to other men scattered along the length of the train. After he had performed this duty for four or five trips, Maxwell was "promoted" to looking out for the gendarmes who examined travellers' papers before the border was reached and another boy was taken along to buy the food. By now Hitler had invaded Poland on September 1 and war with Britain and France had begun. Maxwell says he was well paid to buy food; it wasn't a wage but, nevertheless, he hadn't previously eaten so well. The inevitable disaster struck in December 1939. The escape route and the escapers were betrayed to the Hungarian police by the guide who was supposed to lead them to safety in Yugoslavia.

Maxwell and the other men were arrested at the border, taken back to Budapest and accused of spying. For four months he was kept in a window-less cell manacled hand and foot and beaten by day or by night with rubber truncheons and bicycle chains, three Hungarian policemen taking it in turn to interrogate him. One blow across the face broke his nose; today he can barely breathe through his right nostril. The questions never varied:

Who had recruited him?

How much was he paid?

Who were the French officers who were helping the escapers?

Who was going to meet them in Yugoslavia?

Maxwell repeatedly said he knew nothing, which was almost the truth, for he knew very little.

After some weeks he was informed that he had been tried under military emergency powers regulations and had been sentenced to death, though he had made no appearance before a court or a military tribunal. He was asked if he wished to appeal and he said he did. The French embassy in Budapest, which was looking after Czechoslovakia's interests in Hungary and which seems to have been more staunch in defending the freedom of Czechs than France's Government had been earlier in the year, protested to Admiral Horthy that Maxwell had been wrongly tried under the articles of war because he was under 18 and a minor. A trial was ordered and Maxwell was due to appear in court in January 1940.

His guard in a van taking him to his trial was an old soldier who had lost his arm in the First World War. Maxwell was handcuffed, but his feet were free. He brought his manacles down upon his veteran escort's head and escaped. He has been quoted in the past as saying that he may have killed the man, but he doesn't believe that he did, he only knocked him out. He hid under a bridge where his handcuffs were removed from his wrists by "a gipsy lady", though he says that to this day he doesn't know how she did it. He then jumped a train - the one he had regularly taken before his arrest - which took him from Budapest to the Yugoslavian border, made his way across where he got a lift to Belgrade and went to the

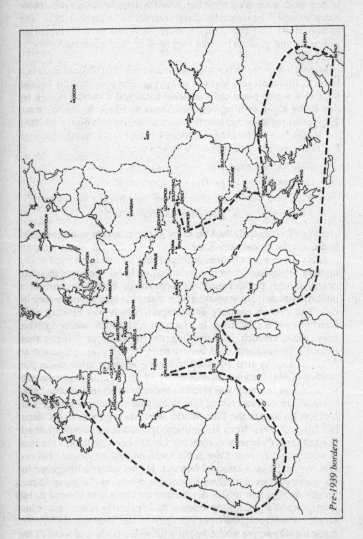

Maxwell's escape route.

French consulate there, joining another group of young Czechs intent on reaching the West. He told me:

> I then went on to Sofia and across Bulgaria by train organised by the French, and along the escape route of Salonika, Istanbul (Haydar Paşa, the Asian part of the city with a magical view across the Bosphorus) and Aleppo, all third-class travel on wooden seats. In Syria we were camped in the French Foreign Legion barracks, given food and eventually sent on what seemed an endless journey to Beirut where we stayed in a Foreign Legion camp. For the first time in my life I was given a wine and cigarette ration. I touched neither. Then we boarded ship for Marseilles.

That was in March 1940. Ever since the previous October, Czech volunteers for the Foreign Legion had been assembling at a military camp at Agde-sur-Mer, near Marseilles, and groups of young Czechs continued to arrive there until May. Maxwell had joined the Legion after lying about his age (he was not 17 until June 10, during the thick of the fighting). After the German invasion of the Low Countries on May 10, the Allied military situation rapidly became desperate; new recruits were being sent to the front almost immediately upon arrival at the camp.

The Czech forces in France at the time of the German offensive totalled some 10,000 men and were formed into the 1st Czech Division. Maxwell was transferred to it from the Legion. On June 6 the French Supreme Command ordered two of the division's infantry regiments, 5,200 men in all, to the front. The second of the regiments was incorporated into the French 239th Division and sent to defend a crossing of the River Marne near L'Ourcq and La Ferté sous Jouarre. At first the Czechs were successful in stopping the Germans; but nowhere in France were defences holding for long. The commander of the 239th soon ordered it to retreat and the men marched 100 kilometres to Vilbert-Rozoy where they entrained to the Loire and occupied defensive positions near Orléans until June 18. Before joining the division Maxwell had been hurriedly trained as a machine gunner in the sidecar of a motorcycle, and he was a private in a motorised brigade dispatched to assist his fellow-countrymen in the battle for Orléans. He was slightly wounded in the knee by shrapnel, but not badly enough to keep him out of the line. For a few hours during the thick of the fighting he was captured by the Germans, but in the confusion of battle he easily made his escape.

The actual fighting for Maxwell lasted only two or three days. The

German advance on the Loire, as everywhere else that summer, was irresistible and the Czechs continued to fall back before being marched to Sète, near Marseilles.

Many of the soldiers arriving there were bitter at what they claimed was the desertion of their officers while the battle was at its height. That desertion was to have its consequences soon afterwards when the remnants of the division reached Britain.

Winston Churchill's Government had promised Dr Beneš, who was heading the Czech Government in exile, that any Czech units which wanted to fight on would be evacuated, and four Royal Navy ships and three Egyptian transports were waiting off-shore to embark them.

Maxwell told me:

> I was then offered by a United States vice-consul, through an interpreter, the chance of a scholarship in the United States. The interpreter said, "Your Government says you are a bright young man and so you can be educated and, after the war, help in the reconstruction of your country." I said that I had heard that Churchill had said on the radio that England would carry on the war against Germany. I said I wanted to fight the Germans. The vice-consul said everyone would give their right arms to go to America and that I was a fool.

Only about 4,000 Czech servicemen reached Sète in time to be evacuated and only 1,600 of those who had been fighting were among them. The rest were part of a formation which had never been at the front. The fate of those left behind was dire. The German High Command had issued a directive that Czechs captured while fighting for the Allies were to be shot. Any identified as Jews were to be handed over to the Gestapo for execution, which was as certain as shooting but not likely to be as swift. This order remained in force throughout the war, which is why Private Hoch adopted British pseudonyms several times before finally settling upon Maxwell in 1945.

Maxwell was taken aboard a British destroyer where he was given white bread - the first time in his life that he had tasted it - Gold Flake cigarettes, and tea and marmalade before being transferred to the *Mohamed-el-Kebir*, one of the Egyptian ships pressed into service as a troop transport (and later in the war to be sunk by a U-boat). The voyage from Sète to Liverpool, via Gibraltar, took almost two weeks. Maxwell arrived on Merseyside in the last week of July - "with a rifle in my hand", he says; "I wasn't a refugee" -

wearing French Army uniform and not knowing a word of English, not even "Goodbye."

* * * * *

Though he never realised it at the time, a new life was beginning. He was never to live in Czechoslovakia again and only once was he to visit Solotvino.

Maxwell wrote in 1968:

> I was born in that part of Czechoslovakia which was pinched from Hungary by the Treaty of Versailles and has now been pinched by the Russians from the Czechs.

For many years after the war he tried to go back to see his birthplace, if only to exorcise the memories of his poverty and to find out what he could about the people he had known. The Soviet authorities persistently refused permission. Maxwell asked Nikita Kruschev personally to allow him to return, but the Soviet leader refused, his veto apparently stemming from the fact that an attempt on his life was once made in Solotvino. Eventually, Kruschev's successor, Leonid Brezhnev, relented and Maxwell made the journey in September 1978, together with his wife Betty. Mrs Maxwell noted in her diary written for her children:

> We were extremely privileged and honoured guests of the Soviet Union, for no foreigners were allowed nearer than three miles from the border and certainly not in that area [access was restricted, apparently, because it was now a sensitive military zone]. They say it has been worked out that Solotvino is the very centre of Europe. What I saw was a grey landscape, very flat with some low, undulating hills [and] far away high mountains to the right in Romania and a long, straggling village. I was pointed out the shaft of the modern salt mine, then modern, low, indifferent houses; all, I was told proudly … had been built in the last twelve years. I thought it could not be Daddy's village … then after about two miles we made a complete U-turn and retraced our steps lower down. I could then see some older buildings and sparsely built houses on a generally sloping landscape down to the Tisza river.

The chairman of the local Soviet welcomed the Maxwells and said he would not find the village he knew; it had all been rebuilt. But after visiting the new salt mine and a new hospital, they finally reached the old and poorer part of Solotvino where Maxwell had once lived. Mrs Maxwell recorded:

> (We passed) old wooden log houses (and) a biggish courtyard which

had once been the market place, then some more wooden houses. In that street there were only houses on the right side. The left was the top of a swift falling slope which ran down to the Tisza river and the Romanian border.... (Maxwell) walked up very determinedly to where the house of his grandfather was. There he met a Romanian man of about his own age but who looked twenty years older. They had a chat ... and the man said, "I know who you are; I recognised you when you arrived at the town hall. I thought it was you. I was at school with you." Then all of a sudden these two men hugged each other. He explained that the shack which had been Daddy's house [Yankel's] had been demolished and that the synagogue at the back had been turned into a bakery and that the street which had been a cul-de-sac had been opened, which was why the house proper could not be found. The houses were old, made of wood and all looking as poor as in Daddy's time. The streets were muddy and, really, in that corner of the world nothing had really changed....

Despite meeting one old face, the visit was a disappointment and an anti-climax. He knew no one else and he recognised very little. Now he has no desire to go back there again. Certainly, he has never regretted his leaving.

Immediately after Solotvino, the Maxwells were guests at a dinner in Novosibirsk, Siberia, to celebrate a British Week there. The Russian Minister who was among the guests toasted Maxwell and several other Britons present, including the British Ambassador to the Soviet Union, Sir Curtis Keeble, and Sir Fitzroy Maclean, soldier, author, diplomat and former Conservative MP for North Ayrshire and Bute. Referring to the fact that Maxwell's home town was now part of the territory of the USSR, the host said that Great Britain's gain had been the Soviet Union's loss. Maclean interrupted to ask what would have happened to Maxwell had he stayed in Czechoslovakia after the war. The Minister said that he thought Maxwell would be living not far away from where they were at that moment - i.e. Siberia. But whether he would have been above or below ground, the Minister said, he was not prepared to offer an opinion.

* * * * *

It was the singular fate of the Jews of Czechoslovakia and Hungary to have been the victims of two of the most evil men in the history of mankind, compared with whom the Goths and the Vandals and the Mongolian hordes of Genghis Khan were innocents abroad. Reinhard Heydrich, Heinrich Himmler's No. 2, and Adolf

Eichmann, the most infamous mass murderer the world has ever known, were the originators and executors of what is now known as the Holocaust, whose purpose was to exterminate all the Jews of Europe and which, in large part, succeeded.

Auschwitz, in the Polish province of Galicia, was one of the most notorious of the concentration camps where millions of Jews were experimented upon, gassed and hideously cremated during the operation of the "final solution". It was established on the orders of Himmler in 1940 and staffed by German criminals. It was comparatively small and held only a few Jews until 1941, when an extensive range of wooden barracks was built and called Birkenau or Auschwitz II, though "Auschwitz" is the name commonly applied to both.

The decision to begin the extermination of the Jews was, apparently, on the suggestion of Heydrich, and the commandant of Auschwitz was instructed by Himmler in June 1941 - the month when Hitler attacked Russia and Hungary entered the war on his side - to start the preparations for their systematic mass murder. How many died there in the end is unknown. The number of registered inmates who were murdered in the camp was 261,000, but the vast majority were unregistered. The figure for the period between February 1942 and November 1944 is believed to be about one million Jews and 250,000 others, mainly Poles, but including some gipsies[12].

The mass murder of Hungarian Jews was masterminded by Eichmann, but it did not begin until late in the war, well after he had set about the destruction of the Jewish community in Czechoslovakia. That began in earnest after two Czechs, dropped near Prague by the RAF, had assassinated Heydrich in the summer of 1942. First, there was the atrocity at Lidice, a village outside the capital, where all the men and youths over 16 were cold-bloodedly murdered; then virtually all Czech Jews were rounded up and consigned to their deaths.

Among those who died in Auschwitz were Maxwell's beloved mother, Chanca, her three youngest children, Zissel, Tzipporah and Itzak, and Grandfather Yankel. They were in the first convoy to leave Solotvino for Auschwitz. The second convoy took Jews, including some of the Hoch family's relatives, from the surrounding villages who had been brought into the ghetto at Solotvino. Just how and when Mehel died is unclear. He is believed to have been shot, though whether immediately on arrival at Auschwitz or some time afterwards is not known.

Maxwell was told after the war that his father had been seen and he went to Prague in 1945 with authority to bring him out if he could find him, but there was no trace. Another report said that his father was one of the victims of a ship which went down in the Baltic soon after the war's end, but that rumour was no more substantial than any of the others. There is no reason why the Germans should have treated Mehel any differently from all the other male, middle-aged Jews they rounded up. Mehel's most likely fate is that he did not survive his wife and family for long, if at all, though able-bodied Jews were often "selected" to labour for the German forces and were not killed until they were too exhausted to be of any further use.

The Solotvino ghetto was established in the lower part of the town, between the river and the first hill, where most of the town's Jews lived. The war years had made life even more unbearable for them; there was no flour for bread and they had to grind peas and beans to make an ersatz form of it. But life in the ghetto was even worse because of the overcrowding. There was little or no food except for those who were able to pay the Romanians to smuggle it in.

There was a strict 5 pm curfew. No one was allowed to leave home for any reason, even to go to the lavatory. Two young girls who attempted to do so were thrashed by Hungarian soldiers who said they would beat them "until the ocean split and Moses could come across it".

After a month in the ghetto, the Jews, some 4,000 in all and mostly near starving, were put into the convoys for Auschwitz. They were rounded up on May 20, 1944 - the Sabbath - marched to the station, packed into cattle trucks and departed the next day. The second convoy left three days later. The first train to Auschwitz arrived at midnight on Tuesday, May 23. The Jews had been packed in, 70 to a wagon, with two pails - one for water and one for slops - and two loaves of bread to each wagon. They were told that they were going to work as labourers upon the farms.

On arrival at the camp, the older men and women and the children were separated from the able men and women. The "weak" were taken immediately to the gas chamber. It is certain that Chanca, Zissel, Tzipporah, Itzak and Yankel were murdered in the early hours of Wednesday, May 24. Laishu, a first cousin of Maxwell who survived the camp, has told him so. Her own mother and four brothers and sisters died with the Hochs that day.

Shenya, Brana and Sylvia were all working in Budapest at the time of the round-up of their family in Solotvino. Brana was arrested outside the railway station, where she had gone to see Sylvia safely aboard a train to Solotvino, and sent to Mauthausen concentration camp and subsequently to Buchenwald. Sylvia was dragged off the train, but was able to escape being shipped to a camp and sheltered in a Red Cross home in Budapest. Among the other children there were three from Romania. When their mother collected them in January 1945 she took Sylvia with her to help with the children on the journey back home and then invited her to stay until the war had ended.

Shenya was employed as a nanny/housekeeper by a Gentile actress in the Hungarian capital and she carried Gentile papers. But eventually, she, too, was arrested on the streets of the city in the winter of 1944, in the last round-up of the Jews, disappeared and was never heard of again. She most likely suffered the fate of other Jews seized at the same time: they were roped together, hands tied behind backs, and thrown over the parapet of the bridges across the Danube. The only alternative was to be shot on the spot. An article by an Auschwitz survivor, Isabella Leitner, graphically described how her own sister died in Budapest:

> They marched her, tied to 400 other Jews, from her building. They marched them naked, in the middle of the night, in the winter ... and they shot them into the Danube. And they did it the next day, and the next, and the next....

Sylvia wrote to Maxwell in 1983:

> Brana and I returned home after the war to see what was left of the family. Brana came from the concentration camp in Buchenwald and I came from Romania. By good fortune we arrived in Slatina (Solotvino) at the same time, which made our return less painful than it might have been. At least the two of us had survived and we were optimistic that you were safe and well with the British Army. With our house ransacked and derelict and our field and orchard handed over to our Hungarian neighbours by the Russian authorities, we could see no future for us in Slatina. We had to look for a new country and a new home.

The first thought of the sisters was to make their way to Palestine and they travelled, with a number of other young Jewish survivors, through Hungary, Austria and Germany under the auspices of the United Nations Relief and Rehabilitation Administration (UNRRA). But before leaving Europe they decided to try to find their brother. Sylvia says that a "bush telegraph" system grew up among refugees which helped in tracing missing persons. They enquired continually about their brother and at last found someone from Solotvino who had seen him in Prague - searching for them.

After Sylvia became seriously ill with septicaemia in a camp near Munich, Brana decided to make a determined effort to find Maxwell. She travelled to Berlin in November 1945 to ask at British Army Headquarters there if anyone knew anything of his whereabouts. Astonishingly, they did: She was told he was an Interrogation Officer at the Intelligence Corps HQ at Bad Salzuflen, near Iserlohn. Brana found him there. Maxwell boarded his sisters at the home of a German family, the Bruchs, in Graz, where his regiment was stationed, until he got permission for them to enter Britain eight months later. In return for their "hospitality", Maxwell kept the Bruchs supplied with coffee and food at a time when the average German ration was below the level which had been authorised by the Nazis for concentration camp inmates. Sylvia told Maxwell:

> I shall never forget the joy of seeing you again; and what was even more wonderful, you seemed just as pleased and happy to have found us again. We found a brother who really cared about our survival and our well-being and who was anxious to make up for the deprivations we had suffered during the war. Our plans to emigrate to Palestine were put aside and we accepted with great enthusiasm your invitation to settle in England.

Maxwell arranged for Sylvia to complete her education at a private school in Devon. She now lives with her husband in North London.

3

From Private to Captain

If any question why we died,
Tell them, because our fathers lied.
Rudyard Kipling

Maxwell arrived in Britain at a time when it had been deserted by
the ally with which it had entered the war, when its army had
forsaken most of its equipment in the fields of France or on the
beaches of Dunkirk and when Hitler was daily boasting of the
invasion of the British Isles which would swiftly end the war. The
anglophile President of the United States, Franklin D. Roosevelt,
was doing all he could to help within the limits of his constitution, a
Congress where anglophobia was still a force and the isolationist
tendencies of a people unready to believe that Britain's fight was
their fight too. The entry of Italy into the war when it appeared to
have been won by its Axis ally had considerably worsened Britain's
strategic position in the Mediterranean, the Middle East and Africa,
though not by as much as was feared at the time, the deficiencies in
the Italian fighting qualities not having then been exposed by the
Greeks and Wavell's tiny army in Libya and Cyrenaica. It was a
desperate, almost impossible, moment in Britain's history. Her
empire stood stout in support of the war. There was no one else.
Franco's Spain still hesitated about intervening directly on Hitler's
side, but it seemed likely that it would. States like Hungary,
Bulgaria and Romania were tempted by the promise of a share in
the victor's feast but still nerving themselves to take the plunge. The
British people under Churchill's leadership had no option but to
fight on and hourly waited for the long-threatened terror bombing
to begin as a prelude to a full-scale invasion. If they had no choice,
neither did the members of the Polish and Czechoslovakian forces
who were escaping from Hitler's continent in any boat or ship
seaworthy enough to carry them. Were Britain to fall, then their

deaths were certain; if not in battle, then before a firing squad or in a fashion unspeakably worse.

The Jewish soldiers from the occupied territories were at the greatest risk. The war for them was a battle for survival in its most literal form. They had seen at Sète the desperation of hundreds of Czechoslovak civilians, men, women and children, many of them Jews, trying to board the ships taking servicemen to England. The commanders of the Czech division had taken the harsh, if inevitable, decision to leave most of them to whatever malign fate the Gestapo had in mind to mete out, though in the event some 500 Czech civilians did make their escape. At the same time, according to a Jewish historian[1], officers commanding some individual units were authorised to exclude from those to be evacuated any military personnel whom they considered to be "politically unreliable" or who "because of their behaviour and personal qualities, do not deserve to remain in our ranks".

That was an opportunity for a number of Czech officers to parade their own anti-semitism and many Jewish soldiers, as well as their relatives, were forbidden access to the transports lying off Sète. This account goes on:

> There were heart-rending scenes.... Desperate people tried to jump aboard the boats as the landing bridge was raised. They fell into the sea and were drowned. Among the Jewish civilians who were turned away was Dr Ludwig Levy, the aged chief rabbi of Moravia. He was left to die in occupied France....

The last troops to be evacuated left Sète on June 27, three days after hostilities officially ceased following the capitulation of France under the palsied leadership of the aged, anti-semitic Marshal Pétain who had assumed the premiership six days earlier. Some Czechs still managed to escape via Marseilles to Yugoslavia after that date, but most of those left behind were trapped. Most important of all for the developing struggle for air supremacy, only 28 of 932 Czech airmen in France were not evacuated to the United Kingdom. The rest played a gallant part in the Battle of Britain. But for the remnants of the Czech army there was no heroic role to fill.

As the Czech troops arrived from France and the Middle East they were housed in tents at Cholmondeley Park, near Chester. Some of them were in a mutinous mood and denouncing their officers for their arrogance or for their cowardice or for their anti-semitism or for all three. The situation rapidly worsened. By the time Maxwell arrived at the camp, the men were in a ferment and were refusing to obey the orders of their officers. When those opting for this defiance were asked during parade to step forward, nearly 500 did so, Maxwell among them. They were immediately surrounded by guards and held in another part of the camp. On July 26 President Beneš visited the camp and assured a delegation of eight Jewish soldiers that he would not tolerate anti-semitism. On July 27 an order from the Czech High Command in London announced that all the mutineers had been discharged from the Czech army. The next day Maxwell was among a group of 539 Czechs who were handed over to the British military authorities and taken by military policemen, bayonets fixed, to an internment camp at Oswestry in Shropshire.

Many of those discharged were Communists, mainly veterans of the International Brigade who had inspired the revolt at Cholmondeley Park. They were led by Vladimir Clementis, a former communist MP, later Czechoslovakia's Foreign Minister from 1948 to 1950, who was hanged in Prague in 1952 after "confessing" to being an agent of "Western imperialists". He was rehabilitated in 1963 and his party membership was posthumously restored. In addition to his group, about 150 Jewish soldiers left the army of their own accord because they found the anti-semitism intolerable.

The group of "mutineers" sent to Oswestry were later transferred to another camp on York racecourse and then to a third at Sutton Coldfield, near Birmingham. Most of them, and a substantial number of those discharged from the Czech army, applied to join the Auxiliary Pioneer Corps - the only unit in the British army open to foreigners in 1940 - and 460 were accepted, Maxwell among them. His enlistment in the Corps is dated October 9, 1940. The form he had to sign warned that anyone giving false information would be punished, which did not prevent his lying once more about his age, giving the year of his birth as 1921 instead of 1923. Thus he began his career in the British army as No. 12079140, Hoch, Private L. (Later, as Private L.I. du Maurier, his no. was 13051410; as Private Leslie Jones it was 5050000 and as an officer in the Queen's Regiment it was 342170.)

The Pioneer Corps was hardly what Maxwell had been looking for. It was nearly the most unglamorous unit in the British army. It did sterling and essential work and after the war was honoured by the prefix "Royal" being added to its title, but it was an award for digging, not for fighting, as exemplified by its badge which displayed a pick and a shovel. Maxwell says he was misled: that in Europe, pioneers were engineers, not labourers. But being misled was irrelevant; there was nowhere else for him to go.

He was bored, always hungry and didn't like the pay of two shillings (10 pence in decimalised currency) a day. His time was spent in physical labour and he found the work - digging either roads or the foundations for barracks and the like - hard and tiring.

A very large number of the other recruits to the Corps were foreigners or from the colonies and dependencies overseas - people thought either too untrustworthy or too incapable to be allowed into fighting units, at least not straightaway. There were over 1,000 Germans in the Corps in July 1940, some of them highly-skilled doctors who were only permitted to work as medical orderlies with the rank of private. Suspicions of these "aliens" were high among government officials as well as the man in the street and intensified by the prospect of an invasion and fears of a fifth column being admitted to this country under the guise of refugees. According to an official history of the Pioneers[2], one Assistant Director of Labour, when pressed by the officer commanding an "alien" company for his men to be given weapons, replied:

> It is possible in an emergency that the men of the company, if armed, might overcome the British element in it and take possession of the arms if they felt so disposed.

The history records that aliens from enemy countries "were far from being contented with their lot" and were eager to serve in a more aggressive role. That desire is the story of Maxwell's military life.

After a few weeks in the Corps he began to complain of pains in the stomach. The army had a remedy for such afflictions and his appendix was removed at the hospital in Ely in December 1940, though it seems uncertain whether it was actually inflamed. He spent most of the next three years in the Corps, stationed in various areas of England and Wales, including Ilfracombe in Devon, Diss in Norfolk, Newmarket in Suffolk, and Sennybridge in Breconshire, where he broke stones in a quarry and helped build a major artillery range.

It was, he says, boring and backbreaking work. His lasting memory of his time in Wales is that he never saw the sun. He coped by voracious reading of Penguins and Pelicans, the original paperbacks, and, on average, got through one a day.

A fellow Pioneer private who served with Maxwell at Ilfracombe, Mr Bedrich Flesch, of Cambridge, recalled in a letter to Betty

Maxwell being on kitchen duty with him and peeling potatoes. "Although we were billeted in an hotel," he wrote, "we slept on mattresses on the floor." He went on:

> Your husband was a very good soldier and his buttons and badges were always nicely polished, although he made it clear to all that he had come to fight the Nazis - not to clean buttons and badges! As you can imagine, we had regular kit inspections and when other soldiers lost their knives and forks they took from your husband [probably the youngest member of the platoon], so when inspection took place he was short of equipment....

The first essential for Maxwell had been to learn English. He picked it up quickly. In 1982 he told Terry Coleman of *The Guardian* that he had learned to speak the language in six weeks, taught by the lady owner of a tobacconist's shop in Sutton Coldfield who had befriended him in 1940. Coleman asked if he was saying that he had learned English in the best possible way, that is from an English mistress? Maxwell replied:

> I was too young to have a mistress. I was very innocent in that respect. No; we talked a lot, and walked and read.

Coleman asked if Maxwell had ever seen her again. He replied, "No."

For nearly three years the war passed Maxwell by. Russia was invaded, Moscow and Leningrad besieged, Pearl Harbour bombed. Singapore fell and Tobruk was taken, lost and taken again. Greece and Yugoslavia were overrun and in Czechoslovakia the campaign to wipe out the Jewish population was intensified. Romania and Bulgaria, where fascist régimes had assumed power, entered the war and, decisive to the fate of Maxwell's family and to the fate of the other Jews of Ruthenia, so did Hungary, a few days after Hitler began his onslaught on the Soviet Union on June 22, 1941. Then came what Winston Churchill designated as the turn of the tide. The Germans were thrown back from Moscow and stalemated before Leningrad. The entry of America into the war meant that a flood of men and materials began to enter Britain. Mass bombing by day and night by the RAF and the USAF took the war home to the heart of Germany. El Alamein began the process of expelling all Axis forces from North Africa. Italy surrendered and Mussolini had to be rescued by Otto Skorzeny from the ignominy of being imprisoned by the people he had led for 20 years.

While all this - and much more - was happening, Maxwell was

experiencing the most frustrating and tedious time of his life. He
says:

> Until October 1943 I was in the Pioneer Corps building roads and
> huts and unloading and breaking stones in Welsh quarries or charging
> ammunition and loading petrol trains. All told, it was a very
> unpleasant experience.

After the convalescence which followed his appendicitis
operation he broke his thumb in a fight with another soldier and
found himself back in hospital, this time at Cambridge, and then in a
second spell of convalescence at Bedford. If the war offered him no
excitement, his off-duty hours provided compensation. At Bedford,
he recalled in a note dictated in 1952:

> I met a Mrs Tillard [Mrs Leila Tillard, daughter of a major-general
> and widow of a colonel in the Gurkha Rifles; she died in 1970], a
> charming lady who had just suffered a terrible bereavement, losing
> her only son in a night raid on Essen. She took a great interest in me
> and acted as a mother to me for many years. Through her, I met the
> headmaster of Bedford public school [H.W. Liddle, M.A.] and
> through him I met another lady, a widow, who was to play a leading
> part in my life for the next two years. We met in the bar of the Bridge
> Hotel and talked for half the night. We fell in love at first sight. She
> was a very beautiful and intelligent woman and although she was
> much older than me, I was very much in love with her. She
> represented the dream of my youth - I was then only 18 years old....
> Although we severed all connection in 1944, I cannot look back on
> those years without seeing her vividly. She was the turning point in
> my first life. With her I turned from an adolescent into a man and
> with her I left behind all that was unsettled in me, all my youth.

Through this widow, Sylvia, he met Brigadier M.A. (Gary)
Carthew-Yorstoun, DSO, CBE, of the Black Watch, a regular
officer since the First World War and commander of the 176th
Infantry Brigade, who was to become Maxwell's mentor. The
brigadier, who died in 1968, took an immediate liking to the young
Czech who he found was eager to discuss military tactics and
strategy and welcomed him into his home. He was instrumental in
starting Maxwell on the military career which was to lead to a
commission and the Military Cross. On June 3, 1943, a week before
Maxwell's birthday, Brigadier Carthew-Yorstoun wrote to Ivan du
Maurier - a surname borrowed from the cigarettes Maxwell smoked
- with the good news that his ordeal in the Pioneer Corps was nearly
over:

> I have been held up waiting for a letter from your CO which only
> reached me two days ago. Now that the business has started, I do not

think it will be long before we can get things through. I hope to see someone in the War Office on Sunday with the object of getting a move on [with] the normal procedure. Don't worry; we'll get you out quite quickly now.

Brigadier Carthew-Yorstoun's influence was a considerable one for Maxwell to have on his side. He had been on Montgomery's staff in the 1930s. When Mrs Betty Montgomery died in October 1937 he cared for the couple's only son, David, after Monty accepted a posting in Palestine in 1938, and continued to give a home to the boy until his own wartime duties made it impossible. This close personal relationship with Monty, however, did not extend to the brigadier's military career. When the victor of the desert war returned from Italy at the beginning of 1944 to take command of the British invasion forces, he relieved Carthew-Yorstoun of his post on the grounds of medical unfitness. Later in that year the brigadier was appointed commanding officer of the British troops in Paris, yet another coincidental circumstance which was to prove to be to Maxwell's advantage.

Carthew-Yorstoun ensured that Maxwell was transferred from the Pioneer Corps first, and briefly to the Somerset Light Infantry stationed at Colchester and then to a battalion which was under his command, the 6th North Staffords, stationed at the Beckenhall Hotel, at Cliftonville, near Margate, on the Kent coast. With the S.L.I. he was asked to lecture other soldiers about the Czech struggle and a page or two of his notes remain. "We [the Czechs] wait," he said, "ready whenever called upon to pay our debt to you." He went on:

> The world decided to sacrifice our country in order to preserve the peace it was longing for. They took our frontiers - our mountains - they deprived us of every possibility of defending our land. Our army was ready and determined to fight. The whole nation was on guard, and its soldiers were standing under arms on its frontiers. Our cry was "Ne dame se" - "We shall not give in." At Munich, we sacrificed a part of our country for the sake of peace and for the well-being of Europe.... Events culminated in March 1939. The Nazis swept over what was left of our country. It was too late to think of defence.... Our towns were occupied, our forces disarmed and day by day our country was robbed of its supplies in order to provide hungry Germany with food.... Many of us were convinced that war was inevitable. Therefore, we hastened to take our place in the struggle for a better future, for a free Czechoslovakia in a free Europe, at the side of our friends, wherever and whenever we might find them. We forgot the sacrifice we had been forced to make by the Allies....

There is nothing startlingly original about those words, but they
show a clear grasp of affairs and a remarkable command of English
for a 20-year-old who three years before had never travelled beyond
the boundaries of his native country and whose studies had been
largely religious.

Maxwell is remembered by his North Staffordshire battalion
comrades, who knew him as Leslie du Maurier, as "a tall, skinny,
but handsome lad" with an Adolphe Menjou moustache. He arrived
with only half his kit and shared a room with Private L. Kent,
nicknamed "Bow-legs". Later, Maxwell, Kent and another soldier,
Private Harold Thorley, were to win the divisional prize for a
10-mile run and walk in full battle order across the South Downs in
one hour and 42 minutes. As Maxwell now says, he was "as fit as a
flea" in those days.

Soon after arrival at Cliftonville, Maxwell was made a lance-
corporal and was seconded to take charge of a sniper section of
between 12 and 15 men. By the time the D-Day landings took place
he had become a sergeant. Corporal Walter Smith and Lance-
corporal Sam Mitchell were two of the snipers who served with him
throughout the Normandy campaign and both attended a reunion in
Derby in September 1987 when Derby County, the First Division
club of which Maxwell is chairman, played (and lost to) Oxford
United, the club of which he was formerly the chairman.

Mitchell remembers Maxwell particularly well because when they
first met Maxwell shouted at him and Mitchell decided that if this
Czech newcomer was going to be put in charge of the section he
would ask for a transfer. Later, in the stress of war, the two became
good friends.

Mitchell's recollections of his new comrade tally with several
others of the period. Maxwell was not, he says, "very regimental",
but he "got away" with things. He seemed to get on well with
colonels but not sergeant-majors and he was disliked by junior
officers. Mitchell also recalls Maxwell shouting at a brigadier and
the brigadier replying, "Do what you want, du Maurier." Mitchell
found this familiarity - and the fact that Maxwell could indulge in it
without reprimand - "unusual". The antipathy of sergeant-majors
towards Maxwell was reciprocated. When Mitchell was helping to
carry a wounded sergeant-major on a stretcher after the crossing of
the Orne river in August 1944 Maxwell's only comment was: "That's
one less, Sam."

Brian Straton-Ferrier says that his mother's home in South
Kensington, London, became Maxwell's off-duty base towards the

end of 1943. The family had "somewhat adopted this attractive and impressive youth", partly because he had no one else to turn to and nowhere else to go. Straton-Ferrier says he was jealous of Maxwell's good looks and charm and he dismissed his self-assurance as "arrogance".

> There was something dominant, almost domineering, about the man even then, which offended my highly-refined training in the British public school tradition of hiding a sense of superiority behind a façade of stiff-upper-lip self-deprecation. I wonder if his sons, educated as I was, find this same problem with him.

Early in 1944 Maxwell was recommended for a commission. He attended a War Office selection board lasting three days, but failed to pass the exam. However, his career was now progressing. He was made a full corporal in April and a sergeant in May and put in charge of the sniper section of the battalion.

Captain Edward Abbotts, OBE, former Intelligence officer of the 59th Infantry Division and known to other servicemen as "Crash" Abbotts, remembers first meeting Maxwell in 1944 before the Normandy landings when he was still Sergeant du Maurier. One of Abbotts's duties was the supervision of the training of snipers and, accordingly, he arranged to meet the sergeant in charge of training the division's marksmen:

> I expected to encounter a hard-bitten regular soldier who had probably served part of his time as an instructor at the Small Arms School or some similar establishment. In the event, I found myself confronted by a slim, athletic-looking twenty-year-old who, at first glance, looked as if he could have come straight from school rather than be charged with the destinies of a Division's marksmen. At second glance, however ... his strength of character and dedication came through.... If he had not made me aware of his Central European origin, I would have classified him as a native-born Englishman who spoke standard English with no trace of a regional accent. He outlined his training programme and I realised at once that there was nothing I could add to it. He already had a good team and his whole emphasis was on motivation. His war aims were the same as mine but a thousand times more intensely personal. The best I could do in the circumstances was to let him get on with the good work without outside interference.

The 59th Division did not sail for Normandy until June 27, 1944, three weeks after D-Day. Maxwell's battalion, the 6th North Staffords, completed its concentration on July 1 and moved up to Basly between July 5 and 7 to carry out reconnaissance for the divisional attack on Caen from the north. Regimental notes record that the battalion began its attack on the village of La Bijude, north of Caen, on July 8. Fighting throughout the day was bitter and confused but by the evening La Bijude was captured and the 7th South Staffords passed through the battalion to attempt to take Malon. They did not succeed and the following day at 10.30 am the 6th North Staffords attacked the village. It was strongly defended by entrenched Tiger tanks and 75mm anti-tank guns but by 2.30 in the afternoon it was taken. The battalion's losses for the two days of fighting were heavy: two officers and 41 other ranks were killed and 12 officers (one of whom later died from his wounds) and 135 other ranks were wounded. Maxwell came through unscathed but he remembers the fighting for La Bijude as his first "real trial" in battle and says he was "scared all the time". Nevertheless, he was recommended (without immediate result) for a commission in the field, so he believes his commanding officer thought he had done "rather well".

On July 11 the battalion moved to a rest area to reorganise, but it was in action again on July 16 when it was ordered to capture Haut des Forges as part of 177th Infantry Brigade's objective to cut the road from Villers-Bocage to Caen, the most heavily defended section of the German front in France. The attack was a preliminary to the launching on July 18 of Operation Goodwood which was designed to smash German resistance and open up the way for the British 1st Army to break out in Operation Cobra on July 20.

Montgomery had predicted his two-pronged offensive would "set the Normandy front aflame"[3], but his attack was more of a damp squib. However, the North Staffords played their small part and Haut des Forges was taken, at a cost of eight British dead, including an officer, and the wounding of 24 other ranks. Five German officers and 285 other ranks were taken prisoner. For the next three days the battalion was dug in at Haut des Forges. Casualties were light, despite enemy shelling and mortaring: two soldiers were killed and two others, one a lieutenant, were wounded. For the 10 days after that, the battalion's duties largely consisted of patrolling. Eight officers and men were killed in this period and 35 wounded.

On August 4 the battalion was ordered to Villers-Bocage and took up defensive positions south of the town. It met little resistance. But on August 6 it was given instructions to cross the River Orne, and did so that same evening behind two companies of the South Staffords.

Earlier that day Abbotts had received a "disquieting" intelligence report that the Germans were not treating prisoners from occupied

Robert Maxwell's family in 1925. Back row, third from left, Grandfather Yankel Slomowitz. Fourth from left, sister Gisl. Fifth from left, father Mehel Hoch. Middle row, second from left, Grandmother Slomowitz. Third from left, mother Chanca Hoch. Bottom row, fourth from left, Robert Maxwell (Ludvik Hoch) and fifth from left, sister Brana.

The village of Solotvino in 1936, where Robert Maxwell was born.

Robert Maxwell, in profile at the bottom of the picture, at Cholmondeley Park in 1940 with fellow soldiers of the Czech army.

Convalescing at Ely, Maxwell plays cards with fellow patients.

Private on parade: Maxwell, aged 17, in the Pioneer Corps at Ilfracombe.

Young Maxwell in the Pioneer Corps in 1941, on washing-up duties.

Private Maxwell with his first football team, B Company, 6th North Staffords, at Cliftonville in 1943.

The family that 'adopted' Private Maxwell: John, Eileen, Jack and Brian Straton-Ferrier, pictured in London.

Robert Maxwell, as Sniper Sergeant du Maurier talking to French civilians in Normandy in 1944.

The photograph Betty kept with her while Maxwell was away at war.
Inset: The photograph of Betty which Maxwell carried with him during active service.

2nd Lieutenant and Mrs Robert Maxwell, MC, on their wedding day in Paris on March 14, 1945.

Betty Maxwell's father, Capitaine Paul Meynard, pictured in 1917.

Betty Maxwell's Mother Colombe, pictured in 1915 when she was decorated with the Croix de Guerre.

Lieutenant Robert Maxwell and his men ready to go into action in spring, 1945.

MODERN BATTLE: THE VICTORY OF THE ROER TRIANGLE BY THE BRITISH 2ND ARMY.—No. 2: THE GALLANT FIGHT IN SUSTEREN.

BRITISH INFANTRY OCCUPYING TWO CORNER HOUSES AT A VITAL ROAD JUNCTION IN SUSTEREN, HOLDING ON GRIMLY AGAINST PANZERS WHILE AWAITING THE HELD-UP BRITISH TANKS.

Detail from the Illustrated London News, February 17, 1945, showing action in the Roer Triangle, the battle in which Maxwell won the Military Cross.

Field-Marshal Bernard Law Montgomery decorates 2nd Lieutenant Robert Maxwell with the Military Cross.

Time out of war: Bob and Betty pose for a snapshot on a London rooftop in 1945.

The final triumph: Lieutenant Robert Maxwell, MC, leading his battalion during the Victory Parade through Berlin in September, 1945.

With his platoon in 1945.

Sisters Brana and Sylvia, pictured after they were reunited with their brother.

Captain Maxwell pictured with Barry, the dog that came from Hitler's personal kennels.

Maxwell tries on civilian clothes, with Betty in Berlin in December, 1945.

In Berlin with Fritz Neuman, head of the SDP, Berlin and Arno Scholz, Editor of the German newspaper *Der Telegraf* in 1945.

Brigadier General Carthew-Yorstoun, Major Christopher Rhodes, Major Nick Huysmans and others at Michael's christening, Berlin, 1947.

The twins Christine and Isabel at two weeks, 1950.

In France, 1957, Betty with Ian on her lap and, moving to the right, Isabel, Christine, Philip, Anne and Michael.

countries as prisoners of war but were despatching them to concentration camps as traitors or political prisoners. He was instructed to warn any refugees serving in the division of the dangers and to do everything possible to ensure they would not be put unduly at risk. That meant withdrawing them from the line. He says:

> I sent an urgent message to the 6th Battalion of the North Staffordshire Regiment, to which du Maurier was attached, asking for him to be sent immediately to see me. An hour later he stood before me and I gave him the news that he was to be withdrawn from the forthcoming action and explained the reason for this decision. He looked at me in utter amazement ... and pointed out that his own first-hand experiences of Nazism had left him with no illusions about sportsmanship, rules of war or any such refinements. He knew only too well the sort of enemies we were fighting....
>
> He finished by asking permission to ignore the instruction to go to the rear.... In the circumstances I released him from the constraints of a direct order but repeated that I was advising him, most earnestly, that as he ran risks additional to those of his colleagues he should take advantage of the directive from Corps. He thanked me and left without saying whether he would take the advice or not.

Captain Abbotts never saw Maxwell again for nearly 40 years, but he remembers the sequel. A few days later another Intelligence officer said to him: "I thought you told du Maurier to withdraw?" "Yes," replied Abbotts, "I did recommend it."

"A fat lot of notice he's taken of your recommendation", said the other officer. "He's there on the bridge, in the thick of it."

Abbotts commented:

> I noted it, without surprise. It was inevitable. At the age of barely 21 he had set himself a mission and he was moving to fulfil it.

The crossing of the river was made before dark, took the Germans by surprise and encountered little opposition, but the calm was not to last for long. The regimental notes describe what happened next to the 6th North Staffords:

> In spite of very heavy and continuous mortar and 88mm fire, they secured their objectives and dug in by 23.30 hours, taking some 40 prisoners. [From] August 7 until the afternoon of the 9th, the battalion maintained their positions in the Orne bridgehead in spite of the fact that a very heavy counter-attack by SS troops with Tiger tanks had reduced the battalion down to the battalion HQ and D company, practically intact, and A, B and C companies in skeleton only.... Mortaring and shell fire were both very heavy and continuous throughout the time that they were there and the battalion was

almost constantly standir,g-to. Counter-attacks by the enemy became too numerous to record and it was probably through the magnificent shooting of the artillery that the bridgehead was ever held.

Casualties during this period included two officers and 31 other ranks killed and seven officers and 109 other ranks wounded. Fifty-three other ranks were missing.

The role of the 6th North Staffords in the Orne crossing had been to guard an essential bridging site at Le Bas and cover the necessary bridge-building operations. This was, says Abbotts, crucial to the success of the whole operation, though the 59th Division's role was to be diversionary and of relatively short duration. The main offensive was due to start on the following morning, August 7, when the Canadian army and the Polish Armoured Division were to drive south in an attempt to close the Falaise Gap and prevent the escape of a major part of the German army. The crossing of the Orne was intended to divert German infantry and armour from south of Caen to make that task easier. The Canadian push was to be preceded by a massive air bombardment of the German positions, but at this point, Abbotts writes, "all went crazy".

Not for the only time during the Normandy campaign, the bombing was punctual but the wrong target was hit. The bulk of the barrage fell upon the unfortunate Poles and Canadians. Their offensive had to be called off, but the 59th Division was now committed to a diversionary foray - a bridgehead across the River Orne - "which slowly developed into a mortal combat on unsuitable terrain against an enemy vastly superior in men and armaments and enjoying the advantage of defending terrain of its own choice".

The bridgehead was held for three days despite the fact that the defenders, the 271st Infantry Division, had been reinforced by two panzer-grenadier regiments from the 12th SS Panzer Division, the Hitler Jugend. The panzers made repeated efforts to reach the bridge as the weather closed in and prevented the British commanders from calling up any air support until late on the second day. Finally, it came in the form of a squadron of Thunderbolts. Once again there was a failure to identify properly the bomb line, which was the forward edge of the Forest of Grimbosq, and the bombs were dropped upon the 59th's rest area which was already crowded with casualties from the battle. The 6th North Staffords was one of the units badly hit and, according to one survivor, the casualties from this mistake were "dreadful". Taken together with the losses in the early fighting, the battle for the Orne bridgehead and the struggle to trap the German army by closing the Falaise

Gap, the division was to become gravely weakened. Those members who remained fit for fighting were later dispersed to other units when Montgomery was forced to "cannibalise" some divisions to make up the strength of others.

On the afternoon of August 9 the battalion was withdrawn to rest and reorganise for an indefinite period. The respite was brief. During August 13/14 it moved towards Donnay and the north end of the Forest of Cinglais on the eastern side of the Orne. It went through the forest and finished at Pont d'Ouilly, after what was claimed to be the fastest advance made on foot by any unit up until that time. About 80 prisoners were taken at a cost of practically no casualties. The battalion eventually finished so far ahead of the rest of the brigade that it had to halt for 24 hours until the others caught up.

The battle for the bridgehead over the Orne, at the Forest of Grimbosq, was, for both Maxwell and Captain Abbotts, the most memorable of those early days in France. Abbotts says it was the "graveyard" of the formation with which he had served since 1939. Maxwell says that for 48 hours he thought his "end had definitely come". Abbotts's account of this time says that the Germans were not observing the Geneva Convention:

> The SS, for instance, shot padres and stretcher-bearers as they helped the wounded; in addition to the ubiquitous mines in hedgerows and on roads, the retreating Germans mined the steps leading up to wayside shrines and even attached mines to the bodies of the dead.

One of those killed by a mine was the commanding officer of the 6th North Staffords, Lieutenant-Colonel G. Wilkins, according to regimental records. The belief of some of his men, including Maxwell, that he was killed in the inadvertent American bombing of the rest camp seems to be erroneous.

Anecdotes, as always, abound about the fighting from those who came through it. One ex-private at the Derby reunion recalled how Maxwell, riding a captured German motorcycle, had gone forward with a few of his men, taken cover in bushes and then been confronted by a Tiger tank. Maxwell says that moment was the most frightening of his life.

Maxwell had not drunk alcohol since his chastening experience of it as a child. But the battalion commander's batman had just thrown him a bottle of Gordon's gin. He took a deep swig of it to steady his nerves and then aimed at the tank with his PIAT anti-tank gun, hit it twice and disabled it. A little later, when some British soldiers broke before a German attack and started to flee back across the bridge, Maxwell was witnessed to point a machine-gun at them and threaten to open fire unless they returned to the other side of the bridge. They did so and the bridge was held. On another occasion, men of the battalion were near enough to hear the Germans cursing them. Maxwell cursed back in fluent German; his command of languages appears to have earned the admiration of other soldiers in the battalion. They also thought him brave and that if anyone were to survive the war, he would. "He had a smooth, silky way about him", said Eric Grindley, of Ash Bank, Stoke-on-Trent, then company quartermaster sergeant of B Company to which Maxwell was first attached before being transferred to the HQ Company. An ex-corporal in the 6th Battalion, Harry Shorthose, of Derby, put it more graphically to the Stoke *Evening Sentinel* in 1984, when the newspaper was carrying a series of reminiscences by those who knew Maxwell during his time in the North Staffordshire Regiment. Maxwell, he said, had the kind of personality "which could sell sand to the Arabs".

One of Maxwell's other barrack-room comrades asked him what he intended to do after the war. "I am going to England", he said, "to become a squire."

Sam Mitchell recalled an occasion when he and Sergeant "du Maurier" accepted the surrender of 100 prisoners. Maxwell took all the bank notes the Germans had on them and Mitchell received the small change. None of his former comrades had any doubts about Maxwell's war aims to kill, capture or otherwise defeat Germans, and in pursuit of them he paid little regard to the etiquette of war. At Bayeux, he was furious when six of his men failed to report one evening at 5 pm sharp as he had instructed. The men pleaded that they hadn't known the time because none of them had a watch. The next day Maxwell gave each of them a watch, all of which he had removed from the wrists of German prisoners-of-war. At Villers-Bocage he arrived for reconnaissance duty wearing the uniform of a German officer. He was immediately issued with an identity book in the name of Lance-corporal Leslie Smith in case he was taken prisoner. The subterfuge may not have saved him if he had been captured. The Germans were apt to treat enemies wearing their uniforms as spies and to execute them, anyway, if they fell into their hands. The sequel to the story came some months later when Eric Grindley was working for the 21st Army leave unit in an hotel in Brussels. Two gloved hands were clamped over his eyes from behind and a voice asked: "Guess who?" When the hands were removed he saw Maxwell wearing the uniform of a British army officer and automatically assumed he had stolen it rather than won promotion.

The *Sunday Times*, in an Insight article on October 5, 1969, claimed that Maxwell was not "entirely popular" in the ranks because the other soldiers didn't quite understand where he came from. The article, one of a series designed to do damage to Maxwell's reputation and which, as we shall see, in part succeeded, also quoted an unnamed adjutant as describing him as

> A big fellow. Very dark. A bit of a mystery. Went forward a few days after we landed in Normandy and came back loaded with bottles of Calvados.

One would think that increased his popularity with the other men if nothing else did.

The fighting at the Orne river crossing was the last engagement of the 6th North Staffords. They were moved back on August 20, 1944 for reorganisation and dispersal. The regimental note of their activities concludes:

> Throughout the time that the battalion was in France as such, it has taken part in the major operation which resulted in the defeat of the 7th German army. It has fought against most types of German divisions, including [the] SS [and] Panzer.... It suffered considerable casualties, particularly in officers, but has never once failed to take its objective.... We have fought over most types of country from extremely flattened and very strongly-held areas north of [the] Villers-Bocage-Caen road to country which has almost been untouched by war. Apart from having faced every known form of German weapon, we have also been rocketed by our own Thunderbolts, machine-gunned from the air and some of us have been unpleasantly close to 500lb bombs dropped on the wrong targets.

The final toll of casualties for the battalion was cripplingly high: nine officers and 112 other ranks killed, 29 officers and 347 other ranks wounded and one officer and 57 other ranks missing. Maxwell had been wounded again but only lightly; he was struck in the jaw by either a piece of shrapnel or a spent bullet. He still carries the scar.

Major-General L.O. Lyne, DSO, commander of the 59th Division, wrote on August 10 to Brigadier R.W.K. Fryer, commander of the 176th Infantry Brigade:

> Will you please convey to all ranks of the Brigade Group under your command my tremendous admiration for the magnificent fight which they successfully waged in the Orne bridgehead.

The night advance was skilfully made and achieved complete surprise. It was then up to us to hang on to the Bridgehead we had gained. How successfully this was done the whole world now knows. This achievement not only redounds to the credit of every Officer and man concerned but has had a very considerable bearing upon the whole disastrous situation in which the German Army now finds itself.

You will all like to know that now we have been able to turn to the offensive the Division are once more advancing and have captured over 200 prisoners already today. The Forest is literally strewn with the bodies of men of the 12th SS Division, killed during their repeated counter-attacks, which you so ably repulsed.

Maxwell had been promoted to staff sergeant during the battle on the Orne. One consequence of the fighting was that his then adopted name, Leslie du Maurier, and his unit were mentioned by the Canadian commentator Chester Wilmot, in a radio broadcast which commended him for his bravery and stated his nationality. On the orders of Major-General Lyne, Maxwell was withdrawn from the line and given yet another identity, this time as Private Leslie Jones. He had a spell as an interrogator in a prisoner of war camp at Arras, went with the remnants of his battalion to Belgium, which he thoroughly disliked, then secured seven days' leave and made his way to Paris. There he had two strokes of luck. He found that his old mentor, Brigadier Carthew-Yorstoun, was the commander of the British troops in the French capital and he met Elisabeth Meynard. The consequence of the first piece of good fortune was that he was assigned to intelligence work in Paris while waiting for his recommended commission to come through and he was allowed to wear civilian or military clothes, as he wished. The consequence of the second was that for the second time in a young life he fell in love at first sight and within eight months was a married man.

* * * * *

Even if, after four years of occupation, Paris was not the romantic magnet of its reputation, it was still a haven for Allied soldiers who hadn't slept in a comfortable bed, spent an evening in a woman's company or been served anything but army rations for months. They flocked there in their thousands. Brigadier Carthew-Yorstoun was concerned about his Czech protégé who, by his own confession, had started "dashing my way among the girls". Carthew-Yorstoun thought that the kind of girl Maxwell might meet on his own was not the kind whom he ought to meet and recommended him to a friend who in turn recommended him to a Madame Maloubier, President of The French Welcome Committee, a newly-started club where Allied officers (and those waiting to be commissioned) could meet French families wanting to befriend them.

It is unlikely that the youthful Maxwell, in Paris for the first time in his life, fully appreciated the brigadier's concern for his moral welfare, but, he says, he eventually went to the club hoping to meet people who could describe to him what life had been like under the Germans.

> When I arrived, there was a large crowd of officers and a still larger crowd of civilians, all talking together in an over-populated room. I saw a girl standing behind a large desk. The room was too crowded and I couldn't get in, so I stayed in the doorway, gazing at her. She was pretty, very vivacious, slim, well-built.... Above all, I couldn't take my eyes off her face. There shone the most lovely pair of blue eyes I had ever seen. She had a lovely look of slight childish desperation as she was spoken to by so many people all at the same time. I loved her dearly, there and then. From the minute I saw her I wanted her for my wife.

Not for the first time, he speedily achieved his ambition.

Elisabeth Jenny Jeanne Meynard was born on March 11, 1921 at La Grive, between Lyon and Grenoble. When she began studying at the Sorbonne in 1939 for an arts degree (which she later changed to law, spending three inconclusive years at it), Maxwell was selling trinkets in the streets of Bratislava. Her family was everything Maxwell's wasn't. Her father was a major in the First World War, serving in the Cadre Noir de Saumur, an élite cavalry regiment, an Officer of the Legion of Honour and decorated with the Croix de Guerre with Palm and two stars. He was rich when he inherited some silk factories from his father and his grandfather, but they were closed during the depression of the early 1930s. After that collapse, the family moved to Paris and during the Second World War he was an adviser on fraud in fruit and vegetables at Les Halles, Paris's equivalent of Covent Garden market in London. He read law later in his life and became a legal consultant.

Her mother was a teacher at the outset of her career and then became a supervisor in the telephone service, working in Arras during the First World War. When the Germans occupied the city and the civilian population was ordered by the French authorities to leave, she remained behind in the cellar of the central Post Office and manned a telephone line to the front. For that, she was mentioned in dispatch. Later, after the French had regained the city and then lost it again, she repeated her former courage and was awarded the Croix de Guerre with Palm, a rare honour for a woman.

During her law student days Elisabeth was a "pionne" (a student paid to supervise children) in a reformatory for juveniles from eight to 16. In June 1940, as the German armies advanced on Paris, she accompanied children from the reformatory who were evacuated to Cabourg in Normandy. They stayed there for a month before the Germans arrived and were taken to Flers de L'Orne, and then to Condé sur Noireau, a distance of some 70 kilometres. The children had to walk it.

She spent most of the years of occupation continuing her studies. She got her job at the Welcome Club because she could speak English, having been partly-educated as a child at a convent at Acocks Green, near Birmingham, to where she was sent when the family fortune was mostly lost. She was only at the Club for a month, but it was the month when Maxwell saw her for the first time. After leaving there, she worked as secretary and interpreter for an American colonel at the 48 Hours' Leave Club. When she accepted Maxwell's proposal of marriage, he insisted she should leave. A modern woman might have insisted with equal vigour that it was for her to choose whether or not she left her job, but Betty Maxwell says[4]:

> I always try to weigh up where my first duty lies but, if a choice has to be made, my husband comes first and I decided that very early on in our life together.

When Maxwell was finally introduced to her at the Welcome Club it ended, he said, his life as "an adventurer". Brian Straton-Ferrier, who got to know Elisabeth when she stayed with his mother shortly after her marriage, says that the young Frenchwoman was "rather scared by this wild-looking moustachioed young man who manifestly lacked her own cultural background". If so, she must have stifled any misgivings. The courtship, in the fashion of wartime romances, was speedy, the passion grand and the outcome happy. But, at first, the Meynard family was certainly alarmed at the foreigner who had suddenly erupted into their midst. Betty's elder sister, Dr Yvonne Vittoz, a gynaecologist who later delivered all but one of the Maxwell children, has recorded the fullest account of the days leading up to the wedding, beginning when Betty was asked to look after a Czech sergeant attached to the British army who had been recommended by Brigadier Carthew-Yorstoun. Maxwell had been described to her as "a courageous soldier, deserving to be taken care of".

Said Dr Vittoz:

> Thus she made the acquaintance of ... Ivan du Maurier, tall, dark, handsome, of war-like bearing, wearing superb boots laced right up to the knee and driving a motorcycle and sidecar.

The sartorial perfection of the driver wasn't reproduced in the mechanical efficiency of the brakes of the motorcycle, which Dr Vittoz described as "tricky". As a result, Maxwell only narrowly missed a lorry while being shown around Paris by Betty, who was the sidecar's passenger. She was less fortunate, being struck in the ribs by pipes protruding from the vehicle's back. A stunned Maxwell had to take her to hospital, where she was found to have suffered only heavy bruising. Dr Vittoz went on:

> It was a good reason for the "Czechoslovak" to come to the house to have news of her. My parents and I were not too affable towards him - he had a rather wild look about him, but above all, he had almost killed Betty! Let him depart quickly and have no more to do with her!

When Maxwell returned to his unit, the family believed - and hoped - Betty would never see him again, but he returned to Paris in mid-November and Dr Vittoz's account went on:

> This time, the family was beginning to realise, not without some anxiety, that the foreign sergeant was very interested in Betty. He told all sorts of tales, which seemed a bit dubious to us: how he had succeeded in escaping from a Hungarian prison at the age of 16 by knocking out the night guard; his travels ... to reach France, passing through Yugoslavia, Turkey, the Lebanon.... His enrolment in a Czech unit billeted in the caves of Roquefort (which has led to his permanent horror of cheese made from sheep's milk) and his participation in the battle of Orléans, his exodus as far as Sète, then his embarkation.... This type of escape which has become a legend but which at the time we had difficulty in believing.... He also said at the time he was hunting out Gestapo chiefs who were disguised as insignificant soldiers. He showed us a silver cigarette case, taken from an unmasked German.

> Betty found it difficult to hide that she was in love with her soldier, whilst he seemed more and more worrying to our parents, who thought him a bit of an adventurer, with whom it seemed unthinkable that their daughter should make plans for the future.

> After a few days' leave, he left for the north and the war. Betty soon received a letter in which he confessed to her that after having won many a battle, he had just lost one: that of love. The letter ended with a proposal of marriage in due form.

At home this letter had the effect of a bombshell. We did not know anything about him, except the stories he told, which seemed unlikely, and he dared to ask for her hand in marriage.

Insensitive to those arguments, Betty was radiant. Our father wanted to obtain some information. He received a letter of praise from an English general, which reassured him a little. Ivan, called Ian, obtained from the Czech embassy a birth certificate and a certificate stating that given his youth when he left Czechoslovakia, it was very unlikely that he had ever been sentenced for any crime. The business sorted itself out ... and the date of the engagement was set for the end of the year.

Ian arrived in the very last days of December. This time he had an enormous black dog in his sidecar, a stray which he had found.... At that period, General Carthew-Yorstoun came to visit us and this impressed my father very much. He introduced Ian as his protégé, whose father he was replacing, and he paid Ian such compliments that our parents were immediately won over. He went as far as saying that he had only sons, but, that if he had a daughter, he would willingly have given her to a boy of such worth. The adventurer was "cleared through customs".

The engagement was celebrated with a simple meal.... Ian had slipped a modest ring on Betty's finger. In a great hurry, they had fixed the date of their wedding for the month of March. Very soon Ian had to leave for Holland where the German Army was hanging on. From now on, because of Betty, he held his life dear. Nonetheless he left for tough battles, but, believing in his lucky star, he assured Betty that he would come back with the Military Cross.

The next the family heard was that Maxwell had indeed won the MC. Dr Vittoz continued:

My father, who was a graduate of Saint Cyr [the French Sandhurst] and a former career officer, was particularly proud of the honour which rewarded the bravery of his future son-in-law. During this time, the marriage preparations monopolised my mother and my sister.

On March 14 Betty became Madame du Maurier at the town hall in the 16th Arrondissement and on the 15th the religious service was celebrated in the (Protestant) Church of the Annunciation, rue Cortambert, by Pasteur Maury.

It was, by coincidence, exactly six years to the day since Ruthenia was invaded and occupied by Hungarian troops.

Dr Vittoz concluded her recollections:

The gathering was large and brilliant, lots of uniforms, and among them General Carthew (and) Lady Moorehead, colonel of the Women's Army (WAACs).

> Betty was very beautiful in a lace dress.... There was an abundance of flowers, but the most extraordinary thing was the abundance and richness of the lunch in this period of restrictions which had been going on for so many years.... It was a "good tuck-in" which Mother had managed to organise in our house in rue Desbordes-Valmore, with the precious help of her new son-in-law who had obtained the unobtainable in the way of food, with the complicity of the English Military Supplies office!

The bride added to her sister's account:

> Lace was the only available material which did not require clothing coupons. Its drawback, however, was that it was see-through. Bob managed to let me have a parachute and from it several layers of petticoat were made to obscure the transparency.

Betty recalls thinking "at least with this man, I will never be bored". She could hardly have contemplated at that time that this life without boredom would include bearing nine children.

* * * * *

The mystification which the Meynard family had felt about their new son-in-law was shared by most of those who knew him. As always, his activities while in Paris were shrouded in mystery. The pass allowing him to wear whatever clothing he chose to was issued by the British army staff office in Paris on October 7, 1944 and stated:

> The bearer of this pass, No. 13051410, S/Sgt du Maurier, L.I., is a British soldier and is authorised to be in Paris and to wear any uniform or civilian clothes.

The Allied military authorities feared a communist insurrection behind their lines. The pass was to enable Maxwell to move freely in disguise so that he might observe whether the danger was real or imagined. One day he wore the uniform of a paratroop major; the next he was dressed like a working-man. Throughout his life he has taken pleasure in creating confusion; wartime certainly gave him full and early scope.

There had also at one point, just before Christmas 1944, been a plan to drop him by parachute deep behind the German lines. It was hoped that his fluent German would allow him to report on the measures the Wehrmacht was taking to defend its homeland against an Allied spring offensive.

Maxwell retains a letter from Supreme Headquarters, Allied

Expeditionary Force (SHAEF), dated December 18, 1944, addressed to Staff Sergeant L.I. du Maurier, saying:

> 1. You will proceed by military aircraft (ATC) on or about 20 December 1944 from present station to Paris, France to carry out an assigned mission.
>
> 2. Travel by military aircraft is directed. Baggage allowance is limited to one hundred (100) pounds.
>
> By command of General EISENHOWER

and it is signed by the Assistant Adjutant-General, Lieutenant-Colonel H.C. Chappell.

Maxwell was not anxious to go. He regarded the "assigned mission" as suicidal. In the event, the surprise German offensive in the Ardennes threw SHAEF into confusion and everyone's energies were concentrated on first containing and then throwing back the German attack. The parachute drop was abandoned and Maxwell never heard of it again.

Maxwell also carried with him a certificate from the Czechoslovak Government in exile in London - the one the Meynard family was shown - stating that according to the official records of its Ministry of the Interior "Mr Ludvik Hoch, alias du Maurier, was born on the 10th June 1923 at Selo Slatina, Czechoslovakia." It continued:

> Taking into consideration his age on leaving Czechoslovakia, we think it highly improbable that he has ever been sentenced by any Czechoslovak court. This certificate is issued to him for the purpose of getting a commission in the British Army.

It is equally improbable that the Ministry of the Interior was aware that Maxwell had been sentenced to death by the Hungarians, though such a sentence would hardly likely have been a bar to promotion even if it were known.

In the event, that Christmas Maxwell returned to England to be kitted out as an officer and he officially attained the rank of a second lieutenant in the Queen's Royal Regiment (West Surrey) on January 6, 1945. By then he had accomplished his final change of name and was known as Second Lieutenant Ian Robert Maxwell. He had been reluctant to adopt yet another - he had already discarded Hoch, Jones and Smith, the last two within the previous six months, and now he had to lose du Maurier as well - but the authorities insisted upon it.

Apart from anything else, the frequent adoption of new names was irritating his bank manager. His battalion commander in the North Staffs had recommended him earlier in the year to Grindlay's

Bank at Westminster as a suitable candidate for an account (a more relaxed attitude is taken nowadays towards prospective new clients) and wrote:

> He has been recommended for a commission ... which I have every reason to suppose will be granted provided he is not killed before the War Office make up their minds. His regular source of income is of course his Army pay which is negligible and does not warrant a bank account. His other sources of income appear to be incidental to war and of a non-predictable nature. I discovered that he was carrying some £30 about with him and considered that at his age and with his possible future it was high time that he opened a banking account....

Maxwell recalls:

> The bank manager at Grindlay's was furious when I gave him my new name of Maxwell and he said, "This is the last time. Do not ask me to change again or I will close the account!"

He did, however, marry under the name of du Maurier nine weeks later because his official papers were still in that name. Maxwell has always proudly claimed that his final choice was a good Scottish name - Carthew-Yorstoun, who apparently suggested it, was a Scot - though at the time he simply described it as being "as good as any".

Maxwell was posted to the 1/5th Battalion of the Queen's. His old friend, Brigadier Carthew-Yorstoun, again intervened to give his career as an officer a fine send-off. He wrote to the battalion's commanding officer on January 2, 1945:

> Lieutenant Maxwell is, I understand, under orders to join your battalion after receiving his commission which was gained for gallantry in the field in the battle of Normandy. I have known him for some years, as well as friends of his and he has stayed with my family at home and I have the highest regard and respect for him.... He has a very strong personality, is well-disciplined but will for various reasons give far better results where he has a certain amount of freedom of choice and movement, than in a position where he is surrounded by too many rules and restrictions.
>
> His sense of duty is outstanding and his desire to kill Huns a driving force.... I know you have acquired a most valuable officer.

The Queen's were part of the 7th Armoured Division, renowned as the Desert Rats. For some weeks the division had occupied a front of about six miles on the south-west of the only German position west of the River Roer, a deep salient near Roermond, a Dutch town just inside the border with Germany. The 131st Brigade were on the right of the sector and the 1/5th Queen's to the right of

them, with their headquarters just inside Germany, in the village of
Wehr. The history of the Queen's Royal Regiment[5] says that the
elimination of the salient was an essential preliminary to the move
up to the line of the Rhine. It had been intended to launch an attack
in early December, but it was first postponed by "vile" weather and
then by the desperate German offensive in the Ardennes aimed at
smashing its way through to Antwerp. For a while the situation was
dangerous, but the attack was held and by mid-January Hitler's last
throw had failed. But while the threat existed, the 1/5th remained
on the defensive. German shelling of the British positions was heavy
and there were frequent clashes between British and German
patrols. Winter snows concealed enemy minefields and some patrols
lost heavily.

On January 10 the battalion was relieved and moved back to
prepare for its part in Operation Blackcock which was intended to
take the Allied army right up to the Roer and wipe out the salient.
The 7th Armoured Division was to play the leading part with the 8th
Armoured Brigade and the 155th Brigade of the 52nd Division
under its command. The main attack was to begin on January 16,
but on the 12th the 1/5th was ordered to capture the village of
Bakenhoven so that it might form a firm base. The weather was
"appalling", according to the account of the fighting compiled by
Major H. J. Nangle, DSO, who was temporarily in command of the
battalion. The countryside was covered with snow which had melted
in places and then frozen into solid sheets of ice. Other snow and
sleet had then fallen upon the ice and it had been followed by dense
patches of fog and mist.

Bakenhoven itself was entirely surrounded by a dyke and a canal.
The attack upon it by the 1/5th began in the early hours of the 13th.
A folding light metal bridge known as a Scissors was put in place
across the dyke and flail tanks and other vehicles crossed it, though
with difficulty, and it was periodically mortared and shelled.

All the houses in the village had been heavily booby-trapped
except for those occupied by the Germans, but by 6.30 am it was
firmly in the hands of D Company. Unfortunately, a flail tank
returning across the Scissors bridge had collapsed it and both bridge
and tank ended in the dyke. That meant that the company was cut
off and the Germans counter-attacked that evening. "The timing of
the attack was perfect", wrote Major Nangle. The enemy, young
German air force troops, came in as the light was failing and
wearing snow suits and it was difficult to see them against the white
countryside. But after two hours of fierce fighting the Germans

were forced back, leaving 25 dead. The way was clear for Operation Blackcock to begin. Maxwell's unit, A Company of the 1/5th, under the command of the Durham Light Infantry, crossed a stream, the Vloed Beek, and branched south to occupy a concrete works.

The 1/5th were now to seize Susteren, a strongly defended village across the Vloed Beek. The weather conditions had worsened. A slight thaw had turned the frozen ground into thick mud, it was foggy and at 2 am, when the attack began, it was pitch dark. It was impossible to get the six-pounder anti-tank guns across the dykes, but by 8 am B Company had won a foothold in Susteren. The Germans then counter-attacked and a platoon was overrun and the company HQ severely shot up. But two enemy tanks were destroyed and the British tanks arrived soon afterwards. The Germans withdrew and by mid-afternoon the village was cleared. The British losses were considerable - 39 killed and wounded (including all the officers of B Company) and 29 missing. By now the thaw had increased, making progress even harder. As the official history records[6]:

> Tanks could only work effectively in this country of dykes and swamps in hard frost and these conditions no longer existed.

On January 21 the 1/5th moved up to Echt and then to Aanderberg, north of Montfort, to support other units which were being strongly counter-attacked. The Germans were also infiltrating the battalion's communications and A Company had to clear them, joining the others at Aanderberg on the 25th. The enemy troops were now falling back behind the Roer, but they left a great number of mines behind and the advance was slow. On the 29th A Company moved in to clear the Dutch village of Paarlo. It was here that Maxwell won his Military Cross. The official citation reads:

> During the attack on Paarlo on 29th January 1945 Lieutenant Maxwell was leading his platoon when a heavy artillery concentration fell on and near the platoon, killing and wounding several men.

> The attack was in danger of losing momentum, but this officer, showing powers of leadership of the highest order, controlled his men with great skill and kept up the advance. During the night, another platoon of this company was counter-attacked and partially overrun. An attempt to restore the position with another platoon failed, but Lieutenant Maxwell repeatedly asked to be allowed to lead another attempt, which request was eventually granted.

> This officer then led two of his sections across bullet-swept ground with great dash and determination and succeeded in contacting the platoon who had been holding out in some buildings.

Showing no regard for his own safety, he led his sections in the difficult job of clearing the enemy out of the buildings, inflicting many casualties on them, and causing the remainder to withdraw.

By his magnificent example and offensive spirit this officer was responsible for the relief of the platoon and the restoration of the situation.

The official history says that during the night of the 29/30th about 50 German troops recrossed the Roer in assault boats and, preceded by heavy shelling and mortaring, made an unexpected counter-attack on A Company. It goes on[7]:

The Germans got into the houses held by 8 Platoon (Lieutenant M.L. Baker) and there was fierce fighting in the dark. In one house, Lance-corporal Dennis most gallantly held them at bay with his Sten gun until 7 Platoon, splendidly led by Second-Lieutenant R. Maxwell, counter-attacked with tank support and cleared the enemy from the village.

In his report of the fighting, Major D.J. Watson, the A Company commander, who was later wounded after the battalion crossed the Rhine, described the action after the Germans attacked the house where Lieutenant Baker and his men were holding out. Two Bren gunners posted on the first floor were the first to be wounded and Lance-corporal Dennis took them to the cellar for safety while Lieutenant Baker went to the first floor to post two more men. At that moment the Germans burst into the house, cutting off Dennis from Baker. Major Watson's account goes on:

In an attempt to relieve them I took two sections from another platoon and we tried to crawl up to the house. A wounded German lying in the street started crying, "Please, friends, come and help me." I stood up, but the moment I did so another German a few yards in front blazed at me with a Spandau. He missed me and hit a lance-corporal by my side. With us we had two Brens, but when we got them in action, unfortunately they jammed. In the circumstances, I had to withdraw the sections. I brought up a tank ... and got it to engage the Spandau.... The tank boys did magnificently. They quickly silenced the Spandau and they accounted for another machine-gun directed at the tank turret.

Meanwhile, the rest of the company were more than holding their own. Mr Maxwell, also a platoon commander, sallied out with two sections and with no further interference from the Spandau which had barred our route, he began to clear the Germans from the houses in Mr Baker's vicinity.

That was the turning point of the battle. The enemy now withdrew and as they went the tank gunners and ourselves gave them hell.... To get to our chaps in the cellar we had to wear respirators, the air being thick with smoke from bursting grenades and exploding ammunition. Mr Baker thought we would find them dead, but they all came out safely.

Lance-corporal Dennis said that the men in the cellar had been saved by the fact that it was in three separate compartments, the middle one being a "no man's land" and the one occupied by the British having a curtain stretched across it. Each time the Germans tried to enter the middle section, he sprayed them with his Sten gun. He went on:

Mr Maxwell when he arrived was fortunate not to be shot himself. Thinking they were Germans upstairs, he ordered them to come down [speaking in German]. One of our lads yelled, "Yes, you —" and let go with his rifle. He just missed. Help for us did not come a moment too soon. All the ammo. I had left was half a Sten magazine.

Maxwell later recalled the situation immediately before he went to the rescue of Baker, Dennis and the others:

The platoon on my right was over-run and the battalion commander ordered my company to withdraw. My company commander (Major Watson) ordered me to retreat, saying that the position was untenable, with heavy German fire (machine guns, rifles, mortars and other guns) against us. I told Major Watson that I could not obey his order because I believed that Lieutenant Baker and some of his men in the other platoon may still be alive and was determined to lead a counter-attack to see if we could repulse the Germans and free our comrades. The major left me, saying that it was a stupid enterprise and I might have to face a court-martial if I came out alive. I organised my remaining forces and counter-attacked.

The Germans were so surprised by this unexpected effort that they began to fall back. The British losses were seven killed and wounded. The following day the Germans blew up the last bridge over the Roer and Operation Blackcock was over. The 1/5th Queen's remained in the Paarlo district until February 7, then spent five days in the "comparative comfort" of the barracks at Maesyck, a pleasant little Belgian town with "very hospitable inhabitants". After some routine patrolling, the whole division was relieved on February 21 by an American Armoured Division and moved back to rest and prepare for the attack on the Rhine.

At the beginning of March Maxwell received the news that his mother and a sister had been executed "as hostages" in July 1944. In a brief note to Betty on March 4, giving her the news, he wrote:

> As you can well imagine, I am not taking any prisoners, and whatever home my men occupy, before I leave I order it to be destroyed.

The next day Field-Marshal Montgomery presented the medals won by the division during Operation Blackcock. Major Nangle received a bar to his DSO, Major C.V. Lilley, Lieutenant M.L. Baker and Second Lieutenant R. Maxwell all received the Military Cross. Lance-corporal R. Dennis received the Distinguished Conduct Medal and Corporal F. Dolly the Military Medal. The share of the medals won by the 1/5th Queen's was the largest in the 7th Armoured Division.

Congratulations poured in for Maxwell. Major-General L.O. Lyne, commander of the 7th Armoured Division, wrote: "Well done!" Brigadier Carthew-Yorstoun was effusive, but added:

> Now, whether you like it or not, you have got to pipe down a bit and not exactly go out of your way to obliterate Boches. You have your girl to think of....

He was unaware, of course, that the girl had been promised the Military Cross, though even she must have been astonished that Maxwell had fulfilled the first of the pledges he had made to her within six weeks of making it. It must have strengthened the remarkable act of faith which led her to agree to marry him in the first place. Not that there was time for second thoughts. Four days after the medal ceremony Maxwell was back in Paris with her to prepare for the marital one.

* * * * *

Maxwell returned to the front after an absence of 13 days. The spring offensive, Operation Plunder, the last great push of the war which was to take the Allies across the Rhine, was about to start. Clearing the west bank of the river had taken the 1st Canadian Army and the 9th American Army nearly five weeks. The fields were sodden and, in some places, flooded. Together with dense minefields and the great forest of the Reichswald, this ensured that progress was difficult and slow and it was not until March 12 that the two armies joined up. The 7th Armoured Division remained resting and training in Holland until the assault was due to begin. The role of the 7th Armoured Division was to ford the river at Xanten, one of the main crossing points (the other was at Wesel) on the British front. Its objective was to drive east and north-east to cut across the lines of communication of the German 1st Parachute Army, the only one to escape virtually intact to the east side of the Rhine.

The first assault began on March 23. By the evening of the 26th the 15th Division had a bridgehead five miles deep on the east bank and the 7th Armoured Division crossed the next day. The official history of the Queen's records[8]:

> The [1/5th] Battalion was in splendid fettle, over strength in numbers and in a high state of efficiency and morale after its month's rest and training.

At first, opposition was slight and the regimental records noted that "many Boche were glad to surrender", but on the 29th the 1/5th encountered strong German resistance at Sudlohn where the remaining members of a panzer grenadier division were holding out. The Germans were overcome and 30 prisoners taken. A and D Companies then moved along parallel roads to Ahaus. D Company was delayed by several German bazooka attacks and its column split up. A Company was delayed only by minefields. Together with B Company and D Company which later rejoined them, they occupied Ahaus, which had been totally destroyed by the RAF, on March 31. By April 1 the division had advanced 120 miles from the Rhine to the River Ems. The resistance had been slight; the German army in the west was collapsing, its organisation was virtually non-existent and the expected resistance from civilians and "werewolves" did not materialise. The civilians appeared "mostly surly and apathetic", says the regimental history.

There were occasional pockets of stout resistance, especially by officer cadets and instructors from the Hanover Cadet School, who fought hard and held up two armoured divisions for 48 hours, "a good example of how well-trained and determined infantry in defence can achieve much against vastly superior forces". But the advance generally was inexorable; only its pace varied. On April 5 the 22nd Armoured Brigade, with the 1/5th under its command, swept forward 20 miles, but on April 7 the 7th Armoured was checked again when the Germans blew up all the bridges over the Weser. A and D Companies of the 1/5th, together with the 8th Hussars, made an organised attack on the village of Riede on the road to Bremen, but when they advanced with their tanks the Germans, who had held the village during the day, were found to have fled. The next morning, says the regimental history[9]:

> The Battalion, again with the 8th Hussars, were ordered to attack the two villages of Sudweyne and Kirchweyne, about fives miles south-west of Bremen.... A Company led off successfully and by noon had cleared Sudweyne, held by a newly-arrived company of 20

SS Training Division, 7 Platoon (Lieutenant R. Maxwell) alone
having killed fifteen SS men and taken fourteen prisoners.

Other companies of the battalion ran into strong resistance and an
officer had to be transferred from A Company to C Company
because all its officers were dead or wounded. The history
concludes:

> It had been a very good day for the 1/5th Queen's, who had advanced
> to within fives miles of Bremen against determined opposition from a
> strong SS formation.

The Germans were clearly determined to fight hard to keep
Bremen, so the 7th Armoured Division was switched to another
part of the front and on April 15 crossed the River Aller. The 1/5th
went over at 11 am and by nightfall had advanced 10 miles to take
the town of Walsrode. The next day, C Company liberated 12,000
British and American soldiers and thousands of prisoners of other
nationalities from a large camp south-west of Fallingbostel while A
Company waded across the river to the north-west of the town to cut
off its defenders. But most of the Germans withdrew in time. By
April 20, Hitler's birthday, the 1/5th was ordered to help clear the
Forest of Harburg and on the next day it took up position on the
high wooded ground above Harburg and Hamburg.

Resistance stiffened once more. D Company had one of its
patrols wiped out by a German party shielding under a white flag
and for some days activity was confined to sniping and patrols. But
the war was being lost by the Germans elsewhere. On April 29 they
began to negotiate the surrender of Hamburg, which was
accomplished on May 2. Until that moment the Queen's were still
faced with sniping and by German posts with no inclination to
surrender, but says the history[10]:

> In the morning of the 3rd, after the announcement of the surrender of
> the city, prisoners began to pour in. They were of every age, from
> young boys to old men, and seemed quite apathetic.

At four o'clock that afternoon the 1/5th Queen's, Maxwell among
them, with the 5th Royal Tanks, led the 7th Armoured Division
into the devastated city, the largest captured by the Allies and
Germany's chief port. The 1/5th took over the town hall, the post
office and the police barracks, all of which were in the centre of the
town. That night Germany's surrender was announced. Hostilities
were to cease the next day. Though VE-Day was not officially to be
until May 8, the war in Europe, in which up to 50 million had died,
including six million Jews, among them - though he could not be

certain of it then - most of Robert Maxwell's family, was over. During it the 1/5th Battalion of the Queen's suffered nearly 1,500 casualties, but in its last phase between the Rhine and the Elbe its casualties were comparatively light - nine officers and 69 men killed or wounded.

On September 7 Maxwell led the detachment of the 1/5th which took part in the Allied Victory Parade through Berlin. It was a long way from Solotvino and it had taken him five years to get there, but no moment in his military career was sweeter.

* * * * *

Throughout the fighting of the first four months of 1945 Maxwell wrote to his wife-to-be and then his wife-that-was. Much of the correspondence was what is to be expected of the newly-affianced and newly-wed, but almost every letter also described the fighting in which his unit was taking part. They show a confident, at times conceited, ambitious young man, never doubting his ultimate survival, though occasionally aware of the anxieties of a wife who must have dreaded daily the arrival of a telegram from the War Office which began, "I deeply regret to inform you...". The letters, all written in idiomatic English which betrays no trace of his central European origin and addressed to "Betushka", demonstrate a detestation of the Germans and a ruthlessness in fighting them which was all the more striking because it was unquestioned: though he conceded occasionally that war was beastly, there is no doubt that he relished his part in it. Thus, he could casually inform his wife that he had shot the mayor of a German town without apparently wondering whether she might think summary execution was a harsh punishment for an official who had misled him. The letters, written in the last weeks of the war, have a cumulative impact and extracts from them are reproduced in sequence rather than interspersed in the narrative. The first was written soon after he joined the Queen's in January:

> *20 January 1945*
>
> Before leaving Brussels, I had an interview at Army HQ and was told that the Divisional Commander who commanded the Division in which I was serving in Normandy is commanding the Division to which I am going and that he asked that I be posted there after having written a very complimentary letter about me which will be very useful in my military career.
>
> Both the horse and the dog are happy and are just itching to get to

grips with the hated Boches. [The "horse" was a motorcycle and sidecar. The dog was a labrador which Maxwell had acquired in Paris. In the style of a First World War English officer, he took it to the front with him, hidden beneath a blanket in the sidecar. It was killed when it went ahead of Maxwell and ran onto a landmine.]

26 January 1945

... You my love have been given the harder task, that of anxiety and waiting and fear of what the postman may bring next day ... to me, this period is but like a nightmare which has to be and will be forgotten, but what it is doing for me is that it's steeling me for my future responsibilities and cleansing me so that I am worthy to become the husband of you, my star.

28 January 1945

I am in Holland. I am commanding about 30 men and this time tomorrow I shall take them into attack ... when talking to them or giving orders I am my usual strong and confident self, but inside I am anxious. Will I do well? I pray to God so that he may give me wisdom and strength so that I may come out victorious of the ordeal ahead. The chaps I am commanding seem to be a hard and difficult lot ... all that I have got to show them tomorrow is that I am also a good fighting fellow and the rest is easy [in] this beastly game which people call war.

31 January 1945

I have stood the test. I am now sitting in a house and trying to write a letter to you. I have to make a great effort not to drop the pen as I am still suffering the effects of the previous battle. We took a village on the morning of the 29th after some opposition. We made our hole and now we have to hold it. Apart from the usual artillery and mortar fire, nothing happened during the day, but at night round ten o'clock after a stiff barrage the Boches put in an attack with orders to retake the village. [This was the fighting which earned Maxwell his M.C.] This I learned from prisoners which I interrogated after the battle, which lasted till 2.30 am. Most of the men were very brave.

1 February 1945

I have just finished censoring my platoon's mail. One chap writing to his fiancée says that "this mob", meaning this regiment, seems as though it wanted to win this war on its own and I am inclined to agree with him.

Later the same day

It's midnight, and a strange sinister quietness prevails in this surrounding countryside broken at this moment only by the distant sounding hum of a night-fighter on patrol. This peace is unbelievable

and foreign to the usual din and noise of a battlefield; war is a very
strange game and, as you see, it has also got its peaceful minutes
which are very welcome. Your photo in the shadow of my hurricane
lamp by which I am writing looks more beautiful than ever. I can
never tire looking at it. I always seem to discover something I have
missed in the face which I adore.

5 February 1945

The house which I left not so long ago has received three direct hits;
as usual, they waited until I left (Keep it up, Adolf). I am glad I
ordered the civilians to evacuate the place, otherwise they would
have had it.... Can you as my military subordinate report all
[wedding] preparations ready and complete? Because Lieutenant
Robert Maxwell has already made a name for himself here by not
liking things done slowly and halfway. So you keep a sharp lookout,
otherwise you will have to answer several charges which you may find
difficult to explain, even though you are a lawyer.

12 February 1945

We are once more off to the line and the weather is simply too bloody
for words. I wish God wouldn't help Hitler every time and to make
things worse. We blew the Roer dams, thus making it still more
difficult for everybody.

16 February 1945

I shall consider no labour too hard nor exertion too difficult for the
attainment of the one and cardinal aim, which is happiness for us and
our children. I believe that all other things which we hope to attain in
life depend upon whether we have the will and character to attain
complete unity of purpose, which automatically will reward us with
the happiness that we are striving for.

23 February 1945

I am now in a town in Holland.... During the day I do training with
my men. At night I read whatever I can lay my hands on and sleep as
many hours as I can.

27 February 1945

I don't think I shall be going back to the front before our marriage as
I have got to attend a parade where Montgomery presents me with a
medal ribbon.

28 February 1945

I have just had a personal letter of congratulations from the
Major-General commanding the Division on my immediate award of
the MC and on this coming Monday I will be decorated by
Montgomery.

6 March 1945

I was decorated yesterday by Montgomery. He asked me all sorts of questions and was apparently pleased with my answers.

[Maxwell returned to Paris on March 9, and was married five days later, three days after Betty's birthday. They honeymooned at Versailles from the 15th until the 19th.]

22 March 1945

I have just finished my day's work, which consisted of training my men in street fighting. I feel very tired, as I had to do a lot of running about and shouting; the weather here is just like summer, which is a great help to me because it helps me to overcome my loneliness.... I am happy because of the certainty of all this soon being over and we shall then be able to start on the road of happiness together as one strong and unbreakable unit, a unit which can weather all storms and which in the end is bound to emerge triumphant....

27 March 1945

I am quite well and very much in love with someone you know perhaps and miss her as much as I miss thirty tons of armour around me, because for the last half an hour all hell has broken loose over here. It's misty and it's cold but that and more will not stop me from finishing my letter to my wife. Over here the going is pretty hard but it can't last very much longer now because the foe is getting a hell of a time, too. Shells are falling all around me but I have got a very nice and deep hole which some German must have spent at least two days to dig and so I am not worried.

28 March 1945

We got the Germans on the run at last ... the Germans are at the moment nowhere to be found.

1 April 1945

My company commander has been wounded in the arm. I got a piece of shrapnel in the knee, not very serious. [This was similar to the wound he received in the fighting in 1940 but this time it was in the other knee.]

3 April 1945

I had a very amusing day yesterday. I will now give you a report of it. I and my men captured a bridge and crossroads on the night of the 1st; next morning when it got light I saw a village about one kilometer in front of my positions. I decided to go and have a look at it with my batman and one machine-gun; the first house I came to I asked the German living there how many soldiers were in the village and where are they? He told me there are 16 and he pointed out the houses which they occupied, so I sent him to tell the German soldiers to come out with a white flag or else. A few minutes later I saw them running out of the houses and we started firing at each other. I got two of them and came back to my positions and I ordered the mortars to shell the village for a few minutes. A few minutes later the white flag was hoisted on the village church, so I picked all my men up and we marched into the village. At the end of the village begins a town of about 8,000 inhabitants and I thought perhaps I could repeat the same game, so I sent one of the Germans to go and fetch the mayor of the town. In half an hour's time, he turned up and I told him that he had got to tell the Germans to surrender and hang the white flag otherwise the town will be destroyed. One hour later he came back saying that the soldiers will surrender and the white flag was put up so we marched off, but as soon as we marched off a German tank opened fire on us. Luckily he missed, so I shot the mayor and withdrew. I saw my colonel and asked him whether our artillery could fire on the town. He said Yes, if I could direct it by wireless. I said Yes, so back I went to the village. The only place from where I could observe and direct the artillery was the church spire, so up I went, got my wireless working and ordered the artillery to open fire. For half an hour I directed them on different targets; believe me, it was quite a sight.

I could see exactly every shell's exploding point. Meanwhile, the Germans suspected that somebody must be directing the artillery, because it was so accurate. They knew the only place you could observe the town was from the church spire, so they tried to shoot it down. Of course they missed.

6 April 1945

I am fit and well, and very deep inside Germany advancing along a main road. I don't know where they are, but nor do the Germans know where we are and so you keep going until somebody starts shooting, then you have to fight a little battle or a big battle, it all depends how many Germans there are; as usual, we win and we get on our tanks or trucks and move on. I wrote to you about how the town has been taken at last. It was defended by about 600 officer cadets from the school of officers, Hanover, all of them fanatics, so most of them died.... I am dead tired. I haven't had my clothes off for weeks now and no sleep for 72 hours, but still it will not last very long now.

9 April 1945

I am well and still fighting. There is a very difficult job for me to do. We have got to rush a bridge across a biggish river. We hope to go that fast that the Boches will have no time to press the lever and blow the bridge whilst we are getting across or just after we are on the other side. But I know that God is looking after us.

Later the same day

I am sound ... in good health and in most excellent spirits after a very successful day of fighting a few miles from Bremen. The Germans have brought up SS formations to defend the town and this was our first encounter with them. I was leading my platoon into a village. I had to fight for nearly every house and the hardest fight I had was in the cemetery. The outcome was that I took the village after four hours' fighting. I lost one man killed and one man wounded. We killed over 20 and took 19 prisoners. I have ordered the Germans out of a very nice house and installed my HQ in it....

12 April 1945

21 Army Group HQ turned down the recommendation to my promotion to Captain on the grounds it would cause bad feelings between the other officers of the brigade if I was promoted so quickly, because after all I have only been commissioned three months. I am not unduly disappointed because, after all, the army is not my career....

13 April 1945

I am writing this letter in a German house from which I have evicted the occupants on 10 minutes' notice, which they didn't like very much. So I reminded them of 1940-41-42 and what they used to do to other people when they were winning....

17 April 1945

I am fit and well and if the Boches don't decide to put in a counter-attack against my positions, I may be able to get a few hours sleep.... Blast it, damn it, the shooting has started again.... It's a counter-attack all right, so if I post this letter then you will know that I managed to beat it off.

20 April 1945

This last week we have been fighting or advancing continuously and we are now very close to Hamburg and the going is harder the closer we get to the darned place.... At the moment, I am sitting in a farmyard and writing this letter on my knee, the sun is out and it is nice and warm. A few hundred yards from here a wood has been set on fire, a little way over to my left you can see our tanks and artillery knocking down another German village and so it goes on until the last Boche has either been killed or laid down his arms.... All I ever seem to write about is this beastly war.... But as long I am doing what I am, war is all I can write about.

23 April 1945

I had a very lucky escape last night on patrol, a big shell landed half a yard in front of me and failed to go off! Believe me, I felt very weak at the knees for a few minutes after that, but I got my few Jerries for the day and returned to my positions at 05.30 this morning....

26 April 1945

This morning I had an interview about my job as liaison with the Red Army, it was quite successful and I shall be notified as to whether I have been accepted within the next three weeks. We are very near Hamburg and the Germans have succeeded in halting up our advance. For the last three days we haven't advanced an inch, we are in defence and the Boches on our front are very aggressive, they keep on jabbing at our lines, attacking here, attacking there, as if they didn't know that half of their country has been occupied already. Sometimes, I begin to think that I should have joined another regiment, because somehow or other the Queen's always seem to attract all the Nazi fanatics on its front, but never mind, we have beaten them quite a few times before and we shall no doubt shift them from here shortly. And here is exactly what's happening on my little part of the front. At the moment there is a German plane overhead and our guns are firing at it and here come some shells; our own guns have opened up and now it is like Dante's Inferno. The air is filled with all sorts of noises, whines, cracks and booms.... I was just going to write that it is quiet again but our artillery has opened up again.... It's all quiet now except for distant explosions of the shells somewhere in the Boche lines....

27 April 1945

You simply must write to me every day ... because I must have this little bit of daily happiness to save me from getting drowned in my surroundings which consist only of hate, fear and destruction.... I have now been moved to a more dangerous part of the front, still near Hamburg, but the Boche is only 150 yards away, which means you have to be awake all night and sleep in daytime if you can. My feet are burning like hell and it is exactly a month today since I had my boots or clothes off and I am really beginning to feel the strains of it all. I must have a bath tomorrow even if I have to get the water under sniper fire....

All shooting has just started. My platoon is being attacked. I must go.... It was a German patrol trying to take some prisoners but we saw them off for a little while, anyway. This is why any talk of V Day which one can read about so much in the papers these days doesn't make any sense for me. Do you remember when I told you last December that it will not be over till June, well, that still stands.

29 April 1945

It looks like we are going to stay here in a defensive role for a few more days, so I decided to have a big hole dug where I can put in the whole of my HQ staff, my wireless and telephone. Myself, my batman and wireless operator worked on it for 12 hours non-stop. It's 1.70 [metres] deep, 2.50 long and 2.20 wide, it's got a very strong roof on top and on top of the roof is all the soil which we dug out. That makes it a very good foxhole and only a direct hit by a heavy calibre shell could do me any harm whilst I am down here....

I must go and see my sentries, whether they are awake and doing their duties. I have got 12 men on guard during the whole night and it is a very good thing from the point of view of my men's morale to show them that even though it's gone midnight I am not afraid to go and inspect the most forward sentries of my platoon which is about 60 yards from the Huns' positions.

Later the same day

I am well, but in the same place, and especially at night it's rather nerve-wracking ... they put in a counter-attack with 200 men, one tank and several self-propelled guns. Fighting went on all night and by the morning they had had enough. They lost 47 killed, 56 captured and no doubt quite a few were wounded, but the Germans managed to evacuate them - we lost seven killed, 20 wounded and 18 got captured.

4 May 1945

The war is over!!! It's just been announced, 8.20 pm, it's true, it's over and I am still in one piece.... I have just been told we are pushing on to Kiel right away. Look out for the newsreel about Hamburg, you will see me in it issuing orders and carrying my faithful stick.

4

Berlin, Barter and Books

I have been poor and I have been rich.
Rich is better.

Sophie Tucker

The end of the war, when it finally came, was almost an anti-climax. There was no drama, no sudden collapse as there had been in 1918. The defeat of Germany had been a foregone conclusion for months, even among the Nazi hierarchy. Hitler's suicide merely cheated the death which those who had suffered from the Third Reich were preparing for him. Most soldiers not in the Allied armies wanted to get home as quickly as they could and were willing once more to place the future of Europe back into the hands of the politicians. In Britain and America those families with sons, brothers and fathers serving - or imprisoned - in the Far East wanted the fighting there to be brought swiftly to an end. Britain, in particular, was anxious to begin to repair the devastation which war had delivered both to its cities and to its economy, and to that end was within two months to sweep Winston Churchill and - more precisely - the Conservative party from office. The gratitude of the people for what Churchill had done did not extend to the party he led. The voters, and especially the servicemen, were not prepared to leave the winning of the peace to a party whose pre-war policies had helped lead the way to war.

Maxwell had already decided that his future lay in Britain and had sent Betty to stay in London with the Straton-Ferriers until he could provide a home for her and start to make his fortune. That he was determined to achieve outstanding success, in one field or another, is beyond doubt. What that field would be was uncertain on May 8, 1945. The election of the Labour Government that July seems to have passed without comment by him. Because he didn't have a vote, had no experience of the British electoral system and didn't even have British nationality at that point, the radical nature of the domestic change may have evaded him.

His own political leanings had been shaped in his teens by his mother. He was of the European left, hated appeasement and counted himself an enemy of the class which had condemned his father and millions of others to poverty, and unable to provide a proper home, education or sustenance for their families. But there was no sign at that stage, other than in the promise in his proposal of marriage, that he was contemplating a political career.

But he was certainly thinking of his civilian career. On May 10, two days after VE Day, he wrote to Betty:

> We have now become static and doing guard over the beaten Boches. The job is very simple ... and it gives me more time to think of our future, for which I am now making careful and detailed plans.... I shall let you know them all as soon as I have decided which course of action I am taking, either to do my two years Army of Occupation or to get my discharge papers as soon as possible. That at the moment is my big problem ... if I stay another two years in the army, then all the best jobs will have gone.

In a sense, he seemed almost reluctant to let go of the war. Perhaps it was too soon to shake off the first five years of his manhood, all of which had been spent in uniform. He was writing again to Betty on May 11:

> To divert my mind away from that terrible longing that I feel for you, I went out and took eight of my men with me on a security patrol and check-up in my area. I searched quite a few houses and when I had finished I had found three rifles and ammunition and nine German soldiers, four in uniform, the rest in civilian clothes and one Gestapo, not a bad bag. The Germans in the area are dead scared of me and have already nicknamed me the Black Hurricane and there isn't a thing they wouldn't do for me. The Herrenvolk, they make me laugh.... I have got to prepare a lecture tonight on how to be a useful citizen because tomorrow morning I am talking about it to the troops ... now that there are no longer any Germans to fight we have still got to keep the troops occupied and the best way of spending the time before demobilisation is definitely in preparing for their responsibilities in civilian life; I contribute to that end by giving lectures on various subjects and I have also become a teacher for part of the day in that I teach languages for two hours daily. What a change from digging-in and shooting.

Again, on May 13, still longing for home, still missing his wife, still only slowly letting go of the war:

> Sometimes that pang of loneliness hits me so hard that its weight

becomes almost unbearable.... When there were Germans to fight I
could turn that loneliness to hate but now whom else can I come to
for consolation but you.... [Describing photographs taken
immediately after entry into Hamburg] The three tanks you see are
under my command and my men ride on them. They saved our skins
quite a few times.

Towards the end of May he snatched a few days' leave in London,
laden, like most returning servicemen, with presents which were
usually described as "souvenirs" and a number of china figures and
vases which he had bought. Some were later sold, others the family
still has.

Betty was living at Eileen Straton-Ferrier's home in South
Kensington. She had arrived in late April, according to Brian
Straton-Ferrier, looking "exhausted, half-starved and thin as a
needle". She hadn't seen rice or sausages for four years, he recalled,
and ordinary British rations, which were spartan enough at that
time, "seemed to her like a feast".

Mrs Straton-Ferrier remembered Maxwell's sudden, un-
announced arrival on leave. Though he had written regularly to
Betty, the letters must have been delayed and she had "feared the
worst". Betty ran down five flights of stairs from her attic room to
throw her arms around Maxwell before he had time to unload his
pack.

Brian Straton-Ferrier, speaking many years later to his mother,
reminded her of the day when a large, heavy parcel arrived for Betty
at the Straton-Ferrier home. It was from Maxwell and "it stank to
high heaven". He said:

> We opened it and found inside the uncured pelts of two magnificent
> silver foxes. Betty had them treated and turned into a pair of very
> ritzy wraps.

Mrs Straton-Ferrier then told her son of the sequel. Some years
later she was due to be presented at Court and meet the Queen, now
the Queen Mother:

> Impecunious as my mother then was, the agonising problem of what
> she was to wear assumed earth-shaking proportions. The day was
> saved when Betty loaned her a smart hat she had bought on a recent
> trip to Paris, a pair of long, black suede leather gloves and - two
> magnificent silver fox furs.

When Maxwell returned to Germany after his first home leave he
began to lead a life which, he said in a letter on June 7, "is much too
easy for me". He filled in his time perfecting his Russian. On June

26 the 22-year-old groom of little more than three months was
philosophising on marriage and divorce and writing to Betty:

> If you ask me why so many marriages end up in the divorce court, it is
> because most men don't put forth the same effort to make his [sic]
> home a going concern as he does to make his business or profession a
> success ... although to have a contented wife and a peaceful and
> happy home means more to a man than to make a million pounds,
> not one in a hundred ever gives any really serious thought or makes
> any honest effort to make his marriage a success. He leaves the most
> important thing in his life to chance and he wins or loses, according to
> whether fortune is with him or not and that ... is one thing I shall
> never do; and that's why I am so certain that with your help ... we
> shall make our life worthy of our dreams and promises and at the end
> of it all we shall most certainly be able to stand up to our children as a
> perfect example of happiness attained through sacrifice, effort and
> goodwill.

The next day he carried his philosophy of marriage into its
practical realities, writing:

> Here are my six rules for the perfect partnership.
> 1. Don't nag.
> 2. Don't criticise unduly.
> 3. Give honest appreciation.
> 4. Pay little attentions.
> 5. Be courteous.
> 6. Have the utmost confidence in yourself and in your partner.

On July 1 Maxwell was posted to Berlin as part of the advance
party to take over the British section of Berlin from the Soviet army.
Four days later he was writing lightly to Betty:

> Have you read, darling, that Carpathian Ruthenia is now officially
> USSR, which makes us Soviet citizens?

Maxwell's job was to get his battalion billeted in Berlin. From
morn till night, he said, he had been working to get its barracks into
a fit condition. They had previously been occupied by Soviet troops
who had left them in "a most filthy state". To put matters right, he
ordered the Burgermeister to send in five hundred women to clean
the barracks, but "although they have been at it for four days the
job is still not finished". In addition, he had to find labour to
connect the water and electricity supplies, acquire furniture and
"hundreds of other things". At the end of it all, he said, he was left
very tired. On July 9 he was writing sombrely:

> Berlin is in a shambles. You can ride in a car for an hour without

being able to see one house intact. The people are on starvation rations and no doubt before the year is out thousands of them will perish of hunger.

Maxwell's command of languages made him much in demand and he became adjutant to the Military Government with offices in Berlin's Spandau prison. It gave him work to do and allowed him to use his initiative, but he didn't like it for several reasons:

Firstly, in doing my job I am helping the Germans, secondly, most of the time I have to spend in my office interviewing people and writing out orders ... and I can't stay for long a chair-bound soldier ... and I am already thinking of trying the field security police.

His political thinking at this time did not match his military experience. The aftermath of victory bathed the Western world in a rosy optimism which the facts were not to warrant. He wrote to Betty on July 21:

About Potsdam ... I think that the three major powers will come to an agreement about getting a working peace for Europe in spite of the terrific difficulties to be surmounted, because if they cannot find a form of agreement between themselves and at the same time acceptable to the whole world, then the greatest-ever disaster will embrace the world as well as themselves and I am sure that Churchill and Truman, as well as Stalin, are aware of all that and that's why I am certain that a lasting peace as well as agreement on all important economic questions will be reached at this most momentous of all international conferences in the whole history of statesmanship, and I am also sure that from its success the whole of mankind will gain immensely by the establishing of peace and order right throughout the world.

In fact, Potsdam didn't achieve much at all. It began on July 17, but Churchill returned to London on the 25th so that he might be on hand for the expected Conservative general election victory. Instead, there was a Labour landslide and Clement Attlee, who had been with Churchill at the conference, returned without him, despite an invitation to the wartime leader to remain with the British delegation. Attlee arrived on the 28th. Eight days later the atomic bomb was dropped on Hiroshima and the world changed again. The Allied victory parade through Berlin, in which Maxwell proudly took part on September 7, was already part of a different age, the nuclear one.

Meanwhile, his personal future was of more immediate concern than the future of the world. He left his post with the Military Government and returned to his battalion where, he told Betty on

July 23, he was "doing nothing", though he went on to protest:

> I am not wasting my time, I am making money, instead. I will give
> you a closer account as soon as I can. My profits since I got back here
> must be nearly £100, which is not so bad. My prospects for further
> profit are quite good and I am doing nothing illegal.... I have at most
> one more year to serve, during which time I shall perfect my French
> and Russian and, if I have the time, I will also learn Spanish, as it is
> imperative that I speak Spanish if I want to do business with South
> America. [In fact, Spanish was to be one of the world's few principal
> languages which he never learned.]

In another letter he repeated his prediction about the dire
prospects facing the people of Berlin. They were "most certainly
starving" he said, and unless the food situation improved rapidly - of
which there was no chance at that moment - "then thousands will go
kaput of hunger".

He was still awaiting word of his family in Solotvino. He had
heard a year earlier that his mother and a sister were dead, but he
knew no more, though by that time he feared that none of them had
survived. That knowledge could move him to anger. His hatred of
the Germans was never far below the surface and he wrote:

> It is appalling to see all these Englishmen walking arm in arm with
> these Hun women. I am simply disgusted to see how short their
> memory really is....

Today the ferocity of the hatred and bitterness which consumed
him during and immediately after the war has eased. He says:

> The sorrow of the loss of my family is ever before me. It is not for
> me to forgive, only the dead can do that. I cannot forget. But I find
> the German people are making excellent efforts to redeem
> the irredeemable. I do not hate the Germans today. But they are
> thorough to the point of pedantry. They were educated to follow
> orders to the point where they would kill deliberately. The vast
> majority of the British would rebel against having to do that. You
> could not in Britain have farmers living next to a concentration camp
> and keeping it secret.

By July 29 he was writing to Betty saying that he was going for a
job with the Control Commission in Germany because, otherwise,
he was likely to be posted to the Pacific, which he was not anxious
should happen. "Don't worry, dearest", he reassured his wife, "I
shall get out of it, somehow." Meanwhile, he continued with his
Russian lessons:

> I am learning to read and write Russian two hours a day, I am making
> excellent progress and I should be able to write to you a letter in
> Russian in a fortnight's time.

Whether Mrs Maxwell would have been able to translate such a letter was not a matter he dealt with. His thoughts were now concentrated on returning to Czechoslovakia to find out what had happened to his family. He had arranged to leave for Prague in early August but his brigadier refused him permission to go for fear that the Russians would arrest him if he tried to pass through their zone without authority. His mind, however, was not excluded from dealing with other questions. He wrote to Betty on August 4:

> I have sent you with one of my soldiers five paintings which I hope you received. Look after them and especially the ones without frames. You must be very careful not to damage them. I will let you know shortly what you should do with them.

The paintings were later examined by experts and turned out to be skilful copies of little value. The Maxwells still have one of them.

On September 7, still preoccupied with personal matters, he wrote:

> I am worried about my future, speaking in material terms, and last, but not least, my surviving sisters. Where are they? What are they doing? Are they to have survived the indescribable horrors of Auschwitz in order to die of hunger and cold in the so-called liberated world?

At that time he had no sure knowledge that any of his sisters were alive. Through the Red Cross, he had managed, in 1943, to send a telegram to his family in Solotvino and had received a reply saying that all were well. But he could not know what had happened after that, except that Hungary's Jews had been rounded up and most of them sent to Auschwitz. For their part, Brana, who survived Mauthausen and Buchenwald, and Sylvia, who sheltered in Budapest and then Romania, could not be certain whether their brother had come through the war unharmed.

Maxwell was made Intelligence officer for the 1/5th on September 17 and he wrote to Betty:

> It means I shall have a lot more to do; besides controlling 130 Germans who work for us in camp, I have also got to look after the running of the battalion farm which consists of pigs, chickens, ducks and geese. Add all this to the normal regimental duties and you will see that your husband will have very little time to get lazy.

But three days later came news that the battalion was leaving Berlin at the beginning of October. He wanted to be posted to the Intelligence service in the British zone so that he might later apply for an Intelligence liaison job with the Control Commission. That would be a civilian post, paying about £1,000 a year, a considerable salary for those days. More important, though, was the fact that he thought the job would help him to gain British nationality, which was crucial to his whole future.

On September 20 he was gleefully writing that a Czech colonel had promised to try to trace his sisters for him in return for petrol with which Maxwell had supplied him:

> When they are found I intend to bring them here to Berlin, and for as long as I am in Germany I think that they should stay with me, especially if I volunteer to stay another year here, in which case you would be here to help me look after them.

On October 14, at last, he left for Prague, armed with a certificate authorising his father to leave Prague for Berlin "to assist with the return of Czech citizens to their country". The certificate's validity had expired, but it was a vain quest anyway. Mehel Hoch had been dead for at least a year and probably longer. But that visit to Prague was to lead to Sylvia and Brana hearing on the refugees' grapevine that their brother was alive and well and looking for them.

In November 1945 he started a new job as an Intelligence interrogation officer at Iserlohn, to where Brana traced him on the 21st and where the three surviving Hochs were at last reunited. The good news he had for them was that they would soon become aunts. Betty was pregnant and their first child was expected in the early spring.

* * * * *

On January 7, 1946 he was writing mysteriously to Betty that Major Willi Johannmeier "who had the third copy of Adolf's testament was here with us but I am not allowed to discuss this subject any further". In fact, Maxwell had been within an ace of getting his hands on Hitler's last will and testament, at the time probably the most sought-after historical document in the world. Johannmeier had been in the Fuehrer's bunker in Berlin until April 29, the day of Hitler's suicide. He and an SS officer, Wilhelm Zander, Martin Bormann's personal assistant, had been entrusted with copies to take to the outside world. Zander was to deliver two copies, plus the certificate of Hitler's marriage to Eva Braun, to Admiral Doenitz, who briefly succeeded Hitler, and Johannmeier was to pass his to Field-Marshal Ferdinand Schoerner, newly-appointed commander-in-chief of the army. Maxwell had interrogated Johannmeier, whose possession of the last will and testament had been disclosed to the British by a Propaganda Ministry official, Heinz Lorenz, who had also been in the bunker until the end and who had brought Joseph Goebbels's last testament out with him. Johannmeier, says Maxwell, refused to part with Hitler's testament unless he was given his freedom in exchange. Maxwell was not empowered to offer that. General Sir Brian Horrocks, his corps commander, told Maxwell that he had failed and that a superior Intelligence officer would be sent out from London. He was to be Hugh Trevor-Roper, later Lord Dacre, expert on, and author of, *The Last Days of Hitler*. Maxwell asked Horrocks for an assurance that Trevor-Roper would not be given the authority to offer Johannmeier what he was unable to - his freedom. Horrocks readily gave the assurance.

From this point, the accounts of Maxwell and Trevor-Roper become irreconcilable. Maxwell says that Johannmeier was an SS officer and in a letter on another matter, sent to Professor Trevor-Roper in July 1962, he referred in passing to the fact that he had been one of the 1st Corps interrogators at Iserlohn of Major Johannmeier, "Hitler's SS adjutant". Trevor-Roper, in his book, described Johannmeier as "a straightforward soldier, of unconditional loyalties and unpolitical courage"[1] - qualities which would not normally be ascribed to an SS man - and he wrote of him:

> At first, he denied all knowledge of the Bunker, then, finding it impossible to maintain this position, he insisted that he had merely been sent as a military escort to Zander and Lorenz, to guide them through the Russian lines. What their mission was he did not know: it had been none of his business to ask. Nothing could shake him from this position, and in spite of the discrepancy between his evidence and that of Lorenz, he almost convinced his interrogators.

But Maxwell clearly was not convinced. He insists that Johannmeier wanted freedom from arrest and prosecution. Trevor-Roper mentioned no kind of bargain at all. He said that Johannmeier was "actuated merely by loyalty ... impervious to fear, indifferent to reward, it seemed that nothing would move him except reason", which, in the end and unsurprisingly, was to prove to be the reason of Trevor-Roper. Its power so overwhelmed Johannmeier that he "capitulated" and handed over the testament. Maxwell says that despite Horrocks's assurance, Trevor-Roper offered Johannmeier his freedom. Certainly, Trevor-Roper made no reference to Johannmeier being arrested, though both Zander and Lorenz, his companions in the bunker, were taken into custody.

Trevor-Roper's picture of a simple, loyal, unpolitical soldier merely doing his duty seems at odds with the fact that he was in the Fuehrer's bunker until the end, when all had been given the opportunity to leave several days earlier and most had taken it; that he maintained his loyalty long after Hitler's death had been accepted by the world; that he was, according to William Shirer[2], Hitler's military adjutant and a "much-decorated" officer, and, by the description of John Toland, author of the authoritative biography of Hitler[3], the Fuehrer's army adjutant. Hitler's close aides were always required to be politically loyal and no one, however simple a soldier, could have been that close to the Fuehrer and been unaware of the crimes committed on his orders.

Nearly 30 years later there was a satisfying sequel for the young Intelligence officer who had seen his interrogation taken over by the superior officer from London. While waiting in a BBC studio to take part in a television broadcast he saw the late Charles Douglas-Home, editor of *The Times*. "Hullo", said Maxwell. "What are you doing here?" Douglas-Home replied that he was announcing the biggest news: the discovery of Hitler's diaries. Maxwell told him not to be stupid; they did not exist. Douglas-Home said he was satisfied that they did. Their authenticity had been certified by Lord Dacre. Maxwell then recounted the story of the interrogation at Iserlohn. He may not have dented Douglas-Home's belief in the existence of the diaries, but Lord Dacre himself did that within hours when he recanted on his previous conviction that the diaries were genuine.

There were other excitements while at Iserlohn, where the work was so secret that every Intelligence officer was known by another name, a practice which had become commonplace for Hoch-du Maurier-Smith-Jones-Maxwell. This time his pseudonym was "Captain Stone", though it was a name designed only to be used to conceal his true identity.

One of the Germans whom Maxwell personally detained was Herr Friedrich Flick, probably the most important German industrialist after Krupp, who later appeared before the War Crimes Tribunal at Nüremburg. Flick was a steel magnate, an active financial supporter of the Nazi party who was rewarded by being allowed to take over a plant in occupied Lorraine for a song. He was found guilty on three charges - the use of slave labour, spoliation and co-operation with the SS - but found not guilty of crimes against humanity. He was sentenced to seven years' imprisonment.

When Maxwell had arrived to arrest Flick, an elderly man, at his castle near Düsseldorf, he found him in bed with a 16-year-old girl, enjoying the fruits of Nazi power to the last. It was the rule that those leading Nazis arrested for suspected war crimes had to be thoroughly searched for the possession of cyanide pills. Given his nakedness, there was only one possible place where Herr Flick might have been hiding the means to suicide, but he refused to bend over until Maxwell "slapped" him with his officer's stick. Nothing was found.

More important was the interrogation of Lieutenant-Colonel Herman Giskes, chief of German counter-espionage in the Low Countries and Northern France from 1943 until the end of the war. Giskes had run an Intelligence operation codenamed North Pole, the truth about whose success is still not fully explained.

In July 1940 the British Government set up the Special Operations Executive, a secret service department designed to encourage and support resistance movements in the German-occupied territories. The section covered by Giskes was probably the most essential, especially as it was the area in which the Allies would have to make their re-entry into Europe. But the Dutch section of the SOE was captured and used by the Germans from its early days. According to *SOE*, by M.R.D. Foot[4], a Dutch agent called Zomer was arrested in the late summer of 1941 with enough cipher material on him to enable the Germans to break the MI6 cipher system. As a consequence, fake messages were sent to London by the Germans purporting to be from genuine agents and members of the resistance. Either through a catalogue of errors so gross that they would make the post-war Intelligence services appear a model of efficiency, or by deliberate intent, which would raise callousness to a new height, scores of agents continued to be dropped into Holland only to find the Germans expecting them. As a result of what Giskes called Englandfunkspiel, more than 50 agents parachuted into the Netherlands were put to death. The German deception continued until near the end of 1943. Once it was blown, Giskes cheekily sent a message - *en clair*, not in code - to London thanking the SOE for their "long and successful co-operation", adding:

> Whenever you will come to pay a visit to the Continent you may be assured that you will be received with the same care and result as all those you sent us before. So long.

On the surface, it was the most successful German Intelligence operation of the war. Not only were the agents parachuted into their

net but also, according to *Secret Agents, Spies and Saboteurs*, by
Janusz Piekalkiewicz[5], a huge quantity of arms and materials,
including more than 15 tons of explosives, 3,000 automatic pistols,
5,000 small arms, 300 machine guns, 2,000 hand grenades, half a
million rounds of ammunition, 75 transmitter sets and a great mass
of miscellaneous equipment.

The question remains whether SOE in fact knew that its
operation in Holland had been turned and continued with it,
knowing it meant certain death for the agents, as part of a huge plan
to deceive the Germans about the Allied plans for the invasion of
Europe. One consequence of the information they obtained was
that German troop concentrations in Holland were designed to
meet the threat of an Allied landing in the Pas de Calais area, a
belief which was central to the deception plans and which led to a
fatal delay by the German High Command in countering with all
their forces the main invasion thrust. Maxwell's conclusion, in a
report he submitted after completing his interrogation of Giskes,
was that the double deception theory was correct and that the agents
had been knowingly sent to their death by the SOE. His report was
dismissed as "foolish" at the time, but subsequently its conclusions
were shared by many others, including Piekalkiewicz.

Giskes was later sent to London for further interrogation over a
period of several months. After deciding there was no evidence to
link Giskes with war crimes, the British handed him over to the
Dutch authorities, who released him in September 1948.

* * * * *

Despite the excitement of the interrogations of Johannmeier,
Flick and Giskes, much more important to Maxwell's future during
his time as an Intelligence officer was that his interest in science,
which would become the foundation of his reputation, his success
and his fortune, was aroused. He was to say in later life that the
bombing of Hiroshima and Nagasaki focused his mind upon the
revolution in science which the war had brought about, but the more
immediate application of that realisation came in his job at Iserlohn.
As he explained to *Computer Weekly* in 1981:

> I was involved in interrogating German scientists and discovered that
> most problems in science are only capable of solution if the people
> working on them have the access to the right kind of information.

Though the Intelligence job clearly had its attractions and

distractions, his eyes were increasingly fixed upon the day when he would be demobilised and would have to find his own way in a post-war Britain struggling to recover from the most devastating war in history. He wrote to Betty:

> A man with my linguistic knowledge and personality should have no difficulty in getting a good job in the export trade, since this trade is bound to flourish in England as the only industrial country in Europe capable of supplying its insatiable needs.

Early in the New Year he was recommended for promotion to captain, a development which aroused the ire of other officers who protested that Maxwell had only been at Iserlohn for a few weeks and had been commissioned only a year earlier. "So", he grumbled, "in order to avoid a delicate situation they are delaying my promotion for a little while, which means me doing a captain's job for a lieutenant's pay". His promotion, however, came soon afterwards and he became Captain Maxwell.

A role in the regular army was offered by Major-General Lyne, his old 7th Armoured Division commander, and there was an opportunity for further promotion to major and to be in charge of film production and distribution and the control of all cinemas in the British zone of Germany, but he rejected both. Betty's pregnancy was occupying his mind and he was anxious to gain British nationality - the first essential to a successful career in civilian life - and get out of the army.

He wrote constantly to Betty about the child-to-be:

> It's just something which I honestly fail to be able to put on paper. The only thing I know is that every time the thought of you and our child comes to mind (which is quite often), a sort of mellow, sweet and divine happiness spreads itself all over my mind and body.

As the day approached, the anxieties grew: would it be a boy or a girl? Would Betty suffer? Would she love him as she did before? Could he be a good husband and a father at the same time?

His first son, Michael, was born on Betty's birthday, March 11, and his letters to her were bursting with exuberance. He wrote three days later:

> First, let me congratulate you from the bottom of my heart and, secondly, let me tell you that I love and worship you beyond anything that you may imagine ... let me tell you how proud and happy I am ... tremendous desire to embrace you both.... Did you have to suffer a great deal? I was so glad to read that our son weighed only five pounds because I hope that by being so small he will have given you less pain.

The birth of Michael in a London hospital automatically gave him British citizenship in advance of his father. But Maxwell was doing everything possible to change his nationality.

The British Government had suspended the granting of naturalisation in 1940. Five years later the backlog of applications was huge and priorities had to be decided. Fortunately, the highest priority was given to those who not only had "the qualities ordinarily expected of a good citizen" but had also given "good service in the Forces of the Crown", as the Home Secretary, Mr James Chuter Ede, explained to Parliament on November 15, 1945. This was clearly to Maxwell's advantage, but, as usual, he was impatient to get on. He was more seriously worried than he had been about his current nationality because of Carpatho-Ruthenia's absorption into the Soviet Union, and, at the suggestion of his commanding officer, had already sought the help of a Tory MP, Sir Jocelyn Lucas. A Home Office official wrote soothingly to Sir Jocelyn:

> I am making inquiries from the Foreign Office about the question of Mr Maxwell having to acquire Soviet citizenship. I believe the position is that he need not do so unless he wishes, and that he will have an option to remain Czech....

In fact, he wanted neither of the options. But once again the good fortune of coincidence was with him. Major-General Lyne had been promoted to be Director of Staff at the War Office. When he invited Maxwell, at the beginning of June 1946, to make the army his permanent career, Maxwell pointed out that he was not a British citizen. Lyne immediately telephoned the Permanent Secretary at the Home Office, Sir Alexander Maxwell (no relation), and asked him to come to his office, which Sir Alexander obligingly did. He immediately started the arrangements to give Maxwell British citizenship, though, in the event, Maxwell decided that an army career was not for him.

The formal news of his naturalisation came on June 13 when the Home Office informed him that a certificate of naturalisation would be forwarded to him "on receipt of a fee of Ten Pounds". The money was speedily sent off and the certificate came through a few days later on June 19. On July 2 a friend at the War Office wrote congratulating him, saying:

> I see from the first return of grants your name appears at the top.

Maxwell from then on was British. Mrs Maxwell later acquired citizenship and has remained of dual nationality, French and British, ever since, as have the rest of their children.

* * * * *

In March 1946 Maxwell was appointed to the Berlin Information Control Unit and on July 20 he was offered an appointment with the Control Commission for Germany as "a Temporary Officer Grade III, Information Services Control Branch of PR/ISC Group", which effectively made him censor of the newborn free Berlin press. The letter of appointment stipulated that he would be required to serve until September 30, 1948. The pay, including a Control Commission allowance of 25% of his basic salary and a Foreign Service allowance of £90 a year, amounted to £620 a year, undreamed-of riches in Solotvino and reasonable in immediate post-war Britain. He had arranged for his sisters to go to Britain and the process of his release from the army was under way. On July 17 he had begun 80 days' leave ending on October 5, when he was to be released from military duties. Major-General Lyne again provided him with a generous reference:

> Captain R. Maxwell, MC, served under me both in the ranks and as an officer during the greater part of the campaign in North-west Europe and after it.

> Captain Maxwell is a born leader of men and some of his exploits were quite remarkable. He certainly earned his Military Cross several times over. He inspired the men under him to great feats of endurance and bravery, and was quite one of the most successful young officers whom I met during the whole course of the war.

> I can confidently recommend him for any position demanding self-reliance, leadership and initiative.

A letter from the War Office later that year thanked him for the "valuable services which you have rendered in the service of your country at a time of grave national emergency" and granted him the honorary rank of captain.

The Director of the Press and Publicity Branch of the British Information Services in Berlin, and Maxwell's immediate boss, was Major George Bell, Sandhurst-trained and a Tank Corps veteran. He and his wife Anne lived in a block of flats on Kastanien Allee in Charlottenburg, a suburb reserved for British army personnel. Above them lived the Maxwells, Bob, Betty, their infant son Michael, and an Alsatian dog called Barry whose acquisition by

Maxwell was in the bizarre fashion which attaches itself to so many
of his activities. Maxwell had needed dental treatment and, wanting
the best, went to Dr Eibisch, the surgeon who had previously
treated Hitler. While he was attending to Maxwell's teeth, the
dentist told him about the kennels from where the Fuehrer used to
get his dogs. Maxwell went there and obtained Barry, the last stud
dog left. The departure of the Alsatian was too much for the
breeder and he committed suicide. The dental bridge which Dr
Eibisch provided within 24 hours was made of platinum and
vanadium and is still being used today.

When the Maxwells left Berlin they gave Barry to Mrs Maxwell's
parents in Paris rather than leave him in quarantine for six months,
the mandatory requirement before he could be allowed into Britain.
Later, when the Meynards moved to a smaller house, Barry was
given to a customs officer in the French Alps. When last heard of
he was helping to rescue those trapped in the snow, harbouring
delusions of grandeur and thinking he was a St. Bernard.

Mrs Bell, in her 60th birthday tribute to Maxwell, said:

> [He] was already a bit of a legend in Berlin when I arrived, something
> of an enigma to fellow officers and consequently the subject of lively
> discussions amongst themselves, tinged with a little jealousy....
> George was glad of his services on his staff.... Bob's flair for
> languages, his astonishing ability to assimilate new facts, to read
> rapidly and to retain what he had read and his good relationship with
> German journalists and publishers was invaluable.... There was,
> even in those early days, a charm, a charisma, about him and he had
> vision. I've often thought of Bob in these words of John Cowper
> Powys, "Brain is common enough, imagination is what is rare." ...
> Sometimes it was these qualities that made kindly-intentioned, often
> brave but dull people suspicious of him.

Detlev Raymond, the trainee-editor of *Der Berliner* - later
renamed *Der Telegraf* by the Germans in order to show some sign of
independence - recalls a Maxwell of the Control Commission
unrecognisable to almost any other person who has ever known
him:

> Betty had not yet arrived [in Berlin] and Bob Maxwell, believe it or
> not, was not working. He wasn't doing a damn thing ... nothing. I
> think he played cards a lot with the other officers and on occasion I
> believe he drank.... He just loafed. He came into the office at 11 am,
> looked a bit hung, chewed the fat with the editor, told him what to
> print and what not to print - the editor got madder than all hell, but
> what could he do, the Allies ruled the roost? -[and] disappeared at
> noon. He maybe poked his head in again at night ... he tried to upset

the make-up and so on, but the typesetters usually wouldn't let him.

Raymond says that as soon as Mrs Maxwell arrived that winter with the baby Michael, Maxwell became "orderly, industrious, almost punctual":

> He didn't argue with the editor any more. He just dictated to him....
> He had no time to play cards any more.

Raymond tells a colourful story of Maxwell's first involvement in international politics. Both West and East were struggling for the control of Berlin and elections were due to be held on October 20, 1946 for the city's assembly. Effectively, they would decide whether the city was to become part of the Russian zone, as the Russians claimed was their right, or be divided between East and West. Each of the governing powers was to supervise the vote to ensure that it was free and each power was entitled to send observers to the other sections of the city to ensure that the poll was being conducted scrupulously. Maxwell was chosen to be the British representative in the Soviet sector and set up his headquarters there on the Thursday before polling day, which was a Sunday. Raymond was instructed to arrive on Sunday morning and report to Maxwell. He says:

> What confronted me there defies any rational description.... Here was a large ballroom-like affair in what used to be an affluent German home in East Berlin, containing a U-shaped table of considerable dimensions, on which were perched endless plates of hams, boiled eggs, breads, vodka, butter, more vodka, cakes, sausages, and other goodies in a wild disarray. Unbelievable. At the head of the table sat a giant Russian colonel who was eating an equally giant plate of freshly-fried eggs. Next to him sat [Maxwell] obviously not in the best of shape; but he had sat there, miraculously, throughout three days of continuous feasting (so he told me loudly and with glee, pointing to both his French and American observation colleagues who lay on the carpeted floor, fully, if untidily, dressed, fast asleep or beyond consciousness).... I looked at the poor American lieutenant who was neither black nor white, as was customary for American officers, but was positively green and I asked Bob whether we should not call an ambulance. He just laughed and made some grand gesture with his arms, implying that we should let the "dead" rest in peace, and he told me again to fill up on whatever was offered.

As the afternoon wore on, Maxwell began to insist that the task of supervising the elections should be carried out. The Russian colonel pointed to his prostrate Allied colleagues and shrugged his shoulders. Maxwell was adamant. A Soviet officer then reported that all transport had broken down. Maxwell insisted that they should all use his jeep, in which Raymond had arrived, and eventually they descended upon the polling station.

Raymond writes:

> We entered, Bob looking a bit wild. I think he had battle dress on, paratrooper boots of sorts, a greatcoat hung loosely over his shoulders, no insignia thereon, a British officer's cap on the back of his head, his dark hair a bit disorderly and partly on his forehead. At the polling table sat two election officials ... both with a fat SED (Communist) party button in their lapels. This was strictly illegal.... Bob talked to them in German and pointed this out. I was standing next to Bob and heard the reply, "But don't you understand, we are Communists." "So I see", said Bob. "Now please remove these party buttons." But they kept repeating their plea that they were Communists and it gradually dawned on Bob and me that they were mistaking him for a Russian officer....

Despite his rigorous insistence on fair play, Maxwell had himself defied an instruction to British Military Government officers that they were not to give any assistance to any political party. The Social Democrats needed petrol and paper and the funds to purchase them and Maxwell ensured that they got all three. Later the SPD leader, Dr Kurt Schumacher, and his deputy, Erich Ollenhauer, went to Berlin and personally thanked Maxwell for his help.

The final result of the election gave the Social Democrats 63 seats, the Christian Democrats 29 and the Communists only 26. It was an overwhelmingly pro-Western vote, which demoralised the Berlin Communists but hardened the Soviet resolve to hold on to part of the city. Berlin was divided and the seeds which were to grow into the Berlin Wall had been sown.

Early in 1946 the United States Secretary of State, James Byrnes, proposed to the British Government that the United States and British zones of Germany should be merged. The motive was primarily economic, though it undoubtedly had political advantages, not all of which were clearly seen at the time. The British Foreign Secretary, Ernest Bevin, was not keen, but, as Alan Bullock says in his biography of Bevin[6], the practical advantages were "overwhelming". The conditions of the people in the British zone in the coming winter threatened to be disastrous and Britain could not afford, with its own dire economic position, the drain upon its resources needed to keep the German population alive. The bi-zonal plan was intended to restore West Germany to economic well-being within three years, but the more immediate short-term aim was to prevent the people from starving. The

Americans brought a dowry of some $400 million to the "marriage" and a Joint Export-Import Agency was set up, charged with reviving the (West) German economy by importing the necessary food for the hungry and the raw materials with which to restart German exports.

So desperate was the German plight that the whole of the $400 million was allocated on a crash basis over 30 days and the respective zonal commanders-in-chief were asked to select officers to take charge of the purchasing required. Maxwell was one of 12 British officers chosen for the task. His particular role was to buy sugar, coffee, cotton waste (for cleaning locomotives), paint for the painting of bridges and railway equipment and pigs' bristles for the paint brushes. The American general who briefed him and the other officers on their task warned them that when they opened for business on the Monday morning "every crook in Christendom" would be at their door to sell them what they didn't need and to offer them bribes.

Maxwell's office was in the IG Farben works in Frankfurt, on the 14th floor. On the Monday morning the queue stretched from his door, down the stairs and to the street. The American general had not exaggerated.

The first man Maxwell saw was a Hungarian "who looked like a bishop". He remembered:

> He said he represented the Hungarian Government and had two trainloads of sugar waiting at the Austro-Hungarian border. His price was X dollars per ton. I said, "Thank you, please leave it and we will get in touch." But he refused to leave and said he had something else to say. He was also instructed, he said, to offer me $6 a ton commission in a Swiss bank account. I had the man arrested and bought the sugar from elsewhere.

> At the end of the exercise, I was interviewed by my commanding officer. Many of the people handling the business had been found to have taken backhanders. I was asked, "Why weren't you taking bribes?" I said if he had offered me 25 cents a ton I might have fallen for it. But a sum of that size was beyond my comprehension.

The Control Commission and JEIA work undoubtedly prepared Maxwell for the whirlwind business life on which he embarked even before he left Germany for good.

Julius Springer, cousin of the elderly German publisher Ferdinand Springer, had gone to him to complain about the inadequacy of the Springer paper ration compared with the generosity shown to the newspapers which were under Maxwell's control. Though Maxwell was not in charge of paper for books, Julius said that unless it was increased he would further complain to Sir Stanley Unwin, President of the Publishers' Association in Britain. Maxwell threw him out of his office. In due course Unwin wrote to the Foreign Office and the Foreign Office complained as well. Maxwell says he deposited its missive into his wastepaper basket. But the Springers came back; Julius introduced Maxwell to Ferdinand and the two men became friends. Before the war Ferdinand Springer had been the world's leading publisher of scientific books. He was part-Jewish but had survived the Third Reich's extermination programme because of the representations made on his behalf by the German scientific community. When the Soviet forces occupied Berlin he had been detained but allowed by a friendly Russian interrogator to go to West Berlin, which is where he met Maxwell. Springer's Hungarian wife had concealed some of her jewellery, the sale of which provided the German publisher with the finance to restart his business, and Maxwell helped him to set up in Heidelberg.

As a result, a large consignment of the back numbers of Springer's journals, said by Brian Straton-Ferrier - but disputed by Maxwell - to have been labelled "waste paper" (and which had been hidden in a castle) was sent to London, an early Maxwell miracle in the days when transport of any kind but military was almost impossible to obtain. They were invaluable to the Western scientific community. Maxwell stored and then sold them for Springer, through a company which he established called the European Periodicals, Publicity and Advertising Corporation. His career in scientific publishing and distribution had begun. Later, in 1949, EPPAC was succeeded by another called Lange, Maxwell and Springer (which became I.R. Maxwell and Co. Ltd. in 1955, and is currently trading as Bumpus, Haldane & Maxwell Ltd., a wholly-owned subsidiary of Hollis plc). Maxwell's role was to sell the company's books and journals throughout the world. Within two years it was to have a staff of 120. Lange was a Prussian who, according to an in-house history of Springer-Verlag, New York, "was largely instrumental in securing the survival of the company during the difficult period of the Third Reich", probably the most euphemistic description of Hitler's 12-year dictatorship which has ever been penned.

While still working for the Control Commission, where he was rapidly gaining an expertise in barter trading, and on release leave from the army, Maxwell became a director of Low-Bell, Ltd. -

which he usually referred to as Low Ball, Ltd. - engaged in the export-import market. Low-Bell had been established at the end of 1945 by another Czech, Arnold Lobl, whom Maxwell had met in London, but Lobl was barely making a living from it. On September 12, 1946 Maxwell acquired 90 shares in the company and a few days later took another 300 and became a director, together with Jack Straton-Ferrier, husband of Eileen.

Low-Bell's offices were at 113 Grand Buildings, Trafalgar Square, right in the heart of London. The name of the block was the only grand aspect of the company and it was, in any case, a misnomer. The rent was cheap (about £80 a year) because most of the light which should have struck the windows of the poky little office was obscured by a billboard outside advertising Ivor Novello's *Perchance to Dream*. Low-Bell dealt in anything and everything, including caustic soda, cement, dyes, eucalyptus oil and peppermint, leather, cider taps, Turkish carpets, coal, cinnamon, vanilla, feather dressers, boots and shoes, furniture, neon signs, pepper, kapok, sardines, ginger, beads, safety pins, pencils, deer skins and dried peas. Everywhere in Europe in those days of rationing, shortages, quotas and a scarcity of foreign currency, the key to success lay in the ability to barter and an ability to provide goods which others found impossible to do. This talent had been developed by Maxwell during his time with the Control Commission, but its seeds went back to his first days as a salesman of cheap jewellery in Bratislava. Brian Straton-Ferrier says:

> All my family became involved in the hunt for half a million pairs of boots wanted, I think, by someone in Turkey.... A Venezuelan wanted bathroom tiles, sanitary ware and cement. I myself earned a fiver by finding a few tins of unobtainable caustic soda....

Later, Lobl left the company and its name was changed in October 1947 to Low-Bell and Maxwell, Ltd., and in April 1959 to Maxwell Scientific International (Distribution Services), Ltd.

Maxwell left the Control Commission on March 15, 1947. Seven days later he registered his new company, EPPAC, and engaged another Czech, John Kisch, whom he had first met in Germany. Kisch had been a press officer responsible for providing supplies for the new German newspapers. In 1985 he recalled those days:

> All our printing works were bombed to bits and the equipment decimated. To make the new newspapers operative, all sorts of materials were necessary. One particular item was in more than average demand and not available. "There is only one man who can help you", said [a] major. "In Berlin, there is a press officer by the

name of Captain Robert Maxwell. Give him a ring." I did, and after a few preliminaries he asked me where I came from. I told him Prague and we continued the conversation in Czech. That was the first time I talked to him and true to his reputation, and after extensive haggling, I got what I wanted .. having established we both liked efficiency and drive, we decided to get together after demob.

Kisch says that Maxwell had a corner in the import of German newspapers and they decided that their best customers would be German prisoners of war still held in Britain. Maxwell owned a large Dodge which he had somehow acquired in Berlin and brought back with him. Kisch used it to search for buyers of their papers. It still carried a Military Government, Berlin, licence plate. According to Kisch, a £50 profit which Maxwell made on selling a ton of caustic soda was the foundation of EPPAC's income. As the German prisoners returned home, so the circulation of the imported papers fell, but Maxwell was now more concerned with importing scientific journals:

Bob found very nice offices in No.3 Studio Place, just off Kinnerton Place [Knightsbridge]. But now the rent was £350 and I did not know where the money was coming from. Neither did he.

Later that year Kisch felt that he was no longer as close to Maxwell as he had been and returned to journalism. But the office was expanding. Victor Sherwood, later managing director of one of Maxwell's companies and who died in 1987, joined him. He wrote of his employer:

From the early days when he did not know where the next £1,000 was coming from - although it always did materialise - it was obvious he was going places.

Vernon Baxter, who worked with Maxwell for the next five years, first met him in Berlin, just after he had been demobilised:

He offered me a position at £6 a week for some unspecified work but I felt I owed it to my former rank of staff-sergeant to ask for at least £8. He looked at me with eyes half-closed for a while as though he was not quite sure whether I would be worth all that money, but in the end he agreed.

What followed then was a pattern still familiar today. Baxter reported for duty at Kinnerton Place at 9 am sharp. Nobody there had ever heard of him. "Nobody" consisted of Victor Sherwood and "an attractive secretary who smoked cigarettes of such strength that she suffered from dizzy spells and twice walked straight into the glass pane of the door leading to the chairman's room". The chairman was Jack Straton-Ferrier, who received Baxter with "the utmost kindness" despite the fact that he hadn't the faintest idea who Baxter was. A cable was sent to Berlin; within three hours Baxter was confirmed as a member of the staff.

Shortly afterwards, says Baxter, Maxwell returned from Berlin with a dozen agreements appointing EPPAC as sole representatives of some of the most distinguished German scientific, medical and technical publishing houses. This was the beginning of his active business co-operation with Ferdinand Springer. Maxwell, with no background in science and technology, had been presented with an opportunity by his good fortune in being in the right place - Berlin - at the right time - when the scientific world was desperate to learn the work of German scientists which had been denied to them for years - and in finding the right man. It showed an insight bordering on genius, however, for this former Czech peasant, whose entire adult life had been spent in the British army and who was still only 24, to recognise that opportunity and to seize it.

The *Sunday Times* Insight investigation of Maxwell published in August and October 1969 examined his life from Solotvino onwards and took a year to put together. Under different owners and editors, the paper has been obsessed with Maxwell for 20 years and more. All the articles at that time were permeated with innuendo, but all fell short of outright accusation, not least because of a strenuous legal battle with writs and injunctions taken out by Maxwell. The residual effect, nevertheless, was damaging. Among many other things, the article of October 5 dealt with Maxwell's early post-war career and said:

> Springer-Verlag ... received on January 1, 1946, the first British-issued licence to restart publishing. But getting started again was not as simple as that: the firm's stock had been scattered through Germany for security from bombing, its export trade was frozen and its plant was in disrepair. It is very clear that Maxwell played a crucial part in getting the business going again.

> Springer executives have told us that Maxwell was, in the line of his PRISC duty, helpful to them when he was on the Commission....

Of course, when Springer-Verlag received its licence, Maxwell was an interrogation officer at Iserlohn. He did not join the Control Commission until more than six months later. The *Sunday Times* quoted a memorandum written by a Springer executive in 1959 about the assistance the company got from Maxwell:

> It was a time when there was no telephone and no petrol, and no spare parts for printing machinery, or other vital things that were

necessary for the revival of a business such as Springer-Verlag. Captain Maxwell always knew the answer, solved the hardest problems ... it was largely attributable to him that the road to the reconstruction of the business was cleared.

The *Sunday Times* could also have quoted the memorandum as saying (and underlining for emphasis):

Springer-Verlag will never forget the help given by Captain Maxwell at that time.

The paper went on:

Maxwell's first contract with Springer was signed in December 1947.

The implication was clear, even if the charge was not explicitly made. But if Maxwell had a role in restarting the Springer business, it lay in encouraging Ferdinand to begin all over again. He was in no position in January 1946 to assist, properly or improperly, in the granting of licences. His duty as press officer related to newspapers. It was another officer who was in charge of book publishing. His contract with Springer came nine months after he had left the Control Commission and begun trading as a civilian in London.

For its part, there was nothing to stop Springer's from dropping Maxwell once the wartime restrictions upon German business were ended in the early 1950s, but he remained an active partner until the beginning of 1959, when Lange wrote to say that the distribution agreement would not be renewed. Maxwell replied to Lange saying that the decision had caused him "a great deal of anguish":

Anguish, because it means official notice to sever our special relations which have existed over a decade and which have been so dear to my heart. Everything I know, everything that I have built up, everything that I have learned and acquired springs in one way or another from the joint fountain of Dr Ferdinand Springer and yourself and the splendid House of Springer-Verlag.

In the 10 years from 1948 in which the co-operation existed, the total net turnover of EPPAC, Lange, Maxwell and Springer and I.R. Maxwell and Co. amounted to more than 20 million Deutschmarks. The memorandum referred to by the *Sunday Times* was a draft report, dated July 11, 1959, to Dr Lange, which was critical of many aspects of Springer's relationships with Maxwell and which prepared the ground for the break; it is clear from it that he drove a hard bargain, demanding the highest discounts on Springer's journals and books and controlling their exports so that all had to go through London. Nevertheless, the memorandum admits, again and again, that Maxwell's help was crucial to

Springer's and that re-establishing its business would have been impossible without him.

Springer-Verlag had been desperately anxious to resume its export trade but in the post-war conditions deliveries of its journals to individuals was impossible. When it began discussing, in October 1947, with the British authorities the possibility of exporting its books there was no official exchange rate for the Deutschmark and every single price had to be authorised by the British export authority, the Joint Export-Import Agency. The Lange memorandum went on:

> During this most difficult situation we had the first offer from Maxwell and his drastic and highly successful method ... contributed to smoothing the way in a very short time and made our first struggling exports very much easier.

What Maxwell achieved for Springer-Verlag was an extremely favourable (for the time) exchange rate of 21 Deutschmarks to the £1, much to the annoyance of the American administration in Germany. It meant that the German publishers were selling their journals cheaply, but selling them at all mattered more than the price. But eventually Springer-Verlag were to resent the Maxwell connection and the report states tartly:

> The assistance which he received from Springer-Verlag as antiquarian, bookseller and publisher in the long run far outweighed his help to us, which arose due to the needs of the post-war era and thus was of a temporary nature.

The German publishers had become impatient with EPPAC's "unprofessional and tedious" business procedures, mainly due to a lack of skilled personnel when Maxwell was not able to devote all his time to their affairs, and on September 1, 1949 Lange, Maxwell and Springer was established and in December Maxwell was appointed managing director for a term of 10 years at a salary of £2,500. But, said the report to Dr Lange:

> The increasing failure to promote Springer products from London led to business relations beginning to drift apart and to final alienation.... The reason, perfectly understandable from a human point of view, which led to this alienation has to be looked for in the fact that Maxwell's aims went far beyond Springer-Verlag's requirements. Springer's whole existence was for Springer; but for Maxwell they were a means to an end. His purpose was to create for himself an important business position in London.

As the West German "economic miracle" got under way, Springer-Verlag was anxious to be free of its connection with

Maxwell. It wanted to resume its pre-war eminence and regain its old customers, especially in the United States, and it felt Maxwell was not able to do that for it.

But in the years up to 1952 Springer's needed Maxwell because he was their outlet to the world. He had been their choice and they had rejected an approach from a Swiss firm which had made a similar offer to Maxwell's in favour of doing business with him.

As the company's internal memorandum summed up (not quoted by the *Sunday Times*):

> The collaboration with Maxwell between 1947-50 brought Springer-Verlag many successes as no direct exports from Germany were then possible and Maxwell knew how to obtain advantages for Springer in every respect. He cleverly used the difficulties which existed in Germany to Springer's benefit. Without his intervention, this would not have been possible.... Our association with Maxwell at a time when it again became realistic to export direct from Germany was disadvantageous and of little interest to Springer who had experience of foreign dealings lasting for decades....

> The close relationship with Springer-Verlag has (from 1950 onwards) not only brought him great financial advantages but has enabled him to lay the foundations on which he could build his publishing house, Pergamon Press.

> In no way do we wish to state that Maxwell was not entitled to concentrate his own efforts on his publishing company and in his own interests; at the same time, it is also obvious that from then on his interests were no longer and in no respect tied to Springer's interests and here we find the explanation for the intended ultimate separation.

The company which was to become Pergamon Press was, in fact, founded jointly in 1948 by Butterworth and Co. (Publishers), Ltd., one of Britain's oldest publishing houses, and Springer-Verlag. It was called simply Butterworth-Springer, Ltd., and incorporated in April 1949. But its origins went back to November 1946, when the British Government suggested to Butterworth's that it should enter the field of scientific publishing. The Butterworth history[7] says:

> [The Government's] emissary was Count [Frederick] Vanden Heuvel, a shadowy and influential person, described as "the epitome of a diplomat with his imperial whiskers and black homburg". Also involved were some of the best-known scientists of the day; and, at a later date, a young British army captain, of Czech origin, who had adopted the name of Maxwell. With these auspices, it deserved to be more successful than it was.

The scientists who met Butterworth's in government offices in

Great George Street, just off Whitehall, were all famous names: Sir Wallace Akers, Sir Charles Darwin, Sir Alfred Egerton, Sir Richard Gregory, Professor R.S. Hutton and Sir Edward Salisbury. Also there were a representative of Butterworth's and Sir Charles Hambro, chairman of Hambros Bank. A Scientific Advisory Board was set up with Professor Hutton as its secretary. Sir Alexander Fleming, the discoverer of penicillin, joined the board at its second meeting. Sir Edward Appleton became a member in 1949. The Butterworth representatives were John Whitlock, their joint managing director, and Hugh Quennell, both of whom were directors of Butterworth-Springer when it was formed. Quennell and Whitlock, "novices in the world of science", leaned on Vanden Heuvel for advice and support. The Butterworth history goes on:

> John Whitlock used to refer to the Count as the cloak and dagger man. He was called by his friends Van, but those who had known him longer, and perhaps a little better, than Whitlock referred to him as Fanny the Fixer.

Vanden Heuvel (or Huyvel), a Dutchman by descent, was a Count of the Holy Roman Empire and died in 1963 at the age of 78. In reference books he was described as being a member of the British diplomatic service in Switzerland during the war - in fact, he was the station chief of the Secret Intelligence Service (MI6) in Berne - and was awarded the high honour of the C.M.G. in 1945. He did not know Maxwell at that time but was to play a part in the ill-fated purchase of Simpkin Marshall a few years later.

The purpose of the Scientific Advisory Board was to develop British scientific publishing through Butterworth's, using the expertise of Springer's. Dr Paul Rosbaud, who was also at the initial meeting and a Springer protégé, was to edit the journal which the board proposed to publish. Rosbaud was another of those who had lived in the sinister world of espionage and he had been introduced to Butterworth's by Vanden Heuvel. According to a book published in the United States in 1986[8], Rosbaud had been seen, apparently, as "a pillar of Nazi society" when he was, in fact, a spy for Britain, with the codename of "Griffin". The book credits him with the first information to reach Britain about the German V-2 rockets which brought terror attacks on London in late 1944, and it was from him that the British Government first learned of the German intention to build an atomic bomb. His only motive was a burning hatred of Nazism. He was smuggled out of Berlin at the end of 1945 and brought to the West. His supporters in the Butterworth-Springer project included Sir Charles Hambro and Vanden Heuvel. After leaving Butterworth-Springer he was for many years Scientific Director of Pergamon Press until a fundamental row with Maxwell about the expansion of the company eventually led to his resignation.

The development of the Butterworth-Springer company was of labyrinthine complexity in its financial and company arrangements, and by 1948 Butterworth's were becoming concerned about the links between Springer and Maxwell. The Butterworth account says[9]:

> Rosbaud was at this time not on the Butterworth payroll, but working for them freelance. His reports on visits to Springer tended to reach Quennell via Vanden Heuvel, who got to know Robert Maxwell through Whitlock. Rosbaud transferred his considerable editorial talents to Maxwell at a later stage.

In the summer of 1950 the Scientific Sales Manager of Butterworth's, Ron Watson, believed that "Butterworth-Springer worked more to the advantage of Springer than Butterworth". As a consequence, and after discussions in Berlin with Dr Lange and Ferdinand Springer, Butterworth's decided to pull out of the partnership. In May 1951 Butterworth's agreed to sell its interests to Maxwell for £13,000 net and to a change of name for the company to Pergamon Press, Ltd. (an original intention to change it to Parthenon Press was abandoned). Butterworth's waived a debt of £23,547 owed to it by Butterworth-Springer, which meant it emerged from what it calls an "adventure" showing a loss of £10,547.

The stock of titles published by Butterworth-Springer and handed to Pergamon, thus forming the beginning of Pergamon's book list, were:

Progress in Biophysics.

Progress in Nuclear Physics.

Progress in Metal Physics (except Vols. I and II).

Introductory Statistics.

Metallurgical Thermochemistry.

In addition, Pergamon acquired three journals:

Spectrochimica Acta (bought by Vanden Heuvel for Butterworth's from the Vatican).

Journal of Atmospheric and Terrestrial Physics.

Geochimica et Cosmochimica Acta.

Today's catalogue of the books and journals published by Pergamon is three inches thick. In a history of the company, Maxwell explained its purpose:

> Leading British scientists and government persons concerned with scientific affairs were disturbed that in the inter-war years the Germans' scientific work enjoyed a higher prestige than our own, although, in quality, the British work was better. In analysing the problem, they concluded that one of the factors behind this was that the Germans had in Springer an aggressive publishing house which was helping to disseminate the results of German science much more effectively than our university presses were doing at that time, with the result that they encouraged Butterworth's and Springer-Verlag to join hands. The idea was to set up a joint company so that the Springer know-how and techniques of aggressive publishing in science could be made available for the publication and dissemination of the results of research of British scientists.

Maxwell had no financial interest in Butterworth-Springer, but Lange, Maxwell and Springer, Ltd. (LMS) was appointed distributor of its publications.

Tom Clark, an accountant who joined Maxwell early in 1951 when he was operating from premises in Neal Street, off Covent Garden, London - next door to a wholesale potato merchant - and still works part-time for him today, recalls:

> The company was always short of money at this time and up to the top of its overdraft facilities with the bank, but was frequently rescued by the receipt of large sums of money, usually about £30,000 a time, which came out of the blue from China, with instructions to purchase vast quantities of back issues of periodicals.

In fact, only one large cheque - for £25,000 - was received from the Chinese, but there is no doubt it was welcome. Indeed, any order was.

During 1951 Butterworth's became increasingly unhappy about its partnership with Springer's. The trouble with the joint company was that it required a great deal of capital investment without any assurance of profitability. Springer-Verlag, for its part, wanted to develop their own publishing in the English language unfettered by a partner and to end the "anomaly" of the LMS monopoly on distribution which forced all its foreign customers to order its publications through London.

The £13,000 by which Maxwell and his family were able to buy control of the company seems today a laughably small sum. It gave them 75 per cent of the shares while Dr Rosbaud owned the balance. Nevertheless, £13,000 was more money than Maxwell possessed at that moment, so he borrowed. He went first to Sir Charles Hambro, who had been introduced to Maxwell by the Board of Trade, had been impressed with him and was now sufficiently persuaded by his ideas to instruct his chief cashier to give Maxwell a cheque book with authority to draw cheques up to a total of £25,000, a gesture for which Maxwell, understandably, has remained ever grateful. Sir Charles was to say later that it was the job of a banker to trust his judgement, but the loan was not just a whim on his part. An article in *King* in 1967 quoted another director of Hambros as saying:

> He [Maxwell] has always appeared to know where he was going. More important, he could explain how he proposed to get there. He's thought out the whole journey from switch-on to switch-off.

Maxwell got the loan of more money from relatives in America (Uncle Nathan, who had helped the Hoch family to buy its house in Solotvino in 1937, obliging again), as well as some help from his wife's family, and obtained a contract from His Majesty's Stationery Office to supply it with out-of-print wartime German scientific material. HMSO could not, because of the Byrnes-Bevin agreement and the establishment of the Joint Export-Import Agency, import these works without a licence; what is more, it would not have been able to purchase them at the favourable rate of exchange which Maxwell had managed to secure. It therefore turned to him and advanced £7,000 to ensure the purchase. He then borrowed a further £5,000 from the Westminster Bank, bought the documents for £12,000 and sold them to HMSO for £20,000, netting him a profit of about £8,000. With this, a few hundred pounds from his army gratuity and the sale for £200 of some crystal beads which he had bought in Czechoslovakia when he returned to Prague in the autumn of 1945, he now had the capital to start making his business grow.

Maxwell took the name for his new company from a Greek town in Asia Minor, famous for a great work of art, the Altar of Pergamon, dedicated to the goddess Athena, and for a library unique in the civilised Mediterranean world. The company's colophon, or publisher's imprint, was taken from a head of Athena shown on the back of a coin of about 400 B.C. Board of Trade approval for the new name came on July 17, 1951. When Maxwell acquired Butterworth-Springer it had only the few journals and books listed above. Up to the end of 1987 Pergamon Press had published some 11,000 books, had 4,000 or so titles in print and was publishing new titles at the rate of 365-400 a year.

The original germ of an idea that the crying need of education in the future would be for international scientific publishing of all kinds now began to take commercial shape. Maxwell realised that scientists and academics were desperate to get their basic research work into print; the fees which they were paid were of secondary consideration. Other scientists were just as desperate to read of the work their colleagues were doing. University and other libraries were only too eager to buy, at almost whatever price, the reports of the studies in which the scientists were involved. Maxwell was taking a risk - though with hindsight it was small - that he would make a loss. The scientists for their part may not have been making much money, but they were making their reputations. But when he published a *Dictionary of Physics* and it sold better than expected, he doubled his payment to the contributors, adding a £30,000 bonus to the £30,000 due under the contract.

In an interview in 1964[10] he explained the secret of Pergamon's success in two sentences:

> The central theme is speedy production and world-wide dissemination. I believe that scientific research is an international thing not confined by national boundaries.

Maxwell was now firmly on the highway to becoming the world's second largest scientific publisher - far and away his greatest achievement besides which his newspaper interests, though more exciting and glamorous and newsworthy, are of little importance. But before he achieved that position he was to run into a roadblock which brought him the first serious setback in his career since he was arrested on the Yugoslav border in 1939.

In the spring of 1951 he was asked by some of the leading figures in Britain's publishing trade to rescue an ailing book wholesaler's which was of considerable importance to the trade but which was operating at a loss. It was called Simpkin Marshall. His involvement with it was to set other book publishers against him for a generation. It was the first time that his optimism, his belief in his own ability to overcome any obstacle, to pick up any wreck and turn it into a gleaming new model, was to let him down. He found that his demonic energy, his habit of working 18 hours a day, his determination to succeed where others had failed was not enough. It was to be an expensive lesson, not only for him but for everyone else involved. But he, at least, was young enough to benefit from it. When the book publishers approached him to save Simpkin Marshall he was still only 28. Had they come 10 years later, the conditions which he would have imposed might have been stringent and both his reputation and his bank balance would have been healthier because of them.

In the first of the examinations of Maxwell which were to continue for a decade, the *Sunday Times*, on December 27, 1964, quoted an (anonymous) accountant who had studied the history of the Simpkins episode as saying of Maxwell:

> He was pretty nearly murdered. He was in the wrong place at the wrong time. But it will dog him all the days of his life. He is like the rogue elephant of the book trade.

The true importance of the Simpkin Marshall affair lies in that comment. He should have walked away from the company, not embraced it. When, some 15 years later, the Leasco controversy blew up, critics returned to the ʻSimpkins affair" and made a connection between the two, especially between the complex financial arrangements which were integral to both. The accusations levelled at him at the time Simpkins went bust were clearly remembered; the facts behind them more hazily so. He was the wrong man to try to save the skin of a trade notorious for its amateurism and incompetence in meeting the needs of its customers and the aspirations of its authors. (He was to write in *Time and Tide* in 1964: "British publishing is still largely regarded as an occupation for gentlemen"). No doubt, as an anti-establishment man, he was flattered to be asked by the establishment of the trade to rescue them. He would have been wiser to have made his excuses and left.

Maxwell's involvement with Simpkins began at a moment when his career was taking off. LMS was making money, he had acquired Pergamon and the size of his staff was beginning to expand in keeping with his ambitions. For the first time since he returned from Germany, he felt he had time to spare for other pursuits. The wholesaler, for its part, was in deep trouble and was looking for a white knight. The dashing Maxwell seemed to be just what Simpkins was looking for. The company was owned by a distinguished printing and publishing house, Sir Isaac Pitman and Co., Ltd., run by James and Christopher Pitman. The Pitman brothers had neither the money nor the managerial skills available to revive Simpkins which had never recovered from the destruction of its premises and stock of books during the air raid of December 29, 1940, when the Luftwaffe devastated the City of London. They wanted to dispose of it and as quickly as possible. Most British publishers - there were important exceptions - were anxious to ensure that Simpkins was kept in being because it performed an invaluable role for them. It did what they were abysmally incapable of doing - it was able to supply single copies of almost any book in print. But its boast that it could do so within 24 hours had long become more theoretical than real.

John Whitlock of Butterworth's introduced Maxwell to the Pitmans. He thought that Maxwell's intimate knowledge of the German book industry, in which wholesale book distributors had thrived, plus his phenomenal energy, would be able to revitalise Simpkins. Maxwell was tempted by the challenge. At a Reform Club lunch for eminent publishers, Sir Stanley Unwin, the most distinguished of them all, strongly encouraged him to take over the company and promised his full support. With that, plus an auditor's report which advised that Simpkins could be run profitably from new premises *with the co-operation of the main publishing houses*, and after further meetings with the Pitman brothers, Maxwell decided to go ahead and buy the business. He expected to make it a success - and to supply single copies again within 24 hours - because he had been promised the support which the publishers had previously denied to Simpkins - a larger discount - on their books.

The report of the Official Receiver, after Simpkins went into liquidation in 1955, recalled that the company had been wound up voluntarily in February 1941, after the German bombing. But the need for the wholesaling services which Simpkins provided led the Publishers' Association to approach Pitman's so that a wholesale bookselling business could be carried on co-operatively, with the publishers supplying their books to the company on sale or return. Simpkin Marshall (1941), I ʻᵈ was set up in March of that year and two nominees of the publ. er nd booksellers were appointed to the board (and served on .. ..til 1948), which demonstrated its importance to the trade. By September 1941 Pitman's had advanced £50,000 to the new company, without security. In view of what was to happen to the company after Maxwell took over, the account of the Official Receiver, J. Melville Clarke, when he reported in 1955 about the subsequent events in 1941, was revealing:

> It was clear that losses were being incurred due mainly to the inability of the company to increase its turnover, as the supply of books was not available owing to war-time restrictions and *to the reduced rates of commission allowed by publishers*. [My italics] It would appear that the previous company earned a gross profit equivalent to a commission of 14% to 15% whereas, on the bulk of its purchases, the company could not obtain more than 10% commission on sales.

A further difficulty arose because, contrary to the expectation of the board, many publishers would not co-operate on the basis of supplying stocks on sale or return but insisted on the company buying firm.

After the co-operative scheme was dropped, said Clarke, the company carried on the business of a competitive wholesaler and "some improvement" in the terms of trade was obtained from the publishers upon an undertaking by Simpkins not to sell to retailers at a greater discount than the publishers would allow. Simpkins traded at a loss of over £14,000 in 1942, but for the next four years made small profits, varying between £1,728 and £4,946, though they were miserly returns on a turnover which totalled £811,000. During the next four years turnover grew to £1,121,000, but profits were replaced by losses amounting to over £130,000 for the period. One of the principal causes of these deficits, apart from higher overheads, was an arrangement entered into by the company during the war whereby it undertook to purchase the whole output of some of its suppliers; but when books of better quality became available after the war, Simpkins could not dispose of its stocks. In January 1948 the Publishers' Association told Simpkins that it did not wish to exercise the option to take over the business which had been given by the company in 1941.

By 1950 the Pitmans had had enough. They had financed Simpkins without security and free of interest to the tune of £344,000 and in June that year they told the Simpkins board that they were unable to make any further advances and wished to sever their connection with the company. To avoid it going into liquidation, it was decided in November 1950 to try to sell the company as a going concern. The trading results for 1950/51 were an improvement. Turnover had risen to £1,178,739 and the gross profit for the year was £147,370 (net, £17,216) and the debt to Pitman's reduced to £282,475. Nevertheless, the outlook was bleak and negotiations began in June 1951 for Maxwell to acquire this company. The Official Receiver's report went on:

Maxwell ... states that prior to his acquiring control of the company's affairs, he made a thorough investigation of its business and financial position and had discussions with leading publishers and booksellers. He arrived at the conclusion that the company was indispensable to the book trade and that the majority of the publishers would support his scheme to rationalise the book distribution in the United Kingdom within the framework of the company. His aim was to persuade booksellers to concentrate their single-copy business with the company and to arrange for the publishers to supply to the company their complete range of titles on a consignment basis.

Maxwell's ambitions for Simpkin Marshall were huge, but their weakness was that they depended upon the wholehearted co-operation of British publishers. "On consignment" meant that the publishers would send him their books and he would not pay for them until they were sold. This had advantages for both parties. The publishers would not have to store their volumes in their own, often unsuitable, premises and Maxwell would not be involved in a heavy capital outlay with the risk that he would be left with large numbers of unsaleable books.

He outlined his plans in an open letter to booksellers in March 1953, nearly a year after he took over an abandoned brewery (renamed Maxwell House) in Marylebone Road, London, for conversion to a warehouse, and five months after it opened for business. He admitted that all was not yet well: floors still needed to be fitted and temporary and makeshift arrangements had "to be made the best of". But when Simpkins was taken over from Pitman's, the new Board had to take a "fundamental decision":

> Was Simpkins to remain much as it stood, with perhaps improved organisation and service, or was it to attempt the altogether more vital and ambitious task of stocking every British book in print?

Far-sighted booksellers had long called for a central clearing house for books, he said. Simpkins had had to move and had fortunately found a building of a size to meet every possible demand, and so:

> We have decided, with the support of our financial backers, to build a new Simpkins *in which we shall be able to carry stock of every single book in print*....

> The advantage to the bookseller, beset by ever-increasing carriage costs and soaring overheads, is obvious. For all the publishers whose lists are carried under the scheme the whole of the bookseller's daily needs can be condensed into one order and supplied *from stock*, with answers, in one parcel. Think of the postage, the cheque stamps, the correspondence saved! Think of the simplicity in following up outstanding orders!

Equally, he said, the scheme was attractive to publishers, for whom single orders were a bugbear and involved packing, addressing, invoicing and subsequent accounting. A large number of lists of important publishers were already upon the Simpkins shelves or in the process of being installed. He listed some of the most famous names in British publishing: Allen and Unwin, Black's, Jonathan Cape, Chatto and Windus, Collins, Peter Davies, Faber, Harrap, Heinemann, Methuen, Murray's, Odhams, Oxford University Press, Secker and Warburg and many others.

Admittedly, the constructional work in the new building had meant that "the speed and accuracy in attention to orders, at which we aim, has been adversely affected". He added, in words which showed he knew the risks he was running:

> We have taken on a job which we have been told by the largest firms in the trade couldn't be done. If it *was* done, they said, it couldn't be made to pay. We shall see!

He then outlined how the ambitions were being realised:

> On the four vast floors at Maxwell House there are 150,000 square feet of superficial space. On this great area we are erecting some 30 miles of shelving. About 27 miles are already complete. When all is complete, Simpkins can house some 9,000,000 volumes. On the stock already on the shelves some £450,000 has already been invested.... By the end of April, we shall be streamlined; the builders and fitters will be out of the building....

But he had not allowed his ingrained optimism to disguise the reality of what Simpkins was trying to do:

> Once this great machine is complete, once it is really under way, we shall have perhaps two years in which to justify our faith and confound the cynics. In that time, if we are to succeed, it will become the rule with every progressive bookseller to send all his daily orders to Simpkins.... There are probably £7,500,000-worth of single-copy orders every year in the British book trade, whose total sales now amount, if we include export, to over £45,000,000. The vast majority of these single-copy orders are at present expensively and reluctantly handled by publishers. Are we expecting too much if we ask for another £3,000,000 of this business in 1954?

The short answer to that was Yes. Maxwell explained to the booksellers that he had no wish to extend his control of Simpkins, where he was managing director. His interests, he said, lay more in the technical field, "but I took on Simpkins, partly perhaps because I was challenged by a friend, as something which needed doing and was worth doing", but once the company was established as a vital part of the machinery of the British book trade, then it would be

> an undertaking which should be controlled and managed by the people who profit by its activities. This is looking, perhaps, beyond a formidable array of fences and water ditches to the winning post a long way ahead. But I wish it to be clear that when we do reach that

post the future will be in your hands [the booksellers'], jointly with the publishers, and not in mine.

His intention to stay no longer with the company than it took to put it on its feet was thus explicit. Had his plans for Simpkins been realised, he would have been a hero to the trade to this day and awarded whatever is its equivalent to the Victoria Cross. But in the end there was never enough money available, for which Maxwell has always and unswervingly blamed the publishers. Maxwell could not, and would not, place his two growing companies, LMS and Pergamon, in peril in order to make a success of a business in which he had no intention of staying, though his large personal shareholding would have been greatly enhanced in value if it had succeeded and he had been able to realise it. The financial arrangements for his acquisition of Simpkin Marshall and his subsequent means of providing it with further cash were complicated and, as in most matters which are best understood by readers of the *Financial Times*, suspected by those who couldn't follow them, though they couldn't be blamed for that.

The Official Receiver's account of them, beginning with the negotiations in June 1951, was the most objective, but it also captured their complexity:

Overdraft facilities were arranged with fresh bankers and Maxwell says that it was his intention to dispose of the company's stocks which were of a value of about £250,000 and to replace those stocks by consignment supplies which the company would not pay for until sales were made. In this way, the monies advanced by the company's bankers should have been repaid in about two years.

By an agreement dated 31st October, 1951, between Pitman's and Maxwell, it was provided (inter alia) that:

(a) of the company's indebtedness to Pitman's then amounting to £268,217, £160,000 should be assigned to Maxwell in consideration of an immediate payment of £50,000 and nine half-yearly instalments making up the balance of £110,000.

(b) payment of £72,590 by the company by instalments was to be accepted by Pitman's in settlement of the balance of £108,217, these instalments to be paid out of similar amounts to be received by the company from Book Centre, Ltd., for services to be rendered by the company.

(c) the issued share capital of the company (£109) was to be transferred to a nominee of Maxwell.

Maxwell states that he personally paid the £50,000 to Pitman's in respect of the assignment of the debt of £160,000 and Maxwell's account in the company's private ledger was credited with £160,000 on 1st April, 1952. On the same date, Pitman's agreed with Maxwell that, upon the immediate payment of £90,000, plus £8,000 on 31st March, 1953, the balance of £110,000 due under the agreement should be considered as fully satisfied....

On 8th July, 1952, 50,000 preference shares were issued for cash (45,000 to the company's bankers' nominee company ... and 5,000 to Maxwell) and 44,891 ordinary shares for cash to Maxwell and 5,000 to the nominee company (paid for by Maxwell), making the total issued capital £100,000. On the same date, the company repaid Maxwell £54,891 (which sum he had paid for shares) in respect of his loan account.

It would appear that as a result of these transactions Pitman's received £50,000 from Maxwell personally and £98,000 in cash from the company. The company received £99,891 in respect of share capital and repaid to Maxwell on the same date £54,891. The debt due to Pitman's, viz. £268,217, was extinguished but the company's liquid resources had been reduced by £53,000 and £12,000 remained owing to Maxwell.

During February or March 1952 Maxwell loaned £13,500 to Captain Peter Baker, MC, printer, publisher and financier, Tory MP for South Norfolk and a former prisoner-of-war. Though they were politically apart, they had many other things in common, including military rank, the publishing trade and the same decoration for gallantry. It was a friendship which was to be used against Maxwell later in the Simpkins saga and when he first tried to enter the House of Commons.

In 1954 Baker, if not an alcoholic, was drinking heavily and, as a voluntary patient, entered a Surrey mental home, where he was arrested by Fraud Squad detectives. He was later convicted at the Old Bailey on charges of forging the signatures of two industrialists, Sir Bernard Docker and Sir John Mann, for sums totalling over £100,000. He was sentenced to seven years' imprisonment and expelled from the House of Commons. When Maxwell took over Simpkin Marshall, Baker controlled the British Book Centre in New York and was also a director of Falcon Press, Ltd., of London. In 1951 Maxwell had loaned £8,500 to those companies through Baker. The MP promised to repay the money by December 15, but did not. He wrote to Maxwell on January 21, 1952, humbly grateful to him for not enforcing repayment:

I know how difficult things are for you (and me) at the moment, and I am, therefore, more than grateful that you are trying to get through without it. I do not think that in the long run it will do you anything but good, but in the meantime if I can expedite matters to help you without renewing it, I will certainly do so.

Eleven days later Baker wrote to thank Maxwell again, this time for extending the loans, promising "I will come to you next week" with proposals for repayment. Baker was in a financial mess. The Assistant Official Receiver, reporting in 1954 on a deficit of £290,000 for The Falcon Press, said that it was "pretty clear" by March 1950, the year before Maxwell made his loan to Baker, that the company was "on the rocks". He added:

> The sheriff's officer was so constantly in attendance that when he died the staff clubbed together and bought him a wreath. There seemed to be some doubt as to whether he was a member of the staff.

By an agreement dated May 2, 1952, Maxwell bought 1,215 of the 2,500 issued shares in the British Book Centre for £11,800 which, said the Official Receiver of Simpkins, was satisfied by the release by Maxwell of Baker's indebtedness. In his book, *My Testament*, published soon after he went to prison, Baker said he and the other directors of the Book Centre were "very relieved" to sell it to Maxwell, "the new and remarkable tycoon of the book trade in Britain"[11]. Baker estimated that Maxwell had made £200,000 in business before buying Simpkin Marshall, which no doubt explained why he went to him for a loan. He described him thus:

> He was one of those able, quick-thinking, flamboyant tycoons who, also having the power to annoy you immensely by his actions, could charm all anger out of you in a five-minute meeting with a glass of sherry. Whatever cross words we exchanged, we always ended up friends again. I was very glad to hear that he had phoned my father while I was awaiting trial to say that, whatever the facts, he felt for me in my troubles.

Maxwell's sympathy for Baker did not, however, extend to any further business involvement with him. In February 1960 he wrote to Baker:

> I, too, am very sorry that I had to change our appointment at such short notice.... As I told you, I am so pressed for time that I cannot take on any outside interest of any kind, and so I must decline taking up any shares in your syndication company.

The new directors of the Book Centre included Maxwell and Arthur Coleridge, managing director of Simpkins when Maxwell took over, and Hambros Bank's representative in New York. An announcement said arrangements were in hand for over 30 British publishers to continue to co-operate with the Centre which would, in addition, be able to draw upon "the comprehensive resources" of Simpkin Marshall and Lange, Maxwell and Springer. The Book

Centre was in debt, but after Maxwell acquired it agreements were made between it and its British publisher creditors to pay 25 per cent of their claims, and promissory notes maturing in 1957 and guaranteed by Simpkins were issued for the balance of 75 per cent. In return, the publishers agreed to supply the Centre with books through Simpkins on a consignment basis.

Maxwell told the Official Receiver that he was aware that the Centre was insolvent when he took it over, but he envisaged that by allowing Simpkins to grant it extended credit it would become an "invaluable outlet" for the company's export trade and prove a profitable business once sales in the American market built up. In fact, for the year ending December 31, 1954 the Centre made a small profit of £3,000. But at the date of the winding-up order for Simpkin Marshall it was in debt to the company for £117,260, of which only £14,839 was recovered in full and final settlement, though the company was freed from the liability for the guarantees it had given to British publishers on the Centre's behalf.

On October 1, 1952 Simpkins issued to its bankers a debenture creating a floating charge on its assets to secure all monies due to them (£74,000) or about to become due, at an interest rate of five-and-a-half per cent a year. Then a further complication intervened when Whitlock introduced Maxwell to Dr Kurt Waller, or William Kurt Wallersteiner as he was alternatively known. Dr Waller, a German-Jewish refugee and an organic chemist, owned or controlled an international group of companies, including a London merchant bank, the Anglo-Continental Exchange, Ltd., and the Watford Chemical Co. (which Maxwell nicknamed and invariably called the Watford Comical Co.). He was the leading expert in bartering, the trade phenomenon which flourished in the conditions of currency restrictions and rationing which dominated business life in post-war Europe and he was looking for a young, dynamic businessman who could help him sort out his mounting problems, mainly of cash flow. After meeting him, Waller decided that Maxwell was that man.

One of Maxwell's favourite anecdotes concerns Waller's genius for trading. After the Chinese communist victory over Chiang Kai-Shek in 1949, the new Government of China was in need of every kind of raw material to restore the country's war-shattered economy. Because it came to power at the height of the cold war it could not deal with the West through the regular trade channels. For ideological reasons, the experienced businessmen who had been responsible for China's trade had been sacked and replaced by inexperienced, but ideologically-sound, apparatchiks. Waller did "phenomenally well" in dealing with the new Government, but most particularly when it wanted to order a hundred tons of indigo blue dye. Unfortunately, a crass Chinese official added an extra nought to the quantity required and Waller was asked to supply 1,000 tons, which was roughly equivalent to the world's output at the time. Waller combed the world to fulfil the order, shipped it to China and made a vast sum from it. Maxwell says:

> One of the consequences of the error was that when the Chinese troops invaded South Korea, the British and American troops found to their astonishment that the Chinese infantry was clad in blue uniforms which made them easier to see and to shoot. The other consequence was that for 25 years until the cultural revolution almost everyone in China wore blue.

Waller made "millions" out of the Chinese trade and used them to invest in what he did best, which was bartering, swapping large consignments of cement, egg yolk, silk, tinned pork, wooden houses, anything that someone had for what someone wanted. After Maxwell joined Waller's organisation he went to Vancouver, Toronto, Atlanta and various other cities to complete Waller's deals. There was a minor disaster at Vancouver where the Canadian dockers refused to unload a liberty ship's cargo of cement because of its East German origin. The ship was leaky and the cement set. In Atlanta 500 wooden houses were found not to measure up to the local fire regulations and were left to rot.

Maxwell had agreed to help Waller, but only if Waller, in turn, agreed to become involved in the financing of Simpkin Marshall, a relationship which was to make the understanding of what happened to Simpkins, and why, even more complicated and difficult to understand.

Maxwell told Waller that working for him would mean spending a substantial time away from the affairs of Simpkins. Hambros, the Simpkins bankers, were pressing for a reduction in the company's debt to them, some £320,000, and Waller agreed to pay off the loan and take over the debenture at a fixed rate of interest of five-and-a-half per cent for five years, expiring in August 1958. In addition, it was agreed that Maxwell would receive 20 per cent of the net profits of the Waller companies as his fee, worth, he was assured, about a million pounds over the first two years. Most of Waller's money was tied up in goods and materials which he had received in exchange for other commodities. In all, the stocks he held were valued at well over £10 million and Waller wanted to realise a large part of it. Maxwell says:

> I saw in this arrangement a source of providing a substantial medium-term capital for Simpkins, which was just what was needed to get them over their difficulties while I completed my re-organisation of the business in co-operation with the British publishing industry. It was my intention at that time that sums due to me from Waller should be partially offset by sums due from Simpkins to him and his companies.

Before the heads of agreement between Maxwell and Waller were signed in July 1953, the Watford Chemical Co. agreed to pay £50,000 to Simpkins as an advance payment against Maxwell's future earnings. After the signing of the heads of agreement, two of Waller's nominees joined the Simpkins board and the Anglo-Continental Exchange loaned a further £80,000, unsecured, having also repaid Hambros.

The *Sunday Times* of October 5, 1969 described John Whitlock, a former major, as an "Intelligence veteran", presumably to add colour to their theory that Waller was a victim of the cloak and dagger brigade when he was "induced", as the paper put it, to concede 20 per cent of his profits to Maxwell. It argued:

> Part of Wallersteiner's business was trading in chemicals and dyestuffs with East Germany and Communist China. This was not illegal in Britain, but it was subsequently to involve him in serious difficulties with the American Government. He was afraid it could incur the displeasure of the British authorities, too. His relationship with Maxwell makes sense only if it is understood that - rightly or wrongly - he really did believe Maxwell could protect him from trouble with various Secret Services.

It was an intriguing read for lovers of spy thrillers. But Waller was no fool. He was a businessman on a large scale. Why should he believe he should be in trouble with "various" secret services for trading legally with East Germany and China? And which secret services? The American? What could they do to him covertly that their Government could not do openly? The United States was going through the most violent anti-communist phase of its history, but what Waller was doing was not breaking any law in the area where he was operating. If he thought Maxwell could protect him from action initiated by the British Government under legislation not then enacted - and which if it were enacted could not be retrospective - why did he think so? Whitlock and Maxwell may both have been former Intelligence officers, but Maxwell had been

one for a period of only a few months. If Waller believed that
ex-officers who were now in the publishing trade could prevent legal
action being taken against him by the British authorities when he
was not breaking the law, then he hardly deserved to be allowed out
on his own, let alone run several companies including a merchant
bank.

Waller's real problem was that he wanted to exchange his
commodities for cash and Maxwell's reputation, dating back to his
days in the Control Commission, was as a born negotiator, an
ingenious provider of the impossible, whether it was coffee or a
currency bargain, a charmer who could sell nail varnish to the Venus
de Milo. It makes more sense for Waller to have seen Maxwell in
that light rather than as a major figure in the mysterious world of
MI5 and MI6. His need to dispose of his large stock of barter goods
was also growing more urgent as the world began to climb out of the
aftermath of war. The West German economic miracle was under
way and rationing was ending throughout Western Europe. What
Waller had to sell would only retain its value while there were still
shortages. Once there was plenty, millions of shoes or hundreds of
wooden houses or thousands of tons of dyestuffs would become a
drug on the market.

The Official Receiver stated that Simpkins was continually short
of liquid capital and that between July and December 1953
Anglo-Continental advanced a further £100,000, none of which had
been repaid at the time of the winding-up order. In January 1954
Anglo-Continental advanced a further £20,000 to Simpkins,
unsecured. On March 30 a further £30,000, at an interest rate of
seven per cent, was advanced by an insurance company as a
mortgage on the premises at Marylebone Road and Dr Waller
agreed that this mortgage should have priority over his own
company's debenture. At about the same time, Maxwell, on tax
advice, asked for his original agreement with Waller to be varied so
that payment would be made direct to Simpkins, in return for the
company allowing his services to be used by Waller.

This agreement also stipulated that Maxwell would act as
"confidential manager" to Waller for three years from March 3,
1953, that Simpkins would receive 20 per cent of the net profit of
each of Waller's companies from that date, that the security for the
debenture would not be enforced unless the assets of Simpkins were
in jeopardy, that the £50,000 advanced by the Watford Chemical
Co. the previous June should be regarded as payment for the
transfer of 50,000 preference shares, and that the rate of interest

paid by Simpkins on all finances provided by Waller's companies
should be reduced to four per cent a year. It looked a good
agreement for Simpkin Marshall, less so for Dr Waller's companies;
at least, that is how Dr Waller and his financial adviser, Todd, saw
it.

Maxwell says:

> No sooner had the ink dried on this agreement than there was an
> argument with Waller. He felt (so he said) that Simpkins would be
> earning too much money as a result of the work I had done for his
> companies and wanted me to agree that the total remuneration
> should be less. Of course, I saw no reason to agree this, but Waller
> tried to make me. His main tactic to bring pressure on me was
> suddenly to "discover" that his investment in Simpkins was in
> jeopardy and he threatened to call in the debenture. This would
> obviously have closed Simpkins, with all the loss of jobs and
> incalculable harm to the British book publishing industry.

The Official Receiver says that Todd advised Waller in May that
it was his opinion that the assets of Simpkins were in jeopardy. Todd
then told Maxwell that he intended calling a meeting of its creditors.
Maxwell responded by successfully applying for an injunction
preventing the meeting from being held, following which new heads
of agreement were drawn up, this time between Simpkin Marshall,
Waller, Maxwell, International Services Trust (a Maxwell company)
and others, whereby Simpkins and the Trust were respectively
entitled to a sum equal to 20 per cent of the overall profits of the
Waller group of companies for a period of 17 months from January
1, 1953. Those sums were to be set off against the £100,000 due to
Anglo-Continental from Simpkins and the debenture. But the
company was no longer liable to pay part of its profits to Waller. A
Waller nominee, Brigadier-General A.C. Critchley, a Canadian,
noted golfer and briefly a Conservative MP before the war, who had
lost his sight the previous year, was appointed chairman of the
board of Simpkins, and Anglo-Continental undertook not to
demand repayment of the debts to it until August 1958, provided
repayments of £5,000 were made every half year from December 1,
1955. Maxwell declares:

> Effectively, I was severing the connection with Waller as a result of
> this final agreement and I felt that Simpkins could not expect more
> from Waller's companies than was owed to those companies because
> I was already suspicious that when the accounts of Waller's
> companies were produced, Waller would ensure that they were
> produced in such a way that the sums due from Simpkins would
> appear to be much greater than the sums due to Simpkins.

Furthermore, I could not expect any more advances from Waller's companies and, therefore, Simpkins was once again short of liquid capital.

At the time the Official Receiver's report was published the accounts of the Waller companies had not been submitted, but Todd stated that they had made an overall loss and there would not, therefore, be any payment to Simpkins under the agreement with it. Maxwell contested this statement, declaring that there was a substantial sum due. But it was not going to materialise and he was fully aware of the company's serious financial difficulties. Maxwell immediately arranged for Chalmers, Wade and Co., the auditors to the Publishers' Association as well as to Simpkins, to investigate the trading arrangements of the company, especially its margins of profit on the books it sold. Chalmers, Wade reported on November 16, 1954, recommending:

Development of single-copy business.

Improvement of publishers' terms to give Simpkins a 20 per cent margin.

Extension of consignment stock arrangements to all publishers as far as possible.

Copies of the report went to the publishers' and booksellers' associations asking for an early decision. It came on January 21, 1955. The publishers said No. Maxwell says:

I had no alternative but to invite Waller to appoint a Receiver.

The history of Simpkin Marshall from the days of its resurrection in 1941 after the bombing of its premises had been of the publishing trade willing the ends but unwilling to provide the means. It wanted the services of a large book wholesaling company but it declined to grant it a profit level which would make it possible. With hindsight, the decision of the publishers in 1948 not to exercise their option to acquire Simpkin Marshall seems a serious mistake.

In the time since he had taken over, Maxwell had been trying to place the wholesaling business on a co-operative basis and by October 1953 he had concluded agreements with 35 publishers to supply Simpkins on consignment. Although this meant that the company did not have to buy the books, the publishers still required it to make deposits with them on a revolving basis. When the receivers were appointed on April 1, 1955 these deposits amounted to some £68,000. The fact that the publishers required them, says Maxwell, was one of the reasons why Simpkins was short of capital.

The need to convert the new premises to meet what he saw as the needs of the trade was another.

After January 21, 1955 Simpkins incurred no new liabilities and traded on a cash-only basis. Tom Clark, who had joined Maxwell early in 1951 before the purchase of Pergamon and worked closely with him in Simpkins, recalled:

> I remember André Deutsch coming into my office with his solicitor, Rubinstein, and refusing to leave until his debt had been paid. He said Simpkins had helped him to start up his business and he wasn't going to allow Simpkins to kill it off.

In February the larger publishers held two meetings at which they decided not to take any action to enforce their claims against the company and on February 8 appointed a committee to investigate its affairs. The committee considered further proposals for reconstructing Simpkins put forward by Maxwell, but decided on March 28 that the company had to go into liquidation and on March 31 the company, the debenture holder (Anglo-Continental) and others agreed that, because of Simpkins's insolvency, a receiver should be appointed. All the secured creditors of the company were paid in full, but the unsecured creditors, the debts to whom amounted to some £656,000, received only 19 pence in the pound.

The publishing trade, in large part, blamed Maxwell for the failure of Simpkin Marshall. It thought he was too ambitious. He, for his part, put the blame wholly upon them. He told the Official Receiver the insolvency of the company was due to:

> Loss of its bargaining power and retail outlets compared with the previous company.

> Loss of incentive for retailers to buy through Simpkins because the publishers offered them better terms.

> Objections by the publishers' and booksellers' associations to the company opening its own retail outlets.

> The tendency of certain publishers to insist upon the company buying substantial quantities of their titles when granting wholesale terms, which often led to substantial losses through stock depreciation.

Maxwell refuses today to admit to any error on his part. The lessons he had learned from the failure of Simpkin Marshall, he said, were two:

> Never again allow anyone else to set the profit margins for your businesses.

> If a gentleman of the establishment offers you his word or his bond, always go for his bond.

The Official Receiver spread the blame equally in his report:

> The failure of the company is due mainly to (1) insufficient capital
> throughout; (2) small differences between publishers' prices and the
> company's selling prices which was insufficient to cover overhead
> expenses; (3) expenditure on the premises at Marylebone Road and
> (4) the financing of British Book Centre, Inc. in New York.

> It appears doubtful whether the company was at any time solvent.
> The directors concerned were at fault in acquiring the Marylebone
> premises and financing British Book Centre, Inc. at a time when
> the company was insolvent without making satisfactory arrangements
> for the introduction of sufficient further capital. Moreover, as the
> company was unable to obtain a larger margin between the
> publishers' prices and the company's selling prices and as its overhead
> expenses continued to increase, it would seem that the directors
> should have considered and decided upon liquidation at a much
> earlier date.

James Pitman, who became Conservative MP for Bath, always
exonerated Maxwell from any blame and defended him against his
critics. When the Simpkin Marshall affair was raised during
Maxwell's attempt to win Buckingham as a Labour candidate in
1959, he wrote to the *Sunday Express*, which had revived the issue:

> It is certainly my view that no stigma attaches to Captain Maxwell....
> Rather, he made a most commendable and generous effort to
> continue a service which enemy action had totally destroyed ... and
> had been re-created largely by the Pitman organisation.

But the row rumbled on and on. After the *Sunday Times* article of
October 5, 1969, an embittered publisher, who had lost £300 in the
crash, wrote a vicious letter to Maxwell:

> The future looks black for you, and your friends must be minimal
> while your enemies increase.... I wonder how much longer your luck
> can hold out.

For his part, Maxwell told the publisher that he had deprived
Simpkins of more than the £300 he had not been paid:

> Hence, you, along with the rest of the publishing industry, cannot
> divest yourself of your share in closing down Simpkin Marshall.

Maxwell rejected the *Sunday Times*'s chronicle of events. The
paper had mentioned that four years after he had acquired Simpkin
Marshall it was half a million pounds in debt; he responded by
saying that when he took over the company its overall debts were
more than that. He denied that the acquisition of the British Book

Centre (which went into liquidation a few years later) was responsible for the Simpkins collapse. He said:

> It is simply not true that Simpkins advanced any cash [to the Book Centre]. It had substantial old stocks which could not be sold in the United Kingdom and it was decided to see whether there might not be a better market in the United States. No-one in the United States would buy these books other than on consignment, but there were two objections to this: the first was that Simpkins would have no control over the books once they were shipped and the second was that there would have been administrative problems under the then Exchange Control regulations which imposed strict requirements on overseas consignment sales.

> The solution (to sell them to the British Book Centre on extended credit) appeared the only commercially feasible thing to do. British Book Centre then shipped the books out on consignment to bookstores all over the United States; I believe very few of them were sold. Eventually, huge quantities were returned to British Book Centre, who offered them to the Receivers to take in return for the sum originally invoiced. The offer was rejected by the Receivers, who accepted a payment of 42,000 dollars instead and the books were then remaindered or wasted.

In his report to the creditors, Maxwell defended the purchase of the British Book Centre. At the time he acquired Simpkins, the Centre had been in financial difficulties, having lost over £100,000. It had not paid British publishers for some time and the publishers had ceased to supply it:

> It seemed to me then proper that I should rescue this shop window for British books in America. From experience, I knew that there were good possibilities for marketing British books in the States, and concluded that the BBC, New York, with the facilities and backing of Simpkins behind it, could, in time, be turned into a successful business. This has, in fact, proved to be the case; for the year ending December, 1954, the Book Centre has, for the first time since its inception, made a small profit. Nevertheless, the cost to Simpkins and me, as events have turned out, of getting this organisation to this stage has been a very heavy one.

The gravamen of the charge against Maxwell then and subsequently, especially by the *Sunday Times* in its campaign, was that he had done very nicely out of a collapse in which others had suffered. But he told the creditors:

> I have never drawn any salary or expenses for my time and effort put into the business and over the years my other companies have made substantial financial contributions to help Simpkins along.

Indeed, he revealed that in the abortive negotiations with the Publishers' Association which preceded the calling-in of the Receiver, he had offered to put up substantial sums of "fresh money" as well as to hand over the equity and management of the company to trustees appointed by the publishers' and booksellers' associations, "provided the trade assured the continuance of the business in one form or another", and he added:

> All along I have been firmly convinced that it would be a calamity to the whole book trade if this opportunity were not taken to rationalise the trade for the ultimate benefit of all in the trade.

Arthur Coleridge, who had been managing director of Simpkin Marshall before the arrival of Maxwell and stayed with the company until mid-1953, wrote to the trade magazine *The Bookseller* accusing a majority of important booksellers of putting the whole of their worthwhile business direct to publishers, but traditionally relying on Simpkins for all their difficult, odd and unidentifiable items.

It is profitless now to speculate on what might have been, but it seems sensible that the Pitman brothers should have been allowed by the trade to put Simpkin Marshall into liquidation when they wanted to in 1950. The publishers who approached Maxwell to save the company did neither him nor themselves a favour. Nor did he in listening to them. In view of the publishers' past record, it was over-optimistic to believe that they would grant Simpkin Marshall the profit margins it needed to succeed, especially in view of the heavy capital costs involved in leasing and fitting-out new premises to provide the service the trade required. But they had touched him at his weakest point; he finds it impossible to resist a challenge. Sometimes the results of his falling for temptation are spectacularly successful. Relieving a small group of beleaguered British soldiers in 1945, after his company commander had told him he was stupid and would probably be court-martialled, even if he were successful, is one example. There are many others. He was still behaving in exactly the same way 35 years after Simpkin when he agreed to try to save the Commonwealth Games in Edinburgh from collapse; when in 1982, 1984 and 1987 he stepped in to rescue, respectively, Oxford United, Derby County and Watford football clubs; when he became chairman of the House of Commons Catering Committee in order to stem the losses which were becoming a public scandal; when he sought to use his rich resources to launch an international campaign to help the sufferers from AIDS; when he tried to save Aston Martin from collapse; when he tried to rescue Craven

Assurance. The list is endless. To put it all down to vanity would be
superficial. His curiosity is unquenchable. He delights in being a
problem solver; it is a kind of Solomon complex. But it is not a
selfish one. It is the situation which requires a solution for a public
benefit which attracts him most of all; but he would often be
disappointed were he expecting public acclaim.

5

Rise of Pergamon

Science is vastly more stimulating to the
imagination than are the classics
J.B.S. Haldane

With the end of Simpkin Marshall, Maxwell returned full-time to the affairs of his brain-child, Pergamon Press, the company built on the rock of a single, simple, clear conviction that the post-war world would be dominated by the scientific developments - the control of the atom, the jet engine, radar, rocket technology, antibiotics and the like - which the needs of the war had accelerated. His business was rapidly expanding as the demand for scientific textbooks, journals and papers, especially the pre-1945 German publications and the new information and discoveries they contained, multiplied over and again. In January of the previous year, 1954, he had begun a series of overseas visits, which was to last for more than a decade, to acquire new publication rights for the company and to recruit scientists as editors and advisers to the growing number of journals he wanted to produce. He went to Moscow for 10 days as part of a 30-man trade delegation whose mission was to achieve a new two-way traffic of scientific and technical publications between East and West. But while he was there he told Nikita Kruschev it was time the Russians started to pay royalties on the British books which they had shamelessly - and freely, in the literal sense - pirated for generations. It was a concession which they had been notoriously refusing to make since the days of the Czars. When Kruschev asked why they should pay for what they could get for nothing, Maxwell replied that in that case he would take Russian publications and pay no royalties. He returned with the British publication rights for some 50 Soviet scientific, technical and medical works and a promise to buy a substantially larger number of British books. He also got a promise from Kruschev that he would look into the copyright question. True, it was a look which was longer than it was hard; in fact, it was to become one of the longest looks in history. But eventually it bore fruit.

Within 24 hours of his return from the Soviet Union Maxwell was off on a 17-day visit to Canada, as part of his commitment to Waller to sell off bartered East German cement and to negotiate the resumption of trading with the Soviet Union which had virtually ceased during the cold war. He told the Canadians that the Russians were "definitely interested" in buying at least $20 million-worth of Canadian goods for a start, with more to follow later.

But his first overseas visit after the Simpkins collapse was to Peking as a member of a delegation led by S.A. Lane of the Brush Group, invited by the Chinese Import and Export Agency at the request of Sir Anthony Eden, the recently-installed Prime Minister. The journey to China in those days was by slow plane to Hong Kong and then by the infinitely slower and even more uncomfortable train to Peking, a discomfort made worse by the loudspeakers which incessantly blared out Communist propaganda. They could not be turned off, so Maxwell ripped out the one in his compartment. It didn't help. He was threatened with ejection from the train and its journey was delayed until the damage had been repaired. The party had no choice but to listen to the barrage for the rest of the journey.

Negotiations with the new régime were novel. Maxwell represented the book, periodical and film interests on the delegation. His meetings with the Chinese Minister of Education were regularly interrupted by the Chinese team leaving the room to practise their callisthenics. Towards the end of the talks, which produced very little, Maxwell said he couldn't stand another journey on the Chinese "torture" railway and asked to be allowed to fly home via the Soviet Union. It was the height of the cold war and he was told it would be impossible to achieve. But a friendly Russian consul swiftly obtained visas for him and Lane, the others having to go back the way they came. They travelled in a Chinese National Airways plane via Irkutsk (the last one in had to close the door), which pursued a zig-zag course for most of the way. When Maxwell asked why this was happening, the Russian Deputy Minister of Foreign Trade, Kirmikan, who was also on board, said they were not going to show to foreign capitalists the great things which were happening in Siberia. An argument developed. Maxwell told the Russian that the Chinese liked them even less than they did the Americans and British and that within two years the Russians would want the Western allies to protect them against the Chinese. The argument caused a commotion in the plane. When it landed he was briefly arrested by the secret police, the NKVD.

The sequel to Maxwell's first visit to China came many years later, in the early 1970s, when he was invited to visit the country again. Once more he met the Minister of Education, whose first words were to apologise to Maxwell for not replying to a letter Maxwell had sent to him in August 1955. The delay, he explained, was due to the Cultural Revolution. Maxwell complimented him on the efficiency of his filing system.

On his return from Peking Maxwell flew to Geneva for the first United Nations International Conference on the Peaceful Uses of Atomic Energy, whose official publisher he became, and where he attended - invited or not - every reception which was held so that he might recruit new authors and editors to work for Pergamon. Maxwell was to say later:

> I was so impressed by the future prospects for, and the importance of, nuclear energy for peace as well as war that I agreed there and then to publish a substantial number of journals covering the entire field of nuclear energy.

There was almost an explosion of new journals from Pergamon: *Inorganic and Nuclear Chemistry*; *Annals of Nuclear Energy*; *Applied Radiation and Isotopes*; *Progress in Nuclear Energy* (in 12 separate series); *Health Physics*; and many others. All were successful and in great demand among scientists and university libraries, and most of them still exist.

The current executive editor of the *Annals of Nuclear Energy*, Professor M.M.R. Williams, Professor of Nuclear Engineering at the University of Michigan, has recalled what he was told about the Geneva conference:

> The various delegations ... vied with each other to give the most magnificent receptions and, of course, Bob Maxwell attended all of these (either invited or uninvited) to make his contacts. In one instance, the French decided to hire a boat and serve a meal whilst sailing around Lake Geneva. The numbers for this event had to be limited and invitations were carefully scrutinised as people came aboard. As the boat pulled away from the quayside and there was about five feet of clear water, Bob ran to the edge shouting, "Wait for me", and jumped across. The sailor who helped him was too concerned for his safety to check his invitation - rumour has it he did not have one and this was a ruse planned well in advance....

The work of gatherings like "Atoms for Peace", though mystifying to even the intelligent layman and of little or no concern to anyone else, was of all-consuming interest to scientists throughout the world, and the right to publish the papers presented to them was invaluable to Pergamon. The journals of the conferences themselves were profitable and each contract which was obtained helped the growing reputation of Pergamon and made future contracts easier to gain.

But the most important of the contacts Maxwell made in Geneva was the head of the Soviet delegation, Academician Topchiev, who, besides being a leading petroleum chemist was also the secretary of the USSR Academy of Sciences. Maxwell recalls:

> I, like everyone else, was surprised by the quality of some of the research work in this field disclosed by the Russians at this conference ... and I accepted an invitation from the Academy to discuss with their leading scientists the possibility of having some of their research work translated and published in England by Pergamon.

With his remarkable energy, his ability to impose his ideas on people whom he had never met, his - for want of a better phrase - sheer cheek, Maxwell was putting Pergamon on the scientific map. He was 32, full of life and the company was prospering. He had cornered one of the potentially most lucrative markets in publishing. He was on top of the world. But then, almost immediately after his return from Switzerland, disaster struck.

Suddenly, and without previously feeling ill, he began to suffer sharp pains in his chest. His own doctor prescribed hot poultices to relieve the discomfort, but when there was no improvement and the pains got steadily worse X-rays were recommended and taken and tumours were detected in both his lungs.

Dr Ogilvie Macfeat of the Department of Radiodiagnosis at the London Clinic reported on October 7:

> Two, fairly large, rounded opacities are present in the upper left axillary region and a small, oval shadow overlies the intersection of the fourth and seventh right ribs.... The lung markings, generally, are normal, and the heart is normal in size and shape.... The appearances are almost certainly due to secondary malignant deposits in both lungs - most probably from a Seminoma [a cancer of the testicle].

A report from Dr Macfeat four days later said that the two large opacities were composed of "multiple rounded tumour nodules". A leading authority on lung cancer, Sir Stanford Cade, was consulted, and he diagnosed secondary cancer of the lungs. The world which had been opening up for Maxwell was now closing in with terrifying rapidity. Betty still recalls the horror of the day when she heard Sir

Stanford's verdict: She says:

> I remember only too well when, in an icy-cold and detached manner,
> the "great man" delivered his message to Bob. Sir Stanford said that
> as Bob had an important business and six children he felt it was his
> duty to tell him he had four weeks to live so that he might put his
> affairs in order.
>
> When I was brought in, my first reaction was of revolt, followed by an
> intense desire to do something about it. Bob was devastated.
>
> It was then that, one day, on looking at some flowers that had been
> brought to him, he realised the beauty of nature and the fact that he
> had never had time to appreciate the design, colour and fragrance of
> a flower, and now he never would.

Whether or not it derives from that experience, it is a fact today
that displays of flowers are never absent from his office or his home,
or wherever he is working, even in the depth of winter. Betty
Maxwell continues:

> The nursing staff were in tears that such a handsome and attractive
> young father of six should be condemned to such a short life. They
> allowed me to sleep in his room at night, which I did on a mattress on
> the floor near his bed. We talked endlessly and made plans. I kept
> holding his hand all night so that he could go to sleep knowing that I
> was watching for Death and would not let her take him away without
> his knowledge.
>
> Although Bob had gone through the most hair-raising experiences
> during the war and been close to death many times, it was different to
> be told in cold blood that he was going to die soon. In the war, he had
> been single and his priority had been to defeat Nazism and avenge his
> family in Czechoslovakia. Now he had a wife and six kids of his own
> whom he adored.

At first it didn't occur to the Maxwells to question Sir Stanford
Cade's diagnosis. Their eldest son, Michael, who was then aged
nine, was brought from his preparatory school to say goodbye to his
father and the other five children - Anne, Philip, Christine, Isabel
and Karine, who was herself to die two years later - were brought to
the clinic by their nanny, Marion Sloane, to do the same.

Betty says:

> You must realise we were still very young and we had no reason to
> suspect the veracity of the verdict of such an eminent man as Sir
> Stanford. But while I was living at the clinic I started to move heaven
> and earth to see if anything could be done.

The first move she made was to telephone her sister, Dr Yvonne
Vittoz, the Parisian gynaecologist who had delivered all but one of

her children. Dr Vittoz advised Betty to call in a French specialist in phthisiology, Dr Roger Kervran, for a second opinion. She and Dr Kervran then flew to London for him to examine the X-rays which had been taken of Maxwell's lungs. He said he was not convinced that Sir Stanford's diagnosis of cancer was correct and he recommended that a new team altogether should be asked to investigate Maxwell's condition. At such a desperate time, the Maxwells were ready to seize upon any sliver of hope and Sir Clement Price Thomas, the surgeon who had operated on George VI in 1951 for lung cancer, was consulted. He recommended that Mr (later Sir) Peter Kerley, who had been the king's radiologist, should be asked to take new X-rays.

Kerley performed a tomography, a radiography which shows in clear detail a particular part of the body. He identified a small tumour in the top left lobe of the right lung, but he said that the secondary tumour in the lung which had been detected by Sir Stanford Cade did not exist. It was, apparently, no more than the shadow of an "excrescence" on the rib. As a result of these new X-rays Sir Clement Price Thomas advised an exploratory operation. This he performed himself at the University College Hospital, London and removed the upper left lobe in Maxwell's right lung. A biopsy then showed that the tumour was non-malignant.

Kerley remained a friend of the Maxwell family until his own death some 20 years later. He had been so appalled by the original diagnosis of Maxwell's condition that he refused to make any charge for his services, either then or for the subsequent X-rays which he took, first every three months, then at six-monthly intervals and finally once a year. For his part, Maxwell, a two packets a day cigarette smoker until his illness, gave up the habit. He now hates cigarettes and only the addicts on his staff - and highly-regarded addicts at that - would dare smoke in his home or office.

It was a long time before Maxwell allowed himself to be convinced that he did not face an early death and the illness probably added to the urgency and impatience with which he has always dealt with any issue. For years it became his practice to preface any remark about the future with the words, "If I am here...". Ann Robertson, his secretary from 1948 until 1958 when she emigrated to South Africa, recalled visiting him in hospital just before the operation:

> [He was] interviewing a Christian Science leader to try to find some truth which he could accept with his analytical mind for the hereafter. I then had to read him pages of a Christian Science charter, but he

could find nothing to satisfy him and in turn he tried the Chief Rabbi and the Catholic priest; and even the Church of England padre tried to play his part, but I don't think any of them provided an acceptable solution.

But Mrs Maxwell says her husband never consulted a Catholic or an Anglican priest; she only remembers his talking to a friend who was a Christian Scientist. Outside the immediate family and friends, there was a strictly business-like, even mercenary, approach to Maxwell's illness. It was recounted by Tom Clark:

> Bob's illness caused a certain amount of consternation in certain quarters because in 1952, at the request of Hambros, the company had taken out an insurance policy for £100,000 on his life. Bob had purchased this policy from the Receivers of Simpkin Marshall and there was a lot of to-ing and fro-ing as to who should have the benefit of the policy if Bob did die. Some of the creditors thought the policy should not have been sold and that any ultimate benefit should be distributed among them.

There was a bitter tailpiece to the whole terrifying experience. On a visit to Japan in 1949 Maxwell had brought back a large opal as a present for Betty. After the operation, and because of the superstition of ill-fortune which attaches to the stone, Betty decided to sell it, through a friend, for the "ridiculous" price of £92 and was paid in cash for it. A few days later Sir Stanford Cade submitted his bill for his services. The temptation was to tell Sir Stanford that he wasn't going to get a penny, but Betty resisted it. His bill was for £92 and she gave it to him - with the cash which she had got for the opal.

* * * * *

After five weeks' convalescence in Jamaica, all the time half-expecting the death sentence to be reimposed, Maxwell returned to the building up of Pergamon. He was determined to multiply the growth of the company which was already under way. In January 1955 he had told the board it should aim to publish 100 books a year by 1957 and in March it agreed to embark upon a systematic expansion, with the aim of doubling output within a few years. Tom Clark analysed the reasons for the company's success:

> One of his major attributes was the ability to seize the heart of a problem and give an immediate decision - one that sometimes appeared inappropriate but nevertheless turned out to be workable.

To have a chief who appeared to be able to solve all problems gave immense confidence to the senior staff; his ability to inspire confidence even in the darkest days was quite extraordinary. He never showed doubt, never considered retreat or defeat. If anything went wrong he expected to be told immediately and would give his advice without recrimination. If he discovered an error third-hand there would be trouble.

He had an odd trait. If someone lost a fiver he would be severely reprimanded. However, if the sum was considerable, say £1,000, there would be the inevitable storm but afterwards the story would be told with roars of laughter. His great theme was that he wanted "value for money". No expenditure unless there was a good benefit. No purchase unless obtained at the lowest price. Money was not to be wasted.

An impartial report on Pergamon Press, drawn up in 1978 by a team at the Imperial College of Science and Technology in London, said:

The early rise of Pergamon can be attributed to the recognition of the potential post-war market for the dissemination of scientific knowledge and to the break from the traditional approach of dealing in Europe and the Commonwealth only.

That recognition was Maxwell's supreme achievement. Hurried and harried by him, Pergamon moved in March 1955 to larger offices in Fitzroy Square, London, which were to remain its headquarters until the move to Headington Hill Hall, Oxford, in 1960. An extraordinary general meeting of the company - held on the day after Maxwell's first chest X-ray - had increased its capital from £10,000 to £50,000 by the creation of 40,000 £1 shares. But this galloping expansion was resisted by Pergamon's science director, Dr Rosbaud, who was, after Maxwell, the most important man in the company and one who, because of his reputation with Springer-Verlag, had the trust of many of the scientists whom Maxwell had recruited. Rosbaud doubted the wisdom of such a vaulting ambition and such rapid growth as Maxwell was demanding. Friction began to grow between him on the one hand and Maxwell and the rest of the board on the other. The row simmered for months before reaching a crisis in May 1956. Rosbaud had written a letter to Hugh Handsfield, editor-in-chief of the American scientific publishers McGraw-Hill, telling him that Pergamon could not fulfil his order for copies of *Principles of Optics* in the time required, nor could it possibly quote him a price. But the time and the price were paramount in a deal which had already been negotiated by Maxwell.

"Surely there must be some misunderstanding", Rosbaud wrote to Handsfield:

> I don't think there will be any hope for the sheets to be shipped for twelve to fifteen months, and with regard to price, we cannot possibly give you a quotation as we don't even know the size of the book....

Maxwell exploded. There was an acrimonious meeting with Rosbaud on May 25, two days after that letter had been sent, and then a formal letter from Maxwell to his science director later that same day:

> This is to confirm our discussion this morning when I informed you of the immediate suspension from your duties as science editor.... I regret to have to take this step but I am afraid that your letter of May 23 addressed to the editor-in-chief of McGraw-Hill leaves me no alternative ... having regard to similar acts of disloyalty in the past about which you have been reprimanded. I would remind you also that in September 1955 you assured me, on your word of honour, of your loyalty, support and co-operation. I am afraid that I am unable to accept your apology and explanation that you have acted impulsively. I regard your letter to McGraw-Hill, together with many other recent actions you have taken, as constituting a definite breach of your service agreement with the company.

Rosbaud protested, in a reply written that day, that he had in no way been disloyal and said the suspension ordered by Maxwell was "entirely unjustified". But at a special board meeting of Pergamon four days later Maxwell set out his case. He had, he said, earlier in the year agreed that publication of *Principles of Optics* would take place towards the end of 1956 with a view to getting a firm order from McGraw-Hill. He had also agreed with them a maximum price for 2,500 copies. When Rosbaud had seen the order he had taken "unilateral action of a most disloyal and harmful nature". The only object of his action, said Maxwell, must have been to encourage McGraw-Hill to negotiate directly with him, thus "seeking to discredit the veracity as well as the authority of the Managing Director" (Maxwell).

Dr Rosbaud admitted, again, that he had acted impulsively, but denied Maxwell's allegations about his motives. The chairman of Pergamon in those days was Harry Siepmann, previously an executive director of the Bank of England, who was recruited by Maxwell. According to Tom Clark, Siepmann was

> ... a man of outstanding ability and well known in the international banking world, but he was always very short of money himself which led to a few problems.

The board's minutes précis Siepmann's summing up: he said that at first he had been convinced that there was nothing underhand or secretive in Dr Rosbaud's action, but as the meeting progressed it became clear that Dr Rosbaud had had every opportunity to raise the matter or consult Captain Maxwell. It was clear that he had acted independently, behaving as though he were the watchdog of the board. This he was not entitled to do.

Siepmann then delivered to Rosbaud an extraordinarily back-handed finding of innocence on the charge of having been disloyal. The minutes record him saying:

> He would categorically acquit Dr Rosbaud of disloyalty to the Press, though at the same time he considered him to be constitutionally unable to be loyal to any one person. He did not appear to realise that being loyal to a company meant being loyal to the individual members directing that company.... The letter should never have been written....

The suspension of Rosbaud was then confirmed. After negotiations, Rosbaud gave "undertakings about his future conduct", but his days were numbered. By October the board was agreeing to pay him £2,500 for loss of office and Rosbaud formally resigned and sold his shares. He faded from view after that and died in 1963. Maxwell says of him:

> He was an outstanding editor of the European type from whom I learned some of the trade in the early days.

After Rosbaud's departure there was nothing to hold Maxwell back and the way was open for the company to grow in the way in which he envisaged. If he made Pergamon, it is also true that Pergamon was the making of him. Post-war Britain did not have many lasting success stories, but Pergamon was one of the few. Whatever else he has achieved in his life, nothing can surpass his success with it. Equally, whatever business disappointments and defeats he has suffered, nothing ever hurt more than losing Pergamon for five years to Leasco.

In his career he has taken over many loss-making companies and made them profitable; he has also started a number of new enterprises - like retail booksellers in the 1960s and the *London Daily News* in 1987 - and when they proved not to be profitable closed them down.

But Pergamon was unlike any other. The old Butterworth-Springer company was little more than a small-time experiment in partnership which had failed. He turned it into Pergamon Press, building it from almost nothing with almost nothing except an obsessive energy and a vision. It was his baby, his creation, and he nurtured it from birth. Without any scientific or technical training at all, with no education in the subjects which fascinated him or, indeed, with little formal education of any kind, he saw what no one else had seen: that the thirst for scientific knowledge and technical information would grow and grow and that the other publishers of scientific journals were not equipped, either physically, mentally or mechanically, to cope with the demand. In an interview with Sheridan Morley[1] he explained why he was different from other publishers, saying:

> I've taken less than the 150 years they thought it would take to achieve.

He had a formulation which he loved to quote in those early days:

> From the year 1 A.D. it took 1,750 years for knowledge to double for the first time. It doubled for the second time by 1900; for the third time by 1950 and for a fourth time 10 years later, by 1960.

By 1975 it was to double again and Maxwell's intuitive awareness of what was happening in the world of science, technology and medicine was the single main cause of the success of Pergamon. Lady Elizabeth Wilson, wife of a former British ambassador to Moscow, recently recalled going to him to propose the publication of an English-Russian dictionary:

> I ... said a small dictionary is not going to make sense - it will have to be quite a big dictionary. Are you happy to accept this as I have no degree in Russian? I will always remember his answer: "I'm always ready to back my hunches." I'm happy to say that the resulting dictionary has been widely acclaimed both here and in America as the best (though not the most comprehensive) English-Russian dictionary so far.

When everything else in his business life is put into the balance, the development of Pergamon will always be enough to ensure that the pros outweigh the cons. The tributes paid to him by the scientists who have worked with him will always be greater than the libels for which he so frequently has issued writs.

For the past 40 years he has given his life to it. He has travelled the world on its behalf; the passenger miles run into millions, the nights away from home and family run into thousands. Betty estimates he has spent 80 per cent of his time away from home, but accepts it with remarkable resignation.

The result of this ceaseless global activity was that he took the

ambition which had made Dr Rosbaud flinch even beyond his own
early dreams. Pergamon became the jewel in a crown which at times
must seem to him to be composed of thorns. Ironically, it is also the
side of him of which the British public - who know him mainly from
almost-daily headlines about Maxwell bidding for this or Maxwell
buying that, of Maxwell in a baseball cap photographed at Derby or
Oxford or some other sporting scene, or angrily litigating against his
latest detractor - has rarely seen and knows virtually nothing.

The first objective in the Pergamon expansion programme was to
recruit to its ranks the authors and editors who were the best in their
respective scientific fields and then, more or less, to give them their
heads. After the founding of Pergamon it was that decision which
was crucial to its success. He was loyal to his editors and they, in
turn, were loyal to him when he needed friends most and they struck
the decisive blow in returning Pergamon to his control at a time
when the political, publishing and financial world was writing him
off once and for all. That loyalty still supports him today.

About 300 editors of Pergamon journals contributed to a
privately-printed volume of tributes for presentation to Maxwell on
his 65th birthday. In it, they set out their memories and their
experiences of their publisher. What is striking about this praise,
even for a festive occasion, is the unanimity of the scientific view
about his vision in recognising the need for journals in a bewildering
range of specialties and the freedom which he gave the editors to
establish and develop them. The tributes are an extraordinary
contrast to the publicity which he endures because of his other
activities. Because of the rarefied fields in which they work, most of
them are unknown outside their science and the universities. They
are Maxwell's anonymous fan club.

Professor A.L. Copley, editor of *Biorheology*, for example, told
of how he was approached by Maxwell in 1959 to start a new
international journal of biorheology and to become its editor-in-
chief. Copley and a colleague, Dr George Scott Blair, head of the
Physics Department of the National Institute for Research in
Dairying, near Reading, tried to caution Maxwell about the venture
and pointed out that an earlier American attempt to produce one
had failed. Copley went on:

> He [Maxwell] commented that whoever published the journal
> apparently did not know how to go about it. Bob stressed that he
> anticipated to lose money for about the first five years. Only after this
> time would he expect Pergamon Press to break even and only after
> some additional time would he hope to make a profit.... What I

admired in Bob ... was his recognition of the significance of this new science, his readiness to risk money on it, and the enthusiasm he showed as a publisher for a scientific discipline which at that time was known only to the very few who practised it.... [He is] a daring non-scientist with exceptional insight into the future of science.

The editor of *Ocean Engineering*, Professor M.E. McCormick, declared:

The foresight of Mr Maxwell contributed significantly to the establishment of post-war science and technology since he supplied the background materials upon which scientific and technological advances are built.... Through [his] guidance, both direct and indirect, the journal has become the international standard of literature in ocean technology.

The editor of *Insect Biochemistry*, Professor L.I. Gilbert, said:

There are only a few hundred subscriptions to *Insect Biochemistry* and its publication by Pergamon Press is more of a service to the field than good business practice.... Maxwell continues to publish the journal using high-quality printing techniques, makes it available to investigators at a nominal subscription rate. [His] company, in a monetary sense, profits little from its sales.

Professor Harry Messel, head of the School of Physics at the University of Sydney, first met Maxwell 35 years ago. He recalled:

Our friendship was immediate and never faltered. He had great plans for publishing scientific books and journals; I had plans for a top-class School of Physics.... Maxwell needed top-quality material to publish and we needed a reliable, well-known and fast publisher. This combination has resulted in Pergamon Press publishing in excess of 40 books and monographs emanating from my School of Physics.

Messel remembered how in 1969 he needed a sponsor with £10,000 for the 13th International Science School for high school students on "Nuclear Energy Today and Tomorrow". He phoned Maxwell, who simply asked: "Where do we send the cheque?" Then he required the publication of the lecture material for the school within four weeks. It was 473 pages and Maxwell met the deadline. Messel commented:

I love the decisiveness of the man; he has no time for changing his mind. He makes decisions (and usually correct ones) and then carries them out at great speed.

Professor W. Johnson, editor of the international journals *Impact*

Engineering and *Mechanical Sciences*, reacted similarly to Maxwell:

> He seemed to be in a rare class of competence which was all his own -
> a sharp mind, ability in several languages and a capacity for
> nearly-instantaneous decision-making....

> Without Robert Maxwell's establishment of a special relationship
> with the USSR for technical translation rights, the West would have
> been the poorer for knowledge about the Soviet Union's
> achievements and contributions in the field of applied mechanics.

The director of the World Development Institute and chairman of
the editorial board of *World Development*, Professor Paul Streeten,
wrote:

> One hears many people virulently criticising Robert Maxwell....
> Innovation implies the removal of deadwood and the deadwood
> sometimes is alive enough to squeak. But they are puny squeaks
> against the powerful and imaginative innovations that Bob
> initiates.... He has given enormous encouragement to young scholars
> to find publishing outlets, even if old fuddy-duddies occasionally
> complain.

A more personal note was offered by Professor Neville
Postlethwaite, editor of the *International Journal of Education
Research*, who didn't meet Maxwell until 1980 and expected
something different from what he found:

> He met me at the front door of his Oxford home. All that I had heard
> about him before was that he was originally Czech and a show-off. In
> fact, I met a man who spoke beautiful and mellifluous English (better
> English than mine, and I was born and raised in England!), who was
> extremely courteous and who insisted on carrying my bag and
> showing me to the room where I would sleep. This was a very
> different image from the one that I had received from the media....

> I have not the slightest hesitation in stating that, in my perception,
> Maxwell has been at least two moves ahead of anyone else ... at any
> given point in time....

> Many people complain of his dictatorial and bombastic manner. This
> has not been my experience, but then I do not work for him. He
> considers bla-bla as stupid. One has to express one's ideas concisely
> and quickly. If this is not the case, he becomes impatient and, shall
> we say, testy.

The renowned lateral thinker Professor Edward de Bono believes
that in 10 years time "thinking" will be taught in schools covering
more than half the population of the world and that Maxwell has
played the "key role" in making this a possibility. The Soviet Union,
Japan, China, the United States, Canada, Australia, New Zealand,

South Africa, Britain, Bulgaria, Ireland, Sweden, Malaysia, Singapore and Israel have all shown an interest in putting thinking in the curriculum or have already done so. In Venezuela, says de Bono, every youngster must spend two hours a week on thinking skills and Ecuador is considering doing the same. In his tribute de Bono said:

> The whole success of the project has depended on two key contributions from Robert Maxwell.

The first was a meeting at Headington Hill Hall in June 1979 when Maxwell arranged a dinner for a Venezuelan professor, Dr Luis Alberto Machado, to meet de Bono. De Bono told Machado about his Cognitive Research Trust programme to develop intelligence. Since then 105,000 Venezuelan teachers have been trained in his methods. More fundamental, de Bono added, was that his brother, Peter, who was in charge of publishing his CoRT programme, was looking for an established firm to take it on and couldn't find one:

> I mentioned to Robert Maxwell that I was looking for a publisher. He immediately offered.... Then and there, a decision was made. I regard this sort of behaviour as the ultimate justification for people like Robert Maxwell ... such people can make decisions based on their own enterprise and vision without having to go through layers of timid and conservative committees terrified of making mistakes.... This project to teach the world to think could just be the most significant and most enduring of all [his] considerable contributions to the world.

Sir Derek Barton, Nobel Prize winner, an early adherent to Pergamon and a founder-member of the board of one of its most renowned journals, *Tetrahedron*, wrote of Maxwell in 1983:

> He foresaw the revolution in scientific publication, and especially its internationalisation, a decade before it really happened.... I am not competent to judge the role that Bob Maxwell has played, and might play, in national politics, but as a scientist I hope that he will not be elected again to the House. It would be a waste of his unique talents. If not elected, he can spend more time devoted to his real work in the encouragement of scientific publication.
>
> I think that what I most admire about him is that fact that, lacking a formal education at more than a modest level, he yet manages to understand perfectly the world of the university. He recognises that professors are not all equal and that a few, whom he seeks out and encourages, are exceptional.

Professsor Harvey Brooks of Harvard University was persuaded by Maxwell in the autumn of 1955 to become editor of the *Journal of Physics and Solids*, which at the time was no more than the glimmer of an idea in Maxwell's mind. He baulked at the thought and wrote:

> I didn't know quite what to make of this energetic and forceful young man, only just turned 32, who was a rising star in the technical publishing world. Was he just a flash in the pan? Was he really serious...? Was it really right for me to invest the time and effort in such an enterprise, and a profit-making enterprise at that?

He decided it was and never looked back. But the scientific tradition at that time was that the work of the eminent members of professional societies was largely published in the journals of those societies. Profit was not part of the societies' motive. Indeed, as Professor Brooks said, there seemed to be something "faintly disreputable" about such an incentive. The same fears struck Professor Elias Burstein of the University of Pennsylvania, who was approached through Brooks to become a member of the International Advisory Board of *Physics and Solids*.

> I was obviously interested ... but somewhat hesitant because of concerns that had been raised ... in the United States regarding the publication of a scientific journal by a "commercial" publisher.

But he joined and has never since regretted it. Professor Jack Christian, of Oxford, editor of *Progress in Materials Science*, had his initial doubts:

> As an author and editor, I have enjoyed for many years ... a "long, cordial but slightly adversarial" relationship with him, the tension in which has arisen from the sometimes conflicting interests of science and business, but has been relieved by Bob's geniality, generous spirit and willingness to accept another point of view. Scientists are often suspicious of commercial scientific publishing and I shared these reservations initially, but ... the services which Pergamon provides are essential....

From the University of Liège, Professor Zénon Bacq, chairman of *Biochemical Pharmacology*, a Pergamon journal which has been successfully published for 30 years, wrote:

> Bob is at the disposal of anyone with a valid idea.... [He] represents audacity, the pleasure of beginning and completing an action that others, even tough and well-informed competitors, hesitate or refuse to undertake ... represents as well an acute sense of management ... stopping in time a project which is going badly ... accepting his mistakes, changing partners.... In truth, Bob is a world you can never completely travel round.

Professor John Coales, of Cambridge, says:

> In the 50s, all my friends in the publishing world told me he was the greatest villain unhung, taking over technical journals here and killing them there.... I reached the conclusion that his reputation was inspired by the envy of his competitors and their irritation caused by a young man coming in and beating them at their own game.

To beat them, Maxwell poured every ounce of energy, 18 hours a day and seven days a week, into the task, but stayed his hand in one vital area. In 1955 he had founded the *Journal of Nuclear Energy*, which has continued for more than 30 years and is today the oldest publication to specialise in nuclear science and engineering. Its editor since 1972, Professor M.M.R. Williams, says:

> One thing Maxwell does not do is interfere in editorial decisions; in that respect, he is the ideal person to act as a publisher of scientific journals.

Other scientists have heaped even more fulsome praise upon Maxwell's head. Those quoted above are only a small selection of the whole; but by the very nature of their occupations, their views are seen by only a tiny section of the population compared with those who read, say, the criticism of him when he is accused of trying to kidnap Association Football in England for his own personal satisfaction.

Throughout the growth of Pergamon - and especially after he lost control of it - Maxwell's staunchest allies were to be these scientists or others like them. Those who envied his success sneered that he got the scientists to work on the cheap - though it is clear from the scientists' evidence that they recognised there was often a loss involved in production of the journals - and that he charged too much for what he produced. The criticism overlooked the fact that for the scientist, the fee for publication was not paramount. What Maxwell gave them was the opportunity to publish and disseminate their work and to read and absorb the work of others. What is more, such was his speed of production that the scientists whose work was published in a Pergamon journal had the advantage of getting into print first, a consideration which was vital to them. There was a two-tier subscription system for the journals, but it was slanted in favour of the individual subscriber, who paid the lower price, and against universities and libraries who had to pay the higher rate, a strain which they were more easily able to take. This system was much criticised when Maxwell first introduced it, but later it was adopted by other publishers. The best test of the scientists' regard is the action taken by their community after Maxwell lost control of Pergamon. It was the loyalty of the scientists which made his return to the chairmanship of the company the only alternative to its collapse as a scientific publishing house and its eventual disappearance.

* * * * *

One of the problems of keeping up with Maxwell is his bewildering habit of suddenly striking out in a new direction when he seems to be fully occupied elsewhere. The greenness of new fields is a constant temptation and his career in films, a distraction into which he had been enticed by Siepmann, is a classic example of it. Siepmann had introduced Maxwell to Paul Czinner, film director and husband of the celebrated pre-war film star Elisabeth Bergner. Czinner was looking for an "angel" to finance a film of Wilhelm Furtwängler's last performance as a conductor, the 1954 Salzburg Festival production of *Don Giovanni*. Pergamon had little money to spare in those days, though Czinner was in a far worse state, not even being able to pay his telephone bill. But Maxwell believed in the project and formed a company, Harmony Films Ltd., to back it.

Though the reviews were mixed, most were glowing. The *Daily Telegraph* said the experiment was "wonderfully successful" and *The Observer* described it as "an interesting experiment in film making". *The Spectator* thought it "musically magnificent" and the *New Statesman* said it was "an occasion not to be missed". But *The Guardian* found the sound-track "distorted". For the *New York Daily News*, on the other hand, the showing of the film at Carnegie Hall was "exciting and unprecedented" and "a rare musical treat". The *Daily Telegraph*'s New York correspondent found it "marred by the use of the wrong amplifiers and speakers", though that was hardly Harmony Films' fault. *Don Giovanni* was a success with audiences in France, Japan, the United States and Canada as well as Britain. Even today it is being produced in cassette form. It was also shown in the Soviet Union, where German artists and conductors who had performed under the Hitler régime were not popular.

Later it was followed by another Maxwell-Czinner colour production, *The Bolshoi Ballet*, which included a complete performance of *Giselle* with Ulanova, filmed in two all-night sessions at the Royal Opera House, Covent Garden, London, after the audience for the public performance had left. Tom Clark recalled:

Sunday
nov. 21

Dear Captain Maxwell,

The accompanying package contains
forty five grams of streptomycin.

Today I had an emergency call from London
from the wife of my war time British Military assistant,
Colonel James Gault of the Scots Guards. She states
that Colonel Gault is desperately ill and that
the local supply of this drug is almost
exhausted; it is needed at once in his treatment
and I am cabling to the family to say that
you will leave it at the military attaché'
office in London about noon on Monday.

I was informed by the brother of Colonel
Gault that, before your arrival, he will have
secured any necessary authority for import, etc.

I do hope this errand causes you no great
trouble. I am most concerned about the case
and I assure you of my lasting gratitude for
your cooperation.

Most sincerely,
Dwight D Eisenhower

A letter from Eisenhower, 21st November, 1949.

Celebrating Ferdinand Springer's 70th birthday at Heidelberg.

With Tonjes Lange at Heidelberg, 1950.

Maxwell mountain climbing with Sir Robert and Lady Robinson on the Swiss side of the Matterhorn

With Sir Robert Robinson for the launch of Tetrahedron.

The picture taken for Maxwell's
political campaign posters.
It proved to be a winner.

Welcoming Hugh and Dora Gaitskell at the Bletchley Labour Party hall in 1962.

At the Kremlin with Nikita Kruschev, Anastas Mikoyan, Ambassador Frank Roberts and Reginald Maudling.

Laughter with Margot
Fonteyn.

Doctor Kervran, the
French doctor whose
advice saved Robert
Maxwell's life during his
illness in 1955.

With Galina Ulanova, 1956.

With David Frost at
Headington Hill Hall in
the early Sixties.

With Betty at the
Worshipful Company of
Gardeners' banquet,
Mansion House, 1960.

Victory march after winning Buckingham in 1964.

Bob and Betty after winning Buckingham in 1966.

Maxwell arrives at the Commons as MP for Buckingham.

With Edward Heath and Horace King in the newly reopened Annie's Bar
at the Commons.

With George Brown on the terrace of the Commons in 1964.

With Professor Theodore von Karman, the father of rocketry.

Meeting Valentina Tereshkova, the first woman in space, 1964.

With Harold Wilson and the Mayor of Bletchley in 1965.

Maxwell presenting Leonid Brezhnev with a copy of his book, Moscow 1978.

With King Faisal of Saudi Arabia, 1967

With Indira Gandhi, Prime Minister of India, 1967.

Robert Maxwell with Lord Mountbatten in 1978.

Betty with Michael, Anne, Philip, Christine, Isabel, Ian and Kevin, 1959.

Karine.

> All the seats in the stalls were taken out, cameras installed and
> *Giselle* was performed again with Czinner directing the photography
> and the irrepressible Bob frequently up on stage telling Ulanova in
> Russian what to do and how to do it. This went on all through the
> night until about 8 o'clock the next morning.

The world's leading prima ballerina was said to have been
annoyed by this instruction, but *The Bolshoi Ballet* was another
winner and was included in a list of the top ten films for 1957. The
Manchester Guardian described the film record of Ulanova dancing
as "superb", which is probably the last recorded instance of the
paper saying something favourable about anything connected with
Maxwell. The première at the Royal Festival Hall in London was
attended by the Duchess of Kent and the Countess Mountbatten,
with the proceeds going to the Royal College of Nursing. *What's On
in London* rhapsodised:

> Our grandchildren will bless the name of producer Ian Maxwell.

After a gala performance at London's Haymarket, it played to
capacity houses, broke box office records in the capital and the
provinces and was entered for the San Francisco International Film
Festival. For a while the idea of creating a new form of film art
excited Maxwell. He was taken with plans by Lady Robinson, wife
of Sir Robert Robinson, the chemist and Nobel Prize winner, for a
series of cartoon films entitled "Dodo, the Kid from Outer Space".
At one point he envisaged producing 120 of them; eventually 52
were made.

There were other plans for what the United States *Film Daily*
called "artistic" pictures, including a Sadler's Wells ballet, a Gilbert
and Sullivan opera, a film of Maria Callas at the La Scala in Milan, a
Stratford-on-Avon production of *A Midsummer Night's Dream* and
a ballet by the Royal Siamese Ballet in Bangkok. But there was a
falling-out with Czinner in 1958 when he attempted to negotiate a
film of the Sadler's Wells ballet, financed by Rank's, and cutting out
the Maxwell company, even though he was director of it. Legal
proceedings were taken against Czinner and Elisabeth Bergner and
these projects too never developed. A performance of *Swan Lake*
and a Hungarian production of the opera *Hary Janos* were filmed in
the 1960s and presented by Maxwell, but they were not box office
successes and other, more important matters, supervened. In a way,
it was a pity that this side of Maxwell's talents was never allowed to
flourish. Maxwell as a full-time film producer would have been in
the style of Hollywood at its most outrageous and, perhaps, at its

most successful. Still, abandoning the production side after *The Bolshoi Ballet* enabled him to spend every waking hour again on the affairs of Pergamon Press.

* * * * *

The pace continued to quicken in 1956. In March he took up the invitation of the Soviet Academy of Sciences and visited Moscow, where he was given the room of the Vice-President so that he might interview leading Russian scientists.

Among them was Academician Kapitza, a Nobel prizewinner and director of the Institute of Theoretical Physics, who had worked before the war with Rutherford at Cambridge. Kapitza introduced him to Professor Lev Landau, who had been imprisoned in a gulag under the manic purges of the Stalin era. In 1939 Kapitza had protested to Stalin and to Beria, the head of the Soviet secret police, as well as to Molotov, then the commissar in charge of internal security. Molotov said that Landau was a confessed German spy, but eventually the physicist was released by Beria into Kapitza's care. He told Kapitza he had confessed to being a spy because he had a horror of physical violence. In February 1988, 49 years later, Kapitza's letters were released for publication under Mikhail Gorbachov's glasnost policy (see Appendix 6).

Maxwell said of his visit:

> As a result, I became convinced that we in the West were making a grievous mistake in underestimating the value of Soviet research in many fields and I resolved to start a major five-year programme of translation of their books and journals....

Three years later the director of the National Science Foundation in Washington (the top United States government agency concerned in scientific research) allowed him to convene on its premises a meeting of representatives of learned societies and relevant government departments. Maxwell goes on:

> The day before the meeting, the Soviet Union launched Yuri Gagarin into space.... By this simple act, no one could any longer deny the urgent necessity of the Western world getting to know Soviet scientific literature. The meeting was not only a success but the level of officials attending was upgraded from middle range to the highest executives, including White House advisers to the President on scientific matters.

The result was that the United States Government decided to spend millions of dollars on the translation of Soviet scientific, medical and technical literature and Maxwell was requested to set up a non-profit-making organisation - which became the Pergamon Institute - designed to "encourage the teaching of Russian and disseminate scientific, medical and technical literature". Maxwell wrote to Sir Alexander Todd:

> Unless the UK moves fast in this field, we shall only be left to translate periodicals of second- or third-rate importance.

To a Russian scientist he said the Institute would be "forging a powerful bridge of friendship and understanding between scientists of our two countries".

Various United States government agencies funded the huge translation programme, spending about $10 million over the following three years. Maxwell told the agencies and the scientific community that the Pergamon Institute, in conjunction with Pergamon, would do the work for five years. In that time hundreds of thousands of pages were translated from the Russian and led to the publication of hundreds of different titles. Sir Robert Robinson, one of the most-honoured, nationally and internationally, British scientists of all time, became president of the Institute and its first large-scale translation programme was in aeronautical sciences. But there were problems in establishing it as the force Maxwell had envisaged; not least that of finding adequate translators. However, the Institute began to undertake an increasing amount of work for governmental and industrial bodies and by August 1958 Maxwell was forecasting to Sir Robert that it would be out of the red by the end of the year. In 1959 it moved to Headington Hill Hall, but it gradually became of lesser importance; in 1963 Pergamon reduced the programme drastically; its own journals had to come first. Despite his unbending anti-communism, Maxwell had never ceased to try to promote better Anglo-Soviet relations. The Institute was part of that philosophy, but in the end it, like all Maxwell organisations, had to justify itself, even if it didn't pay its way, and it failed to do so. It became one of the old soldiers of the company. It wasn't killed, but it slowly faded away. But as Maxwell admitted:

> Pergamon gained an immense amount of prestige and much gratitude throughout the scientific world and this helped immeasurably in its huge expansion and in its credit in dealing with the scientific community and government departments responsible for science throughout the world.

Enterprises like the Institute only added to the pace of Maxwell activities. He continued to attend almost every international scientific conference that was held, introduced to them often by the scientists who were working for him, and tendering for the publication of their proceedings.

In January 1957 he and Betty attended President Eisenhower's inaugural ball in Washington. The Maxwells may have seemed surprising guests, for he was still, in the United States, a comparatively unknown British publisher of almost wholly unknown British books. But in 1949 Colonel James Gault, an Old Etonian and Scots Guardsman who had been Eisenhower's military assistant during the war, had been seriously ill with an internal complaint and needed the antibiotic, streptomycin, which in those days was scarce. Gault's family appealed urgently to Eisenhower for his help in securing the drug and he was able to get 45 grams of it. Maxwell was in the United States and about to leave for London and he was asked to deliver it. Eisenhower had sent a personal letter expressing his "lasting gratitude for your co-operation".

From Washington the Maxwells went to the Oak Ridge Symposium on Atomic Energy at the University of Puerto Rico, and then on to Barbados for a brief holiday. Sadly, this was cut short when they were urgently recalled from the island because their youngest daughter, Karine, had been taken seriously ill. When the Maxwells left England there had been no suspicion that there was anything wrong with their child. But Karine was found to be suffering from leukaemia and it developed with frightening rapidity. Desperately, the Maxwells wrote to a long list of leading cancer specialists asking for their help in saving their daughter's life. Today, with the great advance in treating leukaemia in children, she might well have recovered. But survival then was rare and she died on February 8, 1957, aged three. The Maxwells were devastated and he said it was the worst blow he had ever had in his life.

Nevertheless, in March Maxwell was off on his travels again, this time to the Nuclear Congress in Philadelphia; other conferences followed, including the International Conference on Radio-Isotopes in Paris in September. This breakneck activity worried Sir Charles Hambro and at the beginning of 1958 he wrote to Betty Maxwell:

> I do hope Bob will take warning and make a good resolution to rest and consolidate during 1958. He will kill himself and his business at the pace he works.

The advice was ignored. In March 1958 Maxwell appeared in Palermo at the Agard (Advisory Group for Aeronautical Research and Development) conference, a NATO organisation, at the Fifth Assembly for the International Geophysical Year in Moscow (July) and Fusion '58, the Second United Nations' Conference on the Peaceful Uses of Atomic Energy in Geneva (September), where he rented a château to throw a lavish party to celebrate Pergamon's tenth anniversary.

Tom Clark has recalled the family drama which surrounded the frequent Maxwell visits abroad:

> There was always a particular flurry when he was about to set off on one of his foreign journeys. The secretaries would be running around collecting papers together, Bob would be telephoning and shouting for this and that - Where's my hat? Where's my bag? - the chauffeur would say that the car was ready and that it was getting late for the plane. Finally, Bob would dash out to the car. The children would gather outside the house ringing a large ship's bell which hung by the front door and as the car sped up the drive there would be yells of "Goodbye."

> Then peace would descend until his return.

In October 1958 Pergamon suffered from the first of a series of disturbing fires which was to plague the company for nearly 20 years. A blaze at the Fitzroy Square offices in London badly damaged two floors and destroyed an 80,000-page secret Russian bibliography of all the books and pamphlets produced in the Soviet Union for the previous 20 years. Maxwell had negotiated the right to publish it during a visit to Moscow University and had had to supply out-of-print Western publications and undertake to provide future Western books in exchange. It was a substantial setback. Other fires were to follow in 1973, 1976 and 1978. All were at Pergamon offices in Oxford. After the 1976 fire Maxwell flew back from Russia and launched a full-scale inquiry into it, but it discovered nothing. The 1978 outbreak was almost a carbon-copy of the previous one and the one of 1973 and the cost of the damage ran into many thousands of pounds. The police said that they believed an arsonist was at work, because the last two fires seemed to have been started with an incendiary device. If so, it was clearly someone with a grudge against the company. Maxwell offered a £1,000 reward to find the culprit, but he was never found.

In the middle of 1959, responding, more than a year late, to Sir Charles Hambro, Maxwell wrote to him:

> My various businesses are flourishing. I have paid up all my debts and borrowings, including income tax, and our cash at bank since the beginning of the year has fluctuated between £70,000 and £100,000. I feel sure that you will be pleased to know that the business which you helped me start is doing so well....

This was a period which saw the publication of *Tetrahedron*, the

Metallurgy Abstracts Journal, *Physics of Metals and Metallography*, *Vacuum*, and the *Proceedings of the Fourth International Conference on Biochemistry* in Vienna, as well as many other journals, monographs and reference works. At the beginning of 1959 Maxwell published a list of 120 books he intended to produce by the middle of the year, a catalogue of scientific and technical publications and two medical textbooks. In addition, he went to Poland, Budapest, Vienna and attended another Agard conference, this time in Athens. His youngest son, Kevin, was born in February.

His success in winning the nomination at Buckingham and the general election campaign of 1959 briefly interrupted his devotion to Pergamon, but after it was over the transfer of the company from Fitzroy Square to Headington Hill Hall took place in January 1960 and he took a full-page advertisement in the local paper seeking to recruit staff.

A mansion house has been on the site at Headington since the late 18th century and a Tudor building was there before that. Recent work on the kitchen of the Hall uncovered what appears to be evidence of an even older site, but the present house was only built in 1861 by James Morrell, an Oxford brewer. His descendants lived there until 1946 and Oxford City Council bought it from them in 1953 for £13,700. By the time Pergamon acquired the lease of the Hall in 1959 it was in a state of near-ruin and the extensive gardens had been plundered. At one time complete demolition was contemplated by the council, but it was considered too expensive. Maxwell had the Hall and its grounds completely rebuilt and landscaped (at his expense, it is a full repairing lease) and the house is now a listed building. The original lease on the house and grounds of some 15 acres in all was offered by tender by the council in 1958. Only four replies were received: one for part of the property at £350 a year; a second for £500 a year; a third for £550; and the fourth, Pergamon's, for £2,400 a year for 21 years. The council jumped at it. In September 1962 Pergamon asked for a longer lease and offered a substantially increased rent. A new lease was agreed for 75 years at £3,000 a year, rising to £4,500 when a new office building was erected. In 1965 the lease was amended again, Pergamon this time agreeing to pay £5,050 a year. Today, after further negotiations in 1978, Pergamon holds a 99-year lease on the house and grounds. For this, Maxwell offered a capital payment of £10,000 plus graduated rent increases rising to £15,540 in the middle of the next century.

The deal caused a minor outcry among Oxford residents, who

complained that the property had gone too cheaply. But Maxwell pointed out that apart from spending £1,250,000 on restoring the property, he was paying £40,000 a year in rates, directly employing 700 Oxford workers and making provision to employ a further two to three hundred. Today the rates for the office, house and other premises are over £110,000 a year.

By the time of the move to Headington Hill Hall, Pergamon was growing stronger almost by the day. It acquired several new companies - including Newnes and Bletchley Printers, Ltd. in the Buckingham constituency - published, with Chicago University and Pergamon Press, Inc., the first atlas of the other side of the moon and doubled its share capital to £100,000. While all this was going on, Maxwell and Betty found time to help a charity appeal for the Royal College of Nursing. A letter of thanks on behalf of the College to Mrs Maxwell for "working like a black for two days" would not be repeated in these days of racial sensitivity, but the same writer added that Betty and her husband were "the best friends the College ever had".

Each month saw new books and new technical journals being published, new developments and new ideas. In 1961 Maxwell was in Moscow again, to meet Yuri Gagarin, the first man in space, and Nikita Kruschev. This was the meeting with the Soviet leader at which he asked to be allowed to visit his birthplace in Solotvino and which Kruschev refused to permit. Also that year another Maxwell initiative was launched, this time the Commonwealth and International Library of Science, Technology, Engineering and Liberal Studies, whose purpose was to provide a library of 1,000 low-priced original educational textbooks by 1967. Arrangements were made to translate the Library's titles into French, German, Russian and Spanish. The list of titles was literally an A to Z, ranging from Aeronautical Engineering to Zoology, and the hundreds of honorary members of the Editorial Advisory Board of the Library read like pages from a world's Who's Who of the great and the good among educationalists, employers, politicians and scientists.

Maxwell went on a world tour in 1962 to promote the Library, repeating in various countries "I want to help the man in the factory who is anxious to educate himself and get on", and despite an early setback a month before the official launch in May, when a fire destroyed several hundred thousand pages destined for the Library, it got off to a flying start.

The project's readership ranged from infants to graduates and the subjects covered from rural studies to nuclear chemistry. The Indian Prime Minister Pandit Nehru - whose sister had attended the launching of the Library at Oxford - wrote to Maxwell thanking him for the Library, saying there were 47 million to 48 million Indian boys and girls undergoing higher education for whom there was the urgent problem of finding books. He invited Maxwell to visit him in New Delhi. The two men met in a small room, but as soon as Maxwell began to talk Nehru yawned, started to fiddle with a balloon on his desk and then yawned again. Maxwell, peeved, said:

Prime Minister, in my opinion, you were the aggressor in Kashmir.

Nehru, startled, stopped yawning and put the balloon down. For the next four hours he and Maxwell argued about the fighting which had caused a million deaths and where the responsibility for it lay. It wasn't so much that Maxwell was convinced that Nehru was the guilty party, but that he was not going to accept the treatment which Nehru apparently reserved for those whom he expected to bore him. When Maxwell saw India's Minister of Education the next day the minister had with him a six-page memorandum from Nehru on Maxwell. Mrs Pandit later explained that as Prime Minister her brother was compelled to meet many tedious people and the balloon and the yawning were his technique for cutting an interview short.

In those early days after the launch the potential for the Library seemed enormous. Its prospectus stated:

The Library is designed to provide readers, wherever the English language is used or can be used as a medium of instruction, with a series of low-priced, high-quality soft-cover textbooks and monographs.... It is a bold and exciting adventure ... at a time when the thirst for education in all parts of the world is tremendous.

In an earlier interview Maxwell had declared that "books must replace bombs in the affairs of men" and in another in 1963 explaining how the Library would address itself to its task, he said[2]:

Until recently, the countries of Africa were using textbooks written really for British schoolchildren. For instance, a textbook in arithmetic: a child in Nigeria would be given a problem to work out - an express train meets another express train travelling on a separate line and they pass each other in a tunnel ... now what speed were they doing? To a Nigerian child this is absolute nonsense. They haven't got double-track railways and they have no tunnels. The kind of books now being written for the Commonwealth and International Library are written from the point of view of the local situation. If they are meant for Nigerian or Jamaican children, then the examples ... will be set in something that the child meets in everyday life.

Some of the Library's books were outstandingly successful. One on practical commerce sold 20,000, as did another entitled *Exercises in Modern Mathematics*. A volume on biology sold 12,500, one on logarithms 11,000.

At the 1962 annual general meeting of Pergamon at Headington Hill Hall the shareholders received an impressive report. In the financial year which had ended the previous October Pergamon had published 213 books and 600 separate issues and volumes of its 90 scientific, medical and technical journals, and 80 per cent of its production was being exported. The net profit for the year was £69,000, some £24,000 more than the year before.

Another ambitious project connected with the Soviet Union was launched in September 1962 when Pergamon and the Macmillan Co. of New York combined to publish a 1,000-page work on the USSR which Maxwell confidently forecast in a letter to Kruschev would "become the standard work of reference on the Soviet Union" in the West. He wrote in the preface:

> It is impossible to estimate what the Russians are going to do in the future unless we know their past, their aspirations and their claims. The time has now definitely come when every intelligent individual must learn to think globally, beyond the horizon of a narrow, nationalist point of view. This can only be achieved by learning about the history, life and culture of other peoples.... Ignorance is the worst enemy of peace.

But the encyclopaedia was not well received, the general opinion being that it reflected too much the Soviet version of history, in whose reliability not much faith has ever been placed.

The expansion of Pergamon led to a continuing expansion of staff and to increased demands upon those already working for him, especially his personal staff. Sometimes the pressure upon them boiled over. When he called, peremptorily, over his inter-com to a secretary to make him a cup of tea, another secretary told her: "Don't forget the sugar", to which she replied, "The arsenic, you mean." Unfortunately she had forgotten to switch off the connection and Maxwell heard every word. When the tea was brought in he asked her, politely but to her dismay, "Did you remember the arsenic?"

In 1962, when he was seeking a new personal assistant, a harassed secretary drew up a spoof advertisement for the post which has survived in the Maxwell archives. Written with obvious feeling, it said:

> A highly-desirable post as Personal Assistant to a Publisher is offered

to a person complying to [sic] the following qualifications: he, she or it must be unmarried, with no outside interests, brown-haired and slightly deaf, with eyes in the back of the head. Must have a skin like a rhinoceros, be impossible to insult, with a tough stomach and able to take shorthand sitting on the floor of a moving car. The physique is important and should incorporate a large, strong backside for holding open heavy doors while holding in one of three pairs of hands a very heavily-laden tray.

The applicant should be clairvoyant, with the patience of Job, suffering from permanent insomnia and a shrunken stomach which does not need any food. Needs stamina, must be able to type letters at speed without reading the original correspondence, be able to run a mile in four minutes when telex machine starts up, read unintelligible scrawl, reincarnate destroyed papers and work for long periods without supervision but without any initiative.

Must have strong anti-capitalist tendencies but be able to drive a Rolls Royce and be sympathetic towards hordes of children and muddy spaniels. The build required should be impervious to peacock mating cries and the kicks of small ponies, must be able to find telephones covered by several layers of bedclothes. Must be confidently able to ignore all instructions with an innate disbelief in the veracity of others and able to keep a steaming kettle ready and suitable for opening confidential envelopes.

Anyone answering the above description, please telephone Oxford....

Despite the pressures, the draftswoman of this "advertisement" remained with Maxwell for another 25 years.

An even more difficult time was had by Mrs Wade, his Irish office cleaner at Headington Hill Hall. Maxwell had a practice of throwing discarded papers into a heap on the floor. Mrs Wade, whose habits were much more tidy, would collect the papers and replace them neatly upon Maxwell's desk. Maxwell frequently told her not to do so, but to no avail. Eventually he grew angry. "Mrs Wade", he exploded, "nothing I say seems to have any effect. You are not to put things back on my desk or I will fire you." Mrs Wade trembled and said she wouldn't do it again.

At this time Maxwell was preparing to go to a publishers' conference in Madrid and the night before he left he called for all the files relating to it. There were so many of them that he couldn't get them on his desk. So they were all left in a pile on the floor.

Maxwell arrived at his office early the next morning to do the necessary reading. The files were not to be seen anywhere. Maxwell called in his cleaner. "Mrs Wade", he said, "what have you done with my files?"

"You told me, sir", replied Mrs Wade, "that anything on the floor had to be thrown away, so I have thrown them."

In those days Pergamon had a practice of burning all discarded material every other day. That particular morning, unfortunately, was the one for burning. At the cost of singed eyebrows, the personnel manager, Mr Bertie Upstone, rescued the files, warm but not incinerated, in the nick of time. An exasperated Maxwell sent for Mrs Wade again.

"Mrs Wade", he asked resignedly, "don't you understand the difference between heaps and piles?"

* * * * *

Nineteen-sixty-three saw Pergamon financing a scholarship at Keble College, Oxford, to enable graduate scientists to take courses in arts subjects (and a fellowship in politics was established two years later at Balliol). The opening of Maxwell's bookshop in the city, just beyond Magdalen Bridge, was a grandly-ambitious project, with a lecture and exhibition room, with separate bookshops for paperbacks, children and teenagers. There was also a secondhand textbook department, invaluable for impoverished students, and an office equipment and stationery department. It was designed also to be a meeting place and incorporated a coffee house where dons and students could meet on equal terms. It lasted for some eight years, but it was the kind of project where Maxwell's heart ruled his business head. In the end it had to go, as its last manager, Dennis Murphy, explained:

> It had everything, acres of space, miles of bookshelves.... A sumptuous coffee bar served what was, by common consent, the finest cup of coffee in Oxford, and a really fetching record department with private booths featuring a large selection of new releases both classical and pop. To cap it all, there was a really breathtaking stairway, worth of the Czars of Russia, which led from the ground floor to the coffee lounge and record department.

> But the location was on the wrong side of Magdalen Bridge and never prospered, apart from the coffee lounge.... The shop was losing money and I had to advise the Man accordingly. However, sources close to him told me to tread lightly - the bookshop was his pride and joy....

> I was ushered into the presence, who was flanked by four or five sombre-looking gents. They were accountants. The Captain was in his most friendly and expansive mood (this is his most dangerous mood - the cobra is about to strike).

"Murphy", says the Captain, "you were wrong in telling me that the bookshop was losing X pounds per week. It is losing three times that amount. So, it has to close." "Sir", says I, "when?" "Now", says he. Within half an hour I was back at the bookshop. The doors were closed forever and I informed the assembled staff of 20 or so that it was all over.

Bookshops were also opened in Glasgow, Edinburgh, Stirling and Lancaster. They too failed and were shut down. According to Tom Clark, the Pergamon secretary at the time, it wasn't only a problem at Oxford of being on the wrong side of the track or, more strictly, Magdalen Bridge. Pilfering by students was one of the main causes of its unprofitability. The son of a millionaire who was caught thieving said:

Stealing books from Maxwell does not cause me a bad conscience because it is only a tick in a millionaire's ledger.

By 1964 Clark was reporting Pergamon's sales and profits up "substantially", the first by 22 per cent and the second increased to £160,000. Maxwell wrote in the annual report:

Scientists and engineers are at present unable to digest the volume of new knowledge becoming available.... So desperate is the problem that it is now becoming far cheaper for certain research workers to go back into the laboratory and repeat the work, if necessary to re-invent things, rather than laboriously and time-wastingly to struggle with the floods of professional journals, books, magazine articles and Ph.D. theses.

By that year the 100th title in the Commonwealth Library had been published, though the goal of 1,000 volumes had been put back a year to 1968 (it was eventually reached in 1971). A dividend to shareholders of 10 per cent in 1963 was raised to 50 per cent in 1964 and profits had jumped again, this time to just under £234,000. Pergamon was now no longer a private company. Maxwell, like most other politicians, had been expecting a general election in the spring of 1964. When it was announced that it wouldn't take place until the autumn, he seized the chance, on the suggestion of the chairman of Henry Ansbacher and Co., "Boy" Hart, to go public.

A report by Ansbacher's on the prospective share offer was glowing: exports had now risen to 85 per cent of output; branch offices were maintained in New Delhi, Sydney and Tokyo, as well as agencies in many other countries. The Commonwealth Library already had 120 volumes in print; Pergamon had published 1,000 books in three years, 500 of them in 1963 alone. A new printing works, Buckingham Press, had been built at Bletchley; an agreement had been reached with Macmillan of New York which

made Macmillan's the exclusive distributor of Pergamon books in
the Western hemisphere and the Philippines for a period of five
years (this agreement ended in 1965, when Pergamon's New York
President, Mr Majthenyi, accused Macmillan's of trying, "by a
crooked deal", to dispose of Pergamon's books to its own
subsidiary); agreements had also been reached for the distribution
of Pergamon products in Malaya, Kenya and Rhodesia. The
freehold premises in Fitzroy Square had been sold for £165,000,
leased back for £13,000 a year to Pergamon, which then sub-let part
of the premises for £10,000 a year, which seems a bargain.
Ansbacher promised that Maxwell would enter into a service
contract as Managing Director for a period of five years, "during
which time he will undertake to spend such time as necessary on the
company's affairs", but Ansbacher's went on to warn:

> Although Mr Maxwell is clearly the driving force and has been
> responsible for the entire concept of Pergamon Press, he claims that
> the company can, and has at times in the past, operated in a
> completely satisfactory manner without his supervision. As Mr
> Maxwell is standing as a Labour candidate at the General Election in
> October, it is imperative that the management of the company should
> be ensured in the likely event that he is returned to Parliament and,
> hence, unable to devote the whole of his time to the company's
> business.

The *Financial Times* was concerned about the reliance Pergamon
placed upon Maxwell, and its columnist "Observer" wrote the week
before the share issue[3]:

> The City will have to make its own attempt to assess the most
> controversial figure in British publishing. For all its seven-man board,
> its 200-odd editorial workers and its legions of professional advisers,
> Pergamon is a one-man show; and Ian Robert Maxwell collects more
> news coverage, more abuse and more envy than any publisher since
> the copyright acts were passed.

It added, after recalling - again - that he was the son of a Czech
farmworker, that "his foreign origin is one of the standing charges
against him".

The share offer was in July 1964 and it closed within 60 seconds.
The success was overwhelming and the issue of 1,100,000 two-
shilling (10 pence) shares at 17s 6d (87.5p) each, amounting to $27^1/_2$
per cent of the ordinary capital - the rest was retained by the
Maxwell family interests - was oversubscribed 21 times. Within days
the shares were showing a profit on paper of 20 per cent.

In his first report to the newly-public company Maxwell said that
for the year ending in July 1964 sales and net profits had again

reached record heights. The pre-tax profit had beaten the forecast of £500,000 by £54,000 and the dividend was to be 50 per cent, compared with a forecast of 45 per cent at the time of the share offer. The company was expanding in every corner of the globe and the 200th volume in the Commonwealth Library series was published in April 1965. That too was another year showing record profits - this time up to £848,000, 53 per cent up over the previous 12 months - and the dividend went up to 70 per cent. In the January the company had acquired the share capital of Pergamon Press, Inc., its United States arm, and profits from it boosted the total. Most significant of all, Pergamon had begun to move into information storage and retrieval through the use of computers, an arid field except for the enthusiast, but one which was to fortify the present prosperity of the Maxwell Communication Corporation.

By 1966 the estimated value of Pergamon was £7 million, its annual turnover was £5 million and it was employing 2,500 in publishing 600 new titles a year and 120 journals. It won the Queen's Award to Industry for its export performance and George Brown, effectively deputy Prime Minister and officially deputy leader of the Labour party, went to Headington to open the company's new offices and warehouse built in the grounds of the Hall.

Maxwell's ceaseless travels in search of new business now passed the two million-mile mark. At the end of the year, when he was presented with a special copy of *Tetrahedron* to celebrate his 80th birthday, Sir Robert Robinson wrote to Maxwell:

> Your contributions to the dissemination of scientific knowledge have been outstanding and I am sure that this will be recognised more and more in the future.

In fact, that contribution meant that by 1965 100 journals had been launched in 15 years; the figure was to grow to 200 by 1976, 300 by 1982 and 400 by 1988 (see Appendix 4).

But meanwhile the restless search for new acquisitions went on. In February 1966 Pergamon entered a new field when it bought the old-established Exeter-based company Wheaton's, a main supplier of educational textbooks. A takeover bid for Aberdeen University Press was rejected, but Maxwell acquired C. and E. Layton, Ltd., the blockmakers - and, to improve morale, gave a firm guarantee of at least a year's employment to every man on the payroll - Equipment Comparison, Ltd., which specialised in testing equipment and management services, the Religious Education Press, Bumpus, the famous old booksellers, Haldanes, and the

Book Society before embarking at the end of the year on his world tour to sell *Chambers's Encyclopaedia*, which he had bought with the Subscription Books Division of George Newnes Ltd. in December 1965 for £1 million. An article in the *Financial Times* said[4]:

> A competitor not unkindly described Maxwell as the Henry Ford of publishing, but he has been more astute than Ford in looking to his markets.

The *Investors' Guardian* said he was a "super-salesman". The *Daily Telegraph* said after Maxwell's return that there were "around a dozen countries still reeling from his whirlwind, fact-finding encyclopaedia selling tour", but it asked about Pergamon's profit growth[5]:

> Can all this continue, or will the present level represent, in retrospect, a high watermark in Pergamon's fortunes?

The publication of the new edition of the *Encyclopaedia* in 1967 - celebrated by a lunch at the Savoy Hotel, London, with Anthony Crosland, the Secretary of State for Education and Science, as the guest of honour - was described, not over-modestly, by Maxwell as "the most important publishing event of the decade". It almost led to a partnership which, if it had developed to its full potential, would have had repercussions beyond the dreams or fears of anyone engaged in any part of the printing and publishing trade. He discussed an agreement with a Mr Rupert Murdoch, of News Ltd., an Australian company, under which Murdoch was to buy a half-share in Pergamon of Australia, which would have given him the exclusive distributorship of the *Encyclopaedia* throughout most of Asia. In a letter to another Australian businessman, Maxwell described Murdoch as "a natural for the job". But it was not so much a partnership as a brief encounter.

In 1967, among many other business and political ventures, Maxwell increased his holding in the History Book Club to 90 per cent and acquired Speedwriting Ltd., the Thomson subsidiary which was formed to establish in Britain the American form of alphabet shorthand which, while inferior to Pitman's, attracted those secretaries who were not inclined to devote the time to learning which Pitman's demanded. He also took 61,250 shares in Thomson Press (India) and bought a 50 per cent stake in International Learning Systems for £486,000. He was said to be interested in buying *The Spectator*, the (then) liberal Tory magazine owned by Sir Ian Gilmour, but nothing came of it. And a multi-million pound

offer for Butterworth's, the company from which he bought the
origins of Pergamon Press, was rejected. The Butterworth history
said:

> Fear of Maxwell was rife, though there were some who would have
> welcomed his drive, and discounted any danger to their careers.

But the official Butterworth reaction to the bid led to a libel
action and a grovelling apology in the High Court. After hearing
from Maxwell that he intended to try to acquire the company,
Butterworth's asked one of its employees, a Miss Kekwick, to
inquire in the publishing trade generally, and among former
Pergamon employees in particular, to discover whatever she could
about Maxwell. She then arranged a meeting with the managing
editor of the Hamlyn Group and asked him, according to a
statement made in open court, a question whose implications
"impugn the reputation and integrity" of Maxwell and Pergamon.
Butterworth's accepted that the implications were "wholly
unwarranted", admitted the "falsity" of the allegations and
recognised "the gross impropriety" of what they had done. Its
counsel added that the suggestions made were "entirely baseless and
improper", paid all costs and thanked Maxwell for his generosity in
waiving his claim for damages. Butterworth's was eventually bought
by the International Publishing Company, the group which sold
Chambers's to Maxwell. Maxwell was later asked why his bid for
Butterworth's failed. He replied[6]:

> It was unsuccessful because IPC decided to pay £2 million more than
> I was offering and it turned out to be £2 million more than the
> business was worth.

But his most significant purchase in 1967 - because of its
consequential, far-reaching effects - was the acquisition of Caxton
Holdings, publishers of educational and technical books and,
through its wholly-owned subsidiary, Caxton Publishing, the *New
Caxton Encyclopaedia*. Caxton's was a well-established company,
founded in 1901. It sold almost entirely through door-to-door
salesmen and very little to dealers and booksellers. The British
Printing Corporation bought a half-share in Caxton Publishing to
become partners with Pergamon in retail bookselling. The takeover
of Caxton was part of the natural expansion of Pergamon and made
sense for the owners of *Chambers's Encyclopaedia*. Caxton's had
long had export markets in Australia and New Zealand and had
recently developed new ones in South Africa, Sweden, Norway and
Denmark, Greece, Turkey, Finland, Malaysia and Singapore.

The name of the new joint company was changed to the International Learning Systems Corporation, Ltd., and Maxwell envisaged it as an ideal springboard for an attack on the world market for encyclopaedias. He told *The Guardian*[7]:

> I see this new company developing as a serious competitor to the American encyclopaedia publishers. They are, at present, sharing a £200 million a year market entirely among three companies, not because *Chambers's Encyclopaedia* and the *New English Encyclopaedia* were not equal to or better than anything the Americans can put up ... but because of the lack of British salesmanship and the failure to provide the necessary financial and marketing resources to match the opportunities on the world market.... With this new company the target of having a five per cent share of this market is easily attainable.

And so it may have done, except for the fact that he and BPC had fallen among thieves and were extensively cheated by the men they had engaged to sell their encyclopaedias. The chairman of Caxton Holdings at the time of the Pergamon takeover was Hedley Le Bas, whose grandfather had founded the company 66 years earlier. Le Bas had the familiar twin problems of drink and money - too much of the one and too little of the other. Le Bas freely admitted his problem. He wrote to Maxwell on June 6, 1967:

> I understand that you may terminate my contract at your own discretion should I not remain permanently teetotal.

There were two other directors of the Caxton company, Rodney Jenman, who was no more to be trusted than Le Bas, and Peter Carter-Ruck, the company's solicitor and well known today as a libel lawyer.

Jenman, a sporty-looking man in his mid-forties and slightly younger than Le Bas, was in charge of overseas operations and his employment agreement with the joint company was through a Bahamian Corporation of which he was a major shareholder and which was supposedly responsible for overseas sales. In fact, the company was a tax haven and repository of monies Jenman was receiving - legally as well as illegally - from Caxton without incurring the notice of the auditors. Both Le Bas and Jenman received kickbacks in commission from their salesmen and the commission was paid without regard to the fact that the subscriptions for the book sales, on which the commission was based, had frequently not been received. The game was up for Le Bas and Jenman when one of their accomplices, Victor Abbott, who was at least as dishonest as the others and had worked as personal assistant to Jenman in

London, fell out with them and told Maxwell how he and BPC were being cheated. The men were putting in fraudulent expenses, receiving illegal commission from the sales of all encyclopaedias and generally taking their employers for a ride. Jenman was also said to have been blackmailing some of the company's salesmen. He had a flat maintained for him (at ILSC's expense) in London, in which his mistress lived. This lady would bestow some or all of her favours upon visiting salesmen and had, for the future advantage of Jenman, placed a tape machine under or near her bed.

When Maxwell discovered in 1968 that he was being systematically defrauded he immediately sacked Jenman and Le Bas, who both prudently decided not to sue for the compensation to which honest men would have been entitled. The story of Caxton, Jenman, Le Bas and Abbott formed part of the investigation which the Department of Trade and Industry subsequently carried out into the affairs of Pergamon in relation to the proposed merger with Leasco. Le Bas took his revenge and gave evidence to the inquiry to Maxwell's detriment. He and Jenman were among the "informants" of the *Sunday Times* which led to the paper's damaging articles about Maxwell in 1969.

But Caxton's was only one part of the increasingly intriguing life which Maxwell led. A fellow-publisher urged him in April 1967 to write his autobiography, but he turned down the idea, saying it wasn't likely "for a long time in the future". André Deutsch wrote to him later saying that he too would like to publish "that book" and even offered an advance, a supererogatory gesture if ever there were one. But the answer was No to him as well. Instead, the reading public had to be content with the profiles in abundance which continued to be published about him. He told one interviewer[8]:

> I would have been a success in anything. But I chose an activity that was socially useful, and that aspect gives me extra satisfaction. I don't know why other people didn't get hold of it. But it came to me after the war and I knew it was right.

To another reporter he revealed his objections to inherited wealth, saying[9]:

> I do not plan to leave my children an inheritance. The money left after taxes will go back to the scientific work I have taken money from.

He told *The Sun* in January 1968:

> I have no sense of property. I am not interested in ownership.

In 1968, despite occasional gloomy forecasts in some newspapers about the ability of Pergamon to continue to increase its profits, *Management Today*'s British Profitability League showed the company to be 19th in the list of the 200 top companies, with Marks and Spencer 18th. In June Maxwell began preparing a bid for the British Printing Corporation, but by the next month it was clear he had failed to acquire 10 per cent of the group and he decided not to bid for any more shares. He also made his abortive bid to buy the *News of the World*, which is dealt with fully in a later chapter.

Inevitably, Maxwell's political and business lives overlapped. Politics gave him an outlet and a platform for promoting his dedication to the advancement of science and technology. He saw this most likely to flourish under a Labour Government, but his thinking about it was not determined by a political or ideological approach. Pergamon gave him the opportunity to put his beliefs into practice at a profit and the base from which he could attempt to spread them more widely. In 1963 he had told the Labour party working party on science and industry (which he chaired) that the translation of science to use by society was not well understood or practised. He put forward major proposals for a future Labour administration to make drastic changes in Britain's approach to scientific development and in 1967 published a lengthy study on the need for the Government to pursue a public purchasing policy which would benefit industrially efficient firms (see Appendices 2 and 3). It was an incredibly detailed programme for a major change in government policy, with over 600 recommendations in all. Maxwell advocated that the Labour Government should establish a Public Sector Purchasing Board to advise on and co-ordinate all buying by public bodies. He also urged the creation of a City of London liaison committee, a "star rating" scheme for exporters, larger profit margins for government contractors and savings by local authorities and hospital boards by more efficient purchasing. Throughout the 1960s he continued, inside and outside the House of Commons, to press his ideas on an unresponsive Government and an apathetic public.

In September 1968 he was urging the purchasing policy upon a wider market. In a speech at the Dorchester Hotel, London, he declared[10]:

> European airlines, air forces, nuclear reactor power and computer users must give preference to procuring their equipment from European firms, and the manufacturers must be persuaded to integrate and merge across frontiers, otherwise £10,000 million-

worth of orders will be lost to America within the next decade in these fields alone. The development and competitiveness of these technologically highly advanced European countries are inhibited by the fragmentation of public purchasing and the division of development contracts on national lines, and by duplication. United States producers dominate world markets in aviation, nuclear power and computers, partly because of the size and homogeneity of the American market, both public and private, and partly because of their concentration of effort. For instance, in the United States fast breeder reactors are in the hands of one giant company, but in Europe we have three separate programmes by Britain, France and Germany....

In twenty years since, little has changed on the European front and the co-operation he was advocating is still absent, even though Britain long ago joined the EEC.

Though many of his ideas for the positive use of public purchasing powers were warmly welcomed by the Wilson Government (see Wilson letter, Appendix 3), putting them into practice was a different matter. Many of them were eventually adopted - but by Conservative governments, first the Heath Government of 1970 and then, more particularly, by the Thatcher administration. The magazine *Purchasing and Supply Management* wrote in December 1984:

> It was not until 1979, with the election of the most radical Conservative Government this century, that Sir Keith Joseph announced an "enlightened public purchasing initiative". Its aims, and many of its stated tactics, were lifted directly from the Maxwell report, albeit with changes of phraseology, to fit Tory notions of the "survival of the fittest" rather than the "white heat of technology" approach....

A letter from the Department of Trade and Industry to Maxwell's office in March 1985 agreed that "there is quite a bit of common ground between the ideas in the [Maxwell] report and current policy" although there were "also certain differences ... naturally enough". The principal difference, however, was clearly one of political ideology. Maxwell had wanted to try to co-ordinate purchasing with the nationalised industries and local authorities and, as the DTI said, there was "no question" of the Government trying to do that.

Proposals he made in 1968 for European co-operation in space research never bore fruit, though similar ideas are still talked about. As the Council of Europe's *rapporteur* on scientific matters, he pressed Wilson to ensure Britain remained associated with a joint European programme of space research. In a report to the Council of Europe in January 1969 he said[11]:

> The only way to make real progress in European space matters will probably be, to begin with, by the setting up by the Ministers of a European Space Commission consisting of experts nominated by the Ministers themselves, preferably by some form of qualified vote, who would not receive any instructions, but, on the contrary, would be under an obligation to consider all problems referred to them by the Ministers from the point of view of Europe as a whole. Eventually, the Ministers themselves will have to adopt a qualified majority voting system in any case, but the first step in this direction would be the promotion of a European Commission on the lines I have suggested.

Lord Gladwyn, an ardent pro-European, enthusiastically quoted Maxwell's report at length in a speech in the House of Lords. He said that in the European context Maxwell was a visionary - if the definition of a visionary was one who had dreams which were not realised for a long time, if ever.

* * * * *

Looking back, those concerned with Maxwell the publisher may think he paid too much attention to the political side of his career or to matters which were not strictly of concern to the future of Pergamon Press. But that would be to misunderstand him. He is never content unless he has half a dozen projects, negotiations or developments in hand all at the same time. He can concentrate on a single issue to the exclusion of everything else and then, when that question is concluded, concentrate on something else to the total exclusion of whatever he has just been dealing with. Nevertheless, the *Financial Times* had warned that Pergamon looked like a one-man show and if it were right, it is clear that the one man was doing too much in such a large organisation or others were doing too little. Alternatively, both theories may have been true, the second being a consequence of the first.

On the other hand, it seemed that nothing could arrest the advance of the Press under his guidance, even if he were unable to devote all his time to it. The report on the company's progress in 1966 showed profits before tax at £1,331,992 (after tax, £710,427); a dozen new companies had been taken over, the share capital had been increased and Pergamon was producing 131 periodical and serial titles, compared with only 10 less than a decade earlier, and the Commonwealth Library was making "a good contribution" to Pergamon's profits. The recommended dividend for a 14-month period was 74.5 per cent. For the year ending December 31, 1967 things were even better. There were now 152 periodicals, etc., being published. Profits had risen to £1,449,740 (net £809,511) and the company's net assets totalled more than £5,500,000, an increase of more than £2 million over the previous year. Allowing for a scrip issue during the year, the dividend was up by eight per cent. The first edition of *Chambers's Encyclopaedia* - 15,000 copies - Maxwell reported, had been completely sold out in just over one year. There were now 6,000 book titles on Pergamon's list and the 1,000th volume in the Commonwealth Library was scheduled for March 1970.

Inevitably, the report and accounts for 1968 were even better. Some 125 countries were buying Pergamon's products, and the number of journals, etc., being published had risen to 185. Profits before tax and debenture interest were £2,181,922. Maxwell reported to the shareholders (of which he was far and away the most substantial):

> In addition to the increase in our established business, we have continued our policy of growth through acquisition.

Pergamon had taken over Sun Engraving, D.R. Hillman and Sons, Ltd., and a major printing unit at Bletchley and arrangements were being made to purchase further companies during the year, including one belonging to a Maxwell family trust, Maxwell Scientific International, Inc. There had been one disappointment during the year:

> Most shareholders must have been aware last autumn of Pergamon's protracted efforts to effect a merger with the *News of the World* organisation. Many may have wondered whether it was wise to devote substantial management effort, as well as considerable expense, to what may have appeared a fruitless and bitter battle. However, nothing that has subsequently occurred has changed the view of your board that a merger of Pergamon and the *News of the World* would have produced an international printing and publishing organisation of great strength....

Rupert Murdoch would have agreed with that. But apart from the failure to buy the Sunday newspaper, all still seemed rosy. Maxwell forecast:

> Subject to unforeseen circumstances, the profit for 1969 will be in line with the forecast of not less than £2,500,000 made at the end of 1968.

The one circumstance that neither he nor anyone else could possibly have foreseen was that this was to be his last chairman's report to Pergamon for five years, because by the time the report and accounts were next presented he would have been ousted.

6

Out and In

*I chose to be British - you are British
by accident* - Maxwell to a heckler.

Maxwell's entry into British politics, like so much else he undertakes, was sudden, spectacular and surrounded in controversy and had that tinge of luck or destiny which seems to accompany him on every enterprise. For 15 years he was the candidate in Buckingham and for six years he was its MP. After he lost his seat in 1970 he strove to get back into the Commons, despite his concern with the loss of Pergamon Press and the legal and boardroom battles to regain it. He even sought nomination to the European Parliament, a body with little or no power but which symbolised his belief that it was in a wider Europe that Britain's political and economic future lay. But after he failed there, he abandoned his political career.

In the end, what did it all add up to? By the criterion of the young man of 21 who promised his wife-to-be that he would become Prime Minister of England, not much. He never attained junior or senior ministerial rank, which is one of the standards by which success in politics is judged. As a backbencher, he promoted a useful Parliamentary Bill, the Clean Air Act of 1968, which helped considerably to clear Britain's pollution-ridden skies. And he was chairman of the Catering sub-committee of the Services Committee of the House of Commons; in other words, he was in charge of the Commons kitchens, not normally a task on which to build a political reputation.

But if a man is judged by the anecdotes told about him, then Maxwell certainly left a mark upon the House of Commons which many a Cabinet Minister would envy. Today, 18 years after he left it, he is still remembered there. He argued, he questioned, he interrupted, he barracked, he speechified. There was no subject in which he wasn't interested or on which he had nothing to say. His ruthless elimination of the loss on MPs' catering cost them dear, or so they never stopped complaining. But he did what he set out to do. His concentration upon his political career adversely affected his business one, for all his ability to keep several balls in the air at once. Had he not spent so much time on parliamentary affairs, he might have been able to prevent the loss of Pergamon which set him back several years and nearly destroyed him. On the other hand, the causes which he cherished - partnership with Europe and the development of Britain's scientific and technological resources - could best be expressed in Parliament, not through publishing, though with him the two were intertwined.

If he was always in the news or under attack, or even the subject of praise, he throve on it. Agreement he finds dull, unless it is reached after a satisfying struggle. Obscurity he would have found boring. If he was to find, after being adopted as a candidate, that the politician's greatest burden is the newspapers' cuttings libraries, nevertheless, he supplied the cuttings. Those which Mrs Maxwell has collected about her husband's activities over the years, together with his personal papers, now weigh over 350 kilograms.

In politics, nothing has ever been said too often not to be repeated; no dish is too old not to be rehashed; no deed is ever forgotten - or forgiven - and no sentiment, once expressed, can be unexpressed. The British do not put their politicians upon a pedestal so much as under a spotlight, as John Profumo and countless others can testify.

The nature of the British press means that the fallibilities, real or imagined, of Labour politicians are revealed with a greater zeal and dedication than those of any other party, but those are the rules of the game. If they spring, in large part, from the political views of press proprietors, it is also the case that Labour is a morally censorious party, swift to denounce, as Harold Wilson did memorably, those who make money rather than earn it. For a party founded on principle, it is inordinately concerned with personalities and Maxwell is undoubtedly a personality. Though its record in defending the cause of refugees and emigrants in general was always an honourable one, the traditional working-class suspicion of foreigners is shared by many of its middle-class leaders and supporters, as Maxwell was to find. Xenophobia has long been the unifying passion of privately-educated socialists, especially those on the far left. The Labour party was also in the 1950s - and to some extent still is today - wary of rich men, though not hostile to the benefits of their wealth. Rich foreigners are in double jeopardy.

What is more, dynamic individuals like Maxwell are uncomfortable to accommodate; witness George Brown and Aneurin Bevan. Flamboyance somehow betrays a lack of sincerity, or supposedly so. Individuals who go their own way, unconscious or uncaring of consensus, or who believe that democracy can be taken too far in committee, are the awkward squad of politics. Labour is a nonconformist party which distrusts nonconformists.

Labour constituency parties have always been ready to choose to represent the working-class those who do not spring from it. They have always also been ready to send to Parliament a sprinkling of millionaires like Sir Stafford Cripps, George Strauss and Harold Lever, to advance the cause of equality. The representatives of the genuine working-class - dockers, miners, railwaymen, lorry drivers - have fallen away steadily over the years, not only because their numbers in employment have diminished but because the choice of constituency parties has fallen more and more upon the middle classes.

But Maxwell's was a unique selection. That he was working class was beyond doubt: few people in Britain could have been born into greater poverty. On the other hand, he was undoubtedly rich. He had proved his loyalty to Britain on the battlefield. Nevertheless, he was a foreigner. What is more, since he left the army he had never been employed. He had always been an employer. It was a paradoxical mix which was offered to the Buckingham constituency Labour party.

Maxwell had been known to sack people. He was suspected of not always consulting the trade unions about those decisions which he thought he should make; and if he did consult them, there was no certainty that he would accept their advice. There was also a further difficulty. Though he claimed to have been an active supporter of the Labour party since 1945 and was a member of the Fabian Society, Maxwell only joined the party in 1958, the year before he sought the Buckingham nomination. In the minds of some, this confirmed him to be a Johnny-come-lately, an adventurist and a careerist who had not performed the minimum mandatory number of years knocking on doors and licking envelopes. (This entrance has long since been bolted. Today no candidate can be adopted for a parliamentary constituency unless he or she has been a member of the party for at least two years.)

It was inevitable that Maxwell should go into politics because he is attracted to where the power lies. He also had, and has, a genuine social conscience; had he not, the Conservative party would have been a natural choice for a wealthy, self-made man always irked by restrictions. But it was also inevitable that he would find life as a politician abrasive and frustrating. He admits that as a cabinet minister he would probably have been a disaster. His impatience would have been detonated by the cautious ways of the Civil Service. He would have had his permanent secretary perennially at his door complaining about the way he was treating his staff, about his habit of dealing with issues on the telephone instead of by paperwork and by his tendency to take and announce decisions first and to consult afterwards. Nor would he have been a good team man. He would have had opinions on every minister's subject and he would have voiced them, much as Mrs Thatcher used to do when she was a member of Edward Heath's Cabinet. As a junior minister, life would have been even more difficult because the permanent secretary would have had a senior minister to whom he could complain. In any case, to whom might he have been the junior? His main governmental interest was in developing Britain's scientific and technological capacity. Labour's first Minister of Technology was Frank Cousins, the former general secretary of the Transport and General Workers' Union and a leading unilateralist with whom Maxwell clashed spectacularly at the Labour party conference at Scarborough in 1960. They wouldn't have lasted five minutes together in office. Cousins's successor was Anthony Wedgwood Benn, as he still was in 1966. It would have been easier to mix oil and water.

For his first 18 months as an MP Maxwell assiduously worked for his constituency and his rapidly-growing business interests took second place. He invigorated his local party and made them about the richest in Britain through successful money-raising schemes. He captured the headlines in his local papers and the nationals; he intervened in Commons debates to an extent which left other newcomers gasping and the old-timers resentful. It wasn't an act. It was the way he behaved all the time. Consequently, when after Labour's landslide victory in 1966 he spent more time on his business - including a six-week tour abroad winning orders for *Chambers's Encyclopaedia*, of which he was the publisher - the backlash was more considerable than if he had neglected his constituency from the start.

He was neither on the left nor the right on political issues, though he was to become president of the Left of Centre Group. He supported a better deal for farmers, who are traditionally Conservative voters, but strongly defended the nationalisation of steel when many Labour MPs were uneasy about it. He was out of tune with the free-thinking on moral issues which marked the 1960s. He was never in favour of the permissive society; he was too stern a parent for that. His involvement in giving evidence for the prosecution of *Last Exit to Brooklyn* made him unpopular with politicians and publishers of the left. He demanded trade union reform long before the Labour party was ready to contemplate it. He urged the sale of council houses to their tenants even before the Conservatives proposed it. His "I'm Backing Britain" campaign had a sparkling beginning, but it embarrassed those who thought it smacked of narrow nationalism. Yet he is an internationalist and was strongly in favour of Britain's entry into Europe at the very time when the Labour party was moving strongly against. He wasn't a maverick, but he was often out of step.

He undoubtedly made an impact upon Westminster, even if it was a bruising one. His regard for the niceties and conventions of House of Commons procedure was, at times, perfunctory. But he had fun and was a remarkably effective constituency MP. After he left the Commons he retained his interest in, and allegiance to, the Labour party while remaining in fundamental disagreement with it over defence, over the latent and sometimes overt opposition to the Common Market and over the party's failure to tackle the menace of the Militant Tendency until the eleventh hour. In the 1987 general election campaign the Mirror Group Newspapers were the Labour party's most powerful and reliable supporters. Maxwell provided, without stint, the money and resources to finance the papers' campaign. He was daily involved in its planning and execution. That all the effort and expense was in a cause which could not be won was understood but never openly acknowledged. It was something which had to be done.

* * * * *

It is astonishing that the Buckingham general management committee swept aside all the traditional Labour inhibitions and chose Maxwell to fight the seat; after all, and apart from anything else, he was the youngest of the five hopefuls on the short-list and in those days youth, and the apparent omniscience which its possession bestows, was not regarded with the automatic awe which is its birthright today. The ritual objections to the new and the foreign were to come later from some members of the party's National Executive Committee; the covert racialism and open nationalism was to be the prerogative of his Conservative opponents. It was only those whose job it was to choose a candidate who might win the seat for the party who ignored such issues.

The Buckingham party in the summer of 1959 had been faced with a sudden crisis. Its much-respected prospective candidate, Dr Gordon Evans, who had been defeated by Sir Frank Markham (Con) in 1955 by only 1,140 votes, had been badly injured in an accident and could not fight the seat. A general election was thought to be imminent - in fact, it took place on October 8, little more than six weeks after Buckingham's selection conference - and a replacement for him was urgent. An original list of 15 possible candidates had been cut to five and the GMC met on Saturday, August 22 to make its final choice. Maxwell's opponents were a local railway worker, a London solicitor, a railway goods train guard from Grantham (Margaret Thatcher's home town), and Hugh (now Lord) Jenkins, assistant general secretary of the actors' union Equity, and an active organiser of marches and meetings for the Campaign for Nuclear Disarmament. Another local man who wanted to win the party's nomination, Tom Mitchinson, had failed to make the last five. Though he cast his vote for Maxwell at the selection meeting, he subsequently signed Sir Frank Markham's nomination papers, which was the kind of internal party squabble Maxwell's first election campaign could have done without. Mitchinson, a building trades worker, was in no doubt about his reasons for opposing Maxwell when he spoke to the *Daily Mail*[1]:

> I believe that real Labour chaps should represent the party - not all these barristers, journalists and so-called intellectuals.

The other "real Labour chaps" on the management committee disagreed with Mr Mitchinson and later expelled him from the party.

The candidate selection committee meeting took four-and-a-half hours to come to a decision, which is about par for the course in a marginal constituency. They sweltered, literally as well as metaphorically, on a hot afternoon and Maxwell was the clear victor on the third ballot. At his first real attempt to win a nomination - he had considered earlier trying for a vacancy at Aylesbury in the same county, but the procedures were too far advanced for him to join the contest - he had succeeded.

He and everyone else guessed that time was short. Though the Parliament which had been elected in May 1955 still theoretically had nine months to run, all the signs were that the Conservative Prime Minister, Harold Macmillan, intended to make an early dash to the polls. He had restored his party's morale after the humiliation of Suez and had brought his old friend, President Eisenhower, over to Britain for the first British political TV spectacular. The two of them appeared together, parading as the living symbols of the special relationship between the two great democracies. Macmillan's flair for showmanship was never seen to greater advantage. It was an era when Britain still had something to contribute to international affairs - though not as much as the politicians would have the voters believe - and Macmillan played up the visit of the wartime Allied Supreme Commander for all it was worth. Labour made the mistake - and Maxwell was no exception - of fighting Macmillan on the ground of his choosing instead of upon those policies where it was strongest. I witnessed one instructive incident in the Glasgow constituency of Kelvingrove during that election campaign when the Labour candidate stood on the back of a lorry and began her speech, "I want to tell you why it is essential that Hugh Gaitskell [Labour's then leader] should represent Britain at the Summit." "Bugger the summit, Mary", said one of the audience, "when am I gonna get a hoose?" It was a lesson which was never understood by Labour in 1959 and was still imperfectly understood in 1987.

In his speech to the selection committee, Maxwell had begun on international affairs, stating baldly:

> I disagree with the leadership of the party on their present nuclear disarmament policy. The proposal by them to set up a non-nuclear club [a compromise painfully worked out by Gaitskell to bridge the gaps between his views and the party's pacific wing] has been a non-starter right from its inception. The reason why it has been a non-starter is that most people who really and truly believe that Britain ought to give up, unilaterally and immediately, her stock of hydrogen and atom weapons know that the present policy is insincere and unrealistic and will find no backers anywhere in the world.

Instead, Maxwell had his own policy, which became known as the "Buckingham Plan", which was that a Labour Government returned after the general election would unilaterally give up the use of nuclear weapons and turn them over, with their delivery systems, to the United Nations and ask the Russians and the Americans to do the same. He described it as "not only an honest policy but also an absolute election winner". It may have been honest, but it was as unrealistic as the policy he was denouncing. A better reason for proposing this "solution" was that it distanced him from a policy to which he was then, and still is, totally opposed, without leading to accusations that he was splitting the party. Though he was new to active politics he was already old in the ways of campaigning.

The rest of his speech was taken up with the conventional statements expected of Labour candidates, including a defence of nationalisation - "not for any dogmatic reasons but simply and solely to ensure and guarantee full employment to every person on these islands who wants to work". He asked, prophetically as it was to turn out 20 years later:

> If the Tories really believe that nationalisation is bad for the nation, why haven't they denationalised British European Airways, the Central Electricity Board, the Gas Boards and the railways, to mention a few?

He promised there would be no return to rationing or unnecessary controls by a Labour Government, except to ensure the building of hospitals, roads, schools and factories and to protect Britain's gold and foreign exchange reserves from "the speculations of unscrupulous bankers and City and foreign gamblers".

The last Labour MP for Buckingham had been Aidan Crawley, a former county cricketer who later switched sides and joined the Conservative party (his daughter, Harriet, only narrowly failed to defeat the London Left's ambitious standard bearer, Ken Livingstone, in the 1987 general election). Crawley's defection was clearly in the minds of some of Buckingham's Labour activists and at the end of his speech Maxwell announced:

> I should now like to make a statement of a personal nature. Two comrades in this constituency ... said ... We promise you our wholehearted help and feel certain that if you are selected you will be able ... to win this constituency. We should, however, like to know this: are you a careerist? ... we had an awful disappointment with Aidan Crawley. I affirmed I was not a careerist.... I come from a very humble farm-labouring family and would rather cut off my arm than betray my class. In any case, Aidan Crawley was in need of a career and I am not - for mine is made.

Once selected, he threw himself into the fight with his usual breathtaking gusto. Three days later he was attending and disrupting an open-air meeting of Sir Frank Markham's and then writing to the Tory MP explaining that he had only done so because of the "innuendoes, half-truths and complete untruths" which Sir

Frank had delivered to the audience. He then demanded that Sir Frank should appear on a public platform with him to debate their respective parties' policies. Sir Frank, who was not the most quick-witted and articulate of the Tory knights of the shires, wisely declined.

There was still the problem to be overcome of Maxwell's endorsement by the National Executive Committee of the party. He was strongly assisted by Dr Evans, who wrote to the party's national agent, Len Williams, denouncing the attempt by some local party people to see that endorsement was denied. Dr Evans was particularly concerned about an article, culled from the cuttings library, by the *Sunday Express*'s political columnist Crossbencher. There were a poisonous few paragraphs about Maxwell, though by the paper's standards it was a pretty mild poison. The Simpkin Marshall affair had been revived; his recent membership of the party had been pointed out; the fact that he was of Czech origin and had been born Ludvik Hoch was inevitably printed; and reports that Maxwell had been seen in a Rolls Royce were natural grist to Crossbencher's mill (and the only new item in it). Dr Evans was anxious to refute all this: he was convinced the party had made "a very wise choice" and he had found Maxwell to be "frank, open and sincere".

In the event, the NEC endorsed Maxwell's candidature on September 14 by a two-thirds to one-third majority - with, it was said, Richard Crossman, James Callaghan and Anthony Greenwood among the dissenting minority - though it did little to help his campaign, sending only the worthy but dull Patrick Gordon-Walker of its national figures to speak on his behalf. The expected protests that an inexperienced and recent party member had been chosen for a "plum" seat came from trade union members of the NEC, but Maxwell answered these critics by declaring[2]:

> Most of the members of the NEC were aware of the work I had done for the party since 1945.... Although neither I nor they were very pleased or proud of the fact that I had not got around formally to joining the party until 12 months ago, the reasons were that in the Esher constituency, where I live, the Labour party is most inactive and there was no local party in Esher itself in recent years until I organised one 12 months ago.

Esher is part of the lush Surrey stockbroker belt, immovably Conservative. At the previous general election the Tory candidate had a majority of more than 20,000 over his Labour opponent.

Local Labour parties in such areas were often surprisingly flourishing, but there were many exceptions.

Having secured his back against his comrades, Maxwell now had to fight the Tories, who, taking Crossbencher as their benchmark, began to smear him thick and fast. An allegation in the *Daily Telegraph* said that in the constituency there were complaints - though the complainants were not identified - that Maxwell had concealed his Czech birth. Maxwell retorted that he had confirmed that at a meeting of district party secretaries three weeks before the selection conference. Seeing that almost every national and local press reference to him described him as Czech-born, it would have been a futile hope to disguise his origins even if he had intended to.

More serious was a confidential bulletin sent out by the Conservative agent for Buckingham, Frank Smith, to Sir Frank and Lady Markham and to all district officials urging them to ask Maxwell questions about:

> His experience in the Czech army.
>
> His name when he received the MC.
>
> His business dealings, "which were recently the subject of an article in the *Sunday Express*".
>
> Whether he employed non-union labour at the Pergamon Press.

Smith ended his bulletin with a warning:

> Please read this carefully and ensure that it does not go astray. Each copy is numbered.

However, one Tory recipient was sufficiently disgusted by the proposed campaign as to send Maxwell a copy of the bulletin. The first Tory supporter to ask the questions, plus one about his alleged association with the former MP, Peter Baker, received a libel writ, as did Mr Smith and the *Buckingham Advertiser*. Later, Lady Markham and the *Northampton Chronicle and Echo* received writs for a letter from her which the paper had published. A local doctor, chairman of the Olney, Bucks, Conservative Association, was moved to drive his car at an audience being addressed by Maxwell and was fined £25 with £15 costs. It was certainly a campaign of fierce passions.

Maxwell wrote to the *Advertiser*, quoting James Pitman, chairman of the former owners of Simpkin Marshall, as saying - in his letter to the *Sunday Express* - that "no stigma" attached to Maxwell's character in connection with the closing down of the wholesaling firm. A "Maxwellgram" set out the facts in greater

detail and included a quotation from Sir Frank Markham saying he
would rather win the election on the Conservative party programme
"than by any scurrilous tricks and defaming his opponents".

In a letter to the voters Maxwell denounced Sir Frank's appeal to
"bigoted prejudice" by quoting a Mr Bill West of Buckingham who,
in answer to the question "How can you vote for a foreigner?"
replied:

> Captain Maxwell is no more a foreigner than Prince Philip. Like him,
> he was born abroad, came here as a boy, fought for this country and
> has been working for its interests ever since.

But, according to the *Daily Telegraph*, three days before polling,
there was a sign on a wall in Buckingham stating:

> Bucks people do not need to be represented in Parliament by an
> insulting foreigner, so let's put a check on this over-confident Czech.
> A real Englishman as Member for us.

The constituents of Buckingham were bombarded with speeches,
statements and "Maxwellgrams" from their Labour candidate,
beginning with an appeal to all Liberal voters to vote tactically in
order to defeat the Tories until such time as the Liberal party
replaced the Tory party as the second party in Britain:

> I therefore appeal to Liberal voters to use their vote effectively
> against the Tory candidate by voting Labour and not to throw away
> their vote by supporting the hopeless case of [the Liberal candidate].

There was certainly no attempt to talk down to the electors of
Buckingham. They all received his adoption speech in the form of a
nine-page "Maxwellgram", in single-space typing, setting out his
policy, demanding more money to be spent on science and
technology and space research, a more scientific use of manpower
and machinery (the policy which Harold Wilson turned into an
election-winner five years later), equal pay for women and all the
other party nostrums of 1959. Several of the pages were devoted to
the Buckingham plan for nuclear disarmament, including a detailed
description of the effect of the explosion of a 10-megaton hydrogen
bomb. Copies of the plan, he said, had been sent to Mr Gaitskell,
President Eisenhower, the Soviet leader Nikita Kruschev, and the
general secretary of the United Nations. He never did do things by
halves.

More percipiently, his election address promised that every
council tenant would be helped financially to buy his home, a policy
which, if it had been adopted and extended by the Labour party in
the years after 1959, might have changed the face of British politics.

During the course of the campaign his agent, Bryan Barnard, calculated Maxwell addressed 179 meetings in 16 days, touring the constituency in a red and white caravan which he used as a mobile office. This was described by the local paper as an "innovation" in electioneering.

There was a nationwide swing to the Conservative party on polling day. The Tory majority in Buckingham went up from 1,140 in 1955, in a straight fight with Labour, to 1,746, with a Liberal candidate taking over 4,000 votes, but losing his deposit. Maxwell, despite disappointment at being beaten, could count it as a good result. He refused to shake Sir Frank Markham's hand at the declaration of the poll because "he fought a dirty election". The full result was:

Sir Frank Markham (Con)	22,304
Robert Maxwell (Lab)	20,558
Evan Richards (Lib)	4,577

Bryan Barnard, however, was bitter and did not mince words in his report to the party upon the campaign. Maxwell, he said, had stood out far above the other 14 would-be candidates who wanted to represent the party at Buckingham, "but he also had exceptional disadvantages - he was Czech-born and had only been a member of the party for a few months". Nevertheless, he said, the constituency party had been quick to see "the qualities, ability, personality and sincerity of the man". However:

> Little did we know that another fight was also on. Disloyalties were quietly taking place in our own camp by one or more of the unsuccessful candidates.... A smear article appeared in a Sunday newspaper ... one of the disloyal members of our camp, Tom Mitchinson, one of the unsuccessful candidates and former president, signed the Tory nomination papers.... Never have I seen a single personality in politics rally more enthusiasm or create greater interest than did Bob Maxwell. Politically, he murdered the Tories and they knew it - only one thing would save them from defeat. They must intensify the smear campaign.

Did it work? Barnard had no doubt that it did. There had been a last-minute "filthy" campaign, he said, about "Maxwell's prison sentences, affairs with film stars and the rest". The weekend after the election he had toured the constituency and asked 35 people unknown to him how they had voted. Five wouldn't say. Five were Conservatives. Three were "staunch" Labour. Nineteen confirmed their support for Labour or Maxwell, but had changed their minds at the last minute when they realised "what a terrible man he was".

He couldn't decide what the other three might have done. Barnard's judgement was that "the bitter smear campaign had worked and at a modest estimate it had cost Maxwell at least 3,000 votes and had deprived Labour of an outstanding victory".

His disappointment was understandable, but Labour won only one seat from the Conservatives during the 1959 campaign and that was in Scotland. The chances are that Maxwell would have lost come what may, even if more narrowly than he did. Though mud sticks, it frequently sticks to the throwers as well and during the course of an election campaign the damage is roughly equalled out.

Later Barnard wrote to Maxwell saying he had never known a candidate create such an impact upon a constituency and thanked Betty Maxwell for her "tremendous volume of hard work" during the campaign. Maxwell responded by giving Barnard a watch. Agents do not expect tangible thanks from their candidates and Barnard was overjoyed. Patrick Gordon-Walker - who five years later was to lose his seat in Smethwick in a campaign which was notorious for its appeal to racialism - wrote to Maxwell saying he had watched his fight against "a sinister and dirty campaign" with admiration; nevertheless, Maxwell had lost and that was what mattered. He had been expecting to win and had privately forecast a "handsome majority" of up to 6,000. He had - and has - no interest in coming a good second in anything.

But two months later, confidence undimmed, he declared in a speech in the constituency that the electorate would turn to Labour "the next time they have a chance to do so". In that he was right. But it was to be another five years before he was to be proved so. In the meantime he gave the red and white caravan in which he had fought the election to a farmworker with two young children who had been evicted from his tied cottage.

* * * * *

During the waiting years until the next general election a Maxwell weakness - getting too involved in matters of detail from which he should distance himself - manifested itself in Buckingham and Buckinghamshire. He became the president of the Buckingham constituency party long before the re-adoption procedure for a parliamentary candidate could begin. He became chairman of the Buckinghamshire Federation of Labour parties. He regularly attended executive meetings of the Buckinghamshire party - 12 out of 13 in 1960 - stood for election to the County Council - losing by only 107 votes in a safe Tory seat on a 70 per cent poll - and became entangled in constitutional squabbles with a faction - including a railway worker, Ray Bellchambers, another whom he had defeated for selection in August 1959 - which had never reconciled itself to his arrival.

On the credit side, he undoubtedly galvanised an already active party into incredible achievements. Party membership went up when elsewhere in Britain it was falling; new offices were opened in various parts of the constituency; a party newspaper, the *Bucks Courier*, was launched (chairman of the editorial board, I.R. Maxwell); and the party's profit from its main money-raising scheme, the Tote, was over £14,000 in 1960, a sum which, even today, would be beyond the imagination of most local Labour parties and would not disgrace a vigorous local Conservative party. He even persuaded Betty Maxwell, whose hard work had endeared her to most of the party's members, to stand at the last minute in the County Council election at Newport Pagnell. She lost by a two-to-one margin, but without her the party would have been unrepresented in the contest for the town's seat. Unfortunately, a row between her husband and members of the Newport Pagnell party - in which Maxwell was undoubtedly in the right but with which he ought not to have become involved - leading to the suspension of its chairman, Arthur Leary, deprived her of the help of several key workers.

An old-fashioned knockabout speech in February 1961 attacking the squirearchy in Buckinghamshire - the Viscounts, the Lords and the Ladies who passed on their county seats from one generation to another - and especially a gentleman luxuriating in a name which seemed a parody of aristocratic nomenclature - Alderman Sir Everard Digby Pauncefort Duncombe - brought a sharp reminder in a letter to a local paper that hostility to his "foreignness" would not be overcome. "Captain Maxwell should realise", wrote an indignant voter, "that this attempt to introduce electioneering tactics which were normal in Central and Eastern Europe before the last war are unlikely to appeal to the electors of North Bucks who have learnt from experience that many members of the old-established families have rendered outstanding service to the county." There wrote the true pen of English county deference, knowing nothing of elections in Central and Eastern Europe, such as they were, but believing that local government in England was not only immeasurably superior to any other form of administration which existed but was reserved for native-born Englishmen only.

Nationally, Maxwell declared for Hugh Gaitskell in the fight against the tide of unilateral disarmament which was sweeping through the Labour party. For the first time the Left, propelled by Frank Cousins, had achieved a major victory over the party leader. Cousins was the kind of man who arises occasionally in all movements, from the extreme Left to the far Right. His combination of an electric conference oratory and muddled thinking produced a dangerous instability within the party. Politically he was naïve, as were many of his contemporaries and successors in the trade unions, but the naïvety was buttressed by power. He controlled the biggest block vote at the annual party conference; bestowing such a political weapon upon an individual who is not answerable to a political electorate was, and is, an abiding failing of the Labour party's constitution. Consequently, the Scarborough conference of 1960 produced the gravest split in the Labour party since the defection of Ramsay Macdonald in 1931, with the delegates voting for a unilateralism which it was impossible for the leadership to accept. Maxwell spoke to the conference the day before the vote, moving a resolution calling for party unity, which in the circumstances was about as effective as a prayer for world peace on September 2, 1939. Cousins was his target, but as his resolution deplored personal attacks, he made no mention of him by name. No one listening had any doubt, however, who he had in mind when he denounced "those members of our movement who have advocated disunity and treachery". If "the wreckers and destroyers" persisted, the Labour party would be annihilated just as surely as mankind would be annihilated in a nuclear war. He went on[3]:

> Last Sunday night I was watching Mr Grimond [Jo Grimond, leader of the Liberal party] closing the Liberal conference at Eastbourne. He taunted us by saying that there was no need for him to attack the Labour movement - we were doing it very nicely for him. The Liberals are hovering in the wings of history like vultures waiting to take our place if we give them the chance.

And for those who sought to replace Gaitskell as leader, Maxwell made it clear where he stood[4]:

> If we were to elect a new leader, he would not be able to unite our movement as well as Hugh Gaitskell did prior to and during the election. This movement has no finer leader than Hugh Gaitskell and we stand by him. Let those of you who put personal ambition before the unity of this movement beware. We have got the ability in our constitution to deal with you.

That kind of menacing sentence was commonplace coming from trade union leaders. It was less acceptable to the conference coming from an employer. The Gaitskellites applauded and the Cousinites slow-handclapped as Maxwell left the rostrum.

The conference at the Yorkshire seaside resort that year was the most dramatic in the turbulent history of Labour party conferences. None since has equalled it for drama and passion. It was an extraordinary quality of Gaitskell, allegedly the target of Aneurin Bevan's wounding phrase about "a desiccated calculating machine" - though Bevan denied it - that he aroused greater emotions of loyalty and hatred than any other Labour leader in modern history. He and Cousins had nothing in common. Nor did Cousins and Maxwell, except brute political instincts. Cousins responded to Maxwell's attack[5]:

> We are not debating whether Hugh Gaitskell and I like each other. That has never been in question [laughter]. That is not an issue.

He was speaking, he said, because his delegation had agreed he should do so in order to answer the "unfair criticisms which a certain gentleman made". He went on:

> Nobody is entitled to tell us that, if we don't agree with each other, we are going to be treated rather roughly. I thought that was the nicest speech for disunity we have heard for a couple of days.

Nevertheless, the Maxwell resolution was carried by an overwhelming majority and the Gaitskell defeat on unilateral disarmament was comfortably reversed the following year.

When Maxwell returned to Buckingham to make his report on the conference, he continued his attack on the general secretary of the T & GWU[6]:

> The split in the party is the outcome of Frank Cousins abandoning the trade unions and meddling in politics.

Four years later, after Hugh Gaitskell's death, Cousins and Maxwell sat in the same Parliament, supporting the Government of Harold Wilson. The irony was that Cousins was in the Cabinet as Minister of Technology, the subject on which Maxwell was by far the greater expert. Politics is like that.

The Maxwells had intended to move home to the Buckingham constituency but their eldest son, Michael, was gravely injured in a car accident during the Christmas holidays of 1961, and lay in a coma at first at the Radcliffe Infirmary, Oxford, and then at the Churchill, where Mrs Maxwell would visit him every day. The plans to move were abandoned in favour of making a permanent home at

Headington Hill Hall, where Pergamon Press was already installed. But they did keep a house at Bletchley. Maxwell retained his chairmanship of the Buckinghamshire Federation of Labour parties but gave up his presidency of the constituency party.

With Maxwell pushing them, the local party finances were growing stronger and stronger and in 1962, at Bletchley, a new headquarters was opened by a genuinely-amazed Hugh Gaitskell, delivered to the site by helicopter, the latest Maxwell innovation for politicians like himself with little time to spare. The building cost £20,000 and stood in grounds of one-and-a-half acres. Maxwell set up a Fund-raising Foundation, run by Bryan Barnard, to help other constituencies do the same as Buckingham, but the scale of that success was never repeated elsewhere.

In June 1962 Maxwell was re-adopted by Buckingham to fight the next general election. He took the occasion to announce that he was dropping his army rank of captain and wished to be referred to as "Mr" Maxwell. It indicated, he said, his belief that military power on a national scale was now outdated. Maxwell promised that he would win the next contest and Sir Frank Markham declared that he wouldn't, but shortly afterwards he announced his retirement from politics. The local Conservatives chose Mrs Elaine Kellett, an academically brilliant but politically shrill former MP, to succeed him and to defend the seat against Maxwell's challenge when the general election finally came.

Maxwell, meanwhile, disturbed many of his supporters by declaring himself in favour of Britain joining the Common Market, a cause which had little popularity in the party and which was opposed by Hugh Gaitskell. But within a few months Gaitskell was dead and Maxwell returned from a tour of India and Australia to denounce those Tory journalists and politicians, including the Prime Minister, who had denigrated the Labour leader while he was alive but praised him highly now that he wasn't. Maxwell said he was "nauseated" by them.

Nineteen-sixty-three was the year when almost everything happened in British politics. Gaitskell's death had plunged the Labour party into gloom, but his successor, Harold Wilson, arrived on the scene with ideas flying in all directions. The Profumo scandal was not only shocking in itself; it showed that the Prime Minister who had carried all before him as Supermac didn't appear to know what was happening or how his War Minister spent his time when he wasn't at the War Office. Then Macmillan, having decided to resist party pressure upon him to retire, suddenly resigned when faced with a prostate operation - a more serious ordeal then than it is today - and from a scramble of the power-hungry to succeed him, the Earl of Home stepped down from the House of Lords to do so, metamorphosing into plain Sir Alec Douglas-Home.

The effect so far as Maxwell and other aspiring Labour party candidates were concerned was that the general election which was universally expected to take place in the spring of 1964 was put off until the last possible moment in the autumn. They all had to wait six months more. Maxwell spent the time fatefully by turning Pergamon Press into a public company.

* * * * *

Maxwell's fast-growing business in scientific publishing and his enduring belief that Britain's future lay in applying the latest science and technology to British industry chimed perfectly with Harold Wilson's promise to lead the nation into "the white heat of the technological revolution". The trouble was that Maxwell was devoting his life to the advancement of science and Harold Wilson had only decided at the last minute to adopt the theme for his first party conference speech as leader. No one was more surprised than he to discover he had struck a chord with an exactitude which occurs only once in a political generation. The "white heat" phrase became the platform to launch an election campaign; it was not intended to start a revolution. Wilson's interest in modernising British industry was genuine enough, but in government the new vision gave way to the old traditions and the white heat cooled.

Nevertheless, in one of the many innovative moves he made in his early days as leader, Wilson set up a working party on science, government and industry. It was to report to Richard Crossman, a politician whose principles were no match for his need to be admired, and Maxwell was appointed chairman. Crossman was to write later[7]:

> Maxwell is a very strange fellow - a Czech Jew with a perfect knowledge of Russian, who has an infamous reputation in the publishing world as the creator of Pergamon Press. Throughout this work on science, where I regretfully let him set up a group of very powerful scientists, he has been unfaultable. I can't find him putting a foot wrong. The paper he and his group have produced is by far the best.

Maxwell threw himself into the committee's work with enthusiasm and discussed it with President Kennedy's scientificadviser, Jerry Wiesner, and several other leading scientific personalities in Washington, as well as officials at the Pentagon. In Britain he had discussions with the chairman of the Advisory Council on Scientific Policy, Lord Todd, the former Chief Science Adviser to the Ministry of Defence, Sir Frederick Brundrett, and many others. Many of the working party's subsequent recommendations were implemented by the Wilson Government, but the essential determination to create a science-oriented administration was never there. Scientists like Lords Bowden and Snow were brought into the Government with a fanfare and departed with barely a murmur. But that letdown was still in the future. At the 1963 party conference, again at Scarborough, Maxwell won warm applause for a speech outlining what had to be done.

The growth of the national economy, he argued, followed closely the resources devoted to research and development. To the extent that these were channelled by decisions of government, so the whole thrust of the economy was determined. He urged that the next Labour Government should create a Cabinet-level minister responsible for higher education, science and research (it didn't; there was a Minister for Education and Science, but it was principally the old Ministry of Education with a new title), the setting up of a Technological Grants Commission and the creation of a free science and engineering advisory service for industry, especially for small and medium-sized businesses.

For a man not yet an MP, Maxwell was making a mark. For the fifth conference running he had been called to speak at the party conference (and he was to do so for every year in which he was a candidate or an MP). The deputy leader of the Labour party, George Brown, went to Bletchley in February 1964 and declared that Robert Maxwell was bound "to play a very major role" in the next Labour Government. The science correspondent of the *Daily Express*, Chapman Pincher, said roughly the same thing. Despite the fact that he subsequently said to me that he would have been a disaster in the Cabinet, at that moment his hopes must have been high.

But in the constituency, the campaign of veiled innuendo against Maxwell's foreign birth continued. The Liberal candidate for Buckingham, Jack Wallis, told a local paper that the unpopularity of

Robert Maxwell was "a fact of political life". He added, primly:

> It is not my place to go into the reasons for this. Indeed, as a Liberal,
> I deplore some of the reasons put forward by the Tories to denigrate
> the Labour candidate. As a Liberal politician, however, I must take
> note of them.

It is a hackneyed political tactic to remind the voters of the
presence of mud in order to dissóciate from it and Maxwell was to
meet it often in the weeks leading up to polling day on October 15.
Indeed, an organisation calling itself the "National Campaign for
Free Speech" entered the fray with a simple poster demanding, in
large capital letters:

ASK YOUR MP ABOUT THE FOREIGN PHONEY JAN
LUDWIG HOCH!

From the start Maxwell announced that he would win. The other
candidates, Mrs Kellett and Mr Wallis, were notably less confident.
There was a mood for change in the political air. Sir Alec
Douglas-Home seemed a man born out of his time; whatever his
other qualities, he did not possess the drive and dynamism which
Labour presented to the electorate. Mrs Kellett said she had
detected "a sniff of victory", but it was a scent which eluded other
political noses just as keen.

The contest for Buckingham was fought along predictable lines
and Maxwell stayed close to party policy, even on defence. Both he
and Mrs Kellett promised that the election would be conducted
cleanly, without smears and personal abuse, while Wallis vainly
asked why, if Labour was the party of equality, it had adopted a
millionaire to be its candidate. Maxwell, as ever, was the most
mobile and announced that he would visit the 179 villages in the
constituency during a tour of some 3,000 miles. This time, instead of
a caravan, his "wheels" were a Land Rover fitted with a half-inch
thick pile carpet, cushioned seats and a desk. Inevitably, there was a
loudspeaker on its roof. Bryan Barnard had returned from the
Fund-raising Foundation to be his agent. By a coincidence, Barnard
had been the Labour agent in north-west Norfolk in 1955 when the
Labour candidate there notched up his party's only gain of that
general election - by beating Mrs Kellett.

Even Tom Mitchinson, the man who had signed Sir Frank
Markham's nomination papers in 1959 and been expelled from the
Labour party in consequence, announced that he was supporting
Maxwell. He had opposed him in the previous election, he said,
because he thought Maxwell was an outsider and wouldn't stay in

the constituency. But he had. Now the Conservatives had brought in an outsider and he proudly disclosed that he had refused to sign Mrs Kellett's papers. Election campaigns always open the door to prodigal sons, though Mr Mitchinson admitted he didn't expect to be re-admitted to the party.

Maxwell's daily itinerary read like a ride through rural England, with "whistle stops", for example, on September 30, at Rowsham, Aston Abbotts, Cublington, Dunton, Hoggeston, Little Horwood, Nash, Whaddon, Haversham Village, Little Linford, Great Linford, Old Bradwell, Shenley, Loughton, Calverton, Beachampton and Thornton, followed by meetings in the village square at Great Horwood, at a public house in Mursley, by the Post Office at Drayton Parslow and at the crossroads of Newton Longville. On other days the Land Rover roared into Botolph Claydon, Water Stratford, Barton Hartshorn, Chetwode, Preston Bissett, Newton Blossomville, Stoke Hammond and scores of other villages and hamlets with idyllic names.

Promises, as always, abounded from all candidates, though the most diverting was one by Maxwell to eat a Liberal councillor's hat if the Liberal candidate did not lose his deposit. (The deposit then was £150 and was forfeited if a candidate did not receive one-eighth of the votes cast.) Once again, the subterranean campaign about Maxwell's origins came into the open in the last days of the campaign, with Maxwell protesting, at his eve-of-poll meeting on October 14, at the manner in which Mrs Kellett introduced herself in her leaflets and on public platforms - as being 40 and British,

> ... implying, thereby, that I am not, and her supporters, taking the lead, go about whispering that the Labour candidate is a foreigner. If I am a foreigner, so is the Duke of Edinburgh. He, too, was born abroad but from what we can see he seems to be quite popular.... Is it not right to ask this lady candidate and her friends whether in being born British they had any choice in the matter or were required to make any effort? I was involved in both. I have had several reports [of] Conservative canvassers, when being told that the elector will vote for Maxwell, saying, "Oh, are you? We are extremely worried about the Labour candidate - he keeps disappearing behind the Iron Curtain." So does Mr Chambers of ICI and many other people as well as Mr [Reginald] Maudling.

For good measure, Maxwell also pointed out other similarities with Prince Philip. They were both born on June 10 and they both had a wife called Elizabeth, even though Mrs Maxwell's name was spelt with an "s" and not a "z". The speech was accompanied by the uproar traditionally invoked for eve-of-poll meetings, with the inevitable shout of "You are a Czech." The following day was devoted to a frenzied effort by all parties to get every possible vote out. Because of the size of the constituency, the counting of the votes did not begin until 9 am on the following day, Friday, October 16. The delay made the Buckingham result crucial. Labour's expected majority was melting overnight into single figures. If seats like this one could not be won, it would disappear altogether. But Buckingham came up trumps. On an 86.5 per cent poll (astonishing seeing that the register had been compiled exactly a year earlier), Maxwell became a Member of Parliament by a majority of 1,481. The result was:

Robert Maxwell (Lab)	23,085
Elaine Kellett (Con)	21,604
Jack Wallis (Lib)	5,578

Mr Wallis lost his deposit and Robert Maxwell did not have to eat the Liberal councillor's hat, which had been displayed in the window of a local shop in the hope that he would be compelled either to swallow it or his words. The swing to Labour was about 3.3 per cent, higher than in some marginal seats in London. Betty Maxwell was the postal votes officer for Buckingham and, largely due to her efforts, Buckingham Labour party registered 1,750 such voters, which was 269 more than her husband's majority, and the second highest total in the country. The overall Labour majority in the United Kingdom as a whole was only four and in a speech to party workers that Friday evening Maxwell predicted another general election within 12 to 18 months.

* * * * *

Maxwell made his entrance to the Commons at the same speed at which he did everything else. On his first day there, shortly after the Queen's Speech, Bryan Barnard introduced him to an old friend, Dr Horace King, then deputy Speaker of the Commons and later Speaker. Said Barnard, another June 10 baby, in his tribute on Maxwell's 60th birthday:

> Within seconds you asked Horace how you could go about making your maiden speech. Horace diplomatically replied, "You should seek a good attendance record, listen carefully to experienced debaters and then, when a subject you know something about is for debate, you make your maiden speech." Your immediate reply was: "I haven't come here to be a rubber stamp. I want to make my maiden speech this afternoon." Horace was taken aback and then

> remarked: "Are you serious?" and you said: "Yes, of course I'm
> serious." Horace walked back a couple of paces and then said: "I'll be
> in the chair at about 4.30 pm - I'll call you then."

That gave Maxwell two hours in which to write a speech. Various
hurried drafts were thrown away before he decided to combine his
notes with speaking off-the-cuff, becoming the first Labour MP to
make his maiden speech on the first day of a new Parliament.
Maxwell's political secretary for 10 years, Judith Ennals, said:

> Some wags remarked: "There's our Bob, hardly waited for Her
> Majesty to sit down!"

Though he had been impatient, Maxwell's speech followed
ancient tradition. He praised his predecessor, Sir Frank Markham,
for his "courage" - tactfully omitting to recall how he had refused to
shake hands with him at the declaration of the poll in 1959 - and
concentrated the first half of what he had to say on the problems
of his constituency. That was not only conventional, it was
commonsense. The air at Westminster was already thick with talk of
the next election. But the second half of his speech was devoted -
again - to a plea for government assistance to apply science to
industry and criticism of the waste of scientific and engineering
manpower - as well as taxpayers' money - on defence research
programmes.

Charles Longbottom, an elegant young Tory MP for York,
followed Maxwell and commended him for "a remarkable and
fluent maiden speech". Later speeches were not to be received so
warmly by the Conservative benches. A rather more backhanded
compliment came from Charles Pannell, the newly-appointed
Minister of Public Building and Works:

> Dear Bob - It was a good maiden speech indeed - I wish I had heard
> it. All the best, Charles.

The magazine *Nature* reported Maxwell's remarks about science
and industry almost in their entirety, but added perceptively[8]:

> The opinions and ideas of Mr Maxwell are what we have been
> awaiting for a considerable time. However, one cannot help but feel
> that much that is talked about development of scientific progress into
> industrial practice is so much political ammunition, and only the next
> few months will show if the present Government is successfully on the
> way to taking full advantage of scientific research.

Maxwell quickly implemented a promise to bring more work to
his constituency and located the Pergamon warehouse, a printing
works and a library supply business in it. And though he approved

of a pay rise of £1,500 a year for MPs - which aroused a public outcry when it was paid before old age pensions were increased - he gave his first year's increase to needy pensioners in the constituency. He found time to become treasurer of Centre 42, the left-wing theatre project, and founded the Michael Maxwell Memorial Fund for Brain Research, with a gift of £2,000 a year for research at Oxford, where Michael still lay in hospital in a coma after his road accident four years earlier. He threw himself enthusiastically into his new role, touring his constituency every weekend and putting his business affairs in second place. He sponsored an appeal for funds for a children's home so that it might help a dozen children crippled by the disastrous thalidomide drug and he even answered an appeal from the steward of the Conservative Club at Bletchley to be saved from eviction from his flat there. Maxwell went to the club, argued with the Conservative committee and got the eviction postponed.

Mrs Ennals recalled "a Saturday jaunt" through Marsh Gibbon, Poundon and Twyford before heading for Stony Stratford, Maxwell in his Rolls and she in her Mini:

> We came to a Halt sign at a country crossroads. I hesitated at the sign and went across, trying to keep track of the Rolls. Seconds later, a police motor-cyclist flagged me down.... He was not satisfied that my hesitation constituted a real stop and took out his book. Ever alert, [Maxwell] had caught sight of my dilemma in his rear view mirror and come back. He greeted the officer and enquired after his wife and children by name! The officer was as flabbergasted as I was. "Come on, Judy, don't waste the officer's time arguing", [he said] and off we went. It is this fabulous memory of his which floors both friend and foe.

She might have added "cheek" as well.

Cheek was certainly a description applied to Harold Wilson in his first few months as Prime Minister. He had an almost totally inexperienced Cabinet, most of whom had voted against him as leader, a Foreign Secretary (Patrick Gordon-Walker) and a Minister for Technology (Frank Cousins) without seats in Parliament, a majority of only four and an impending financial crisis which threatened devastation to the economy within a month of taking office. Maxwell had no doubt about the gravity of the crisis. Speaking to a trade union conference in Buckingham in November, he declared that if the Government had not been able to arrange a loan facility of more than a billion pounds "this country would have been bankrupt within a week". It was, he said, a crisis just as serious as the one we had faced in 1940. Like Wilson, he was tempted into using the Dunkirk analogy. Wilson for his part regretted it afterwards; it was not a miracle which Britain needed but a long and sustained effort for economic recovery.

They were certainly hazardous parliamentary days, physically as well as politically. MPs near to death arrived within the precincts of the Palace of Westminster to cast their votes while lying semi-conscious in an ambulance (provided there is a physical presence within the Palace, an MP is not required to register his vote in person: a whip will do it for him). Any MP looking to be under the weather could be certain to be plagued by inquiries about his health from other MPs, concerned not so much with his well-being as the possibility of the Government's majority being dissolved by death, thus precipitating a general election. The hearts of the Prime Minister and the Chief Whip must have jumped a beat or two when they read that Maxwell had been fined £25 for careless driving of his Rolls, the carelessness amounting to shaving while travelling at a speed of between 60 and 75 miles an hour The prosecution was brought privately by a company director - and Conservative - and was adjourned three times, the first occasion because it was three days before polling day, which may have frustrated its intention.

A political fright came over the nationalisation of steel. The Tories were bitterly opposed and were relying upon Labour defections to deny the Government its will. Two Labour MPs, Desmond Donnelly and Woodrow Wyatt, were threatening to vote against the measure which would, theoretically, have produced a dead-heat. The steelmasters were hoping that Maxwell would join them. In 1963 Maxwell had been asked by George Brown to approach the bosses of the steel industry to see whether a compromise could be reached between them and the Labour party which would enable a bill to be passed which, if not having their approval, would at least be reluctantly accepted. The bosses were not prepared to enter into any discussions with the party, even informally through Maxwell, in advance of a general election which all of them hoped - and some believed - Labour would lose. The Queen's Speech of 1964 made it clear that the Government intended to go ahead with nationalisation and a White Paper setting out its proposals was debated in the Commons on May 5, 1965. Representatives of the steelmasters came back to Maxwell and urged him to support Wyatt and Donnelly. Though he did not agree with old-style nationalisation, he refused to listen, saying that Labour had been elected on a clear mandate to nationalise the industry and that its bosses had missed their opportunity. In the event, after George Brown had appeared to make concessions to Wyatt and Donnelly, the two potential rebels voted with the Government and steel was nationalised in the next Parliament when Labour's majority was secure against any conceivable desertions.

Maxwell's energy and industry were phenomenal. Harold Wilson, who in later life became a warm friend, used his appetite for facts and statistics to calculate Maxwell's impact on parliamentary affairs during his first year as an MP. In his contribution to the 60th birthday book he said Maxwell made speeches on:

> Charolais cattle, eggs, factory farming, hormones, the Agricultural Price Review, the P1154 and the HS681 aircraft, Sea Slug and Sea Dart, the Warsaw Convention and The Hague Protocol, Soviet aircraft in Berlin, five separate interventions on the business of the House (highlighting issues to which he felt Parliament should be giving priority), the computer industry (in which he was a pioneer), the publication of the parliamentary voting division list, the regional planning boards, the state of the economy in south-eastern England, the use of synthetic oestrogens in agriculture, church schools, the College of Further Education in Bletchley, part-time teachers, schoolchildren, religious education, the teaching and research costs at universities, Mr Speaker's conference on electoral law, the Railway Board's design office and staff, export awards, exports generally, speeches and resolutions by farmers and farmers' organisations, health and medicine, disposable syringes, electrically-operated house-chairs, questions of general medical practice, hormones in poultry products and their "effects on man", new drugs, the activities of the Home Office in respect of telephone tapping, hospitals, cervical cancer, Clare Hall hospital, Bletchley maternity hospital, Chelmsford St John's hospital, service costs and professional advice, housing building standards, the sale of council houses, houses for Londoners, British service personnel in Kenya, interventions chasing the Ministry of Labour on training facilities for girls, on the TSR2 aircraft project and redundancies there, land reclamation, local government and air pollution, the brick industry, the Board for Prices and Incomes, decimal currency, housekeeper allowances, purchase tax, teaching aids, corrections to the Official Report (*Hansard*), British overseas diplomatic commercial offices, pensions and the national income, together with family allowances and appeals on industrial injury cases.
>
> Post Office - letters, delivery delays in North Buckinghamshire, the nuclear power programme of the Ministry of Fuel and Power. There were questions on the steel industry, on prices and incomes policy, on discussions with the Prime Minister of Israel, on a prime ministerial visit I paid to President de Gaulle in Paris, the issue of private hearings on prison committal orders, brick supplies, the Queen's Award for Industry, which I set up, railways and the services they

provided, British Rail's central design establishment at Derby, proposed rail closures - ahead of his time, here - and railway pensions.

Under the *Hansard* heading for Technology, we find his interest concentrates on the computer industry - years before that became fashionable - the Computer Advisory Unit and medical engineering; then there were questions on the telephone service, with particular local reference to the Bedford exchange, a query relating to the United Nations' Trade and Development Board's secretariat and a question on Vietnam.

The rest of his time, said Wilson, was his own, except for his speech on the Queen's Speech, four separate speeches on the Budget, the Judges' Remuneration Bill, the Monopolies and Mergers Bill, a motion of censure on the Government, the bill to abolish the death penalty, the Science and Technology Bill and eight times briefly and once at length on general and specific matters relating to technology. Wilson counted over 200 contributions in that first session of the 1964 Parliament. In addition, and almost in passing, he said there were 221 interventions by Maxwell at question time and in debates. Maxwell's own calculations were that in 12 months he had made 92 speeches or lengthy interventions in the Commons, asked 65 questions, written 215 letters to ministers, led 20 deputations, sent an average of 35 letters every day, addressed 115 public meetings in his constituency, interviewed more than 780 constituents, travelled 15,000 miles, made more than 6,000 telephone calls and sent out 2,500 letters of thanks to loyal supporters.

* * * * *

As usual, Maxwell's contemporaries were divided about him. Some of his colleagues in the Parliamentary Labour party were hostile, some of his opponents were friends. Tommy (later Lord) Balogh, the Hungarian economist who was himself subjected to an unremitting hostility which sprang in large part from his foreign birth, was to write of him:

He is a real, ardent entrepreneur, a species the number of which seems to have slumped to single figures in Britain today.... He produced a surplus in the accounts of the refreshment department in the House of Commons, a feat hardly ever equalled. It is easy to understand that he sometimes arouses opposition instead of help in his soaring success.

Tony Benn, with that distant distaste which the upper-class Briton reserves for Europeans, wrote into his diary[9]:

> He [Maxwell] really is rather a thrusting man who regards the House of Commons as a place where he can push himself.

That, of course, is not a quality which is commonplace among politicians nor expected of them.

In September 1965 Benn recorded that he met Maxwell at the Labour party conference and was told by him that he was determined to take up the question of modernising the Labour party machine[10]:

> Frankly, I don't want to get mixed up with Maxwell because it's really just a part of his campaign to get on the National Executive and he was honest enough to say it. On the other hand, he has got the resources and though I would never take a penny from him, if he does get some facts and figures out it certainly would be helpful.

Three days later he confided to his tape-recorder:

> I know Bob Maxwell is intending to do serious research and he is a potential ally. The big struggle with Maxwell is whether you allow him to use you or whether you use him. My firm intention is to keep some sort of control myself. But when you're wrestling with a millionaire you do start with something of a disadvantage.

The diaries suggest, however, that Mr Benn's biggest struggle was with his conscience. He wanted the advantages of Maxwell's resources but did not want to be obligated to him, an attitude with which Maxwell was to grow familiar over the years.

Jack Dunnett, a right-wing Labour MP for Nottingham and later President of the Football League, put his finger upon the difficulties Maxwell faced in the Commons when he wrote:

> It was quite clear from the outset that Bob would make his mark in the House of Commons because he was a vigorous speaker with something to say and he usually attracted quite a lot of attention. I for one always went in to listen to his speeches. Nevertheless, the House of Commons does not take kindly to those, who, notwithstanding their undoubted ability, attempt very early to impress such ability upon the House. It is regarded as usual to undertake a very long apprenticeship before expecting to achieve any success or to make any progress and this was something Bob soon discovered much to his obvious frustration. As he was not likely ever to surrender his habit which he had from the outset of stating facts purposefully, it was no mystery why he did not progress towards the Ministerial rank to which his talents and energy undoubtedly entitled him. But even if he had taken a more subdued role, while still showing that he had real

talent, I think that his independence of spirit would probably have prevented him from attaining high office.

Richard Crossman, another of Labour's inveterate diarists - though his diaries were usually composed at the weekends and were not truly daily records of events - accorded Maxwell a reluctant admiration, mainly because he got Crossman out of a hole when he was Leader of the House of Commons and therefore responsible for the services of the House. For some years the catering services of the Commons had made a substantial loss and it was growing. There were some excuses. Staff had to be paid for 52 weeks of the year when the House was in session for only 32 or 33 weeks, which meant that for a large part of the year the only revenue coming into the Catering Department was from the canteens, which served a depleted press, secretarial staff and others employed in the buildings. But it was also the fact that MPs dined and wined - especially wined - extremely cheaply and were determined not to end the arrangement which enabled them to do so. Maxwell, with reservations, took over the chair of the Catering sub-committee from the ailing Bessie Braddock, the Labour MP for Liverpool Exchange, more noted for her enthusiasm for professional boxing than the kitchen.

It took a lot to win the gratitude of Crossman or to wring a compliment from him, and even then it was certain not to be unalloyed. After the devaluation of November 1967 the Government was desperately keen on a Buy British campaign to keep up employment at home and reduce the costs of imports which were, of course, now higher. Crossman wrote in February 1968[11]:

> ....I had to ... see Bob Maxwell.... What a miraculous man that fellow is. However much people hate him, laugh at him, boo him and call him a vulgarian, he gets things done. If it wasn't for Bob Maxwell we would have got nowhere with this campaign. He was rebuked and got a terrible snub from the CBI - who said this was an anti-export campaign - but then he modified it to a Help Britain campaign and persuaded the CBI to support him.

Maxwell, he was writing a month later, was "that adventurous erratic creature", which was as near, probably, as he ever got to understanding him.

(Incidentally, the editor of Crossman's diaries, Janet Morgan, wrote in the first volume that Maxwell did not stand at the 1970 general election after an inquiry had been set up into "the financial dealings" of his company. Like much that Crossman himself wrote, that was inaccurate. He stood but was defeated.)

Sir Geoffrey Rippon, a Conservative opponent but later a close business colleague of Maxwell's, said of Maxwell's time in the Commons:

> No one could fail to be affected by his warmth and charm, his gift for personal friendship, and the range of his interests. The Refreshment Department in the House of Commons has never been the same since he shook it and its foundations.

But perhaps his best friends and greatest admirers were the Silkin brothers, John, Chief Whip in the first Wilson Government, and Sam, Attorney-General in the second. Maxwell had, they said, "the alliance of ability, courage and driving force" which had propelled their own father, Lewis, "from the obscurity of foreign parentage and the poverty of London's East End over obstacles which broke many but merely served to spur him on into the highest councils of the land". (Lewis Silkin was a member of Clement Attlee's post-war Labour Government. As Minister of Town and Country Planning he did more than any other individual to end the haphazard development which was disfiguring the face of Britain and he was the "father" of the new towns which were planned or started after the war.) In their contribution to the 60th birthday book, the Silkins wrote:

> Two generations of the Silkin family have received and welcomed the friendship of Robert Maxwell. Between them, they have acted as his solicitor, his counsel, his fellow directors, his deputy chairmen, his chief whip, his delegation leader, his personal adviser and his draftsman. They have seen him in his moments of apparently irretrievable disaster, his years of carefully planned and executed reconstruction and his ultimate time of triumph. They have been the recipients of the hospitality and the generosity of a friend and of he sharpness and determination to drive a hard bargain of the businessman at arm's length. They have fought him and fought for him and sometimes in fighting him they have fought for him. They have exhausted themselves for him, despaired of him, laughed with him and at him, and taken pride in him.... They have seen him grow from a big man with his feet on a foothill to a giant astride a mountain peak.... In the whole of Bob's complex character there is not an ounce of malice or viciousness. It is surely that which makes one willing to accept from him, sometimes with a feeling of amused resignation, that which from others would be beyond the normal claims of friendship....

None of this, of course, impressed his old adversary, Crossbencher in the *Sunday Express*, who predictably called him a "gasbag" and repeatedly advised him to "belt up", advice which, however heartfelt, would, if followed by all those upon whom Crossbencher bestowed it, leave his column half empty on most Sundays.

On the other hand, the *Daily Mail*'s parliamentary correspondent, Eric Sewell, who was later a Conservative parliamentary candidate, put Maxwell among the Top Ten "who can delight or surprise or who are apt to be in the centre of the trouble". He went on[12]:

> Mr Maxwell came into the Commons with flattering promptness on the first day of the present Parliament, made his maiden speech two-and-a-half hours later and hasn't stopped talking since.
>
> He has speechified, questioned, interrupted, attacked, and defended, with passionate relentlessness, on topics from cancer to brick supply. Equipped with a self-confidence verging on brashness, and a deep, powerful voice that can outcry all irritated protests, he has yet to find a parliamentary situation into which he fears to put his foot.

* * * * *

In his tribute to Maxwell, quoted above, Wilson tactfully overlooked one intervention by the MP for Buckingham which infuriated him at the time and which irritated most of the rest of the Parliamentary Labour party, not least because it delayed a speech by the Prime Minister, speaking second at the start of a two-day debate on foreign and defence matters, well beyond the deadlines of the evening newspapers, leaving whatever late space there was for the Conservative spokesman, R.A. Butler.

Maxwell had been appointed to the Estimates Committee of the Commons when it was set up in November 1964. The Committee's function is to scrutinise government spending, and it should keep a particularly beady eye on supplementary estimates over and above the promised government spending limits for the year. In theory, the House can reject the estimates. In practice, it never does. Over the years, supplementary estimates were presented to the House as a formality and were used as the pretext for a general debate relating to one of the issues contained within them. But the estimates themselves and the reason for them were never considered by the House as a whole. On December 16, 1964 supplementary estimates totalling some £60 million were presented for agreement "on the nod". But Maxwell rose to complain:

> The Estimates Committee has had very little time, if any, to consider them. We are talking about £60 million. I regret very much that, by

arrangement between the two Front Benches, an opportunity is not being given to debate these supplementary estimates. Contrary to general belief, backbench Members of Parliament have no real opportunity to control Government expenditure.

In particular, he singled out a request by the Foreign Office for an extra £9.7 million when it was not doing enough to promote British exports. The official record of parliamentary debates, *Hansard*, neutralises the cat-calls, heckling, jeers and ribaldry of the Commons which has become familiar to radio listeners by inserting a single word [Interruption] into its report, especially when an MP's words are drowned by the noise. By the end of Maxwell's second paragraph the House was getting restless (so were the journalists, of whom I was one, in the Press Gallery above the chamber; we were all there to hear the Prime Minister, not the MP for Buckingham). So when he continued, *Hansard* recorded:

> There is a fiction abroad that Members of Parliament control the money spent by Government Departments. [Interruption] I knew that some of this was wishful thinking, but I did not realise until I came into the House [Interruption] how much of a rubber-stamping organisation the House of Commons had become.

> The Chairman: Order. I hope that the Committee will give the Chair an opportunity to hear the hon. Gentleman.

> Mr Maxwell: The House of Commons in its function of controlling Government expenditure has become something which is shockingly exemplified by the procedure for these supplementary estimates. Hon. Members will have noted in paragraph 2 of the Estimates Committee's memorandum —

> Mr Thomas Steele (Dunbartonshire, West, Labour): On a point of order, Dr King. Is it in order for the hon. Member to read his speech?

Strictly it isn't, but as Dr King reminded MPs, it was in order to use "copious notes", and Maxwell retorted that the last time Mr Steele had spoken he had read his speech too. And so it went on. There was another [Interruption] followed by a Tory MP, Anthony Fell, protesting:

> There is such a noise coming from the other (Labour) side that I cannot hear what the hon. Gentleman is saying.

Dr King told him the noise was coming from both sides, something which Mr Fell knew perfectly well. His only desire was to make matters worse and increase the Prime Minister's obvious annoyance and he promptly repeated his complaint. Maxwell restarted and had reached his third sentence when another Conservative, Sir Rolf Dudley Williams, contributed a totally mystifying point of order which Dr King ignored. At the end of his next sentence [Interruption] was recorded again and Dr King told the House:

> Disorder and noise only prolong the time taken by the present speaker and make it more difficult for us to get on.

Another Labour MP, Eric Ogden, intervened and Nicholas Ridley, later a member of Mrs Thatcher's Cabinet, tried to do so. Finally, John Biggs-Davison (Chigwell, Con) rose to praise Maxwell for "the courage and temerity" with which he had made his speech. It had been one of those interludes which frequently give the Commons a bad name to an uncomprehending public outside Westminster.

But it did nothing to halt the flow of Maxwell's speeches, questions - especially on constituency matters - articles, ideas and actions which continued to fall, inexhaustibly, upon willing and unwilling ears and eyes alike. He accused the Conservative former Chancellor, Reginald Maudling, of inviting businessmen to start a run on sterling and Maudling demanded an apology. Maxwell refused. Maudling's friends in the City of London, he said[13],

> will all testify to the fact that his actions have encouraged British businessmen in buying sterling forward in such quantities as to do us incalculable harm.

And Maudling had to be satisfied, or dissatisfied, with that. Mr James Ramsden, a former junior defence minister, fared no better on March 10, 1965, after Maxwell had accused him of making a significant change in the *Hansard* report of a speech he made during the closing months of Sir Alec Douglas-Home's Government six months after he delivered it. Ramsden said it was a reporter's error - as it was. Maxwell said he hadn't accused Ramsden of doing anything dishonourable, but he described him and his colleagues in the former administration as "incompetent twerps" and declared that there was evidence that in defence matters "they cooked the books to suit their party instead of making sure that our country was adequately defended". The charges blew up into another classic House of Commons row, with Sir Alec and other former ministers rising indignantly to complain, but the really poisonous contribution came from Sir Rolf Dudley Williams, one of the most unpleasant MPs to sit in the Commons during the post-war period.

Rising on a point of order, he said:

> I was only going to say that I agree that we must accept remarks from the hon. Member for Buckingham which are foreign to the House....

The Tories wouldn't let go of the issue and it was raised again the following day by Anthony Kershaw (Stroud), who repeated Maxwell's words about "cooking the books" and received a shout of "hear, hear" from the Buckingham MP for his pains. The Paymaster-General, Mr George Wigg, a former colonel, supported Maxwell, but claimed that he was the author of the phrase, having used it some seven years earlier. The row rambled on, as Commons rows do, for another 40 minutes that day before the supply of bogus points of order ran dry. Eventually it spilled over onto the Commons Order Paper, where a motion of censure upon Maxwell was tabled by Kershaw and a number of other Conservative MPs and countered by another from Michael Foot and 16 other Labour MPs. In the end it all faded away, and neither Ramsden nor his ex-ministerial colleagues got an apology. *The Times*'s parliamentary correspondent had no doubt what the uproar was all about:

> Mr Maxwell relaxed, smiling gently. He had set out to anger the Opposition and succeeded beyond his dreams.

This overlong turmoil was succeeded by other, more minor, rows with Edward Heath and a host more Conservative MPs, week after week and sometimes day after day. Maxwell was, in the strictly literal sense of the word, irrepressible, though the Liberal MP for Orpington, Eric Lubbock, did his best when he followed a 36-minute speech by Maxwell during a debate on technology by saying[14]:

> I am most relieved to be able to get into the debate at last. The hon. Member for Buckingham signalled to me before he rose to speak that he would make a short speech. I dread to think what it would have been like if it had been a long one. I hope that Crossbencher has been sitting with his stopwatch in the Gallery.... I hope that, in the next Honours List, the hon. Gentleman will be offered a seat in another place [the House of Lords] so that other people will have to suffer him instead of us.

History spoiled the jest. It was Lubbock who went to the Lords, inheriting the title of Lord Avebury. Maxwell remained a commoner.

An article in the *Illustrated London News* - now edited by his old colleague in post-war business, John Kisch - quoted Maxwell as saying[15]:

> I've come into the Commons as a moderniser - to halt the retreat of this country which has been going on for the past 50 years.

The magazine said there was "growing evidence" that a lot of people, including Maxwell's Labour colleagues, did not want to hear what he had to say, to which he retorted:

> I've got everything I want. Nobody can bribe me into silence.... The obstacles I have met since I have been in Parliament are beyond belief. But there's one difference between me and a lot of other members - I'm prepared to shout out.

And shout he did, especially on behalf of the ordinary soldier whom he thought was being over-stretched in Britain's still world-wide role. Though with the benefit of hindsight he might have amended his peroration to one speech in a debate on the Defence Estimates[16]:

> The poor bloody infantryman is the Queen of the battlefield.

Ever proper, the *Hansard* (official report) record of the debate changed "Queen" to "King".

But in a private letter to a scientist at the Department of Scientific and Industrial Research, he confessed:

> Having regard to the small majority, I am having to spend 60 to 70 hours a week at the Palace of Westminster and at times I am not terribly pleased with my success.

Though it is an ancient cliché, the House of Commons was then, and to a large extent still is, a club where the rules are understood rather than written down. Maxwell broke them. He denounced the all-night sittings as "an absurd way of running the country", but that was how the club liked to run the country. He did not display the patience which is required of a young man wishing to succeed; he did not observe the courtesies beyond the bare minimum; he used language ("incompetent twerps") which was regarded as vulgar; he was insensitive to interruption or murmurs of distaste; he intervened in debates he hadn't attended; and he won more publicity in one week than long-standing members had achieved over a period of years, which made him an upstart too. The House of Commons is generous towards failures and sympathises with those who are going nowhere. Conversely, it distrusts those whom it suspects are going somewhere. An MP only finally acquires genuine popularity when he is seen to have discarded all personal ambition. One political observer wrote of Maxwell in June 1965[17]:

> He came new to the House last October and sat himself down on the front row beyond the gangway with the mavericks, the clowns and the orators - the Marcus Liptons [Labour MP for Brixton and an amazingly successful self-publicist], the Emrys Hugheses [Keir Hardie's son-in-law and the only MP with a certificate proving his

sanity, given to him when he was discharged from an asylum], the
Michael Foots [15 years later, the leader of the Labour party].
Promptly, on the very first day, after the Prime Minister and the
Leader of the Opposition, up got Maxwell and made his maiden.
He's that sort of man. He breaks all the rules, has no idea of tact. He
has avoided being typecast as being on the Left or Right. The Left
can dislike him because he's rich. The Right because he's rude. The
Tories because he's not one of them. But the funny thing is many
Labour people have gradually come to feel, almost in spite of
themselves, a certain grudging respect. For one thing, he attacks the
enemy....

* * * * *

Outside the House, Maxwell tried to stampede the Labour party
into modernisation after disastrous results in the 1965 local
government elections, especially in the south of England, appeared
to doom the Government in the general election which could not be
long delayed. His prescription was sound, but the patient stubbornly
refused to accept it, as others both before and after him discovered.
In an article that year in *Tribune*[18] he attacked the lack of promotion
prospects for the staff of the party's headquarters, then Transport
House, the fact that only some 200 constituencies had full-time
agents (at the 1987 general election the figure was no more than 70),
the failure to commission professional surveys to discover why
different regions swung differently (not done until after the 1987
election), the lack of research facilities for MPs (not corrected for
another 10 years) and the failure to raise individual subscriptions
paid by party members. He concluded:

> Only a better-financed Labour party, modernised and reorganised
> from top to bottom, can be sure to maintain a Labour Government in
> office with a working majority for a sufficient number of years to
> enable our Government to implement fully the socialist policies for
> which our party stands.

It took another 20 years for that process of modernisation to
begin.

Maxwell helped to raise £10,000 for a new inquiry into the
workings of the party organisation. But the one that was held was
not, and was never intended to be, the radical inquiry he was
looking for. It was put into the safe hands - safe, that is, not to rock
the boat - of a foundrymen's union official and NEC member,
William Simpson. Simpson agreed with Maxwell that Labour MPs
should make a contribution towards the cost of servicing the

Parliamentary Labour party, but his report, essentially, was for not doing a lot about anything.

In a debate on the recommendations of an interim report by Simpson during the 1967 party conference - the last at Scarborough - Maxwell asked how the National Executive Committee could be trusted to carry out party reorganisation when they were the very people responsible for the inefficiency. They had not invited outsiders to sit on the committee and they had not asked constituency parties to submit evidence or make recommendations. He was scornful about those recommendations which had been made[19]:

> They have come forward with a recommendation for a graduated subscription for members. I wonder how many of them would like to go canvassing and would like to ask people to join the Labour party and be told, "Certainly, how much?" and then have to say, "I cannot tell you until I know how much you earn." What a lot of silly nonsense!

He urged that the party should consider setting up a commercial organisation to do its own printing, a publishing department which could make a huge profit, and a travel agency. There were all kinds of services which were needed by the trade unions, such as a design department which could bring union journals up to date and the party could provide them.

But Transport House was determined not to listen. Three weeks before the conference Maxwell had written an article in *The People* describing the party headquarters as a "ramshackle affair". He asked[20]:

> How can we persuade people that we are capable of modernising Britain when we can't even modernise ourselves? The truth is that the Labour party has been run in roughly the same way, and with the same rusty rule-book, for more than half a century.

The faults he identified were still there 20 years later. *The People* article continued:

> Labour has nobody working full-time on political education, nobody working full-time devising new election techniques, nobody organising cheap bulk-purchase of supplies for the constituencies. There is only one full-time TV and radio officer and only one person to help all the Labour council groups in the country. The research department, under-paid and understaffed, has a complete turnover of staff every five years because there is not a proper career structure.... At every level there is a shortage of equipment - cars, copying machines, teleprinters, tape-recorders, addressing machines, TV

aids. Harold Wilson's "rusty penny-farthing" crack [made in an inquiry report 12 years earlier] is an under-statement. In comparison with the Tories we haven't even invented the wheel.

Transport House - which Maxwell offensively renamed Heartbreak House - retaliated by refusing Maxwell a list of addresses for which he had asked, and which they had agreed to furnish, of Labour MPs, constituency parties and trade unions to whom he was intending to distribute copies of a pamphlet - written by Clive Bradley, a former senior official of the party - describing how Scandinavian socialist parties raised funds. Matters were not helped by Maxwell rejecting the Simpson inquiry report as "old-fashioned and inept" and adding: "I can tell them how to raise a million pounds without this", by which he meant his proposals for printing, publishing and travel agency services.

* * * * *

Nineteen-sixty-six was certain to be an election year. The Labour Government's tiny majority was disappearing as the strain of maintaining the Government in office became too much for some of the less robust members of the Parliamentary Labour party. The only question was whether it would be in the spring, summer or autumn. Relief came from a by-election in North Hull in January when Labour retained the seat with a greatly increased majority when most politicians, including a large number on the Labour side, expected it to be lost. Maxwell, however, won money in bets with Tory MPs and gave it to the Socialist Women's Circle which Betty had set up in the constituency. (I, too, struck a number of successful bets on that by-election, but all of mine were with gloomy Labour MPs.) The success was seen as making an early election inevitable, but defeat would have made it even more so because it would have reduced the majority to one at a time when it was known to the Prime Minister and the Chief Whip that another Labour MP, Harold Hayman (Redruth and Camborne), had little time left to live.

In the run-up to the election Maxwell's Commons activities continued without pause. He asked questions or made speeches about the site for a new town in North Buckinghamshire (eventually Milton Keynes was chosen), speed limits, exports to Africa, milk tests, defence, therapeutic abortions (he wanted abortion law reform), a Boeing 707 freighter crash at Tokyo and compensation for dispossessed tenant farmers.

Maxwell had had astonishing success with his local farmers, members of an industry notoriously hostile to Labour Governments, despite the fact that the post-war Attlee Government did more for its security than any administration before or since. Speaking to the Bucks branch of the National Farmers' Union, Maxwell was reported as saying:

> Gentlemen, I am on the side of the farmer, not because I like your blue eyes but because you have saved Britain £250 millions this year in foreign exchange.... There should be no problems for Britain today if other industries had expanded their production in the same way as you have done.... Farming deserves a fairer return for the capital invested and the hours worked. In the past, you have not been fairly rewarded for the increase in productivity you have achieved.... Gentlemen, the aim of the Government is to raise farm incomes....

The chairman of the branch hoped that Maxwell would speedily become the Minister of Agriculture. After he had received a deputation of Bletchley farmers incensed about the annual agricultural price review, its leader confessed:

> I am going to make a remark I never thought I would make in public. I would like to thank Mr Maxwell.... He was the only MP who would receive a delegation, knowing full well that not many of us would vote for him.

He was a guest at the NFU's annual dinner and attended the Police Ball and the opening of a new branch of his local newspaper; he welcomed a stream of government ministers to his highly marginal seat and heard the deputy leader of the Labour party, George Brown, the second most important man in the Government, say of Pergamon Press[21]:

> If every industry sold abroad such a high percentage of its output, there would be no balance of payments problems.

It was announced in February that the Queen would be visiting Maxwell's constituency on April 4 (as it turned out, four days after the general election, which had not then been confirmed) and that Maxwell would be among those presented to her, which could not have harmed his vote when the time came. The date of March 31 for polling day was announced on February 28, exactly 500 days after the previous one. Everywhere there was the usual scramble to adopt candidates and get the local campaigns under way. A Maxwell slogan - "Back Harold and Bob to finish the job" - brought the retort from Mrs Kellett that it was "rather typical of that retiring, shy violet". She would, she said, fight to bring back truth, honesty and decency into politics. Maxwell was unanimously re-adopted to fight the seat and promised:

> Under no circumstances will I indulge in personalities or smears.

A local newspaper reported the news that he would again be contesting the seat for Labour with the headline:

> The man the Tories love to hate adopted as Labour candidate.

Maxwell had to fight the election with a different agent, Bryan Barnard having relinquished the post some months earlier in the hope of getting a parliamentary seat himself. The new agent, Jim Lyons, one of the most experienced in the party, said he hoped to help Maxwell increase his majority.

The Liberal candidate was John Cornwall, whose hat Maxwell had promised to eat if the Liberals hadn't lost their deposit at the previous election. Mr Cornwall made the fatal mistake of announcing that he hoped, at least, to come a good second. In the event, he came a bad third and the Liberal deposit was forfeited again.

The promise of a clean fight was maintained, leading one Buckinghamshire reporter to write:

> Those people who live in the Buckingham constituency and who remember the 1959 general election - the first in which Mr Robert Maxwell took part as a Labour candidate - must be wondering what has happened this time because EVERYONE IS TOO NICE REALLY! Seldom, if indeed at all, does one hear the "foreigner" slur on the Labour candidate. Nowadays, it is, "Where's your Rolls Royce?".... There is nothing more vicious than that. In those years ... since 1959, Mr Maxwell has matured. No one can deny that during his short term in office, Mr Maxwell has done a good job as a "local" MP.

Though the opinion polls favoured Labour - the new Tory leader, Edward Heath, had failed to make an impact on the voters - Buckingham was bound to be a hard fight. Heath himself, in an infelicitous remark, was reported by local Tories as saying that if there was a place where a man ought to be replaced by a woman, it was in the general election at Buckingham.

The number of voters in the constituency had gone up by over 6,000 since 1959 and the newcomers were certainly not all Labour. The south of England was at the start of its swing against the Labour party which was by 1987 virtually to wipe out all Labour representation outside London. One of the biggest worries was the weather. March was its usual self, a mixture of sunshine, winds, snow and blizzards. Maxwell made few speeches and concentrated on answering questions, despite the risk that involved with hecklers. Dealing with them, he explained, "is like marriage - it cannotbe described, only experienced". Mrs Kellett was angered by an accusation he made that the Conservatives would put up prescription charges and called Maxwell a liar. He retorted that he had no intention of replying in kind to her "shrill abuse". She declared that she was in favour of restoring capital punishment, knowing that Maxwell had voted against it. She also said that she was not worried about the ever-shortening odds on a Labour victory.

Seeing that those odds had reached 20-1 on Labour with the leading election bookmakers, Ladbroke's, her optimism owed more to blind faith than a knowledge of betting. Maxwell himself was quoted at five-to-one on. Mrs Kellett's final claim, at her eve-of-poll meeting, that she would win by 100 votes was virtually an admission that she couldn't win. But to help remove any doubt, government ministers came to the constituency in good number, headed by George Brown - a far cry from 1959 when Maxwell received the minimum support from the party's Front Bench. At his eve-of-poll meeting Maxwell was asked why, as he was a millionaire, he was a socialist and answered:

> The fact that I have made a couple of bob, the fact that I have made good in business life, has not, and never will, turn me against my class.

On polling day itself the weather was perfect and the electors flocked to cast their vote. The percentage poll was slightly down compared with 1964, 85.7 instead of 86.5, but the numbers voting for the Labour and Conservative candidates was up. Maxwell showed an increase of 1,769 and Mrs Kellett 996. Result:

Robert Maxwell (Lab)	24,854
Elaine Kellett (Con)	22,600
John Cornwall (Lib)	4,914
Majority	2,254

The total cost of Maxwell's campaign was just under £943. Mrs Kellett spent £879 and Cornwall £504, which included his lost £150 deposit. The swing to Labour was only one per cent this time, less than the average for the country as a whole, where Labour's majority of seats over the Conservatives was 110. Mrs Kellett decided not to contest the seat a further time. Maxwell had once again wagered profitably with Conservative Members of

Parliament. James Dance (Bromsgrove) sent him a cheque for £25, "which is what I think I owe you for our bet on the result of the election", Frank Taylor, a Manchester MP, sent another £20 and Sir Charles Taylor (Eastbourne) contributed £10, via his secretary.

George Brown had told an election meeting that Maxwell would be important to the next Labour Government, but 12 days after the election Maxwell wrote to a friend:

> I have let it be known in the proper quarters that I am not available for junior office, not because I am big-headed but because I have considerable commitments to Pergamon and to our export drive, and I have not been long enough in Parliament to deserve senior office. Therefore, you can rest assured that the result of this massive win for Labour will be that I shall once again be able to devote the bulk of my time to Pergamon.... The Government must now use its mandate to recover and restore the economic well-being of the country and I am very optimistic that with a little bit of luck we will be successful.

That luck was not forthcoming. Within a few weeks the catastrophic seamen's strike had begun. Before it had finished, irreparable damage had been done to the economy, to foreign confidence in the pound sterling and to the future electoral prospects of the Labour party. Exports were held up but imports continued to come in. If devaluation were not already inevitable, the strike made it so and Maxwell probably regretted that before it was over he had confidently predicted there would be no devaluation, even though it was still 15 months away.

There was a more immediate consequence of the strike which was to confound Maxwell. In the debate on the Queen's Speech opening the new Parliament he had commended the Government for preserving the voluntary principle in relation to Prices and Incomes and he illustrated his thinking on employee and employer relations which was to develop over the years and cause several angry confrontations with the trade unions. He told the Commons on April 21 that while he welcomed the Government's new Prices and Incomes Bill which preserved "the vital voluntary principle" of negotiations between employers and employees, it would require a change of attitude on the part of the trade unions:

> Success can be achieved only by striking a bargain with the trade unions to accept a new and important principle for themselves, namely, that they also have a responsibility for productivity. Until now, the trade unions negotiators have said that they are paid by their members in order to ensure that their members receive maximum wages, and to ensure that conditions of employment are improved. When management speaks to the trade unions about

productivity, the trade unions say that this is the responsibility of management. In the past, that attitude of the trade unions was quite understandable, because all along they have feared, and still fear, a return to unemployment.

But the Labour Government, he argued, by introducing redundancy payments and retraining and maintaining full employment, despite a severe economic crisis, had a right to ask the trade unions now to accept responsibility for productivity increases.

Wage negotiations should be conducted on a national basis only for minimum national scales and any additional increases should be achieved by negotiations on a plant-to-plant basis.

Maxwell rejected the Conservative party's proposals for solving industrial relations problems by "introducing legislation which would fine members of unions" who struck unofficially. "Our jails would not be big enough", he declared.

(When he assumed control of Mirror Group Newspapers, nearly 20 years later, he insisted upon higher productivity from the beginning. Ironically, though, he was only able to achieve it without much greater disruption because of the Conservative Government's legislation to limit the opportunity of trade unions to strike or take some other form of industrial action.)

But the voluntary principle which Maxwell commended in May was abandoned by July. Harold Wilson returned from an official visit to Moscow to introduce the most drastic restrictions to save the economy which was on its knees because of the strike. Among other measures, he announced a six-month pay and prices freeze. Voluntaryism was out and compulsion was in and it stayed in until 1969. Relations with the trade unions were so badly impaired that when Mrs Barbara Castle sought, in her White Paper, *In Place of Strife*, to introduce modest reforms of union practice, the unions refused to co-operate (and suffered much more under later Conservative Governments as a consequence). The seeds of the 1970 general election defeat were liberally sown within weeks of the 1966 victory.

But few were looking that far ahead that summer. Despite promising to devote more of his energies to his business - and he bought several small companies during 1966 - Maxwell found time to join the NATO parliamentarians, which involved trips to Europe, as well as becoming involved in the Left of Centre group of MPs, to raise £10,000 for the hoped-for intensive inquiry into the Labour party's organisation and become treasurer of the Attlee Appeal Fund. The number of questions he asked of ministers scarcely abated, and ranged from his support for Britain's entry into the Common Market to the new town for North Buckinghamshire.

He also significantly retreated from his earlier rejection of capital punishment. After the murder of three London policemen, he said he would support the re-introduction of hanging for the murder of policemen and prison officers on duty, arguing that the death sentence would be a deterrent; however, confining hanging to those who murdered police or prison officers has no logic (what if they are off duty or in plain clothes at the time of their death?). If it is a deterrent to one type of murder, then it must be a deterrent to other classes. In fact, hanging has never been convincingly shown to be a deterrent to any type of murder; policemen were killed by criminals both before and after the death penalty was abolished. But instinctively, as opposed to rationally, he believes in an eye for an eye. He is tempted today to advocate the execution of terrorists, but recognises the dangers in creating martyrs and the fact that retaliation in the form of taking hostages as an insurance against the death penalty would almost certainly follow. He had little support from the Labour side for his change in position, but he was loyally backed at that time by his agent Jim Lyons.

Less contentiously, in 1966 Maxwell published a new book on Chequers, the country home of Prime Ministers in Buckinghamshire, and sent proof copies of it to former Prime Ministers, including Lord Attlee, asking if they would like to contribute any of their thoughts about it. Lord Attlee's reply was as economical in the use of notepaper as he customarily was in the use of words. It was on a sheet headed "The Countess Attlee". The word "Countess" was struck out and "Earl" inserted. The address at the top of the notepaper was the Attlees' old one at Great Missenden. That was deleted with a large "X" and his current address, a flat in King's Bench Walk in the Temple, had been scrawled in the top right-hand corner. He had gone to the Temple after his wife's death in 1964 and clearly thought that at 83 it was not worth getting any new notepaper printed. The reply said:

Dear Mr Maxwell,
Thank you for sending me the proof of the book on Chequers. I think that the extract which you already have from my book is an adequate contribution from me. More would be presumptuous.
  Yours sincerely,
  Attlee

* * * * *

In November 1966 Sir Cyril Black, Conservative MP for Wimbledon, a Baptist, and a strict and unwavering upholder of an unyielding concept of Christian morality, launched a private prosecution against a book, *Last Exit to Brooklyn*, by a then unknown American author, Hubert Selby, jnr. Sir Cyril was a type of MP rare in his own day and unknown today. An unkind but not unfair portrait of him by Jon Bradshaw in *Queen* magazine described him thus:

> Sir Cyril is very much an Old Testament Christian, in the oldest, the purest, biblical sense. An eye for an eye. A tooth for a tooth. He knows that within the last twenty-five years there has been a lamentable decline in the country's moral and spiritual values. And knowing he holds the minority view, he has nonetheless taken to the field to do battle. Sir Cyril believes in capital punishment and in birching; he is a lifelong teetotaller and non-smoker, strongly disapproving of gambling, mini-skirts, liqueur chocolates, homosexuality, socialism, fornication, the laxity of Sunday religious observance, strip clubs, modern morality, the immorality of television, divorce, psychiatry and pornographic literature. He is, he believes, on the side of the angels.

> Sir Cyril is the perfect Puritan, a spiritual throwback…. A burly, singularly pale and hairless man … he laments the demise of piety and fights, with vigour, against the profane. His is the old ethic damming the rising tide. Toying still with God's final purpose, Sir Cyril Wilson Black is in prim pursuit of his ends, pious and purse-proud, this long-pated patriarch, the last, perhaps, of his sallow tribe.

Sir Cyril's legal action led to *Last Exit to Brooklyn* being accorded a literary merit which it did not possess. Its writing was of a better quality than the soft and hard porn books which were to flood the market from the 1960s onwards, but not significantly so. It was not of the same quality, say, as *Tropic of Cancer*. The publication of even more explicit novels and collections of short stories than *Last Exit* is commonplace today. The book was published by the small London firm of avant-garde publishers Calder and Boyars. Sir Cyril was appalled by it and sought an order from the magistrate, Leo Gradwell, at the Marlborough Street Magistrates' Court for its seizure, forfeiture and destruction under the terms of the Obscene Publications Act of 1959. Among those whom he asked to give evidence on behalf of the prosecution was Robert Maxwell. There was no doubt that Maxwell shared Sir Cyril's views about pornographic literature, though not on everything else. There was no doubt, either, that he believed Britain was facing a moral decline. His early rabbinical studies and strict upbringing helped form his character and his outlook on such matters. He had also fathered nine children and was fiercely protective of them. *Last Exit* was not a book which he would have wanted - or, indeed, permitted - any of them to read. He agreed to Sir Cyril's request to give evidence.

Should he have done? Was it right? And if it was right, was it worth it?

His attraction to Sir Cyril was not that he was the father of a large family, nor the fact that he was a Labour MP, though both mattered. The essential point was that he was an important publisher of a large number of books. But for a publisher to assume the role of censor was bound to bring the wrath of other publishers, as well as authors - including Samuel Beckett and Brigid Brophy - down upon him. He would answer that this was of no concern to him. The book was sufficiently "dirty" for it to be banned. He told the court that he was "horrified" at this "brutal and filthy" book, saying[22]:

> I am against censorship, but what I do feel is that a publisher is given a privilege ... to disseminate information and literature and also has a responsibility to censor himself to prevent this kind of muck being traded under the respectable imprint of a publishing house and holding up his membership of the Publishers' Association to do so ... a halt has got to be called.

The defence naturally argued that the book was of literary merit - a defence under the Obscene Publications Act, though, logically, it would seem that a pornographic book of literary merit was more likely to "corrupt and deprave" than a book without it - and its counsel had the following exchange with Maxwell[23]:

> Would you consider that the Decameron should be censored?
> What is the Decameron?....
> From what you know of New York does it sound a true picture?
> Not from what I know of New York.
> Does it depict any kind of social condition that you recognise?
> All it depicts to me is that it is the dirty book of the month....
> What do you think happens to someone reading the book?
> I can only answer for myself. As a publisher I am horrified to be a member of the same association as your client; that he uses this honourable profession to disseminate this kind of muck for profit. I am horrified that any one of my eight children may be exposed to this kind of filth.

After Mr Gradwell ordered the forfeiture and destruction of *Last Exit*, Calder and Boyars decided not to appeal, but John Calder said he would continue to sell the book in Britain. Eighteen eminent publishers, though declining to comment on the merits of the book, wrote a letter to *The Times* about Maxwell's statement that he was horrified to be a member of the same association as Calder and Boyars. They declared:

> ... We would like to affirm that we are happy to have Messrs Calder and Boyars as colleagues.

Maxwell cared nothing for what his fellow-publishers thought of him. He had had no time for them since the Simpkin Marshall affair. He told the London *Evening News*:

> I don't withdraw a single word. I am astonished that a group of distinguished publishers should refuse to admit that if the community gives them the privilege to disseminate information and entertainment they also have a responsibility to discipline themselves not to distribute pornography under the guise of literature.

Nor did he worry about *The Spectator* describing him as a reactionary. His denunciation of *Last Exit* as a book written "only for profit" induced Bernard Levin, among others, to point out that profit was the reason why Maxwell was a publisher; but that was a fallacious argument unless he means profit at any price.

Today *Last Exit* would barely be noticed on the bookshelves and the claim that it had literary merit might find few advocates. It sold well because of its notoriety. Had Sir Cyril Black said and done nothing, it would have reached a far more restricted audience. Maxwell had entered a battle which, though temporarily successful, could not in the long run be won. In the end, that which is censored achieves a wider publication, as the revelations of the former MI5 agent, Peter Wright, in his book *Spycatcher* testified in 1987. In most cases the most effective answer to those who say "Publish and be damned" is "Let them publish and be silent."

But Maxwell had no regrets and refused to accept any expenses from Sir Cyril's solicitors. A proposal by him that the book trade should itself set up a committee to vet allegedly-pornographic books before publication was overwhelmingly rejected by publishers, authors and others concerned. He did receive a large number of letters from those, including headmasters, who supported him, but it was an episode which many of his friends found it difficult to understand.

In and Out

With all the temptations and degradations that beset it, politics is still the noblest career that any man can choose.

F.S. Oliver

Maxwell wrote in a 1966 Christmastide report to his constituents that he had "attended regularly at the House of Commons and have played my full part in debate". The *Hansard* volumes for the 1966-67 session bear that out, but his trips abroad gave him a bad record in the division lobbies. In 435 divisions he voted on only 124 occasions, the worst performance of the 24 members of Labour's Home Counties group of MPs. His absence provoked one of his local newspapers, the *Wolverton Express*, into a stinging criticism. In a leading article early in 1967 it said:

> More than one-third of the area of the Buckingham parliamentary constituency and over one-half of its electorate are directly affected by the Milton Keynes New Town.... Those with problems, however, are quite unable to turn to the member, Mr Robert Maxwell, for advice or assistance. He is at present halfway through a globe-trotting tour selling encyclopaedias. Mr Maxwell's six-week tour has been described as an important attempt to boost the export of British books. If successful, it will also have the effect of increasing his personal fortune as well as adding to the welfare of the company's shareholders and employees.... When the pay of MPs was paltry it was claimed that they could not exist without a background job. Now that they receive a realistic salary, their fulltime allegiance should be with the people they represent.

The cry that Members of Parliament should have no outside paid occupation is as old as it is illogical. It would debar lawyers, journalists, authors and businessmen from continuing using the skills which might have won them their seats in the first place. But it has always had a superficial attraction to the voters and when it is voiced by a local newspaper against a local member it can be damaging. In fact, the attack was grossly unfair, but the effect was to ensure that a suspicious eye was kept on Maxwell every time he went abroad.

The trip the paper complained about had taken Maxwell to India, Thailand, Japan, Hong Kong, Indonesia, Malaya, Singapore, Australia, New Zealand, Mexico, Canada and the United States and had mainly taken place during the Christmas recess. The itinerary had been arranged before he had secured a "pair", a Conservative MP with whom he could have an agreement not to vote while he was away. The justification for the mission - that it would earn £2 million in foreign currency at a time when every penny was needed - was not one likely to impress even his old friend John Silkin, the Government's Chief Whip. It certainly gave ammunition to his enemies in Buckingham. The Liberal candidate at the previous year's election, John Cornwall, complained that Maxwell had only made five speeches in the Commons in the previous 10 months (in four of which the Commons had not met). That was the opposite of the complaint of the Liberal party in the Commons who thought Maxwell's interventions were too frequent. The new Conservative agent in Buckingham, Joseph French, piously protested that letters in the local press - largely written by Conservative supporters - about "the absence of a certain MP" had been "a little bit nasty", but his further thought that Maxwell could have "flogged" his encyclopaedias around the world by using "paid stooges" suggested that the sympathy was synthetic. Maxwell's area whip, Will Howie, a Luton MP, later wrote to complain that he had voted in fewer than half the divisions since the previous April and suggested he should pair "less frequently" in order to improve his voting record. But he vigorously defended himself upon his return, telling constituents at Bletchley:

> If only 50 more people were doing for the country what I have been doing, there would not be a pay-freeze nor a balance of payments problem.

Despite the criticism of his absences, even John Cornwall had to admit, "As yet I have not found fault with Mr and Mrs Maxwell's work for individual constituents." Week after week the local newspapers detailed Maxwell's activities. He urged a new further education college for Bletchley, saw deputations from teachers wanting salary increases, attacked the closure of Buckingham hospital, attended a railwaymen's reunion, led a deputation to the

Ministry of Transport about the closure of Castlethorpe station, defended radio amateurs against new wireless telegraphy legislation, won a payment from an insurance company for a constituent who tripped over a broken manhole, got an automatic Mini for a disabled ex-serviceman, fought the closure of a local foundry, supported petitions on air pollution and noisy fire sirens in a quiet village, attacked a water price rise and council rent increases, and compelled British Rail to start a (successful) search for a missing artificial leg belonging to an old age pensioner. When one of the parish councils in his constituency complained that he hadn't answered a letter from it, he won an apology when the council found that the clerk hadn't sent it.

Most effective of all was his intervention in September 1967 in a damaging pay and productivity dispute at Vauxhall Motors, Luton, where thousands of Buckinghamshire men and women worked. Twenty-five of them, all Maxwell constituents, turned up at the Labour Hall in Bletchley one evening and asked him to try to settle it. The next day he negotiated a truce and got deadlocked talks reopened. Some of the workers concerned even went to their local newspaper, the *North Bucks Times*, to express their gratitude. The East Midlands organiser of the National Union of Building Workers, Arthur Leary, wrote to Maxwell:

> I could not let the occasion pass without ... expressing my personal appreciation for your efforts during the last week....
>
> Circumstances were such that they needed a strong character with the right kind of background and drive to make the company face up to reality. You were obviously the right man in the right place at the right time....

The irony was that Leary had been the man who, because of a dispute with Maxwell, had denied to Betty Maxwell the help of key party workers when she stood at Newport Pagnell as Labour's candidate in the Buckinghamshire county council elections. Soon afterwards Leary was sacked from his post in the union. Maxwell protested and he and Will Howie were instrumental in getting him reinstated.

Also during this period, when he was being accused of neglecting his public duties for his private business, he organised the raising of desperately-needed finance for Centre 42, of which he had become treasurer. The number in the Centre's title derived from resolution 42 of the 1960 Trades Union Congress which urged the unions to play a more active part in cultural activities. Under Arnold Wesker, it ambitiously tried to raise £600,000 - and achieved less than

£40,000 towards its target, and some of that was in promises, not cash. An even more ambitious attempt to raise £750,000 was quickly abandoned and it set its sights on getting enough money - £27,000 - to acquire the freehold of its premises, the Round House, at Chalk Farm, London. Maxwell asked the Prime Minister and Mrs Wilson to host a reception for Centre 42 at 10 Downing Street - he and another socialist millionaire, Harold Lever, footing the bill - and Maxwell sent out the invitations. All references to money were struck out of the letters to prospective guests and (wealthy) patrons of the arts, but they did not need to be told what the function was about. Ten days after the reception the £27,000 was in the bank.

No wonder that his party agent in his report for 1967 was able to say:

> In addition to giving his usual outstanding service to his constituents, Bob Maxwell has, during the last 12 months, come rapidly to the fore in national affairs. Besides being Treasurer of the Earl Attlee Memorial Fund, investigating the possibilities of a national daily Labour newspaper and numerous other activities, he is now the secretary - and doubtless the driving force - of the "I'm Helping Britain" movement. I doubt if any other backbench MP of any party has appeared so often on television or is so well-known.

In a message to youth in his constituency, Maxwell dwelt once more on ethics and morality and the advantage of character over formal education[1]:

> The important lesson for all to learn is that the achieving of their maximum must always be their aim and that character and determination count in the long run quite as much as anything else. Whether we like it or not, much of life is a battle and a struggle (even for the sons of the wealthy) and children must be taught to persevere and hold their own ... there is a virtue in determined, consistent hard work and effort.

> Even with effort, however, not everybody can achieve academic success and a parent whose children try hard but meet with little recognition should not feel disappointed. Unfortunately, clever children have become a status symbol for their parents, so that having a son with nine O-levels or an IQ of 140 is almost as good as having a second car or a swimming pool. This attitude is more than unfortunate, it is dangerous and damaging to the bright and the less-bright child, both of whom are forced more and more to the conclusion that nothing is really as important as academic success: that qualities of character, courage, persistence, determination, honesty, loyalty and self-discipline are not valued as highly as O-level passes.... It is all too easy to equate an aristocracy of brains with a university degree.... It is this false standard which contributes so

much to the preservation of a class-consciousness which is so wasteful of the country's talents.

It is easy to see that in that speech Maxwell was talking about himself and his own origins and lack of formal education.

While Maxwell laboured and philosophised, the local Conservatives chose a new candidate to fight for the seat, William Benyon, a 37-year-old farmer and landowner, who naturally - and rightly, as it turned out - claimed "We can win this seat."

* * * * *

Maxwell made a strong attempt in 1967 to win one of the vacant seats in the constituency party section of Labour's National Executive Committee created by the decisions of Jim Callaghan and Richard Crossman not to seek re-election. (Callaghan stood, instead, for the post of Treasurer and easily beat Michael Foot.) At a time when the party, under the pressure of unpopular government measures, was moving strongly to the left, he had no real hope of succeeding despite promises from parliamentary colleagues - including Bob Mellish, who pledged him 4,000 votes from Bermondsey - to give him their support. What little chance he may have had disappeared with his advocacy of entry into the Common Market, which was not to the way of thinking of constituency party activists, and by a speech he made at the party conference in defence of the public schools on the very day that delegates were casting their votes.

The abolition of all fee-paying schools is an article of faith for most rank-and-file members of the Labour party. They don't expect it to happen, but they will not accept the heresy that there might be any merit in them. Maxwell told the conference he was in favour of "integrating" the schools into the public system, not abolishing them. A vote for abolition, merely because Labour envied and hated the schools, would send hundreds of thousands of voters flocking to the Conservative party at the next general election. He warned:

> If you decide to say, "Let's destroy these schools", you would be making a very grave error, indeed.

He was hissed and booed and interrupted with shouts of "shame" and "disgraceful" when he went on to say that he had eight children and would send to public schools "those in need of going there". (In fact, two had gone to fee-paying schools and five to state schools, and Michael, the eldest, had never recovered from his road accident in 1961.)

When the results of the voting were announced the next morning, Maxwell's vote was only 54,000, nearly 300,000 below what he needed to win. (The following year he did better and got 92,000 votes, but it was still a long way below a winning total.) The public schools speech must have at least halved his prospective support.

Earlier in the year his speeches about the Common Market had begun to get him into trouble. The Labour party's Director of Publicity, Percy Clark, refused to circulate to newspapers and the broadcasting services the text of one of them. He delivered it, nonetheless, telling his constituents on April 29 at Bletchley:

> From 1954 to 1955 Britain was offered by the present Common Market and EFTA (European Free Trade Association) countries the leadership of Europe and we turned it down contemptuously time after time because of the mistaken belief that we still had the resources and the power to play alone in the super-power league…. Our bargaining power is less today than it was at the time of the Heath negotiations (1963) because the Common Market position has got stronger and ours, unfortunately, weaker. It is exceedingly dangerous for the Prime Minister and other influential people to allow it to get about that if it had not been for de Gaulle our application would have succeeded last time. This is just not true. The difference is that he had the guts to bring the negotiations to a close and many European and Common Market Governments secretly applauded him for it. There is a large body of European opinion, which we ignore at our peril, which believes that we are anti-European and that we only wish to join the Common Market as a way of maintaining our standard of living and world power influence…. There are very few leading politicians in the Labour party who have given serious thought to the French case or who are not patronising or contemptuously hostile to her. Unless we make a more serious attempt to understand … our second attempt to get into the Common Market will fail no less miserably than the first….
>
> I hope that the Government will invite the Parliamentary Labour party to vote on the application so that the whole country and the world should know and see how strong is the backing for the Government's decision to apply to join the Common Market. I doubt that Mr Shinwell [Emanuel Shinwell, the octogenarian former chairman of the PLP who was the most outspoken advocate of staying out of Europe] could muster more than 30 votes in the PLP for his old-fashioned and most harmful anti-Europeanism…. I hope those senior members of the Government who are against Britain joining Europe will do the Government and the country a service by

resigning because they oppose our application ... such a demonstration would go some way to convincing the Europeans that our application is a serious political decision and is not just based on commercial considerations.

Maxwell had emerged as one of the most forthright supporters of Britain's joining the EEC at a time when a substantial minority of the Labour party, especially on the backbenches, was reluctant to vote for it. The speech was not helpful to the Prime Minister who, in any case and in private, was often "patronising and contemptuously hostile" to France. Maxwell had already irritated Harold Wilson a few days earlier after the Prime Minister had announced there would be a series of three meetings of the parliamentary party for the Government to hear its MPs' views before the Cabinet reached a final decision. Maxwell remarked at a private PLP meeting that he couldn't see the point of the exercise since the Government had already made up its mind to go into Europe. Wilson said that remark was "mischievous". Politically it was. But it was also true. A local newspaper had the right word for the intervention: "tactless". The suggestion in the speech that the party should, after all, vote was no doubt an attempt to be constructive. But it was the advice to dissenting members of the Cabinet to resign which took the headlines and which led to the refusal to circulate the speech.

One course Maxwell was not in favour of was a free vote in the Commons when the final decision whether to apply was taken on May 10, 1967. He told a private parliamentary party meeting, according to a report I wrote for my then newspaper *The Sun* (the broadsheet successor to the *Daily Herald*, not the Murdoch *Sun*):

I am sick and tired of the Left wing coming up with their bleeding hearts arguing for their consciences and free votes.

I described him on that occasion as "extraordinarily insensitive, brusque and brash".

In the event, the Government had a majority of 426 for the application to join the EEC. Only 36 Labour members voted against. But once again de Gaulle was to apply his veto. Britain did not become a member of the Common Market until 1973, under Edward Heath's leadership and after a monumental split in the Labour party. By then Maxwell had ceased to be an MP.

* * * * *

Parliament, like an army, does its best work on a satisfied stomach. It will never erect a statue to the chairman of the Catering sub-committee of its Services Committee for providing its gastronomical needs, but it will always be ready to consider constructing a gallows for the one who doesn't. Maxwell's acceptance of the post was one of the more diverting episodes in his political career. He was offered it because Richard Crossman, who, as Leader of the House, was also chairman of the Services Committee, didn't have the nerve to admit publicly that the Refreshment Department was making heavy losses without being seen to be doing something about it. The general public had only one view about such a deficit: that MPs were feeding their faces cheaply because the man-in-the-street was subsidising them, a view which, whatever the qualifications which could rightly be made about the loss, was basically correct. The most redeeming quality of Crossman was his brutal frankness, even about his own failings. In March 1967, he recorded, he had to go to the Services Committee to get agreement on how to meet a £60,000 deficit on the kitchen account. He wrote[2]:

> We just dare not publish the report of the accountants or the Treasury O and M until we have a concrete policy. What we finally decided was to bring Bob Maxwell on to the Committee and put him in the chair. When I first heard the idea I was shocked, but John Silkin swallowed it and persuaded Bob Maxwell to accept and to my amazement the Tories on the Committee accepted him too, in particular Willie Whitelaw and Selwyn Lloyd [both former Leaders of the Commons]. I think they realised that one has to get a businessman of experience and courage and that Bob is the only businessman in the House who will be prepared, out of sheer vanity and ambition, to spend a couple of years saving the House of Commons kitchen from corruption and bankruptcy.

In other words, Crossman wouldn't face public criticism of the mounting losses on catering without being seen to be doing something radical about it. Appointing Maxwell was certainly that. The position was that the deficit for 1966 alone was £34,000 and the accumulated loss, which was costing £175 a week in interest charges, had reached £60,000. The Services Committee wasn't able to do anything about the mismanagement which it knew existed in the Refreshment Department, and it had to turn to someone ruthless to get it out of the hole. The Tories accepted Maxwell's appointment because they had no alternative. They could not be seen to be partly responsible for the loss and unwilling to take steps to remedy it.

Though there was no ideological content in the splendid menus and extensive wine lists with which the House was accustomed to sustain itself, it was better that unpopular measures should be taken by a socialist businessman. Whether the Services Committee quite realised what it was doing is doubtful. If it thought, like Crossman, that Maxwell would take a couple of years quietly to inject more business-like methods into the Department and reduce the loss on catering to an acceptably scandalous level, though perhaps not eliminating it altogether, it could hardly have been more wrong. Had he been in charge, Maxwell would have wanted to create the world in fewer than six days. Today, 20 years afterwards, the Maxwell era is still remembered and the anecdotes about his chairmanship are still retold.

Whoever dubbed Maxwell Chairman Ma - the Foreign Secretary, George Brown, seems to have been the first to do it publicly - must have had an inkling of the revolution to come. His first pronouncement, after giving a pep talk to a mass meeting of catering staff, was to tell Crossbencher[3]:

In my first year, we shall not just break even. We shall make a profit.

Said Crossbencher, cautiously:

And to dynamic, self-confident Mr Maxwell I wish the best of British luck.

The Treasury investigation which forced Crossman to act had found "serious shortcomings" in the Refreshment Department. The cost of materials was "very high" and represented more than 57 per cent of turnover; there was no adequate system of control for purchasing or for recording the number of meals served; the over-production of food against a demand which frequently had not materialised had led to "excessive waste" and there was unhygienic, time-consuming and inconvenient distribution of stores and cooked food. The "first and most urgent step" was the institution of proper financial and administrative control.

Armed with those findings, the whirlwind struck, though to begin with it seemed but a balmy breeze. Maxwell immediately got the press on his side by announcing that he was going to reopen Annie's Bar, a legendary watering hole where political correspondents and Members of Parliament could meet on equal terms (even if the cost of most of the drinks fell unequally upon journalistic expense accounts), which had been destroyed in the wartime bombing which badly damaged the House of Commons. This honeymoon didn't last long. By July the Press Gallery was threatening a 24-hour boycott of all the catering facilities because of unresolved problems over conditions and facilities. It was only called off after Maxwell promised that "positive steps" would be taken to improve matters. The catering staff was asked to suggest ways of improving the catering and saving money, with prizes of £10 for the best idea, but a proposal to combine the dining rooms of Lords and Commoners was not pursued. Many of their Lordships had gone to the Upper House to escape their former colleagues in the Commons. They certainly didn't want to eat with them. The most hideous proposal, which was also not developed, was to place vending machines in the most historic building in England, Westminster Hall, where kings and princes and statesmen had lain in death and where Charles I was tried and condemned by Cromwell's court. Even Bob Mellish, the Minister for Public Building and Works, a former dockers' union official and not generally regarded as a deeply-cultured man, was moved to protest. In a letter he wrote to Maxwell, clearly drafted by civil servants, he said he was "shocked" at the suggestion. In a personal, handwritten footnote, Mellish, a great admirer of Maxwell, added:

> You must be stark raving mad to think of this one!!

Changes in administration and control were started immediately, which is the recognised pattern of all Maxwell reforms. The dining room walls were repainted blue, white and gold and the chef was sacked. The new colour scheme offended some MPs who preferred the old dun-coloured décor. Even less palatable, in an epicurean as well as a financial sense, reforms were also put in hand. Prices went up and MPs began to squeal with pain. Maxwell regularly had to answer questions in the Commons about the work of his sub-committee and the damage it was doing both to members' pockets and palates. For example:

> Bryant Godman Irvine (Con)[4]: Will he now introduce a moderately priced menu so that in future Members will not be precluded from entertaining the majority of their constituents?

> Maxwell: Banqueting charges have recently been reviewed ... which resulted in the need to introduce prices comparable to those elsewhere. I cannot ... accept the inference that they are prohibitive.

> Irvine: In my constituency, 32s 6d (162.5p) is regarded as a very high price indeed for lunch.

> Peter Bessell (Lib)[5]: Are you aware of the decline over the last three months in the quality of the food served in the Members' and Strangers' cafeteria?

Maxwell: I am aware and regret that the quality of the food ... has deteriorated recently.

William van Straubenzee (Con)[6]: What is his policy in relation to booking charges? Does he feel it equitable that the booking charge for a dinner which I cancelled ... and which was to be held next May, should be retained by the Catering Department although it was cancelled in September?

Maxwell: ... the answer is yes....

van Straubenzee[7]: Why are avocado pears no longer available in the Members' Dining Room?

Maxwell: Avocado pears have been available at the Buffet in the Members' Dining Room for the past three weeks.

van Straubenzee[8]: Why is *oeuf en gelée* not available in the Members' Dining Room?

Maxwell: The demand for *oeuf en gelée* does not warrant it being placed on the menu.

And so on. The tireless gourmet van Straubenzee also wanted to know why he couldn't get cold lamb cutlets. Maxwell told him he could, provided he gave 24 hours' notice. John Rankin (Lab) demanded that all food supplied to MPs should come from animals reared under free range conditions. Arthur Lewis (Lab), a man of enormous girth and appetite, wanted to know the individual prices of the components of a two-shilling (10p) ham sandwich, the wholesale cost and the retail price of a pork pie and the cost price of a single sausage. To the last, Maxwell solemnly replied that prior to July 1966 the price had been one shilling (5p) but had now risen to one shilling and twopence (nearly 6p). Mr Lewis got a similar detailed answer on the prices of tea, coffee, a slice of bread and butter, a scone, grapefruit cocktail, roast lamb and two vegetables, cold chicken/tongue and a corned beef salad. Even in March 1969 James Dance (Bromsgrove), a persistent critic, was still complaining[9]:

The food is less warm and less good and there is less choice than there used to be. I was even charged 4d (less than 2p) the other day to put the pink in my pink gin.

Dick Crossman, who was fastidious about his food if not other matters, also had a serious complaint. He recorded in his diary[10]:

... Bob Maxwell blew in at my urgent summons because in the tea-room this morning I discovered that instructions have been given by the fellow who runs the Catering Department to serve powdered milk in tea. We'd already had foreign cheese forbidden in our own

restaurant but powdered milk was going a long way. I asked Bob how
he could allow this to happen and he explained, "I've given the chap a
commission of £200 a year for any savings he got and he made a
saving of £100 a week on powdered milk." "Well, you can't make that
saving", I said. "Off with it this afternoon", and I'm glad to say it
went.

Other real howls of rage came from the staff when Maxwell
announced that any of them accepting tips would be dismissed (he
said he thought them "degrading" and instituted a service charge
instead) and from MPs at a decision to sell off the bulk of the fine
wines which had been bought cheaply (and were being sold cheaply)
by the Refreshment Department over the years and to substitute
wines which were less grand and more expensive.

The ban on gratuities was not, in fact, new. It had first been
resolved in October 1945 that tipping should be abolished and the
words "No tipping, please" be printed on the menus. This decision
was reaffirmed in 1946 and in 1949, accompanied by the threat of
instant dismissal. In 1953 it was agreed to add 10 per cent to all
banqueting bills in lieu of tips. But in spite of all the resolutions,
tipping continued. The only difference - but a vital one - between
the past decisions and the one implemented by Maxwell was that the
ban on tipping was incorporated into contracts of employment.

Members of the staff were badly paid - Maxwell said their wages
were "pitiable" - which is why they resented losing their tips.
(They would also have known that other members of the staff at the
Commons, including policemen and messengers, received
substantial "Christmas boxes" from MPs and, more especially,
journalists for services rendered.) The Government's incomes
policy made wage increases impossible to backdate nor could they
be treated so generously that the job would be comparable with the
wages paid outside. Nevertheless, by the standards of those days the
increases eventually paid were large in order to compensate for the
fall in income from tips which they shouldn't have been receiving
anyway. But at a time when there was full or overfull employment in
London, the officials of the Department found it almost impossible
to recruit labour. I knew from my own experience as a one-time
member of the Press Gallery's Catering Committee that at times
staff had been taken on from among the down-and-outs on
London's Embankment. The new wages had to be paid for, and that
could only be done by increasing the prices of meals. A new notice
was printed at the bottom of each menu:

By the decision of the Services Committee, tipping is not allowed

and a surcharge of 7.5 per cent is incorporated into the menu price as
a contribution towards an increase in wages and to cover gratuities.

It was cheap at the price.

As for the wines, *The Guardian* reported under the headline
"Château Pergamon"[11]:

> Captain Robert Maxwell, new Tsar of Commons catering, is
> presently clearing out Westminster's old and distinguished wine
> cellars in order to rent the storage space to merchants. One of the
> ways he is doing it - very quietly - is to sell off genuinely good stock
> (château-bottled clarets of pedigree) over Commons bar counters by
> the glass - at normal parliamentary plonk prices. Thus far, shamingly,
> not one MP has noticed any difference - a sad reminder that most
> Westminster wine drinkers are only portly beer men on an enforced
> diet.

However, the paper was able to report on another occasion that
Maxwell had revoked a decision by Mrs Braddock that the MPs'
Dining Room should not have table cloths, which showed that the
last vestiges of civilisation had not been lost.

Away from the publicity, Maxwell set out in a letter to Crossman
on July 18, 1967 the difficulties he had found in his new post:

> When some four months ago I most reluctantly agreed to replace
> Bessie Braddock ... I do not think anybody realised the terrible mess
> and complete lack of financial or any other management control in
> the Catering Department....

> Since I took over the chairmanship of the Catering sub-committee I
> have spent some 400 hours on dealing with its problems, which is
> more than the total number of hours I have been able to spend on
> behalf of Pergamon Press and the rest of my parliamentary work.

> Over the past decade or so, chairmen of the Catering sub-committee
> have been unwilling or unable to spend that kind of time on the
> affairs of the Department. This may explain the reasons why the
> Department had got into such a deplorable state ... which has now
> been spelt out in considerable detail in the ... report drawn up for me
> by a top team of five experts from Forte's who have spent three
> weeks in the Department.

Maxwell recalled a promise given in the previous year by the
Chancellor of the Exchequer, James Callaghan, that he would make
a grant to the Department equivalent to a third of the loss sustained
by it during the parliamentary recesses since 1964, plus an
interest-free loan, and said that Callaghan had repeated it in an
informal discussion before Maxwell accepted the task of wiping out

the losses. He then listed the steps he had taken to achieve that end:

> He had ended over-expenditure on materials and reduced wastage.
>
> He had improved security (and dismissed four employees for "misfeasance").
>
> He had hired, for the first time, an experienced catering financial controller as deputy to the general manager.
>
> He had replaced the Personnel Manager "who was most unsuited for the job and was quite ineffectual".
>
> He was going to appoint a Banqueting Manager to ensure that the loss of many thousands of pounds "through sheer inefficiency" in the booking of banqueting rooms would be avoided in future.
>
> He had raised prices.
>
> He had halted "over-investment" in wines and liquor and realised "locked-up" capital.
>
> He had stopped the hiring of casual labour on Fridays [when the House sat only briefly] and tightened up on overtime.

As a consequence, he said, the losses, which had been running at £3,000 a month, had been halted. The Department was now forecasting a profit of £10,000 for the year ending December 1968, though he expected it to be higher. He estimated the profit for 1969 to be not less than £20,000, and he would have no difficulty in repaying any loan the Chancellor agreed to make. He added:

> I have promised, at your request, that an increase in wages will be granted immediately the Government's standstill is over. This promise needs to be implemented urgently.... I will need to offer substantially increased wages in order to obtain the right quality of staff....
>
> So that you may appreciate the serious trouble the Department has got into, I must bring to your notice that we have at present on our staff 25 people with a prison record [because] the Department has been unable to recruit people at the present low rates of pay and took what they could get. I am sure it is not in the best interests of the Department or the House of Commons that such people should remain in our employ.

What Maxwell wanted was for the Chancellor to fulfil his promise of an interest-free loan by providing £50,000, repayable in three equal instalments, in which case he would stay on as chairman until the Department was on a sound footing. He sent a copy of his letter to Crossman to the Chancellor together with a formal request for the loan. But the economic climate had changed since the sunny days of the previous year when Callaghan first made his promise. The Chancellor wrote back saying an "interest-free loan at the present time would prove embarrassing and would set a precedent which I should not like to see". In short, he was reneging. Instead, he offered the loan at the Government's normal rate of interest. Maxwell replied rejecting that proposal as "quite insufficient" and warning of industrial action being taken by the staff unless the promises made to them, on the basis of Callaghan's previous undertakings, were implemented. But the Chancellor would not be moved and Maxwell was forced to accept the loan on the terms offered.

By December Crossman was telling his tape-recorder[12]:

> The Catering sub-committee under Bob Maxwell is making a profit.

But Crossman proudly claimed the credit for restoring Annie's Bar.

In December newspapers reported that a loss of £1,000 a week had been turned into a profit of between £400 and £500 a week. It was the first profit since a surplus of £1,029 in 1961. Not even Crossman could claim the credit for that. The columnist Henry Fielding wrote in *The Sun*[13]:

> What has made the change? The new broominess of Robert Maxwell.... [He] rooted out casual workers, started a clocking-in system, cut down on overtime but increased wages by 10 to 15 per cent, demanded more rational buying systems and stopped the nicking and embezzling....

The Observer reported[14]:

> There must be an awful lot of unlined pockets around ever since Robert Maxwell ... set about the thieves' kitchen in SW1. One ex-member of the staff, according to Maxwell, was making so much on the side that he was in danger of overtaking the Prime Minister as Westminster's top earner.

As for the Press Gallery, which had in the summer been threatening to boycott its catering facilities, its secretary wrote at the end of November thanking Maxwell for the "substantial improvements" which had been made, adding:

> As a result ... many more members of the Gallery are now eating [in the cafeteria] instead of going outside for their meals. This, of course, has put additional pressure on our very limited accommodation....

But the sniping from disgruntled MPs went on. Sir Knox Cunningham, Ulster Unionist MP for South Antrim and former parliamentary private secretary to Harold Macmillan, attempted to get Maxwell removed from the chairmanship of the sub-committee because he was "high-handed and dictatorial" and did not consult other MPs. A hundred MPs, including Maxwell's five Labour colleagues on the sub-committee, responded with a Commons motion deploring Sir Knox's "personal attack".

Mrs Margaret McKay, Labour MP for Clapham, went public with her outrage at the change in the dining room décor. Unspeakable, horrible and repulsive, she called it. The wife of a Tory MP, Philip Holland, claimed that her wish to hold her son's wedding reception on a Saturday in the House of Commons had been frustrated by Maxwell. She was certainly not going to invite him, she said, to the function which she held across the road from the Commons[15]:

> Apart from the fact that he is the last person we would invite, he doesn't even belong to the same party.

Another formidable Tory woman, Dame Irene Ward (Tynemouth), complained that since Maxwell's arrival decent, plain biscuits had disappeared and only "nasty, cheap sugary ones" were available, and Mr van Straubenzee protested again that he hadn't had his deposit returned after he had cancelled a dinner.

Maxwell said:

> If my enemies attack me the way they do, things must be improving.

After that the sub-committee moved into calmer waters and on March 25, 1969 Maxwell resigned the chairmanship. His colleagues on the sub-committee recorded their "deep appreciation to Mr Robert Maxwell for his great services" and the Services Committee, under Fred Peart, who had succeeded Crossman, resolved warmly to thank Maxwell "for the work he has done in reorganising the Refreshment Department and placing it on a profitable basis". Peart himself, in a private letter, then thanked Maxwell on behalf of the Services Committee, saying:

> They do not forget the great amount of time, experience and sheer hard work which you devoted, amongst all your other concerns, to this, one of the most thankless tasks in the House, and which you carried out with such marked success.

All this achievement, however, was questioned by the *Sunday Times* in its notorious article about Maxwell's career on October 12, 1969. The references in it to his conduct of the chairmanship of the Catering sub-committee led to a complaint by Maxwell to the Privileges Committee of the House of Commons. The article, which is examined more fully elsewhere, was damaging to Maxwell in almost every field of his public activities. It said, in part, in the florid prose which, it was imagined in that era of investigative journalism, gave an added authority but was often deployed to disguise its absence:

> Maxwell's success is achieved by applying a certain technique to one situation after another. The pattern can be observed in microcosm through one recent episode: the ballet of Robert Maxwell, caterer extraordinary to the House of Commons. It displays all the classical movements in the Maxwell repertoire - the Amazing Leap from the Wings, with Loud Promises of Modern Efficiency; the Masterly Treatment of Accounts; and the Rapid Disappearance, just before the audience starts to throw things.

The *Sunday Times* agreed that had Maxwell made the Commons catering pay its way it would have been "no mean achievement" and admitted that in the year before Maxwell had taken over what it miscalled the "Refreshment Committee" there had been a loss of £33,000. It said that the chairmanship of the Committee was "a government appointment" - it is not, as Richard Crossman's diaries showed - and that "Maxwell was given the job by a Labour party nervously trying to find a use for his tycoonish reputation". This was probably more ignorance than malice. Journalists unfamiliar with politics were unlikely to know how the Services Committee operated or to be able to distinguish between a government and its party, though the distinction is clear. More important, the article set out to show that in fact no profit had ever been made. It declared:

> From Maxwell, there was talk of results analysis and profit targets. Professional advisers were imported from Forte's. The wine cellar was sold off to provide capital, and a brewing-group subsidiary was given an exclusive contract to supply all liquor. So far, the Maxwell reforms, although probably not to the taste of active wine-fanciers, had achieved some improvement in the financial position, albeit at the price of complaints about standards.

> But such marginal economies were not going to produce the profit Maxwell wanted. Help from the public purse was necessary for that, as Select Committee reports show. The £61,000 overdraft was an embarrassment, and was costing £3,000 a year in bank charges. Maxwell persuaded the Treasury to lend the Refreshment Department £50,000 with the interest being met from money from the grant-in-aid, itself Treasury money.

> By December 1967, Maxwell was mentioning the heady figure of £20,000 as the profit he would achieve in 1968 ("profit", as it happens, was being used in a peculiar sense - even if the forecast had been accurate, the profit would have been almost exactly equal to the increase in the Department's subsidy which Maxwell had negotiated

with the Treasury to increase from £10 a year to £21,000).

Maxwell quoted in support of his forecast a current weekly profit running at between £400 and £500. It was true - but the pre-Christmas weeks are exceptionally rich in parties and demands for wine and spirits.

On the 1967 figures, he had wiped out the overdraft, with the Treasury's help, and by reducing stock, hustling MPs to pay their bills, and delaying payments of the Department's bills. The gross loss had been reduced by £5,000. But there was no actual profit.

All this and more was before the Committee of Privileges, but the Committee was not concerned with inaccuracies in the article, only whether the privileges of the House of Commons had been breached by the paper obtaining possession of draft documents which had not been reported to the House. The suspicions which the paper trailed were all nonsense. Maxwell had not "persuaded" the Treasury to lend the Refreshment Department £50,000 as part of a creative accounting exercise. That was the sum which the Chancellor of the Exchequer had promised to a previous Leader of the House, Bert Bowden, the year before Maxwell was ever mentioned as chairman of the Catering sub-committee. It was then to be interest-free, a promise which, as mentioned above, the Chancellor felt compelled to break. The grant-in-aid had also been promised by the Chancellor at a meeting with the Committee when it was chaired by Mrs Braddock. It was clearly stated then to be "to help with the loss which was due to the period of Dissolution". It might not have been necessary, and certainly would have been less, had the Chancellor not retreated from his previous position. Two general elections within 18 months had worsened the deficit substantially and the Chancellor accepted that the loss should not fall upon the Refreshment Department. This had been announced by Callaghan in the summer of 1967 in response to an "arranged" question from Maxwell. What is more, this procedure had been publicly outlined by Maxwell himself in the House of Commons nine months before the article appeared[16]. He listed the deficits which had occurred from 1962 onwards (when a Conservative Government was in power and Conservatives held the majority of seats on select committees), including a deficit of £33,044 in 1966 and one of £28,181 for 1967, and added:

The accumulated deficit of the House of Commons Refreshment Department on 31st December, 1968, was £106,121. This deficit has been met by reduction in stock, etc, Grant-in-Aid and a loan of £50,000 from the Treasury.

It was also the case that grants-in-aid had been under negotiation between the Treasury and various Catering sub-committees since 1963, as Maxwell pointed out in his evidence to the Privileges Committee. Between 1947 and 1959 the grant-in-aid had averaged over £12,000 a year. Maxwell took the Privileges Committee through the *Sunday Times*'s allegations point by point. An accusation that he got the Treasury to "jack up" the subsidy to £23,000 was "a complete fabrication". The *Sunday Times* claimed that a profit of £1,787 declared in the draft accounts for 1968 turned into a loss of £3,400 after Exchequer and audit accountants discovered "errors of substance", which meant that the true position was a loss of £3,400. Maxwell told the Committee that this was "not true, insofar as it implies that there had not been continuous discussion ... during the months prior to the submission of the accounts". The paper went on:

> Part of the catering "profit" derived from a further payment of £2,850 which he [Maxwell] claimed the Treasury had promised. But as it had not been formally agreed, and certainly not handed over, the accountants removed it from the books. Another part of his "profit" depended on his having changed the basis of provision for replacing equipment, normally a steady sum spreading uneven expenditure over several years and latterly a figure of £6,000. Maxwell had only provided for £1,665, the amount actually spent in 1968.

Maxwell told the Committee:

> This statement is false. In fact, the provision for depreciation was approved by the sub-committee on the initiative and recommendation of the General Manager and the Financial Controller of the Refreshment Department, who had pointed out that the Department already had an unexpended reserve of £13,000.

The *Sunday Times* concluded:

> There remained only the exit. Early this year, the other members of the Refreshment Committee found that a major policy directive had been issued entirely without their knowledge. The committee, it seems, were not amused. In April 1969, Maxwell resigned.

If the readers of these passages are meant to infer anything from them, it could only be that Maxwell had cooked the books in order to show a non-existent profit and that he got out before he could be found out or was forced out because of his high-handed behaviour in taking policy decisions without consulting his sub-committee. The "major policy directive", in fact, was an instruction Maxwell had given between meetings of the sub-committee that a decision of July 1967 on manpower budgeting should be adhered to.

The more serious implication was that this was his normal way of conducting his business affairs. If it didn't use the word "shady" or something similar, it was because it didn't dare to for fear of a writ. But a great deal of investigative journalism is of the "nod and wink" variety, implying that there is a great deal more that could be told if the law were not so restrictive. The readers are expected to understand that, and they do. It is a perfectly legitimate approach for a serious journalist to adopt - provided there really is more in the issue under investigation than is allowed to meet the eye. Muck-raking is an honourable pursuit. Muck-making isn't. John Silkin and Richard Crossman (see Appendix 1) were so angry at the *Sunday Times*'s reporting that they wrote to its editor-in-chief, Denis Hamilton, a man with strict views about what was journalistically proper. Hamilton wrote back to Crossman saying he was "personally shocked". He said that while he was editor-in-chief the journalists would not be allowed to use the paper for "personal vendettas".

The leading article in the *Sunday Times* the week after the Privileges Committee reported said it accepted that Maxwell's conduct as chairman was in no way "improper". It added: "It is not, incidentally, a word we have ever applied to it." Yet, if his conduct was not meant to seem improper, there was little point in the passages about the Catering sub-committee.

The weakness of the *Sunday Times* Insight team on this occasion was that it had no insight. It displayed a total ignorance of how the House of Commons conducts its affairs. The accounts of the Refreshment Department had to be drawn up professionally, not by Maxwell, and examined and agreed to by the sub-committee and the Services Committee, both of which were and are all-party in their membership. It is not possible for one man or woman consistently to run the whole show without consulting his colleagues. It might be done in some businesses, but not in Parliament. MPs do not allow themselves to be used to further the advancement of another MP. They are not going to help someone else in a game which they all want to win.

The Committee of Privileges, whose members included the Attorney-General, Sir Elwyn Jones, the former Foreign Secretary, Patrick Gordon-Walker, the Leader of the Conservative party, Edward Heath, and the Leader of the Liberal party, Jeremy Thorpe, as well as several former Cabinet ministers of both major parties, issued its report in March 1970, three months before the general election. It found that the privileges of the House had not been breached and therefore no question of contempt of the House arose. But it said:

> The article contains an attack upon the chairman of a Select Committee of the House of Commons in language which in parts is by implication derogatory. Your Committee consider it right to report that they heard no evidence that Mr Maxwell's conduct as chairman of the Catering sub-committee was in any way improper or departed from normal procedures in compiling the accounts.

* * * * *

Another spiteful episode in Maxwell's public career came in November 1967, illustrating the venom which he aroused, especially among Conservative supporters. A former Conservative MP, Colonel Frederick Gough, MC, a member of an old army family, wrote to the *Illustrated London News*:

> Sir: In your issue of November 4 ... you give a detailed biographical article on the career of Robert Maxwell, MP. Inter alia, you mention, without giving any details, that he is the holder of the Military Cross. It would be in Mr Maxwell's interest if you could deny with authority the persistent rumours that Mr Maxwell has not been so honoured, and to do this perhaps you would publish the relevant details of the *London Gazette* in which his award was published. It is a comparatively small band of MPs and ex-MPs who can boast this particular distinction and it would be appreciated by us all to know for certain whether or not Mr Maxwell is qualified to join us.

It would not have been difficult for a colonel with access to the library of the House of Commons to have found out the information for himself - unless he was so certain that Maxwell's claim was fraudulent that he didn't think it worth bothering. It was a reckless allegation to commit to paper and Maxwell issued a writ for libel.

In a letter to his former colleague, John Kisch, editor of the *ILN*, Maxwell wrote:

> May I hope that the publication of the citation and the photograph, together with the date on which it was officially gazetted, will answer Colonel Gough's "prayer" and will be considered by him and his friends as authoritative evidence sufficient to satisfy them that the MC has not been awarded to me unofficially by foreign friends for trundling so many tens of thousands of barrels of cement in our glorious Pioneer Corps.

Maxwell's ex-army comrades flocked to his support. His old company commander, Major Watson, wrote:

> If you should require either written or verbal evidence of the detailed

circumstances in which you were awarded your MC, I am at your disposal. After all, I wrote the citation!!

Major-General Freeland, Maxwell's former regimental commander, wrote to say that he had confirmed to a *Daily Mirror* reporter that Maxwell had won the MC "and that it was well and truly earned by your brave actions and fine leadership of your platoon in that battle".

Mr J.W. Bogg, a former orderly with the Queen's Royal Regiment, said he remembered the award well "and the boost it gave to our morale" and Captain Henry Kerby, right-wing Tory MP for Arundel and Shoreham and, like Maxwell, a fluent Russian speaker, wrote:

I am delighted to see that you are about to put on the spot that tiresome Establishment figure who has now had the bloody cheek to question your MC.

Colonel Gough wrote to his lawyer on November 28 to thank him for "working like a beaver and bringing a proper balance to a wretched misunderstanding". He went on:

I accept that a lot of it could have been avoided, but I really was trying to do something for a fellow-victim…. I was crucified some years ago…. If you would care to arrange it, I'd like to meet Maxwell and shake him by the hand.

The reference to his being "crucified" dated back to the Suez crisis of 1956 when petrol was rationed and the colonel was discovered to have a private petrol tank at his home, leading, as he complained at the time, to "unfounded and malicious rumours" that he was hoarding it and a promise by him that he would not withdraw any petrol from the tank until rationing had ended. He did not get a good press.

A month after his letter to his lawyer Colonel Gough apologised in open court, admitting that the letter to the *ILN* could only have been understood to mean that Maxwell, if not an imposter, claimed a medal the award of which could not be readily substantiated. The colonel's lawyer said that his client deeply regretted the distress he had caused and offered his sincere apologies. He also paid all Maxwell's costs.

* * * * *

The devaluation of November 1967 devastated Labour party morale and made the Government more unpopular than it might ever have imagined 18 months earlier when it had swept to its general election victory. Maxwell strongly defended the Government's decision, not least because it compelled Britain to withdraw from East of Suez and to cancel the purchase of F-111 aircraft from the United States, which he had been urging for some time. But an announcement by him that he was increasing the price of his books for export to retain the sterling equivalent after devaluation brought estimates that he had, literally, "made a million" out of devaluation.

His greatest success in the chamber of the Commons, as distinct from its private committee sessions, came in early 1968 when he used his luck in the annual ballot for MPs to introduce bills of their own, choosing to bring in a bill to tighten up the restrictions on air pollution. The Clean Air Bill, as it was called, was debated on February 2 after a notably conciliatory speech by Maxwell in which he promised to consider seriously each and every objection to it. The bill was designed to give local authorities and the Government greater powers to control the emission of grit, dust and fumes from industrial premises and give the responsible minister power to direct local authorities to carry out programmes of smoke control. It also made it an offence to deliver or to buy smoke-producing fuel for consumption in a smoke-control zone. After a fortnight's adjournment of the debate, the bill was given an unopposed Second Reading on February 16.

However, it ran into obstruction from then onwards. Further progress was prevented by Conservative MPs shouting "Object!" each time it came before the House on a Friday (This is an old stratagem employed to defeat private members' bills. Its excuse is that it is used to ensure that no legislation passes through the House without adequate debate. Often it is used in order to stop a measure which has popular support but which is secretly opposed.) Maxwell's conciliatory mood disappeared. When the Government made special provision for his bill to be debated in order to get round the obstructors, Maxwell bitterly complained that although the Conservative party had assured him that it had no objection to his bill they "nevertheless put up stooges" like the MP for Bristol West (Robert Cooke) to shout "Object!" He then went on to describe Cooke as "a little quisling", an unparliamentary phrase which he had to withdraw. Eventually, on May 10, the bill passed its committee stage in the Commons. A large number of amendments were made to it. All but one came from Maxwell; he successfully resisted a great many others from Tory MPs. After an easy passage through the House of Lords, the bill became an Act of Parliament later that summer.

Nothing he did at Westminster ever earned him greater praise.

But another of his enterprises earned him far greater publicity. It was more exciting, more spectacular and certainly more sensational than the Clean Air Act, though, in the long run, it was nowhere near as beneficial. And it all began, as the brightest ideas should, from the unlikeliest of sources: five secretaries from Surbiton in Surrey. It also contained all the elements of a good story. It had attractive girls, patriotism, a new idea, a simple cause, and an effective slogan. It was the "I'm Backing Britain" campaign.

* * * * *

Devaluation and the drop in national morale which followed began it all. In the first week of January 1968, no doubt as their collective New Year's resolution, five typists at the Colt Heating and Ventilation Co. in Surbiton decided to work an extra half-hour a day without pay in order to help Britain. It was a genuine, selfless gesture by five non-political girls who wanted to do something to get their country out of its mess. It simplicity was quickly obscured by the publicity which followed. As one of them said[17]:

> We got mixed-up when asked horrid questions about trade unions. Thanks to all the interviews and things we just didn't get any typing done.

That seemed to defeat the purpose of the exercise from their point of view, but the spirit was undoubtedly right and it caught the mood of the moment. It was also a godsend to an embattled Government. As the late Nicholas Tomalin reported in the *Sunday Times*:

> By January 7, after the Prime Minister had noticed it, newspapers had exploited it, unions had begun to sabotage it and Colt's (overwhelmed by its fervour) had asked the Department of Economic Affairs to institutionalise it, I'm Backing Britain was forced to come to terms with real national life.

Two rival organisations were set up to develop the campaign: the Industrial Society and Bob Maxwell, "who decided", said Tomalin, "that he could do the job better" and:

> In some ways, Maxwell was right. The Industrial Society is accustomed to scrupulous, small-scale persuasions ... the vibrant Maxwell used the opposite method....

The Industrial Society was quoted as saying that it was used to doing good by stealth and a spokesman added:

> Maxwell might be interested in doing good, but he certainly isn't interested in doing anything by stealth.

In fact, if the campaign was to succeed at all, stealth was useless. Publicity was all. Maxwell sprayed quotes around, never disguising his intentions of making a Big Bang in a few weeks in order to get the campaign off the ground. He told the director of the Industrial Society, according to Tomalin:

> The trouble with you is you're all trying to be virgins, whiter than white. I've succeeded in raping you.

He readily admitted to another campaigner that he intended to leave the campaign "within six months".

What was undoubtedly true was that Maxwell had had the idea of a Buy British campaign around about the same time as the typists decided to Back Britain. It wasn't a gimmick, even if it looked like one. He has always preferred to buy British goods for his own businesses. His enormous car fleet is almost entirely British. He did everything he could to encourage British print machine manufacturers to produce the new colour machines he needed at Mirror Group Newspapers and only went to Germany for them when the British manufacturers could not match the specifications, even at a higher price than obtained in Germany. He was censured by Labour's National Executive Committee at the instigation of the hard-left Mrs Audrey Wise, who was ignorant of the facts.

The almost incredible fact about the 1968 campaign was that it was an idea which he developed with his old adversary, Frank Cousins, now once more general secretary of the Transport and General Workers' Union. (Cousins had resigned from the Government in the summer of 1966 because of his fundamental disagreement with the prices and incomes policy.)

But had he attempted to do it without the adventitious help of the Surbiton Five, it would never have got off the ground. The typists, above all else, were non-political. What they were doing was for Britain. What Maxwell and Cousins wanted to do would have been seen, rightly or wrongly, as something to help a besieged Labour Government. The Industrial Society announced on January 8 it was taking on the campaign. Three days earlier Maxwell had approached David Frost, through the journalist Clive Irving, for help to launch his campaign. Frost donated £1,000 and Maxwell appeared on the Frost Show.

An inaugural meeting of the campaign at the House of Commons on January 10 was supported by Sir William and Robert Butlin of Butlin's, Ltd., Lord Byers, chairman of the Liberal party, Jim Conway, general secretary of the Engineering Workers' Union, Cousins, and Michael Sieff, of Marks and Spencer, Ltd., among others. The others included Joe Hyman, of Viyella International, who arrived just before the meeting closed and later became involved in an acrimonious squabble in the letters columns of *The Times* because Maxwell assumed his backing for the campaign and Hyman repudiated the assumption. It ended, however, in mutual expressions of admiration and goodwill.

The objectives of the campaign were set out soon afterwards[18]:

> To explain in specific terms to the population at large what they can do as individuals to help Britain improve its economic position.

> In particular, to stimulate a small but critical shift in consumer expenditure (i.e., 3.5 to 4 per cent of total expenditure on imported goods) from imported goods to home-produced goods.

> To make very visible to the consumer the opportunities for personal action that will contribute towards this shift and to educate the consumer into effective decisions and actions.

> To think of people in their consumer roles as the prime target, whilst recognising and demonstrating the wider context in which they operate and live.

Maxwell had originally placed his emphasis on Buy British-Sell British as the theme of his campaign. This quickly ran into trouble. A number of leading exporters were keen on the second half of the slogan but not the first, fearing that if other nations adopted a similar policy it would harm their own manufactures.

Lord McFadzean of British Insulated Callenders Cables summed up their feelings. In a letter to Maxwell he said he admired the initiative and the hard work put into the campaign but he couldn't support it:

> There are several reasons for this, the main one being ... I do not agree with any public "Buy British" campaign. On several occasions during my career I have objected like hell to other countries doing this and have publicly stated in many countries my belief in the removal or avoidance of any restrictions on the freedom of world trade.

Spillers, Ltd. said it would distribute car stickers among its workforce but didn't want to take an active part in the campaign, though it wished it success. The Co-operative Wholesale Society and its Scottish counterpart joined in enthusiastically, but the House of Fraser took the same line as Spillers. Bernard Delfont, the impresario, sent what seemed to be a heartfelt letter of support, but was upset when that support was made public by Maxwell in an advertisement without informing Delfont first. Seeing that the advertisement committed Delfont, among others, to paying for the cost of it, this was, at the very least, an unfortunate oversight. Another of those named as supporting it was Beaverbrook Newspapers, Ltd. Its then chairman, Sir Max Aitken, was incensed by a remark by Maxwell that the campaign would help make Britain fit to enter Europe. The whole political weight of the Beaverbrook Newspapers, though slight, was devoted to attacking any idea of Britain doing any such thing.

But the public response was amazing. British Rail said they would only sell British-made matches after a constituent had complained to Maxwell that BR only sold foreign ones. A Nottingham department store told Maxwell that it and its whole staff would support the campaign. Girls began to wear clothes with a Union Jack motif and all the staff of Littlewood's stores were asked to wear Union Jack lapel badges, supplied by the Industrial Society, which planned, altogether, to distribute two million of them. A building firm in Scotland decided to freeze its house prices for six months and gifts poured into Her Majesty's Treasury. A Leeds worker donated a week's wages, an old age pensioner gave £86 and a clerk declared he would regularly give 10 per cent of his earnings. Shop stewards at the Colt Ventilation Co. decided to defy their union which had ordered its members there not to work extra hours for no extra money. Blackpool hoteliers decided to buy British food and a wigmaker urged long-haired youths to sell their hair and reduce the need to import hair from abroad. Enoch Powell said it was all "ineffably silly", but for once he was out of touch with the popular mood.

The mayor of Bootle, in north-west England, announced the promotion of a "Bootle Backs Britain" movement and the Government, not to be outdone, ordered Whitehall departments to Buy British whenever possible. Gerald Nabarro (Worcestershire South - Con), who, in appearance, was a caricature of a wicked English squire, denounced the BBC for showing a TV programme which dwelt on the advantages to be found in a Mercedes car. Prices in 600 Tesco supermarkets were pegged for two months and at Warwick University the entire catering staff decided to work an extra hour a week for nothing. Ladybird, the biggest manufacturer of children's clothing in the Commonwealth, decided to hold its prices steady for six months. Sir William Butlin and nine of his directors decided on cuts in their joint annual income totalling £50,000, giving the money to a scheme to encourage people to take their holidays in Britain. Butlin's holiday camps, of course, were the biggest single supplier of holidays in Britain. For those who believed that in Britain everything stopped for tea, the news that fitters at a firm of Dundee vehicle distributors had decided to forego their tea break must have demonstrated just how seriously Britons had taken to the cause.

The wave of populist support even affected the language of Sir Derek Pritchard, chairman of the British National Export Council, who, according to the *Daily Mirror*, declared:

> We have got to get up off our fannies, stop moaning and get out and sell.

In the middle of it all, Maxwell took over as chairman of an ailing insurance company, Craven, and promised to put in £200,000 in new capital, enough to give him voting control. But his intervention only staved off the collapse by less than three months. The company had provided figures to a High Court judge showing that it was solvent. But, in Maxwell's words, it was "hopelessly insolvent". Hundreds of thousands of pounds'-worth of claims against the company had not been listed. He added:

> This is the answer really why I have been caught and why everybody else has been caught.

Had he known the truth, he said, he and his colleagues would have been saved the embarrassment of liquidating it. The reports of the take-over and the descriptions of his Backing Britain campaign as often as not reminded readers that he was Czech-born. Maxwell answered them by saying:

> I'm foreign-born - therefore I'm more patriotic than the natives.

By February Maxwell had dropped the "Buy British" part of the campaign and retitled it "Sell British, Help Britain, Help Yourself." The Industrial Society, meanwhile, continued its efforts almost unnoticed by anyone. Some of Britain's best-known politicians - even if their fame was in part due to a reputation for being awkward - like Michael Foot, Quintin Hogg and Enoch Powell, denounced the whole thing. Hogg (later to resume his earlier title of Lord Hailsham) advised the campaigners to "Belt up", fastening on unfortunate suggestions that mothers who didn't need family allowances should give them up and that schoolchildren should think twice before taking their school milk. He denounced the "gall" of "rich men" who dared to suggest such things, though he was later to serve long and loyally under a Prime Minister who virtually ended the supply of milk to schoolchildren and was a member of the Cabinet which reduced the value of the child benefits which replaced family allowances. Maxwell said Hogg and the others were cranks and aimed full-page advertisements at them by name.

The *Daily Mirror* gave the campaign its editorial support but its columnist, George Gale - who, nearly 20 years later, was to be re-employed briefly on the paper after Maxwell had bought it - was scathing[19]:

> I loathe and despise the Back Britain campaign in all its wretched manifestations. Its most squalid aspect yet is now being displayed in advertisements in almost all the country's principal newspapers [including, though Gale was apparently unaware of it, the *Daily Mirror* that same day]. A motley outfit of the rich ... are paying for these advertisements.... I trust no one ... will pay any attention to them whatsoever, except to laugh.

But a Tory MP, R. Gresham Cooke, gave unexpected support, saying[20]:

> Despite its having been run by a Labour MP, there was much good sense in the full-page propaganda of the "Help Britain" campaign. The situation is too serious to yield to a "do nothing" attitude or to every niggling criticism of anything constructive ... we must conserve our foreign exchange by "Buying British" at home....

A background note compiled for the campaign neatly summed up its purpose and the early reaction to it:

> The reason for the campaign was a recognition that there was a genuine desire among millions of people in Britain to do something themselves to help Britain. This desire was frustrated because there was no guidance on what they could do and no central point to co-ordinate activities. It was agreed that this was not a government campaign ... and Robert Maxwell, acting as Campaign Manager, put the show on the road.... Mr Maxwell raised a number of sponsors, a good deal of money and considerable hostility....

The note listed the "enemies" and "fence-sitters" who stood in the way of the success of the campaign:

> Those who see it as a Harold Wilson plot - i.e., a spirit of National Unity behind a Help Britain theme would benefit the Prime Minister at a time when his stock in the country is low.
>
> Those who see it as a Robert Maxwell effort and who do not like Robert Maxwell.

Those who see it as a "millionaires' benefit" and think these people are interested only in a "Buy British" motivated consumer boom.

Editors and columnists who object to the ads. either on the basis of style or content.

Professional "knockers" ... being smart in public print and vindictive and vitriolic about their pet hates.

Trades unionists who see the whole thing as a plot against trades union productivity bargaining.

Pure economists who see our crisis as one which is the sole concern of Government, industry, the trades unions and the Treasury.

Industrialists, businessmen, trades union leaders who are waiting to see how things work out and who have been alarmed by the "anti" publicity and have not yet decided to declare themselves publicly.

To counter this hostility it was decided to "take the personal vendetta element out of the campaign by avoiding public argument on a personality basis"; to demonstrate by maximum editorial coverage the broad base of public approval; to dovetail the various campaigns running; to give the unions and their shop stewards and ordinary trade unionists as much space as the millionaires; to encourage the setting up of Help Britain centres and committees by using the thousands who had written or telephoned their support and getting them to distribute literature; to establish a "band wagon" feeling; to try to isolate the "knockers" as "anti-patriots"; and to try again - Hugh Cudlipp had already said No - to "tie in" the *Daily Mirror*.

In March Maxwell announced the setting-up of national action centres, staffed by retired people who had offered their help, which would act as "a clearing house" for complaints about shoddy goods, poor after-sales service and delivery delays. A special telephone number - 160 - was provided for people to call and hear a Backing Britain message, given by a popular entertainer rejoicing in the distinctly un-British pseudonym of Engelbert Humperdinck. Maxwell also announced that he would give up as campaign manager in the summer, having devoted, as he promised from the start, six months of his time to the post. The campaign had been so successful, he said, that he would no longer be needed after August. It would not die because his personal involvement had ceased. He had nothing but scorn for his prospective opponent at Buckingham, Bill Benyon, who had condemned the campaign, and he forecast a "dramatic" cut in imports when the next figures were printed. In fact, later in the year exports did rise and imports fell, though how much of the improvement was due to the campaign was impossible to quantify. The Industrial Society's campaign flagged badly. By May the full-time staff of 25 which it engaged in January had fallen to four. A dejected campaign adviser said[21]:

> People always think that we are something to do with the Labour party. Without its political flavour, I am sure the campaign would have been taken a lot more seriously.

Maxwell, according to the *Financial Times*, was unwilling to gloat, saying only[22]:

> Their task was a lot more difficult. I'm only sorry they didn't accept my original offer to pool forces.

* * * * *

Benyon's prospects of winning Buckingham were increasingly bright. The Government's popularity had fallen to an all-time low in 1968, especially in the south of England. It was being humiliated in every by-election and after disastrous local government elections in the spring Cecil King, chairman of the Mirror Group of Newspapers, the only group which had consistently supported Labour since the war, demanded Wilson's resignation. This led to his own departure shortly afterwards, in a coup led by Hugh Cudlipp, who became chairman in his place, but it did nothing to improve the Government's poll ratings, even if it gave Wilson immense pleasure.

Maxwell's chances of holding his seat were not helped by a decision of British Rail to close the Oxford to Cambridge railway line which ran through his constituency. A survey of Oxford's favourite politicians which appeared in the undergraduate magazine *Isis*, which Maxwell owned, showed him to be placed at No. 35, which was not too bad seeing there were more than 600 to choose from. He was now so well-known that a local newspaper's main front-page story carried the simple headline across three columns:

> Robert Maxwell, MP will be in town tonight.

The justification was that it was an important meeting. Maxwell had agreed to the paper's suggestion that he should hold a no-holds-barred meeting with his constituents, which enabled them to devote a second "splash" story to him the following week, this time over four columns, under the headline:

> Mr Robert Maxwell, MP drew a full house.

Unfortunately, its story began: "Forty minutes late and amid boos and a slow handclap from an audience angry with waiting, Mr Robert Maxwell...." The paper admitted, however, that Maxwell was "unruffled" by his reception. His first step was to pin "I'm Backing Britain" posters at the wings of the stage of the Buckingham town hall. He then apologised for being late and blamed the delay on the traffic conditions on a Friday evening in London. The questioning was hostile, but Maxwell was unbending. To complaints that Buckingham was not being developed, he retorted:

> Give me an assurance that you want to develop and I will help you.

Nevertheless, he was as assiduous as ever in his constituency work, ranging from getting a weedy patch of ground developed to winning a grant for a new sewage works at Bletchley. But nationally Labour went from one catastrophe to another. The Foreign Secretary, George Brown, resigned from the Government on March 15 - the Ides of March - petulantly and suffering from a hangover. The Chancellor, Roy Jenkins, introduced a Budget which put up taxes and results in three by-elections in government-held seats saw comfortable Labour majorities dissolve into substantial Tory majorities. Maxwell told his local paper that the results "couldn't be worse". He went on[23]:

> There is plenty of time for the Government's economic measures to bring stability and growing national wealth in time for Labour to win the next general election.

In a speech to constituents in April he spelled out some of the issues which had been so damaging to the party:

> We have been disillusioned by equivocation in Vietnam, zig-zagging on Rhodesia, and a prices and incomes policy where prices are encouraged to rise and incomes remain virtually frozen.

Nevertheless, he continued staunchly to defend the Government's policies, convinced that the Government only needed time for the stern measures it had taken to succeed. But that time was running out and he and other Labour MPs in marginal seats knew it. When the Buckingham borough council elections were held in May, the local Labour party was only able to field one candidate for five seats to be contested. Bill Benyon continued to attack Maxwell on every possible occasion and equalled him in at least one matter. He was fined for speeding.

* * * * *

Nineteen-sixty-eight was of special significance to Maxwell. It was the year in which the troops of the Soviet Union and its satellites invaded Czechoslovakia, moving in on August 20 to crush the liberalising Government of Mr Dubcek. The House of Commons was recalled for an emergency debate. Naturally, Maxwell spoke, beginning:

> As is well known, I was born in Czechoslovakia, in fact, in that province of Czechoslovakia that the Czechs were made to cede to Russia after the last war, Ruthenia. I remember well the betrayal that I, though very young, and the whole nation of Czechoslovakia felt at being let down by Great Britain and France at Munich. There followed the dismemberment of Czechoslovakia, in due course, and I found myself being harassed by Hungarian troops.... It was not just German officers who probably participated in the same invasion of Czechoslovakia; there were also Hungarians and Poles who participated in it and I will not be surprised if some of their senior officers and NCOs were the very same people who did it then who repeated it this time.

But he attacked those on the Conservative benches who were using the debate to "fan the embers of the cold war" and he urged the Government "not to be panicked into that kind of situation".

> Whereas we, together with most of the world, condemn the Russians for their dastardly act in invading by trickery this defenceless country, that invasion has not altered the status quo.... It would be utterly wrong to give up the détente for which we have all fought, worked and made sacrifices, merely because of this ghastly Russian invasion. It would be no service to the Czech people - not to mention us - to do this....

The reason for the Russian invasion, he said, was that the Soviet Union feared that the Czechs were about to sweep all their old Stalinists out of office and that "a completely revived, reconstituted and refurbished Communist party would come into existence", opposed to the Russian concept of centralised democracy. The Russians had decided that unless they nipped this development in the bud "they would never again be able to stop some of this freedom from seeping into their own party, their own army and their own satellite forces". He went on:

> They were afraid to let the shaft of light into their own party. After 50 years of communism they felt unwilling or unable to talk any other language but that of the tommy-gun and the tank. They may well have gained for themselves a few years' respite in which their kind of dictatorship can prevail....

But what could be done to help the Czech people?

> In my opinion, it must be as little as possible in the form of Government action. Any attempt to turn the heroism and suffering of the Czech people into a weapon of the cold war for stiffening the posture of NATO against the Warsaw Pact would harm the Czech people…. What the Czech people really need is action by individuals.

> In view of the illegal and treacherous invasion … any persons who have booked holidays, tours or visits to the Soviet Union or to the countries which are assisting them should consider cancelling or postponing such visits…. Ordinary citizens should avail themselves of every opportunity to protest against this invasion in the strongest possible way…. British businessmen seeking Russian trade, ballet or music lovers seeking Russian culture, or even simply tourists seeking Polish or Russian holidays cannot carry on as if this rape of Czechoslovakia had not happened.

It was a journey back in time for Maxwell. His argument that governments of the West should not be panicked into extra defence spending but that individuals should display their outrage seemed to some Tory MPs to be weak. But his analysis that the true Soviet fear was of freedom seeping into their own country, though not generally shared at the time, even in the Labour party, was in the event shown to be correct.

On behalf of the British Youth Council he opened a centre for stranded Czechoslovakian students in Britain. In all, there were some 3,000, of whom about 100 would not be able to return to their own country because they had taken an active part in opposing the Soviet occupation. He also led a successful deputation to the Supplementary Benefits Commission to secure financial help for Czechs arriving in London.

* * * * *

In 1969 Maxwell voted for the first time against the Government and in defiance of a three-line whip, over its alleged "mishandling" of the Soames affair. In January our ambassador to Paris, Christopher Soames, had had a startling interview with General de Gaulle which he related to the Prime Minister and the Foreign Secretary in a secret telegram. De Gaulle had said that he had no part in the creation of the Common Market and had little faith in it. He preferred to see a looser form of association replacing it, with a small inner council consisting of France, Britain, Germany and

Italy. The Foreign Office, which was going through a Francophobe phase because de Gaulle was frustrating Britain's attempts to join the EEC, circulated the Soames telegram to its overseas posts.

Inevitably, the news began to leak in a garbled form. The Foreign Office wanted to reveal the whole story through an Italian newspaper so that it would appear innocent of breaking the confidentiality which attached to the de Gaulle-Soames meeting and to the telegram. I told the Prime Minister of this plan and he vetoed it. Instead, against his express instructions, the Foreign Office leaked it in total detail to the British press. It was a mammoth piece of stupidity by diplomats who were too clever by half. The subsequent outcry was a gift to the Conservatives and a disaster for a government which had enough troubles from its enemies without more being added by its officials. The Tories were rightly critical. Wilson, who could not tell the truth about the Foreign Office's intrigues, had to defend an indefensible position. In a vote in the Commons in February Maxwell went into the division lobbies with the Conservatives. His commitment to the European cause was total and the damage done to Anglo-French relations by the Foreign Office seemed to him to have set it back by years.

At the end of March a letter from Edward Heath invited him to join others concerned with "promoting the European idea" to attend a fund-raising dinner at the Guildhall at the end of July. Money, of course, was not mentioned: only the hope that Maxwell would find it possible "to attend and support this cause". In fact, the intention was to raise £750,000. The venture was nearly wrecked when the Prime Minister discovered that the company promoting the dinner, Arrow Enterprises (proprietor, Jeffrey Archer), was to take 10 per cent of the proceeds. Because Wilson threatened to pull out and reveal why, Arrow Enterprises had to be content with a flat fee, substantial though it was.

In June Maxwell gave an unusually fractious but revealing interview during a profile of him on the Eamonn Andrews programme *Today*. Sandra Harris asked him[24]:

> Mr Maxwell, while you're surrounded by tremendous wealth, do you still think about poverty?

He replied:

> I can never be separated from my origins. I came from a working class and I'm part of them and will continue to support them.
>
> Did you ever consider being a member of any other party?

It's a scurrilous suggestion and quite untrue. Just because I've made a couple of shillings, I'm not about to change sides.

You've also been described as a tremendously ruthless man - as a man that is very, very difficult to cross. Does what other people say about you worry you at all?

No, it doesn't.

Later Miss Harris asked:

A lot of people find it hard to reconcile your socialist principles with all the splendour that surrounds you. How do you explain this?

Why should I have to explain it?

If you did, what would you say?

I've nothing to explain because the question itself is impertinent. It has no point. It implies just because somebody has made money that he cannot be a socialist, or to be in favour of profit is something that's wrong....

Does property mean a lot to you?

Quite unimportant. I merely have property as a means of getting things done that need to be done. I'm completely unattached.

Margaret Laing, a journalist, was frequently interposed into the profile and her comments were hostile:

He's very primitive and having achieved supremacy, he will just mark out his terrain like some old lion and walk around it, I think. A jungle man.

In a studio discussion afterwards, Clive Jenkins, general secretary of ASTMS, protested:

I think it was a bloody awful profile, tendentious, unfair, even malicious. I like him and I think he's done a great deal for Britain - for publishing. He's transformed it from a cottage industry.

Three Labour parties - two in Leeds and one at South Kensington, London - sought to nominate Maxwell for the treasurership of the Labour party at the 1969 party conference, but he declined on the grounds that the current treasurer, Jim Callaghan, was "doing a splendid job". Politically, as the next general election drew nearer, his constituency affairs continued to dominate. The proposal to build a new London airport in Buckinghamshire found him among the leaders of the opposition though, unusually for him, he was accused of being too cautious by the more fervent after he counselled them not to fire off all their ammunition at once. Reports that he wouldn't stand at the next general election if he won control of the *News of the World*, which he had been seeking, dissolved when he didn't. But Conservative confidence in wresting the seat from Labour was high. The Shadow Chancellor, Iain Macleod, went to Bletchley and declared: "It's no problem." With some exceptions, Maxwell continued to get a good press; one local paper in August described him thus[25]:

> To the world at large, a ruthless tycoon, a millionaire with a flair for hitting the headlines, an ambitious man loved by few, but for whom most people have a grudging admiration.

> Yet this is the same man who shook off derision and scorn, even from members of his own party, to show that courage, loyalty and organisation can win a marginal seat like North Bucks. The man who was not afraid to don the cloth cap - metaphorically and physically, to talk to his electorate, to take set-backs and be proved wrong without batting an eyelid; and to deal with the problems and complaints of constituents of all political persuasions with an efficiency that bears favourable comparisons with the very high standards set by his Conservative predecessor.

The paper asked Maxwell what effect being MP for Buckingham had had upon him. He replied:

> It has matured me, certainly.... Ten years ago I used to be impatient and not look for other people's good points....

The news that he had ceased to be impatient must have astonished those who didn't know him when he was.

* * * * *

Maxwell entered 1970, which was expected to be general election year, in a spirit of optimism. In a Christmas message to his constituents he forecast that in 1970/71 Britain would be able to repay its foreign debts and reduce the heavy burden of taxation, make progress with equal pay for women, increase pensions, build more homes and roads and raise the salaries of teachers and others who had not been receiving their "fair share". The decade of the seventies, he said, was going to be Britain's decade.

The publicity surrounding Pergamon Press and Leasco and the *Sunday Times* articles was of serious concern as the general election neared, though the Conservative agent for Buckingham, Joe French, said in January he thought it had done Maxwell "not very much" harm. Unknown to any of his colleagues, the Prime Minister had already decided that an election after the introduction of decimalisation in February 1971 would probably end disastrously; the only question was whether it would be June or October 1970, and he was strongly inclining towards June. Maxwell himself thought October was the more likely and told his supporters so. He continued loyally to support the Government's retreat on trade union reform which had taken place in the previous June and forecast victory again when polling day finally came. Meanwhile, he pursued his constituency interests as vigorously as ever, fighting for road signs near a children's school and trying to improve a grant to be paid to a pre-school play group. He was heartened by two victories at Bletchley in the county council elections in Buckinghamshire in April and amended his forecast of the election date to June or July.

The formal announcement of the election date was made on May 18. The Buckingham Labour party seemed, as usual, to be efficient. Betty Maxwell was again charged with the task of securing the maximum postal vote and her eldest surviving son, Philip, was responsible for the canvass. Publicly, Maxwell was confident. But privately, the atmosphere within the party had soured. Maxwell did not have the same relationship with Jim Lyons as he had had with Bryan Barnard. The emergence of a hard-left opposition to Maxwell's kind of Labour party had begun within the local party. But at his adoption meeting he told his supporters:

> As at the last election, I intend to play the ball and not the man.... The Tories are on the run.... The opinion polls without exception show that at last people are coming to realise that the rather strong measures the Government had to impose are paying off in a big way.

Alas, the opinion polls had it all wrong.

Maxwell made a stout defence of Labour's policies, concentrating this time on those things which concerned the voters - the cost of living, housing and other domestic matters. Benyon, the Conservative candidate, did the same, with one unpleasant passage in his adoption address which showed the venom with which many Tory candidates approached that election. If there was one question on which Maxwell could not be challenged, especially by a man who was only 15 when the war ended, it was his patriotism. But after the routine attacks on the "dishonesty" of socialists, Benyon went on:

> All this brings into question the patriotism and integrity of certain sections of the Socialist party. Do you honestly believe Will Owen stands alone? Undoubtedly, both inside and outside the House of Commons, there are those socialists who either actively or passively support international communism to the destruction of their

judgment and patriotism.... If a socialist Government is re-elected,
you can be sure of one thing - the power of this particular element will
increase....

Will Owen was the Labour MP for Morpeth and had been
charged with offences under the Official Secrets Act relating to the
passing of classified information to another country in return for a
payment of £2,500. The evidence was thin and he was acquitted
three weeks before Benyon made his speech, though a listener to it
might not have thought so. The country to whom he was alleged to
have given the information was Czechoslovakia. Benyon did not
mention Maxwell by name, nor did he suggest Maxwell was among
those whom he suspected, nor did he mention Czechoslovakia. But
everyone knew Maxwell was a socialist who had been born in
Czechoslovakia and it would not have been surprising if those who
heard or read Benyon's speech put two and two and two together
and made a lot more than six.

Benyon's concluding words about the election campaign - "it will
probably be dirty; this depends upon our opponents" - were thus
particularly nauseating.

The big guns were more ready to fire for Maxwell in the 1970
elections than they had been previously. George Brown came to
speak again and so did the Home Secretary, Jim Callaghan, and the
Lord Privy Seal, Lord Shackleton. As before, Maxwell energetically
toured every village and hamlet in his constituency, visiting up to 18
a day, greatly aided by a summer which offered almost unbroken
sunshine. The bombardment of the electors with *Maxwellgrams*,
this time more sharply written and headlined, was unceasing.
Maxwell made effective use of an editorial in the *Sunday Times* (of
all papers!) which, while endorsing the Conservative party of
Edward Heath, had declared four days before polling[26]:

> There are at least two Tory candidates who would positively blot the
> Parliamentary scene. Brian Rathbone at Smethwick and William
> Benyon at Buckingham have made such extreme pronouncements on
> race that they should be positively voted against.

That could only be an invitation to vote for Maxwell, which must
have been painful to the Insight team. But the electors of
Buckingham were not listening. As in the rest of the country,
though on a less scale, there was an astonishing, unexpected and
late swing to the Conservative party. A Labour lead in the national
opinion polls of over 12 per cent six days before polling disappeared

altogether. Maxwell increased his vote by over 700 compared with 1966, but Benyon took the seat. Result:

Benyon (Con)	28,088
Maxwell (Lab)	25,567
Cornwall (Lib)	5,475
Con. majority	2,521

Mr Cornwall lost his deposit again. The percentage poll was well down on previous years - 81.5.

The result was a bitter disappointment for Maxwell, who was afterwards inclined to blame the difficulties within the Buckingham party for his defeat. But a *Guardian* writer seemed to have it right in an article shortly before polling day when he said of Buckingham[27]:

> In theory, it is ridiculous that Labour should ever have taken a constituency which is richly ripe hunting and shooting country from one end to the other.

Among the warmest letters of condolence to the Maxwells were from Dick Crossman and Jim Callaghan, both of whom had objected to his selection for Buckingham 11 years before. John Silkin wrote that the Commons "will not seem the same without you". That was unquestionably true.

Recriminations over the defeat at an inquest held by the executive committee of the Buckingham party were unusually virulent. Its President, Arthur Leary, reported he had made numerous requests to the agent (Jim Lyons) from February onwards asking him to convene an urgent meeting of the party officers and the MP to discuss detailed plans for the election, but he had failed to do so. Leary's catalogue of accusations against Lyons was lengthy:

> Even after the general election was declared, the agent failed to produce a detailed plan; Buckingham did not have the minimum organisation necessary for a successful campaign; the agent failed to convene meetings to enthuse supporters or to instruct local parties to do the same; willing workers had never been contacted by him in the four years between the two general elections; he failed to obtain up-to-date electoral registers and some canvassers had worked on registers three years old; no election material was ordered from the party's headquarters in London; one local party was allowed to "fold up" just before the election; another was so upset by the agent that it had become "ineffective". In addition, several members of the party had complained of "insufferable rudeness" by the agent to voluntary workers and staff and a survey costing up to £4,000 which he had been authorised to undertake had never been carried out.

The agent responded that he had decided to keep an election organisation in being only in urban areas in which he thought the party could win seats. He had therefore "written off the villages as not being worth bothering with". He declared that the deficiencies in the organisation were due to the fact that he considered Maxwell wanted to be in charge and he denied he had been rude to anyone. The committee "noted the agent's statement that he refused to serve in future as election agent to Mr Maxwell".

Leary suggested that the agent should find another job and six local parties passed votes of no confidence in Lyons. Lyons refused to go and the Buckingham party asked the NEC to conduct an inquiry into why the election had been lost. But the NEC widened the inquiry to look into the constituency party's affairs. The majority of witnesses at the inquiry supported Leary rather than Lyons. But, not surprisingly, the NEC came down heavily in favour of Lyons, who was strongly backed by his union, the National Union of Labour Organisers. It found:

> The party was "generally well administered".

> The statements to the inquiry by Mr and Mrs Maxwell and by Mr Leary were directed at the deficiencies and criticisms of the agent to which Lyons had given "reasonable explanations" and many of the complaints about him were "exaggerated beyond limits that could be substantiated".

> That not every member of the organisations which passed motions of no confidence had been invited to attend, nor had the agent.

> That there had been "undue influence and interference in party administration by the candidate" and difficult situations could arise if the candidate's wife held senior office in the party (even though she was a member of it). It excused the agent from responsibility for letting village organisation lapse and for not conducting the survey which had been agreed.

The NEC's decisions were savage. Although it said Lyons should be censured for failing to provide in written form a satisfactory plan in advance of the general election and for not putting in hand the essential preliminary work - the two main complaints against him which had led to the inquiry - it "severely censured" Maxwell for his "interference in the administration" of the constituency and warned him as to his future conduct; and "severely censured" Betty Maxwell, Arthur Leary, Ray Bellchambers and D. Holt, the four senior officers of the party, for failing to deal with the situation.

Mrs Maxwell retorted that since Mr Lyons had failed to do his job, someone else had to do it. Bob Maxwell concurred, saying[28]:

It is both illogical and unjust of Transport House to censure other people who are unpaid voluntary workers for doing the election work that had to be done by them because Mr Lyons failed to do his duty.

Arthur Leary said the findings were "undeserved and unfair". At the annual general meeting of the party in September 1971 Mrs Maxwell and Leary were re-elected vice-president and president respectively. But the disputes within the party were growing week by week. Throughout the country there had been a surge of left-wing influence in local Labour parties during the last years of the Wilson administration. Party activists passionately rejected the Government's tacit support of, or failure to condemn, the American war in Vietnam; they hated the Government's mild attempts to restrict the unions' rights to strike; they bitterly opposed restrictions on immigration, especially for Ugandan Asians; they did not want to enter the EEC. A number of MPs were to fall before these influences in the years ahead. Maxwell, foreign-born, an employer, a millionaire and now identified as a right-winger, was an obvious first target. A polytechnocracy was wielding its power inside the Labour party. The man who was to emerge as Maxwell's principal opponent, Geoff Edge, was a lecturer at the Open University, and a newcomer to the Buckingham party.

Short of giving away all his money, living in a squat and becoming a full-time research worker for community projects, there was no way in which Maxwell might have placated the new left. Eventually it was to be shown that he had the support of the vast majority of the officers and delegates to his party's management committee. But in the years that took to be demonstrated, irretrievable damage was done.

The Wolverton local party passed a vote of no confidence in Maxwell in October that year - the first public criticism made of him in 12 years as a candidate. Barnard said of the rise of the critics:

They didn't understand him. He's a "Go for it" kind of man who won't tolerate barriers to progress.

Betty Maxwell added:

Bob tends to see things his way…. He sees faster and farther than the rest of us. It is his strength. But it can antagonize. There were certainly people who felt threatened inside the local party. They wanted Bob out at all costs - even to the death of the party itself.

Maxwell pointed out that the secretary of the Wolverton party who had called a special meeting to condemn him had been defeated in the vote for election to the Buckingham executive committee whereas he had been elected by an overwhelming vote. Maxwell then lost his executive seat when the Bletchley party, advised by Lyons, who sympathised with the newcomers, "reorganised" and deprived him and four others of their places on it. Maxwell called for Lyons's resignation and the split widened as pro- and anti-Maxwell factions carried it into the local newspapers. The constituency party's general management committee condemned the Wolverton party by 34 votes to 21 and in December Lyons announced that he had decided to retire early and would leave within a month.

The struggle for supremacy went on throughout 1971, 1972 and 1973. But in all those years Maxwell continued to act on behalf of his former constituents and to speak as if he were already the chosen candidate for the next election, an MP in exile. He was chairman of the North Bucks Unfair Rent Committee, harried the Secretary of State for Social Security over burial grants, forecast a wage freeze, supported Britain's entry into the Common Market and denounced Richard Nixon's import surcharge for the effect it had upon local industries. As Buckingham finally moved in the late summer of 1973 to choose a parliamentary candidate - Bryan Barnard had already been reappointed as the agent - Geoff Edge made the mistake of saying that an independent Labour candidate might stand if Maxwell was chosen again. That is, short of leaving the party for another, the ultimate sin, and it rebounded badly upon him, with calls for his expulsion or suspension from the party.

Barnard described Edge as "a nasty bit of work". He went on:

> He never had the courage to stand up to face-to-face argument. Instead, he went round crawling to people behind Maxwell's back, drumming up bitterness here, pouring in the poison there.... He only became a member of the Labour party in the year before he settled in the constituency.

Mrs Maxwell still feels bitter about Edge's activities:

> He had a warped political brain, but there was a brain there. He set out to topple Bob and couldn't, but in the process he demolished the party. I remember tackling Edge and asking him why he hated us so much. But he merely said, "I can't tell you now but you'll understand later." Yes, I do understand now. People can be just plainly malicious and he was. Such people should never have been allowed to infiltrate the Labour party and destabilise it.

When the Buckingham selection conference was finally held at the end of September, Maxwell was overwhelmingly the choice, beating Stuart Holland, the left-wingers' nomination (and now MP for Vauxhall, London), by 82 votes to 29. A third candidate received only four votes. Maxwell had received 30 nominations from local parties, women's sections and trade unions; Holland received one from a local party (Wolverton) and five from trade union branches, including the Communist-dominated Bletchley Trades Council. Maxwell made a principal plank of his re-election speech his opposition to the nationalisation of Britain's 25 leading companies - he described it as "idiocy" - a proposition which was supported by Holland.

This had been approved late one evening by little more than a bare quorum of the NEC and had already been rejected by Harold Wilson. A complaint to the NEC against Maxwell's nomination was made by Bletchley Trades Council by six votes to four with two abstentions. It later transpired that the six who voted for it were all Communists. Maxwell said those opposing him were the "same small, unrepresentative minority". The president of the party, Jim Cassidy, who had opposed Maxwell's nomination in 1959 but now said he was a "100 per cent Maxwell man", told dissenters either to "Back Bob" or leave the party altogether.

Maxwell went straight to the Labour party conference where he spoke once again, this time on equality for women, and was rebuked by the chairman, Bill Simpson, for advocating that the party should withhold payment for use of the Winter Gardens, Blackpool, because of its scandalous underpayment of its women workers. Official NEC endorsement for his selection came in December as industrial action by the miners took increasing effect and the country began to move towards power blackouts, a three-day week and a general election. Election fever rose rapidly in January 1974, as Conservative politicians and the newspapers which supported them began to chorus the theme of "Who Governs Britain?" It was a fatally-flawed slogan, because the Heath Government had a satisfactory majority of 30 in the Commons and if it couldn't govern with that it was unlikely to be able to govern with double or treble it. Nevertheless, it had a powerful appeal in the affluent shire counties around London where there were no miners.

Heath stood out against the majority in the Cabinet who wanted a snap election - not because of the miners but because the Treasury's secret projections for rises in the cost of living from April onwards were horrendous - but eventually caved in and on February 7 announced a general election would be held on the 28th of the month. Maxwell and other Labour candidates in the south of England wisely chose to fight their campaigns on the cost of living.

For the first time in more than a generation the Liberal party looked to be in with a chance of saving more deposits than it would lose.

Buckingham had undergone various changes to its boundaries and there were some 7,000 more voters than there had been in 1970, most of them emigrants from London. These were thought largely to be Labour voters, though it has since been shown that many people who change their homes also change their votes. Certainly, none was a miner and the strike was a handicap as Labour struggled through the early days of the campaign. Maxwell, plumper than in earlier electoral battles, embarked on the same strenuous tour of the villages of the constituency, though the blackouts which the power cuts brought were a handicap to him as to everyone else. All the same, he was confident of winning, even over-confident, calling Buckingham a "safe Labour seat".

Heath was sufficiently concerned about Buckingham to go to Bletchley and make a speech there to party workers, while Maxwell made his speech from a Land Rover parked outside. When Heath came out, Maxwell tried to secure an untroubled path for the Prime Minister through a noisy crowd. He was unsuccessful. His efforts were not appreciated anyway by Conservative supporters, one of whom screamed:

> They're the extremists. There they are. They ought to be shot, the lot of them.

Another told *The Guardian*[29]:

> That man Maxwell is appalling. It simply is not done to disrupt another candidate's meeting. It shows you what five years of Wilson would be like.

It was hardly fair. Maxwell had arrived first.

On polling day the opinion polls put Heath back into power. The *Daily Mail* proclaimed, under the headline "A Handsome Win for Heath"[30]:

> Mr Heath will be back in Number 10 tomorrow with a heavily increased majority of 50 to 60 seats. Over Labour alone his lead will be 70-80.

The *Daily Express* said simply: "It's Heath by 5%."

In the event, Heath was out, after failing to negotiate a deal with the Liberal leader, Jeremy Thorpe, which would have kept a Conservative Government in office. Harold Wilson, as leader of the largest party, resumed the premiership. But Maxwell was not in the

Commons to support him. The Buckingham result was:

Benyon (Con)	27,179
Maxwell (Lab)	24,056
Crooks (Lib)	15,519
Con. majority	3,123

The percentage poll was high again, 85.1, and the Liberal kept his deposit comfortably.

Throughout the country the Liberal vote had soared, but in Buckingham it had clearly benefited Benyon rather than Maxwell. Benyon's vote was down by 909 compared with 1970 and Maxwell's by 1,511. The Liberal vote was up by 10,044. It was impossible to be sure whether the strife within the Buckingham party had fatally damaged Maxwell's chances of winning in an election whose circumstances were unique, but it certainly hadn't helped. Ironically, the man whom the Maxwell camp identified with the sapping of party morale, Geoff Edge, had been elected MP for Aldridge-Brownhills, a seat he held in the second election of that year, but he was defeated in 1979. He made no impact in his time in Parliament and has never returned to it.

Bryan Barnard in his election report had no doubt that Labour had lost the seat rather than the Tories had won it:

> We must not hide from the fact that to win elections in marginal constituencies it is absolutely necessary to have good organisation ... we were beaten by better organisation by both the Tory and Liberal camps. This is the agonising penalty we had to pay as a result of the unforgivable events surrounding 1970 and the subsequent period of almost four years when we were denied the right to organise. The whole of this period was taken up with party in-fighting....

Maxwell was glum, but predicted another election soon. *The Times* dismissed a Tory claim that he had antagonised a sizeable proportion of Labour voters, saying[31]:

> The extraordinary personal success story of this former Czech soldier impressed many ordinary people.

The *Milton Keynes Express* was sympathetic[32]:

> Mr Maxwell fought hard in the face of critical publicity which would have shattered the confidence of a less tough and urbane campaigner. To drop only 1,500 votes in the circumstances is quite a remarkable achievement....

Because of the imminence of another election, local parties were authorised to go ahead with choosing a candidate. Buckingham again chose Maxwell, in the same week in April in which he regained the chairmanship of Pergamon Press after an absence of four-and-a-half years.

On October 10, 1974 he faced the electors of Buckingham for the sixth time and with his third agent Peter Allison having replaced Bryan Barnard. Labour had ended the miners' strike and restored full-week working, but the cost of living was rising sharply. The Government hoped to win with a clear and large majority, but though the Conservative party had failed to make an impact in its seven months of opposition, Labour had failed to generate the enthusiasm which it needed if its majority was to be secure. The campaign in Buckingham was a repeat of February's, with the same three candidates. The Chancellor of the Exchequer, Denis Healey, another robust politician, went to Buckingham to speak for Maxwell and a local opinion poll gave him a slight lead, but with too many "Don't Knows" to give it any validity. In the event, Maxwell lost once more:

Benyon (Con)	26,597
Maxwell (Lab)	23,679
Crooks (Lib)	12,707
Con. majority	2,918

The percentage poll was disappointing for Buckingham - only 79.7. All the candidates received fewer votes than in February. It was small consolation that Maxwell lost fewest of all.

The remarkable thing was not that Maxwell lost Buckingham in 1970 and then twice failed to regain it in 1974, but that he won it and held it in 1964 and 1966. A tidal electoral change against Labour had begun in southern England which the sweeping victory of 1966 disguised. After 1974 it continued to strengthen. In the next general election after 1974 - May 3, 1979 - with an electorate increased by nearly 25,000, Benyon's vote rose by 13,500 and the new Labour candidate's by only 4,000. In June 1987 Benyon switched to the new town of Milton Keynes, where his majority was 13,701 over the Alliance candidate, with the Labour candidate a further 5,500 votes behind. At Buckingham the Conservative candidate had a majority of 18,526 over an Alliance candidate. Labour came third, with only 9,053 votes, more than 23,000 behind the victor.

After the second disappointment of 1974 Maxwell decided that he would not contest the seat again, to the joy of the minority of hard left-wingers, who remained unforgiving to the end, and to the distress of many ordinary members of the party who wrote to him of their tears. Bryan Barnard, now the party secretary, said of Maxwell in his annual report to the party:

> True, he was a glutton for publicity and perhaps he made enemies just as easily as he made friends and he was frequently controversial. Whether you liked Bob or disliked him, whether you agreed with him or disagreed with him ... the fact remains that he served his constituents well and in so doing he frequently penetrated the barriers of bureaucracy and red tape, an achievement which is beyond the capabilities of most men. We thank him and we wish him well.

Maxwell remained on Labour's list of prospective candidates and showed interest in a number of seats, including Brixton, London, and, especially, Kettering, Northamptonshire. He made a determined bid to win the seat there after the sitting member, Sir Geoffrey de Freitas, announced in 1977 that he would not contest the next election. But left-wingers on the local party's executive committee were determined to keep out anyone from the right. Though both Maxwell and Tom McNally, Jim Callaghan's political adviser who later defected to the SDP, received 10 or more nominations, their names were kept off the short-list of candidates. This rejection of Maxwell infuriated the local party secretary and agent, Henry Nairn, who resigned, saying that the "grass roots" of the party had been ignored. But no change was made. Kettering in those days was thought to be safe for Labour, but it is now a safe Conservative seat. Labour came third there in 1987.

When his attempt to gain the nomination for a seat in the European Parliament failed in 1979 - he would have stood as a supporter of Britain's membership, not an advocate of withdrawal - Maxwell abandoned his active political career. Even if he had secured the nomination for a winnable seat, it is doubtful whether he would have succeeded. After the second general election victory of 1974, it became almost impossible for Labour to retain any seat in a by-election. Losses in them meant that the Callaghan Government's majority quickly melted and it had to do a deal with the Liberals to stay in office. Its incomes policy broke down before union opposition. Then it was forced by defeat on a motion of confidence in the House of Commons to call an election in May 1979, in the worst possible circumstances, after a winter of heartless public service strikes. The Labour party activists of those days had little in common with most members of their own Cabinet; and least of all with the Prime Minister.

The party's opposition to the Common Market, the joining of

which Maxwell placed above any other domestic issue, grew with the election of Michael Foot as leader. The grip of the unilateralists tightened and Labour went into the next general election in 1983 pledged to unilateral disarmament, withdrawal from Europe and no incomes policy. Had Maxwell still been an MP he would constantly have been in trouble. It would have been impossible for him to retreat on the issues of defence and the EEC; and while he would have "privatised" differently and wanted to make changes in the Government's trade union reform laws, he could not have opposed either as a matter of deep principle. His support for the sale of council houses, which preceded the legislation by more than 20 years, would have been a further source of disruption. The new Labour party procedures for deselecting MPs were tailor-made for constituencies with members like Maxwell. Had he regained a seat in the House, the tumbrils would have been waiting.

William Davis wrote in *Punch* in October 1983:

> Robert Maxwell is perhaps the classical example of a businessman who tried his luck in politics and decided that it was a waste of time. He became an MP but failed time and time again to get promotion to ministerial rank because he was considered to be "too pushy". His ability was not the issue; his impatience with the political game most certainly was. He is now running a large corporation and is much happier.

Davis was wrong on his main count. Few men spend 20 years of their lives, certainly not a Maxwell, and then decide it was all a waste of time. Politics were, are, and will always be an integral part of Maxwell's life. Part of his success in business he owes to the fact that he thinks like a politician. He has always done so. He is not a businessman-turned-politician. He is a politician-turned-businessman.

Though Maxwell ceased to play an active public role in politics after 1979, his membership of the Labour party still rankled with those who believed that millionaire-employers had no place in it. He had a series of highly-publicised clashes with the printing trade unions. Almost every time there was an industrial dispute in one of his plants there was a demand for his expulsion from the party. The argument appeared to be that if he were not prepared to submit to any demand made by the unions - whether it was reasonable or outrageous - his membership should be forfeit. Sogat '82 and the National Graphical Union tried to get him expelled from the Oxford East constituency party because he had taken the unions to court. A West Country Labour party branch asked for his expulsion after a dispute in a factory near Bristol, even though the majority of union members there were not in dispute. Ron Brown, MP for Leith, whose eccentric support for Colonel Gaddafi was itself an embarrassment to the Labour party, wanted Maxwell's expulsion because of a dispute at the *Scottish Daily Record* of which Mr Brown appeared to know nothing.

A more thin-skinned man might have forestalled any action by the party and left it in a temper. But Maxwell shrugged it off, ignored the threats of the Oxford party, put Mrs Audrey Wise and Labour's National Executive in their places, and continued to support the party financially and publicly. When he bought Mirror Group Newspapers he committed them unfalteringly to continue their support for the Labour cause. With his encouragement, Mirror Group employees designed the publicity material for the Fulham by-election in 1986, which recorded a rare Labour victory. More than once he rejected informal soundings about a place in the House of Lords, which, for their Lordships' sake, was both a pity and an escape. The old place would never have been the same again had he fallen for the temptation.

In July 1986 Maxwell looked back on his political career in an interview on TVS. To the question "What did you achieve?" he answered:

> I suppose the most important thing was getting through a bill, the Clean Air Act of Great Britain.... It has been emulated or copied now by more than 100 countries throughout the world. I am very proud of that achievement.

But he had failed, he said, to achieve a better harnessing of science to industry. It would have been an easy thing for governments to do: all that was lacking was their political will. As for his experience of the House in general:

> I used to think I was the cleverest thing on two legs when I went into the House of Commons, but within six weeks I discovered that on the only thing I knew something about there were at least ten people who knew 100 times more. It's a very sobering experience.

8

Pergamon Lost - Pergamon Regained

Saul, Saul, why persecutest thou me?
Acts of the Apostles

The failure to win control of Butterworth's and the *News of the World* had been a severe disappointment to Maxwell, but his appetite for building up Pergamon's book and journal publishing and expanding it into the exciting new fields of information retrieval and data banks was unaffected. Indeed, the defeats he had suffered made him even more keen and that keenness, in turn, made him incautious. When, in January 1969, he received a call from Saul Steinberg, chairman of the Leasco Data Processing Co., one of the fastest-growing young businesses in the United States, suggesting a deal between his company and Pergamon, Maxwell jumped at the chance.

Superficially, Steinberg and Maxwell had a lot in common. Both were self-made men who had become millionaires in their twenties. Both were Jewish. Both were daring. Both their businesses were founded on a single bright idea which had not occurred to anyone else. Both were ambitious. Both were regarded with suspicion by the conservative financial establishments of their respective countries. Both wanted to expand. Both had suffered a major frustration. But there the similarities ended.

Steinberg came from a middle-class American family living in Brooklyn, where his father, Julius, ran a small household goods company. Steinberg said of his father[1]:

> He was unusual in that he was always satisfied with what he had and never wanted more.

It was not a case of like father, like son.

While he was still at business school Steinberg conceived a plan to undercut IBM in the leasing of computers by buying IBM's own

machines and then renting them out more cheaply. At first he had
no capital to put his theories into practice and worked for his father.
But eventually he persuaded Julius to put $25,000 into the Ideal
Leasing Company and signed up his first customer in May 1961,
interrupting his honeymoon to do so. Within two years the revenue
of the company had reached $2 million. By August 1965, when
Ideal, now renamed Leasco, became a public company, those
revenues had quadrupled and Steinberg was making profits of
around $225,000 a year. Like Pergamon when Maxwell floated his
company in 1964, the buyers were eager, even at $90 a share. At 26
Steinberg was a millionaire, even if only on paper. His offices had
moved to Park Avenue from Brooklyn and he and his family (wife
and three children) had moved to Long Island, where he began an
art collection which included a Matisse, a Picasso and a Renoir.

But the increasing speed of the advance in computer technology
soon meant that the machines Steinberg was leasing were becoming
obsolescent long before their contracts ran out, leaving him with
worthless computers left on his hands. Others had seized on his
original idea and were competing in leasing with him. There were
further problems too. Philip Jacobson, then the financial
correspondent of *The Times* in the United States, detailed them[2]:

> Like other leasing companies, Leasco has been criticised over
> accounting techniques. In particular, around the end of 1968, the
> financial weekly, *Barron's*, made some pointed observations about
> the group. It noted that although Mr Steinberg had previously
> enthusiastically aligned Leasco with the "financial" method of
> operating - where full investment plus profit were returned during the
> life of the first, unbreakable lease - and had also stated that all leases
> were insured for 85 per cent of receivables, things had subsequently
> changed radically.
>
> Leasco documents disclosed, none too prominently, a switch to the
> "operating" approach, where the group could not expect to recoup its
> full investment on first leases. *Barron's* also noted that Leasco no
> longer insured its leases, and that it had changed depreciation
> procedures to its advantage. *Barron's* felt that these important policy
> changes could have been given greater prominence by Leasco in its
> reports to shareholders.

Ironically, Leasco's complaints about Maxwell's accounting
techniques were to lie at the heart of the subsequent split with
Steinberg and the report of the two inspectors appointed by the
Department of Trade to investigate the Pergamon-Leasco affair.

In May 1968 Steinberg struck out in an entirely new direction,
buying up an old-established American insurance company,

Reliance, which was sitting on assets and investments which were undervalued. It added enormously to his financial power. Next he tried to buy the Chemical Bank, but the Wall Street establishment, it was said, did not want him in the banking field and organised his defeat.

There was a substantial selling of Leasco shares which forced down its price by 34 points within two weeks. Steinberg's chief advisers, White, Weld, left him and so did Lehman Bros. Jacobson says that at least one of Leasco's major clients threatened to take its business away if Leasco did not abandon its bid. Then both New York State and Congress rushed through bills to block the takeover of banks. Steinberg conceded defeat. Instead, he turned towards Europe for his further essay in expansion.

Steinberg's offer was to make Maxwell President of Leasco's operations in Europe, following an acquisition by Leasco of Pergamon Press. He and his lawyer, Bob Hodes, subsequently met Maxwell and painted a rosy picture of the burgeoning Leasco business and the likelihood of the company's share price continuing to rise. Steinberg told Maxwell he had been investigating Pergamon for several months and that he particularly wanted to join up with a major scientific publishing house. Pergamon, he said, was "ideal". Leasco wanted to link the scientific information held by Pergamon with their computer storage facilities, the marriage of software to hardware. At first Maxwell would not commit himself, but he continued discussions with Steinberg and his advisers throughout April and May of 1969. Finally, on June 17, after four days of negotiations in New York, an agreement was reached and signed. By it, Maxwell undertook to accept on his own behalf the offer for shares in Pergamon made by Steinberg and to secure the acceptance of members of the family for theirs. The effect was that Leasco was making an agreed £25 million takeover bid for Pergamon, pricing the company's shares at 37s (185p), about 11s (55p) higher than the price then obtaining on the London Stock Exchange. Leasco would buy from Maxwell 34 per cent of the Pergamon shares held by him and his family and he promised to recommend to the 3,000 other shareholders that they also should sell to Leasco. The major part of the purchase price would be paid for in Leasco stock. For shareholders outside the Maxwell family the offer was to be either Leasco stock or cash. Maxwell was told that the Leasco stock (then standing at $37) would rise to $50, that the company had 60 million Eurodollars on deposit and would get $100 million from its purchase of Reliance. Maxwell subsequently declared, in an affidavit for an action against the *Sunday Times* which, in the end, was settled without an action being heard:

> The Leasco representatives did not produce any current financial statements, saying that the figures were unavailable, and I over-ruled the worries of my advisers and their advice not to sign the agreement until further information about Leasco had been provided. I should have observed advice on this occasion.

Though agreement had been reached, the first seeds of future trouble had been sown. There is no doubt that Steinberg was intending to take over Pergamon. But despite the fact that he was to become the majority shareholder in the company, it was probably at that time he began to suspect that Maxwell's intention was to take over Leasco in Europe. *The Times* reported that when it telephoned Steinberg at his London office on June 18 a "surprisingly English voice" answered. *The Times* went on[3]:

> It was Robert Maxwell … breathless to know how the press was reacting to the big proposed sell-out.

The Times was also surprised by the press conference which was held that day:

> Normally at a press conference summoned to announce a takeover bid, it is the bidder who does the talking…. The meeting lasted 50 minutes in which time Robert Maxwell did 90 per cent of the talking.

Before the agreement was signed the President of Leasco, Bernard Schwartz, and the head of its Corporate Planning Department, Michael Gibbs, came to Britain to meet Maxwell and look at the books of Pergamon. Gibbs told Maxwell that it was on his recommendation that Steinberg had approached him. There was a further examination of Pergamon's books by Leasco representatives at Oxford on July 3 and 4. They stated they were satisfied in every respect. Maxwell's affidavit went on:

> At about this time, unknown to me, Leasco had already begun to purchase large blocks of Pergamon shares on the open market although I had been given to understand that Leasco would not acquire more than 10 per cent of the shares before they made a formal offer. I expressed some concern, although I cannot remember whether it was to Steinberg or to Rodney Leach of Rothschild's, Leasco's merchant bank. In any event, the reply was that I should not worry as the purpose of the acquisition was solely to save money as the shares could be purchased at a price less than the proposed offer price of 37 shillings (185p).

On July 10, the Bank of England gave permission for Leasco's bid to proceed and on the 18th the Board of Trade said that it would not be referred to the Monopolies Commission. Leasco continued to buy Pergamon shares until they held 38 per cent of them, bought at a cost of £9.5 million, over and above the shares which had been pledged to them by Maxwell.

There were further investigations by the Leasco auditors, Touche Ross, in Oxford and London between July 16 and 24. They were given full access to all Pergamon's papers and they asked for more information about the Maxwell family's various private companies. Maxwell then attended a meeting in New York on August 7 with one English and one American partner of Touche Ross and representatives of Maxwell Scientific International, one of Maxwell's companies. Again, Touche Ross's accountants were given access to any records which they wished to see.

On August 13 Steinberg wrote to "Dear Bob", cordially inviting him to a meeting at the Pierre Hotel, New York, "to make a thorough examination of where we are and where we want to go". Steinberg had now begun to question the Pergamon profit forecasts. He said he wanted to create a "retention fund" into which he would pay half the price for the Maxwell family shares until the forecast profits were realised.

At first Maxwell was reluctant to agree, but raised no fundamental objection, beyond insisting that:

> This will not be disclosed and that nothing will need to be published in the offer document that is likely to be harmful to Pergamon's or my credibility.

But later, on August 18, after discussions with his solicitor, Paul Di Biase, he decided that certain conditions had to be imposed, the main one being that he had to retain management control in order to ensure that Leasco did not deliberately fail to meet the profit targets and thus be able to refuse to pay the second half of the agreed price of the shares.

Steinberg had flown to London and was staying at Claridge's Hotel. In a lengthy letter to him there on August 19 Maxwell said that he had agreed to Steinberg's proposals to retain $10 million against a net profit of $3 million for 1970 and 1971 because he had felt Pergamon would easily earn it. Indeed, he was prepared to forego the whole of the retention fund if that figure were not reached, provided that the other half of the agreement - no publication - was adhered to. But Rothschild's and Pergamon's advisers had met and were unanimous that if the retention agreement went ahead it would have to be disclosed. In that event,

Maxwell said, it would inevitably damage his and Pergamon's credibility "no matter how it is wrapped up".

Rodney Leach had told him, he wrote, that the retention proposals were "untenable, should not have been made by you nor accepted by me and had he been present at that part of our meeting … he would have dissuaded us…". Maxwell told Steinberg he was concerned about "the damaging rumours" stemming from the delayed issue of the offer document. He also complained that Steinberg's accountants did not fully comprehend the nature of Pergamon's business:

> The figures have been got up to show the most pessimistic results without giving Pergamon credit for the things which they are properly due under British or American accounting practices…. Bona fide book sales to Maxwells and MSI, the bulk of which have already been sold to third parties, are also improperly eliminated.

Maxwell said that deductions from the 1968 profit figures had been erroneously made and he listed his objections which made the retention agreement unworkable, including:

> The damage to the credibility of himself, his advisers and Pergamon by any implied or tacit admission that the 1968 accounts did not give a true and fair view of the profits.

> The destruction of one of the major assets for Leasco and the incentives for him of the merger - his mission and responsibility to look after Leasco's international business.

> The fact that he would, of necessity, need to retain complete control over management and investments and would be compelled to take a narrow Pergamon and short-term view.

> The impossibility of going back to the various trustee funds and getting them to agree to the retention fund.

> The problems involved in drafting the legal document, including the difficulty of defining profits.

> Provision for changes in tax rates and devaluation of any currencies.

He told Steinberg he was confident that Pergamon's profits would not only be more than $3 million but would exceed £3 million and he saw no reason why his family should be treated any worse than any other shareholder.

This "late and substantial change" proposed in the price would also mean that undertakings which Leasco had given to the Board of Trade, the Ministry of Technology and the Treasury would be difficult, if not impossible, to fulfil and government consent for the merger would need to be reapplied for. In addition, Maxwell was also disturbed by what he described as a sudden "high-handed and undiscussed" proposal from Steinberg to cut his service agreement with Leasco from five years to 15 months:

> This is bound to diminish my authority within the Pergamon Group and with all of the organisations, editors and authors with whom we deal, thus completely prejudicing my ability to earn … the profits required by Leasco.

Maxwell offered to meet Steinberg and Rothschild's in a final attempt to find a "mutually satisfactory solution". He added:

> Should this not be possible I can see no alternative to our terminating the negotiations.… I do hope you can bring about a last-minute miracle that will enable us to fulfil our dream of creating, over the next five years, a world-wide business corporation that will earn as much money overseas as Leasco currently earns from all its operations in North America.

A complication arose on August 20 when Maxwell learned that the trustees for a trust formed for his children had sold 600,000 shares in Pergamon on the open market. Maxwell authorised Robert Fleming and Co., his advisers, to make the news public. Next day he appeared before the City Takeover Panel to explain the situation. He told it that the settler of the trust concerned was a Mr De Pfyffer, the American attorney for some relatives of Maxwell in the United States, and that the discretionary beneficiaries were nephews and nieces and his own children, though not Maxwell himself. He had met De Pfyffer only once and he had not known in advance of the sale.

That same evening Rothschild's announced that the merger was being called off by Steinberg, citing among his reasons the position of ILSC, the company jointly owned by Pergamon and BPC which had suffered from the depredations of its crooked directors - who were in place at the time Maxwell bought the company - the trading relationship between Pergamon and MSI, and the composition of the published forecast of earnings by Pergamon for 1969. Maxwell claimed that Leasco had pulled out because it didn't have the money to complete the bid[4]:

> They were between two evils - having to announce they hadn't the cash or attacking Pergamon. They chose the second.

Steinberg said that was "rubbish" and that his company had $100 million in cash. Maxwell retorted that the $100 million was locked up in Reliance Insurance and belonged to Reliance's policy holders. Maxwell's merchant bank advisers, Flemings, immediately resigned, saying Maxwell had not consulted them about the statement. His stockbrokers, Panmure Gordon, also ceased to act for him. *The Times* said[5]:

> The withdrawal of the stockbrokers, perhaps even more than that of Flemings, will give Mr Maxwell the impression that his City friends are deserting him in the hour of his greatest need.

At a hearing of the Takeover Panel on August 25-27 Maxwell withdrew his allegation, but said that if Leasco did have the cash the only reason for its withdrawing from the bid must be to get control of Pergamon more cheaply. Rothschild's told the Panel it was greatly disturbed by the sale of Pergamon shares by De Pfyffer. It said it had asked Maxwell five times during the night of August 18-19 whether he could guarantee delivery by the trust and he had replied in the affirmative and the news of this sale had been regarded by Leasco as the last straw that broke the camel's back. During the hearing it was clear that the gulf between the two sides, who by then thoroughly distrusted each other, was growing by the minute. It was also clear that Maxwell wasn't making a good impression on the Panel. It was his misfortune that he was the last victim of the previous pusillanimous Panel (in his takeover bid for the *News of the World*) and the first victim of the new one which was determined to demonstrate its strength.

Maxwell rejected a suggestion that he should invite the Board of Trade to conduct an inquiry into the circumstances surrounding the takeover, saying that inquiries had a connotation of fraud and as such would be damaging to Pergamon's credibility. The chairman of the Panel, Lord Shawcross, disagreed; though he would bear the factor in mind, he said, the public interest was paramount.

On the night of August 26-27 Steinberg made a new bid to acquire Pergamon, under which Leasco would purchase Pergamon shares for what Hodes admitted to the Panel was likely to be "significantly less" than the original 37s. The director of the Panel, Ian Fraser, said that someone would have to guarantee that the offer would not be less than 37s, but neither Maxwell nor Leasco was prepared to do so. Steinberg, from New York, dug in his heels and refused to make a further offer.

The Takeover Panel, in a statement on August 27, said[6]:

> [It] is satisfied that Leasco's decision to withdraw from the proposed offer was the result not so much of any single factor as of the cumulative effect of a series of difficulties and doubts which eventually destroyed their confidence. The agreement between Mr Maxwell and Leasco involved the former's employment by Leasco as

Chief Executive in charge of their foreign interests, including Pergamon, and his appointment as vice-chairman of the parent board in the United States. The arrangement contemplated was, therefore, one to the success of which personal confidence was essential ... this breakdown of confidence was mutual....

The Panel examined whether there had been a full disclosure by the board of Pergamon of all relevant matters. It went on:

In view of what follows, it is right that the Panel should state at this point that nothing in the information before it casts doubt on the standing or future prospects of Pergamon, a company which under the energetic leadership of Mr Maxwell has made notable progress. Nor is there any suggestion at all of personal misconduct on Mr Maxwell's part.

In the opinion of the Panel, however, there are substantial grounds for questioning whether the shareholders of Pergamon were in fact given at the appropriate times all the information about the affairs of their company which, in the circumstances, they would reasonably be entitled to expect. The Panel emphasises that it is the information made available to Pergamon shareholders rather than to Leasco with which it is in the present context mainly concerned.

Those concerns related to ILSC and the relationship between Pergamon and companies owned by what Maxwell had described as "Maxwell family interests".

The Panel repeated that there was "no suggestion of any personal misconduct" and that a full investigation might well show all the transactions in question had been conducted with complete propriety:

But having regard to all the circumstances ... the Panel considers that the public interest does require that the true position should be established by an independent investigation.... The Panel has, therefore, decided to call the attention of the Board of Trade to these matters with a view to that Department exercising its power to inquire whether in fact the members of Pergamon have been given all the information with respect to that company's affairs which they might reasonably expect to receive.

Meanwhile, Steinberg flew to London from New York to reopen negotiations with Maxwell. On August 29 they agreed to reshape the Pergamon board with Steinberg and four Leasco nominees and Maxwell with four of his nominees, plus two others to be named by Rothschild's and agreed with Maxwell, serving on it. Steinberg said in a BBC interview:

I think that Pergamon is a good, sound company.

The talks quickly broke down. By September 5 Steinberg was demanding that his nominee, Peter Stevens, should be given full powers of management of the merged company. Maxwell said he wasn't prepared to surrender it.

On September 13 Leasco announced that it had again withdrawn from the bid talks and would ask the Pergamon shareholders to sack all their seven directors and put in seven directors nominated by Leasco. Steinberg said he would consider reappointing some Pergamon directors, but they all rebuffed him, saying that unless Leasco got control by making a successful offer to shareholders they would not work under Leasco management. Steinberg was then reported in the *Wall Street Journal* as having said that Leasco had[7]

accomplished its purpose of taking over the British concern without having to pay the $60 million it had expected it would cost.

Maxwell said[8]:

Perhaps people will now believe what I have been saying all along: I have been trying to stop Leasco buying Pergamon on the cheap.

Rothschild's said that the *Wall Street Journal* had misunderstood and misquoted Steinberg. The *Journal* reporter said, in true American tradition:

I stand by my story.

A Pergamon shareholders' meeting was called for October 10, at noon. At that stage Steinberg, who had promised the Takeover Panel not to purchase any more Pergamon shares for 12 months, held 38 per cent of the shares and Maxwell 28 per cent. The 15 per cent held by the City institutions - Pearl Assurance and ICI and its pension fund among them - was thus crucial.

Rothschild's said Leasco wanted a new board for Pergamon consisting of an independent chairman with overriding executive powers, an additional independent director and three Leasco and three Pergamon full-time executive directors, other than Maxwell. He would merely be invited to act as a consultant. Bankers acting for the City institutions accepted these proposals and nominated Sir Henry d'Avigdor-Goldsmid, banker and bullion dealer and Conservative MP for Walsall South, to be the independent chairman. Sir Henry agreed to become so for "a limited period".

Maxwell's new bankers, William Brandt, declared[9]:

That Mr Maxwell is of essential importance to the business is accepted by all concerned.

On the day before the shareholders' meeting Rothschild's secured a High Court injunction restraining Maxwell from adjourning the meeting, a step he described as "arrogant and stupid", in view of the fact that Lord Aldington, a distinguished former Conservative MP and Board of Trade minister, representing Brandt's, had promised that the meeting would be conducted according to "Marquis of Queensberry rules". Many years later Lord Aldington explained why Brandt's had agreed to become Maxwell's advisers:

> I had a strong streak of admiration for him. He was intensely patriotic and a go-go man, something we needed in British business. He was sometimes difficult but always a positive man.

There was a large turnout for the meeting, which at times had uncanny echoes of the *News of the World* EGM called to prevent Maxwell acquiring that company. The shareholders present were overwhelmingly on Maxwell's side and slow-handclapped Leasco representatives who tried to speak. But Steinberg and his representative, Stevens, were elected on a show of hands. Maxwell told the meeting:

> I am in a position to ... make an offer for all the non-Leasco shares held by the institutions and the public for cash at a price of 25s (£1.25) a share.

To their later regret and cost, the institutions spurned the offer.

A resolution proposed by Maxwell leaving the existing management to run the company was carried on a show of hands by 228 to 67. But when a poll was held the institutions' vote, added to Leasco's, gave Steinberg a decisive victory - 61 per cent to 33 per cent with six per cent abstaining. Nine Pergamon directors, including Maxwell, were removed from the board and seven Leasco nominees, including Steinberg, were elected in their place.

The company which Maxwell had built from nothing and whose success had for 20 years seemed unstoppable had cast him out. Messages of sympathy flooded in. Woodrow Wyatt wrote:

> I am sure that your energy and brains will secure victory from defeat in the end ... although the campaigning against you has often been very unpleasant ... the British sense of fair play will ensure that it is eventually counter-productive.

Professor Ronald Belcher of Birmingham University said in a letter:

> Obviously there was too much dirty work in the backstairs department for you to cope with, without resorting to the same tactics.

Professor Boris Ford of the University of Sussex declared:

> It simply isn't possible to think of Pergamon in your absence.

George Scott Blair wrote angrily:

> Your many friends all over the world will be shocked and
> disgusted.... I'm afraid that your fate shows the rottenness of the
> whole system.

And Professor Sir Nevill Mott wrote from Cambridge:

> Robert Maxwell's Pergamon has become part of our scientific life and
> we will not think much of it in any other way.

Despite the sympathy, at the time it seemed as if Maxwell had
reached the bottom of the pit. But even worse was to follow.

Nevertheless, at a time when the City and the financial press had
mainly written him off, he kept his head. He remained the tenant of
Headington Hill Hall, part of which had included the Pergamon
offices. That meant that his dominating physical presence was
always there. He also kept control of the American offshoot of
Pergamon, Pergamon Press, Inc., despite the fact that Leasco
owned, through Pergamon at Oxford, 70 per cent of the shares.

The Board of Trade inquiry into Pergamon's interest in ILSC and
Maxwell Scientific International was conducted by Owen Stable,
QC, and Sir Ronald Leach, senior partner in the firm of chartered
accountants Peat, Marwick and Mitchell. They were appointed
early in September 1969 and declared they wanted to complete the
inquiry with as little delay as possible, a commendable ambition but
one which was to lead them into errors; those errors, in turn, were
to be compounded by a procedure, established in 1890, which was
amply demonstrated to be unfair, inadequate and inefficient.
Nevertheless, when the inspectors made their statement Maxwell
agreed with them and promised his full co-operation. But then
Leasco brought proceedings against him in the United States' courts
claiming $22 million compensation for Pergamon shares which it
had bought on the open market (a hopeless suit, though enlivened
by hilarious attempts by the Sheriffs' officers in various United
States' cities trying and failing to serve the writ upon him) and by
the fact that having lost Pergamon he no longer had access to its
papers and records. He was also concerned that the inspectors'
report, published or not, would be sent to Pergamon, which meant
Leasco. His lawyers therefore advised him not to appear before the
inspectors until he ascertained the procedure they intended to
follow and whether he would be given notice of any allegations
made against him. The inspectors declined to give the assurances
and Maxwell and several other former directors refused to appear
before them unless ordered to do so by a court.

The inspectors did go to law. In April 1970 Mr Justice Plowman ordered that although the inspectors were bound by rules of natural justice (which their counsel had argued they were not), Maxwell's demands went too far. In the Court of Appeal, when ordering Maxwell and the others to answer the inspectors' questions, Lord Denning, then Master of the Rolls, declared of the inspectors:

> They must be masters of their own procedure. They should be subject to no rules save this: They must be fair.

It was a phrase to assume great significance later in the saga, when it became manifestly clear that they were not. Another statement which grew in importance as matters developed contained a commitment made by Owen Stable to two Pergamon directors. It greatly impressed the Court of Appeal:

> If, after we have listened to the evidence and have studied all the documents supplied to us, we came to the conclusion that there were certain matters on which we thought certain individuals were at fault, it would be right to recall those individuals before us, put to them broadly what the criticism is and ask them if there is an explanation. I think that natural justice requires that.

Lord Justice Sachs, sitting in the Court with Lord Denning, said that statement showed that the inspectors were going to do exactly what was right:

> To give at the appropriate later stage to anyone in danger of being criticised notice of the potential criticism in general terms sufficient to enable him to know what the allegation was....

In the event, Maxwell gave evidence to the inspectors on a dozen occasions between August 1970 and June 1971. In the affidavit mentioned above, Maxwell said of Lord Justice Sachs's statement:

> I had this particular passage very much in mind when I was giving evidence to the inspectors.... I had been worried by rumours that I had heard that the inspectors had completed a report which was very hostile towards me and I pointed out to them my concern.... As it happens, the inspectors had indeed signed their first report on June 2, 1971, so ... I no longer had the opportunity of making further representations to them on the matters contained in the first report although the inspectors did not point this out to me.

The first report was published on July 13, 1971, despite efforts by Maxwell and Sir Charles Hardie, chairman of BPC, to have it deferred or amended. It was 100,000 words long and substantially flawed by the acceptance as reliable of the evidence of witnesses who had been proven to be dishonest and who had been sacked by

Maxwell. It concentrated on the acquisition of Caxton Publishing, and especially its business in South Africa, and accused a former director of BPC, Michael Pickard, of advising Hedley Le Bas to accept the Pergamon-BPC offer without disclosing BPC's interest; it further accused Maxwell and, in one instance, his bankers, Ansbachers, of making inaccurate, untrue or misleading statements. All of these were later to be rebutted by Maxwell, but they led the inspectors to their notorious attack on Maxwell's conduct of his business affairs:

> ... in reporting to shareholders and investors he had a reckless and unjustified optimism which enabled him on some occasions to disregard unpalatable facts and on others to state what he must have known was untrue....

> We regret having to conclude that, notwithstanding Mr Maxwell's acknowledged abilities and energy, he is not in our opinion a person who can be relied on to exercise proper stewardship of a publicly-quoted company.

Maxwell responded with predictable fury. First he and BPC issued writs against the Department of Trade seeking to have the report declared null and void, claiming that the "purported report" was written in breach of the inspectors' obligations. His solicitors, Lewis Silkin and Partners, said:

> Abuses of procedure took place and were such as to make it impossible for Mr Maxwell and others to have a fair opportunity to explain the matters on which the inspectors have reached wrong conclusions.

BPC said that the inspectors[10]

> had acted contrary to the principles of natural justice in the conduct of their investigations and the report in its present form cannot stand.

Maxwell called a press conference and said:

> I wasn't looking for a whitewash, but I'm not accepting a smear. The inspectors have virtually deprived me of earning my living. They accuse me of being optimistic. I plead guilty. Of being reckless. Not true. Of telling untruths. Not true.

The inspectors, he said, had followed a Star Chamber procedure. The promise they had made - that if individuals were found to be at fault they would be recalled and the criticisms put to them - had not been fulfilled. Even if his legal action were successful, he said, it was doubtful if he would ever be able to eradicate the stigma of the report.

It was "a great injustice, a great sin", he declared.

In his more measured affidavit he said:

> The inspectors had formed the view that I was to blame for virtually every single transaction which had been investigated. They made a number of criticisms which were totally unrealistic, but in particular my criticism was that they preferred the evidence of other witnesses (in particular people I had dismissed) without giving me any idea that they proposed to do so, which meant I was not able to bring before them documents which not only showed that their conclusions were wrong but that the evidence of the people they were relying on indicated, at best, those people had faulty memories and, at worst, that they were blatant liars.
>
> I was stunned by the first report and after studying it carefully I gave instructions to my advisers to consider what action (if any) could be taken.

One aspect of the inspectors' report which is heavily open to criticism but which received little notice at the time is the fact that they placed a great deal of weight upon the evidence of Hedley Le Bas in considering their findings about Caxton Publishing. Le Bas, as Maxwell had already discovered, was a crook and a drunk and Maxwell had fired him. He and his accomplice, Jenman, who was not a drunk, had given evidence to Maxwell's detriment to the inspectors. Had Stable's undertaking to abide by the rules of natural justice been adhered to, Maxwell would have had the opportunity to rebut the evidence which Le Bas and Jenman had given against him. But it was not and he could not. Samuel (now Lord) Silkin, QC, who was later to become Attorney-General, acted for Maxwell in the eventual trial of his action against the inspectors. He told me:

> Mr Le Bas clearly became most bitter against Mr Maxwell and made to the inspectors accusations intended to be to his discredit.... These accusations were denied by Mr Maxwell but were substantially accepted by the inspectors. It is clear they regarded Mr Le Bas as a reliable witness and Mr Maxwell as an unreliable witness....
>
> In the course of the hearing before Mr Justice Forbes a number of documents which Mr Maxwell had received from Mr Le Bas were produced. These documents had not been referred to in the inspectors' report and it is not known whether they had studied, or even seen, them.
>
> Mr Le Bas had said to the inspectors that ... ILSC was "skint" and said "there could be no reason why we had £200,000 to pay out in profits. There were not any accounts." In his contemporary letters to Mr Maxwell and reports to the board, Mr Le Bas painted a very different picture from that which he gave, some years later, to the inspectors. The forecast profits of £200,000 would, he said, have been

realised if the auditors had not handled write-offs "in an abnormally harsh fashion ...". He followed this with his general assessment: "When I took over the managing directorship of the joint companies, the turnover was around £3 million a year. It is now running at £6 million to £7 million per year."

Lord Silkin commented:

Trying to be as fair as possible to Mr Le Bas, it is hard to follow the basis on which his evidence could reasonably be preferred to that of Mr Maxwell.

The hearing before Mr Justice Forbes, to which Lord Silkin referred, took place in September 1970 when Maxwell applied for an interlocutory injunction seeking to prevent the inspectors from continuing with their inquiry. The judge was the only member of the Bench to have read the full transcript of the evidence given to the inquiry. Though he declined to award the injunction, he was severely critical of the inspectors who, he said, had moved from an inquisitorial role to an accusing one, and asked:

Once they decided they were not merely investigating and finding facts but were going on to make criticisms, should they not have informed Mr Maxwell?

What really disturbs me is that these last paragraphs in the report are paragraphs which say, "We form the opinion that Mr Maxwell was the person who was doing everything and not listening to anyone", leading up to the resounding final conclusion that he is unfit to be in control of a public company.

The last paragraph, said the judge, "was entirely gratuitous". Raymond Kidwell, QC, for the inspectors, replied:

It was a general conclusion, it was an opinion which they formed.

The judge commented:

An opinion which they formed which was highly damaging and practically business murder as far as Mr Maxwell was concerned.

Mr Justice Forbes said that the inspectors should have asked Maxwell why he sacked a number of senior executives over a short period, because they had criticised him for it:

There may be no dispute on that finding, but when the inspectors go on to make a criticism of Mr Maxwell and his stewardship, that is a matter which should have been put to Mr Maxwell. He might have had some explanation for it.

The following day he returned to the same point, saying that the "swingeing" criticisms of Maxwell would be "a black mark against him for ever", and asking:

> Should not the inspectors have given him an opportunity to defend himself?

In his judgment on the ninth day of the hearing, Mr Justice Forbes said:

> It will be seen that the inspectors, though they clearly have the power, have no duty to criticise anybody. They may, in the course of their investigation, or at the end of it, feel it their duty to make criticisms of the conduct of certain persons, but if they do so it seems to me that they abandon their role as finders of fact and assume a different role - one of accusation....

> The inspectors' report, when delivered to the Department, will form the basis on which the Department will decide whether criminal proceedings should be instituted against anyone concerned with the company under investigation.

> If such proceedings are started, the defendant in those proceedings will have the opportunity not only of knowing what the precise charge against him is, but of hearing all the evidence on which that charge is based and of testing it by cross-examination. He will also be able to put before the tribunal evidence and argument to counter the prosecution's case....

> A criticism by inspectors in a report which is published to the world may have much the same effect as the punishment that a criminal court could impose, but that criticism is subject to no challenge and no appeal.

The judge said:

> At no stage did they indicate to Mr Maxwell that they were minded to make or ever might make any criticisms themselves, let alone give an indication of the form that the criticism might take. I have been through the entire transcript of the evidence of Mr Maxwell and that is the summary of the manner in which the inspectors carried out this investigation.

On the final paragraph of the report, the judge commented:

> This conclusion stands against Mr Maxwell's name and amounts to banning him permanently from business life, for no body of shareholders would be wise to appoint as a director a man against whom this criticism stood. It is a fundamental rule that before being convicted of any offence a man should know the substance of the charge made against him. For myself, I cannot see how this rule can be satisfied unless a man knows both the fact that he is being charged and the identity of the charge that is being made.

In order to satisfy this rule, the charge must be formulated with some precision. It is also necessary to acquaint the man with the substance of the evidence against him before asking him to make his defence....
It seems to me insufficient merely to put to the witness possible criticism of his conduct. They must bring home to him that he stands to be criticised by the inspectors in a particular fashion and inform him of their reasons for reaching that provisional conclusion. I think that this point was at one time clear to the inspectors.

His last remark related to Stable's promise quoted above:

It is impossible to read that passage as meaning anything other than that there should be three stages. First, the hearing of evidence (including Mr Maxwell's) and the study of documents. Secondly, the inspectors coming to a conclusion (necessarily tentative in the circumstances), and, thirdly, putting the substance of that conclusion to the witness....

It follows that, in my judgment, the probability is that the trial judge would find a failure by the inspectors to direct themselves properly as to the rules of natural justice which should govern their investigations. My decision in this matter most emphatically does not mean that the inspectors have been unfair, as that term is often used. It merely means that in my judgment it is likely that at the trial of this action they may be found to have taken a wrong decision in a field where the landmarks are few and the terrain confused.

In refusing the injunction, he said that to grant it would mean that two years' work by the inspectors would be wasted. But they had undertaken not to deliver a further report until the Court of Appeal had decided upon Mr Maxwell's application, provided he moved quickly. If the Court decided that he (Justice Forbes) was right and that there was a real likelihood of Maxwell succeeding at the trial of the action, it would be tantamount to saying the inspectors had made an error in the conduct of their investigation. In that case he thought it inconceivable that the inspectors would do other than suspend their inquiry.

Maxwell said the judge had "fully vindicated" his view that the report had not been prepared in accordance with natural justice, but wanted to go ahead with an appeal. Silkin advised him not to; in his belief, the words of Mr Justice Forbes would ensure that natural justice would prevail.

At that moment all appeared to be going in Maxwell's favour. Anthony Bambridge wrote in *The Observer*[11]:

I bet he wins. I can see the headlines now. Pergamon quote restored. Maxwell makes cash bid for Pergamon shares. Maxwell wins. Chairman Maxwell comes home. Vote of confidence from loyal employees. "He's my Mr Wonderful", says office cleaner.

Apart from the office cleaner, whose reaction was not recorded, Bainbridge was right in every respect, but he was not to be proved so for a long time and the delay between forecast and achievement was to do considerable damage to Maxwell's reputation and to the fortunes of Pergamon Press. The *New Statesman* declared[12]:

> By his vigorous counter-attack against the Department of Trade and Industry, Mr Maxwell may already have ensured that he will be the last person to be subjected to this kind of administrative "fishing expedition" masquerading as a legal process.

Maxwell's decision not to appeal against the refusal of an injunction left the inspectors free to publish their second report, which they did on April 11, 1972. This concentrated on the affairs of Pergamon's subscription book division which was, they said:

> a history of the overstatement of its normal trading profits and exaggerated claims of its sales ... both must have had a material effect on the value of Pergamon's shares in the stock market.

Maxwell was abroad when the second report was issued. He expressed his surprise that the DTI had issued a further report without prior notice and again without giving him a chance to refute hearsay accusations. His solicitors announced further proceedings against the Department and the inspectors to have "this ... tainted document set aside".

Maxwell's first action against the inspectors was heard before Mr Justice Wien in the High Court at the end of November 1972. Unfortunately for Maxwell he took a diametrically opposite view from Mr Justice Forbes about the way in which the inspectors had acted and how they should act in the future. In his view the needs of natural justice were served if Maxwell was made aware of the fact that on certain matters he might be open to criticism. After that it was up to him to follow up those matters by producing further material which might exonerate him. If he didn't, he could not, in the judge's opinion, complain of unfairness. In the hearing of Maxwell's application for an injunction Mr Justice Forbes had considered the argument whether the public interest required a speedy conclusion of the inquiry and commented:

> It cannot be right to suggest that injustice should be done because to do justice would be a tedious and lengthy process.

But Mr Justice Wien disagreed. He said that an inquiry of this kind was of such complexity that to adopt the procedure Maxwell wanted would indefinitely prolong it and was impracticable.

Maxwell had engaged Lord Silkin to conduct his case, but at the end of the fourth day he dismissed him and decided to conduct it himself. Lord Silkin told the judge that he was withdrawing because of "an amicable difference of opinion between us on a matter about which Mr Maxwell feels strongly", which was a question about which witnesses to call. Maxwell says:

> Mr Justice Wien viewed the case (so far as I am concerned) in an extremely narrow way and effectively said that the only relevant point was whether the inspectors had questioned me in such a way as to indicate that I stood to be criticised. The first three days of the trial were quite stormy in that Mr Silkin [as he then was] continually tried to draw to the attention of the judge matters of fact which showed the inspectors to have been wrong, but Mr Justice Wien was not having any of it. He finally said in no uncertain terms that he would not listen to such matters and would not allow Mr Silkin to refer to them…. Mr Silkin said to me that he could no longer attempt to draw the judge's attention to such matters, bearing in mind the very clear direction he had been given.
>
> We agreed amicably that the only way for witnesses to be called and for an attempt to be made to show that the inspectors had been wrong in their conclusions would be if I conducted my own case because the judge would have to allow me as a litigant in person rather more latitude….
>
> In the event, the judge continued to ignore all these points [showing that the inspectors were wrong] and gave me a very rough time although, as I envisaged, he did not refuse to let me bring whatever evidence I chose.

At the end of the 13-day action Mr Justice Wien ruled that Maxwell had failed to substantiate any allegation of unfairness:

> I cannot accept that the rules of natural justice in an investigation of this kind required the inspectors to put the substance of their conclusions to a witness whose words or actions were to be criticised.

But he did agree that Maxwell had no other course open to him but to try to prove that the inspectors had reached the wrong conclusions:

> He has no right of appeal and if the inspectors acted in accordance with the principles of natural justice he cannot take the matter any further. Parliament has made no provision for his so doing and I express no view whether Parliament ought to do so.

Maxwell went to the Court of Appeal, but it upheld Mr Justice Wien's judgment, as opposed to Mr Justice Forbes's. Maxwell was then asked by the inspectors to give further evidence and he appeared before them on several occasions in May and June 1973.

He found them "totally hostile" and declined to see them again.
They then gave him a further 14 days to make any written
submissions he wanted to; he found the time short, but made
submissions on as many subjects as he and his lawyers could in the
days available. When the third and final report of the inspectors was
published in November 1973 he was outraged. The inspectors had
made a basic and simple error which seemed incredible coming from
a QC and one of the foremost accountants in the country. In
examining the books of Pergamon and another Maxwell business,
Robert Maxwell and Co. Ltd., they had mistaken a credit entry for a
debit entry. They had to publish a note to their report stating:

> We regret that we were in error in stating in paragraph 714 that at
> 31st October 1968 R.M. and Co. owed Pergamon £50,809. That sum
> was in fact owed by Pergamon to R.M. and Co. All references in the
> report to that debt and the state of the account between Pergamon/
> MSI and R.M. and Co. at 31st October 1968 are inaccurate and the
> opinion expressed in paragraph 823 should be disregarded.

Altogether, the admitted inaccuracy involved a difference of
some £240,000; a sum which should have been placed in Maxwell's
favour had been placed against. Their note notwithstanding, the
mistake seemed indicative of the attitude which the inspectors were
taking towards Maxwell; they had formed an opinion and their
hearings appeared to be designed to substantiate it.

An unexpected and unprompted defence of Maxwell came from
Professor Richard Briston, Professor of Accounting and Finance at
the University of Strathclyde, writing in the chartered accountants'
journal *Accountancy*. He criticised the appointment of Sir Ronald
Leach, who at the time of his appointment as inspector was
President of the Institute of Chartered Accountants. Professor
Briston wrote[13]:

> In view of the vested interest which the Institute had in this affair, it
> was unfortunate that he should have been appointed as an inspector
> ... however conscientiously he applied himself to his task, it would
> not be easy for him not to be influenced subconsciously by the
> criticism of his Institute in the financial press resulting from a series of
> cases culminating in the Pergamon affair.

Professor Briston scrutinised the criticism of the inspectors that
Maxwell had tried to "maximise" the share price of Pergamon:

> In recent years ... the maximisation of short-run share price has been
> a necessary objective for all but those companies which are large
> enough to be free from the fear of takeover....

A growth company such as Pergamon would find itself faced with a grave dilemma if it invested in a project which would have heavy set-up and promotional costs, but was ultimately expected to show high profits. If conservative accounting principles were adopted … this would cause a set-back in reported profits and, almost certainly, a drop in the share price. A take-over bidder might well then appear.…

The whole weight of the [Takeover] Panel's belated attempt at self-assertion was … directed against Pergamon. Although both the City and the Institute of Chartered Accountants should have been on trial for allowing lax accounting standards to prevail, they were instead enabled to interpose Pergamon as the defendant. In so doing, the Panel clearly extended its scope from that intended at its inception.

Of the criticism that Maxwell was not a person whose stewardship of a public company could be relied upon, Professor Briston commented it could be argued that that criticism could be aimed at several entrepreneurs. He added:

In any case, their conclusion is by no means self-evident … he was, at worst, excessively optimistic about the prospects of ILSC. For a long period he was genuinely optimistic about the current prospects.… The conclusion from reading the evidence of the first report is that, whatever else he may have been, Maxwell was unlucky.

In an examination of the criticisms in the second report about the reported profit figures of Pergamon, Professor Briston said:

The accounts had received a clean certificate … many of the treatments adopted by Pergamon turned out to be justified, and the inspectors had the advantage of hindsight.…

He [Maxwell] adopted commercial practices which were far more common than the City or the Institute cared to admit, and which on an academic analysis were forced upon him by the obsolescent reporting practices adopted by the City. When the City, in order to postpone the threat of an SEC [Securities and Exchange Commission], had to make an example of somebody, it turned out through a series of unfortunate circumstances to be Pergamon and Robert Maxwell.

In their third and final report the inspectors reiterated their accusation, which Professor Briston had refuted, that Maxwell had tried to inflate the Pergamon share price and said:

We have no hesitation in attributing the primary responsibility for the rise and fall of Pergamon to Mr Maxwell.

The report also corrected the inspectors' misreading of the accounts in their second report, from which they had concluded that

Pergamon funds were used to finance the purchase of the company's own shares, and they withdrew the allegation.

Maxwell issued more writs against the inspectors and the Department of Trade, this time claiming damages for libel and negligence and seeking an injunction halting circulation of the report. He also, on the same day, issued a 141-page reply to the inspectors, drawn up by him and his lawyer, Michael Ogden, QC, one of the leading figures at the English Bar.

It was a detailed refutation of almost every finding made by the inspectors. It catalogued their errors, which were considerable, their failure to abide by the promise of natural justice which led to Maxwell not knowing what the charges were against him, or by whom they were made, and the reliance on witnesses whose unreliability was amply documented. Maxwell's reply borrowed its title from what Lord Denning had said in the very first action in July 1970: They must be fair.

As an example of the inspectors' inaccuracies, Maxwell wrote:

> At paragraph 1180 the inspectors quote hearsay evidence given by Sir Henry d'Avigdor-Goldsmid which they present in a way derogatory to me. They did not question me about Sir Henry's evidence and they ignored sworn testimony which contradicted it. After I received the report, I drew Sir Henry's attention to the inaccuracies of his evidence, and he wrote a letter to my solicitors explicitly withdrawing his statement in this regard.

As a comment upon the inspectors' criticism of his "stewardship" he quoted Norman Freeman, chairman of the Institutional Shareholders' Committee, who had said:

> We are unimpressed by the statement "Mr Maxwell is not a fit person, etc", largely because it is a value judgment by reference to undisclosed principles, masquerading as a statement of fact. Scientists tend to ask: is this a statement that is amenable, even in principle, to proof or disproof? And we cannot see that it is. No one could prove it because the basis of fitness is not disclosed; equally, and for the same reason, no one can defend himself against such a charge. It is not, of course, that we are insensitive to ethical questions. Thus, we find it highly unethical to make unprovable but damaging statements, or to depart even in the smallest particular from the principle that a man is to be deemed innocent until proved guilty by due process of law.

In his general condemnation of the inspectors' reports Maxwell declared:

> The inevitable effect of these reports has been very serious damage to

my personal and professional reputation. In more specific terms, the two earlier reports have prevented my re-election to the board of Pergamon, as well as causing me and my family terrible anguish and great material loss.

In short, the consequences of the inspectors' reports could not have been worse, in terms of punishment and suffering, had I been charged with, and convicted of, a criminal offence regarding the Pergamon affair.

Yet the inspectors who conducted the investigations and the DTI who published the reports have afforded me no opportunity to defend myself. I was not allowed to hear the evidence that was given against me, I was not able to contest such evidence as tended to show misconduct on my part, and above all at no stage did the inspectors inform me of their specific allegations or their potential criticisms against me so as to enable me to rebut them ... had I been afforded an opportunity to reply to the allegations made in the reports, as promised by the inspectors, I would have been able to disprove them....

Instead of writing an even-handed report setting forth objectively the facts that were presented to them by both sides, and rational conclusions drawn from those facts, they have written a report which completely distorts the facts.

The inspectors could not have written this report had they adopted their promised procedure, which would have enabled me to answer their potential critical allegations or to point out that their preliminary critical conclusions were inconsistent with the evidence in their possession....

The inspectors accuse me of lack of disclosure to shareholders and in the published accounts. However, they cannot and do not quote any rules, regulations or norms established by the Companies' Act, the Stock Exchange Council or the City Panel on Takeovers and Mergers that I have broken.

Nor have they quoted a single Pergamon professional adviser telling them that I have refused to follow their advice on disclosure or on accounting matters.

Surprisingly, I alone am blamed for virtually everything - this, in spite of the fact that the inspectors know and admit that accounting standards at the time were "to some extent undefined", as were the rules of disclosure....

I am left with the feeling that if a witness had said that he had heard that I had robbed the poor box, these inspectors would have solemnly recorded the statement in their report as testimony of "a reliable and convincing witness".

Towards the end of his response Maxwell asserted:

One of the main purposes of the inspectors' report and conclusions is

clearly designed to prevent once again my re-election to the
Pergamon board.... I reject totally and deny most emphatically the
inspectors' allegations. The motivations ascribed to me by the
inspectors for the apparent wrongdoings are as childish as they are
baseless....

I do not propose to let the inspectors get away with it. I will continue
my fight to clear my name from these unfair and unfounded charges.

He has never stopped fighting since.

* * * * *

But while the inspectors were spending years in trying to unravel
the events of 1969 and earlier, dramatic changes were taking place
at Pergamon. The company started going downhill from the
moment Maxwell left it. Leasco had neither the loyalty of the staff
nor of the journals' editors. It lacked anyone with the
entrepreneurial skill which had built up the company and it had no
one who could see an opening for a new journal and exploit it. Sir
Henry d'Avigdor-Goldsmid, the independent chairman, never
settled happily in his new role from the moment he arrived at
Headington Hill Hall on October 10, 1969. His first question to
Brian Moss, general manager of the transport, shipping, purchasing
and establishment services of the company, was to ask the
whereabouts of the chairman's office. He was told it was in
Maxwell's home and he had to be content with a small office used by
one of the managers in the building on a hill 100 yards from the
house. Sir Henry's next call to Moss was to ask where he could find
the chairman's Rolls Royce. Moss explained that the Rolls Royce
belonged to Maxwell and not the company. A despairing Sir Henry
then asked to be told where he could find the bar. "There isn't a
bar", replied Moss. The only drink available was in the Hall itself
and that was the Maxwells' private supply in their private house. Sir
Henry had to ask Moss to send out for a bottle of gin and some tonic
water and take the money from the petty cash.

Steinberg's attempts to get control of Pergamon Press, Inc.,
the American subsidiary, were a failure. After Maxwell had been
deposed from the Pergamon board he and Betty went on holiday to
East Africa, suggested and arranged by Lord Aldington. Jean
Baddeley, Maxwell's personal assistant, who went to Malta at the
same time, recalls:

The Maxwells had hardly arrived in Kenya before they had news that
the recently-appointed president of PPI, Jim Ross, had been

"nobbled" by Leasco and was attempting to call a PPI shareholders' meeting so that Leasco (not content with Pergamon Press Ltd., the British company) could also take over control of PPI. Mr Maxwell hopped on the next plane to New York and took control of the situation. The matter went to court and we lost. Against his lawyers' advice, Mr Maxwell insisted on going to appeal. This involved getting a judge to sign an order that night to prevent the shareholders' list being handed over to Leasco-PPL. The United States legal firm acting for PPI said it was not possible to get a judge at that late stage; needless to say, it was nevertheless done, by tracking down a judge and dragging him from his bed (to where he had repaired, having imbibed well at his club) and persuading him so to sign.

The appeal court ruled that Ross had no authority to call a meeting because he had resigned from his appointment beforehand. It also held that Ross had been induced by an executive employment agreement with the Steinberg-controlled Pergamon company "to seek to repudiate his prior resignation" in order to get Maxwell out. A key figure in the struggle was an American merchant banker, Sigmund Wahrsager of Bear, Stearns & Co., who represented the public shareholders of PPI. He received a telegram from Leasco telling him to resign. He refused, saying that if Leasco thought he would resile from his public duties it was mistaken. After being defeated over the shareholders' meeting, Leasco tried to serve a writ for $22 million on Maxwell. The process-server went to the Pierre Hotel suite where Maxwell was staying. Jean Baddeley helpfully told him where Maxwell - who was hiding in the suite - could be found later that day and the official happily went off to wait for his quarry. Maxwell and his entourage then hastily packed their bags and fled to Washington and thence to London. The only scare came at Dulles airport when a man approached Maxwell and said "You're Robert Maxwell", an accusation to which Maxwell did not reply. "Well", the man went on, in words which caused his listeners' hearts to falter, "I am a lawyer." Then he reassured them:

> I've been following what's been going on and I want to wish you all the best and I hope you win.

Sir Henry d'Avigdor-Goldsmid was also embroiled in the attempt to serve the writ on Maxwell and a process-server arrived at Maxwell's offices in Fitzroy Square, London, demanding to see Maxwell. Miss Baddeley told him her employer wasn't there. The man decided to wait. He was still there the next morning, but Maxwell had left the night before through a rear exit. Two days later he returned, again through the back door while the writ-servers monitored the front. But they soon realised they had been fooled and covered the back entrance as well. Miss Baddeley completes the story:

> On that Monday evening there was a very important free vote in the House of Commons on capital punishment. Maxwell was determined to vote.... Since he now was not able to leave the building without being accosted, he telephoned Sir Henry, also an MP, apprised him of the disgraceful behaviour of Pergamon's solicitors whom he could only assume were following Sir Henry's instructions and informed him that if the writ-servers had not been removed within 30 minutes he would call a press conference at Fitzroy Square to explain how he was being prevented from participating in an important vote. The siege of Fitzroy Square crumbled very quickly.

> Months later, Mr Maxwell and Sir Henry met in the corridors of the House of Commons. Maxwell said: "Good afternoon, Henry. Anything I can do for you?" Sir Henry's voice echoed despairingly down the corridor in his wake: "Resign, resign, resign."

But later Sir Henry was to realise that Pergamon without Maxwell was like a racehorse without legs. By mid-August 1970 his unpaid job as caretaker chairman was getting him down. He said[14]:

> I have known nothing like it since the retreat from Belgium in 1940 [Sir Henry had a distinguished war record and held the DSO and MC]. I did not for a moment imagine that a company about to change hands for £25 million could be so destitute of means.

By September Maxwell was talking of mounting a takeover bid for Pergamon, but he was no longer considering offering 25s (125p) a share as he had the year before. Now he was valuing the company at between 12s 6d (62.5p) and 17s 6d (87.5p), commenting[15]:

> The company has been without its sales drive for over a year. I am sad to see what has happened to this great company but very hopeful for its prospects.

For his part, Steinberg said in November that he had been naïve and his Pergamon venture was a $24 million mistake. In January 1971 John Silkin, Maxwell's friend, parliamentary colleague and solicitor, was appointed to the Pergamon board to represent the Maxwell family interests of 28 per cent. Maxwell was appointed the alternate director. As Silkin was conveniently absent from most board meetings Maxwell was able to attend them. In April Sir Henry offered Maxwell a place on the board in return as part of a deal under which Maxwell would concede control of PPI and buy

Pergamon's stock of back-numbers. A joint press statement announced:

> Pergamon Press Ltd. have now reached agreement both with Pergamon Press, Inc. and Maxwell Scientific International, Inc. Pergamon Press, Inc. has agreed to restore the relationship with PPL that existed prior to Mr Maxwell's leaving the chair in October 1969 and to recommend the appointment of Dr Felix A. Kalinski, managing director of PPL, as its chief executive. The board of PPI will be reorganised with Mr Maxwell remaining as chairman, PPL having a majority on the board.

Maxwell's company, MSI, agreed to pay $1 million immediately and a further $500,000 over the next seven years to purchase Pergamon's back number stock; further purchases of back numbers at a minimum rate of $250,000 a year for five years and $200,000 a year for the 15 years following were also agreed. Pergamon may have needed the money - the beleaguered Sir Henry admitted on April 27 that the company's 1970 results would be "ghastly" - but the back numbers were rising in value all the time. The access to this kind of stock after the war had helped Maxwell to his success. Maxwell was co-opted onto the board of Pergamon as consultant on publishing affairs (at a fee of £16,200 a year). He was back, if only tenuously. In a statement he said:

> All outstanding differences between Pergamon and the Maxwell family companies have been settled amicably. I look forward to co-operating with the board to help restore the company to its previous prosperity and pre-eminence in the scientific and educational publishing field.

But those who knew him must also have known that he would inevitably return to full control. There was no way in which he would allow his baby to stay with foster parents forever. The about-face by Pergamon was because the board realised that without Maxwell the company would face collapse. According to the *Daily Telegraph* of May 15, 1971, Steinberg had already written down his investment in Pergamon to $1 in his books. Even so, he was still vehemently opposing Maxwell's return; but without institutional support he could not command a majority. The large City investors who had ensured Maxwell's defeat in 1969 saw the value of their investments melting away and they were glad to see his presence in the company again, even though they were not prepared at that stage to see him in full control.

In February 1972 Sir Walter Coutts, the last Governor-General of Uganda, replaced d'Avigdor-Goldsmid as chairman of Pergamon.

In June the following year he called a special shareholders' meeting to elect Maxwell back on the board, praising him for his "talents and enthusiasm" and commending[16]

> his unique personal contacts with a large number of editors and authors on whose continued efforts the whole life-blood of the company depends.

But the meeting came to no conclusion. The small shareholders backed Maxwell, as he pointed out afterwards, but Leasco with its 38 per cent of the votes remained adamantly opposed and the City institutions did not want the position to change until the final Department of Trade report was published. Maxwell refused to concede that this was a defeat[17]:

> If things were half as bad as some people persist in believing I'd have retired with a bottle of Scotch and a pistol a long time ago.

In November 1973 Coutts wrote to Pergamon shareholders saying that those who had worked so hard to pull the company through four troubled years still found themselves "bogged down in eternal squabbles between contesting parties". He had read the Department of Trade inspectors' reports but he believed Pergamon needed Maxwell's "entrepreneurial flair". He added that in recent months 40 or 50 journal editors had stepped up their demands for Maxwell's return and that the future of Pergamon rested primarily on those editors.

The editors, in fact, were Maxwell's handful of aces. They believed in him and no other. They saw the opportunities he had given them for speedy and learned publication of the work of their scientific communities being destroyed.

A meeting of the editors was convened in the staff common room at Imperial College, London, on October 31, 1973, with the purpose of rallying support for Maxwell and to ensure he regained his place on the board. Steinberg decided to fly to London from New York to attend it, but his plane was delayed for several hours by fog at Heathrow.

Professor Brian Spalding, mechanical engineering scientist and editor of the *International Journal of Heat and Mass Transfer* who took the chair at the meeting, said:

> I was telephoned by Maxwell some weeks before the meeting. He didn't say he was in trouble - that's not the way he talks - but he solicited my assistance.... He wanted myself and other leading editors to let Sir Walter Coutts know we wished to stay with Maxwell and not with Steinberg.

Our biggest stumbling block was Norman Freeman of ICI who represented the institutional shareholders. He called us to a meeting on October 26, five days before Steinberg was due. This City gent's tone was extremely unpleasant. He was saying that the chances were that Maxwell would end up in jail, was a disreputable man and he couldn't understand why we wanted anything to do with him. But we had nothing against Maxwell. He had brought us into being and we didn't want any change. He established those journals, but they were ours. We considered ourselves free to take them to other publishers if we wished. The editors, we believed, created the prestige for Pergamon. Maxwell knew this. He pushed the idea. He flew in editors from abroad and he made us believe that we held the cards.

Professor Sir Harold Thompson, the eminent physicist, began the meeting with a plea for Maxwell's re-election to the board. By now Freeman's position had softened slightly and instead of completely opposing Maxwell he asked only that the appointment should be delayed until the publication of the third and final DTI report. Professor Sam Eilon, a management scientist at Imperial College, said:

Steinberg arrived at last. He began by claiming that Leasco would ditch its former "passive role" in the company and emphasised that he wouldn't under any circumstances acquiesce in Maxwell's return. I stressed the editors' view, which was that Maxwell had played a key role in making the Pergamon journals a great success.

Steinberg was plainly quite contemptuous in his reply. He did not need the current editors, he said. Editors were two a penny and he could line up dozens to take their places. If Steinberg had any chance of projecting an image of credibility to the journal editors, he lost it completely at that meeting.

Professor Spalding commented:

Call us pig-headed or idealistic, but we wouldn't move. Steinberg was a smooth man, smallish, rather rotund, very confident, with a winning way - but not with us. We came away from the meeting knowing that Maxwell had won the day.... Our loyalty to Maxwell was sincere. We did not have to be pressed, bullied or bribed to support him....

Maxwell is not an academic type. Many academics may not find his public image very appealing. But he recognises what makes us tick and that, with his large-mindedness, outweighs his lesser defects.... Of course, he is a businessman. He is there to make a profit.... But it doesn't appear in a calculating way. Projects become adventures and adventures are fun.

Professor Harold Liebowitz, now Dean of Engineering and Applied Science at George Washington University, remembered meeting Maxwell in New York in 1969:

> He told me about his plans to go in with Steinberg and I advised him against it. These were two strong personalities and I told Bob he was too good to be number two.... He went ahead and came close to losing everything. But I backed him because Pergamon Press was one man, Maxwell. Without him - nothing. In all my life I can honestly say I've met no one who works as hard as he does. He is a workaholic, 24 hours a day. He even lives above the shop at Headington Hill Hall, the place we American editors call Triple H ranch, and he has devoted his life to his work. Sure, he's had a good life, but it has always been tied to a vision of establishing a worldwide communications network. Other businessmen profit in a selfish way ... but there's much more to Robert Maxwell. Though it sounds too fulsome, I believe he genuinely wishes to obtain a higher quality of life for society.
>
> Even in his darkest days, that optimism never left him. One looks at Jewish people like him and one sees a people who have had to go on, regardless. They are taught strength, courage and how to bounce back. That is Maxwell. There are few people who have had such a great effect on my life.

Professor Harry Wasserman, Professor of Chemistry at Yale, another of the scientists who attended the Imperial College meeting, said:

> Bob may well have been pulling the strings of that editors' rebellion, but there was no doubting that the way we closed ranks behind him was purely spontaneous and completely successful.

Maxwell was, in fact, three floors below where the meeting was taking place, dictating press releases about it to Professor Spalding's secretary, Colleen (now his wife), and irritating her by putting his feet on Spalding's desk.

Professor James Hartnett, now Head of Mechanical Engineering at Illinois University, was yet another American editor who flew to London. He said:

> I had no hesitation in coming. I was indebted to Maxwell in so many ways.... Thank goodness we carried the day ... all organised, of course, by Maxwell himself. He is a genius. There is no question about that. He is able to see opportunities where other people don't.... But he damn near blew the whole thing in the Leasco business.

Professor Alan Sartorelli, Professor of Pharmacology at Yale and one of America's leading researchers into cancer, recalls:

> My feelings were the same as most other Pergamon editors. We knew
> Maxwell really cared about science and scientists, while we suspected
> Leasco was just out to make a buck. I became a stockholder in
> Leasco, which entitled me to have a say in the running of the
> company.... I told [Steinberg] I would withdraw my journal from the
> Pergamon stable unless Maxwell was allowed back. Bob, you see,
> had been very clever. He had never claimed copyright for the
> journals, so technically they were ours to take wherever we pleased.
> But he knew that as long as we enjoyed our unique relationship with
> him, there was no other publisher we would want.

The month before the scientists' meeting Maxwell had started
talks to buy Tinlings, an ailing printing firm in Liverpool which
could have, if he wished, given him the opportunity of a new
publishing base. It must have been clear to the Pergamon board that
if he did so he could resume publication of most, if not all, of the
scientific journals on which Pergamon depended. The board's
dilemma was that Steinberg still wouldn't have Maxwell at any price
and the City institutions were still staying their hand.

But they were being worked on by, among others, Robert Perrin,
management consultant and editor of the Pergamon journal *Long
Range Planning*. He said:

> I had meetings with the City shareholders at which I hammered home
> the central point - no Maxwell, no Pergamon. I told those City boys,
> "If you remove Maxwell, Pergamon will collapse like a stack of
> cards." He dominated the company completely. He was a desperately
> bad delegator with a second-rate staff in those days. Here, in short,
> was this giant with thousands of ideas and contacts, surrounded by
> poor calibre people. I could not pass judgment on the DTI inspectors'
> famous report but I did tell the shareholders that they wouldn't have a
> company if Bob went, and you can imagine what shareholders do
> when they are given that kind of advice. In those circumstances, with
> the leading academic editors in rebellion and strong financial advice
> in favour of Maxwell, we were able to stage an effective fight-back.
>
> The whole Leasco affair was a nonsense. Here they were, trying to
> ditch Maxwell from Pergamon, while he was sitting smack in the
> middle of it at Headington Hill Hall.

Perrin was not an uncritical admirer. None of the top staff, he
said, could travel abroad without their cheques being signed by
Maxwell. Indeed, "nobody, it seemed, could breathe" without him:

> Of course, it was a fault. Pergamon had a dreadful management style.
> Incredibly autocratic, not a well-run company then, but presided over
> by a bloody genius.

In December 1973 Leasco (by now renamed Reliance) proposed

to put 13 new directors on the Pergamon board, men whom John Gillum, of the bankers Samuel Montagu, described as having "the sort of names Damon Runyon would have been proud of". Coutts protested that he had been kept in the dark by Reliance and complained[18]:

> We have been treated rather like a bunch of schoolboys who perhaps do not even deserve a lollipop.

* * * * *

It was now nearly all over. On January 9, 1974 Maxwell announced that he was making a bid for the Pergamon shares, pricing them at 11p each; altogether, his offer was to pay £1.5 million for a company for which Steinberg had been prepared to pay £25 million in 1969.

Though few could have realised it, Maxwell was nearly broke. The legal actions on both sides of the Atlantic to try to clear his name had cost him nearly £2 million; as ever, the lawyers had benefited. Since 1969 he had gone through the most traumatic years of his business and political life. He had lost his cherished seat in Parliament. He had been accused by two government inspectors, one a Queen's Counsel and the other the President of the Institute of Accountants, of being unfit to run a public company. The enterprise which he had built from nothing had almost returned to that state during his absence. Its shares, of which the Maxwell family still held 28 per cent, were practically worthless. The only hope for Pergamon and for Maxwell was for him to return to the company and to recreate, at the age of 51, the company to which he had devoted most of the hours of every day of his youthful business life and which had virtually been destroyed. There was nothing he could do but to start all over again. The £1.5 million he needed to do that was all borrowed by Microforms International Marketing Corporation, a newly-formed American-based company owned by a French lawyer acting for Betty Maxwell's family and set up with the consent of Leasco. By a wounding (to Steinberg) twist, most of the money came from the Chemical Bank, whose attempted purchase by Steinberg in 1968 had been frustrated by Wall Street, and which no doubt was only too pleased to advance it; another willing lender was Fleming's, the merchant bank which had resigned from the position of adviser to Maxwell back in the late summer of 1969.

A few days after his first offer Maxwell increased his bid, but only to 12p a share. Coutts informed shareholders of the terms, admitting that they were "disappointing". But, he said, they had to

measure it against the fact that Pergamon's assets were by then
worth only 2.68p or 4.22p a share, depending upon which figure was
used in the calculation. He added:

> Pergamon may provide a convenient arena for shareholder factions
> to fight each other, but even if the board felt these engagements -
> interesting though they may be to spectators - were not totally against
> the interests of the company as a whole, the plain fact is that the
> financial position of Pergamon is not strong enough for the company
> to be able to afford such luxuries.

The Pergamon board decided to recommend acceptance of
Maxwell's bid. More than 90 per cent of shareholders, including
Steinberg and the City institutions, accepted an offer which was only
one-tenth of what they could have achieved earlier, and Maxwell
restored the company to its former private status. John Gillum,
whose bank was advising the Pergamon board, has told of the final
meeting of shareholders at the Connaught Rooms, London. One
small shareholder asked him:

> How on earth can you say 12p is a fair and reasonable offer. Do you
> know I paid 35s (£1.75) for my shares?

Gillum replied:

> It is not the offer which is losing you money. It is what has happened
> to the company in the meantime. If you did not have an investment in
> Pergamon today, would you buy shares at 12p?

The angry shareholder retorted:

> Nothing would induce me to have anything to do with this company
> ever again.

Gillum said:

> You have answered your own question.

Gillum says that 12p was a fair price at the time, especially as it
seemed unlikely that the Stock Exchange would allow Pergamon
shares to be quoted again in the foreseeable future. Maxwell says he
still wonders why the institutions accepted the 12p when they could
have held on for a couple of years and seen the shares worth £2 once
the company was profitable again. Gillum says that is hindsight.

Having regained Pergamon, Maxwell went with Coutts to the
National Westminster Bank, which has been his staunchest
institutional friend throughout his career and to which Pergamon
was in debt for several million pounds. Coutts asked Alex Dibbs, its
chief executive, whether he had any objection to Maxwell becoming
chairman again. Dibbs replied:

Object? I'm delighted. Now that Bob has returned the bank will get its money back.

Within the first year of Maxwell's restoration Pergamon Press made a profit of £2 million. A curiosity of his acquisition was that the holders of nearly 130,000 Pergamon shares never sought to receive their money. It still resides in the MIMC Acceptance Account at the National Westminster, awaiting applications.

The final word on the governmental inquiry into Pergamon came from the Solicitor-General, Mr Peter Archer, in the House of Commons on May 13, 1977, in answer to a question about the Director of Public Prosecution's investigation into the company. He said that Counsel had carefully considered the results of lengthy and extensive police investigations and had prepared a series of opinions for the Director of Public Prosecutions:

> In these opinions, Counsel came to the conclusion that proceedings against anyone concerned would not be justified. The DPP agreed with that conclusion. Having studied the opinions and relevant papers and discussed them with Counsel and the DPP, I am of the same opinion.

Maxwell was in Peking when the reply was made, talking with the Chinese Book Import Corporation and officials of the Academies of Science and Medical Sciences. He said simply:

> I am delighted.

Ten years later Robert Hodes, Steinberg's lawyer, wrote of Maxwell for the birthday book:

> We were embroiled in a raucous controversy in which light fell on the participants' worst facets. Nevertheless, through it all I remained sensible of parts of him [Maxwell] which I admired and still do now. Pluck: at the darkest moments he deployed a spirit of dauntless optimism and determination, including a lift of the chin, which, given the setting, was often infuriating but somehow preventive of hatred. His care and affection for the family was a genuine and consistent part of his life which never was far from his thought or expression, however discordant were the events of the commercial day.

It was a generous tribute from a former foe.

* * * * *

Not only were no criminal actions brought or even contemplated, but no shareholder took a civil action. Nevertheless, the stigma of the report remained. For that reason alone - though there were others - the Department of Trade inquiry into the affairs of Pergamon was a perversion of justice, whatever the merit, if any, of its individual conclusions. It was the only time the Takeover Panel ever asked for such an inquiry to be held, and then for purposes more to do with proving its own virility than for probing any possible improprieties. The Panel had only just been established when the attempted merger collapsed. It had risen from the ashes of the previous weakling and it had to prove it was strong.

The result was calamitous for Pergamon, Maxwell and the authority of such inquiries. Maxwell and Pergamon have recovered, spectacularly. The inquiry system has not. The inspectors, legally under the law as it stands, delivered quasi-judicial opinions but without any of the judicial safeguards. All the witnesses were heard in secret. The "accused" - Maxwell - was not to know what the charges against him were, nor who had made them, nor on what "evidence" - hearsay, speculation or otherwise - they were based. There was no opportunity to know which witnesses had testified or to what; nor whether their testimony was buttressed by documentary evidence; nor whether that evidence, if it existed, was genuine, forged, or mistaken. There was no opportunity, therefore, to cross-examine those witnesses. The dictum of Lord Denning - They must be fair - was ignored in all but a narrow, legalistic sense. The inspectors can be faulted for their errors which, in the end, added up to an iniquitous catalogue and disqualified their findings, but they did prepare their reports within the framework laid down by Parliament and in the end it is for Parliament to legislate for a procedure which ensures justice is done. Certainly, the present framework is inadequate, designed as it was for a different age of commerce. Even the Soviet constitution purports to operate more even-handedly. The inspectors were police, prosecutors, judges and jury. Humpty-Dumpty like, natural justice was what they decreed it to be. Though a firm promise to abide by its rules was given, it was clear from the judgments of Mr Justice Wien and the Court of Appeal that that promise could not be enforced in law because there could be no appeal against the inspectors' conclusions.

Maxwell could take his own witnesses to speak on his behalf, but he could not compel the reluctant; nor could he call for the production of documents. Affidavits and documents presented to the inspectors demonstrating their acceptance of inaccurate testimony was ignored. The inspectors' finding that annual financial reports certified by the chartered accountants were "distorted" did not lead to any criticism of the accountants. Instead, Maxwell was criticised for allegedly persuading them. Were a judge in the High

Court to adjudicate in that manner the Court of Appeal would be amazed. Above all, there was no right of appeal and there still is not.

Maxwell has not been the only victim of this system, though he might have suffered the most. In 1976 a DTI inquiry into the Lonrho company controlled by Roland (Tiny) Rowland was critical of Angus Ogilvy, husband of the Queen's cousin, Princess Alexandra, and a member of the Lonrho board. Ogilvy and Lord Duncan-Sandys, Winston Churchill's son-in-law and a former cabinet minister, were savaged by the report. As with Maxwell, the inspectors chose to make a personality judgement, pronouncing Ogilvy not to be a strong character. They accused him of being "negligent" in fulfilling his duties as a director "to an extent that merits severe criticism". Though he rejected the criticisms - partly based, as it emerged later, on a letter making allegations of which he had no previous knowledge and which turned out to be false - he felt honour-bound, in view of his close relationship with the royal family, to resign all his company directorships. A friend of his was quoted as saying[19]:

> He would have fought tooth and nail to remain in the City if he had not been married to Princess Alexandra.

Ogilvy himself said at the time[20]:

> I believe the allegations made by the inspectors are based on a number of incorrect assumptions and errors.... Because I have no legal redress there is no way that I can effectively clear my name.

The law is still the same. Both Maxwell and Ogilvy have to live with the fact that judgements were passed upon them which they feel deeply were fundamentally unjust and inaccurate. Whenever stories and profiles are written about them the respective inspectors' findings are revived. The rebuttals rarely are. When Maxwell sued *Private Eye* the magazine sought to introduce what the inspectors had said about him in order to demonstrate that he had no reputation which could be damaged. The judge refused to permit it to be introduced, but if he had, who's to say what influence it might have had upon the jury? At the very least, it would have prolonged an already lengthy and expensive action.

An attempt in 1986 by Lord Silkin in the House of Lords to amend the law so that an aggrieved person might have the right to appeal to the court for a report to be disregarded if it breached natural justice did not succeed. But significantly, after Maxwell returned to the control of Pergamon, the Department of Trade and

Industry issued new guidance to those appointed as inspectors to conduct inquiries into company affairs, though it was too late to mitigate the criticism of Angus Ogilvy. They were warned to refrain from including in their reports references to individuals of the kind which were made about Maxwell, and to give any individual likely to be criticised an opportunity to reply to the allegations. The guidance sets out how far inspectors may go in passing judgements upon people examined by them and makes it clear that if those limits are exceeded then their reports may be edited. It did not, however, amend the basic failings of a system which is not fair, not just and not open and from which no appeal to a higher court can be made.

9

Reflections in the Mirror

I have climbed the greasy pole at last
Disraeli

At a minute to midnight on Thursday, July 12, 1984 the phone rang in the ninth floor Holborn Circus office of the Mirror Group Newspapers' chief executive, Douglas Long. He, Tony Miles, the Group's deputy chairman, Roger Bowes, No. 3 in the hierarchy, and Mike Molloy, then editor of the *Daily Mirror*, all directors of the company, had been dining, appropriately enough, in the Blue Room a few yards away, with Dr Alcon Copisarow, a scientist and former member of the Press Council, and Victor Paige, director and deputy chairman of the National Freight Consortium. The chairman of MGN, Clive Thornton, former chief general manager of the Abbey National Building Society, should have hosted the dinner but had cried off, pleading a headache, and gone home. Copisarow and Paige were there because they had been expecting to be appointed non-executive directors of the Group in preparation for its public flotation later in the year. That prospect had suddenly vanished. They were in the position of those who had booked passages for the *Titanic*'s return voyage from New York: they were never going to know what it was like to be aboard ship. Not surprisingly, they left at about 10 pm, early for a newspaper dinner. Miles and the others sat and gossiped and drank around the Blue Room table, knowing that sooner or later a call would come. When it did, Miles left the room to take it, was heard to say "Well, dash me" - or stronger words to that effect - and put down the phone. Immediately another one rang. This time Long answered it. The two calls had come from Sir Alex Jarratt, chairman of Reed International, which owned MGN, and Les Carpenter, Reed's chief executive. Long and Miles returned to the Blue Room and Miles announced to the others:

"Well, that's it. Maxwell's bought the *Mirror*", which is what they had been expecting to hear all evening.

Miles said that the other MGN board directors had better be called in. Then the phone rang for a third time. Molloy answered it. It was Robert Maxwell, who had spent the day at a suite in the Ritz Hotel, opposite the Reed headquarters building, negotiating the takeover with Carpenter. Maxwell asked politely for Miles. Molloy told the deputy chairman: "It's Robert Maxwell - he wants to speak to you", but Miles, a proud and stubborn man, who had already had Thornton, who knew nothing about newspapers, imposed above him, replied: "I don't want to speak to him. Tell him I've gone home." Molloy went back to the telephone, but Maxwell had already rung off. Miles then said "I'm off." He went first to his own office farther along the corridor and then to his home. From there he telephoned me with the news that Reed's had broken its oft-repeated pledge not to sell the paper to any individual and had done a deal with Maxwell. I said how much I despised the executives of a company which put the pockets of its shareholders before the guarantees it had given to its employees - or stronger words to that effect - and tried to go back to sleep. Miles made several more calls and then returned to the *Mirror*.

Meanwhile, as everybody in the paper kept telling each other, it was now Friday the 13th. At 12.20 am the phone in Long's office rang yet again. This time the call was from the night newsdesk of the *Daily Mirror* on the third floor of the ugly, characterless building which houses the Group's papers. It was to say that Maxwell had arrived and was on the editorial floor and was about to make his way up to Long's office. Long and Molloy went to the lift to greet Maxwell, with rather less enthusiasm than that with which Stanley had greeted Livingstone.

It was a warm and sultry night which later turned, but only meteorologically, into a stormy one, and Maxwell was in his shirt-sleeves. They said "Hello", and he said "How do you do, this is a turn-up for the book, isn't it?" which, for a man not given to under-statement, was a classic of its kind. The three men, together with Richard Baker, deputy managing director of BPCC, went into Long's office. Maxwell and Baker had been on their way by Rolls Royce to Maxwell House, in the City of London, where a meeting of the MGN board had been convened, and where Maxwell's best friend among Mirror Group executives, Bob Edwards, editor of the *Sunday Mirror*, was already waiting. But the road from the Ritz to Maxwell House ran past the *Mirror* building and the new proprietor

Fireworks at Headington Hill Hall for Maxwell's 60th birthday celebrations.

Celebrating Betty's D.Phil. degree at Oxford in 1981. Back row: Anne, Bob, Ghislaine, Isabel, Kevin. Bottom row: Christine, Ian, Betty and Philip.

President Ronald Reagan greets Maxwell at the White House, 1987.

Australian Treasurer, Paul Keating meeting with Maxwell at the *Mirror*, London 1988.

Informal talks: Maxwell with Shimon Peres, President of Israel.

Mutual applause: with Deng Xiaoping in 1986.

President Jimmy Carter and Ryoichi Sasakawa shake hands with Maxwell.

Talking politics with Michael Foot.

Global discussions with Henry Kissinger in Tokyo.

Maxwell and team, about to leave Ulan Bator in the Mirror jet.

Familiar sight over Maxwell's London HQ - the Mirror helicopter.

Left, Robert Maxwell, centre, lion (stuffed) and President arap Moi of Kenya in October 1986.

Laughing press barons Rupert Murdoch, Yosaji Kobayashi and Maxwell.

In Moscow visiting Mr A.N. Yakovlev, (centre) Secretary of the Central Committee of the C.P.S.U. and Politburo member with Mr Afanasyev, Editor-in-Chief of *Pravda*.

The man on the right is Terry Wogan.

Cordial greetings to the Aga Khan.

Fraternal greetings to Neil Kinnock, Leader of the Labour Party.

An informal presentation for the Princess of Wales.

Lady Ghislaine, Mirror Holdings ocean-going yacht.

Discussions in Ulan Bator with Mr J. Batmunkh, head of the Government of The People's Republic of Outer Mongolia.

New *Daily Mirror* newsroom in 1988, equipped with the very latest in newspaper technology.

With Her Majesty the Queen at the Edinburgh Commonwealth Games.

Talks with Dr Silva, Prime Minister of Portugal, in 1987.

A private word with President Mitterrand in Paris in 1988.

With King Juan Carlos of Spain in 1987.

Hand signals: from President Soares of Portugal in 1987.

The Publisher with his Editors: Monty Court, Sporting Life; Ernie Burrington, The People; Eve Pollard, Sunday Mirror; Joe Haines, Group Political Editor; Mike Molloy, Editor-in-Chief; Richard Stott, Daily Mirror; John Blake, Associate Editor, The People.

Red Square, 1987, with son Kevin.

Family fun: Bob and Betty with son Kevin and daughters Anne and Isabel.

Daughter Christine Maxwell at work in
America.

- or publisher as he insisted upon being called from the start - couldn't resist the temptation to call in. When the group reached Long's office Maxwell went straight to the cocktail cabinet and said:

I am going to have a drink. Anyone else want one?

The offer was much more than an act of courtesy. Maxwell may not even have particularly wanted a drink. What Long and the others assembled there thought he was demonstrating was that it was *his* drink in *his* cocktail cabinet in *his* building which housed *his* newspapers and their acceptance of *his* hospitality was also an acceptance of that fact.

* * * * *

The journalists on the *Mirror* staff had been in turmoil for days. A few, a very few, including myself, had been ready to stop the paper publishing to prevent Reed's reneging on its promise not to dispose of the Group other than by its long-planned floating of the company on the London Stock Exchange. Almost at the last minute the National Union of Journalists' chapel made an unprecedented public offer to Thornton in order to assure Reed's that the flotation could be a success: it was to refrain from taking any disruptive industrial action against the paper other than through the agreed procedures. A similar promise had been made by the Sogat '82 machine room chapel, valid for a period of 12 months. Sogat, in a letter to Thornton, added a rider designed to help him in his struggle with Reed's, which had been fervently wishing it had never appointed him in the first place. It said:

If you cease to hold the office of chairman this undertaking ceases to be operative.

In retrospect, the unique concession which two of the most powerful chapels in the company were offering to the management was to do no more than abide by agreements into which they had freely entered. It demonstrates just how far into the jungle of anarchy Fleet Street had journeyed and how the bizarre had become the normal. Nevertheless, it seemed generous at the time and, indeed, in the climate in which the newspaper industry had operated for as long as anyone could remember, it probably was.

For most of its employees, MGN had long been a good group to work for. It wasn't the highest-paying company in Fleet Street, but those on expenses, who were not only the journalists, did exceedingly well. The four-day week or the nine-day fortnight was customary in most departments. Holidays and sick leave were liberally offered and taken, often to excess. If the management stepped out of line (in the opinion of any muscular section of the workforce) a short strike would quickly bring it back. Indeed, the anarchic working practices in Fleet Street at that time can only be understood if it is realised just how appalling the managements were. It was the boast of some *Mirror* executives that it was the most efficient management in Fleet Street. If that were true, then the inefficiency in other offices would not have qualified any of them, in Hugh Cudlipp's famous phrase, to run a whelk stall.

The political policies of the Group's flagship, the *Daily Mirror*, remained firmly in the tradition which had been installed during and after the war. Within that tradition, the day-to-day opinions were agreed, more or less democratically, by Miles, Molloy, Terry Lancaster, the political editor, Geoffrey Goodman, the industrial editor, and myself as leader writer; though Molloy, as editor, always had the right to outvote everyone else, it was a right he used sparingly. The paper was radical, non-establishment, and of the Left, though not under the influence of the leaders of the Labour party, with whom, in fact, contact was sparse, even at general election times. An enlightened approach to national issues was reflected in a civilised conduct of the paper's affairs.

Though the *Mirror* was a journalists' newspaper, at least one of the senior management was known for his hatred of journalists. They, in turn, had a contempt for those in the management who had never been journalists. The editorial staffs of the papers were capable of producing as good a tabloid newspaper as anywhere else in the world. The fact that for some years the *Mirror* had largely been a one-edition newspaper was not due to its writers, but to a combination of print union avarice and management appeasement which made it impossible to produce a fully-editioned paper without incurring prohibitive costs. An attempt at one time regularly to produce a 40-page newspaper had to be abandoned when the bonuses which had been negotiated to facilitate it turned out to be larger than the return from the extra advertising.

There were hardly any members of the staff who couldn't produce horror stories from their own experience. On one occasion, when BBC Panorama wanted to film an interview with me in my office, the electricians' union demanded that it should have 10 days' notice of the request, which, for a current affairs programme, was absurd. On another occasion, when an ITV company asked to record a discussion with me for an educational programme, it was only able to go ahead on a promise by the management that two electricians would be paid two hours' overtime each while the cameras were in my office. The fact that the electricians' services were not required, that no additional lighting was used and that they worked no extra hours - indeed, they sat on the floor outside my office and did no work at all - was irrelevant. Even worse, in its way, was when I went to the office early one morning to write a special series in a nearby building and was told that my typewriter could only be moved by a typewriter mechanic who would not be available until the afternoon. I risked trouble and carried it across the road myself. But such idiocies were commonplace and unresisted by the management.

In the circumstances it seemed no one could enter the newspaper business and hope to make a profit; the surplus declared by MGN in the year of Maxwell's arrival was less than the amount of overtime paid to the small, if excessive, number of electricians it employed. Ridiculous sums were paid out in wages throughout the industry. Some compositors on *The Sun* were said to be earning close to £50,000 a year. Some on the *Mirror* were earning more than assistant editors. The four-day week in many cases was also a four-hour day. At least two chapels had a roster for sick leave. Extra money was demanded - by journalists as well as by National Graphical Society and Sogat members - for whatever new wheeze was dreamed up. At one time journalists who did not work on bank holidays, which was most of them, were all paid extra on the grounds that it was unfair for those who hadn't come in not to be paid the same as those who had. It followed, therefore, that any magnate or millionaire buying his way into Fleet Street could only be doing so because he had enough money to satisfy a power-lust or because he was going to upset the apple-cart, sack a third (at least) of the staff and cause the paper to be closed down, as *The Times* and *Sunday Times* had been closed down for nearly a year under Kenneth Thomson. What is more, closed down to no avail. The chances of anyone actually tackling the problems of Fleet Street without creating more of them seemed slender. Even the ruthless Murdoch was reported to have settled an electricians' dispute at *The Times* by agreeing to pay the men more than they had struck for in the first place. Though he could afford to fight, he was usually the first to cave in.

The journalists had contributed to the parlous financial condition of the Mirror Group by a disastrous strike in 1977 which caused the paper's circulation to plunge from just over 4 million to little more than 3 million, a situation from which it has yet to recover. The strike was shortsighted, but it was born of their resentment that the printers, who set the copy in type, were being paid substantially more than the editorial staff who wrote it; the men who made the frame were doing better than those who painted the picture. The journalists' attitude towards the papers being sold stemmed from their belief that a change in ownership from a benevolent absentee landlord like Reed's to a malevolent single proprietor, whoever he was, would lead to a confrontation with the printing trade unions which, up to that point, *had never lost a battle* in Fleet Street, though they had suffered a stinging defeat, for which they were seeking revenge, at Maxwell's hands earlier in the year when he had finally closed down the printing works at Park Royal. The fear was that confrontation would lead to trench warfare which, whatever the outcome for the owner or the print unions, would mean that the papers - and their journalists - would lose.

But there was more to it than that so far as journalists were concerned. The whole question of buying and selling newspapers as though their place in society was no different from a string of ironmongers is rejected by them, even if the general public does not care less. The advantage of working for a group like the *Mirror* was that there was no proprietor, no Beaverbrook, no Murdoch, not even a tax-exiled Rothermere, whose will or whim could suddenly descend upon it. If the old order wasn't going to prevail and Reed's would not take seriously the offer by the journalists' chapel to find the money to buy the paper, then the flotation was much preferred. Thornton's proposals to prevent anyone possessing more than 15 per cent of the shares of the company would have ensured that there would be no single proprietor to dread. Maxwell's coming would certainly certainly end all that. My own belief, freely and frequently stated, was that he would act quickly and ruthlessly and sack 2,000 people within a matter of weeks. It never occurred to me that Maxwell would have the patience to wait until the print unions behaved so outrageously that they sacked themselves. That 2,000 - between a quarter and a third of the staff - would have to go no one doubted. But Thornton had promised to take five years to do it through natural wastage. It was, as it is easy to see now, pure fantasy. If Maxwell hadn't made the first move in cutting staff at the end of 1985, then Murdoch would still have transferred his papers to Wapping, in London's dockland. He had retreated too often. Another step backwards and he might have found his News International company in the Thames. And once he had decided to fight, the *Mirror* would have had to follow; more decently, perhaps, and less drastically, but inevitably.

The journalists at the *Mirror* were not well disposed towards the printers, whom they regarded as greedy gangsters, and the printers were not well disposed towards the journalists, whom they regarded as pampered alcoholics. Nevertheless, there was a logical solidarity in the attitude which opposed anyone being sacked. Over-staffing was rife in every department. Once a clear-out began it would affect all; and not all had the skill and opportunity of the journalists and printers to be able easily to find another job. Not all the motives were selfish.

It wasn't only the poor return on its investment - often or not no return at all - which made Reed International want to get rid of its newspaper interests, even if that was its prime reason. It did not interfere with the running of the newspapers, but its board, Tory almost to a man, was embarrassed by them. Jarratt, in his one attempt to influence the political staff, had told them in 1978 that his ideal government was a Conservative one headed by James Callaghan. But if he had tried to dictate a change in policy, the chances are that no-one would have paid any attention; board members were constantly having to explain to their friends that what the *Mirror* said was nothing to do with them. They had responsibility without power, the prerogative of the scapegoat throughout the ages, though I haven't any doubt that for a good profit that particular board would have swallowed any political discomfort. Reed's vacillations, which even by Fleet Street's standards were contemptible, showed that this word was worth no more than one of the rolls of wallpaper which it also produced.

But by July 1984 its swivellings had finally halted. It decided to abandon the flotation if a better offer came along, which was becoming increasingly likely. Again and again Reed's had turned down Thornton's ideas to prevent any individual gaining control. Though those ideas were largely supported by the staff, they reduced the flotation of the company to an investment opportunity only. And who in his or her right mind would have invested hard-earned savings in a newspaper in 1984? There was not a newspaper in Fleet Street where the managers were allowed to manage, even if they had been competent to do so, which most of them weren't. Consequently, the estimated value of MGN fell almost daily. At the crisis point, the company's Stock Exchange advisers were estimating that it was worth about £48 million, the value of its numerous properties, furniture and fittings. The estimated value of the papers themselves was nil. The figures were ludicrous. The *Daily Record* in Glasgow, which was modern and highly successful, and the *Sunday Mail*, its sister paper, alone were worth the stockbrokers' valuation of the whole. Matters were made worse by the decision of Thomsons to close down their plant at Withy Grove, Manchester, where the northern editions of the MGN papers were printed. Thornton was talking about spending sums ranging from £20 million to £50 million on replacing the capacity. These costs and the gloom from the stockbrokers put Reed's into a panic: the incubus had to be ditched, along with Clive Thornton.

Among those who opposed the sale, there was no doubt that once it was accomplished there would be nothing that could be done about it. The only hope was to forestall it. The journalists, supposedly, were the most powerful, but they hesitated, as usual. Their senior executives, all but two of whom - Bob Edwards and Terry Lancaster - opposed the sale to Maxwell (or, indeed, to anyone else), were torn between finding a way of getting rid of Clive Thornton, whom they found hopelessly at sea with the reality of the industry, and frustrating Maxwell.

Thornton was almost totally isolated among the management. The jokes about him became more cruel. He and Roger Bowes, who had to work closely with him, were known as Buttons and Bowes. Even his loss of a leg in a road accident in his teens inspired humour and he was known as Hopalong. The most celebrated remark of all about him came from an anonymous sub-editor. "In the land of the legless", he said, "the one-legged man is king."

But he was very rapidly to become a king without a throne. Thornton's basic instincts were decent. He was one of nature's Social Democrats; had he remained at the *Mirror* I have no doubt that he would have wanted the papers to show sympathy towards the Gang of Four's party. But making him chairman at the *Mirror* was like putting Red Riding Hood in charge of a pack of wolves. He could not understand, for example, why men earning £500 a week should want to go on strike. The simple answer, that they wanted £600 a week, was outside his building society experience and he couldn't accept it. When the management offered a derisory wage increase (something between nothing and 85 pence a week) to secretarial and clerical staff, Thornton went down to the consequent picket-line and promised to do something about it. It may have been right in principle, but it was wrong in practice. The only conclusion of the strikers was that he was a pushover. It also infuriated his senior management and showed that the new broom could no more run the whelk stall than any of his predecessors.

In retrospect, the *Mirror* was an accident waiting for Maxwell to happen. When it came to it, he was too fast, too decisive and too secret for anyone to stop him. The moment, if there ever were a moment - which today looks doubtful - had passed. The choice facing everyone was to work with Maxwell or work somewhere else. In the event, only Miles, a former editor of the *Daily Mirror* and chairman before Thornton's arrival, chose the latter option. One journalist, John Pilger, was to say 18 months later, when he was among a number sacked by the *Mirror*'s new editor, Richard Stott, that he was about to resign anyway because he could no longer work for it. His principled stand did not prevent him, however, from asking for - and getting - a much more generous payment - £63,000 - from Maxwell than that to which he was entitled under the redundancy agreements negotiated with his union. It was what a reporter of lesser imagination than Pilger might have described as having his cake and eating it.

* * * * *

After the sudden shock of Maxwell's arrival, the *Daily Mirror* news desk, properly professional, had sent a reporter and a photographer to the ninth floor to report and record his presence, while he got to know his new employees, an acquaintanceship which, for some of them, was to be brief. He asked Mike Molloy what he knew about him. Molloy replied, "Very little", but quoted what Sir Tom McCaffrey, press secretary to James Callaghan when he was Prime Minister and subsequently a publicity adviser to Maxwell, had said about him - that "he is a bastard but a fair one".

Maxwell called an immediate meeting of the MGN board there in Long's office, starting at 3 am. Tony Miles came in from his home in West London and Bob Edwards came back from Maxwell House. It was largely formal, designed to state his authority more than anything else, and he gave notice that there would be another meeting later in the day. For this, there was a fuller turn-out. Maxwell asked what everyone did. Douglas Long replied: "Chief Executive". Roger Bowes replied: "Chief Executive". Vic Horwood, who ran the *Record* and *Mail* at Anderston Quay, Glasgow, replied: "Chief Executive". It was not a good start. The real chief executive was asking the question. Horwood, a distant man in height and manner, said to Maxwell:

I must tell you that the entire staff of the *Daily Record* and the

Sunday Mail have taken a hall in Glasgow for a mass meeting to decide whether they are going to work for you.

Maxwell replied:

You had better get on the first available plane, mister, and tell them that if they don't return to work I will close down their papers and they won't open again.

There was a strained silence. Long said:

Can't we give them a day?

Maxwell replied again:

No. They do it now.

Horwood left.

Maxwell took his three editors, Edwards, Molloy and Richard Stott of the *The People*, and Miles to lunch at Claridge's. Edwards travelled in Maxwell's Rolls Royce, the others by office car. Knowing Maxwell's predilection for getting from A to B in less than the shortest possible time, an apprehensive Edwards privately instructed the Mirror Group driver not to travel at speed. The editors and Miles were told Maxwell's plans for the papers and he delivered a Cudlippian phrase which greatly eased the editorial hostility to him. In future, he said, the journalists at the *Mirror* would be on top and the management would be on tap, a declaration for which the journalists had yearned for years (and which the management has resented ever since). The *Record* was published the next morning, despite its mass meeting, and so was the *Mirror*, which didn't have one. Though several of us who had opposed the takeover expected the sack - it was clear from the beginning that Maxwell's sources of information within the paper were impeccable, including reports on private chapel meetings, and so he knew what had gone on - no one was asked or told to empty his desk. The journalists just got on with producing the next edition, with its new slogan Forward with Britain. That was also its main headline on the front page where, in a signed article drafted for him by Lancaster in the short, stabbing sentences which is the *Mirror*'s style, Maxwell set out what the change meant. It said, in part[1]:

The Mirror Group Newspapers have changed ownership. Their policies will not change.

I am proud to be the proprietor of this group of publications which holds such an important position in the life of the nation.

I certainly hope to make the papers more efficient and thereby more profitable.

My aim is to earn the resources which will enable our newspapers to regain their rightful places as the leaders in their markets.

The *Daily Mirror* and I already have one thing in common. We have supported the Labour party in every election since 1945.

That support will continue. But the *Mirror* has never been a slavish party paper.

It will not be a Labour party organ now. We treasure our independence....

We stand for a modern Britain - a country which truly needs modernising, with industry and trade unions alike prepared to face the hard facts of survival in the Eighties....

I have been in a position to buy the *Daily Mirror*.

But what I cannot buy is the loyalty of its readers.

That will have to continue to be earned.

To me, the *Mirror* has always meant something special.

I believe it means something special to those who work for it and you who buy it. The British people.

This is why the *Mirror* today carries our new slogan: "Forward with Britain".

That slogan is my policy.

* * * * *

Maxwell's ambition to own a national daily newspaper went back more than 20 years. In 1964 he had plans to save the *Daily Herald*, the Labour-loyalist paper whose dreary pages couldn't capture the new and younger audience it needed for commercial success. He failed to get it off the ground and it was succeeded in the autumn of that year by *The Sun*, a broadsheet which made a brave attempt to succeed but which could never shake off the *Herald*'s image.

In 1965, when *The Sun* was already struggling, he contemplated trying to revive the *Herald*, but there was no enthusiasm for that either. He was looking then for a paper upon which the Labour party could rely, not trusting the *Daily Mirror* to fulfil that role. When the *Sunday Citizen* (formerly *Reynold's News*), the newspaper of the Co-operative movement, closed in June 1967, he described it as a disaster. It was the last paper, he said, which was openly committed to and fully supporting the principles of the Labour party[2]:

We cannot forget what happened with the *Daily Mirror* after the '59 election. The masthead, FORWARD WITH THE PEOPLE, vanished overnight; political columnist Dick Crossman was sacked and for the next three years the *Mirror* toyed with promoting the Woodrow Wyatt, Desmond Donnelly kind of Lib/Lab alliance. Had Labour lost in '64, can anyone doubt that the *Mirror*'s break with the Labour party would have been anything but final?

But he put his finger on the problem which had led to the demise of the *Herald* and the *Citizen* - despite all his efforts to save it - and which only the *Mirror*, despite his criticisms of it, has ever managed to solve:

> ... it is not enough to provide a newspaper loyal to the Labour cause. It has to be an exceedingly good newspaper.

Maxwell described the kind of editor which such a newspaper had to have:

> If an editor of a Labour paper feels that he must slavishly support every twist and turn of Government policy, which is often far removed from the general principles of the party and concerned only with temporary exigencies, he will produce an insipid journal that no one will want to read. That was the moral of the death of the commercial *Daily Herald*. He must win respect for daring and courage and have the ability, which all good editors must have, to make enemies.

The following year, on May 10, 1968, his fears about the *Mirror* and *The Sun* were realised when Cecil King, chairman of the International Publishing Corporation which owned the papers, wrote and signed an article published on the front pages of both of them, and of the *Daily Record* in Glasgow, entitled "Enough is Enough", and demanding the resignation of the Prime Minister Harold Wilson. The stratum of madness which ran, in varying thicknesses, through his family, his belief that he was more than King and was a king-maker, is revealed in his own diaries[3] and by Hugh Cudlipp in his sympathetic portrayal of the man he usurped only three weeks after King's démarche[4], and is not part of this book. But it convinced Maxwell that Labour had to acquire a paper it could trust. He wrote to Sir William Richardson, the former editor of the *Sunday Citizen*, on May 16 saying:

> Since Mr King has declared open war against Mr Wilson and the Labour Government, I have decided to accelerate our plans for the launching of a Labour daily. I would be grateful if you would ask your colleagues to assign to me the titles *Reynold's News* and *Sunday Citizen* with a proviso that they can only be used in connection with the launching of a non-profit-making Labour party daily.

As an earnest of his serious intent, Maxwell purchased the general and picture libraries of the *Sunday Citizen* for £2,100, to be used by the staff of the new daily, as well as acquiring its printing presses. But nothing came of that project, though the attempts to resuscitate the paper lasted for several months.

The attempt to revive the *Sunday Citizen* was merely a prelude to Maxwell's first major bid, a few months later, to enter into the league of proprietors of national newspapers by buying the *News of the World*. It was to fail after an acrimonious dispute with the Takeover Panel, a forerunner to the one which was to end disastrously for Maxwell in the Leasco affair. William Davis has racily recounted[5] the origins of the battle.

A professor of spectroscopy at Oxford, Derek Jackson, owner of a quarter of the *News of the World* shares, had just married for the sixth time at the age of 63, and wanted to make the proper financial arrangements should his new wife be quickly widowed and face British death duties of 80 per cent. He decided to sell his shares and invest the proceeds in "external" gilts which would be free of estate duty. He asked Jacob Rothschild's merchant bank to dispose of them. Jackson's cousin, Sir William Carr, was shocked. He made a "fair and generous" offer for the shares - that is, he was willing to pay for them the price at which they were quoted on the open market, which was 28 shillings (£1.40). Jackson didn't reply, because Jacob Rothschild had already contacted Maxwell as a likely buyer and he would certainly pay more. Davis wrote[6]:

> Maxwell was the terror of the publishing world.... When he heard that Jackson's *News of the World* shares were up for sale he leaped into immediate action. He contacted Rothschild and offered 37s (£1.85) a share if he gained control. Rothschild, concerned only with getting the best possible financial deal for their clients, accepted. Maxwell was cock-a-hoop. A 25 per cent share stake seemed to him a pretty good jumping-off point, as indeed it was.... The total value of the offer was nearly £27 million - a tidy sum by anybody's standards.

Carr, who controlled about 30 per cent of the shares in the company, was in bed with 'flu when the announcement of the bid was made. He described it as "cheeky" and asked Hambros Bank to act for him. It moved into the market and started buying up *News of the World* shares while Carr urged other family shareholders to unite, as Davis put it, "against the common foe". Maxwell was confident that his bid would succeed and that there would be no counter-bidders - indeed, Hugh Cudlipp, for IPC, and Associated Newspapers both quickly said they weren't interested - and announced that if it did he would not stand for re-election when the next general election arrived because the roles of MP and newspaper proprietor were "incompatible". He also promised that the paper would retain its political independence, though no doubt it would have been left-leaning independent instead of right-leaning independent under Carr and his egocentric editor, Stafford Somerfield. The organisation, he said, in an interview with *Campaign*[7]:

> ... has got so many other problems that need to be tackled first. To begin with, I would want to make sure that the printing works turn in a higher profit than they do at present and then go out and get some orders to fill their capacity. The organisation's paper mill needs additional orders. There are some serious technical problems there as well ... this is a company which only a few years ago returned 35 per cent on its capital but now there are debts and the return on capital is dismal. The *News of the World* itself is highly profitable and its formula satisfies 16 million readers. Why should I interfere with it?

Nevertheless, it was widely suspected that the paper's news values would be in for a spring cleaning once he was installed in the proprietorial chair. The man who had long argued, years before the *Last Exit to Brooklyn* case, that book publishers should censor themselves and not publish "dirt" could hardly have lived with the Carr-Somerfield *News of the World*. (Michael Gabbert, whose brief editorship of *The Star* in 1987 drove away advertisers and readers who were disgusted by a daily diet of soft porn, was an assistant editor of the paper.) A front-page story the Sunday before Maxwell made his bid was headlined "Royal Biographer in Shock Sex Change", and reported that a man who had written a book about Princess Margaret had had an operation, had become a "woman" and was about to marry "her" butler, who was a Negro. It had nearly all the elements of a *News of the World* classic - royalty and race, sex and servants. Only the cleric and his catamite were missing.

But the *NoW* organisation was much more than a Sunday newspaper which filled its pages with rehashed court stories of sleazy sex, a formula which had made it the most popular paper in the history of journalism. It also owned a famous golf course, Walton Heath in Surrey, and a chain of local newspapers and had extensive printing interests, which were of more value to Pergamon Press than the paper itself. Fleet Street, however, was only interested in the paper. The bid led to a proliferation of profiles about Maxwell. Margaret Laing, no friend, recalled his once saying he was "a jungle man" and indicated four times in the same article that he was not British-born[8].

Anthony Harris, in the *Financial Times*, described a typical Maxwell evening. In between meetings with his board and his takeover advisers, he had a shorter meeting with the clergyman who ran Pergamon's religious books division to discuss a new Pergamon project, an ecumenical Bible, inquired about the sales figures for a primary school series, set up a dinner to mark the retirement of a life-long servant of a company he had only recently acquired and dealt with various other topics[9]:

> Here, in short, was the familiar Maxwell who baffles and enrages his rivals - grandiose projects (the budget for the new Bible is likely to run into six figures before it is published), the almost gatecrashing approach to the top authorities in every field he enters, the personal concern of a well-briefed constituency politician. It is all a bit Flash Harry on the face of it, not at all publisher-like. But - and this is what above all enrages rivals - it works.

The Economist said the bid was[10]:

> ... the sort of challenge to an industry's establishment which the newspaper business needs and which Mr Maxwell is so eminently qualified to throw down, having the requisite mixture of boundless confidence, cheek - and a good profits record.

Maxwell's first offer for the shares was seen by the market as an opening bid. The price of *NoW* shares jumped to 45s (225p) and Maxwell was a buyer at that price.

Once again Maxwell's foreign birth was used against him. He had said that if he did succeed in his bid he would not change the editor of the paper (though many people in Fleet Street would have told him it would be a mistake not to do so), but that did not prevent the unpleasant Somerfield from writing[11]:

> We are having a little local difficulty at the *News of the World*. It concerns the ownership of the paper. Mr Robert Maxwell, a Socialist MP, is trying to take it over.

> Personally, I don't think he will, and I, as editor of your paper for more than eight years and a member of the editorial staff for nearly a quarter of a century, fervently hope that his bid will fail.

> I do not propose to write about the financial aspect; that will be made clear by others better qualified. I write only as the man responsible for the contents of a newspaper which, for more than 50 years, has held the highest circulation in the world.

> Why do I think it would not be a good thing for Mr Maxwell, formerly Jan Ludwig Hoch, to gain control of this newspaper which I know has your respect, loyalty and affection - a newspaper as British as roast beef and Yorkshire pudding?

Somerfield then set out his reasons, which reeked of insincerity except when he was making it clear that he didn't want the paper to fall into the hands of a socialist. (At that stage, presumably, he did not know that his next boss would be a man who was in the Oxford University Labour Club at the same time as Gerald Kaufman, then a member of Harold Wilson's staff, and later MP for Ardwick.) Even Maxwell's promise not to interfere in the editorial policies of the paper, leaving the editor free to say and do what he liked, didn't tempt Somerfield. He must have been the only editor outside Eastern Europe to aver that he didn't want that kind of freedom. He said:

> We don't run the *News of the World* like that.... The editor has daily contact with the chairman. We discuss our ideas. We discuss our policy....

> As far as my own position is concerned, I will not work with Mr Maxwell. I do not understand his views or his policy. I do not believe he is the right man to control the greatest paper in the world.

Somerfield then launched into a nauseating song of praise for Sir William Carr, with eulogy tempting him into making a forecast about the future which the future was quickly to prove was inaccurate. He said to his readers:

> Let me tell you something about the Carr family who at this moment run the *News of the World* and who I believe will continue to do so....

> Is there another Chairman in Fleet Street who stands up at the annual Leg O'Mutton supper to laugh and jest with the staff ...?

> This is a British newspaper, run by British people. Let's keep it that way.

William Davis, then financial editor of *The Guardian*, commented that this was "a crass, xenophobic outburst, a typical example of the paper's narrow-minded approach" which offended many people who, although disliking Maxwell, "took a dim view of these kind of tactics". Maxwell himself, when asked about Somerfield's attack, dismissed it as "scurrilous and beneath contempt".

The really disturbing tactics, however, were those being employed by Hambros Bank which, in defiance of the Takeover Panel's code, was buying up shares in the market in an attempt to stop Maxwell. Maxwell's complaint to the Panel was supported by serious financial commentators but rejected by Hambros, which pointed out that the code only forbade a company's board from buying in this fashion; though the *NoW* was Hambros' client, the bank, allegedly, was buying on its own behalf, a transparent excuse which was later admitted to be false and which exposed the weakness of the Panel. Unfortunately, it was that weakness which was to determine the outcome of the battle.

That was defeat for Maxwell, a financial loss for the shareholders who spurned his better offer, the speedy deposition of Carr, who misplaced his trust in Rupert Murdoch - no doubt imagining that a Commonwealth citizen (as Murdoch then was) would be a whiter man than a Czech-born one - a contemptuous humiliation for the Takeover Panel and the sacking of Stafford Somerfield, perhaps the only worthwhile result from a disreputable tale. The editor's confidence, however, that the paper would remain British-owned and British-run did not prevent his ensuring that Lord Goodman, solicitor to the mighty, drew up a contract which would make it too expensive for the paper to sack him. That was another miscalculation.

Professor Jackson probably watched the early stages of the struggle with considerable enjoyment. He was the man who couldn't lose; the only question was how much he would win. He commented sardonically from the sidelines in Paris[12]:

> I find it very curious that Hambros and Sir William, having offered 28s (140p) are now recommending shareholders to turn down 37s 6d (187.5p).

The same edition of the *News of the World* which carried Somerfield's attack on Maxwell prominently displayed what the *Financial Times* described as "an unprecedented paragraph" advising *NoW* shareholders to get in touch with Hambros. The *Financial Times* said that Pergamon and its advisers were studying whether it contravened Board of Trade regulations against advertising for the purchase of securities. Hambros, in the meantime, according to the paper, were providing £750,000 to finance the purchase of shares in support of the Carr-run board. Maxwell, that same day, October 21, raised his bid for the *NoW* shares to 50s (250p) for the voting shares - which Davis described as "generous by any reasonable standards" - and 42s 9d (213p) for the non-voting. Professor Jackson's prospects were improving almost hourly.

On October 23 the financial editor of *The Times* thought it right to warn the City of London:

> There could be grave dangers for the Takeover Panel, and, indeed, for the City, in the *News of the World* affair. If ... the *News of the*

World board, aided by Hambros Bank and stockbrokers Myers, frustrates the bulk of its shareholders from accepting Pergamon's bid or any equivalent or higher bid, the prospect of the City being shackled by legislation is all but inevitable.

It appeared last night that Hambros had been buying shares, largely voting shares, not on behalf of the family of Sir William Carr, the chairman, but for its own account. Hambros is, of course, an associate of *News of the World* and any buying for its own or anybody else's account which led to the defeat of Pergamon's offer and the *News of the World* price falling well below the offered price would be a flagrant breach of the Code.

The Guardian reported that same morning that the Takeover Panel was keeping "a close watch" on the situation. In its view, the takeover code was being "bent if not broken". But the Panel swiftly sent a letter to Hambros, incredibly exonerating the bank from any breach of its code. Meanwhile, the first news of Murdoch's intended intervention burst in the papers the following day. The Carr family, seeking a rescuer to come charging over the hill, had found one in the young Australian newspaper magnate, who the *Financial Times* said had a reputation of being anti-British. Somerfield's roast beef of the previous Sunday was about to acquire the taste of kangaroo meat. But the Carrs were overjoyed - for a while. Never in the history of gallantry had a damsel in distress so mistaken Count Dracula for a white knight.

Through Morgan Grenfell and Co., Murdoch's News Ltd. had bought nine per cent of *NoW* shares. The *NoW* organisation claimed that this purchase, together with 42 per cent of shares controlled or pledged to them, had won the day. *The Times* (not yet inhibited by being a Murdoch acquisition) again voiced its fears in its Business News section of October 25:

... The story of the past three days considerably undermines confidence in the Panel. Morgan Grenfell put in writing to the Panel their proposal to buy voting shares in *NoW* on behalf of Murdoch's group in the share market. Morgans asked the Panel to reply within 24 hours whether this was in contravention of the Code. There was no reply at all, whereupon Morgans went ahead and bought. Yesterday morning the Panel stopped all associates in this bid from buying shares.... The Panel must not be indecisive in this way if it is to succeed. And if it appears in no better light than this by the end of the affair, it will be as good as buried.

The deal which Carr and Murdoch had put together was to give the Australian a 40 per cent stake in the *News of the World* in exchange for the *News of the World* acquiring "certain important

interests of News" in Australia. Murdoch, in a ploy which he was to
repeat with the Monopolies Commission in the years ahead when he
was seeking to buy other British newspapers, said he would have to
"reconsider his position" if the Takeover Panel halted the proposed
deal. Maxwell said:

> This is a disgraceful affair and it is up to the Takeover Panel to do a
> proper job.

Murdoch made it clear that he did not intend to match Maxwell's
bid of 50s a share for the minority shareholders, saying frankly[13]:

> I haven't got enough money for that.

But the Takeover Panel had already decided, according to the
Financial Times, that the *NoW* share price "should not fall
appreciably below the value of the Pergamon bid" after the details
of the new deal had been revealed. The virtual unanimity of the
financial press and financial editors appeared not to influence the
Panel at all. The *Daily Telegraph* said that if the Panel did nothing,
or what amounted to nothing, then the Carr-Murdoch alliance
would defeat Maxwell. But it thought that the arrangements
between News Ltd. and *NoW* was "unlikely" to be worth more to
NoW shareholders than the Pergamon offer. The *London Evening
News* said the Panel had behaved in a "fantastically bumbling
manner". *The Economist* declared that many people would consider
the Panel "a dead duck" unless it exerted itself effectively at the
very last minute. The *Daily Mail* described the deal as "a blatant
example" of the denial of shareholders' rights. From afar, the *Wall
Street Journal* saw the whole affair in a different light[14]:

> Mr Maxwell is a Czech-born entrepreneur who entered the
> publishing business in 1951 with a personal stake of $36,400. In a
> country that still retains strong class feelings, he recognises no
> superiors and is as blunt-spoken as many of the uninhibited
> "exposés" run by the newspaper he seeks to control.

Bill Grundy in *The Spectator* touched on the same theme: he
thought Maxwell was suspect to "English gentlemen" in the City,
many of whom came from families which had been in Britain for
more than two generations.

The Times returned to the attack on October 26 in the severest
words it had used so far, saying:

> It cannot yet be claimed with certainty that the Takeover Code has
> been breached in the *News of the World* affair. But there is strong
> prima facie evidence to suggest that it has.

The paper said that the Panel, in the *NoW* case and in a previous one, the American Tobacco/Gallaher affair, had shown itself to be "a limp rag" and "indecisive". Its "spinelessness" stood out for all to see. Despite the fact that several newspapers had indicated "beyond question" that the action being taken by the *NoW* and its advisers was such that a firm ruling from the Panel was "mandatory", nothing had been done "until the horse appeared to have bolted". The City, *The Times* estimated, had about two weeks to "mend its fences", otherwise it expected the Government would legislate for a Securities and Exchange Commission. There was a "paramount need" for a new regulatory body headed by a man of "outstanding ability and integrity".

Patrick Sergeant, City Editor of the *Daily Mail*, said[15]:

> Mr Murdoch is paraded as the answer to Mr Maxwell's bid. He is, at best, jam tomorrow, at worst, pie in the sky.

The *Sunday Times*'s financial editor Charles Raw said that the *NoW* affair "must be the last bid to be dealt with by the City Takeover Panel in its present form" because it had shown that the Panel was "incapable of ensuring orderly behaviour", and in the same paper Stephen Aris said that Murdoch had not needed to employ "strong-arm tactics" because all the "rough stuff" had been done by Hambros and Morgan Grenfell, the two merchant banks responsible for fighting off Maxwell. Mammon, in *The Observer*, thought that the choice for Carr had been between the devil and the deep blue sea. The *New Statesman*, under the editorship of Paul Johnson, had no doubts that the affair had developed into "a major City scandal", and commented[16]:

> There is an obvious and fundamental contradiction between the preamble to the Code, which demands that the spirit and not merely the letter of its rules should be observed, and the prevailing City assumption - expressed openly the other day by the chairman of the Stock Exchange - that the rules are there to be circumvented by ingenious experts as if they were tax regulations.

Even the *Investors' Chronicle*, which sought to show the Panel was being badly treated by other journals, had to admit that this "conscientious" institution was "ill-equipped".

Almost every commentator came back to the same point. If everything was to be seen to be above board, then the Carr-Murdoch deal had to be shown to be at least as good, if not better, than the Maxwell offer. Hambros had described Carr's original offer of 28s a share to Professor Jackson as a "fair, indeed a most generous price". How, asked Anthony Bambridge in *The Observer*, could Hambros now argue that the shares would be worth 50s once the prop of Maxwell's bid had been removed?

There was little criticism of the Carr family, and it was largely accepted that Hambros, Morgan Grenfell and Murdoch were acting in their own interests, even if those interests were not necessarily to the short-term benefit of the minority shareholders or the long-term benefit of the City of London.

The Takeover Panel met in almost continuous session on October 29. Murdoch came out from a meeting with the chairman of the Panel, Sir Humphrey Mynors, declaring that he was now certain of victory over Maxwell. The Panel said nothing, but *The Times* reported that it had been decided substantially to reorganise the Panel with a full-time chairman. It was clear, however, that what the City was worried about was its own future, not that of the minority shareholders in the *News of the World*, nor whether the deal between News Ltd. and Carr should be stalled, forbidden or unscrambled. The President of the Board of Trade, Anthony Crosland, invited the Governor of the Bank of England, Sir Leslie O'Brien, to meet him to discuss the problem of takeovers, but the Government had more than enough trouble on its agenda without wanting to risk a full-scale battle with the City, to whom self-regulation had become a totem pole, despite the fact that it had been seen again and again to have failed the test when it was required and which, even in 1987, nearly 20 years later, was still failing.

On November 1 the Panel finally came to a decision of sorts and announced it had secured the agreement of Hambros, Hill Samuel (acting for Maxwell) and Morgan Grenfell not to vote the shares they had acquired in the market since Pergamon's first bid at the planned extraordinary general meeting called by the *NoW* organisation to win support for the deal with Murdoch. That decision seemed at first to destroy the voting majority which Carr and Murdoch and Hambros had stitched together. It left the Carr family holding a slightly larger block of committed shares than Maxwell - estimates varied between 32 and 37 per cent for the Carrs compared with about 27 per cent - with something between 20 and 25 per cent uncommitted. But Maxwell was not satisfied: even if he succeeded in winning over enough shareholders to give him a majority among the shares not sold after the bid announcement, those subsequent purchases still constituted a blocking majority. That would still deny the shareholders a free choice. Maxwell and his advisers argued that in the event of the deal with Murdoch not being approved, the Hambros holding should be committed to the Pergamon offer.

The *Financial Times* reported that, despite the agreement with the Panel, the *News of the World* was still receiving written pledges of support from shareholders, apparently paid out in a form of a legally-binding contract, the effect of which would be to circumvent the Panel's ban on either side acquiring more shares. The paper said on November 7:

> The issue ... is one on which the Panel must act. The contract is questionable in two respects. On the one hand it is arguable that the first refusal clauses constitute an agreement to deal, and the Stock Exchange ruling on suspended quotations specifically condemns this. Insofar as it was the Panel that demanded suspension, the Stock Exchange ethic would presumably be extended to Hambros. On the other hand, it is certain that the crucial undertaking over votes contravenes the undisputed City principle that full details of any scheme should be available before the poll. Clearly, any signatory to the contract is effectively voting in advance on the undisclosed deal with News Ltd. The Panel can only assume that the *NoW* board is trying to commit votes now which it fears would otherwise go against it....

The terms of the contract sent by the *NoW* board granted Hambros first refusal on any intended sale and bound anyone signing it to vote for all resolutions for, or on behalf of, the board. Each shareholder, in return, was offered the nominal sum of 10s (50p). Hambros said the contract was only sent to those shareholders who volunteered their support.

On November 8 Maxwell wrote to all shareholders in the *NoW* organisation, pointing out that, despite promises, they had not received any communication at all from their board. He set out in detail his offer, which was a mixture of Pergamon shares and convertible loan stock with a cash alternative for the Pergamon shares if the shareholders so wished. The offer valued the ordinary shares in the *NoW* at 49s 7d (248p) each and the non-voting shares at 42s 4d (221.5p). He urged them not to sign any option arrangement, pledge of support or other form of contract, and if they had already done so, to seek release from it.

The City's nervousness about the failings of the Takeover Panel was increased when the Prime Minister, Harold Wilson, went to the Lord Mayor's annual banquet at the Guildhall on November 11 and declared that if the City didn't act to preserve its "good name" then the Government might be forced to[17]:

> Recent events have cast a shadow over the working of some of our

institutions. There is a demand for action - action by the Government. If this becomes necessary we shall not hesitate to act, but we would vastly prefer that the City itself should provide the discipline - including self-discipline - that is required.

But it was an empty threat. Though it caught the headlines the next day, that part of the speech did not even rate a mention in Wilson's memoirs. It may have helped galvanise the City in its revision of the takeover code, but a new code for some future event was of little use to Maxwell trying to fight the disadvantages of a code as bent as a spiral staircase.

At last, on November 21, the *NoW* board wrote to its shareholders, urging them not to accept the Pergamon offer and promising to give its reasons after it had received the formal offer document. It would also then explain why the shareholders should accept the deal with News Ltd. It signed a provisional agreement with News Ltd. in the second week of December and announced it would be put to the EGM, the date for which was fixed for January 2, 1969. Meanwhile, Maxwell issued a writ in the New South Wales Supreme Court claiming damages of $1 million (Australian) from the *Sydney Daily Mirror*, one of Murdoch's publications, for defamation. The paper, scurrilous enough to make the editor of the *News of the World* blush, had published a series of articles about Maxwell and International Learning Systems Corporation, Ltd. with headlines such as "Racket in Sale of Books" and "Women Warned on Door Sales".

On December 16 Carr announced the terms of the agreement which he had to make with the predatory Murdoch to save himself from the predatory Maxwell. It gave Murdoch 39.7 per cent voting interest in the company and made him managing director, with full executive power, for a fee of £20,000 a year. Carr was to remain chairman. To reach his projected holding, Murdoch undertook to buy 403,000 shares from Hambros Bank at a price between 48s (240p) and 48s 6d (242.5p). Maxwell said that the agreement "made no financial sense whatsoever". The Takeover Panel announced at the same time that dealings would be resumed in *NoW* shares, though News Ltd. and Pergamon were not to participate. The difference between the two rivals, however, was that News Ltd. had a deal with Hambros which Maxwell was unable to make. On the first morning of the resumption in trading, *NoW* ordinary shares were quoted at 46s 6d (232.5p) and the non-voting shares at 35s 6d (177.5p).

On December 19 trustees for Professor Jackson and his brother,

David, took out a writ against the *NoW* board, News Ltd. and Hambros Bank, seeking a series of injunctions to restrain implementation of the agreement between News Ltd. and the *NoW* organisation and sought damages from the *NoW* directors for breach of fiduciary obligations and for injurious falsehood. A similar claim for breach of fiduciary obligations was made against Hambros and damages for conspiracy from all defendants except News Ltd. and the *NoW* corporation. Hill Samuel and Robert Fleming, Maxwell's merchant bank advisers, published a searing attack on the *NoW*-News deal, declaring that the *NoW* board was asking its shareholders to make a sacrifice probably without precedent in the history of major public companies in Britain.

On December 22, under the headline "No News is good news", Anthony Bambridge pointed out that the *NoW* voting shares had now drifted down to 44s (220p) and declared:

> Maxwell ought to win; his chances of doing so are slim.

The likelihood of Maxwell failing was reflected in the share price, which fell again the next day to 41s 9d (209p), an unwelcome Christmas present for those shareholders supporting Maxwell, and he wrote to Crosland asking him to intervene to put pressure on the Takeover Panel to secure the abrogation of the pledges given to the *NoW* board after trading was suspended. The *Investors' Chronicle*, in an end of the year message to the shareholders, said:

> It is still difficult to see any logical reason for Ordinary holders to turn down Pergamon....

Indeed it was, as Hill Samuel and Robert Fleming wrote to the *NoW* shareholders on December 24 pointing out that the Pergamon bid was now worth 51s per Ordinary share (255p) and 42s (210p) for the non-voting ones; they calculated that shareholders who supported their board would certainly lose 10s (50p) per Ordinary share and probably 17s 6d (87.5p).

The air in the last few days before the EGM was filled with insults, Murdoch, in particular, alleging that Maxwell and his advisers had bought Pergamon shares in order to force up the price and make the Pergamon offer more attractive to *NoW* shareholders. At the same time, trustees of the *NoW* pension fund made an emergency application in the High Court to prevent the fund's shares being voted in favour of the deal with News Ltd.

The EGM was held at the Connaught Rooms, Great Queen Street, at 11.30 on January 2, Sir William Carr presiding. After shouts of "can't hear", adjustments to the microphone, more cries of "can't hear", and the chairman promising to do better, the proceedings got under way. The 500 shareholders present - the largest turnout ever, in Carr's estimation - were asked to approve the creation of 5,100,000 ordinary shares to be credited fully paid to News Ltd. "in consideration for the acquisition of certain Australian interests and assets", and to authorise the maximum number of directors of the company to be increased from 10 to 16.

Carr's speech was movingly worthy of the deathbed of Little Nell:

> At the heart of our affairs is a great Sunday newspaper which, despite all the onslaughts on it by its competitors, remains supreme as the most widely circulating Sunday newspaper in the world. To run such a newspaper successfully requires not only editorial and management skill but specialised knowledge and experience. Pergamon have no experience in this field. I must mention the position of our 8,000 employees. They, too, are of the greatest importance. Our relationship with the several trades unions in our highly-specialised operations has been both cordial and delicately balanced. Management and men have always worked closely together. There is good reason to believe - and I say this deliberately - that some unions regard with dismay the takeover attempt by Pergamon.

Carr, more a patriarch than a proprietor, could never have imagined in his most vivid nightmares that the man to whom he was ceding control would one day sack all the employees about whom he was so concerned, deny the trade unions any negotiating rights and move the *News of the World* inside the fortress he had built at Wapping. To be fair, neither could the unions have contemplated such a development either.

Any idea that the *NoW* organisation had rushed into the arms of News Ltd. in order to save itself from Maxwell was a travesty of the truth, he said. For years his company had looked at the possibilities of expansion abroad. He saw the deal as "a unique opportunity" for the *NoW* to "establish a major stake in this fast-growing, fast-developing country [Australia] which has so much to offer the world now". Though he was no doubt sincere, that description of what he was urging the shareholders to do was itself a travesty of the truth.

Carr commended Murdoch - the new managing director was "an energetic young man, full of ideas and enthusiasm" - and then asked for a "personal word":

> If the News Ltd. agreement has your approval, I shall have the honour to remain as your chairman, a position held before me by my father and my grandfather.

What he did not tell his shareholders was that he had had a secret

meeting with Maxwell over breakfast in Sir Isaac Wolfson's
apartment in Portland Place. Carr had asked Maxwell:

> If you buy the company for cash, would you keep me as chairman?
> No.

Carr then said that Murdoch had promised him the chairmanship,
to which Maxwell replied:

> He may have offered it to you but he will take it away from you in less
> than six months.

Carr then asked Maxwell why he objected to him as chairman, to
which he replied:

> Every time I have a haircut at the Savoy late in the afternoon, around
> 4 p.m., I find you and your *News of the World* cronies still drinking
> Martinis and I don't think that is suitable training for any chairman of
> mine.

(In a biography of Murdoch, Simon Regan, for eight years a
feature writer and foreign correspondent for the *News of the World*,
described how Maxwell's prophecy came true. He wrote[18]:

> Sir William Carr, who was very ill, had not been into the office for six
> months since Murdoch's arrival, and Murdoch decided, quite simply,
> that they would have to part company. "I knew the situation was
> getting really hopeless. Carr was on the phone to someone in the
> office almost every day. The only person he never called was me. I
> suppose in a way it's very natural. He had been running the company
> for years and he found it difficult to give up just like that. But we just
> couldn't carry on like that."
>
> He went down and had tea at Carr's country place and told him as
> politely as he could that he did not feel there was room for both of
> them in the firm any more and Carr would have to go. He pointed out
> that he had since bought the Jackson shares in a private deal and
> could now muster over half the voting shares.
>
> Carr said to me, "But you wrote to me saying when you bought the
> shares that it wouldn't change our relationship in any way!" I said
> "That's right. I did. But I've changed my mind.")

But all that was in the future. Murdoch was greeted with
prolonged applause and told the shareholders that they were
acquiring "first-class assets" in Australia. Turning to Carr, he
added:

> Lastly, Mr Chairman, let me say with all sincerity how much I
> personally look forward to doing this job and working to the limit of
> my capacity for this company and its shareholders, and, of course,
> under your continuing chairmanship....

A shareholder wanted to know whether the pledges which had been given to Hambros were still binding. Harry Sporborg, speaking for the bank, said they were, but added that in his opinion had the bank gone through the "formality" of releasing shareholders from their pledges they would not have voted in any different way. Another questioner, who was uncertain how many shares he held and boasted he did not know how to pronounce Pergamon - he may have thought it was an Eastern European word - said he would vote for the recommended resolutions because he had confidence in Sir William Carr - and would there be the usual refreshments?

Question:

> Why was the editor of the *News of the World* given a new contract up to the end of 1976 at an increased salary?

Answer:

> He was going to get it anyway.

Colonel Harry Llewellyn, the Olympic gold medallist and owner of 1,000 voting shares, asked:

> How was it that the Carrs and the Hambros offered Professor Jackson and his family only 28s a share. Wasn't this really asking for trouble?

Carr took a long time to get to the point of the question, but his answer, in short, was that he left it to Hambros to make an offer for the professor's shares and Hambros thought 28s was "a fair and reasonable price" at the time. Another questioner then asked why, if Hambros was selling 403,000 shares at 48s a share to News Ltd. other shareholders weren't being offered a similar opportunity. Sporborg said that the shares really belonged "in equity" to News Ltd. He wasn't sure what the price would be, but Hambros wouldn't make a profit. Maxwell then rose to his feet amid facetious cries of "Name, please", and attempts by a few shareholders to raise objections to his speaking. He began by asking whether Carr would stand by his "kind promise" to give a fair hearing to both sides and allow him to make a brief statement. Sir William replied that Maxwell could have the same time as Murdoch had had, which was three minutes and 10 seconds, a blatantly unfair ruling which brought the expected laughter and applause from his supporters. Almost every sentence was interrupted by Carr and Murdoch adherents, with shouts of "Shame", "Withdraw" and "What about the pensioners?"

When Maxwell said that many members of the editorial staff of the *News of the World* had been invited by the management to take time off and attend the meeting, a "kind of practice [which] may be all right in the USSR and East Germany but not in this country", the official transcript records "(Uproar)". When that died down, Maxwell asked:

> Why did Professor Jackson decide to accept the Pergamon offer for his shares? The answer is … that you asked Mr Sporborg on behalf of yourself and your family to offer him for 750,000 shares 28s a share and the balance one shilling (5p) a share below the market price at the time the deal was consummated. What you failed to go on to say is that in that letter of Harry Sporborg's there is a paragraph which says that the Board consider this offer to Professor Jackson as being fair and generous.…

All this was too much for Carr, who exclaimed that he had been listening to "a great number of half truths from Mr Maxwell", which was surprising, since Maxwell had only been allowed to complete three sentences uninterrupted. A shareholder asked that Maxwell be ruled out of order and another asked that Maxwell should be allowed to tackle Murdoch so that the arguments could be heard. Maxwell challenged Sporborg about the "fair and generous" share offer of 28s. Sporborg defended it as "the market price at the time". Then why, asked Maxwell, was Pergamon's offer a few days later rejected out of hand as being unreasonable and not sufficient? The heckling, of considerably lower quality than would be encountered at a meeting on the hustings, continued unabated. But Maxwell ploughed on, turning to address the uncommitted shareholders:

> If you vote for the Pergamon offer, you will get an immediate increase in income, or shares in a company whose dividends have more than doubled in the last four years. If you vote for the *News of the World* board you will be supporting a board whose dividends were virtually static until the Pergamon offer was made. If you invest in Pergamon you will be having an expanding international company with a record of dynamic growth and well-covered dividends; with the *News of the World* a dismal earnings record and a dividend which is barely covered. (Cries of dissent.)

Carr interrupted:

> Ladies and gentlemen, I have outstretched the time which has been allotted to Mr Maxwell. Would it be your wish to continue hearing Mr Maxwell, or would it be your wish.… (Cries of "No".)

Maxwell wound up his remarks and Carr tried to bring the meeting to the decision he wanted, after explaining to another shareholder the virtual impossibility of producing a daily newspaper at the Bouverie Street premises of the company where the *News of the World* was located:

> Now to start a daily paper, of course, needs a lot of courage. There are not many daily papers that ... are making profits. I am sure the *News of the World* organisation would not want its board to start pouring millions of money away trying to start a new daily paper.

In fact, later that year Murdoch was to buy the title of *The Sun* from IPC and started the new daily paper from the very premises where Carr told the meeting it would be "hazardous" to attempt it. Maxwell returned to the attack, asking Carr:

> If I decide to hold on to my *News of the World* shares how long will it take me till they reach the same price that the Pergamon offer now makes them? Would you care to forecast how long it would take me as a *News of the World* shareholder, if I decide to hold on to my shares - since you have successfully blocked and frustrated this bid - if I hold the shares, how many years do you forecast it will take for these shares to reach the value that shareholders can get for their shares today?

Carr replied:

> I have no intention of giving you any such undertaking: (a) I have not got enough money to give that undertaking, and (b) why should I forecast in one or two years or five years? There are many shareholders who have held their shares since 1891, or certainly from the beginning of the twentieth century, and they are not complaining and they never have complained.... What is, in fact, money when you have had so many other things out of life as well.... If you employ 8,000 you are most probably looking after something like, I suppose, 20,000 or more people and I do not believe in the main - I have never heard until you came along - that there had been any really serious criticism from our shareholders to the board about the lack of dividends which they have received.

It was an extraordinary argument to put to shareholders that money was not all that important. The *NoW* organisation, in that case, must have been about the only limited company where investment had a philanthropic content. Certainly, Carr's argument could only succeed by persuading the shareholders that the *NoW* was a family concern and the shareholders were all part of that family. Beneath it all lay the unspoken assertion that to expose that family to the profit-making of a foreigner would be unpatriotic. (Murdoch, on the other hand, though an Australian citizen at that time, was a descendant of the men who had fought at Gallipoli in the First World War and contemporary of those who had defended Tobruk in the Second, and was, therefore, the next best thing to being British.) The *News of the World*, in Somerfield's words, was as British as roast beef and Yorkshire pudding and they wanted it to stay that way. The resolution in favour of the board's recommendation was thus passed by 4,526,822 votes to 3,246,937. The old metaphor about turkeys voting for an early Christmas was never more apt.

The last chance Maxwell had to swing the vote had, in fact, been lost on the eve of the meeting when the High Court refused to grant the injunction sought by three *News of the World* pensioners obliging the trustees of the pension fund - Carr and two of his co-directors - to cast the fund's 578,000 votes against the board.

But Murdoch and the board had tried to cover against any risk that they might be defeated. According to Regan, Murdoch was worried that if Maxwell sought an adjournment of the meeting it would be decided by a show of hands rather than a count of shares. He quoted Murdoch as saying[19]:

> Maxwell accused us of stacking the meeting, which was half true.... I made sure that the hall was full of our people.... There were several people there who had had one hundred votes or so put in their name a few days before....

Regan asserted that even secretaries at the *News of the World* organisation had been given shares for a few days - and had to sign a contract they would return them when the meeting was over. The Murdoch camp claimed it was "the name of the game" and that nothing illegal was ever done on their side. After the votes had been counted, Murdoch and Carr shook hands and later toasted their victory in champagne; at the time Carr didn't know that he was the biggest loser of all.

Maxwell too shook hands with Murdoch but commented that "the law of the jungle" had prevailed and said he intended to ask the Takeover Panel how it permitted Hambros and Morgan Grenfell to prevent a bona fide takeover bid from going through. A statement from Hill Samuel and Robert Fleming disclosed that Pergamon received acceptances for its offer from 34 per cent of the voting shares and 54 per cent of the non-voting shares. The price of the voting shares fell immediately to 38s (190p), 13s (65p) below Maxwell's offer. Within 24 hours £1 million was wiped off their market value. Shareholders couldn't say they hadn't been warned. Maxwell told them during the extraordinary general meeting:

> If you support your board, you vote for a substantial fall in the market price of your investment.

A concerned *Financial Times* reader wrote to its editor - sending a copy to Maxwell - saying:

> I am not a shareholder in either *News of the World* or Pergamon. No doubt it should not be matter for surprise that the characteristics that typify *NoW* journalism should be found repeated and intensified in its Board of Directors. I am, however, very much concerned with the standards of the City in general and merchant bankers in particular. The technique of the carefully "packed" and rehearsed meeting is certainly highly objectionable on a number of grounds. And is nothing to be done regarding Hambros' public statement, and assurance to the Panel, that all its purchases of *NoW* shares in the market had been on its own behalf, followed now by an admission that more than a third of them were, on the contrary, purchased for the Board's ally, Mr Murdoch?

Christopher Gwinner wrote in the *Financial Times*[20]:

> On the question of the City's Takeover Panel, there can be no doubt that the *News of the World* case sounded its death knell.... Coming so close on the heels of the American Tobacco/Gallaher débâcle, it appears to have damaged its reputation beyond repair.

The Economist succinctly summed up the end of the affair in its headline: Maxwell loses vote, panel loses face.

Harry Sporborg, the Hambros adviser to the *News of the World*, said a week after the EGM that he felt it was now necessary to have a full-time chairman of the Takeover Panel, which was like a burglar demanding more policemen on the beat. He suggested a merchant banker should get the job, which was like the burglar offering to be the policeman. Professor Jackson arranged to sell 1.6 million shares, a large part of his holding, to Rupert Murdoch, which put him £800,000 down on what he might have got, and gave Murdoch 51 per cent of the *NoW* voting shares. Carr's health was not improving, and at the end of January 1969 Maxwell wrote a "strictly private and personal" letter to him saying:

> Whilst naturally regretting the outcome of the recent battle, I do want to send you my best wishes for a full and speedy recovery.

> Don't let the doctors depress you; experience has taught me that whilst expert advice, medicine and surgical techniques are very necessary and valuable, the will and determination of the patient to get well is of far greater value and importance.

At the company's AGM in July Carr announced he was giving up the chairmanship in favour of Murdoch and didn't disclose it was against his wishes. The *NoW* shares fell again, this time down to 25s 9d (129p), barely half the Pergamon offer. Those shareholders who had stood by their chairman had lost him as well as half of their possible capital. The following February Stafford Somerfield was sacked in a three-minute interview. According to Somerfield, no reason was given. Shortly before he died on November 14, 1977 Carr sent a handwritten letter to Maxwell regretting that he had not sold his company to him.

The lasting irony of Maxwell's business life was that the reorganised and tougher Takeover Panel which replaced the one so ineffectual in the *News of the World* affair was to choose him and Pergamon Press as the first target for its newly-bestowed strength.

* * * * *

In May 1969 Maxwell made a formal approach to IPC to buy *The Sun*, the paper of the sixties which clearly wasn't going to survive till the seventies. IPC said such a deal would depend upon "a committee or a board of directors consisting of prominent members of the Labour party" making the approach. A statement from it added[21]:

> What is involved in simple terms is the willingness of IPC to hand back to leading representatives of the Labour party the newspaper which was originally the party's and TUC's official daily journal known then as the *Daily Herald*. Such a transfer would be more appropriate to a group of persons than to an individual.

Maxwell agreed it would be "inappropriate" for an individual to control *The Sun*, but there was no rush from wealthy Labour supporters publicly to declare their willingness to join a consortium. Nevertheless, he still wanted to produce a non-profit-making paper supporting Labour, and carried on trying to get it, despite IPC's stringent conditions, including a guarantee of at least 18 months' publication, which Maxwell was prepared to give. In a letter to Hugh Cudlipp, Maxwell promised that the paper would be "complete, lively and exciting" and its format would be changed from broadsheet to tabloid. He planned to move the editorial staff to the London *Evening Standard* offices near Fleet Street, where the paper would also be printed. The price would be increased and he expected the circulation, which had been hovering around the one million mark, would initially be about 600,000.

But the fact was that no one could believe that Maxwell would succeed where the management of IPC, people steeped in newspaper production for decades, had so palpably failed. Lord Thomson of Fleet, the Canadian proprietor who had rescued *The Times* and the *Sunday Times*, predicted that Maxwell would lose £1,500,000 in the attempt. The chances of the paper surviving in a different guise were severely damaged when IPC gave six months' notice of its intention to close down *The Sun*. That put its readership and its advertising up for grabbing by every other newspaper in Fleet Street and went against the tradition - analogous to devaluation - of denying it was going to happen right up until the moment that it did. It seems clear now that IPC never had any faith in Maxwell's chances of success. Looking back on the episode many years later, Hugh Cudlipp wrote wryly[22]:

> I was certainly in a position to guarantee him the total fulfilment of the non-profit-making aspect of his plan. Journalists were sceptical. Maxwell offered the editorship successively to Robert Edwards, then of *The People*, Geoffrey Pinnington of the *Daily Mirror*, Michael Randall of the *Sunday Times* and William Davis of *Punch*. They were all too busy that month. The printing unions were hostile, in particular Sogat. On September 2, Robert Maxwell withdrew his bid.

But before that happened IPC had begun informal discussions with Rupert Murdoch, the man who had frustrated Maxwell's bid for the *News of the World*. The big differences between him and Maxwell were that he had the *News of the World* presses lying idle for six days a week and, despite Sir William Carr's belief about the difficulties, knew he could produce a daily paper upon them, and that he certainly had no intention of keeping the paper within its tradition of broad support for the Labour party.

Murdoch stressed that he was not a "counter-bidder" for *The Sun*, but said that he was seriously interested if the talks between IPC and Maxwell should break down. Maxwell himself was fully engaged in talks with the City Takeover Panel about the Leasco merger and was not able to devote the time necessary speedily to complete the long-drawn-out negotiations with IPC; nevertheless, he had agreed a price with IPC of £50,000. What he did not expect was that the major printing union would state its hostility to him and favour Murdoch, a decision which its successors must bitterly rue today. There is no doubt that *The Sun* was wasting away. The staff were looking for other jobs and the position had become critical. The National Union of Journalists' chapel at the paper demanded that a deadline of August 31 should be placed on completing the discussions between IPC and Maxwell. That could have been overcome. Far more serious was the announcement by Sogat that it was breaking off talks with Maxwell. In a statement explaining why he had pulled out, Maxwell said[23]:

> It will be a matter of serious regret to millions of Labour supporters and to all radicals in the country that Sogat alone should have taken this unfriendly step, and the full responsibility for the termination of these promising negotiations which had reached such an advanced stage is theirs....

The Sogat decision was taken by its then general secretary, Dick Briginshaw, privately referred to by Fleet Street managers - privately because none dared say it to his face - as Brigandshaw. It is not customary for on-the-record threats to be made by Fleet Street union leaders to Fleet Street proprietors. Instead, warnings of trouble percolate. It percolated through to the IPC management that unless talks were ended with Maxwell, the *Daily Mirror*, then at the peak of its circulation, might face industrial trouble and be unable to print. In effect, that would have been torpedoing the flagship of the IPC fleet. IPC could see no principle involved which was worth that risk.

The Sogat action effectively gave *The Sun* to Murdoch. For well over a decade its members employed by him had first-class seats on the gravy train, but eventually he sacked every one of them. Today Sogat has no representation at his newspapers.

Hugh Cudlipp commented that it was obviously "the end of Mr Maxwell's dream of being the proprietor of a national newspaper"; little could he have suspected that one day Maxwell would own the group of which Cudlipp was then the chairman and that Maxwell would ask him to be his editorial adviser.

Harold Evans, then editor of the *Sunday Times*, Maxwell's inveterate antagonist and later editor of *The Times* (he was sacked by Murdoch shortly after being named Editor of the Year, thus proving that Flavour of the Month is more important), recounted many years later the tactics which Murdoch employed to win *The Sun*. He wrote in his book *Good Times, Bad Times*[24]:

> My first experience of Murdoch was under cover. In April, 1969, four months after Murdoch acquired the *News of the World*, his defeated rival, Captain Robert Maxwell, a naturalised Briton, scientific publisher, propagandist and former Labour MP, offered to take the ailing *Sun* newspaper off the hands of Hugh Cudlipp.... An affable Murdoch rang me to say he had documents on Maxwell. It was all hush-hush and I could have them if I did not announce who had

passed them on. I had not yet met Murdoch. "Why don't you run them yourself?" I asked. "Nobody here", he responded, "can look at it as well as your Insight guys." This was not the whole truth. For a third party to discredit Maxwell was more useful to Murdoch, who had his own eyes on *The Sun*, but was biding his time.

Nevertheless, Evans had the documents collected. He said they turned out to be "flimsy stuff".

* * * * *

Maxwell's next essay in the newspaper publishing business was in Scotland. It began with high hopes and ended in recriminations which have lasted until this day.

Since the war, and despite its "foreign" origins - owned by a Canadian and active Tory, Lord Beaverbrook, and offspring of a London newspaper - the *Scottish Daily Express* had dominated the daily paper scene in Scotland. Like the London *Express*, it was bright, brilliantly-produced and had a flair and circulation none of the other broadsheets could match. At its peak it sold 660,000 copies a day, which in a nation of only five million people was remarkable. (Though the *Daily Record* today sells over 760,000.) But by the early seventies a slide had set in. The *Scottish Daily Express*, like its London parent, was an expensive paper to produce. When its circulation fell to 570,000 retrenchment was the order from London.

Though costs were the major problem, they were linked with, and exacerbated by, industrial problems. The grip which the trade unions had on newspaper managements was as strong in Scotland as it was in London. An attempt to trim staff by 20 per cent in Glasgow by a voluntary redundancy scheme - voluntary because the unions would not contemplate a compulsory scheme - was the laughing stock of the industry. It was open to any journalist to apply - and so the best of them did, taking their lump sum and walking into well-paid jobs elsewhere. The *SDE* was left with those too old or too ordinary to find work in another paper. According to *The Story of the Scottish Daily News*[25], 17 sub-editors on the *SDE* who accepted the terms had to be replaced by 19 others. Forty-one journalists altogether took the pay-off and 43 were recruited to take their place.

It couldn't go on and the thoughts of the Express Group's managing director, Jocelyn Stevens, were already turning towards closure when the *SDE* journalists stopped the paper from publishing one night because a few of them objected to a cold-war cartoon by the stridently right-wing Cummings. On March 18, 1974 - when Britain was still suffering the effects of a three-month-long miners' strike and with a minority Labour Government taking office only two weeks earlier - the closure of the Glasgow works at Albion Street was announced with the loss of 1,800 jobs. The *Scottish Daily Express* would continue to be printed and published - but in Manchester, where the northern editions of Express Newspapers were produced. Stevens claimed that since he had launched a project the year before to "revitalise" the *Daily Express* there had been 56 interruptions in normal work in Glasgow, with a loss of sales of the paper on 40 of them. He added[26]:

> We have continuously attempted to motivate and inspire co-operation with our unions in Glasgow and they have been continuously informed of our financial situation. We have received very, very little understanding....

Scottish trade unions leaders descended upon Downing Street, where I was then working as Press Secretary to the Prime Minister, pleading for government intervention, though nothing but an open-ended subsidy might have persuaded Lord Beaverbrook's son, Sir Max Aitken, to carry on publishing the *SDE*; asked if he would consider a subsidy or a loan, he replied[27]:

> We will look at anything. But if it is a loan it will have to be interest-free. We cannot afford to pay interest.

Apart from being objectionable in principle, a subsidy or loan would have been impossible on financial grounds. Profits were what newspapers had ceased to make. Government assistance to a national newspaper would have had the others demanding similar help before their next first editions were published. In any case, a government and a prime minister which had been so vilified by the Tory press was not going to rush in to save its most virulent voice.

There were only two possibilities: that Express Newspapers might sell the *SDE* to another proprietor - which could not be seriously entertained because of the disastrous impact it would have on the *Daily Express*'s circulation figures and on employment in Manchester - or that the Albion Street works could be taken over by an enterprise which would be able to offer employment to the displaced print workers, or some of them. That idea was already developing in the minds of some of the Glasgow journalists. Thus the workers' co-operative which was to become the *Scottish Daily News* was born.

Express Newspapers quickly agreed to sell the Albion Street plant to their former workforce - it was not a philanthropic act; no one else was likely to buy it - for £1.6 million. The Government cautiously promised to give "the fullest possible consideration" to a co-operative, though the Department of Trade's under-secretary, Eric Deakins, perceptively warned that it was a "possibly risky operation", a caution which was not taken aboard later by the Secretary of State for Industry, Tony Benn, whose enthusiasm for workers' co-operatives which hadn't a chance of survival was to set the co-operative movement back a generation.

An Action Committee of former employees of the *SDE* was set up to prepare a new newspaper, with Allister Mackie, Labour councillor and a former compositor, as its chairman, and a feasibility study was started at Strathclyde University. At this point Maxwell burst upon the scene. On May 15, 1974 he went to Glasgow and told the co-operators that he would put money into the scheme. He warned[28]:

> I don't want to raise false hopes that you are home and dry. You are not. There are many, many hurdles that have to be crossed.

Among those hurdles, he pointed out, was the need for realistic manning levels and disputes procedures. But he demonstrated his support by announcing that he had appointed Michael Cudlipp, a former deputy editor of *The Times* and nephew of Hugh Cudlipp, to assist him in planning the venture.

Mackie said that Maxwell's support was based on political and social motives. He had made two conditions for that support: that the workers should put up some of their own money and that the new enterprise should be owned and controlled by its employees. Maxwell at first promised to contribute 50p for every £1 raised by the employees, but later amended this to agreeing to purchase 100,000 £1 shares in Scottish News Enterprises, Ltd., the company launched the following spring to control the newspaper.

The prospectus for the new company, issued on March 7, 1975, promised a completely new and exciting popular newspaper with which the whole nation would be able to identify. It was a large boast which never looked like being achieved. The paper was dull and unexciting, certainly not popular, and the vast majority of the Scottish nation resolutely refused to identify itself with it. But until the first copies were produced, hopes were high. What is now clear, however, is that some of the attitudes which had contributed, or which the *Express* management claimed had contributed, to the closure of the Glasgow printing of the *SDE* had not died.

The prospectus had stipulated that £475,000 would have to be raised by public subscription by 10 am on the morning of March 28 (Good Friday) if a promised government loan of £1.2 million were to be realised. The workers had contributed £200,000 from their redundancy monies and Maxwell was putting in £100,000, leaving the public to find £175,000, which was not a lot for a paper with which "the whole nation will be able to identify". But by the morning of Good Friday - when the banks were closed - and despite a last-minute contribution of £9,000, the Action Committee was still £25,000 short of the necessary target.

The Story of the Scottish Daily News is revealing about what happened next. The Action Committee met an hour before the deadline was due to expire, "to discuss tactics for dealing with the man they felt confident was going to provide the missing capital", which was, of course, Robert Maxwell. They knew his conditions, a 24-hour newspaper to rival the Scottish mornings and the only Glasgow evening paper, the *Evening Times*, produced with a labour force of only 500, half the size of a conventional daily. The authors of the book continue[29]:

> When the meeting broke up there was unspoken agreement that the Action Committee should accept Maxwell's conditions if only he would agree to invest the missing finance; insuperable obstacles to implementing the conditions could be found after the cash was in the bank.

When Maxwell arrived he set out his conditions for making up the deficit: a 24-hour paper, unlimited (paid) overtime and that he should be made publisher of the paper and co-chairman of the co-operative. One of the members of the Action Committee, Charlie Armstrong, a former stereotyper, recalls leaving the meeting and telling the assembled Fathers of the Chapels (shop stewards):

> Just agree to whatever he says until we get his money.

Mackie reputedly told another man:

> The man's mad. Just nod your head dumbly and we'll get our newspaper.

Maxwell, who was of course unaware of this, addressed a gathering of branch secretaries of the Scottish newspaper unions. *The Story of the Scottish Daily News* tells what happened next[30]:

> "I have spoken to the Action Committee", he announced, "and they are in agreement with certain proposals that I have made." He paused to let that sink in. "I have also spoken to the FoCs about these proposals and they, too, are in agreement." His gaze swept the circle of full-time officials. He went on: "I now want you gentlemen to listen very carefully to what I have to say." From the desk in front of him he picked up a piece of paper. "This is a cheque - my cheque for £125,000." There was a burst of applause and cheering and Allister Mackie ... winked.

Maxwell left the meeting proclaiming "Gentlemen, we have a newspaper." Some of the union officials left the meeting knowing that he wasn't going to get the newspaper he thought he would get but forbearing to say so. The 24-hour paper concept was destroyed by the unions within 10 days. In a TV broadcast on the Good Friday evening Mackie said:

> In case Bob himself thinks that he's going to run the newspaper, then he's in for a disappointment. He's part of a team.

The first blow to the new co-operative came from the Chesters Management Centre of Strathclyde University which had conducted the feasibility study. In short, it concluded that the new paper couldn't succeed because it would get neither the advertising nor the circulation to make it viable. That was the same conclusion which the officials of the Department of Industry had conveyed to their Secretary of State, Tony Benn, the previous summer. Benn had hardly a single supporter in the Cabinet for what he wanted to do to help the co-operative. He succeeded only because a newly-elected Labour Government, faced with another general election within a matter of months of unexpectedly achieving a return to office, did not want to appear to be doing nothing to save jobs in a city where the unemployment rate had risen alarmingly.

Maxwell was opposed to the Chesters report being published, but it was already in the hands of rival journalists and suppression would have done even more harm. Instead, the Action Committee released another report by a firm of chartered accountants which showed that with a circulation of 240,000 and a 40 per cent advertising content the new paper would make profits. But stating what is a profitable level is one thing. Reaching it, as the co-operative was quickly to find out, is another.

The first issue of the *Scottish Daily News* was published on May 5, 1975, proclaiming in a banner headline that it was "Great To Be Alive". Tony Benn, Robert Maxwell and Scottish politicians of all parties were on hand to celebrate the launch. Publication of the paper, whatever its ultimate fate, was an incredible effort. The co-operative had only taken over the old Beaverbrook works three weeks beforehand. But during those weeks the Action Committee had already moved against the interloper from the south who had saved them at the last minute. It was alleged, for example, that £10,000 of the extra £25,000 had been contributed by two journalists so that Maxwell had not met the whole deficit; though, as he had guaranteed it, the distinction might have been thought a quibble. The journalists themselves made it clear, in a letter to *Private Eye*, that on that Good Friday they had wanted to make a temporary investment in the paper and that it had been repaid to them. (In December 1976, in a statement in open court, *Private Eye* admitted that there was no truth in allegations that he had borrowed £10,000 from the journalists, delayed repayment for three months and improperly arranged that his personal debt should be repaid by Scottish News Enterprises, Ltd. The magazine also apologised for suggesting that Maxwell was lying about the circulation figures of the *SDN* and accepted that he had not misrepresented them. The *Eye*'s apology was unreserved and it agreed to pay "a suitable sum" by way of damages and to indemnify Maxwell for his costs. The magazine, at Maxwell's request, made a donation to the *SDN* Welfare Fund. But by then, of course, it was too late to repair the damage.)

A mass meeting of the workforce had agreed to strip Maxwell of his executive powers, though an attempt by the Works Council to sever all connection with him had failed. *The Story of the Scottish Daily News* says[31]:

> The workers deeply resented that Maxwell had imposed last-minute conditions, consolidating his power and imposing his identity on the project. But there was still a residual admiration for the man, for his success and ruthlessness, but principally because he had put in his capital at a time when others walked away.

The first edition of around 300,000 copies was a sell-out, as first editions usually are. The only question which matters is whether those who buy it on the first day buy it on the second and subsequently. The first week's sales, in fact, looked good, but by the end of the month they had dropped to 120,000 copies a day, only half of what was needed for a profit to be made. The Works Council had moved quickly against Maxwell in April and stripped him of any executive powers, though at the first shareholders' meeting on June 4 he was re-elected to the Council as a shop-floor representative. He admitted that there were "disagreements" between him and other members of the Council about how and when to tackle the problems of falling circulation and advertising. These had surfaced, to the consternation of the workforce who had been kept largely in ignorance about the paper's plummeting fortunes, in a lengthy telex from Maxwell on May 20. It recalled that he had given, over a long period, a considerable amount of his time, "free and unstintingly", to the project and recorded his "surprise" at the attempts to remove him from his co-chairmanship of the co-operative so soon after he had been instrumental in helping to raise the necessary money. He went on[32]:

> However, I decided that this was your show and that you should be allowed to run things the way you liked. Several times I pointed out that without me or somebody like me you would find it difficult to launch the paper successfully, to maintain its high circulation and get quickly the necessary advertising. You insisted that you could do all this by yourself and, "in any case you should be allowed to make your own mistakes". As unanimously desired by our workforce, I agreed to keep my peace and not rock the boat and I have adhered to this decision.

> However, in view of the unexpected gravity of the *SDN*'s economic situation, with our sold circulation having fallen as quickly from 325,000 to around 200,000 (which is 50,000 below our prospectus forecast) and our advertising revenue being only 25 per cent instead of the projected 47 per cent of the content of each paper, it would be improper for me to remain silent and sit on the sidelines whilst our workers' co-operative is literally heading for the rocks, with all the loss of jobs that would mean for our staff, the loss of investments to them and to all shareholders, not to mention the embarrassment that this would cause the Government and Mr Wedgwood Benn in particular, were this ghastly situation allowed to happen.

He chillingly outlined the stage the paper had reached: in brief, weekly outgoings £90,000, weekly income £57,000. It was a much larger gap than that which Mr Micawber predicted would cause misery and, in Maxwell's view, only a relaunch of the paper to restore its circulation to 250,000 a day could prevent the remainder of the co-operative's funds running out at some time between

September 15 and October 31. Maxwell said that the situation was
one of the "utmost gravity", rejecting in advance any accusations of
panic-mongering. The figures he had given, he said, could be
verified by the general manager, Eric Tough, or quickly worked out
with paper and pencil. He went on:

> I have some concrete proposals which may just save the situation, the
> key being to make it possible for the editor and his staff to produce a
> much better and exciting newspaper.

His proposals included hiring more journalists and more
caseroom staff to bring about better editioning, and to increase the
number of circulation representatives. He accused the Works
Council of an "unnecessary" appearance on Granada TV's World in
Action programme which had shown the Council's "gross
interference" in editorial affairs; of setting uncompetitive
advertising rates; of charging too high a cover price for the SDN;
and of prohibiting him from organising a meeting with the main
London advertising agencies in an attempt to help the hard-working
advertising manager. He concluded:

> In view of the grave danger which our enterprise finds itself in, I hope
> you will cease your stubborn refusal to comply with the letter and
> spirit of the workforce meeting's decision and agree to let us all work
> together to save the paper and its 500 jobs. We have barely four
> weeks to save the situation because after the end of June we enter the
> traditional period when newspapers lose circulation and when
> advertising is even harder to obtain than at present.

As Maxwell expected, the Works Council rejected his
forebodings and decided that his figuring was wrong and that the
paper was breaking even. The decisions needed to cope with the
crisis were not taken because it was denied that there was a crisis.

By July though, the crisis was recognised. Maxwell was appointed
chief executive of Scottish News Enterprises, Ltd. and on August 18
the SDN was relaunched as a tabloid. The first editor, Fred Sillitto,
resigned, saying he had no experience of producing the smaller-
sized paper but produced a man he thought could do the job, an
Australian, Ralph Saunders. He was appointed at £125 a week, but
the Executive Council, after Saunders's contract had been signed,
instructed Tough and Sillitto to go to him and tell him his salary
would be reduced to £95 a week. Saunders, understandably,
departed the next day.

Maxwell, with the Executive Council, had taken the decision to
reduce the price of the paper from 6p to 5p, which upset the
newsagents, without whom any launch or relaunch cannot succeed,

because it reduced their profit margin. Nevertheless, the first day of the relaunch was a success and all copies printed were sold. Maxwell, as is his wont, was optimistic. There was a print run of 240,000 and he had persuaded 25 government departments to advertise in the paper. He was sleeping on the Albion Street premises, working his usual 18-hour day, but had fallen out irrevocably with Mackie whom he accused of "playing politics" with jobs.

After a good first week, circulation began to fall drastically again. At a meeting of the workforce on September 15 Maxwell demanded a vote of no confidence in Mackie. In a memo to his "fellow co-operators" he said that the circulation of the tabloid of between 170,000 and 180,000 was more than double that of the broadsheet, which had plunged to 80,000. The losses of £30,000 a week had been reduced to £17,000 and he was confident that by the first quarter of 1976 the paper would be breaking even. He promised that he would make a further contribution of capital to the enterprise and stated his optimism that the paper would get further support from the Government.

But that was not how it looked from Whitehall. Tony Benn certainly came back to the Cabinet to ask for more money for the *SDN*, but the Cabinet was determined not to give it to him, reminding him that the original advance from taxpayers' funds had been made on condition that it was once and for all. Mr Benn had backed too many co-operatives which were visibly falling apart and the Cabinet, especially the Prime Minister, had no intention of throwing more good money after bad.

The weakness in Mackie's defence in the debate of no confidence in him was that he admitted that liquidation of the company had been an option which had been presented to the Department of Trade and Industry, even though it was the third option. The fact that he was contemplating the ending of the co-operative had been Maxwell's main charge against Mackie and another member of the original Works Council, Jim Russell. They, together with the chairman of the Scottish National Party, William Wolfe, lost their seats on the Executive Council by a vote estimated at 298 to 12.

Maxwell then announced that he was ready to put in a further £25,000 of his own money provided that the workers raised another £50,000 out of their own wages. The National Union of Journalists' chapel decided that this was, in effect, a wage cut. Its hostility grew when Maxwell contributed a column to the new paper and the chapel committee instructed the editor he was not to print any further contributions from the man who was, in effect, the proprietor but not a journalist.

Matters rapidly grew worse. Beaverbrook Newspapers issued a writ demanding the payment of £59,000 which, it claimed, was still owed by the co-operative for the Albion Street premises and on September 21 Maxwell's eternal enemy, the *Sunday Times*, carried another of its Insight features, this time entitled "How Maxwell Sabotaged the Workers' Dream". It was riddled with inaccuracies and innuendo, but again, as in the rest of the series, it could not fail to be damaging. It recalled the Simpkin Marshall episode and transposed the dates of other events in Maxwell's business career. It reminded its readers of the report of the DTI inspectors (though it did not tell its readers that the *Sunday Times*, frustrated by legal action which Maxwell had taken against it in respect of earlier articles, had supplied to the DTI the information on which the investigation was based), and accused him of "downright lies". It also attacked Tony Benn for not providing, from the taxpayers' purse, an extra £114,000 - its estimate of the Maxwell contribution to the *SDN* - which could have prevented his having any role in the enterprise. (It might also, of course, have suggested that the Thomson family, whose roots were Scottish, which had made a great deal of money out of Scottish newspapers and which owned the *Sunday Times*, should have found the money needed. But it didn't.)

Maxwell responded furiously to the *Sunday Times* and issued a writ which named the three journalists whose by-lines were on it and Bruce Page, the Insight editor, whom Maxwell regarded as the inspiration behind the vendetta which the paper had carried on against him over a period of years. A letter from his solicitors, Lewis Silkin and Partners, denounced the paper for its "many malicious and unfounded attacks, written and/or organised principally by Mr Bruce Page". The editor of the *Sunday Times*, Harold Evans, wrote to Maxwell absolving Page from blame and taking full responsibility for the article, saying:

> I would not want you to be under the misapprehension that I am not in full control of this newspaper.

The editor of the *SDN* and others wrote an eight-page refutation of the article, taking it apart point by point - 18 points in all - disclosing that Maxwell had told the executive that because of his other commitments he could only spare a maximum three months of his time from August 1, denying that Maxwell had acquired assets of

£2 million by spending £100,000 and recalling that it was the Action Committee which had first approached Maxwell for help and the workforce which had recalled him in July and asked him to take charge of the paper as chief executive.

The chairman of the Executive Council, Allister Blyth, called a press conference and declared[33]:

> Without Mr Maxwell the *Daily News* would never have started ... his help, his advice, his financial assistance, have been invaluable to us.

Maxwell, as he has done on other occasions, reacted violently to a description of him as a fascist, a remark reportedly made at an angry confrontation between him and Mackie, and printed in the *Sunday Times*. He told reporters[34]:

> The bulk of my family was annihilated by the Nazis and the last thing you can throw at a person like myself is the epithet of being a fascist.

But he said it as he was leaving Glasgow on October 3, after resigning as chief executive. A mass meeting of the workforce pressed him, by 248 votes to 18, not to give up, but he said[35]:

> I would have liked to have acceded, but given these malicious attacks by the *Sunday Times* and others inspired, at least some of it, by the people inside such as Mr Mackie and Mr Russell and a few others, I really had to remove myself from the battle in order to give the newspaper a chance to carry on its business in calm waters, in a professional way, as it is doing.

The waters may have grown calmer, but they closed in over the head of the *Scottish Daily News*. Its struggles grew weaker and on November 8, after more vain appeals for government help, it printed its final edition, though an "emergency" paper was published for a while thereafter, and some of the old workforce occupied the building to prevent a "piecemeal dispersal" of the assets. For nearly a year Maxwell tried to start a new evening newspaper for the Strathclyde region, offering £800,000 for the Albion Street premises, but the liquidator would not accept less than £1 million. Eventually the works was bought by George Outram and Co. Ltd., owned by the Fraser Group and publishers of the *Glasgow Herald* and Glasgow's only evening newspaper the *Evening Times*.

At an Industrial Society conference in May 1976 Maxwell set out why, in his opinion, the co-operative had failed. In situations where managements had lost control, he said, the only way to get things right was to hand over to workers' control. Workers' co-operatives improved efficiency immediately and abolished any question of overmanning. Work needed to be better organised in British factories and the workers could do this better than others could do it for them. The co-operative movement also eradicated the conflict in industry. But in addition to these advantages, co-operatives needed public sympathy, tough business management and firm financial control, all skills not possessed by the average worker:

> When the co-operative got rid of me [in April 1975] they did not replace my skills by appointing someone else. The £1 million was lost in three months and the co-operative had to vote me back in order to try to save the situation. Among the employed journalists and on the Executive Council there was a strong left-wing element who made life impossible for the editor and tried to edit the paper by committee. The paper became so politicised ... that it lost its goodwill in Scotland and suffered a rapid fall in circulation....

> The Executive Council failed in the primary duty of a workers' co-operative - namely, to make themselves responsible for policy only and to leave day-to-day management in the hands of a strong general manager and financial controller. They tried to run the organisation by committee ... they appointed their own cronies to management positions and so organised the affairs of the trade union chapel that the FoCs, together with the chief FoC, became like Russian trade unions, virtually rubber-stamping everything the Executive Council did.

It was, he added, "a recipe for total disaster".

As one whose advice was sought on the governmental side, I must say that in my view the paper never really had a chance. It was launched at a time of deepening economic crisis, especially in Scotland. Its staff, journalistically, was inadequate. Its preparation was rushed, its purpose and policy unclear. It was not a true workers' co-operative except in the minds of a few activists and Tony Benn. It was invested in by a large number of former Beaverbrook employees not because they believed in an industrial or political ideal, but because they wanted to keep a job, almost any job. Those who wrung their hands the hardest at its demise were those who had ignored its cries for help when it needed it. The national leadership of the printing trade unions never believed in it and gave, in the classical phrase, all aid short of help. Robert Maxwell brought enthusiasm and money to the task, but he could never just be a member of a co-operative team. Nor, I suspect, did he understand the nature of the Scottish workforce, which is unlike any other in the British Isles. Though the Red Clydesiders were part of the history of the 1920s, the spirit which infused them still has its echoes in some industries today, especially the romantically inclined, like journalism. His impatience with what he saw as incompetence or unbusinesslike methods boiled over. Had he been saintly, it is extremely doubtful whether the paper would have had a chance. Its only hope would have been for a sugar daddy prepared to put an unending fortune into buying a high-class staff and quality production facilities; even then it may have failed. It is certain that at least some members of the Works Council thought he was a man to be conned out of his cash - "just agree to whatever he says until we get his money".

That, to understate it by a million miles, was a misjudgement. Though Scotland votes solidly for Labour, businessmen and advertisers do not. The situation grew so bad during the summer of 1975 that the advertising manager could not even give space away in the paper. Other Scottish newspapers, while on the surface sympathetic to the *SDN*'s struggles, had a vested interest in seeing it fail. In that, they were no different from their bigger brothers in London. Until recent years the newspaper industry in Britain only survived through the occasional throwing of its weaker brethren to the wolves. Even if that is no longer necessary, the true reaction to the arrival of a new newspaper is: "How can we kill it?"

A creditors' meeting of the *SDN* was told in December 1975 that the enterprise had been a financial disaster. The Government lost £1.2 million; Beaverbrook Newspapers, a partly-secured creditor, was owed £225,000; and the ordinary creditors were owed £1,291,635. There was nothing left to meet their losses. Robert Maxwell had invested £114,000 and lost it all. More agonising, the workers who had invested the redundancy money received from Beaverbrook Newspapers had lost it. The sceptics who had walked away, saying the co-operative would never work, had been proved right and had their money safely in the bank to prove it.

The action which Maxwell brought against the *Sunday Times* for its article of September 21 was finally settled in 1979, with both sides agreeing to pay their own costs, the *Sunday Times* stating it was "happy to repeat what it had said before, namely that it has never been nor is now their intention to pursue any kind of vendetta against Mr Maxwell". In March 1986, during a dispute at the *Daily Record*, Scotland's biggest newspaper, of which Maxwell is chairman (and of which I am a director), Allister Mackie attacked Maxwell in a TV broadcast in terms which led to an immediate writ for libel, settled in the Court of Session in Edinburgh in December 1986 by a grovelling apology from him for remarks which were "untrue, unfounded and gratuitously offensive". The bitterness over the *Scottish Daily News* has been a long time a-dying.

* * * * *

In October 1980 Lord Thomson of Fleet, younger son of the man who came to Britain and bought *The Times* and the *Sunday Times*, decided he had had enough of the stoppages and disputes which made the production of his newspapers a lottery and announced he was pulling out. The managing director of Times Newspapers, Ltd., Gordon Brunton, declared[36]:

> The major reason behind this decision is the continuing troubled history of industrial relations which goes back over many years. This includes the 11-month suspension of publication in 1978-79 in the attempt to introduce disputes procedures, guarantees of continuous production, a new wage structure, more realistic manning levels and the introduction of new technology.

The fact that Thomson had failed in all these fields, despite a stoppage of almost a year, demonstrated how powerful the printing unions had become. Reform in each of them was essential to the survival of every national newspaper. Thomson's failure was a warning to every other Fleet Street management and an encouragement to every chapel. He and his father had invested £70 million in the two papers and still ended up with an expected pre-tax loss of £15 million for 1980-81. *The Times* and *Sunday Times* were up for sale, and if a new buyer wasn't found by March the following year publication would cease. A deadline of December 31 was set for bids.

Though the prestige and influence of *The Times* had been waning for years (and has since accelerated) it was still, for those who could afford it, the most desirable purchase in the Western newspaper world. When the announcement was made its editor, William Rees-Mogg, said he favoured a consortium to own the paper. He did not, he said, think the problems of *The Times* could be solved "just by a new proprietor with a large cheque book". The editor-in-chief of the papers, Sir Denis Hamilton, saw no future for *The Times* under any ownership unless the new printing technology was used.

Maxwell immediately announced that he was interested in the papers[37]:

> I believe I am the only person willing to make an offer for the entire

package, *The Times*, the *Sunday Times* and the supplements, without breaking them up which, as I understand it, the Thomson organisation is looking for.

Sir James Goldsmith was reported to be a possible purchaser. Lord Weinstock said cautiously that he would be prepared to join a consortium if it did not mean "a ruinous loss". But the Lonrho Group, chaired by "Tiny" Rowland, said through a spokesman[38]:

> We have no intentions towards *The Times* or the *Sunday Times*. We are not interested. They are money losers.

In fact, the *Sunday Times* had been a money-spinner and had only just become a loss-maker. That fact was to be crucial to the eventual sale of the papers to Rupert Murdoch. It enabled the Government, whose loyal supporter Murdoch was and is, to avoid referring the change of ownership to the Monopolies Commission.

Too late, the National Graphical Association said it was willing to make concessions if Times Newspapers would change its mind about selling. The other main printing union, Natsopa (later merged with Sogat), promised no disruption for the rest of the period in which the company published the titles. But one of the specific reasons for disposing of the papers given by Brunton had been the fact that "many of the agreements reached have not been implemented by some of the unions concerned".

Maxwell made a formal approach in confidence to Thomson's for negotiations to begin. He said in an interview in Hong Kong in November that *The Times*'s "main problem" was its print workers, but he thought the decision to sell it might persuade the unions to be more realistic about harsh economic realities. He said he would not include *The Times* in his offer until December 31 because he wanted to give Rees-Mogg the chance to raise the required funds through the consortium which the editor favoured, but he would go ahead with trying to buy the *Sunday Times* and *The Times* supplements. He was reported to be planning to move the printing of *The Times*, if the consortium idea failed, to Oxford. But Bill Booroff, secretary of the London region of the NGA, stated bluntly that his union would fight "tooth and nail" to prevent it leaving Fleet Street (strictly, Grays Inn Road, half a mile from Fleet Street). "We would rather see it close first", he said, prophetically, if unknowingly, forecasting the terms of the battle which was to lead at the end of 1985 to his union being shut out of *The Times* altogether.

Maxwell submitted the formal bid of Pergamon Press for all the shares in Times Newspapers, Ltd. on December 23, 1980. It proposed:

A 125-year lease be granted to Pergamon Press on 200 Grays Inn

Road at an annual rental of six per cent of its current market value
(£12.2 million) with reviews at seven-year intervals.

That Thomson's eliminate from the balance sheet of Times
Newspaper Holdings one half of the inter-group indebtedness,
amounting in aggregate to not more than £40 million and the balance
of the indebtedness to be repaid as follows:

(a) A payment of £5 million in cash.
(b) The repayment of the other £15 million to begin in 1986 at the
    rate of £1 million a year or 25 per cent of TNHL's post-tax
    profits, whichever was the greater, until the balance was
    eliminated.

During the currency of the loan the rate of interest to be paid to the
Thomson Organisation would not exceed five per cent per annum
with varying periods of grace depending upon the profits of TNHL.

The terms of the offer were dependent upon the conclusion of
satisfactory agreements between TNHL and all the relevant trade
unions and the necessary governmental, Takeover Panel and Stock
Exchange consents. In the event of *The Times* or any of its
supplements being sold separately, Pergamon was ready to make an
offer for the *Sunday Times* and its magazine alone. Maxwell's letter
to the Thomson Organisation outlining his bid concluded:

Should Pergamon's offer be accepted, we confirm that such titles that
are acquired by Pergamon will retain their editorial independence as
newspapers of high quality as they have hitherto enjoyed under the
Thomson Organisation....

Though the bid was submitted in confidence, the city editor of the
Evening Standard, Neil Collins, seemed quickly to obtain the broad
details. He described the Maxwell offer as "cheeky", typical of the
man and likely to appeal strongly to the Thomson bosses.
Meanwhile, the staff of *The Times*, under the acronym of JOTT
(Journalists of *The Times*), supported by Rees-Mogg, Lords Swann
and Weinstock and others, were making a serious attempt to raise
the money and buy the paper. Though only Maxwell, apparently,
had made a firm bid, *The Times* reported on January 2 "that if other
serious potential purchasers appear they will not be turned away
despite the passing of the deadline", which made the imposition of
the deadline pointless and a handicap to the only bidder who had
conformed to it. But *The Observer* reported on January 4 that apart
from Maxwell several other bidders, including Lonrho, Goldsmith,
Murdoch and JOTT, had met the deadline and that *The Economist*
and IPC were bidding for the supplements alone. It said that
Maxwell's chances were "slender".

The unions, meanwhile, had called for the current manning levels of *The Times* to be maintained, which was enough to make any potential customer pause. It was those levels, and the disruption inherent in them, which had institutionalised *The Times*'s losses. By January 12 *The Times* reported that Murdoch was giving "serious consideration" to buying both the papers and the three supplements. He did not, at that stage, appear to have made a bid. By the 18th *The Observer* was reporting that Murdoch was leading in the race to acquire the papers and that "a full-blown row over Press freedom and ownership" seemed inevitable. Embarrassingly, the paper recalled what Murdoch had said a year earlier when asked if he would buy *The Times*. He replied:

> No, never. I think *The Times* has been a dead duck since about the turn of the century. To buy *The Times* would be a highly irresponsible thing to do for your shareholders.

Sir Denis Hamilton moved to quieten fears in Parliament and among journalists about the papers' editorial independence. He was chairman of the committee set up to "vet" potential purchasers and he declared[39]:

> I could not personally for one minute allow the *Sunday Times* and, of course, *The Times* and *The Times* supplements to fall into the hands of anyone who would not give binding guarantees of editorial independence and maintenance of the character and high quality of our newspapers.

In the event, the guarantees of independence which the papers got were as binding as those offered to Czechoslovakia after the Munich settlement of 1938.

Rumours abounded about the eventual ownership and journalists, in particular, got more and more worried; there was talk among them of "blocking" Murdoch and of "demanding" safeguards. The then Leader of the Labour party, Michael Foot, vainly tried on January 20, 1981 to get an undertaking from the Prime Minister, Mrs Thatcher, that any bid from Murdoch would be referred to the Monopolies Commission. Mrs Thatcher refused. The writing was writ large on the wall. On January 22 it was announced that Murdoch had succeeded in his bid after giving "extensive" undertakings to protect the editorial quality and integrity of the papers and the supplements. These undertakings particularly safeguarded the position of the editors, who could only be fired by the vote of the majority of the "independent national directors" who were to be appointed to the board. Those undertakings were valid for as long as it suited Murdoch to keep them so, and not a moment longer, as Harold Evans has graphically testified. The only condition attached to Murdoch's offer was that he must, within three weeks, reach agreements with the unions and the staff. There was no referral to the Monopolies Commission. The Government's excuse was that the papers were making a loss and in danger of imminent closure. That made Murdoch, already the owner of *The Sun* and the *News of the World*, acceptable.

The leaders of the the print unions, the NGA, Sogat and Natsopa, appealed to Foot not to continue to press for a reference of the Murdoch bid to the Monopolies Commission. Once more they had given their support to Murdoch and it was crucial. It was estimated, in all, that Murdoch had paid £5 million more than Maxwell had offered, though his acquisition included the purchase of the property at Grays Inn Road, rather than the rental which Maxwell had proposed. *The Times* leader writer knelt before his new master and praised Murdoch's "decision to take on our problems" as "an act of considerable courage". Maxwell, once again, was left without a national newspaper. In 1982 he bought the specialist magazine *Financial Weekly* (and sold it in 1985, at a profit, to a group headed by Clive Thornton) and he was interested in April 1984 in buying *The Observer* from Tiny Rowland, but nothing came of that. But a bigger prize was awaiting him and he secured it with an unstoppable flourish.

* * * * *

Mirror Group Newspapers were delivered into Maxwell's hands by a combination of the attitudes rehearsed above. Reed's, for various reasons, wanted to be rid of them but did not want the odium of a sale to the highest bidder. (They must also have been doubtful whether any individual would be mad enough to take on a company which, with a turnover of over £200 million a year, could only make a minuscule profit if it made a profit at all.) Therefore, the parent company decided to float MGN as a public company. The trade unions were as deeply entrenched in the managerial seats as they ever were. They had a monopoly in the supply of labour and they recruited the workers, not the company. The journalists had a tight grip on the editorial floor. Though they did not choose who would work there, they could certainly prevent anyone being sacked except for the grossest misconduct. It is quite clear that Reed's inability to cope with the industrial problems of Fleet Street dominated its thinking. Its former chief executive, Les Carpenter, admitted frankly[40]:

> We decided to float the *Mirror* in the first place because it lacked profitability. We had the sheer frustration of owning something where we knew what was wrong with it, but didn't think it would be productive to tackle the problems. We faced questions from Reed shareholders at annual meetings about the number of people shown in our accounts as earning over £20,000 a year, about 60 per cent of them *Mirror* employees.... We did not think we could tackle the problems of Fleet Street - like over-manning. We had talks with Tiny Rowland about Lonrho buying it, but he backed off.

> So about mid-1983 we decided to float the *Mirror* and asked Tony Miles and Douglas Long to suggest a possible chairman of the new company.

In fact, Miles and Long went to the *Mirror*'s City editor, Robert Head, and asked him to draw up a list which excluded Maxwell. It was Head's idea to include Thornton upon it. It was immediately seized upon by Reed's and Carpenter invited Thornton to take on the post. He readily agreed.

Thornton was as unlikely a Fleet Street chairman as could be conceived. He didn't look like one, he didn't think like one and he didn't behave like one. Almost his first step as chairman was to halve the size of the huge office on the ninth floor which Cecil King had adorned by having a wall built across it. (It took him three months to get the Services Department to do it, but Maxwell was to have it torn down within 24 hours.) He did not drink alcohol himself and he clearly disapproved of it among his executives. He did not like big lunches. He decided that he would like to eat in the staff canteen to see what it was like. (Rumour had it that none of his executives knew where it was and that a secretary had to lead him to it.) Once there, he sat down at a table with a group of men and introduced himself as the chairman. The men, in the best Fleet Street tradition, rapidly made their excuses and left. They were not even employees of the *Mirror*.

Thornton quickly clashed with his masters at Reed's as the executives there saw him seriously develop his ideas for selling the Group to its employees and its readers with a golden share designed to prevent any one person taking it over. It was that determination which made the value of the company plunge. Carpenter explained:

> Thornton soon fell out with Miles and Long. He didn't trust them. He thought someone was leaking information on the plans for the float.

Every time Thornton opened his mouth and talked of plans to launch a new left-wing newspaper or to give large blocks of shares to the *Mirror* staff it wasn't good news in the City.

Thornton's quarrels with Reed's grew more and more bitter. Though he was suspicious of some of his executives, many of them loyally accepted him as chairman, even if they thought him profoundly mistaken. But others were irrevocably set on getting rid of him or thought that given time he would ensure his own departure.

Nevertheless, few thought that the flotation would not go ahead. Almost until the last minute *Mirror* journalists had not believed that the papers were about to be sold. I had been told some months before by Roy Hattersley, the deputy leader of the Labour party, that Maxwell would buy them. I didn't believe him because Reed's pledge to prevent any one person taking control was unqualified and seemed unbreakable. Maxwell, however, rightly judged that Reed's would not put their promises above profit.

The first firm news of Maxwell's movements, however, was that he had bought a large block of Fleet Holdings, which owned the *Express* papers, from Robert Holmes à Court, the other Australian millionaire well known in Britain. Lord Matthews, Fleet's chairman, welcomed Maxwell's participation as a shareholder. Maxwell said it was "a strategic long-term investment". (As it proved to be. He later sold his shares, at a profit, to United Newspapers, thus making it possible for that company to acquire the *Express* papers. Maxwell had never wanted to own the *Express*; it would not have been possible, he said, for the newspapers' allegiance to the Conservative party to change and he did not want to own a paper whose politics did not agree with his.)

William Phillips in the *Daily Mail* said[41]:

> If Mr Maxwell's identity is plain on Fleet's share register, his ultimate target in Fleet Street is not.

Ivan Fallon in the *Sunday Times* of June 24 thought that Maxwell was interested in *The Observer* and concluded:

> Maxwell thus has three options, with the *Mirror* probably the most likely because of its left-wing slant.

But the speculation about where Maxwell would strike was ended on July 4, when he announced that he had made an offer of not less than £80 million in cash for MGN. If justified, he added, Pergamon would increase its offer to a sum not exceeding £100 million.

Maxwell promised to maintain the Group's political line and added:

> Some people may call me a predator but it is the proposed public flotation which will expose the Group to the law of the jungle. I regard myself as the saviour of the Group against the heavy commercial advantages of its rivals. Mr Molloy, editor of the *Daily Mirror*, has said in a recent article in *The Guardian* that "The Mirror Group has lacked the kind of autocratic player who can take his seat in the Fleet Street poker game." If Pergamon succeeds, then, as Mr Molloy and all his colleagues must wish, power will once again truly return to the ninth floor at Holborn Circus.

Carpenter explained how it was viewed from the Reed boardroom:

> As we got nearer to the float it became clear that Reed would raise only about £48 million from it.
>
> Then Bob Maxwell rang me one Sunday morning. He said he wanted to put a proposal to me or Alex Jarratt. I told him he wasn't going to be welcomed. Reed wanted to float the *Mirror* and had given assurances that this would go ahead. But I would consult my colleagues....
>
> On Tuesday I told him we didn't want to see him. Within hours he had made his first offer and made it public. He sent a letter round by hand. Before we could respond he had leaked it to the press.

In other words, Maxwell had already taken the initiative away from Reed's. From that moment on it wasn't a question of whether but when and how much. The Group had become the Bad Buy of the Year for the Stock Exchange investor and the flotation was looking submersible. Nevertheless, even the most knowledgeable of papers hadn't grasped what was happening. The *Financial Times* thought there was "little probability" that Reed's would strike a bargain with Maxwell and said his cash offer was likely to prove "resistible". Reed's issued a statement saying that it continued to believe that[42]

> the interests of Mirror Group Newspapers and its employees are best served by becoming an independent company with a wide spread of shareholders.

It added that preparations for the Stock Exchange flotation were continuing. But under the headline "Maxwell could pay more for the *Mirror* than anyone else - who can refuse him?" Hamish Macrae wrote in *The Guardian*:

> Reed has a duty to its shareholders which it would be unwise to flout.

Andrew Alexander, city editor of the *Daily Mail*, had little doubt

Maxwell would win and wrote an open letter to *Mirror* journalists, saying[43]:

> Robert Maxwell will get you in the end. Indeed, he will get you soon, I would wager....

> What would he be like as a *Mirror* boss? Not an easy character to work for, or with or under or even over. It would be hard to see him and Clive Thornton lasting in harness for any time at all [in the event, something less than a microsecond]. Admittedly ... Maxwell could end up in a mess, but on balance I would have thought he was more likely to make the Mirror Group highly profitable than the existing management.

Macrae and Alexander proved to be right. Maxwell had made Reed's an offer it couldn't refuse and its major institutional shareholders were beginning to bombard it with demands that a deal with him should be accepted. But its conscience, sensitive to the promises which it had made, continued, briefly, a losing struggle against Maxwell's money; more, I suspect, for the record than for effect. Tony Miles telephoned Mike Molloy and asked him to approach Neil Kinnock - Molloy and the leader of the Labour party are near neighbours - to see whether he would help. Reed's had told Miles that it wanted a statement from Kinnock saying that the party opposed Maxwell's bid. Molloy pointed out to Miles that as a result Maxwell would probably fire him. Miles rang Carpenter and said "You are asking Molloy to approach Kinnock, but he still doesn't have a contract with us", to which Carpenter replied that Reed's would "see Molloy all right". Carpenter's recollection was that "We quite likely said that but I am not sure.... It is always Reed practice to bail out senior executives who come unstuck in such situations."

Molloy and Miles met Kinnock on Friday, July 6, six days before the Maxwell bid succeeded, at Brown's Hotel in London. Kinnock was accompanied by two of his assistants, Dick Clements, former editor of the left-wing weekly *Tribune*, and his press secretary, Patricia Hewitt. No commitment was made by him. He issued a bland statement expressing his attachment to the ideal of press freedom and the diversity of ownership, but almost anything could be read into it. It offered no opinion about whether he favoured Maxwell's bid or not. What was already clear from other contacts was that the former leader of the party, Michael Foot, himself a former Fleet Street editor for whom Kinnock had a great respect, and Roy Hattersley were in favour of Maxwell succeeding.

Yet another former leader, the ex-Prime Minister James Callaghan, rang Molloy to ask what he thought should happen, but did not commit himself to a view. Some Labour politicians undoubtedly feared that Maxwell's acquisition of the Mirror Group would lead to a full-frontal confrontation with the trade unions; others hoped that it would. The National Union of Journalists and Sogat '82 announced it was "totally opposed" to Maxwell or any other individual taking control of the Mirror Group. Sogat also said that such a sale would "diminish press freedom" which was an argument which could only be taken seriously if it came from another quarter.

Carpenter concluded the main story:

> We called a board meeting. We decided the offer wasn't good enough.... Then Bob said he wanted to come to see me. I wouldn't see him until we had an offer from him in writing that we understood and without any bloody caveats.... I remembered that when I sold him Odhams, Watford, we did the deal in a couple of hours and were content at the time - and then spent five weeks arguing about every damn comma in the contract.

> I wanted cash on delivery before we handed over the share certificates.... Alex didn't want to meet him ... he was unhappy and very hung up about the assurances he had given about not selling the *Mirror* to anyone. But he recognised his duty to the shareholders and the rest of the board.... About 50 institutions own 75 or 80 per cent of Reed's shares.... The board agreed we would accept the offer [of £113 million]. There was no vote on it, but I am sure Alex supported it. The rest of the board couldn't turn away an extra £40 million, the difference between Bob's offer and what we thought we might get from the float....

> My last words to Maxwell were: "Whatever you do, don't go down to the *Mirror* tonight." I wanted Tony Miles and his bedraggled colleagues to have time to take it all in. Maxwell assured me he wouldn't go, but he did.

The deal was finally struck between Carpenter and Maxwell at 11.45 pm on July 12 at the Ritz, but not before a final nervous hiccup from Reed's. The price for MGN was £113 million, and Maxwell proposed to pay for it by a banker's draft from the National Westminster Bank. Carpenter refused to accept it. He was afraid - rightly - that Maxwell would go to the *Mirror* and believed - wrongly - that there would then be a strike and the deal would somehow become unstitched. In the end, Maxwell's bankers, Hill Samuel, settled it by giving its cheque for the purchase price to Reed's bankers, Warburg's, after Sir Robert Clark, the Hill Samuel chairman, had been aroused from his bed to OK it.

After trying for more than 15 years, the millionaire publisher was now a national newspaper proprietor, the owner of the *Daily Mirror*, the *Sunday Mirror*, *The People*, the *Daily Record*, the *Sunday Mail* and *Sporting Life*, a small circulation racing newspaper whose most celebrated reader was Her Majesty the Queen. No one imagined at the time of the takeover that it was to be that specialist paper which was to re-ignite his intermittent war with the printing unions over excessive staffing and the right to manage and eventually to defeat them.

The Gravy Train

*Bob Maxwell could charm the birds off the trees,
and then shoot them*

Bill Keys, former General Secretary, Sogat '82

Maxwell acted out of his publicly-recognised character when he took over the chairman's office at Holborn Circus. True, he had his statement of aims filling the front page. True, he squashed the mutterings of dissent in Glasgow and London by warning that if any of his newspapers were stopped by strike action they would never be published again, a statement which was believed so completely at the time that the journalists didn't hold a serious chapel meeting for months and the print workers co-operated, for them, to an astonishing degree. Indeed, one of their leaders was reported as saying[1]:

> There is no point in getting uptight. He is the boss now. We have no intention of being walked over. All we are going to do is wait and see.

But the dramatic action, even explosion, that everyone expected or feared didn't happen. It was like the bombing of London during the 1939-45 war. It may have been inevitable, but it didn't start straightaway. The editors all remained in place and so, for a moment and with the exception of Clive Thornton, did the managers. Indeed, after several years of parsimony the editors found that there was money available to improve the quality of their features and their news coverage. And several journalists who would not have been surprised to be sacked and even expected it - including Paul Foot, John Pilger and myself - were soothed.

The Glasgow print workers published an advertisement in the *Daily Record* for July 13 stating their opposition to the paper's takeover by Maxwell; but the fact of it was announced on the front page of the final edition. The Glasgow journalists were proud of their independence, the profit the paper was making and the circulation records they had achieved with manning levels which they argued were right, but which were undoubtedly a luxury. (By 1988, on much reduced manning levels, profits had quadrupled and the circulations of the *Sunday Mail* (up 10 per cent) and the *Daily Record* (up five per cent) were at an all-time high. Their independence was no less than it was under Reed's, and probably more because their profits were no longer used to prop up the other papers in the Group.)

When I saw Maxwell on the Sunday after the Friday he took over it was obvious he was well-informed about the internal affairs of the Group and about those who had opposed his taking over the papers. The hand of Bob Edwards could be clearly seen. His judgements upon some of the senior figures at the paper showed he had been studying it and them closely for years.

He was with Miles and Molloy and first asked me if I was going to stay. I said my condition was that I would never be required to write anything in which I did not believe and which I was not prepared to defend publicly outside the columns of the paper. He immediately accepted it. Later that afternoon, at the suggestion of Molloy, who told me he had been wanting to do it for some months, he offered me the title of assistant editor. I accepted because there was no point in staying on a half-hearted or churlish basis.

Paul Johnson, writing in *The Spectator*, had welcomed Maxwell's arrival at the *Mirror* and wrote[2]:

> Extremists like Paul Foot and John Pilger are unlikely to be allowed to use it much longer as a platform for their peculiar views.

Even assuming their views were peculiar, he was wrong. Maxwell gave assurances of independence to Foot and Pilger over a glass of champagne later in the week. Pilger's eventual dismissal by the *Mirror* editor 18 months later had nothing to do with what he contributed to the paper and more to do with what he didn't. No one has been dismissed by Maxwell from the paper for his or her political views - extreme left or extreme right - nor has any columnist been censored by him, though there was a brush - quickly smoothed over - with Geoffrey Goodman, the industrial editor, after Maxwell changed part of his column "to make it read better". Maxwell did hire the gruffly right-wing George Gale as a columnist, but it was not a happy signing; his views sat awkwardly in the paper and brought more complaints from the readers than any other writer in memory and he was dropped - again by the editor - after a year.

At times, particularly in the early days, I thought Maxwell was trying to push his agreement with me to the limits of its interpretation, but he didn't go beyond them. We have disagreed on some social and political issues, but provided there is a serious argument to be set against his view he has not been prepared to override the journalist, even when he is not wholly convinced. We disagreed, for example, over the speed at which the *Daily Mirror* would urge Britain's withdrawal from the administration of Northern Ireland - though we were as one on the principle - and further over whether terrorists should be executed. But he did not press disagreement to the point where he asserted his undoubted authority as publisher.

There has been nothing in his reign at the *Mirror* analogous to the instruction the political staff of the *Daily Mail* received when I was a junior member of it in the 1960s, namely, that "in future we support the Tory party 100 per cent, whatever happens". The Mirror Group papers support the Labour party, but not blindly nor slavishly, and certainly not 100 per cent. This leads critics, especially on the far Left, to accuse the *Mirror* of not being "a real paper" any more, reality in their minds being an ability to turn turtle on policy without blushing. But the *Mirror* was never that kind of paper. Before Maxwell bought it it rejected the party's newfound policies on the EEC and defence and took a totally different stance on the questions of Northern Ireland and the sale of council houses. It still has these differences, though Labour's attitude to all but Northern Ireland has, through the force of electoral disadvantage, moderated towards the view from the *Mirror*.

But what was crucial to settling the journalists' minds was Maxwell's declaration about the editorial being on top and the rest on tap. Nothing could have done more to dispel suspicion. Other, symbolic, changes were made at once. The front doors of the Holborn building had been closed at 7 pm for years. Maxwell said it was ridiculous that the public should be denied access to a national newspaper and instructed that they should remain open. The front hall displayed an ancient linotype machine of the kind on which the paper had been printed until a short period before. Maxwell had it taken away. The security guards who had a small television set with which to while away the hours had it removed from them on the grounds that they couldn't watch TV and keep an eye on the firm's business at the same time. Gangs of engineers quickly moved in to improve the telephone system and introduce more modern equipment. Word processors were brought in (though at first Sogat

insisted only directors' secretaries would be allowed to use them).
Overtime - which did not necessarily mean working longer hours -
was stopped throughout the building except when Maxwell himself
expressly permitted it. That was a significant step towards restoring
the company to profit.

Nevertheless, the bigger step had to be taken some time. Paul
Johnson may have been wrong about Foot and Pilger, but he was
basically right, if a little exaggerated in his language, when he added
in the same article:

> Over-manning is universal in Fleet Street but the *Mirror* papers are
> particularly prone to this vice, not least in the journalistic
> departments. Maxwell is a hard man, with a sharp nose for
> extravagance, waste and freeloading of any kind. There will, before
> long, be weeping and gnashing of teeth among the highly-paid, much
> indulged and by no means overworked denizens of Holborn Circus.
> Their late boss, Clive Thornton, threatened to cut down on expenses
> and other old Spanish customs. Believe me, they have seen nothing
> yet.

"Spanish customs" was a phrase to be burned deep into the hearts
of print union workers before 1985 was out. It was one unfair to the
people of Spain. "Sicilian customs" would have been more apt.
Johnson went on:

> Maxwell has many and grievous faults, but no one would deny his
> courage, willpower and, above all, willingness to take decisions and
> give a lead. I don't care a damn about his early business record or
> what the Board of Trade said about him umpteen years ago. That is
> all ancient history. What is relevant is the way in which he turned the
> near-bankrupt British Printing Corporation, a palsied giant sick unto
> death, into an efficient, thrusting, secure and hugely profitable
> concern.

The changes near the top of MGN soon began. Tony Miles
resigned, disagreeing, it was said, with Maxwell's policy of
communicating directly with his editors, but he would have gone
anyway. Douglas Long left. Roger Bowes was promoted into Long's
chair, but didn't last, eventually going for a short while to Express
Newspapers. A legend from the *Mirror*'s past, Lord (Hugh)
Cudlipp, returned at Maxwell's invitation to be the new publisher's
personal consultant. The relationship lasted for a couple of years
until a general election loomed and Maxwell became concerned
about Cudlipp's membership of the Social Democratic Party.

Maxwell also added a new voice to the *Mirror*'s pages - his own.
He accepted that the paper's Comment column was not one with

which he could interfere drastically; instead, he borrowed a pseudonym which Cudlipp had used when he was in the chairman's seat - Charles Wilberforce. Everyone knew who Wilberforce was, and after a few appearances he disappeared from the paper.

Other changes were attempted too. Maxwell had arrived at the *Mirror* hating the need for bingo competitions and disliking the nudes which figured on (or disfigured) page five. He was reluctant to believe that either was necessary to the success of a popular newspaper. Editors and others who knew the effect upon sales which followed when bingo was introduced nationally by *The Sun* persuaded him otherwise. Typically, when he embraced the idea of a game which all could play, he decided to embrace it with enthusiasm. He accepted the idea of a new promotion, "Who Dares Wins", which would rival and exceed bingo in its attraction. He decided to give Mirror Group readers the chance of winning the biggest-ever prize in the history of newspaper competitions - one million pounds. The promotion of the game in the papers' columns was prepared in the greatest secrecy, with only four or five people in the know, including myself and the acting editor of the *Daily Mirror*, Peter Thompson, whose capacity to produce bright ideas for the game's promotion helped gain him the editorship of the *Sunday Mirror* the following year (where, sadly, he did not have the same success).

"Who Dares Wins" was not a winner and news of its birth was bungled. An invitation went to the rest of Fleet Street for a press conference the following day at which the £1 million prize would be announced. It only gave the rival tabloids a chance to jump in first. (When I heard that the invitation had gone out, I told Bob Edwards it was a disastrous decision. "Really?" he said. "Bob Maxwell and I and Bob Head took it." "Well," I said, "it was a dreadful mistake." "What do you think we should do about it?" Edwards asked. "You should tell him he has made a mistake", I replied. "Oh, I can't do that", he said, displaying his customary fear of Maxwell's disapproval. His forehead creased with worry and, grasping his chin, he walked slowly up and down, pondering. Suddenly his face brightened. "I know!" he exclaimed. "I'll tell him that YOU think he has made a mistake.") *The Sun*, the jackdaw of Fleet Street, promptly pinched the *Mirror*'s idea and, in the end, made sure that one of its readers was the first to a million. Maxwell answered cheek with cheek and sent *The Sun*'s winner a telegram of congratulations saying:

We are honestly happy for you. And we are even happier because without us you would never have become a millionaire.

An elderly lady from Harwich, in Essex, Maudie Barrett, was the *Mirror*'s £1 million winner and she was suitably promoted in the paper, along with her dog Trumper. The offer of large prizes temporarily increases circulations, and the Mirror Group's papers jointly put on half a million, but the readers so gained are rarely held. What does seem certain is that bingo is immune to the challenge of all other games. Various newspapers have tried to offer something more exciting (and even the snobbish ones joined in the chase for readers by offering games based on stock market quotations or the like), but in the end bingo is always more popular.

Apart from games, Maxwell was prepared to spend freely to restore the falling circulations of his papers. Features improved and new writers were taken on, including Julia Langdon as the first woman to be political editor of a national daily newspaper, but an attempt to recruit the *Daily Mail*'s gossip columnist, Nigel Dempster, was abandoned when the negotiations about a salary began to centre on a figure more appropriate to an overseas telephone number. Not every promotional idea was a success. A cut in the price of the *Daily Mirror* did not go down well with newsagents because it meant a cut in their profit margin on each copy, even if they did sell extra copies. A seaside gala for the children of striking miners did not please readers who were not from mining families.

The politician in Maxwell tried to settle the miners' strike and he held a secret meeting in Sheffield with Arthur Scargill, the miners' president, and Peter Heathfield, the union's general secretary, to discuss what could be done to present the miners' case and help towards a settlement. I, together with Pilger, Goodman and Edwards, went with Maxwell and spent several hours with him in talks with the miners' team. Scargill was plausible but not convincing, and the talks produced no result. Maxwell also tried during the 1984 TUC conference to bring the two sides - Coal Board and union - together to find a peace formula; indeed, at one moment he thought he had succeeded. But there is a part of Maxwell which is too trusting. He was reluctant to believe Scargill was not genuinely seeking peace. Those of us who thought that a settlement was the last thing which Scargill wanted were eventually proved right, but it was a long time before Maxwell could bring himself to accept it.

The advent of Maxwell to Fleet Street brought new life to the jaded gossip columns of *The Observer*, *The Guardian* and *The Times*, which could hardly let a day go by without the composition of a laborious new joke. *The Guardian*, particularly, insinuated that the *Daily Mirror*, because it was owned by a capitalist, was about to become a supporter of Mrs Thatcher. In the event, the *Daily Mirror* in the election of 1987 was a trenchant advocate of the Labour cause while *The Guardian* offered limp approval of the SDP. As Maxwell pointed out more than once, if the readers of the *Mirror* were all to vote Labour, and no one else, it would form the Government of Britain; if all the readers of *The Guardian* voted Labour, and no one else, the party would lose its deposit in every constituency in the country.

But there was nothing the Mirror Group, or Maxwell, could do which did not bring derision from rival newspapers and their cartoonists. It even followed the papers' appeal on behalf of the starving in Ethiopia, which raised well over a million pounds, and the delivery of supplies to the famine-stricken areas; Maxwell's visit to Ethiopia was portrayed as an ego trip, not a mercy one, and was sneeringly referred to in one paper[3] as "distributing loaves and fishes to the starving". But newspapers are like that. In fact, Maxwell persuaded the Marxist Government of Ethiopia to allow an RAF Hercules to transport relief supplies to the starving. In the event, the Mirror Group's contribution to the relief of distress was greater than the rest of the press combined. Mrs Thatcher wrote to Maxwell saying it was "significant". Neil Kinnock said it was "great".

Other campaigns followed, especially against drugs. The MGN papers devoted page after page - and the *Daily Mirror* most of one issue - towards warning parents and children of the growing menace of heroin and cocaine. Teams of leading *Mirror* writers, led by Maxwell, took to the train for two weeks, travelling to various British cities to meet the readers and answer their questions about the paper. Predictably, people with hobby horses rode in at speed. Equally predictably, *The Guardian* gossip writers exceeded their normal silliness in their reporting of it. But then *The Guardian* is like that too. The success of the brain train was mixed. Success was difficult to come by too on the circulation front. Maxwell had taken over the *Daily Mirror*, in particular, when its sales were inflated by a recently-launched bingo game and kept up by "Who Dares Wins" and its chance of winning a million. When the attractions passed and when the *Mirror* failed to have a further bingo launch the following spring, the circulation began to drop again.

At the beginning of 1985 Maxwell convened a meeting of his several hundred managers at MGN and told them that the future of the papers was "bright", but it was becoming obvious to every employee that the drastic slimming of the staff which had long been forecast was going to have to happen before 1985 was out. Indeed, he told the managers that their numbers would be cut by 25 per cent. (One of the causes of the overstaffing among managers was that under the previous régime at MGN successive national incomes policies were circumvented by "promotion" which allowed salary increases to exceed the decreed limits and "managers" were appointed for that purpose only. Much of the "management" for which the "managers" were responsible was carried out by the union committees. Maxwell's insistence on establishing the "right of managers to manage" was to be at the core of the subsequent industrial troubles at the *Mirror*. The right to manage, unfortunately, when it was gained, was not matched in every case by an ability to do so.)

It was also clear that something would have to be done more quickly about the *Sporting Life*, which was wastefully and expensively produced at Holborn Circus and which was soon to get a rival, the *Racing Post*, which would attempt to break its monopoly among keen racegoers and the betting shops. (the *Post*, in the event, turned out not to be a serious competitor, but it appeared threatening at the time.) *Sporting Life* was losing money heavily. With a daily circulation of about 70,000 its loss was an insupportable £3 million a year, almost as much as the one comparatively successful section of the Group, the *Daily Record* and the *Sunday Mail* in Glasgow, was making. Its profit of between £3 million and £4 million was on a turnover of £55 million, compared with the London papers' profit of well under £1 million on a turnover of £260 million. Maxwell announced that he intended to float the Scottish papers separately from the others and that their staffs would be allowed to buy up to 10 per cent of the shares. But the flotation was too early for City investors who wanted to see evidence that the MGN house, including its Scottish property, was going to be put in order.

Maxwell met Sogat and the engineers' and electricians' unions' representatives to tell them that they would receive a nationally-negotiated five per cent pay increase for 1985, but with the condition that they would "formally undertake to play a positive part in reducing costs in all areas of the company". He added[4]:

> We are the only newspaper group that is genuinely in danger of folding this year. Our staff must understand this. I cannot emphasise too much the seriousness of the situation.

The electricians immediately accepted the five per cent and Sogat said it would recommend acceptance in a ballot. It then scrapped the ballot on the grounds that the MGN staff magazine had published a long article about the offer which constituted an intervention in the ballot by an employer. That an employer should be accused of "interference" by explaining a wage offer to his employees showed how far union control of Fleet Street had gone. The build-up to a confrontation had thus begun. The disagreements which were eventually to lead to an all-out struggle were part of a ritual. Both sides knew that a war was inevitable and both were preparing the ground.

At the end of April Maxwell delivered another warning. The urgency to tackle the MGN problems was greater than he originally expected, he said. The Murdoch newspapers had an "enormous" cost advantage over the Mirror Group and a full colour daily was threatened by Eddy Shah at a production cost only one-fifth of that at the *Mirror*. That competition could only be met by "massive" cost reductions[5]:

> There is now no alternative to this other than to shut down ... a total change in attitude and a major reduction in costs must now be achieved.... It is my aim ... to achieve these changes by voluntary means so as to avoid compulsory redundancies. However, the unions have to be told that, in the interests of job security and the very survival of our newspapers in London and Manchester, they must co-operate in reducing the present gross over-manning and abandoning the out-of-date restrictive working practices which slow down the production and add hugely to the cost of producing the papers. Otherwise, in order to survive, the Board will not hesitate to take all measures needed to this end.... I have not become the Publisher to stand idly by and watch MGN commit suicide....

Mr Bill Miles, Fleet Street national officer of Sogat, responded by saying that the union would be forced to use its industrial muscle unless Maxwell stopped negotiating "by megaphone". The battle-lines were now set, though Sarajevo was still some months off.

* * * * *

As ever, Maxwell made news in other directions. He agreed to step in and save the ailing computer firm belonging to the inventor

Clive Sinclair, then backed out when the full, horrendous situation of the company became clear. He went to Poland to see General Jaruzelski and was reported as saying that the Polish independent trade union movement Solidarity was dead. He threw a party at the *Mirror* to celebrate his first year as proprietor, on the same night as *The Times* celebrated its 200th anniversary. Given the competition, the turn-out for the party was impressive and included Neil Kinnock and his wife Glenys, a fact which was to figure in the following year in a libel action which Maxwell brought against the satirical magazine *Private Eye*, which alleged, falsely, that Maxwell had issued threats against the Labour leader if he and his wife didn't attend. Comment in other newspapers about his first year as a proprietor was universally unfavourable.

Shortly after this first anniversary Maxwell sought to cut costs by offering a number of journalists the opportunity to "work" at home on full pay, the idea being that as the journalists were surplus to requirements they could stay away from the office and release much-needed office and desk space and reduce the need for secretarial assistance. The National Union of Journalists' chapel was hostile to the scheme, but all those receiving the offer were doing little or nothing for the paper and were glad to do it at home rather than journey to the office each day. They did, of course, lose their expenses, which was a further additional saving to the paper's budget. It was a scheme immediately dubbed the "no-day week".

One journalistic enterprise which caused a stir also earned him another enemy. It was a decision to buy the story of Sara Keays, the former secretary to a cabinet minister, Cecil Parkinson. Miss Keays had given birth earlier in 1984 to Parkinson's daughter after he had reneged on a promise to leave his wife and marry her instead. When the news broke, Parkinson had been forced to resign from the Government of Margaret Thatcher, whose favourite he was. Miss Keays burned with anger at the way she had been treated, especially by the Conservative party, and wrote a book to put her side of the story, a decision which almost everyone saw as the spite of the wronged woman, though I think that was to do her a further wrong. One of the attractions of her story to the *Mirror* and its publisher was the fact that it would be available for publication at the same time as the 1985 Conservative party conference in Blackpool, the same conference and the same town where Parkinson had been compelled to leave office two years earlier. It was a natural for the *Mirror* and the timing was right too for some fun.

However, the *Mirror* was in competition with the *News of the*

World, Rupert Murdoch's lurid Sunday paper, which topped the *Mirror*'s final offer by about £40,000. Maxwell said he wasn't going to get involved in an auction and ordered the *Mirror*'s negotiator to pull out. Miss Keays was told, in effect, that if she wanted her story published in that kind of newspaper then she could go ahead. Having ended the talks, Maxwell sat back and prophesied:

She'll ring back in half an hour.

Twenty-seven minutes later Miss Keays accepted the *Mirror*'s lower offer. Some hours later, at midnight, I was at her home between Bath and Bristol with the *Mirror*'s editor, Richard Stott, and its chief lawyer, Hugh Corrie. Maxwell rang and there was a short conversation. Then Miss Keays, who was understandably taut, slammed the phone down and almost screamed:

That man - he is impossible.

But it had been a difficult day for her and she had been outmanoeuvred by a man who uses the telephone as much as a weapon as an instrument of communication. He is a telephone terrorist. He knows what he is going to say when he makes a call, which always puts the receiver at a disadvantage. He also usually ends his calls, whether made or received, with an abrupt "'Bye", which leaves the person at the other end of the line unsettled, frustrated and often fuming.

* * * * *

Over the years Maxwell had had occasional brushes at Pergamon with trade unions - principally the local, Socialist Worker-dominated branch of the National Union of Journalists - but nothing more than was to be expected by any employer in the printing and publishing business. The only reason why disputes in which he was involved made more news than others was that he was a socialist; there was, and still is, an inherent belief among trade unionists that efficiency is the enemy of full employment, because efficiency usually means raising productivity and reducing manning levels. Compelling the loss of jobs, for whatever reason, is regarded as unsocialist behaviour. There were strikes and strike threats after he had sacked two journalists for poor work and bad time-keeping, for dismissing another for trying to obtain money by deception, and for sacking nine more for failing to report for work. There were frequent attempts by trade unionists, in consequence, to get him expelled from the Labour party. Nothing ever came of them.

Maxwell argues that it is only by making companies efficient that employment can be safeguarded and ultimately expanded. It is not an argument which carried much weight with the printing unions over the years which led up to the drastic cuts in newspaper jobs which began in 1985. It certainly was not accepted by them in the most bruising clash any printer and publisher had with the trade unions before 1985, the dispute which became known as the Battle of Park Royal.

In a "dawn raid" in July 1980 Maxwell had bought 11.5 million shares - equal to 29.5 per cent of the whole - in the British Printing Corporation, the biggest company of its kind in the UK and one on which he had long had an eye. BPC did not welcome his interest, but by the beginning of 1981 it was fast heading towards bankruptcy. It was horribly inefficient, its 42 trading companies and their many factories were grossly overmanned and it was making heavy losses. On January 22 Maxwell was asked by the BPC chairman Peter Robinson:

> To work out jointly with our management, in complete confidence, an operational and financial package that would involve restructuring the company. It is recognised that this might lead to Pergamon Press Ltd. acquiring majority voting control of the company.

The force behind the invitation to Maxwell was BPC's banker, the National Westminster, which was owed some £25 million by the company. It also asked Lord Kearton, a successful industrialist who was already a member of the BPC board, to work with Maxwell on a Survival Plan. The bank was to be told by the leading accountants, Coopers and Lybrand, in a report presented to it on February 6:

> If events are allowed to take their course, BPC will have insufficient resources to finance all of its existing activities through the current year.... Fundamental re-organisation and rationalisation of the group is required....

Maxwell immediately began to undertake the task. Radical surgery was required and he used an axe to carry it out. Thousands of jobs had to go if thousands of others were to be saved. In many of the factories the workers realised that there was no future left for them and they accepted the redundancy and pension payments which were part of the survival proposals. But some of the men at Park Royal were not prepared to implement the survival plan because they had one of their own: complete resistance to any change or any reduction in employment. That was what started the trouble.

Park Royal was a purpose-built West London printing works, owned by Waterlow and Sons, which in turn was owned by BPC. The principal work done there was the production of Britain's biggest-selling magazine, *Radio Times*, containing details of all the BBC's TV and radio programmes for the week ahead, and the much-less-popular highbrow broadcasting weekly, *The Listener*. The workers at Park Royal were employed by Waterlow's but the BBC paid all costs of production, distribution and factory and plant maintenance. As *Radio Times* grew in popularity, it was also necessary to print copies of it at the Scottish new town of East Kilbride.

There were two elements at Park Royal which made production of any magazine ludicrously expensive: one was that printing was still done on the traditional hot-metal presses whereas continental competitors had the most modern equipment; the other was that the Sogat members there came under the aegis of the union's Central London branch, which was unyielding, militant, strongly Communist-influenced and all-powerful in Fleet Street, whose managements were firmly in its grip. As a consequence of that branch's involvement, a whole rag-bag of working conditions, pay rates and restrictive practices existed at Park Royal which made it uneconomic. There were well-paid jobs, highly-paid jobs and excessively highly-paid jobs. In addition, there were jobs which were highly paid even though they didn't exist and an insistence on the continued employment of workers who had passed the age of 80, both of which were old-established Spanish customs borrowed from the newspaper industry.

The conditions which were normal practice in the Central London area of the print unions were barely credible to anyone, even print union members, outside it. For example, under Maxwell's Survival Plan a redundancy deal was later agreed with compositors at Park Royal in June 1981 to reduce their department's costs overall by 23 per cent. It was possible to do this by employing more men rather than fewer. The reason was simple: the agreed staffing level up to that time was 60, even though only 40 compositors were actually employed and, in effect, because of the resultant overtime, the wages of 60 men were shared among the 40. The highest-paid were getting just under £25,000 a year. The men's union, the National Graphical Association, agreed that because of the need to cut costs the staffing levels should be reduced to 46. In practice that meant six more jobs. Nevertheless, the 23 per cent reduction in costs was achieved.

A similar system - it is known as "ghosting" - operated in the proof readers' department where 25 men were paid for doing the work of the agreed complement of 30. When their staffing level was cut to 26, an extra reader was taken on, but still savings were made. The men's high incomes did not end at Park Royal: there was always plenty of extravagantly-paid week-end casual work to be had in Fleet Street by its employees, principally those who were members of Sogat. As I stressed in the previous chapter, managements bore an equal share of the blame for the anarchy which existed at that time in the printing industry. If they had resisted excessive demands instead of agreeing to them - or even encouraging them - it would never have been in the state which was eventually and inevitably to lead to a managerial revolution.

The origins of that revolution were in Park Royal.

Gordon Colling, NGA national organiser responsible for negotiating the "buy-out" of restrictive practices and redundancies and new terms for his members, says:

> Maxwell took a strong line. There was bound to be conflict. He was looking for substantial changes and, depending upon the co-operation he got, he was prepared to invest money to up-date and re-vamp the factory. He wanted changes before he invested ... and that is where he ran into a brick wall in respect of Sogat ... Sogat could afford the luxury of a fight ... because they were being subsidised by their high earnings from Fleet Street casual shifts. My people ended up with new agreements for typesetting and web-offset presses. We got some good deals but we lost bodies. That was the price.

The price would never have been paid even then but for the fact that BPC was deeply in the red. The solution which Maxwell produced - the Survival Plan - inevitably meant heavy redundancies and the closure of several BPC plants, but he made it plain that without it the whole company would have to go, with the loss of 8,000 jobs. If it were accepted, Pergamon would make an immediate injection into BPC of £10 million and the National Westminster Bank would advance a further £26 million. The unions' national leaders, after consulting their chapels and branches, said that they would accept. But just as a special meeting of BPC shareholders on April 24 was about to begin, the news came that Sogat had decided to stop all work at Park Royal. The result was that the Survival Plan was approved but the necessary new money on which it depended was withheld.

The next day, a Friday, Maxwell wrote to the general secretaries of all the unions - Sogat, NGA, Natsopa and Slade - with members at the plant. He said:

> The unilateral stoppage by Sogat ... has naturally resulted in totally undermining the goodwill of our remaining customers, who, over the last few months, have kept their orders with BPC companies most reluctantly, and who have been looking forward to a period of relative peace and quiet at BPC.

He warned that without the extra cash he and the National Westminster Bank could provide BPC would be unable to meet cheques totalling £1 million which had just been sent to redundant or retired staff of various of its companies throughout Great Britain. The Survival Plan had come unstuck at the last moment, he said, because of the "brutal" action of Sogat members. He added:

> Our plants may have to close on Tuesday evening because of BPC's inability to meet its financial commitments.

At this point events followed the normal Fleet Street pattern of crisis. A meeting was hastily arranged between Maxwell and the four general secretaries of the unions involved and took place on the Monday.

The only difference from convention on this occasion was that Maxwell had no intention of giving in. He wrote to Lord Kearton before the meeting saying that the general secretaries of the NGA, Slade and Natsopa had agreed to put "maximum pressure" on Bill Keys, the Sogat leader, to ensure that he in turn put pressure on his Central London branch to stick to the Survival Plan. He recalled to Kearton that the London Central branch secretary, George Willoughby, had similarly broken an all-union agreement with Express Newspapers a few months earlier and only a threat to close down the Express papers altogether had brought Willoughby into line. Maxwell told Kearton:

> That did the trick. Let us hope it will do the same for us.... Were they to get away with it, not only would this cost us dearly at Park Royal but it would mean that all our present agreements throughout the group would be unzipped and back again in the melting pot.

Sogat backed down and the money which BPC needed was advanced. But it was only the end of a skirmish not the war. By July 1981 hostilities had broken out again, this time over a modernisation plan at Park Royal which involved a reduction in the staff of 175 out of 682 employed there and the temporary transfer of part of the print run to East Kilbride. The other unions agreed to the proposals, but Sogat's Central London branch again refused, Willoughby ignoring pleas from his national leaders. (One of the enduring problems of the national newspaper printing industry was that the Central London branches were virtually autonomous, as were the chapels. The *Daily Mirror*'s journalists, for example, would no more consider listening to their national officers than they would to the man in the moon.)

Maxwell responded by shutting the factory on July 14. Nine days later the unions, all of them, agreed to accept new technology at Park Royal and Maxwell shelved the plan to print at East Kilbride. There was an immediate cut of 100 in the workforce and an agreement that a further 70 would go in the following year. The special issue of *Radio Times* for the wedding of the Prince of Wales to Lady Diana Spencer on July 29 was printed just in time. The second skirmish was over and Maxwell was winning on points. But there was more trouble to come, even though it was to be delayed; a lack of goodwill made it inevitable, and after a period when only minor disputes affected Park Royal it erupted in the middle of March 1983.

Before the previous Christmas Maxwell had conceded a payment averaging £400 a man in return for a promise by the chapels, given in writing, to restore normal working and to sit down with the management to draw up a new agreement setting out the terms and conditions of their employment - a "house agreement" as it is known in the industry. But he was not prepared to let them have the money until there was evidence that the unions intended to implement their side of the bargain. The unions, as was their wont, were in no hurry to hold the necessary meeting to ensure the settlement was honoured.

Eventually one was held on March 12, but by that time the Sogat machine room chapel had disrupted again. Maxwell said Sogat's "non-co-operation and sheer bloody-mindedness" were almost unequalled in British industry, even in Fleet Street. Those who had stopped work, he said, had dismissed themselves, but those who had honoured the agreements and did not take part in the unconstitutional stoppage and continued to report for work would be paid. On March 20 he closed Park Royal once more and dismissed 400 of the 600 workers. Four days later he dismissed 114 workers at East Kilbride for refusing to handle printing plates which had come from Park Royal.

Willoughby announced that the London Central branch would "black" all BPCC (as BPC had now become) publications, including

TV Times, which printed the commercial television programmes, the leading weekly magazines for women and four colour supplements produced for Sunday newspapers. The *Financial Times* said[6]:

> In a sense, Mr Maxwell is involved in a Fleet Street type of battle and, last weekend, he adopted a Fleet Street style of tactics by dismissing members of Sogat....

On March 29 Sogat lifted the "blacking" after Maxwell warned them the dispute was threatening the jobs of 4,000 workers. Two days later talks between Maxwell and Keys broke down and Maxwell issued a further warning that unless there was an immediate change of heart, Park Royal and East Kilbride would both be finished, along with 750 jobs. He demanded an end to "wildcat" action and a reduction in the costs of production. The BBC, meanwhile, decided to withdraw the *Radio Times* contract from BPCC, prompting Maxwell to say, bitterly[7]:

> The London Central branch of Sogat has achieved the impossible. They have not only lost their jobs, they have now lost the contract as well.

Keys said, in the aggrieved language customarily used on these occasions, that the alternative to industrial action was to "deliver his members into bondage". Instead, he risked delivering them into unemployment for on April 1 Maxwell closed Park Royal and East Kilbride, saying:

> I am relieved that I will no longer be obliged to print *Radio Times* at a loss of £2 million a year.

But, again in accordance with ritual, new talks were convened and took place on the Easter Monday. These agreed on a return to normal working, the transfer, temporarily, of work to East Kilbride, the re-equipment of Park Royal and East Kilbride and an examination of current working practices. It was clearly stated and accepted that in the event of these objectives not being realised within 60 days Park Royal would finally close and, with that in mind, the agreement was recommended to the various chapels. They all endorsed it, except the 123 members of the Sogat machine room chapel and the 17 members of the clerical chapel. Maxwell sacked them. Keys said[8]:

> If any chapel had the right to veto a majority decision of members at both factories [there had been a unanimous vote in favour at East Kilbride] then they put at risk the employment of members

> elsewhere.... To allow such an issue to go unchallenged puts at risk
> the whole democratic structure of the union.

Yet again a return-to-work formula was found and, because of the
interruption of a general election on June 9, the time for the
completion of negotiations was extended to August 12, 1983. After
receiving a report on them, the Sogat National Executive decided to
fight. It resolved to resist the closure of Park Royal, to insist upon
Sogat carrying out its traditional functions in a proposed new
typesetting centre and to declare a national dispute against BPCC if
"meaningful" talks were not entered into. BPCC, for its part, gave
notice of closure. On November 7 Maxwell issued what he called a
"one last chance letter" demanding total participation in the
production of the Christmas issue of *Radio Times*. Five days later he
announced Park Royal would close immediately with the loss of 400
jobs. There had been, he said, "horrors without end" and the loss of
16 million copies of *Radio Times* through wildcat strikes was
"intolerable", both to BPCC and the BBC.

This time it really was the end.

On November 13 engineers moved into Park Royal to dismantle
the printing presses, their principal accessories being 14lb hammers.
Maxwell said the machines were old anyway, and he would replace
them with modern web-offset presses provided the Sogat machine
assistants would operate five-day rather than four-day working. The
secretary of Sogat's London machine room branch, John Mitchell,
complained[9]:

> These are the first negotiations I have attended with 14lb hammers
> being one of the bargaining points.

It was a remark which found its way into the "Sayings of the
Week" column in *The Observer*, leading to an 8 am phone call from
Maxwell congratulating Mitchell on having "arrived".

On November 14 a number of Park Royal employees occupied
the miniature electricity sub-station attached to the factory which
supplied the whole of its power. The sit-in lasted for weeks,
including Christmas, with food and other supplies smuggled in late
at night. It finally collapsed when the electricians realised that Park
Royal was not going to reopen and they settled for talks on
redundancy payments instead. Sean Geraghty, then the electricians'
London press branch secretary and today (1988) a Maxwell
employee at the *Daily Mirror*, said agreement was finally reached at
2 o'clock one morning, but at 7 am, when he was still in bed,
Maxwell phoned to say there was a problem. Geraghty said:

> He explained there was no ceiling on the length of service for those

being made redundant and that there should be one. I said: "We have
a signed agreement, Bob." He said: "I appeal to your better nature."
I replied: "I haven't got one." The agreement stood.

Sogat, however, fought bitterly. Its first step after the
"dismantling" of the presses began was to "black" the distribution of
all BPCC publications, a move defeated by a High Court injunction
awarded to the London wholesale newspaper distributors. On
November 25 it made the Park Royal dispute "official" and ordered
its members at East Kilbride, Leeds and Paulton, near Bristol, to
stop printing Radio Times. A week later an injunction requiring
them to cancel that instruction was won in the High Court by BPCC.
Once again Sogat was forced to comply. Talks between the union
and Maxwell continued throughout December and early January,
accompanied by a further High Court order on January 11 telling
the union to lift new restrictions on the printing of Radio Times.

On January 13 the last round of talks began. Keys complained
later that he had told Maxwell he could not tolerate "his continual
shifting of ground", but he was undermined by other Sogat
members employed by another firm, Hunterprint, at Corby and
Peterlee, who agreed to print Radio Times when the BBC again
withdrew from its London contract. Sogat once more instructed its
distribution members to "black" the magazine. Again it fell foul of
the High Court which granted an injunction against the union to the
BBC.

The fighting, which had lasted for nigh on three years, was now
virtually at an end and the officers of Sogat were instructed to
negotiate the best possible redundancy terms for their members at
Park Royal. The story, on the whole, was much like other industrial
disputes, if rather longer than usual, and only one factor justifies it
being told at length: it marked the first time the Central London
branches of the main printing unions had been badly beaten.
Gordon Colling of the NGA said:

> It was significant in that it was the first time the London Central and
> machine branches had suffered a major defeat.

Sean Geraghty added:

> It was the first loss in the London branches that I could ever
> remember. It gave the employers heart … a taste of things to come.
> The unions were no longer regarded as invincible.

Denis Boyd, the chief conciliator at the Advisory, Conciliation
and Arbitration Service (ACAS), said:

> It was the thin end of the wedge in the employers getting the

upperhand in the Fleet Street power struggle.

Keys believed that Maxwell always wanted Park Royal to close, but added:

> In the final analysis our people gave him the reason to do what he had originally intended.

Keys remained, not surprisingly, aggrieved. He said that negotiating with Maxwell was like being on "shifting sands":

> Even when understandings were reached with him, he would change his mind.

Colling saw it differently:

> He waits until the last possible minute to do a deal to get the last ounce from a situation. But once he has agreed … he spits on his hand and that is it. He has always stuck by his deals with me.

Geraghty said:

> Bob's got a memory like an elephant. But no matter how difficult the dispute or the negotiations, he never bears a grudge. He has never gone back on a signed agreement with me and there have been a lot. Negotiations with him often go on into the small hours but it does not seem to bother him. He is surrounded by Dracula-type people. They are always around in the middle of the night.

Maxwell's victory at Park Royal was complete. By the summer he was able to announce that BPCC's pre-tax profit was up by 78 per cent and that dividends were being restored. A remarkable feature of the agreed rationalisation plan had been an increase in the employees' pension contributions and a reduction in benefits until dividends could be paid again, which it was now possible to do. But the real bastion of print union power, Fleet Street itself, was still to be tackled. What happened in West London made it inevitable, when Maxwell bought the Mirror Group later that year, that an attempt would be made to inflict a defeat upon him. It was difficult to imagine that when the chapels did so they would fight him on a ground of his own choosing and on an issue which they could not win.

* * * * *

For several months after his arrival industrial relations at the Mirror Group were quieter than they had been for a generation. The papers were produced on time, there were more editions and though circulation was falling, morale was growing better. The cancellation by Sogat of the ballot on a five per cent pay offer because of Maxwell's alleged "interference" had been the first sign that the phoney peace was nearing its end. Others were quickly to follow, in Manchester and London, but when war was eventually declared it was over a decision by Maxwell in August 1985 to typeset *Sporting Life* outside Central London in an attempt to stem its losses. The NGA immediately announced that its other branches had been instructed not to negotiate. They followed this with disruption of the early editions of the *Daily Mirror*, losing the paper 750,000 copies. Maxwell failed to get a promise from the union that it would not act in the same way again and announced that 300 NGA members had "dismissed themselves". He suspended publication of the Mirror Group Newspapers. The London regional secretary of the NGA, Bill Booroff, complained that Maxwell had acted outside the normal procedures. He studiously overlooked the fact that his own members had done not only that but by disrupting the *Mirror* because of a dispute on another paper had acted illegally.

The new typesetter for *Sporting Life* - Oyez Press, a Maxwell subsidiary - was offering NGA members £475 a week, but money was not the issue. The union was standing firm on its policy - which was shared by Sogat - that no national newspaper titles would be allowed to be moved from Central London. The weary ritual of claims and counter-claims, with the NGA acting its usual unconvincing role of injured innocent, now began. Its general secretary, Tony Dubbins, accused Maxwell of sacking his members when they were willing to work, a willingness which was patently not present. Maxwell, for his part, said the papers would remain suspended until "managers have the right to manage".

Dubbins described his action as "management by ultimatum". The *Financial Times* reported "sneaking admiration" up and down Fleet Street for Maxwell's stand[10]:

> Many in national newspapers secretly will him to win, not for his own sake but for theirs.

Maxwell used his Scottish paper, the *Sunday Mail*, which was unaffected by the London dispute, to state his case. *Sporting Life*, he said, was losing a £1 a week for every reader it had:

> Surely, all sensible trade unionists must see that this cannot go on.... Disruption of the kind we are suffering at the *Mirror* is a luxury of the past.... This time there will be no traditional Fleet Street fudge....

He pointed out that NGA compositors, none of whom would be

sacked because of the move of *Sporting Life*, were earning a guaranteed minimum of £461.94 for a four-day, 32-hour week, with eight weeks' paid holiday a year. Dubbins accused Maxwell of "wild-cat action" and Maxwell took out High Court injunctions ordering Dubbins not to encourage his members in Manchester to black the production of the *Mirror*. Maxwell announced he was buying, subject to agreement with the unions, the Thomson Withy Grove plant in Manchester, where the northern editions of the paper and its Sunday counterpart were printed. But the attempt to produce the *Mirror* there failed after disagreements about the size of the print run.

The four editors of Maxwell's London papers - Molloy (*Daily Mirror*), Stott (*The People*), Thompson (*Sunday Mirror*) and Graham Taylor (*Sporting Life*) - wrote to *The Times* expressing their support for Maxwell's stand:

> It is a truism in Fleet Street that an editor's first duty is to make sure that he is not the last editor of his paper. Equally, it is the management's duty to run newspapers efficiently to safeguard their future. This is the central issue in the dispute....
>
> Journalists abhor stoppages. They want to get their papers out.... But in this conflict, we unequivocally support Mr Robert Maxwell and his managers.... No newspaper can survive indefinitely if deadlines and editions are missed and if printing standards decline below the quality required....

The NGA let it be known that it had a peace plan; Maxwell told journalists that if there were not an early resumption of work it was doubtful if any printing of newspapers would be done again at Holborn Circus. Meanwhile, he brought out an emergency edition of *Sporting Life* which was produced so cheaply he could give it away to his main customers, the bookmakers. On August 31 Paul Johnson wrote in *The Spectator*:

> The dispute at Mirror Group Newspapers is the opening drum-roll of a sensational season of crisis and innovation which will engulf all Fleet Street.... It is greatly in the interests of journalism ... that he [Maxwell] wins this one.

The *Sunday Times*, a Murdoch paper, gave the lie to subsequent claims by Murdoch followers that their man had led the Fleet Street revolution, when it said that Maxwell had embarked[11]

> on a course which could revolutionise British newspapers.

So he had, but it wasn't yet accepted by the unions. An agreement was reached with the NGA which allowed the resumption of publication of the *Daily Mirror* after a stoppage which lasted 11 days in all. The damage to *Sporting Life* was of no consequence; money was actually saved when it wasn't printing and it still had a monopoly in its field. The damage to the daily and Sunday newspapers was devastating. Inconsistency of supply has a disastrous effect upon circulation and the disappearance of the *Mirror* papers reminded readers of what the editors hoped they had forgotten: that it was one thing to order a Mirror Group newspaper and it was another to be sure it would be delivered. After nearly two weeks off the streets, hundreds of thousands of Mirror Group readers had started to drift elsewhere in search of their daily or Sunday paper.

The terms of the settlement depended heavily upon Maxwell's declared intention to sell his racing paper. That enabled the NGA to claim that it was not retreating on its main contention, which was that no title covered by national newspaper agreements would be transferred outside Central London, despite the fact that printing was resumed in East London. But no sooner had the NGA returned to work than reports appeared that Sogat had expressed its "disquiet" over the agreement. Maxwell said that a number of Spanish practices had disappeared and offered early retirement on full pension to men over 60 and women over 55 in the hope of further cutting costs. He assured Sogat's general secretary, Brenda Dean, who had succeeded Bill Keys, that there would be no compulsory redundancies at Holborn. But they were certain unless the unions co-operated, and there was no prospect of that. Maxwell had not won the decisive victory over them which was necessary for him to complete his revolution and it was inevitable that preparation for the next round of the battle would begin. To quote Paul Johnson again[12]:

> To me, it looks more like a temporary truce than a peace treaty.

It wasn't long before trouble started once more. The *Mirror* resumed printing on September 3 - peace breaking out on the anniversary of war - but five days later Sogat members at *The People* stopped its publication and Maxwell sacked all those involved.

Sunday newspapers are the most vulnerable of all publications. Their staffs are largely composed of men who work elsewhere during the week for high wages. Until 1985 these "casuals" could demand almost anything and get it. The leading Father of the Chapel (shop steward) at *The People* was an employee of Murdoch's *Sun*. For working two days a week, exclusively on union business, his *People* job was worth about £400 to him. He could strike the paper whenever he liked by a wink or a nod. And when he did so, the management could never find him. On one occasion when *The People* was stopped, several of the union committee members first found themselves employment on other Sunday newspapers before giving the order not to print.

Urgent talks were held with Sogat's national officers - Brenda Dean had been the first union leader of consequence to recognise that the national newspaper industry could not survive without drastic changes; her problem was to convince her members and, more especially, the officers of her Central London branch - and a settlement was quickly reached. It promised "guaranteed uninterrupted production and distribution", an inquiry into *The People* stoppage, no compulsory redundancies, an acceptance that *Sporting Life* would not resume production at Holborn and urgent discussions on ending, by negotiation, all Spanish customs. Six days later Sogat members at the *Mirror*, in a ballot, decisively rejected Maxwell's offer of a five per cent pay increase and gave their National Executive Committee the power to start industrial action if a settlement wasn't reached. Miss Dean said Sogat was not seeking industrial action "but it will be considered if needs be". Both the NGA and Sogat - who usually denied any agreement to act in concert but whose ability to communicate telepathically had long been a wonder of Fleet Street - asked that the five per cent pay rise should be made without conditions. Maxwell said, in a message to MGN staff:

> I have to say at once that that is impossible.

Instead he promised to make the payment immediately provided the chapels gave firm guarantees that they would enter talks with the intention of reaching the new agreements which the financial and competitive situation demanded. The talks would, he added, have to have a time limit.

Once again intentions were overtaken by events. A dispute in Manchester which cost the *Mirror* over 500,000 copies led to the London print workers refusing to produce extra copies to make up the shortfall. Maxwell said in a message to the workforce that before the latest trouble the company was facing a crisis of mounting losses:

> Yet some of our national, branch and chapel officers persisted in believing that they could do what they liked, break any agreement and cause any loss, with impunity.... A loss-making MGN saddled with continuing disruptive action could have only one consequence. I must now spell out what that consequence is.

The consequence was dismissal for everyone and an end of publication of MGN's titles from December 31 until the Spring of 1987, when he expected the new colour presses which he had ordered to become operational - unless, of course, new arrangements were made in the meantime. They included redundancy for 2,000 employees, though those taking part in further industrial action would lose their entitlement to any payment. A new company, the British Newspaper Printing Corporation, would print the papers after December 31 and it would engage the staff it needed for the task. Maxwell wrote:

> These are drastic measures.... In my first year as publisher there was little or no disruption.... Then came the disastrous August stoppage which lost us £6 million and, more seriously, circulation on our three main titles. In the Return to Work agreement I received firm pledges of unhindered production.... These have not been honoured by all.... Although I paid the five per cent wage rise for 1985 in advance of improved efficiency, various sections of the workforce would not co-operate.
>
> I fear some union leaders and staff at Holborn Circus thought my warnings ... were a bluff in the tradition of Fleet Street managements.... MGN cannot continue to operate in this kind of atmosphere.... I am ready to negotiate on the details of our future operations but not on the principles or the timing....

Media Week said in November:

> He is now moving in for the kill; and with the titles in their current parlous state, is probably not bluffing when he talks of closing them.... The unions should by now have realised that this is one captain not prepared to go down with his ship.

The air was thick with gloom and talk of crisis. Maxwell excels in such an atmosphere. Warnings crossed each other like swords clashing before the kill. To an extent, Maxwell WAS bluffing, but if he had not been able to see signs of eventual victory he would have closed the papers. Though he had paid £113 million for MGN the year before, the Scottish papers and the MGN property which was his would have brought him in the region of £200 million altogether, a fact of which some of the union leaders were well aware.

Nevertheless, it was necessary for the troops to go over the top one more time, a formal sacrifice to "honour" before serious peace negotiations could begin. Sogat announced that its members would stop work unless Maxwell withdrew the dismissal notices sent to its members. Maxwell, in turn, gave orders for preparations to be made to shut down. The Sogat strike began on Sunday, November

24, threatening the following day's *Daily Mirror*. Maxwell, Mike
Molloy, now editor-in-chief of the Mirror Group, and I went to a
Sogat office in south-east London for talks with the union's leaders.
At one moment he could have had agreement, but he stiffened his
terms. Molloy and I were dismayed, but he was demonstrating to
the union officials that he was prepared to sit it out and that the
financial loss involved in not printing the next day's paper didn't
bother him. Instead he went back to the *Mirror* and did his
desperate best to get a paper printed. He went down to the printing
presses and threatened and cajoled the NGA men working there
(only Sogat was on strike) to produce a paper. They refused. So
Maxwell ordered his managers to do the work. As the publisher of a
mass circulation newspaper, the attempt to produce an edition was a
failure, because only 30,000 copies could be printed. But as a
publisher determined to break the power of the Fleet Street unions,
he had an astonishing success. It was the first time in modern history
that a newspaper had been produced against an official strike by one
of the major unions. Page 2 of that *Daily Mirror* carried a full-page
leading article written by me to which Maxwell added his signature
(see Appendix 5). It said, in part, under the headline "Fleet St. The
party is over":

> For years, the newspapers of Fleet Street have told the rest of Britain
> how to run its business. How to be efficient. Competitive. Modern.
>
> And all the time, Fleet Street has been the most inefficient,
> uncompetitive and old-fashioned industry in the country.
>
> Fleet Street has lectured everyone else about cutting their costs. And
> indulged in a spending spree itself.
>
> It looked as if the good life would never end. But now it is about to.
>
> THE GRAVY TRAIN HAS HIT THE BUFFERS....
>
> The time has come for Fleet Street to face the realities which the rest
> of Britain have known for so long.
>
> ITS WILD AND WASTEFUL PARTY IS TRULY OVER.

In response, Miss Dean said her members had been treated like
"downtrodden 18th century mill workers". But the next day the
strike was called off. In return for Maxwell recalling the dismissal
notices - an empty gesture because they could be sent out again at
any time - Sogat agreed to a timetable for negotiations on job
reductions. It did not agree to accept such reductions, but it knew
they were inevitable. At Miss Dean's request, a clause in the Return
to Work agreement promised there would be no victimisation on
either side. That did not stop the clerical branch of the union later

imposing vicious fines on some of the women secretaries who had reported for work on the day of the strike and threatening to withdraw their union card if they did not pay. In an industry where the closed shop was customary, that would have been tantamount to denying them employment elsewhere should they ever leave the Mirror Group.

After that strike the outcome was ordained, though the negotiations dragged on with some chapels for many months after Maxwell's deadline. It didn't matter that the new model agreements weren't signed, the workers were implementing them. There were no pay increases for those who did not sign, which meant for some workers a delay of more than a year while their chapel officials struggled against making agreements. But most of the negotiations, with more than 50 chapels, were frenzied. At one time nine different discussions between union officials and MGN managers were going on at the same time on the ninth floor. Maxwell hovered around them and intervened when breakdown threatened. The most important he handled himself.

The journalists quickly reached an agreement, giving up their four-yearly sabbaticals and the four-day week. Electricians and engineers and white-collar chapels also reached a rapid settlement. There was difficulty with Sogat, especially over *The People*, where there was a reluctance to concede any jobs at all. Maxwell entered the talks on the paper after deadlock had been reached. He quietly told the union side that he regretted the situation but he understood its position. They, however, had to understand his position, which was that the paper was losing money and that in the absence of an agreement he was going to close it down. Agreement on job losses then followed almost immediately.

One of the interesting Spanish customs to emerge was the existence of a "financial secretary" for many of the chapels; his sole task, for which he was paid by the company, seemed to be to collect union subscriptions. At one point in one set of negotiations Maxwell insisted on the union giving up five more van drivers than it was willing to concede. When the negotiators adamantly refused, he announced he would take instead five jobs from chapel committee members who were full-time on union affairs. That caused consternation and was shelved while the next negotiating point was taken. At the end of the evening only the five jobs Maxwell was demanding from the committee remained outstanding. It was resolved when the union officials offered five other jobs instead - those of the drivers.

Two days before Christmas Maxwell was able to announce that the Survival Plan for the Mirror Group had been agreed and the papers would be produced with 1,600 fewer employees. Compensation payments ranged from a minimum of £2,000, paid to those who had only recently joined the company, to over £70,000 for a long-serving journalist. The pension entitlements of everyone in the company, redundant or not, were enhanced. Some journalists got jobs easily elsewhere and benefited considerably. For others, the future was more difficult, the London branches of the print workers' unions insisting that anyone who accepted redundancy pay would not be eligible for jobs in other newspapers where the unions still controlled the entry. The effect on the *Mirror*'s fortunes were dramatic. After a loss of several million pounds in 1985 the papers were making profits at an annual rate of over £35 million in 1987-88.

While Sogat, the NGA, the NUJ and the other unions were embroiled with talks at the *Mirror*, they were also negotiating with Murdoch over his projected new evening newspaper the *London Post*. Or so they thought. Sogat, in particular, fearing that Murdoch was intending to try to move his main titles - the *Sunday Times*, *The Times*, the *News of the World* and *The Sun* - out of Fleet Street to Wapping, demanded a guarantee of "jobs for life" for its members. A strike was threatened and then implemented. Murdoch's response - Maxwell denounced it as un-British - was even more violent. He moved to Wapping, sacked all the strikers, ended union recognition and produced his papers with members of the electricians' union bussed each day, with police protection, into his Fortress Wapping. Maxwell had started the Fleet Street revolution. While his battle was still being won, Murdoch expanded it. The rest of the newspaper proprietors, having watched from the sidelines to see which way it would go, joined in with enthusiasm.

It was, in effect, the end of Fleet Street as the immovable home for newspapers. There were further attempts to disrupt Mirror Group Newspapers in London in 1986, but much of the heart had gone out of the fight. An attempt to publish the *Daily Mirror* on Good Friday was frustrated by Sogat members and *The People* was not printed in London for two weeks after a walk-out by machine minders; so Maxwell printed the paper in Manchester instead. In September, just as he was due to leave for Bulgaria, Jean Baddeley and I had to abandon plans to go with him and return to the *Mirror* to reach a settlement of a dispute with the NGA which was preventing the paper from being printed. Tactics were discussed with him while he was in mid-air over Europe. The men returned to

normal working eventually, but the *Mirror*'s NGA chapel already
had a High Court injunction against it forbidding further industrial
action. Maxwell's lawyers moved against it for contempt of court
and then, on his instructions, after an agreement was reached with
Dubbins, tried to abandon the action. The judge, Mr Justice
Mars-Jones, sternly pointed out that the contempt was of his court
and that it was not for Maxwell to seek to withdraw it from the
court's jurisdiction. He imposed fines of £10,000 on the leader of the
graphics chapel, Tom Harrison, and £5,000 on his deputy, Billy
Wells. There were no further stoppages; 1987 was a disruption-free
year in the newspaper industry and almost every newspaper began
to make substantial profits again.

Old disputes still produced their difficulties elsewhere, however.
The BPCC survival plan of 1981 had meant substantial redundancies
in many parts of the country, including the small village of Paulton,
near Bristol, where the printing plant of Purnell and Sons was sited.
Substantial cuts in the workforce were proposed and resisted in
almost every year from 1981 onwards. In 1986 it became a bitter
struggle, a six months strike, expensive for the workers and Maxwell
alike. Once again the NGA was at the forefront; it remained
recalcitrant long after the other unions at the plant had accepted the
latest round of job reductions, and the factory teetered on the edge
of closure for months. It was not until talks between Maxwell and
Dubbins took place at the Labour party conference in Blackpool in
October that agreement was finally reached.

There were also disputes just as intransigent at the Glasgow
offices of the *Daily Record* and the *Sunday Mail*, complicated as
they undoubtedly were by the strong feeling of Scottish nationalism
which resents outsiders (i.e. Englishmen, whether native-born or
naturalised) having control over a Scottish institution. Glaswegian
journalists at one time dominated the head offices of the London
newspapers. Every other editor was a Scot and so were many - the
Scots would say all - of the best writers, but that was regarded as
natural.

A substantial amount of new technology had been introduced in
the *Record* and *Mail* early in the 1970s. Both papers are produced in
colour and when Maxwell bought them in 1984 they were making
for the newspaper industry a healthy profit of around £5 million a
year. It was nowhere near the potential earnings, but it was, as
already explained, a lot better than the parent company in London.

In February 1986 Maxwell went to Glasgow to open discussions
with the unions about greater productivity. At that time he had it in

mind to produce a new daily paper for the north of England using
the *Record* presses and perhaps the *Record* title, but there were
production difficulties which caused the scheme to be dropped.
Then he proposed an Irish edition of the *Daily Mirror*, to be printed
in colour in Glasgow. The *Record* journalists refused to work on it,
however, because Maxwell planned to produce the paper without
hiring extra staff. Higher productivity was Maxwell's alternative to
reduced employment and he gave the staff a guarantee to that
effect. But it was refused, the journalists claiming, without a shred
of evidence, that what Maxwell really had in mind was to "anglicise"
the *Record* and the *Mail* to the point that most pages of the papers
would be prepared in London and their "Scottish identity" would be
lost. It was the kind of fantasy to which the Scots are prone; the fact
that there was never a word of truth in it did not lessen the repeated
assertion that it was so. There is nothing so powerful as a rumour
whose time has come.

The journalists were determined to resist job losses at all costs
and, unlike London, the affinity between them and the print
workers was close, a fact which was to make the eventual strike even
more difficult to resolve. Maxwell wrote an open letter to the staffs
in Glasgow, which was printed in the *Sunday Mail* on February 23.
He told them - but, especially, the readers - what the choices were:

> Effectively, I offered a 10 per cent increase in wages and salaries with
> security of employment in return for higher production and lower
> costs.

That meant, among other changes, an end to the four-day week
and the working of five days, though without any increase in hours.
Given the growing threat of competition from the Murdoch papers,
it was an offer which ought to have been accepted. But the National
Union of Journalists and Sogat rejected it totally. (The NGA in
Glasgow had few members comparatively; Sogat and the NUJ were
decisive.) Their rejection brought the other choice into play.
Maxwell wrote:

> We have no alternative but to notify the Department of Employment
> that we will need to declare redundant between 300 and 400 of our
> 1,050-strong workforce.

Those to go were offered two weeks' pay for each completed year
of service with a maximum payment of 20 years at £155. Maxwell
ended his letter with a wounding postscript:

> London printers and journalists have accepted the fact of life that the
> Fleet Street gravy train has finally hit the buffers. The workforce at

Anderston Quay [where the papers were prepared, printed and produced] must also accept that their Flying Scot cannot steam on in the old way.

Matters were not helped by the rest of the Scottish press which stirred the nationalist pot with everything they could find (notwithstanding the fact that, for example, the *Record*'s chief rival, *The Sun*, is owned by Rupert Murdoch, who has been an Australian and an American but not an Englishman or a Scot, and the *Glasgow Herald* is owned by "Tiny" Rowland, a former German). This wish, somehow, to throw off the alien yoke, as the *Record* and *Mail* staffs saw it, was largely bogus. It gave the cloak of high-minded principle to a traditional industrial dispute, but it was to make it impossible to stop and difficult to solve once it was started. On the evening of Maxwell's open letter the journalists and printers refused to print the new Irish edition of the *Daily Mirror* and Maxwell sacked them, which meant non-publication of the *Record*. He said:

> This scandalous overmanning will no longer be allowed to continue.

The journalists and printers turned up for work the next day saying they were prepared to work normally, but normally meant without change of any kind and the *Record* again did not print. The purported fear of "anglicisation" was put into words by an NUJ spokesman[13]:

> Mr Maxwell has thrown a smokescreen over this dispute by saying it is about changes in working practices when, in fact, it is about preserving the Scottish identity of our papers.

As one who had worked for Scottish newspapers for 20 years and as a director of the *Record*, I tried in private talks to convince them that this was ridiculous (why should a newspaper which sold 760,000 in Scotland be remodelled along the lines of an English paper which only sold 15,000 there?), but they were not willing to listen. The rest of the Scottish press continued to report the dispute as if the fantasy was the fact. *The Scotsman* report of it on February 25 began:

> The 1,000 production staff ... dug in last night in a determined effort to prove that they are ready to work and save the separate identity of the newspapers.

The Scottish spokesman for the Labour party, Donald Dewar, said it would be a tragedy if the identities of the papers were sacrificed for "financial expediency". In fact, the threat came from political expediency as the Scottish National party tried to

substantiate the threat from outside Scotland. But after two days the
dispute ended. Maxwell restored the dismissed workers to their jobs
and they, in turn, went back "with the firm intention and
commitment" to start producing the Irish *Mirror* in colour six days
later. It never happened. The firm commitment had the strength
and solidity of a mountain mist when it came to be tested. The
journalists said they had understood there would be no pre-
conditions to the talks which were to precede the new edition;
ironically, their leader was an official from the London
headquarters of the union. In another open letter, Maxwell
repeated that there never had been any intention to insert pages of
the *Mirror* into the *Record*, and added[14]:

> There is no threat of any kind to the *Record*'s independence and
> content and there never has been.

The *Sunday Mail*, in a leading article on the same day, said
bitterly:

> The real bone of contention in the survival plan is that some members
> of the highest-paid workforce in Scotland [the journalists averaged
> well over £20,000 a year] object to giving up a four-day week and
> working the same hours over five days.

The failure, despite the "firm commitment" to produce the Irish
edition, led to a demand by Maxwell for 330 redundancies - his
original alternative to greater productivity. The journalists said they
would oppose any redundancies and Miss Brenda Dean said[15]:

> We are having a gun held at our head.

The dispute took a more sinister turn on March 9 when members
of Miss Dean's union, Sogat, refused to set a leading article which
criticised them unless they were granted a right of reply. It was an
act of censorship and they knew it. It was also a test. If the right of
reply had been granted, they would have had Maxwell on the run.
Instead he fired all the staff of over 1,000, including the journalists
after they went on strike over Maxwell's alleged "refusal to
negotiate". The principal effect of the journalists striking against a
paper which had already been stopped by the print workers was that
they voluntarily gave up their salaries. They spent part of their time
producing their own newspaper, *Your Record*, and established a
picket outside the *Daily Record* offices. I helped negotiate a
resumption of work by Sogat, but then, having agreed terms on
which their members would go back, the Sogat officials refused to
order them to go through the journalists' picket. They had
discovered a way of wounding without striking.

The stoppage dragged on until the beginning of April, enlivened by another ludicrous episode when a short length of barbed wire was placed on a back wall of the building. This was put into position for only 24 hours, after a ladder was found hidden in bushes by the wall. The hysteria which had gripped the Scottish press and broadcasting reporters transformed this into a barrier similar to the hundreds of yards of wire which surrounded the Wapping print centre of the Murdoch press.

The strike was all to no avail. Maxwell wrote to each of the journalists telling them they were free to seek jobs elsewhere and detailing what their pension entitlements were under their employment with him. At last they realised that he really meant to close the papers down and that they were out of work. They promptly agreed to return, accepting the five-day week, and negotiations began on redundancies in every department. Nothing more was heard about the "Scottish identity" of the papers. A Scottish MP, Ron Brown, of Leith, demanded Maxwell's expulsion from the Labour party. Nothing more was heard of that either.

* * * * *

The ambition in newspapers Maxwell has yet to fulfil is the hardest one of all: to produce from scratch a successful and profitable title. The loyalty of readers is notoriously difficult to win away from their habitual reading; they will look at the first issue or two of a new publication and then revert to what they were reading before. For every title that succeeds there are several which fail. One title which did deserve to succeed - but didn't - was a new sports magazine, *Sportsweek*, which Maxwell launched in September 1986. It challenged the generally-held belief that the only thing sports enthusiasts have between the ears is a football. *Sportsweek* was a high-quality magazine, well written, up-market, glossy and aimed at the younger, more affluent, male. A circulation of 75,000 was looked for, though the first print run was nearly a quarter of a million. Hopes were high. The media director of J. Walter Thompson, the advertising agency, said[16]:

> The photography is terrific and there's real substance in the articles.... I think the biggest problem it faces is not in the product but the fact that men are notoriously bad buyers of magazines.

Sadly, he was right. The magazine closed in February 1987. It never held the circulation it needed and lost over £2 million.

Maxwell's major attempt to improve the quality of newspapers available to the daily reading public was the *London Daily News*, launched just as *Sportsweek* was closing. The *LDN* was as good as any evening *news*paper to be produced in Britain; it even perhaps had too much news in it for the readers' tastes. But as the magazine *New Society* said in July 1987:

> For five months London had a newspaper which concerned itself with the same social issues that *New Society* readers find important; and it presented them using mainstream journalistic techniques. It won a core of committed readers, who are now lamenting its passing; but even in an era when new technology is supposed to bring a greater diversity of titles, it simply did not win enough followers.

The *LDN* did not fail because of the editorial content, but because of its editorial and managerial direction, such as it was. Costs seemed out of control almost from the start. It is an inevitable difficulty with any new newspaper - because the casualties among the breed are so high - that to get the right staff to produce the quality needed requires paying them much higher salaries than they are already earning. Men and women who are being tempted out of a secure job into an insecure one need to be insured against the risk they are taking. But the corollary of that is that the paper has to be produced with the leanest possible staff. The *LDN* hired staff as if money were no object. The first budget projections I saw for it, given to Maxwell at Headington Hill Hall in the autumn of 1986, were absurd. They sought to demonstrate that a £6 million-odd loss in the first year of the paper's existence would be reduced to a little over £2 million in year three by assuming an increase in advertising and sales revenue but no increase in wage, paper or other material costs. Maxwell glanced at it for a few seconds and threw it back at the *LDN* team, rightly describing it as nonsense. But the nonsense went on. Some 209 journalists were recruited to the *LDN* when a ceiling of about 80 ought to have been imposed. The ship was so overloaded that on its launch it went straight from the slipway to the rocks and thence to the bottom.

Maxwell must bear part - but not all - of the blame. At a crucial time - November 1986 - in the preparation for the publication of the *LDN* he allowed himself to be diverted from keeping a tight control on its costs by the libel action which he had brought against *Private Eye*. That magazine had alleged, among other things, that he had contributed money to the office of the leader of the Labour party in the hope of getting a peerage. The offer it made of an out-of-court settlement - it had no case - was not acceptable to Maxwell and he determined to let a jury decide. That it did, awarding Maxwell £55,000 damages in all, plus costs estimated at £250,000. Maxwell was vindicated, but the case dragged on for three weeks and his presence was often necessary in court; other issues tended to be excluded or to take a back seat. This meant that at the very time when he should have assumed control of the spending upon *LDN* he did not. It is a standard accusation against him - with some justice - that he is a one-man band and that he gives too little scope to his senior executives. He certainly believes that if he wants something done it is best done by himself. It is a policy which has its dangers. But on one occasion when he did not follow his rule and allowed others greater freedom to decide the project went wrong.

The money he received - and gave to charity - from *Private Eye* was considerable. But the cost of the failure of *LDN* was many hundred times greater.

The men in charge of constructing the *LDN* - Charles Wintour, long-time editor of the London *Evening Standard* who was engaged as editorial consultant to Maxwell, and Magnus Linklater, the *Observer* journalist he recommended as editor - could claim with some justice that the concept of a 24-hour paper, which Maxwell had long wanted to introduce into Britain, required a very large staff. In that case it was a concept which they should have resisted until the paper was on its feet and they did not.

In the event everything that could go wrong did so with unfailing regularity. The paper hit some of the streets of London and the south-east of England on February 24, 1987, but it also missed a great many more. Its distribution was appalling and more than 1,000 sales points in London had no service day after day. The paper was printed at various strategic centres outside Central London and on too many days delivery into it was poor; editions were either so late that the other London evenings - the *Standard* and the *Evening News*, which was resurrected from a long death by the *Standard*'s owners, Associated Newspapers, in order to destroy the prospects of the *LDN* - beat them out of sight, or editions had to be cancelled altogether. Maxwell halved the price of the *LDN* in order to fight off the *Evening News* spoiler action, but whether that was right or not was never proved. It doesn't matter how cheap a product is if it cannot be bought.

It was also clear that those in charge of the paper had no idea what a 24-hour paper should do. The morning editions circulated in the towns in the counties surrounding London, where the competition from the established middle-market papers - the *Daily Mail* and the *Daily Express* - was strongest. Business commuters travelling into London would be presented with a newspaper which was heavy with the capital's news. Readers in Maidenhead or Reading or Tunbridge Wells or Southend had little or no interest in the affairs of the Inner London Education Authority, with which they would frequently be regaled. The readers in London, at whom the evening editions should properly have been aimed, could not rely upon regularity of supply. As the *Daily Mirror* had found out in its strike-torn years, uncertainty of availability is the most damaging weakness of any newspaper.

Magnus Linklater, in a memorandum proposing a change of course which he presented to Maxwell just before the final decision to close the paper, frankly recognised the failings. He wrote:

> The poor circulation figures show that we have failed in our initial objective: to provide a viable alternative to the *Evening Standard* in London. There are three main reasons for this:
>
> 1. Our editorial, advertising and distribution energies have been put into the [morning] edition rather than the evening editions. This has meant not just a division of labour, but an uncertainty about our market - are we a national morning or a metropolitan evening paper?
>
> 2. Ever since the first weeks of our launch we have become an "invisible paper" - we have not been properly sold on the streets of London and people have become unaware even of our existence. I am still dealing on a daily basis with "horror stories" about our unavailability in certain areas.
>
> 3. We set out to appeal to the "intelligent" readership of London ... [and] tended to overlook the real growth area ... regular commuters, young, basically conservative, secretarial or junior management ... who look for an entertaining rather than a demanding or daunting evening paper. We also need more women readers.

The last point was a consequence of an editorial decision taken before the first edition was produced and it was too late, five months after launch, to recover from it. From the start the paper had no women's editor because the women on it regarded such an appointment as "sexist". Linklater accepted their view and rejected the contrary advice from Wintour and Maxwell. The sports pages were abysmal in quantity but lavish in expenditure. Few other papers - certainly not the *Daily Mirror* - would have thought it necessary to send a reporter to a cross-country race in Poland or to cover the Morocco Open Golf championship in Rabat. Yet there seemed to be a feeling that sport was something in which the readers of the *LDN* were not interested. There was an also an obvious disdain among some of the journalists for the *Daily Mirror*, the expertise of whose staff could have cured the *LDN*'s weaknesses within days, and for the publisher who was paying their salaries.

When the end came, it came swiftly. The losses which might have been contained if expenditure had been reined in had become impossible to sustain. The circulation of the *LDN* had plunged so dramatically - aided by the continuing inability to distribute it - that it would have been cheaper to pay the paper's remaining readers a £1 a week not to buy it. Those responsible for the *LDN*'s operation had failed to understand the cardinal rule to observe in dealing with Maxwell: to remember he will never pay for anything more than it is worth. He would have stood a loss of £20 million or more over a period of three or four years provided the paper showed some signs of becoming a success. He would not pay that sum and more for a paper over a period of five months when it showed only the signs of continuing failure and with the journalists formulating a pay claim which would have added at least 20 per cent to costs.

On July 24, five months to the day after the *LDN* was launched, Maxwell announced "with regret and reluctance" that he was closing it. It was, he said, a "good, intelligent, professionally-produced and well-written newspaper", but it had failed to meet its essential minimum sale. Circulation had fallen to below 100,000 when it needed to sell 200,000 to survive. Its disappearance, he added, was a loss to journalism and he remained convinced that London needed an alternative to the *Evening Standard*. He put the blame for closure principally upon the failure in printing and distribution. When he publishes his new paper for the capital - a give-away entitled *The Londoner* is projected - those failures will not be repeated. Nor will his ambitious European daily, which it is intended to publish in 1989, suffer the fatal handicaps of the *LDN*. In the final analysis, Maxwell profits by his mistakes because he has no fear of learning from them.

11

The Family

All happy families resemble one another
Leo Tolstoy

The greatest wealth Robert Maxwell possesses is the love his family show for him. They display their affection openly in a way most English families do not. Each and every one of them is his defender and advocate; if his wife is the more staunch, and the most aggressive, in that defence and more vehement in singing his praises, it is not only because it is part of a nature which values loyalty above almost all other qualities. She believes in him absolutely. It is not a role she plays as part of a marital duty; she has for her husband an undying affection and for his ability an unshakeable admiration. For her, his faults, which she will admit but always qualify, are far transcended by his gifts; his weaknesses are overwhelmed by his strengths. They have their rows, but after 43 years they are still as close as when they wed. On major issues of politics and business she accepts that he will, nearly always, be right. She does not lack opinions, but if there is a disagreement she defers to his.

It would be trite to say that the family which he told her in 1944 he intended to recreate is also her family. After all, she bore their nine children and guarded and guided them while he travelled the world in his restless search for fulfilment. But she stood in for him when he was away, which was often three-quarters and more of the time, while ensuring that the children's awareness of their father never dimmed. She recalled, in a rare article in 1987, one such occasion[1]:

> Bob was away in America and one of my sons, a strapping boy of 15, had been insolent and vulgar at the lunch table. I asked him to leave the room, which he refused to do. I got up, took him by the scruff of the neck, toppled him off his chair and dragged him out of the room

with a strict instruction to come and see me in five minutes in my study. He duly came and agreed he had shown great disrespect, whereupon I told him he could either take "three of the best" right away or wait to hear his father's reaction on his return. I was not at all surprised when he chose the former - which I performed for the first time in my life, albeit very reluctantly....

But when she was needed to travel with him she did so, whatever the difficulties. She accompanied him to international conferences, entertained for him, even represented him at his engagements which he cancelled at the last minute. One of her rare moments of anger against her husband came at the 1987 banquet of the Lord Mayor of the City of London, when he flew off to Paris to see the French premier, M. Chirac, and her son, Ian, was flown in from Paris to escort her instead. But such moments pass. She has become used to them, as she explained in the same article:

> Flexibility and availability to help in his business are the key to our remaining happily married for over 40 years. I may have planned my day meticulously, fixing dentist, hairdresser, attending a charity appeal lunch, shopping and, finally, an outing to the theatre with my grandchildren. As I'm relishing the thought of enjoying *Cats* after a four-year wait for tickets, suddenly I'm asked to drop everything, pack a bag, and take a plane for Washington, Frankfurt or Istanbul that very evening.
>
> A few years ago, I was given just two hours' notice to fly to Japan and deputise for Bob at a pharmacological congress in Tokyo, accompanied by my son, Ian, who luckily speaks some Japanese. Ian was working for Pergamon in New York and I was in London. We met at the airport in Anchorage, Alaska, under the 12-foot high stuffed polar bear, and continued our journey together. I returned six days later, completely jet-lagged and full of raw fish, shark's fin and other "delicacies".

Sharing her life with him, she wrote, was not easy:

> He spins off ideas like a Catherine wheel sprays sparks. He has an instant, detailed and accurate grasp of any situation and opportunity. I am always running behind, trying to catch up.

There she was being too modest. She has a clinical, organised mind and a power of concentration on the immediate issue at hand which are essential complements to a man whose thoughts are forever flying off in a new direction.

Bringing up so many children with such a demanding husband would have been impossible without a nanny. The Maxwells found the ideal one in Marion Sloane, a 29-year-old Protestant Irish girl from County Cavan, herself one of 11 children. Betty Maxwell says of her:

> When I interviewed her and asked why she was leaving her present post, she told me she had been rude to the lady who employed her. I always remember that I engaged her for that very reason because it seemed to me to be so honest, since she could have told me anything else and I would have believed her.

Marion joined when Philip was expected and "had a passion for small children", according to Betty:

> She was enormously experienced and taught me all I ever knew about babies.... Whenever one of our children reached the age of two, she would say: "There are no more babies; we need another one." At times I wondered whether I was constantly having babies in order to keep the nanny! We were partners in bringing up this family ... and I cannot recall one single cross word between us in 16 years.

Marion was, says Betty, "enormously strong and healthy", though a heavy smoker off-duty. But she developed cancer of the colon and died in Betty's arms in September 1964.

When Maxwell embarked on his political career Betty did the administrative work essential for victory in a marginal seat while he grabbed the headlines and made the speeches. When he got elected she stood beside him, but not in the limelight. She worked in the constituency while he attended Parliament. She made speeches and organised the women voters, started a pre-school play group and founded a centre for the elderly. She has always played an active part in the affairs of Pergamon Press and she never lost faith that he would regain it after it was lost. She never considered, even privately, that there could be any validity in the criticisms which were made of the way in which he ran his business affairs. Today she is Director of Editorial Relations at Maxwell Pergamon Publishing Corporation. It is not a sinecure. She works as hard as anybody except her husband.

From the moment she accepted the proposal of marriage from a penniless Czech soldier she does not seem to have had any doubts. If he did frighten her a little at first, she quickly got over it. She is a remarkable woman in her own right, but she lives, willingly and voluntarily, within his shadow. He holds honorary doctorates at Moscow and New York universities; she holds a real one from Oxford. Her intelligence is unquestionable, but she subordinates her judgement, in the end, to his. It isn't a question of her not being a feminist. She is not meek nor humble, but she accepts that he knows best. She is the greatest authority on his life and on his

With Sir Robert Robinson and Giulio Natta, Nobel Prize winner, Stockholm, 1963.

With Professor Hodgkin, Nobel Prize winner.

With Maria Meyer, Nobel Prize winner and her husband.

Maxwell canvassing in Buckingham in 1974.

Ghislaine, director of Oxford United, and team.

Philip speaking at Maxwell's 60th birthday celebration.

Ian speaking in Tokyo at the Pergamon BPCC launch.

At Downing Street with the Duke of Westminster receiving £500,000 from Ryoichi Sasakawa for the NSPCC.

With Edgar Faure and Prime Minister Chirac, Paris, 1987.

Robert Maxwell with Mr Zhivkov, President of Bulgaria.

With James Callaghan, Lord King and Jack Jones.

With Lord Kearton unveiling BPC's survival plan.

Speaking to workers about the BPC survival plan.

With Malcolm Shotton, captain of Oxford United after winning the Milk Cup, 1986.

Doctor of Science at Moscow University, 1983.

Doctor of Science at the Polytechnic Institute of New York, 1985.

Having a drink with Elton John.

A friendly moment with Prime Minister Margaret Thatcher.

Betty with Elizabeth Taylor at an AIDS fund-raising function.

Headington Hill Hall in the Snow.

Greeting Mr Gorbachov in London, 1984.

Fly Past: Publisher, Prince Charles and William watch the Red Devils in June, 1985.

Jak cartoon commenting on the rumour that Maxwell might buy *The Observer*.

Mac's observation on Maxwell buying the *Mirror*.

"THE TROUBLE WITH MAXWELL IS HE ACTS LIKE HE OWNS THE PLACE!"

Comment on the union attitudes to Maxwell taking over the *Mirror*.

"LOOK OUT! — IT'S RAMBO MAXWELL!"

Mac again, with another view of Maxwell.

family's too. She is, by all accounts, a superb cook, which must be frustrating when her husband is always late for meals. She started the collection of press cuttings which today is heavier than that of the Princess of Wales's, though the princess has time to catch up. She has preserved the memorabilia of his army and subsequent careers and built up a photographic library whose index itself is a small book. By comparison, Boswell's task was comparatively short; Betty Maxwell has made the permanent recording of her husband's activities a life's work. It *is* a labour of love, and she freely admits it[2]:

> I feel my life has been much richer with Bob than with anyone else I could have expected to marry. You have to think before you marry, "Where will he go? What is going to happen?" A girl should definitely not marry an ambitious man if she is not prepared to work with him, to take the rough with the smooth, to entertain 30 people at dinner without prior notice.... I am very happy with my lot, although I must admit that sometimes it is hell.

She is free of what the British call "side" and snobbishness. Wealth is a pleasure and a means to an end, but that end is not personal power. Riches are not flaunted, though neither are they concealed. They are a fact of the Maxwells' life. Unlike him, though, she was not born poor. Her ancestry is partly aristocratic. Through her paternal grandmother she shares the family name of the Dukes of Northumberland, de Percy, and through her paternal great grandmother she is a direct descendant of St Louis through John the Good; and through him a cousin 20 times removed of the Queen. Her father's ancestors were Huguenots, the protestants persecuted by the catholics for 300 years until Napoleon gave them the right to worship in their own way. Her great great grandfather was deputy of Vaucluse and an Orleanist and a close friend of Louis Philippe. Some of her ancestors fled to Geneva to escape the persecution. Through the descendants of one of them she is related to protestant banking and diplomatic families, including the wife of the former French Prime Minister, Maurice Couve de Murville. Her mother's side of the family was more plebeian; some of her ancestors fought for the revolution in 1789.

Like all her children, she has dual British-French citizenship and she retains a distinct French accent (indeed, she and her husband frequently talk about family matters in French). She has deeply involved herself in Jewish affairs because of the fate of his family and she became executive committee chairman of the 1988 international conference, Remembering for the Future, on the impact of the Holocaust and genocide on Jews and Christians. She also accepted the chairmanship of the 1988 French Festival at the Barbican Centre, London, celebrating 300 years of French culture. She has also taken charge of the compilation of a volume recording the history of Pergamon Press.

Making a home for a husband who is rarely there has its difficulties, especially when that home also contains a substantial section devoted to offices. The measure of her success is that the towering rooms of Headington Hill Hall still manage to look lived in.

It was from there that she took at St Hugh's, Oxford, as a mature student, her BA Honours degree (in French) followed by a doctoral thesis on the art of letter writing in France between 1789 and 1830. It makes Maxwell himself the only member of the family without an academic honour of any kind but honorary. Three of her sons, Philip, Ian and Kevin, all received degrees at the ceremony at which their mother received her D.Phil. She said at the time:

> All my children were going to university and I thought I could do that, too.

The three boys had all won scholarships to Balliol, equalling the record of three of Herbert Asquith's sons who were there in the early part of the century. Later the family set a new record when the college went co-educational and Ghislaine won a place in it.

* * * * *

The Maxwells fortunately, coincidentally or by design, have children whose life has not been blighted or withered by living in his shadow, as the sons and daughters of so many powerful men have been. The children accept and welcome his decision that they should not inherit his wealth. Each has sought to make his or her way in life without looking to their parents to support them.

In an interview in 1969 Maxwell described, in what would be regarded as sexist terms today, the qualities he would wish on children[3]:

> On a boy, intelligence, curiosity, and the ability to concentrate on the task in hand. And on a girl, kindness, considerateness and conciseness.

But, in fact, there is no sign that he treated his own children differently from each other. All are unanimous about what a wonderful father he has been to them. They were never banned from his presence when he was working at the Hall and it was not uncommon for board meetings or union negotiations to be broken off by a child wandering into the room to be consoled or cuddled or merely to seek the answer to a question. Maxwell was asked in an interview in 1971 whether when he was working at home the children interrupted him. He replied[4]:

> They are invited to interrupt my work if they have got a problem, and encouraged to do so.

He lavished gifts upon them - Anne remembers a huge teddy bear with a red tie; when her father gave it to her there was a growl "which filled the room" and she didn't know whether it came from the teddy or from him - and he displayed a talent for card tricks which mesmerised and entranced them. Today they stand in awe of him, but not in fear. They will seek, respect and defer to his judgement, but not to the exclusion of their own. All but one of the seven who grew to adulthood have worked for him at one time or another, but have also sought careers independently of him; those who work for him now do so by choice, not by order.

His eldest surviving son, Philip, academically the most gifted, worked in Argentina for several years as an economist for the United Nations before returning with his Argentinian wife, Nilda, and his stepdaughter, Marcela, to become managing editor of the *Encyclopaedia of Materials Science and Engineering*, published in 1986. He is currently Pergamon's Director of Research and Development. Ian, the next eldest, was away for some months after Maxwell sacked him. Kevin left his father's employment and proved he could be a success on his own before agreeing to return to the family business at a much higher salary. Anne, the eldest daughter, only worked for her father after a lengthy acting career which never reached the heights and the work rate for which she hoped; after three years with Pergamon she started a new career in teaching. Isabel never worked for her father, making her own career in TV and films almost from the moment she left university, but Christine, her twin, has spent most of her working life with Pergamon. The youngest, Ghislaine, worked briefly in her father's office; then Maxwell helped her develop her idea for selling executive gifts. He has given each of them the opportunity to make their way in life without being their crutch.

There have been two tragedies in Bob and Betty Maxwell's family. It was a black coincidence that, like his parents, he and Betty lost a son and a daughter out of their nine children. The death of their firstborn, Michael, devastated them. He was a youth of great promise - a pupil at Marlborough, fluent in French and learning German and Russian - when, in 1961, three days after Betty gave birth on Christmas Day to her youngest daughter, Ghislaine, the car in which he was a passenger hit the rear of a lorry on the Bicester road, near Oxford. He had been travelling home from a dance. Michael was taken unconscious to the Radcliffe Infirmary, Oxford, with serious head injuries. He was later transferred to the Churchill Hospital, Oxford.

The final report of the consultant neurosurgeon at the Radcliffe was without any hope of any kind:

> It is now five months since my last report on this boy in which I said I could see no prospect of any recovery from his state of total disability; and it is now 11 months since his injury.... I examined him again on the 29th of November.... I should say at the outset that I could see no sign of any significant improvement ... this means that his condition has been static for approximately eight months now. He shows no appropriate emotional expression, no signs of recognition of what is going on around him, and he has made no attempt to talk.... He does not blink in response to a loud noise beside him....
>
> My previous impression has been confirmed and I see no prospect of any further improvement here. As I said in my last report, his expectation of life is enormously reduced as a result of this injury, but it is not possible to say how long he is likely to live in this state; it might well be for many more months yet.

In fact, he lived for more than another five years after that report, dying on January 27, 1968, six weeks short of his 22nd birthday. He had never recovered consciousness.

By bizarre chance Professor Lev Landau, the Stalin purges victim whom Maxwell had known since 1956, also suffered severe head injuries in a car accident a few days after Michael's. While Maxwell was visiting his son daily he received an appeal from the Russians to help find some rare antibiotics which Landau's doctors needed for him. He got the drugs and rushed them to Heathrow airport where a Comet flight to Moscow was delayed to receive them. Landau recovered, though his life, like Michael's, had been despaired of. Eight months later he was fit enough to receive the Nobel Prize for Physics, but he was never able to work as a physicist again. There was not even that limited happy outcome for Michael. By coincidence, Landau died in the same year as Michael, 1968.

For the first year Betty Maxwell went to the hospital every day and Maxwell went there whenever he could, no matter what the hour. Bryan Barnard says:

> Maxwell was a pitiful man at the time because of the accident. I remember returning to Oxford from a conference in London with him. It was quarter to one in the morning. We were just driving into Headington Hill Hall when he stopped me and asked if I minded dropping him at the Radcliffe so he could go and see Michael.... That tragic accident all but broke him. He had tremendous hopes for the boy.

In fact, Maxwell had planned from early on that Michael should take over from him one day and he had made provision in his will three years before the accident for that to happen.

Until the end Betty was an unfailing visitor to Michael, accompanied at times by one of the older children. Though occasionally his eyes flickered and there were slight body movements, Michael never showed any signs of recognising that any of his family was at his bedside.

Damages of £15,900 were awarded to Michael by the High Court in 1963 for his injuries. Maxwell told the court that should Michael succumb, he and Betty would wish to use the damages to provide a fund to encourage the establishment of a Brain Research Institute at Oxford. In 1965 he founded the Michael Maxwell Memorial Fund for Brain Research, with an annual donation from him of £2,000 for as long as Dr W. Ritchie Russell, who had treated Michael, held office as University Lecturer in Neurology. Michael eventually died from meningitis and the inquest returned a verdict of accidental death. The coroner remarked that the road on which the accident happened had "many dangers".

The other tragedy had been just as sudden, shocking and unexpected, though the agony of waiting for death had not been so prolonged. As mentioned in Chapter 5, in January 1957 the Maxwells were in Barbados for a brief break after a lengthy business trip when they were urgently called home because of the illness of their three-year-old daughter, Karine. She had acute leukaemia and there was no saving her, though Maxwell approached every specialist he could in the short time available. A typical plea for help was sent to a Swedish doctor:

> Quite recently my little daughter has been stricken with leukaemia. I am sending you a copy of the report of her case, as well as some slides, and ask you to let me know whether you, or anyone of whom you know, have anything "in the works" of an experimental nature

which could be tried to save or to prolong her life. In the hope that you or your colleagues may soon come up with an answer to this terrible scourge, I, as her father, thank you in advance on her behalf, as well as mine, for whatever you may be able to do.

There was nothing anyone could do. Nine days later, on February 8, Karine was dead.

Maxwell's second child and eldest daughter, Anne, like all the Maxwell children, had first to prove herself academically before starting on a career. After a BA in Modern Languages (Italian and French) at Oxford she spent more than 12 years working as an actress. She appeared in several films, including one, *Ransom*, with Sean Connery, in which she played the part of a terrorist (as she says, for most of the time with a stocking over her face), several plays and in a number of TV series, among them *Yes, Minister*, *Pride and Prejudice*, *General Hospital* and *Hunters' Walk*, before training at the London Montessori Centre to become a teacher. A story is told of Maxwell marching into the office of the director of the Central School of Speech and Drama where Anne was taking a three-year course and demanding[5]:

Tell me frankly - is she making progress or is she wasting her time and my money?

The director replied:

I can only tell you she has the loveliest English voice that has been through this school in 10 years.

Maxwell, reputedly, was astonished:

She has a Czech father and a French mother. How can she have an English voice?

Anne gave up her fulltime film and stage career in 1983 - though she still appears occasionally in TV commercials - and worked for Pergamon Press for three years until she took her teacher training course. But during the school holidays she still works for Pergamon.

Anne remembers what her father said to her when she told him she was going to embark on the Montessori course:

If this doesn't succeed, there'll be nothing left for you to do but to become a nun.

Philip won a scholarship in natural sciences to Balliol when he was only 16, much to his parents' delight. It was a feat unusual enough to be written about in several newspapers. Maxwell rewarded Philip by sending him on an extended tour of North America and wrote a formal letter to his son:

You may find it helpful for me to set out ... the aim and purpose of your visit ... if as I hope you will stick to your promise to keep a daily record of your experiences it will be interesting and probably also very amusing to check your diary against this letter.

   I. I am making it materially possible for you to go to the new world so that you may gain firsthand experience of managing your life outside the discipline imposed by school and family, and so that you may have a long and really enjoyable holiday.

   II. To gain firsthand knowledge and experience of the USA, one of the largest, richest and most powerful countries in the world. Your and everybody else's life and career is influenced greatly by what happens in the USA.

   III. To make friends amongst young and old.

   IV. To do some useful work for Pergamon Press.

   V. Money and other administrative matters.

Herewith some hints that you may find useful in making a great success of your trip.

There then followed more than five single-spaced, closely-typed pages, afterwards known in the family as The Bible. It is a remarkable document, of the kind which was more common a century ago but which now must be rare if not unique. To send a 16-year-old boy on his own on a tour of the USA displayed great trust, but Maxwell made certain that Philip would have his guidance ever present. Though the advice was ostensibly for the immediate visit, Maxwell intended it to have a wider and more lasting application. It was also an intriguing insight into Maxwell's belief in work, a requirement for every member of the family; there is no such thing as a free ride. Philip was being given a holiday as a reward for his success. But the holiday had to be combined with promoting the interests of Pergamon Press from which all his material benefits flowed.

The body of the letter begins with "hints" under the heading **Gaining Experience and Having a Good Time.** Maxwell, clearly thinking of Michael who was then (April 1966), still lying in a coma, wrote to his son:

   (a) You will deprive yourself of an opportunity to gain experience or to live if you do not take good care of your health and avoid getting into unnecessary dangerous situations to health or limb. Always calculate whether the risks you are taking are commensurate with the rewards or whether these risks can be minimised, like, for instance, sitting in the back of the car if there is no safety belt next to the driver's seat.

   (b) You must plan meticulously your days and your entire programme.

This is not only because good planning means good discipline but so that you can get the most out of the time available.... A further major principle which will be useful to you for the rest of your life and not just for this visit is the cardinal principle of living a good life - nothing to excess.

(c) Be genuinely interested in people. Remember every person - be he duke or beggar - has some unique experiences. You encourage them to talk about themselves and their families; wherever you can, you should do the listening rather than the talking. Where conversation flags you can always ask a sympathetic question or make a provocative statement. A great deal of experience in life can be obtained by observing closely the behaviour and actions and reactions of other human beings, measuring their conduct against your own and deciding the standards that you wish to observe and making certain that you do so.

(d) The best way of having a good time, in particular when you are with a group, is to make sure that everybody else participates in having a good time. It is important not to be selfish by not caring what happens to everybody else in the party as long as you are all right.

If the group you are with go in for bad practices either in drink or in sex, or any others for that matter, there is no need for you to participate ... and if some members of the group ridicule you about it you can say that you gave a pledge to your parents ... and you propose to stick to that pledge.

Observing the USA

(a) You will be living with American families, reading their papers and watching their TV. You will find them extremely ignorant about European politics. Their reaction to Labour party policies is likely to upset you because so far as they are concerned they are communistic and no amount of talk from you will convince them otherwise. Therefore, avoid getting into heated political arguments.

(b) Try to meet people of your age and of all classes. I imagine you will best do this by going into youth clubs run by the various denominational authorities or on university campuses.

(c) You should try to learn something of American history which I consider an absolute essential to understanding the USA and understanding its political actions and motivations both at home and abroad.

(d) Finally, this could be a standard request for you to make to your American hosts, saying you are interested in the United States, its history and how its people live and what its future aspirations are and what do they suggest you should do in their locality and neighbourhood to assist you in this respect.

How to Make Friends Amongst Young and Old

(a) By being genuinely interested in people, their problems and experiences; by avoiding selfish and provocative acts and postures; by being considerate and helpful as well as being interesting in one's conversation; by being clean and well turned out.

(b) Remember a listener is always more appreciated than a talker and avoid boasting. On the other hand, one must not fall into the other scale of being too self-effacing or too frightened to intervene in a conversation. Because I know that you do not suffer from this I have not found the need to stress it.

How to be of Use to Pergamon Press

(a) Carry with you our complete books and journals catalogues. The author index in the books catalogue and the list of editors and editorial advisers against each journal in the journals catalogue will be very helpful to you to know what these people have been doing for the Press.... I will also give you a supply of "Publishing with Pergamon Press guarantees you ..." which you might leave behind with anybody whom you have met who is likely to want to know what Pergamon offers to authors.

(b) Give personal greetings from me to each editor, editorial adviser and author of Pergamon Press that you will meet during your journey....

(c) You can say to people who are already associated with the Press, or those that you meet who are not, that Pergamon is expanding very rapidly, that we can offer simultaneous publication in English, French and German and with outstanding books even in Russian.

There followed a list of detailed questions which Philip was to ask about the performance of Pergamon and, where there was dissatisfaction, advice was to be sought on how to remove it. Maxwell then went on:

(d) At each major centre that you visit be sure to telephone and arrange to call upon the university librarian, university bookseller and leading technical booksellers, bring him greetings from me and ask him whether he is satisfied with the services given by Pergamon. If not, what complaints does he or she have and what suggestions about improvements....

Maxwell gave his son £350 in traveller's cheques which, he said, should be more than ample since Philip would have few travelling or hotel bills to pay. But should he become stuck for money he must telephone immediately. To that end:

A card of useful telephone numbers will be given to you before you leave England and you should always carry it in your pocket.

His anxiety about a possible accident was clear again when he told Philip:

> I want you to arrange to carry round your neck an identity tag giving your name ... as well as your blood group. In case of accident, you may get emergency blood transfusion without the loss of time in finding out what blood group you belong to.

Other advice included:

> Whereas air transport is first rate, your greatest problem in the United States will be getting from A to B inside a city conurbation, the reason being the deplorable lack of public transport. Taxis are expensive and few and far between on university campuses. All this you must take into consideration when planning your visits.

> Before leaving your host you must arrange to buy flowers which you present to the lady of the house if you can on the day you leave or have them delivered by ordering them from organisations like Interflora, with a brief message of gratitude and appreciation for their kind hospitality. The value of the flowers could be between $5 to $10. If flowers are not readily available then you must buy the equivalent value in chocolates. In addition, this should be followed up by a brief thank you letter with whatever nice remarks you can make about all members of the family who have participated in looking after you.

> Avoid carrying large sums of money on your person or flashing money about.

> Avoid at all costs going into public parks at night or in any parts of major cities which are seedy or ill-lit. Hooliganism in the United States is quite rife and public safety in their towns is nothing like as good as ours. Don't get into fights because some young Americans can be quite vicious.

> Finally, do remember that people in America - no matter how well-off they are - do not have any servants except the odd daily help, thus what used to be done for you at home by somebody else you must do for yourself in America, like making your bed, doing the washing-up, etc. You must be continually on the lookout not to make additional housework for the family.

Philip took his BA in Physics in 1969, an MA in 1981 and achieved a D.Phil. at Sussex University in 1982 for his thesis on technological learning in the Argentine steel industry. In 1968-69 he was business manager and then co-editor of the Oxford student magazine *Isis* which his father had rescued from closure. In 1969 he and two other students started Third World First, a campaign to raise money from students for anti-poverty projects. Some 20,000 students throughout Britain joined up. After that he worked for

Oxfam in the USA before joining the staff of the Science Policy Research Unit at Sussex.

The twins, Christine (the eldest by an hour) and Isabel, were born on August 16, 1950 and were fortunate to live the summer out. They were six weeks premature and Maxwell chartered a plane for £55 to fly him to Paris when he heard that Betty was in labour. It was the first time he had ever done so, but the twins were already born by the time he arrived. For those days, when incubators were rare, they were extremely small; Isabel was just over 4lb and Christine just under. At first though tiny they flourished and Maxwell went off on a business trip to Berlin, phoning the clinic for a progress report each day. But when the twins were three weeks old Betty, whose own life had been in danger after a difficult confinement, told him they were suffering from what was known then as infantile cholera and is today described as toxaemia. Several other children at the clinic had contracted the infection and one had already died. The twins were dehydrating and rapidly losing weight. As soon as he heard the news Maxwell set off on a 24-hour drive from Berlin to Paris, arriving at the clinic in the early hours. He took one glance at the baby girls and asked Betty's sister, Yvonne, who had delivered them, what she was doing to treat them.

She told him she was trying to get a specialist, but that the best paediatrician, Professor Lamy, was at his holiday home outside Paris and not available. Maxwell immediately jumped into his car and drove some 70 or 80 miles to find the professor and to plead with him to return to Paris. The professor was willing and Maxwell rushed him back to the clinic. Lamy said that the children were dying. He thought "perhaps" he could save Isabel, but that Christine would not survive. The only hope for either of them was to get them at once to his department at the Hospital for Sick Children. Maxwell hustled them all down to the car and drove "like a madman", according to Betty. She was in the back seat holding Isabel and her sister was nursing Christine, while Lamy sat in the front seat with Maxwell. Then the inevitable happened: the Parisian motor-cycle police stopped the speeding car in the Champs Elysées. Professor Lamy told them, "These children are dying; we are rushing them to the hospital." The obliging policemen then went ahead, clearing the way for the Maxwells' car. Mrs Maxwell says:

> When we got there Bob just rushed in, brushing aside the form-filling and the bureaucracy which would have wasted another half an hour. The twins were put into an oxygen tent and onto a drip feed immediately and given aureomycin, then a new antibiotic.

For several days the children's lives were in danger. After a week Professor Lamy was more hopeful; after two weeks he was definitely hopeful; after three the worst was over.

In her contribution to the Birthday Book, Christine wrote feelingly:

> Without your speedy intervention when I was only a few weeks old this piece would never have come to be written.

Her tribute conveyed the sense of discipline, leavened with fun, which all the children experienced with their father. She recalled:

> I remember back to my childhood days to the times when you:
>
> Let me buy and eat three Mars bars en route to a family picnic.
>
> Tried to get me to calculate what seemed at the time impossible sums while I was in bed with a temperature of 103°F.
>
> Roared with laughter as you and I swung up and down on a fairground ride after I had inadvertently chucked my choc-ice bar onto an unsuspecting and thereafter extremely irate Bletchley constituent.

She then highlighted her adolescent days when her father:

> Called me home early from Tante Paulette's because I wrote to you about "seeing a row of bottoms in the moonlight in Bayonne".
>
> Kept me from riding because my school reports were not good enough.
>
> Whistled the end of our parties in the cellars right in the middle of smoochy Beatles records - much to the dismay of everyone.

In 1971, when she was 21, Christine spoke at a meeting of the North Bucks Fabian Society about Women's Liberation. There was no doubt where she stood on the subject:

> There is no greater unfairness than the fact that a man can just flit from woman to woman without incurring any real social stigma; but this cannot be said for a woman since the double standard is still the accepted norm.... The woman is the one with a natural talent for bringing up children. Therefore it is she who must spend several years at home looking after them. She is certainly not expected to be discontented with her lot. But what right have men to make women feel guilty for wanting a fulfilling job? Women ... have as much right not to enjoy cooking, housekeeping or the continual looking after of children.... What women demand is recognition of themselves as human beings in their own right; they want to halt this continual passing off of themselves as consumer goods.

Christine practised what she preached. She took BA degrees in Latin American Studies and Sociology at Pitzer College at

Claremont in California and after that a post-graduate course at the
Lady Spencer Churchill College of Education in Oxford. She taught
for two years in a middle school at Oxford before joining Pergamon
as editor for the school books division. In 1977, with her father's
encouragement, she produced a dictionary aimed at correcting
mis-spelling. But calling it the *Pergamon Oxford Dictionary of
Perfect Spelling* enraged Oxford University Press which successfully
won an injunction to prevent the name "Oxford" appearing in the
title. In 1980 she started Sci/Tech Publishing Services, Inc., a
consulting service, and is its president. In 1982 she was general
editor of *Nuevas Fronteras* (New Frontiers), a bilingual Early
Learning programme in Spanish and English, and the following year
she became chief executive of Information on Demand, a
Californian company providing copies of public documents and
market research, and in 1985 became its president. She lives in the
USA with her husband, Dr Roger Malina, son of a founding editor
of one of Pergamon's journals. They have one son, Xavier, born in
January 1988.

One of Isabel's first memories of her father is of "helping" him,
with Christine, in packing for an overseas trip. While he was out of
the room the twins rolled up his shirts "like sausages", put them into
his suitcase and then tried to do the same with his suits. In 1972 she
graduated from Oxford with an Honours degree in History and
Modern Languages. In the two general elections of 1974 she was her
father's assistant campaign manager at Buckingham. The following
year she started to work full-time in commercial television - first at
Yorkshire TV and then at Southern Television - as a researcher,
associate producer and finally producer. More than any other of the
Maxwell children she was deeply involved in political and union
affairs and for two years was the chairwoman of the main TV union
(ACTT) shop at Southern. The *Daily Express* described her as "an
attractive militant in the Vanessa Redgrave mould" after she
ordered the plugs to be pulled during a dispute with the
management in October 1980. All 240 ACTT members walked out
on her instructions. When she told her father what was happening
he cried:

> Do you realise what you have done? It is the equivalent of standing
> up in front of 500 people completely naked. However, I will attempt
> to put a nappy on you.

Maxwell and his daughter then sat down to draft a "crucial"
statement for the union and to plan the conduct of the strike.

Isabel said in her tribute for the Birthday Book:

> I remember saying at some point "I'm so glad I'm not dealing with
> you as management because I'm sure that we would lose." But we
> didn't lose … after 60 more hours of negotiation we got a great new
> deal.

She added:

> You never held me back from doing what I wanted to do. That is not
> to say that you have not questioned me forcefully in some instances,
> but that was to ensure that I really did know what I was doing, why I
> wanted to do it and what the consequences would be for me if I took
> that particular route. You were very hard when it came to putting my
> ideas down on paper … but it did force me to concentrate my mind on
> what I really wanted to achieve.

In 1980 Isabel met Dale Djerassi, a young American film
producer and son of another founding editor of a Pergamon journal.
In 1981 she went to California with him. Ever since she has been
working full-time for Djerassi Films, Inc., principally producing and
directing TV programmes on education, current affairs,
documentaries, chat shows and drama. They have just produced
their first independent feature film, '68, about a family of
Hungarian immigrants and set in San Francisco. She and Dale
married in April 1984 and have one son, Alexander.

The children Maxwell sees most of - and drives the hardest - are
his two youngest sons, Ian and Kevin. Both are now senior
executives in his business. For them there is no rest. The privilege of
nepotism is unending work.

Ian was the child conceived in 1955 when Maxwell thought he was
dying and wanted another son to bear his name. He is the most laid
back of all the children, with a distinctive sense of humour. For a
long time the best known story about him was that he was fired
because he preferred to meet a girl instead of keeping an
appointment with his father. He recalled the shock of it all for the
Birthday Book:

> I failed to pick you up at Orly airport one weekend and called you at
> the Paris apartment from a roadside phone outside Mâcon at 11 pm
> to make my apologies - only to be told that this was a gross dereliction
> of responsibility, that I was putting love before duty and that I was
> duly relieved of the managing directorships of both our French and
> German offices. I don't know if you can imagine what it was like
> hearing this bombshell that night, stuck in a phone booth, running
> out of money some 300 miles south of Paris. I thought the world had
> caved in - and I'd just been ignominiously jettisoned earlier in the day
> by my then girlfriend to boot!

We buried the hatchet a couple of months later at the Mark Hopkins Hotel in San Francisco. And this illustrates another of your hallmarks: the giving of another chance.... You did have a lot of patience in those days and even today ... you patiently sit with me to explain the basics of business.

Ian said to his father what others fear to say:

You are not a man to hold grudges or to belabour a point. I often think you unnecessarily use a howitzer to shoot a chicken, but when the smoke has cleared the chicken often discovers you were only firing blanks....

You know, of course, that you are an impossible act to follow, but you're a marvellous example to try to emulate in so many ways.... I do wish, however, that you would apply your oft quoted principle of "a pat on the head being worth fifty kicks in the b..." more frequently - not just for myself as much as for the rest of the family and the many people that work with you directly every day.

Ian graduated from Balliol with a BA Honours in French and History. He joined Pergamon straightaway. In 1980, at the age of 24, he was made managing director of Pergamon Press, France and Pergamon Press, Germany (the jobs from which he was abruptly sacked) and in 1981 climbed back aboard as the Vice President, Marketing, of Pergamon Press, Inc. in New York. In 1983-84 he was on full-time secondment to the Prince of Wales's Charitable Trust to help young, unemployed Britons to start up in business. For three years he was chairman of Derby County and saw it from the Third to the First Division of the English Football League, but gave way to his father when he acquired and became chairman of the Agence Centrale de Presse in Paris, where he now spends most of the year. He is a director of TF1, the main French television service. He speaks French and German fluently and Japanese "passably".

Long before the furore in late 1987 over Maxwell's alleged desire to control the Football League, Ian's invariable courtesy led one football reporter to look more kindly upon the Maxwell family. Steve Curry wrote in the *Daily Express* after attending a match at Derby's ground[6]:

Ian Maxwell, for all his privileged upbringing, is one of the lads, as I discovered when he got down on his knees to help me change a punctured tyre.... Perhaps it wouldn't be bad for the game if Maxwell put all his seven children into soccer.

That was not the attitude of the Football League when it called a extraordinary general meeting in January 1988 to stop the Maxwell family extending its influence.

Kevin, two and a half years younger than Ian, is, effectively, Maxwell's deputy in England. He is more intense and more single-minded than his brother. When he graduated from Balliol in 1980 with an Honours degree in French and History he went straight into the family firm and worked for Pergamon until January 1984. After a domestic disagreement with his father that same year he went to work for Holt Saunders, a books and software company, but he returned in September. In 1983, when he was Director of Special Projects, he wrote to his father listing the work he had done since he had taken over the job. Maxwell sent back his congratulations - and his advice:

> If you are to be successful as a publisher ... you must learn to take on only so many projects and ideas at a time which you can genuinely manage ... otherwise you run the danger of being a person with too many ideas but without any finish. As I have told you before, you have got creative talents and time and you must be jealous in the use of both.

> You have prepared the papers well but quite often you have put on one sheet facts and information about two or three projects. That you must never do because it makes it impossible to file them and it causes confusion and extra work and it indicates that you are not thinking as to how your work is to be processed in an orderly manner by others.

These corrections, Maxwell added kindly, did not detract from "the quality and quantity of work" Kevin had achieved.

The *Sunday Telegraph* has labelled Kevin as "The Maxwell Most Likely to Succeed". But Kevin told the paper:

> I am judged on my performance.

In his Birthday Book contribution, Kevin told his father:

> You are a teacher and all my life you have tried to demonstrate the principles underlying every action or inaction even if we were playing roulette or Monopoly or [you were] pushing me off a 30 foot yard arm into the sea - "Hold your breath and keep your feet together" - or writing an essay on Bismarck or Balzac.... Above all, you have given me the sense of excitement of having dozens of balls in the air and the thrill of seeing some of them land right.

Today Kevin is chief executive of the Maxwell Pergamon Publishing Corporation, director of the Maxwell Communication Corporation, and executive deputy chairman of Hollis, the sickly furniture company which Maxwell took over and turned into an engineering giant. He has been given every opportunity to reach the top, but in the end, if he is to succeed, it will have to be on his merits, not because he is his father's son. He and his wife Pandora have two children, Tilly and Edward.

Ghislaine is the glamour girl of the family and, like most youngest children, she has been spoilt, though so subtly that she believes she hasn't. But being spoilt in the Maxwell family is a relative benefit. It did not excuse her from hard academic work, having to learn, as did her brothers and sisters, to speak other languages - she is fluent in French, Spanish and Italian - and having to do the dogsbody jobs in the office while she was still at Balliol and for a period after she left.

She did not stay with Pergamon for long. In 1988 she became managing director of Maxwell's Corporate Gifts, a division of one of Maxwell's subsidiaries, but one in which she has to make her own success. The omens are good. She might even be the first to emulate her father's success and become a millionairess before she's 30. But if she doesn't and she falls flat on her face, her father will be there to help her up and tell her to try again. She says one of his most admirable characteristics is his generosity.

On one occasion she remembers returning that generosity by buying him a Weimaraner puppy. Maxwell was so pleased that he announced he was going to take it for a walk in the Headington Hill Hall grounds. Ghislaine protested that the dog was too young for him to do any such thing.

"Nonsense", boomed Maxwell, and walked out of the house with the puppy on a lead. Once outside it wouldn't - or couldn't - move. Hastily looking around to see if he was being watched - he was, but he didn't detect it - Maxwell picked up the puppy and strode off. Twenty minutes later he returned. "Did the puppy enjoy the walk?" Ghislaine inquired. "Of course he did", Maxwell snorted, as though doubt was absurd.

Ghislaine and the rest of the children are as proud of their father as he is of them. He may be a global entrepreneur, a newspaper publisher, a printer, a TV mogul in Europe and Asia, a workaholic and a figure revered or dreaded throughout his business empire, but his living memorial is his family. All the newspaper and magazine profiles in the world cannot match the one paragraph by which his wife, quoting the French novelist and playwright Henry de Montherlant, pays him her tribute:

> Living alongside you has made me find all other men colourless and other ways of life mediocre.

To be Continued.

Appendices

APPENDIX 1

House of Commons,
London, S.W.1

PERSONAL AND CONFIDENTIAL

October 1969

I am writing to you about the matter which distressed me when I first read the *Sunday Times* last Sunday and which has distressed me still more since the matter has been referred to the Committee of Privileges. I refer to the "Insight" story on Bob Maxwell's career as Chairman of the Catering Sub-Committee here.

As you may remember I was Leader of the House at the time he was appointed and indeed I was responsible, along with John Silkin, for persuading the Tory Chief Whip to join in nominating him to this unenviable job. At the time our financial situation looked desperate and we, as a Government, were saddled with the further awkward fact that Bessie Braddock was Chairman of the Sub-Committee during the period when the disastrous report by a Treasury O and M team had been made to me on the gross inefficiency (to put it mildly) of the department's management and the disastrous losses that had been incurred. I was able, as I knew I could, to persuade Bob Maxwell to take the "suicidal" course of accepting the Chairmanship. His ambition to succeed in politics has always been so immense that I reckoned he couldn't refuse an offer of this kind - and he didn't.

What I did not know was the staggering success he would make of it. He took over a Department totally demoralised, whose staff included a number of prostitutes and thieves, all of whom he sacked without causing a strike. He also took over a restaurant which was incurring gigantic losses in order to provide excellent food and drink to a very few people in the Strangers' Dining Room or in the private rooms underneath at well under cost price. All this he exposed to me with ruthless clarity. He also indicated that in order to destroy the loss we would of course have to lower the standard of choice as well as reducing superfluous staff. Of course he made the most typical Maxwellian mistakes (one day I caught him saving £183 a year by providing powdered milk instead of fresh milk with our tea in the tea room). But nevertheless he did the job we asked him to do. He purged the gross abuse and pilfering; legs of mutton and rounds of beef were being regularly removed under their raincoats by members of the staff. All that is now stopped.

I tell you these few facts in order to introduce the cause of my embarrassment. I got a message that "Insight" wanted me to tell them about Maxwell. I refused. Then I was caught by one of your "Insight" staff early one morning on the telephone and I said, "O.K. I will tell you what I know as Leader of the House. He did a marvellous job."

"But surely there was another side to it?"

"No, I have nothing to add except details to prove that he did a good job."

"But surely, Mr Crossman, you know about the other side?"

"I am telling you what I know and what I should think you would want to print."

And so I told him roughly what I have written to you. When I read the *Sunday Times* this week I found that not one shred or atom of what I had said appeared in print. The article was wholly derogatory and didn't even pretend to give the other side of the case as I had presented it to your "Insight" telephonist. Of course there are papers which use the freedom of the press to run personal vendettas. I should be distressed if I had to conclude that the *Sunday Times* is that kind of paper.

                                                                    R.H.S. Crossman

C.D. Hamilton, Esq., D.S.O.
Editor-in-Chief
Times Newspapers Ltd.

                              TIMES NEWSPAPERS LIMITED
                                  Printing House Square,
                                      London EC4

From the Editor-in-Chief   21st October 1969

Dear Richard,

I was very disturbed indeed to have your letter about Bob Maxwell. I was quite unaware of all this and I shall ever be in your debt for giving me this background.

As the matter is now before the Committee of Privileges and the Editor of the *Sunday Times* is expecting to appear before it in the next few days, it is difficult for me to add anything at this stage but I intend writing you further when the Committee has reported.

In the meantime I can only say how I am personally shocked about your information. I have consistently asked the Editor to check that the enthusiasm and dedication of the staff was not getting out of hand. As long as I am Editor-in-Chief of Times Newspapers there will be no personal vendettas.

                                                                    Yours sincerely

                                                                    Denis Hamilton

The Rt. Hon. Richard Crossman, O.B.E., M.A., M.P.,
House of Commons,
London S.W.1.

TIMES NEWSPAPERS LIMITED
Printing House Square,
London EC4

From the Editor-in-Chief   24th October 1969

Dear Mr Silkin,

Thank you for your letter of October 22. Dick Crossman has written on similar lines, and I have assured him, as I do you, that I would never allow a personal vendetta in *The Times* or the *Sunday Times*.

The Committee of Privileges is now sitting and it is difficult for me to comment further until they have reported, but I assure you that I am investigating the points which you have raised.

Yours sincerely

Denis Hamilton

The Rt. Hon. John Silkin, M.P.,
7, Storeys Gate,
Westminster,
London S.W.1.

SCIENCE, GOVERNMENT AND INDUSTRY
by Robert Maxwell

As is well known, Britain's economic growth rate over the past 10 years has been lower than that of any other highly industrialised country. This is well demonstrated in Table I.1 recently published by T. Balogh as part of his Fabian pamphlet "Planning for Progress: A Strategy for Labour".

Table I.1
Annual Rates of Growth of Gross Domestic Product and of Output in Major Industrial Divisions, 1950 to 1960 (Percentage)

Country	Gross Domestic Product	Agri-culture	Mining	Manu-facturing	Utilities
Japan	9.5	4.7	4.6	18.1	9.9
Germany (Fed. Rep.)	7.6	2.2	3.8	10.1	9.2
Italy	5.9	3.5	10.1	9.0	7.3
Austria	5.9	3.0	5.6	7.1	10.4
Netherlands	4.7	2.3	2.1	6.1	7.4
Finland	4.6	2.4	8.8	6.0	8.0
France	4.3	2.0	6.6	6.5	10.9
Australia	3.9	3.2	-	5.7	7.4
Canada	3.8	1.8	8.7	3.4	9.8
New Zealand	3.5	2.9	-	4.6	7.7
Norway	3.5	-	6.4	5.1	5.9
Denmark	3.4	1.9	-	3.3	8.4
United States	3.3	2.4	1.9	3.6	8.7
Sweden	3.2	-1.0	4.7	3.3	-
Belgium	2.9	2.1	-1.4	4.1	5.4
United Kingdom	2.7	1.7	-0.6	3.5	5.2

Many reasons have been advanced to explain this poor performance. It is, however, more than likely that Britain's failure to grow as quickly as some of its competitors can be traced to a number of partial causes, the major ones being: an insufficient rate of investment to maintain economic growth; neglecting to expand sufficiently all forms of higher education; lack of effective use by British industry of new technology and scientific research; and to a lesser extent the dichotomy that exists in the Government on science for defence and for civil purposes.

There is general public understanding and acceptance of the vital importance of new technology to weapons development but less appreciation of the role that science and technology play in economic growth, and of the need for special arrangements to ensure that new science becomes useful technology, that it spreads throughout industry and the country, and, most important, that people are educated and trained to develop and use it.

The relationships between science, Government, technology and economic growth are not at all clear to most of those engaged in science or Government or to those who participate in the business of building the economy. The translation of science to use by society is not well understood nor practised.

It is accepted that economic growth is desirable and taken for granted that it is one of the Government's functions to foster it in so far as it is compatible with its other major policy aims. It is known that one of the major determinants of economic growth in an advanced society is the speed with which firms are willing and able to use the results of scientific discovery to develop technological innovation, to achieve greater efficiency and higher sales at home and abroad.

The considerable growth of the national scientific and technological effort since the end of the last war has naturally led to intensified discussion of the means by which this vast effort is planned and managed. It is now beginning to be realised that, while government support for research and development expenditure represents a very small fraction of our national economic means, they engage a very large fraction of one of our scarcest national resources, namely scientific and technical manpower. Furthermore, it is now appreciated that points of growth in the national economy appear to follow closely research and development expenditures; to the extent that these are channelled by decision of Her Majesty's Government, the whole thrust of our economy is determined.

It is interesting to note that the N.E.D.C. report refers to accumulated evidence of a correlation between research, development and productivity. They say: "In the past decade the output of the science-based industries has been growing at twice the rate of manufacturing industries as a whole." While the volume of our exports generally during the last eight years has grown by 3.1 per cent, for two science-based industries - chemicals and electronics - the corresponding growth rate has been 10.4 per cent and 7.9 per cent.

In sum, the social and economic leverage of the approximate three per cent of the Gross National Product which is expended on research and development by the Government and industry is many times greater than the actual amount of money involved. Yet the extent of this leverage is only now beginning to be recognised and appreciated.

TENTATIVE OUTLINE ON THE ORGANISATION OF SCIENCE AND ENGINEERING TO ASSIST THE NEXT LABOUR GOVERNMENT IN RELATING SCIENCE AND TECHNOLOGY TO OUR NATIONAL NEEDS AND RESOURCES

The following are tentative suggestions for the organisation of science and technology. The various components that are involved in the overall picture include:

Ministry of Higher Education and Science
Ministry of Aviation
Directorate of Defence Research and Development (D.D.R.D.)
National Council for the Co-ordination of Science and
    Engineering (N.C.C.S.E.)

Defence Research Policy Committee (D.R.P.C.)
Inter Departmental Co-ordination Committee (I.D.C.C.)
University Grants Commission (U.G.C.)
United Kingdom Atomic Energy Authority (U.K.A.E.A.)
Department of Scientific and Industrial Research (D.S.I.R.)
Technology Grants Commission (T.G.C.)
Free Science and Engineering Advisory Service (S.E.A.S.)
Medical Research Council (M.R.C.)
National Research Development Corporation (N.R.D.C.)
Agricultural Research Council (A.R.C.)
Nature Conservancy Board (N.C.B.)
Advisory Council on Scientific Policy (A.C.S.P.)
Social Sciences Research Council (S.S.R.C.)
Central Scientific and Technical Register of Technical
  Manpower (C.S.T.R.)

The creation of a post in the Government at Cabinet level for a Minister of
Higher Education and Science is recommended. The transfer of the following
votes is recommended: the United Kingdom Atomic Energy Authority
(U.K.A.E.A.) (and to end its statutory semi-independent status), the
Department of Scientific and Industrial Research (D.S.I.R.), the Medical
Research Council (M.R.C.), the National Research Development Corporation
(N.R.D.C.), the Nature Conservancy Board (N.C.B.) and the Agricultural
Research Council (A.R.C.) as well as the proposed Social Sciences Research
Council (S.S.R.C.) to this new Ministry, and also suggested is the transfer of
the Central Scientific and Technical Register of Technical Manpower
(C.S.T.R.) from the Ministry of Labour. It is proposed that the University
Grants Commission and the other appropriate bodies responsible for higher
education, i.e. the National Council of Technological Awards, be transferred
to this new Ministry. The U.G.C. is to continue to act as guardian of legitimate
university freedoms.

The suggestions of the Taylor Committee on the creation of a National
University Development Council, whose responsibility it would be to plan for
higher education, are supported. The National University Development
Council should be an independent body appointed by the Minister of Higher
Education and Science, its plans to be published and debated in Parliament.

It is universally agreed that our country is in need of a rapid and continuing
expansion of its facilities for higher education; without this expansion our
entire educational system will become distorted and starved of teachers and
lecturers. The next Labour Government's plans for economic expansion
cannot be carried out without a considerable increase in the number of highly
skilled and professionally trained people. All our short- and long-term national
objectives are unattainable without a continuing increase in the number of
places available in higher education.

It is believed that the creation of the post of Minister of Higher Education
and Science will be most beneficial in achieving the rapid increase in the
number of highly skilled and professionally trained people to cut out waste and
duplication, and to ensure that the nation gets value for the vast sums of money
spent on higher education and scientific research.

United Kingdom Scientific and Engineering Manpower.
(Source: United States Government publication)
Total Number
In 1959 there were 173,000 scientists and engineers in the United Kingdom, of whom 72,000 or 41.5 per cent were scientists, 101,000 or 58.5 per cent were engineers. Thus, there were about two scientists to every three engineers. This is a considerably higher proportion of scientists than in the United States, where the corresponding ratio is about one to two.

Table II.1
Scientists and Engineers in the United Kingdom

	1956		1959		1961	
	Number	Per cent	Number	Per cent	Number	Per cent
Number of scientists and engineers	145,000	100.0	173,000	100.0	186,000	100.0
Number of scientists	61,000	42.0	72,000	41.5		
Number of engineers	85,000	58.0	101,000	58.5		
Per cent of labour force		0.65		0.76		

The most recent survey indicates a significant slowing down of growth, as indicated in Table II.1. In the three-year period 1956-59, the growth in number of scientists and engineers was 28,000; in the subsequent three-year period, 1959-62, the growth was 13,000.

Distribution by Sector
As shown in Table II.2, the proportion of scientists and engineers in the Government sector is about the same as in the United States. The proportion in the industrial sector is less, and the proportion in the education sector correspondingly higher than in the United States.

Table II.2
Distribution of United Kingdom Manpower by Sector, in 1959

Sector	Per cent 100.0
Government	15.0
Industry, including nationalised sector	53.6
Education	24.0
Other	6.6

Research and Development Scientists and Engineers
The proportion of scientists and engineers in research and development is somewhat smaller, but comparable to the United States. In marked contrast to

the United States, however, this proportion is decreasing. Thus (Table II.3) in 1956, 30 per cent, in 1959, 28 per cent, and in 1962, 27 per cent of all scientists were in research and development.

Table II.3
Research and Development Scientists and Engineers in the United Kingdom

Year	Total Number of Scientists and Engineers	Scientists and Engineers in Research and Development	
		Number	Per cent
1956	145,000	43,500	30.0
1959	173,000	48,500	28.0

This unhealthy drop in the proportion of scientists and engineers employed in research and development should be stopped and reversed by the new Ministry of Higher Education and Science.

The creation of a Technology Grants Commission is recommended to perform similar functions for the non-university institutions of higher learning, as the U.G.C. does for the universities. The Chairman of the Technology Grants Commission shall be Deputy Chairman of the University Grants Commission, thus helping to ensure close co-operation and collaboration between these two important Commissions.

NATIONAL COUNCIL FOR THE CO-ORDINATION OF SCIENCE AND ENGINEERING

This Council should be charged with the task of considering our future needs in the light of advancing technologies and changing economic and political circumstances and be responsible for formulating the main strategic lines for the overall government policy on research and development; to settle the major preferences within the broad framework laid down by the Cabinet Defence and Economic Committees for both the defence requirements and the needs of the civilian economy.

The Chairman and its members are appointed by the Minister of Higher Education and Science to work in his office on a full-time basis. Its members must be men and women of the highest quality and capability who shall be seconded, for a period of two to five years, from universities, industry and government departments.

This Council shall replace the A.C.S.P., whose advisory role could best be taken over by ad hoc committees to be appointed from time to time by the Royal Society at the invitation of the Minister of Higher Education and Science.

To give an idea of the size, specialisation and field of work of individual full-time members of the Council, I list below some of the subjects for which they might be responsible.

Defence
Education

Civilian Technology
Science Information
International Science
Physical Sciences
Life Sciences
Natural Resources

The Chairman shall be a scientist or engineer of international stature, and the Deputy Chairman a permanent civil servant who is scientifically qualified. In addition, the following shall be members of this Council: the Chief Scientific Adviser to the Minister of Defence, the Chief Adviser to any new Ministry responsible for central planning, the President of the Royal Society, the Director-General of W.E.D.C., the Chairman of the University Grants Commission, and the Chairman of the Technological Grants Commission.

The Council will appoint permanent or ad hoc panels as necessary, these specialist national advisory panels and committees to advise the Minister and the Council on detailed specialist problems that will arise from time to time. Members of these specialist advisory panels and committees will be drawn from universities, industry and government departments.

Merging of Defence and Civil Science Programmes

The administration of the defence and civil science programmes should be merged and put under the control of the Minister of Higher Education and Science. The Minister of Higher Education and Science shall be responsible, as agent for the Minister of Defence, for all matters of high policy affecting the some forty government defence research laboratories. The present practice of administering the defence and civil sides separately is recognised to be highly unsatisfactory.

The abolition of the Ministry of Aviation is recommended and its functions and staff should be taken over as appropriate by the Ministry of Defence and the Ministry of Higher Education and Science.

The abolition of the D.R.P.C. is recommended and its policy functions be vested in the National Council for the Co-ordination of Science and Engineering.

A further possible advantage of this proposed merger could be that it would provide something that has been lacking for a long time, namely a sharp and independent means for recognising when the mission of a government research and development establishment has lost its validity, and the practical means for redirecting the establishment into more productive channels either within or outside the government department that originally sponsored it. When the independent nuclear deterrent is abolished, the problem of what to do with the Aldermaston Weapons Research Establishment is a good example of the kind of problem we have in mind.

The present system of awarding development contracts tempts private companies to talk their way into a development programme with promises of results which wise technical judgement would deem unattainable, i.e. Sky Bolt, and various other failed home-produced missiles and weapons. The present arrangement does not provide for adequate penalties for failure to achieve promised results, nor does it give sufficient incentives for a high level of technical performance. It also offers incentives to contractors to make systems complex and expensive or to prolong the development work. All this is most wasteful of our vital scientific and engineering manpower as well as of taxpayers' money.

Finally, the present defence research contract arrangement with its built-in competitive incentives and inadequate penalties for poor technical performance leads to the proliferation of many research development groups in private industry of sub-critical size or quality.

Insufficient Long-range Planning and Evaluation

Under current practices, insufficient attention is given to the ultimate monetary costs, manpower and facilities implications of major development programmes at the time these are started.

The present state of maladministration in sciences cannot be tolerated any longer. The imbalance between defence and civil research, of which the Advisory Council on Scientific Policy has so often complained, demonstrates that the present Government does not have a method of dealing with this most vital problem.

The dichotomy between the use and control of scientific manpower for defence purposes and for civil research and development purposes must end.

Directorate of Defence Research and Development

There shall be created in the Ministry of Defence a Directorate of Defence Research and Development. This Directorate, acting on the policy decisions reached by the Cabinet Defence or Economic Committee in consultation with the National Council for the Co-ordination of Science and Engineering, will be responsible for allocating Defence Department resources between basic and applied research and development, the making of longer-term grants and contracts for research, the delegation of management authority and responsibility for major defence research projects and facilities.

They will also be responsible for ensuring good organisation and administration in the some forty government defence research laboratories. In consultation and co-operation with the Ministry of Higher Education and Science, they will ensure that the commercially useful by-products of the defence research programme are identified and developed as quickly as possible.

The Department of Defence expenditures for basic and more fundamental and applied research should be channelled through the Ministry of Higher Education and Science for management and administration.

The Director-General of Defence Research shall be an eminent scientist or engineer seconded from university or industry for a period of five to ten years. In addition to fulfilling his co-ordinating and administrative functions relating to the management of the government defence research laboratories, he will also be the principal science adviser to the Minister of Defence and be a member of the N.C.C.S.E.

The Director-General of Defence Research shall have three Deputy Directors who also shall be eminent scientists and engineers appointed by the Minister of Defence in consultation with the Minister of Higher Education and Science, the First Lord of the Admiralty, the Secretary of State for War, and the Secretary of State for Air.

The Inter-Departmental Co-ordination Committee

The responsibility of this Committee shall be to deal with problems of organisation, administration and co-ordination of research in government establishments and in the nationalised industries. It would further be responsible for relating the reports of the National Council for the Co-ordination of Science and Engineering to specific government programmes.

The Chairman of this Inter-Departmental Co-ordination Committee shall be the Chairman of the N.C.C.S.E. and the Deputy Chairman shall be the Director of the Directorate of Defence Research and Development. This Inter-Departmental Co-ordination Committee shall have a strong Executive Secretary, with an adequate staff, to concern himself specifically with the follow-through on national science and development programmes and to monitor the development of plans and the implementation of the Inter-Departmental Co-ordination Committee's decisions by its member departments. The three Deputy Directors of the Directorate of Defence Research and Development will be members of this Inter-Departmental Co-ordination Committee together with the secretaries and/or directors responsible for research and development of the following organisations and departments: United Kingdom Atomic Energy Authority, Department of Scientific and Industrial Research, Medical Research Council, National Research Development Corporation, Directorate of Defence Research and Development, Nature Conservancy Board, Agricultural Research Council, Social Sciences Research Council, Central Scientific and Technical Register of Technical Manpower, the Ministry of Fuel and Power, the Post Office, the Iron and Steel Board, the Gas Council, the National Airlines, the British Transport Commission.

This Inter-Departmental Co-ordination Committee could also concern itself with the better utilisation of existing capabilities of one department by another when embarking on new or expanded programmes; allocation of responsibility for undertaking new research activities which do not fit clearly within the mission of any one department; to make studies and recommendations concerning long-range research plans of the Government.

How can we best convey the results of research in a form which points the way to its practical applications?

It is now well understood that the growth of our economy, welfare of our citizens, our national security, the aid that we can afford to give to underdeveloped countries, all depend to a growing extent on the effective use our industries make of new technology. In recent years the rate of increase in our Gross National Product per worker (a measure of productivity) and per capita (a measure of standard of living) has slowed down and has been substantially less than those of almost all highly industrialised nations in the world, as shown earlier in this appendix.

Although there has been a rise in the standard of living, that rise has not been uniform throughout the population. The fact of the matter is that there are many areas in our country (particularly those which formerly depended on the exploitation of natural resources and old-fashioned industries such as ship-building, certain types of heavy engineering, textiles, etc.) where the standards of living have not risen and have actually declined. These areas have lacked the effective means to initiate new industrial development.

To improve our competitive position generally we must broaden the technical base of our economy, use technology more effectively and provide the basis for new and better products and services at lower cost. It is important that we decrease not only the direct costs of goods but their indirect costs as well, that is the costs of such services and facilities as transportation, building and construction, plant and machinery. These indirect costs make up a very significant proportion of the costs of all goods and services produced by the nation.

It is apparently not fully realised that scientific discovery followed by technological research and development produces nothing, other than knowledge, for society. They must be followed by their applications through the combined use of capital and equipment and human resources - labour and management - to produce an economic good.

It is commonly accepted that management in British industry, both private and nationalised, by and large has failed badly to make use of science and technology as an aid to increased productivity and profitability. For example, for the first 50 ethical drugs prescribed by doctors under the National Health Service, in order of sales value used in this country, only three were discovered and developed in this country - ordinary penicillin, and the new Beecham penicillins, Broxil and Penbritin. Many other examples of a similar nature can be given, such as computer components, automated office equipment and systems, and certain types of machine tools, etc.

It is generally agreed that one of the major obstacles preventing the wider application and use of science and technology in British industry is that there does not seem to be, at present, an effective organisation or method to convey to individual companies, their management and foremen, the new technology in a form which points the way to its practical applications.

The other major problem seems to be the great gulf and lack of communication that exists between the pure scientists and the applied scientists, the universities, the technical colleges, the trade research associations, industry and Government, and, finally, the gap that exists between management and scientists in individual firms.

The whole issue may therefore be summed up as being a problem in communication of information and the need to change attitudes of mind.

Free Science and Engineering Advisory Service

The creation of a Free Science and Engineering Advisory Service is recommended for technical work and the dissemination of technical information; this should be integrated with the existing services of the research associations. This new service should be most helpful in getting the medium and small firms to use new technology and to introduce innovations that increase productivity.

The service shall be based eventually in the some sixty D.S.I.R. selected universities, colleges of advanced technology and regional technical colleges. It shall be financed through D.S.I.R. grants direct to the chosen institutions. The service will not be concerned with proprietary problems unique to a particular company. Each unit shall be staffed by some ten first-rate applied scientists, who understand and appreciate the significance of what their colleagues in pure science are trying to discover and who keep in close touch with local industry and interpret firms' needs to scientists and engineers in the teaching and research institutions, as well as bringing to the notice of firms, through personal visits, plant demonstrations and seminars, technological developments that will benefit their productivity.

This service could provide the missing link in the communications network between universities, technical colleges, industry, trade research associations and Government. It is estimated that the total number of scientific and engineering staff needed to give this effective free advisory service would be between six to seven hundred, and, together with their supporting staff, we believe that the total annual expenditure would be £2 million. This service will involve the interaction of people interested in science, technology, economics and related fields.

The D.S.I.R. should invite applications from universities and technical colleges to perform this service. The staff of the Free Science and Engineering Advisory Service could also encourage in their region their colleagues in universities and technical colleges and in government research laboratories to carry out industrial orientated basic research, thus helping to increase the supply of technical people experienced in industrial problems.

Finally, they can also be very useful in encouraging firms to support basic technical work both within these firms and outside them either in trade research associations or in some other institution of higher learning or research laboratory.

As a measure of how little use British industry is making of new technological information, the following facts may be of value. There are approximately 90,000 firms in the United Kingdom; of these it is reliably estimated that some 15,000 are members of the various trade research associations. ASLIB, the Library Association in the United Kingdom, records that only 800 industrial firms in the United Kingdom have technical libraries to assist management and staff to keep up-to-date with the latest technical information.

D.S.I.R. - Development Contracts - Industry

The Department of Scientific and Industrial Research should be given by the Ministry of Higher Education and Science an expanded role in the planning, management and support of basic research, including programmes of research which are a blend of basic and applied research.

The Ministry should provide through the D.S.I.R. some £50 million per annum to devote to financing the very substantial growth needed in civilian applied research and development. This money should be expended to finance jointly with industry or alone in universities, technical colleges, research associations or government research laboratories, basic technological problems of importance to industry, i.e. projects likely to have a major effect on industrial productivity contributing significantly to increasing our Gross National Product and exports.

The Government should support the placing of civil development contracts with industry for carrying out applied research of a developmental character in the following circumstances:

a) where the work is recognised as needing to be done in the national interest;
b) where it is too big an operation for a single firm, or a consortium of firms, to undertake it alone; and
c) where the development is too speculative for private enterprise alone.

The F.B.I. recommendations of a target increase of £100 million per annum in the field of research and development, whereby 50 per cent is financed by industry and 50 per cent by the Government, are supported.

The expenditure of substantial amounts of public funds for development contracts in civilian research and development requires that positive arrangements be made for effective accounting, and, wherever possible, for the recoupment, by the Government, of the expended public funds and, where possible, to share in any profits resulting from its support.

Industry itself must find ways and means of redeploying its present scientific and engineering manpower, so as to ensure that fully qualified scientists and engineers are relieved of doing menial jobs that technicians can do for them. The Government should provide tax incentives to industry in order to encourage it or increase its expenditure on research and development. The Government should increase the amount of money available to the D.S.I.R. for research grants and fellowships and establish fellowships and research grants tenable at technical colleges.

Trade Research Associations

It is recommended that a commission be appointed to report on the value and function of trade research associations and how and in what way they can be made more effective, better used and better supported by industry. Our research associations, together with the Free Science and Engineering Advisory Service, should be made a vehicle of information in those industries where the small and medium firms predominate.

Research associations should be enabled to carry out pilot plant development and financing should be done jointly by the Government and industry. Industry and trade associations should be strongly encouraged to appoint consultants from universities and technical colleges.

Compulsory Levy

Most directors of research associations seem to spend a great deal of their time as well as a substantial number of their staff on the problems of raising funds. The introduction of a compulsory levy on industry is recommended wherever this is possible. The advantages of such a levy are that the director and some of his staff will be able to spend their time on research and development instead of raising funds; secondly, there would be a considerable saving on the administrative expenditure; and thirdly, a statutory levy on a horizontally based sector of industry will give the research associations a useful basis to extend vertically.

Patents

Everybody agrees that our Patent Act is very out of date and that our patent system is in need of a radical overhaul. It is recommended that the next Labour

Government looks into the position and examines whether new legislation to prevent the prior assignation of rights in a patent might not be a good way of stimulating innovation in industry. A patent system based on this principle has been working very satisfactorily to all concerned in Germany.

The Social Sciences Research Council

It is strongly recommended that this Council be established to perform the same services for the nation in the social and behavioural sciences as the D.S.I.R. does for the physical sciences and engineering. The social scientists of this country can make a significant contribution to the national welfare and help the country to achieve a faster rate of economic growth.

The establishment of this Council will help to restore a little the imbalance that exists between the resources available for doing research in the physical sciences and the social and behavioural sciences.

It is proposed that this Council shall receive its vote and be answerable to the Ministry of Higher Education and Science.

Science Adviser to Secretary of State for Foreign Affairs

The creation of this new post is recommended. Science and technology play an increasing role in the formulation of foreign policy. Unfortunately this too often is not fully appreciated by policy-makers, thus the primary function of the science adviser to the Secretary of State for Foreign Affairs will be to indicate to top policy-makers when and how scientific and technological considerations bear on foreign policy as it is evolved. The science adviser should be a scientist or engineer or be highly literate in science or technology and should have some appreciation and understanding of foreign affairs. He must be in a position to engage as consultants on specific problems the best technical minds in the country. His staff should be of sufficient size and competence so that he may initiate and provide the guidelines for technical studies important to the Foreign Office and evaluate and interpret for the Foreign Office studies made in other government departments.

A good example are the scientific problems relating to the nuclear weapons test monitoring requirements. A further function of the science adviser to the Secretary of State for Foreign Affairs would be to stimulate relations between British and foreign scientists in furtherance of our foreign policy objectives, a function in which the Foreign Office needs to assume stronger leadership.

Finally, the science adviser should assume authority over the duties of science attachés abroad and assist them in achieving the status of policy advisers on scientific matters to their Ambassadors.

Interchange of Personnel Between Universities, Industry and Government

It is strongly recommended that urgent and positive steps be taken to bring about the development of an interchange of personnel between the universities, industry and the Government. Such interchange will be of considerable benefit to creating the right climate in producing better informed government policies and bringing about closer government, industry and university co-operation which is indispensable to success in scientific economic policies.

Science and Planning

The Chairman of the National Council for the Co-ordination of Science and Engineering shall be a member of the Council of N.E.D.C. or any other senior advisory committee that may be set up by the Ministry responsible for central planning. The secretariat of N.E.D.C. should have a strong technico-economic section which should work in close co-operation with the N.C.C.S.E. In this way the scientific and engineering point of view would take its place easily as part of the wider national planning body.

Science Information

The Ministry of Higher Education and Science could centralise most effectively the important activities relating to science information.

Scientific and Economic Staff in Central Position in Each Ministry

Each Ministry should set up its own scientific/economic department so that in this way science can increasingly help influence policy and action in Government. This forward planning staff with a strong technical bias can be responsible for relating the long-term policy plans of the department to the scope for technological development in the industries on which this department relies. This staff should be given a central position in each Ministry.

An example of how valuable this kind of arrangement can be has been reported to the Gibb-Zuckerman Committee, when it was stated that without the work of the development group in the Ministry of Education on the educational building programme carried out since 1949, the achieved saving of some £300 million on the schools built since then would not have been possible.

New and Powerful Social Tool to Raise the Quality and Standards of Life of the Nation

The Ministry of Higher Education and Science and our scientific and engineering community should make it one of their major joint tasks to employ our newfound ability to combine the great diversity of scientific and engineering skills and disciplines to make a massive assault on very large-scale national problems. The effectiveness of employing this new government tool has been demonstrated during the last war and in the present massive USA - USSR space programmes.

The social innovation and use in peacetime of this new government tool is of even greater consequence in the long run than the scientific and technical innovations on which most of our attention is presently focused. This is the "spill over" from defence of the greatest national and social consequence and we, as a country, have so far failed to use this instrument in peacetime. There can be no doubt that the development of this new capability has endowed us as a nation with great new powers. The new Labour Government should use this social invention for peaceful purposes and not just confine it to the defence sector.

The Government should show the way how to use research and development in the modern inter-disciplinary way through industry to improve and to raise the quality and excellence of the environment in which we work and live.

Familiar examples of the material waste and erosion of the aesthetic environment which are very complex and which can only be solved on a multi-disciplinary basis are congestion and air and water pollution.

Healthy Growth of British Higher Education and Science

The creation of the Ministry of Higher Education and Science will help conserve scarce manpower needed in the effective monitoring and management of the science and development problems of the Government. This new Ministry can help to ensure the continued healthy growth of British higher education and science.

The recommendations made here for strengthening the present organisation and Government at policy level can achieve substantial improvements in the organisation and interrelation of various government departments and agencies supporting science and technology, and provide an overall focus and leadership for their activities. This leadership will reside in the Ministry of Higher Education and Science where the Minister, supported by the National Council for the Co-ordination of Science and Engineering and the Inter-Departmental Co-ordination Committee, can ensure the preparation and review of analyses and plans and the review of the role and responsibilities of the various government departments in science and technology.

Accordingly, the allocation of government support for science would reach up to the Cabinet by orderly examination of needs and aims of both departmental missions and national goals, would include consideration of government priorities and urgencies and would permit a comprehensive balancing of government resources.

In making these tentative recommendations we must emphasise that the strength of British science depends on the initiative, imagination and intelligence of individual working scientists and engineers.

The best possible programme formulated at the top can be made entirely ineffective by the people who are carrying it out. The purposes of organisation for science and engineering in the Government must be to ensure quicker identification and support of new ideas and maintain support for basic research and development to guarantee that the most important national technological jobs are tackled by the most able people.

These proposals are tentative and do not answer all the questions relating to these important problems. Listed below are problems to some of which this appendix has tried to give tentative answers.

(i)   What steps can and need be taken to provide the climate and the support for work in universities and colleges of technology related to the broad practical needs of our civilian economy and society?

(ii)   How can we best ensure that by-products of the defence research programme, once identified, should be developed quickly and exploited?

(iii) What is the best role that Government can play in the encouragement of applying the results of science and engineering to economic growth?

(iv) How can we best get British industry to employ development personnel who may also be working for their competitors and to encourage them to have forward planning for research and development?

(v)   What changes are needed in the machinery of Government to fit its action in detail to the need for (a) proper scientific development in

      industry, and (b) making certain that the administration of the
Government's own expenditure on science is organised to secure full
value for money in the light of our needs and resources?

(vi)   Should there be established in every government department dealing
with industry a scientific/economic staff to act as a forward policy
planning unit, advising the Minister on the technical and industrial
implications of the department's future policy plans, to gather economic
and technical information from the relevant industries, and generally
provide a technical intelligence service to the department?

(vii) How can we best encourage the establishment of the institutions and the
environment that most effectively puts science to practical use, diffuses
the results of technology throughout society and encourages even higher
levels of innovation activities?

(viii) Should there be greater interchange of staff in the Civil Service itself, and
between the Service, industry and the universities; should civil servants
be recruited from industry and the universities on temporary contracts or
seconded?

(ix)   How can we best convey the results of research in a form which points
the way to its practical applications?

(x)   How can we use science more effectively to aid underdeveloped
countries?

(xi)   We need new ways to improve Government-university relationships and
in the conduct of research and development in private industry.

(xii) How far should the Government go in establishing new research facilities
separate from universities and how far should it go to finance them as
part of universities proper?

(xiii) Is it possible to formulate general policies for the support of science and
to institutionalise a long-range planning system? This is perhaps
especially necessary for the support of special fields of research requiring
large and costly facilities, i.e. radio-astronomy, astronautics,
oceanography, high energy physics, etc.

(xiv) How can we raise the status of engineering in this country?

(xv) Can trade research associations, if given the resources, be relied upon to
disseminate technical information and encourage their member firms to
use technical innovations, and should they be provided with funds for
research and training by a compulsory levy on industry?

Government and science are now completely joined together in an
indispensable partnership. Government is dependent on science as an essential
resource for national security and welfare, while science cannot flourish
without government support.

AVERAGE GROWTH RATE (1950'S)
GNP PER WORKER AND PER CAPITA IN SELECTED NATIONS

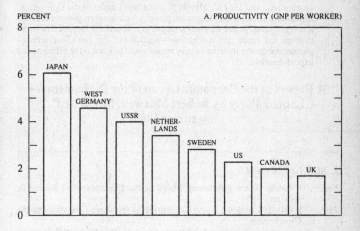

PERCENT · A. PRODUCTIVITY (GNP PER WORKER)

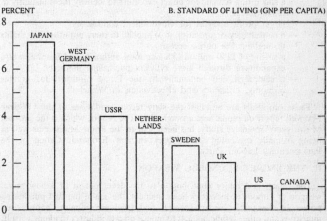

PERCENT · B. STANDARD OF LIVING (GNP PER CAPITA)

Source: "National Institute Economic Review" as quoted in "Economic Report of the President, 1962". "National Accounts Statistics, 1961", United Nations.

PUBLIC SECTOR PURCHASING

During 1963 and 1964 Mr Harold Wilson, then Leader of the Opposition, repeatedly stressed the enormous power which modern government has if it is prepared to use its great strength as a buyer. He intended to comb through the trade and navigation statistics and use the Government's purchasing power in order to save imports and to reward the efficient and export-minded.

A Report to the Economic Group of the Parliamentary Labour Party by Robert Maxwell, M.C., M.P. November 1967

I. MAIN PROPOSALS

First: - a Public Sector Purchasing Board at the Department of Economic Affairs;

Plus: - a City of London Liaison Committee to represent City views to the Government;
- two working parties to report direct to the Prime Minister on Nationalised Industry and local authority procurement policies;
- a star rating scheme for direct exporters to identify them instantly to Government;
- larger profit margins for Government contractors;
- a consultancy organisation in Whitehall to carry out efficiency audits throughout the public sector;
- a saving of £150 million (5%) on local authority and hospital board expenditure through more efficient purchasing methods;
- a campaign, led personally by the Prime Minister, for greater economy, efficiency and effectiveness in Whitehall.

These proposals are amongst the sixty recommendations of the 117-page Maxwell report on public sector purchasing. The report, which is the product of two years' intensive study, has been sent to the Prime Minister as well as being formally presented to the backbenchers' Economic Group of the Parliamentary Labour Party.

II. THE SECRET ECONOMIC WEAPON

The report is a major contribution to the development of a new secret weapon of Labour economic policies: namely, the use of the vast purchasing power of the public sector (central and local government, nationalised industries and other public bodies) to induce private industry to identify itself, in its own interests, with government economic objectives.

III. THE PUBLIC SECTOR

The public sector:
- spends (including transfers) 41% of the GNP;
- directly employs over 30% of the nation's manpower;
- employs two-thirds of those with fulltime higher education;
- owns about 50% of the nation's capital assets;
- accounts for over 50% of the nation's fixed investments;
- finances about 65% of the nation's scientific and technological research and development;
- takes nearly 60% of the output of the construction industry;
- plays a dominant role in not only the electronics and aircraft industries, but also in construction, pharmaceuticals, electrical engineering, telecommunications, power supply, etc.

IV. THEME

The central thesis of the report is that this colossal purchasing power and influence could and should be systematically used under central guidance to promote the Government's national industrial objectives, namely:

FIRST Technological advance
PRIORITY: Export encouragement and import substitution

OTHER: Prices and incomes policy
    Structural reorganisation
    Regional development

V. PUBLIC SECTOR PURCHASING BOARD (P.S.P.B.)

The report's central recommendation to spearhead this new policy weapon is the immediate setting up of a Public Sector Purchasing Board.

It would:
- have central responsibility for advising on and co-ordinating purchasing by all public agencies;
- report to the Prime Minister as overlord of the DEA, which would be the Board's sponsoring department;
- have as full-time chairman a businessman of national stature, assisted by a part-time Advisory Board representing public and private industry, local authorities and the IRC, NBPI and NRDC;
- be staffed by experienced businessmen and civil servants organised into three sections for central government, local government and nationalised industry purchasing;
- provide the "linchpin" of the many proposals in the report.

VI. GENERAL ECONOMIC ARGUMENT

The report's findings are set in the context of a general diagnosis of Britain's economic weaknesses.

"The UK's economic crisis has taken some thirty years to develop and we have three to five years to overcome it."

"British industry cannot be made speedily more efficient and productive by the blunt instruments of deflation and exhortation alone."

"In dealing with the central organisations of industry and the unions, CBI and TUC, the Government is dealing with ... the shadow rather than the substance of power ... at one remove from the actual centres of decision-making ... the boardrooms ... and the shop-floor."

"We have to rely on our own industrial and commercial potential, rapidly modernise it and make best use of it in order to break out from the vicious circle ... to enable Britain to find her role in the space age."

"The Commonwealth countries are of reduced economic or financial importance to us now.... We are unlikely to become full members of the Common Market before the early 1970s, if then. We have to pay off some £600 million in debts to the IMF by the end of 1970.... Our manufacturers and businessmen are having to compete in export markets where we have no built-in or historical advantages, often using lethargic or out-of-date production and sales techniques."

"These comparative export and import statistics (for 1964-67) and our just released September trade figures are most disturbing. They require urgent steps and speedy changes in the structure and sales techniques of our industries ... (they) must give rise to serious doubts about the competitiveness of British industry even in our home market."

"Unless Britain can quickly channel more investment, management and sales effort into export-intensive as well as import-saving industries, our position, still vulnerable, will get worse and *all the squeezing and freezing will have been in vain.*"

This analysis of "our chronic economic predicament" and of the futility of "the blunt instruments" of deflation and high unemployment prepares the way for the major positive premise of the report that "pressure from an important buyer *does* make private enterprise more amenable to mergers, speedy reorganisation and to reducing unit costs through improved efficiency".

Thus it was that when "we interviewed many industrialists and businessmen covering the entire spectrum of British industry and commerce ... they were by a large majority in favour of the Government using its resources in support of national economic policies *even in a directly discriminatory way as between firms*".

VII. CASE HISTORY

This general case for a positive purchasing policy (in contrast with the present laissez-faire freedom of spending agencies - analysed in Section 5 of the report) is powerfully reinforced by a detailed case study. It portrays the complete inability of Whitehall over a long period - despite excellent intentions - to help a British company which pioneered a new microfilm technology and achieved considerable export success. Its chances of achieving a decisive break-through in the face of keen competition from an established American giant in the same field were gravely reduced and almost ruined by lack of Government orders and by the impossibility under Whitehall's non-discrimination rules of establishing a British microfilm standard favourable to the British company. The favourable British standard has at last been agreed and announced, but only after the company had been forced by cash shortages to sell off its US subsidiary, thus sacrificing maximum rewards in the vital American market.

VIII. INDUSTRIAL EXPANSION BILL

The Maxwell report points out that discriminatory public purchasing can be a very important and inexpensive way of achieving the objectives "of this useful Bill", namely putting public money into successful industrial projects and ensuring that the taxpayer gets a fair share of any profits.

IX. PRICES AND INCOMES POLICY

The report suggests how the Government's purchasing power might be used to persuade industry to observe Prices and Incomes Board recommendations. Quite simply, through the DEA as joint sponsoring department for both Boards, the PIB would advise the PSPB which firms in an industry were least likely to co-operate with a PIB recommendation. The PSPB would then ensure that Government contracts were given to more compliant companies. Moreover, "trade unionists would be more receptive to the Government's prices and incomes policy if they could see this kind of discrimination in operation".

X. GOVERNMENT WHITE PAPER

On 25th May, 1967, the Government published its own White Paper (Command 3291) on Public Purchasing and Industrial Efficiency. Although only an interim report, it was greeted in the press and elsewhere as something of an anti-climax after the high hopes of 1964.

The Maxwell report comments that:
- the White Paper is welcome as evidence of the Government's willingness in theory to use its purchasing power to make industry more efficient;
- but, the Government's unreadiness to discriminate between firms "in support of its own major policy objectives" is surprising;
- the White Paper provides no effective support to the Prices and Incomes Policy;
- the White Paper only partly answers the main question, namely, whether Government purchasing should be deliberately used as an economic regulator.

XI. CITY LIAISON COMMITTEE

The idea behind the proposal for a City Liaison Committee is that over recent years the authority of the City's traditional spokesman, the Governor of the Bank of England, has been weakened. "The City is less inclined than ever before to accept that its views can be adequately represented by the Governor."

A permanent City Liaison Committee could:
- advise the PSPB;
- provide the City with a means of formulating, publicising and influencing general economic, fiscal, legal and commercial policies;

- provide a City secretariat;
- make better known and understood the City's worldwide commercial and financial services.

This recommendation takes account of the findings of the Bland Committee's report on "Britain's Invisible Earnings", published in October 1967.

XII. ORIGINS

Hugh Gaitskell, just before he died, asked Robert Maxwell to form a working party to examine how productivity could be increased through better and faster use of science and technology. When Harold Wilson became Leader of the Labour Party he asked Mr. Maxwell to continue the work. This resulted in a background paper, on behalf of a group of eminent scientists and engineers, which Mr. Maxwell presented in the summer of 1964 to a meeting on science, government and industry chaired by Mr. Wilson.

On entering Parliament in 1964 Mr. Maxwell persuaded the Parliamentary Labour Party's backbench Economic Group to study the topic in depth and was himself asked to do the initial work. He convened a working party of leading industrialists, civil servants and academics.

Informal written and oral evidence was also taken from senior and junior ministers as well as many other prominent businessmen, civil servants, bankers, academics, financial journalists and officials of foreign governments. Purchasing practices in the USA, West Germany, France, Sweden, Japan and even the USSR were all closely studied. This evidence is introduced throughout the report as and where it bears upon the argument.

The use of the Government's purchasing power to promote technological advance in industry and to help the export-import balance became an issue in the 1964 election campaign. Mr. Wilson said in Coventry on 6th October, "Nor do I need to stress the enormous power which a modern Government has - if it is prepared to use that power - through its own planning programmes, e.g. in mobilising the demand of our big social service Ministries, not to mention the tax authorities, in placing orders for computers and other modern equipment."

XIII. NEXT STEPS

The Maxwell report will shortly be discussed by the Economic Group of the Parliamentary Labour Party. If it is generally approved it is then likely that the Group will wish to have the Government's comments, including evidence that early action will be taken on the main recommendations.

Meanwhile, the Government has received copies of the report; and it is hoped that its findings will shortly be under study at a high level with a view to rapid action.

XIV. SECOND REPORT

The present report does not claim to be exhaustive. The Maxwell working party is still examining other aspects of the subject. They hope to issue "a second part of this report" later. This will contain the results of additional enquiries of nationalised industries, local authorities, trade associations and other interested organisations.

10 Downing Street
Whitehall

August 25, 1969

Dear Bob,

You wrote to me last February about your concern at our apparent lack of progress in the field of public purchasing and industrial efficiency, following the White Paper of May, 1967.

A good deal of work has in fact been going on under Treasury leadership in the major purchasing Departments and I am now in a position to tell you about some of the fruits of our labours.

It is not, of course, possible for me to tell you in a letter about all the follow-up action which we have been taking, but I would like to outline what we are doing in two broad fields; namely, first, Government schemes for quality assurance and technical evaluation and assistance to industry to improve its efficiency, and, secondly, standardisation and variety reduction in public sector purchasing.

Government schemes which provide assurance as to the quality of products and services include the Burghars Scheme for the assessment of electronic components, the Computer Advisory Service, the Agreement Board which certifies new construction materials, the Central Instrument Information Service and departmentally-sponsored evaluation at hospitals and universities, as well as in Government establishments, of new medical equipment and techniques. The year-old British Calibration Service is an essential service to technologically-advanced industry. As an example of work in this field intended to help exports, tripartite discussions are taking place with France and Germany on the mutual acceptance of certificates of quality and the alignment of technical requirements in such fields as pressure vessels and water supply equipment. Extension of the Burghars Scheme on an international basis is also being discussed. Help to industry provided by the Production Engineering Advisory Service and the National Computing Centre has been supplemented by the Low Cost Automation Centres at Colleges of Technology and Universities, the Numerical Control Advisory and Demonstration Service, and the Scheme for Government purchase of pre-production models of new machine tools and their allocation to representative users, including Government users, for assessment.

Secondly, standardisation and variety reduction in public sector purchasing. More and more, as we have studied these questions of public sector purchasing and industrial efficiency, we have come to see this as probably one of the key factors. In central Government we have already made considerable progress. For example, as a result of variety control substantial reductions have been effected in the number of purchasing specifications in the defence field. 9,500 items under 26 generic headings have been reduced to 2,080. Standard ranges of building and engineering installation components have been developed for use in hospitals. Also in the health field, in which special attention has been paid to export promotion, standard specifications have been produced for surgical appliances and footwear, hypodermic syringes, surgeons' gloves, hospital furniture, and blood transfusion and cervical cystology equipment. International harmonisation of standards in aid of exports is being pursued both through the B.S.I. and, at inter-Government level, through E.F.T.A. and in tripartite negotiations with France and Germany.

So far as co-ordination is concerned, the procurement of about two-thirds, by value, of all Government requirements is already centralised in the sense that one or another individual Department does the contracting on behalf of the others. Some goods bought centrally by Departments are supplied to other public sector bodies - e.g. office furniture and domestic requisites to universities and hospitals, and medical supplies to local health authorities, hospitals and practitioners. Under recent arrangements, a wide range of furniture, furnishings, domestic and kitchen equipment and fire-fighting appliances bought for Government use are being made available to nationalised industries generally and to a limited number of local authorities. The possibility of extending these arrangements to more products, and more authorities, and the possibility of reciprocal arrangements, are being explored.

In addition, departments have, in various ways, helped local authority consortia set up for the design and common use of buildings, pre-fabricated building components, school equipment and scientific instruments. In 1967-68 105 school building projects worth £13 million were started in an industrialised system designed and supplied by a major consortium of local education authorities.

But, of course, this is not enough. We need to extend this work and put it on a more systematic basis. You will have seen the report of the Joint Review Body for Local Authority Purchasing, which was published towards the end of last year. Its recommendations range from short-term measures (like the greater use of specialist purchasing officers and of existing powers for co-operation between neighbouring authorities), to major organisational innovations intended to enable local authorities to work better together, and to facilitate mutual help between them and the Government. Then we have to consider the nationalised industries, which account for a sizeable slice of total public sector purchasing. With this in mind, Jack Diamond has brought forward the proposal, which has been discussed with the Chairmen of all the major nationalised industries, to establish a small ginger group consisting of representatives of the relevant Government Departments, the nationalised industries and, in due course, the local authorities. The tasks of this group would be to invigorate and co-ordinate work on standardisation and variety reduction in the public sector already in progress; to identify candidates for further work on the basis of detailed statistics provided by the purchasing authorities; and to arrange for the necessary detailed work under the leadership of the predominant public purchaser of the products chosen. The objective of each study would be to secure the agreement of the purchasing authorities to buy the standardised product resulting from the study. I am pleased to say that the Chairmen of the nationalised industries have agreed to co-operate with the Government in setting up a high level group of this kind, and the details are now being worked out in the Treasury.

I have written at some length because I share your interest and belief in the importance of these questions. Moreover, if I may say so, we have been both encouraged and spurred on by the work which you yourself have done.

I would, however, like to ask you to treat this letter as written to you personally in confidence, for the time being, since our plans have not yet been disclosed outside the Government circle, save to the nationalised industry chairmen.

Yours,
Harold Wilson

Robert Maxwell, Esq., M.P.

APPENDIX 4

Pergamon Journals — 1988/89

ABSEES - Abstracts Soviet and East European Series
ACCIDENT ANALYSIS AND PREVENTION
ACCOUNTING, ORGANIZATIONS AND SOCIETY
ACTA ASTRONAUTICA
ACTA GEOLOGICA SINICA
ACTA MECHANICA SOLIDA SINICA
ACTA METALLURGICA
ACTA METEOROLOGICA SINICA
ACTA OCEANOLOGICA SINICA
ACTA SEISMOLOGICA SINICA
ACTA ZOOLOGICA
ACUPUNCTURE & ELECTRO-THERAPEUTICS RESEARCH
ADDICTIVE BEHAVIORS
ADHESIVES ABSTRACTS
ADVANCES IN BEHAVIOUR RESEARCH AND THERAPY
ADVANCES IN ENZYME REGULATION
ADVANCES IN OPHTHALMIC PLASTIC AND RECONSTRUCTIVE SURGERY
ADVANCES IN SPACE RESEARCH
ADVANCES IN THE BIOSCIENCES
ALCOHOL (incorporating ALCOHOL AND DRUG RESEARCH)
ALCOHOL AND ALCOHOLISM
AMBIO
ANALYSIS MATHEMATICA
ANNALS OF BIOMEDICAL ENGINEERING
ANNALS OF NUCLEAR ENERGY
THE ANNALS OF OCCUPATIONAL HYGIENE
ANNALS OF THE ICRP
ANNALS OF TOURISM RESEARCH
ANNUAL REVIEW IN AUTOMATIC PROGRAMMING
ANNUAL REVIEW OF CHRONOPHARMACOLOGY
APPLIED GEOCHEMISTRY
APPLIED MATHEMATICS LETTERS
AQUA

AQUALINE ABSTRACTS
ARCHIVES OF CLINICAL NEUROPSYCHOLOGY
ARCHIVES OF ORAL BIOLOGY
THE ARTS IN PSYCHOTHERAPY
ATMOSPHERIC ENVIRONMENT
AUTOMATICA
BANKING WORLD
BEHAVIORAL ASSESSMENT
BEHAVIOUR CHANGE
BEHAVIOUR RESEARCH AND THERAPY
THE BEST OF LONG RANGE PLANNING
BIOCHEMICAL EDUCATION
BIOCHEMICAL PHARMACOLOGY
BIOCHEMICAL SYSTEMATICS AND ECOLOGY
BIOGENIC AMINES
BIOPHYSICS
BIORHEOLOGY
BIOTECHNOLOGY ADVANCES
BONE
BRAIN RESEARCH BULLETIN (incorporating JOURNAL OF ELECTROPHYSIOLOGICAL TECHNIQUES)
BRITISH DEFENCE DIRECTORY (inc DEFENCE ATTACHE)
BRITISH MEDICINE
BUILDING AND ENVIRONMENT
BULLETIN OF LATIN AMERICAN RESEARCH
BULLETIN OF MATHEMATICAL BIOLOGY
CALPHAD
CANADIAN METALLURGICAL QUARTERLY
CARBON
CELLULAR AND MOLECULAR BIOLOGY
CEMENT AND CONCRETE RESEARCH
CENTRAL ASIAN SURVEY
CHEMICAL ENGINEERING SCIENCE
CHEMOSPHERE

CHILD ABUSE & NEGLECT
CHILDREN AND YOUTH SERVICES
REVIEW
CHINA OCEAN ENGINEERING
CHINESE ASTRONOMY AND
ASTROPHYSICS
CHINESE JOURNAL OF MECHANICAL
ENGINEERING
CHINESE SCIENCE ABSTRACTS
Series A
CHINESE SCIENCE ABSTRACTS
Series B
CHROMATOGRAPHIA
CHRONOBIOLOGY INTERNATIONAL
CLINICAL BIOCHEMISTRY
CLINICAL BIOCHEMISTRY REVIEWS
New Series (Published each alternate
year)
CLINICAL HEMORHEOLOGY
CLINICAL PSYCHOLOGY REVIEW
CLINICAL VISION SCIENCES
COMPARATIVE BIOCHEMISTRY AND
PHYSIOLOGY Part A: Comparative
Physiology
COMPARATIVE BIOCHEMISTRY AND
PHYSIOLOGY Part B: Comparative
Biochemistry
COMPARATIVE BIOCHEMISTRY AND
PHYSIOLOGY Part C: Comparative
Pharmacology and Toxicology
COMPARATIVE IMMUNOLOGY,
MICROBIOLOGY AND
INFECTIOUS DISEASES
COMPUTER LANGUAGES
COMPUTER STATE OF THE ART
REPORTS
COMPUTERIZED MEDICAL IMAGING
AND GRAPHICS (formerly
COMPUTERIZED RADIOLOGY)
COMPUTERS & CHEMICAL
ENGINEERING
COMPUTERS & CHEMISTRY
COMPUTERS & EDUCATION
COMPUTERS & ELECTRICAL
ENGINEERING
COMPUTERS & FLUIDS
COMPUTERS & GEOSCIENCES
COMPUTERS & GRAPHICS
COMPUTERS & INDUSTRIAL
ENGINEERING
COMPUTERS & MATHEMATICS WITH
APPLICATIONS
COMPUTERS & OPERATIONS
RESEARCH
COMPUTERS & STRUCTURES
COMPUTERS IN BIOLOGY AND
MEDICINE
COMPUTERS IN HUMAN BEHAVIOR
COMPUTERS, ENVIRONMENT AND
URBAN SYSTEMS
CONTINENTAL SHELF RESEARCH
CONTINENTAL SHELF RESEARCH
with OCEANOGRAPHIC
LITERATURE REVIEW
CORROSION SCIENCE
COSPAR INFORMATION BULLETIN
CURRENT ADVANCES IN
BIOCHEMISTRY
CURRENT ADVANCES IN CANCER
RESEARCH
CURRENT ADVANCES IN CELL &
DEVELOPMENTAL BIOLOGY
CURRENT ADVANCES IN CLINICAL
CHEMISTRY
CURRENT ADVANCES IN
ECOLOGICAL SCIENCES
CURRENT ADVANCES IN
ENDOCRINOLOGY
CURRENT ADVANCES IN GENETICS
& MOLECULAR BIOLOGY
CURRENT ADVANCES IN
IMMUNOLOGY
CURRENT ADVANCES IN
MICROBIOLOGY
CURRENT ADVANCES IN
NEUROSCIENCE
CURRENT ADVANCES IN
PHARMACOLOGY &
TOXICOLOGY
CURRENT ADVANCES IN
PHYSIOLOGY
CURRENT ADVANCES IN PLANT
SCIENCE
CURRENT AWARENESS IN
BIOLOGICAL SCIENCES
DATABASE TECHNOLOGY
DEEP-SEA RESEARCH with
OCEANOGRAPHIC LITERATURE
REVIEW
DEFENSE ANALYSIS
DEVELOPMENTAL AND
COMPARATIVE IMMUNOLOGY
DRUG INFORMATION JOURNAL
ECONOMIC BULLETIN FOR EUROPE
ECONOMICS OF EDUCATION
REVIEW
ECOTASS (English edition)
ECOTASS (French edition)
ECOTASS (Italian edition)
EKOTASS (German edition)
ELECTRIC TECHNOLOGY USSR
ELECTROCHIMICA ACTA
ELECTRON MICROSCOPY REVIEWS

INTERNATIONAL JOURNAL OF IMMUNOPHARMACOLOGY

INTERNATIONAL JOURNAL OF INTERCULTURAL RELATIONS

INTERNATIONAL JOURNAL OF MICROGRAPHICS & VIDEO TECHNOLOGY

INTERNATIONAL JOURNAL OF HOSPITALITY MANAGEMENT

INTERNATIONAL JOURNAL OF IMPACT ENGINEERING

INTERNATIONAL JOURNAL OF DEVELOPMENTAL NEUROSCIENCE

INTERNATIONAL JOURNAL OF EDUCATIONAL DEVELOPMENT

INTERNATIONAL JOURNAL OF PLASTICITY

INTERNATIONAL JOURNAL OF RADIATION APPLICATIONS AND INSTRUMENTATION Parts A B C D & E

INTERNATIONAL JOURNAL OF RADIATION APPLICATIONS AND INSTRUMENTATION Part E: Nuclear Geophysics

INTERNATIONAL PACKAGING ABSTRACTS

JOURNAL OF ACCOUNTING EDUCATION

JOURNAL OF AEROSOL SCIENCE

JOURNAL OF AFRICAN EARTH SCIENCES

JOURNAL OF ANXIETY DISORDERS

JOURNAL OF APPLIED CARDIOLOGY

JOURNAL OF APPLIED MATHEMATICS AND MECHANICS

JOURNAL OF ATMOSPHERIC AND TERRESTRIAL PHYSICS

JOURNAL OF BEHAVIOR THERAPY AND EXPERIMENTAL PSYCHIATRY

JOURNAL OF BIOMECHANICS

THE JOURNAL OF CANCER EDUCATION

JOURNAL OF CHEMICAL INDUSTRY & ENGINEERING (CHINA)

JOURNAL OF CHILD PSYCHOLOGY AND PSYCHIATRY

JOURNAL OF CLINICAL EPIDEMIOLOGY (formerly JOURNAL OF CHRONIC DISEASES)

JOURNAL OF CRIMINAL JUSTICE

JOURNAL OF EMERGENCY MEDICINE

JOURNAL OF INSECT PHYSIOLOGY

JOURNAL OF PHARMACEUTICAL AND BIOMEDICAL ANALYSIS

JOURNAL OF PHYSICS AND CHEMISTRY OF SOLIDS

THE JOURNAL OF PRODUCTS LIABILITY

JOURNAL OF PSYCHIATRIC RESEARCH

JOURNAL OF PSYCHOSOMATIC RESEARCH

JOURNAL OF QUANTITATIVE SPECTROSCOPY & RADIATIVE TRANSFER

JOURNAL OF RURAL STUDIES

JOURNAL OF SAFETY RESEARCH

JOURNAL OF SCHOOL PSYCHOLOGY

JOURNAL OF SCIENTIFIC EXPLORATION

JOURNAL OF SOUTH AMERICAN EARTH SCIENCES

JOURNAL OF SOUTH-EAST ASIAN EARTH SCIENCES

THE JOURNAL OF STEROID BIOCHEMISTRY

JOURNAL OF STORED PRODUCTS RESEARCH

JOURNAL OF STRUCTURAL GEOLOGY

JOURNAL OF SUBSTANCE ABUSE TREATMENT

JOURNAL OF TERRAMECHANICS

JOURNAL OF THE FRANKLIN INSTITUTE

JOURNAL OF THE MECHANICS AND PHYSICS OF SOLIDS

JOURNAL OF THE OPERATIONAL RESEARCH SOCIETY

JOURNAL OF THERMAL BIOLOGY

LANGUAGE & COMMUNICATION

LAW AND MENTAL HEALTH

LEONARDO

LEUKEMIA RESEARCH

LIBRARY ACQUISITIONS, PRACTICE AND THEORY

LIFE SCIENCES

LONG RANGE PLANNING

MAGNETIC RESONANCE IMAGING

MANAGEMENT AND MARKETING ABSTRACTS

MARINE POLLUTION BULLETIN

MATERIALS AND SOCIETY

MATERIALS RESEARCH BULLETIN

MATHEMATICAL AND COMPUTER MODELLING

MECHANICS RESEARCH COMMUNICATIONS

MECHANISM AND MACHINE THEORY

MEDICAL DOSIMETRY
MEDICAL ONCOLOGY AND TUMOR PHARMACOTHERAPY
MICROELECTRONICS AND RELIABILITY
MICRON AND MICROSCOPICA ACTA
MINERALS ENGINEERING
MOLECULAR ASPECTS OF MEDICINE
MOLECULAR IMMUNOLOGY
NEURAL NETWORKS
NEUROBIOLOGY OF AGING
NEUROCHEMISTRY INTERNATIONAL
NEUROPHARMACOLOGY
NEUROPSYCHOLOGIA
NEUROSCIENCE
NEUROSCIENCE AND BIOBEHAVIORAL REVIEWS
NEUROTOXICOLOGY & TERATOLOGY
NEW IDEAS IN PSYCHOLOGY
NONLINEAR ANALYSIS
NUCLEAR AND CHEMICAL WASTE MANAGEMENT
NUTRITION RESEARCH
OCEAN ENGINEERING
OMEGA
OPEC REVIEW
ORGANIC GEOCHEMISTRY
OUTLOOK ON AGRICULTURE
PAINT TITLES
PAPER AND BOARD ABSTRACTS
PATTERN RECOGNITION
PEPTIDES
PERITONEAL DIALYSIS INTERNATIONAL
PERSONALITY AND INDIVIDUAL DIFFERENCES
PETROLEUM CHEMISTRY USSR
PHARMACOLOGY & THERAPEUTICS
PHARMACOLOGY BIOCHEMISTRY & BEHAVIOR
PHOTOCHEMISTRY AND PHOTOBIOLOGY
PHYSICOCHEMICAL HYDRODYNAMICS
PHYSICS AND CHEMISTRY OF THE EARTH
THE PHYSICS OF METALS AND METALLOGRAPHY
PHYSIOLOGY & BEHAVIOR
PHYTOCHEMISTRY
PLANETARY AND SPACE SCIENCE
PLASMA PHYSICS AND CONTROLLED FUSION

POLYHEDRON
POLYMER SCIENCE USSR
PREVIEWS OF HEAT AND MASS TRANSFER
PRINTING ABSTRACTS
PROBLEMS OF CONTROL AND INFORMATION THEORY
PROGRESS IN AEROSPACE SCIENCES
PROGRESS IN ANALYTICAL SPECTROSCOPY
PROGRESS IN BIOPHYSICS & MOLECULAR BIOLOGY
PROGRESS IN CRYSTAL GROWTH AND CHARACTERIZATION
PROGRESS IN ENERGY AND COMBUSTION SCIENCE
PROGRESS IN FOOD & NUTRITION SCIENCE
PROGRESS IN LIPID RESEARCH
PROGRESS IN MATERIALS SCIENCE
PROGRESS IN NEURO-PSYCHOPHARMACOLOGY AND BIOLOGICAL PSYCHIATRY
PROGRESS IN NEUROBIOLOGY
PROGRESS IN NUCLEAR ENERGY
PROGRESS IN NUCLEAR MAGNETIC RESONANCE SPECTROSCOPY
PROGRESS IN OCEANOGRAPHY
PROGRESS IN PARTICLE AND NUCLEAR PHYSICS
PROGRESS IN PLANNING
PROGRESS IN POLYMER SCIENCE
PROGRESS IN QUANTUM ELECTRONICS
PROGRESS IN REACTION KINETICS
PROGRESS IN RETINAL RESEARCH
PROGRESS IN SOLID STATE CHEMISTRY
PROGRESS IN SURFACE SCIENCE
PROTIDES OF THE BIOLOGICAL FLUIDS
PSYCHONEUROENDOCRINOLOGY
PUBLISHING AND NEW MEDIA TECHNOLOGY NEWSLETTER
QUATERNARY SCIENCE REVIEWS
RAPRA ABSTRACTS
RAPRA NEW TRADE NAMES IN THE RUBBER AND PLASTICS INDUSTRIES
RAPRA REVIEW REPORTS
REHABILITATION EDUCATION
REPORTS ON MATHEMATICAL PHYSICS
REPRODUCTIVE & GENETIC ENGINEERING: Journal of International Feminist Analysis

REPRODUCTIVE TOXICOLOGY

RESEARCH IN DEVELOPMENTAL DISABILITIES (incorporating APPLIED RESEARCH IN MENTAL RETARDATION and ANALYSIS AND INTERVENTION IN DEVELOPMENTAL DISABILITIES)

RESOURCES, CONSERVATION &RECYCLING (incorporating CONSERVATION & RECYCLING and RESOURCES AND CONSERVATION)

REVIEWS OF MAGNETIC RESONANCE IN MEDICINE

RHEOLOGY ABSTRACTS

ROBOTICS AND COMPUTER-INTEGRATED MANUFACTURING

SCIENCE BULLETIN (KEXUE TONGBAO)

SCIENTIA SINICA (SCIENCE IN CHINA) Series A

SCIENTIA SINICA (SCIENCE IN CHINA) Series B

SCRIPTA METALLURGICA

SELECTIVE ELECTRODE REVIEWS

SOCIAL SCIENCE & MEDICINE

SOCIO-ECONOMIC PLANNING SCIENCES

SOIL BIOLOGY & BIOCHEMISTRY

SOLAR & WIND TECHNOLOGY

SOLAR ENERGY

SOLID STATE COMMUNICATIONS

SOLID-STATE ELECTRONICS

SOLUBILITY DATA SERIES

SPACE TECHNOLOGY: Industrial and Commercial Applications (formerly EARTH-ORIENTED APPLICATIONS OF SPACE TECHNOLOGY)

SPECTROCHIMICA ACTA Part A: Molecular Spectroscopy

SPECTROCHIMICA ACTA Part B: Atomic Spectroscopy

STUDIES IN EDUCATIONAL EVALUATION

STUDIES IN HISTORY AND PHILOSOPHY OF SCIENCE

SYSTEM

SYSTEMS RESEARCH

TALANTA

TEACHING & TEACHER EDUCATION

TECHNOLOGY IN SOCIETY

TELEMATICS AND INFORMATICS

TETRAHEDRON

TETRAHEDRON LETTERS

THROMBOSIS RESEARCH

TOPOLOGY

TOXICOLOGY IN VITRO

TOXICON

TRANSPORTATION RESEARCH Part A: General

TRANSPORTATION RESEARCH Part B: Methodological

TUNNELLING AND UNDERGROUND SPACE TECHNOLOGY

ULTRASOUND IN MEDICINE & BIOLOGY

URBAN ATMOSPHERE

USSR COMPUTATIONAL MATHEMATICS AND MATHEMATICAL PHYSICS

VACUUM

VERTICA

VISION RESEARCH

VISTAS IN ASTRONOMY

WATER QUALITY INTERNATIONAL

WATER RESEARCH

WATER SCIENCE AND TECHNOLOGY

WATER SUPPLY

WELDING IN THE WORLD

WOMEN'S STUDIES INTERNATIONAL FORUM

WORLD DEVELOPMENT

WORLD ENGLISHES

WORLD PATENT INFORMATION

WORLD SURFACE COATINGS ABSTRACTS

YAD VASHEM STUDIES

ZOOLOGICA SCRIPTA

The following leading article, signed by Robert Maxwell, appeared in the *Daily Mirror* of November 25, 1985. Only 30,000 copies of the paper were printed that day because of an industrial dispute. The article was reprinted the following day.

THE MIRROR   Tuesday, November 26, 1985

FLEET ST.
The party is over

From yesterday's Mirror, the article most of you did not see.

For years the newspapers of Fleet Street have told the rest of Britain how to run its business. How to be efficient. Competitive. Modern.

And all the time, Fleet Street has been the most inefficient, uncompetitive and old-fashioned industry in the country.

Fleet Street has lectured everyone else about cutting their costs. And indulged in a spending spree itself.

It looked as if the good life would never end. But now it is about to.

THE GRAVY TRAIN HAS HIT THE BUFFERS.

The *Mirror* has been the first newspaper group to face the facts. Therefore, it is the first to suffer the backlash.

Like every other Fleet Street paper, we spend too much and employ too many. Mirror Group Newspapers sell over 30,000,000 copies each week and lose money!

Other groups are on the same train. In Mr Rupert Murdoch's *Times* on Saturday, Sir Woodrow Wyatt said that *The Sun*, another Murdoch newspaper, pays over £40,000 a year to its piecework Linotype operators.

Austin Rover may as well pay vast salaries to men to walk in front of the cars it produces and wave a red flag.

The average wage of a Fleet Street print production worker is between £20,000 and £25,000 a year for a 25-30-hour, four-day week, with a minimum of six weeks' holiday a year.

Journalists on the Fleet Street popular papers average £22,000 a year or more. Plus expenses.

For our readers - for the rest of Britain - our industry must look like Christmas every day.

But now the cash flow is drying up.

The *Sunday* and *Daily Telegraph* are in deep trouble. Next year's agreed pay rises have been cancelled.

The Express Group - *Sunday Express*, the *Daily Express* and *The Star* - needs to cut its workforce by at least 2,000.

The *Guardian*, the *Daily Mail*, the *Mail on Sunday*, *The Observer*, the *Financial Times* and the others all face similar problems.

But the popular papers face the biggest.

Mr Eddie Shah will produce his new newspaper in the spring. It won't be as good as the *Mirror*. It may not be as good as the rest of Fleet Street's papers.

But it will cost him only half as much to produce.

After a disastrous dispute last August, none of our papers was published for nearly a fortnight.

It demonstrated that some of our unions weren't serious in joining me in ending the inefficiency and waste of a generation.

In October, workers at Thomson Withy Grove in Manchester, who print the Northern editions of the *Mirror* and *Sunday Mirror*, stopped work in a dispute with their employers - not the Mirror Group.

The general secretary of SOGAT '82 then prevented her members in London - in flagrant breach of the Return to Work Agreement reached after the previous stoppage - from printing sufficient copies of the *Mirror* to make up for the loss on the Manchester print.

Enough was enough.

Action was inevitable if we were to make our papers competitive, modern and profitable and able to safeguard the jobs of most of our employees.

First and foremost, with 11 unions and more than 60 negotiating committees with whom we had to bargain, a strict timetable was necessary.

The immediate necessity was to cut our costs by a third. Eighty per cent of the costs are labour.

That means producing our papers by employing only those we need.

But no one will be harshly treated. Indeed, those who stay with us have been promised a 10 per cent wage rise next year. Those who leave will be treated very generously.

Long-service employees can leave, in some cases with tax-free payments of up to nearly £40,000, plus a pension. Everyone over 50 is eligible for a lump sum plus pension.

The under-50s will be given deferred pensions of much greater value. A man of 35, with only five years' service, would be able to draw a pension of over £13,000 from MGN when he reaches retirement age - whatever job he does after he leaves our employment.

Jobs have got to go. All the unions know that. Costs have got to be cut. Every union knows that too.

The need for decisions is urgent. No one doubts that. Every union at MGN - except the largest, SOGAT '82 - has started positive discussions with us.

And for each of those unions, the dismissal notices MGN was forced to issue have been suspended.

SOGAT alone refused to talk while the notices existed. We offered to withdraw the notices if SOGAT would give a guarantee that negotiations would be concluded by December 7, failing which the Company would have to impose a settlement.

SOGAT said No again. Instead, it called a strike from mid-day yesterday.

It still thinks it can buy an everlasting ticket for the gravy train. Well, it can't and it won't.

Despite the strike, the Mirror Group is determined to publish its newspapers.

We know that is what the vast majority of our employees want to do. They want to work. They want to see the *Mirror* succeed. They want a well-paid job, not social security and the dole.

We are taking this stand for our sake and for the sake of our employees and their families. We are also doing it for the rest of Fleet Street and the country.

The time has come for Fleet Street to face the realities which the rest of Britain have known for so long.

ITS WILD AND WASTEFUL PARTY IS TRULY OVER.

**Robert Maxwell, Publisher,
Mirror Group Newspapers**

---

6 THE GRAVY TRAIN HAS HIT THE BUFFERS 9

From P L Kapitza

28 April 1938, Moscow

To: J V Stalin

Comrade Stalin!

Today a scientific worker of our Institute, L D Landau, was arrested. Although he is only 29, he and Fock are the major theoretical physicists in the Soviet Union. His work on magnetism and on quantum theory is often cited in the literature, both at home and in other countries. Only last year he published a remarkable work, where for the first time he demonstrated a new source of energy in radiation from the stars. This work makes it possible to answer the question: "Why do the energy of the sun and the stars not decrease with the passage of time, and why have they not already been exhausted?" The great future of these ideas has been acknowledged by Bohr and other leading scholars.

There is no doubt that the loss of Landau as a scholar in our Institute will not escape notice both in Soviet and in World Science and will be keenly felt. Of course scholarship and talent, no matter how great they may be, do not give a man the right to break the laws of his country, and if Landau is guilty he must pay the penalty. But I beg you in view of his remarkable talent to give the necessary orders so that his affair can be attended to with great care. It seems to me that one ought to take account of his character which, I have to admit, is simply awful. He is a tease and a bully, he likes to detect mistakes in other people's work, and when he finds it, particularly in the older people, like our academicians, then he teases them in a most irreverent manner. By this he has earned himself many enemies.

It has not been easy to deal with him in our Institute, although he had paid heed to reprimand and has become better. I have excused his behaviour in view of his remarkable giftedness. But despite all his faults of character, it is extremely difficult for me to believe that Landau would be capable of any dishonourable behaviour.

Landau is a young man, there is still a great deal for him to do in Science. No-one but another scholar could write about that, which is why I am writing to you.

P Kapitza

From P L Kapitza

6 April 1939

To: L P Beria

Please release from under detention, Professor of Physics Lev Landau whom you have arrested and deliver him into my personal supervision.

I swear to the NKVD that Landau will not conduct any counter-revolutionary activities against the Soviet authorities in my Institute and I shall take all the measures I can to ensure that he will not conduct any counter-revolutionary activities outside the Institute either. If I hear from Landau any comment harmful to the Soviet authorities then I will immediately communicate this fact to the organs of the NKVD.

P Kapitza

From P L Kapitza

3l March 1940, Moscow

To: V M Molotov

Comrade Molotov!

In connection with the forthcoming elections to the Academy of Sciences I have been asked by O U Schmidt, since Academician Vavilov is ill, to discuss with outstanding physicists like Joffe and Vavilov and to put forward a list of possible candidates. The scientific community has unanimously pointed out Landau as a very strong candidate. But they do not know that he is under my supervision. Since I do not know any of the other comrades in our leadership, except yourself, who are also aware of this, then I have decided to trouble you on this question in order to ask, is this fact an obstacle to my putting him forward as a candidate?

I have to say that Landau's character has improved; he has become a more gentle and more disciplined man and if he continues in this way then, quite possibly, he will become an altogether tolerable fellow. From the point of view of science he is working a great deal and, as ever, brilliantly. In the past year he has completed two good and major works.

In order not to cause you unnecessary trouble, if I do not receive instructions from you by the end of the six days (the period in which the lists must be presented to Schmidt) then I shall conclude that Landau's candidature can be put forward.

P Kapitza

SOURCES AND SELECT BIBLIOGRAPHY

Unpublished Sources

In writing this work I have had full access to an extensive range of private family documents relating to personal, business and legal aspects of Maxwell's life. The family "Birthday book", presented to Maxwell in 1983, and the contributions of editors and authors in 1988 have also proved particularly valuable. In addition, interviews with Maxwell, his relatives, friends, colleagues and associates in his many spheres of activity have been an important basic source.

Published Sources

The published works which I have found especially useful include the family's archive of newspaper cuttings, 1945-88, and radio and television interviews with Maxwell. I include in this select bibliography only books of direct relevance to Maxwell's life story.

Appleton, J.A. *Military Tribunals and International Crimes*, Greenwood Press, Connecticut, 1954.

Baker, Captain Peter, MC. *My Testament*, John Calder, London, 1955.

Bauer, Lieutenant-Colonel E. *The History of World War 2*, Orbis, London, 1966.

Bauer, Yehuda. *A History of the Holocaust*, Franklin Watts, New York, 1982.

Benn, Tony. *Out of the Wilderness, Diaries 1963-67*, Hutchinson, London, 1987.

Bullock, Alan. *Ernest Bevin, Foreign Secretary*, Heinemann, London, 1983.

Cave Brown, Anthony. *Bodyguard of Lies*, W.H. Allen, London, 1976.

Cook, H.C.B. *The North Staffordshire Regiment*, Leo Cooper Ltd, London, 1970.

Cookridge, E.H. *Inside SOE*, Arthur Barker Ltd, London, 1966.

Crossman, Richard. *The Backbench Diaries of a Cabinet Minister*, Hamish Hamilton and Jonathan Cape, London, 1981.

Crossman, Richard. *The Diaries of a Cabinet Minister*, Hamish Hamilton and Jonathan Cape, London, 1975, 1976, 1977.

Cudlipp, Hugh. *Walking on Water*, Bodley Head, London, 1976.

Davis, William. *Merger Mania*, Constable & Co, London, 1970.

Dicker, Herman. *Piety and Perseverance, Jews from the Carpathian Mountains*, Sepher-Hermon, New York, 1981.

Domarus, Max. *Hitler*, Munich, 1962.

Encyclopaedia of World War 2, edited by T. Parrish, Secker & Warburg, London, 1978.

Encyclopaedia Judaica, Jerusalem, 1971.

Evans, Harold. *Good Times, Bad Times*, Weidenfeld & Nicolson, London, 1983.

Fermor, Patrick Leigh. *A Time of Gifts*, Penguin, London, 1977.

Foot, M.R.D. *SOE, 1940-1946*, BBC, London, 1984.

Foster, Major R.C.G., MC. *History of the Queen's Royal Regiment*, Vol. VIII, Gale & Polden, Aldershot, 1953.

Garlinski, J. *The Swiss Corridor*, J.M. Dent, London, 1981.

Gilbert, Martin. *The Holocaust*, Collins, London, 1986.

Giskes, H.J. *London Calling North Pole*, William Kimber, London, 1953.

Herbert, Ivor. *The Way to the Top*, Robert Maxwell, London, 1969.

Hilberg, Raul. *The Destruction of European Jews*, Holmes & Meier, New York, 1985.

Horrocks, Sir B. *A Full Life*, Leo Cooper, London, 1974.

Jones, H. Kay. *Butterworths, History of a Publishing House*, Butterworth, London, 1980.

Kay, William. *Tycoons*, Piatkus, London, 1985.

King, Cecil. *The Cecil King Diary*, Jonathan Cape, London, 1972, 1975

Kramish, Arnold. *The Griffin*, Houghton Mifflin, Boston, 1986.

Kulka, Erich. *Jews in the Czechoslovak Armed Forces Abroad During World War II, The Jews of Czechoslovakia*, Vol. III, Jewish Publication Society of America, Philadelphia, 1984.

Loebl, Eugene. *Sentenced and Tried*, Elek, London, 1969.

Malice in Wonderland, Edited by Joe Haines and Peter Donnelly, Macdonald, London, 1986.

Marmaros, The Book of, In Memory of 160 Jewish Communities, Beit Marmaros, Tel Aviv, 1983, private translation.

McKay, Ron and Barr, Brian. *The Story of the Scottish Daily News*, Canongate, Edinburgh, 1976.

Michel, H. *The Second World War*, A. Deutsch, 1975.

Mills, John. *Famous Firsts*, Weidenfeld & Nicolson, London, 1984.

Moore, H. and Barrett, J. *Who Killed Hitler?*, Booktab Press, New York, 1947.

Patric, John. Czechoslovaks, Yankees of Europe, *National Geographic Magazine*, Vol. LXXIV, July-December 1938, pp. 173-225.

Payne, Robert. *The Life and Death of Adolf Hitler*, Jonathan Cape, London, 1973.

Piekalkiewicz, Janusz. *Secret Agents, Spies and Saboteurs*, David & Charles, Newton Abbot, 1974.

Regan, Simon. *Rupert Murdoch, A Business Biography*, Angus & Robertson, London, 1976.

Rhodes-Wood, Major E.H. *A War History of the Royal Pioneer Corps, 1939-45*, Gale & Polden, Aldershot, 1960.

Rothkirchen, Livia. Deep-Rooted Yet Alien: Some Aspects of the History of the Jews in Subcarpathian Ruthenia, *Yad Vashem Studies*, Vol. XII (1977).

Shirer, William L. *The Rise and Fall of the Third Reich*, Secker & Warburg, London, 1960.

Shirer, William L. *End of a Berlin Diary*, Hamish Hamilton, London, 1947.

Smith, Lorna Steward. *Hungary: Land and People*, Athenaeum, Budapest, 1933.

Street, C.J. *East of Prague*, Geoffrey Bles, London, 1924.

Toland, John. *Adolf Hitler*, Doubleday and Co, New York, 1976.

Trevor-Roper, H.R. *The Last Days of Hitler*, Macmillan, London, 1956.

Trevor-Roper, H.R. *The Testament of Adolf Hitler*, Cassell, London, 1951.

Universal Jewish Encyclopaedia, New York, 1969.

Von Knierem, August. *The Nüremberg Trials*, Henry Regnery Co, Chicago, 1959.

Wiesel, Elie. *One Generation After*, Schocken, New York, 1982.

Wilmot, Chester. *The Struggle for Europe*, Collins, London, 1952.

Windsor, Philip. *City on Leave, A History of Berlin, 1945-1962*, Chatto & Windus, London, 1963.

REFERENCES

Chapter 1: Contrasts and Paradoxes

Contributions from the 1983 "Birthday book" and from the Pergamon editors' contributions of 1988 were useful in the writing of this chapter.

1. Herbert, Ivor. *The Way to the Top*, Robert Maxwell, London, 1969, pp. 146-7.

2. *Daily Mail*, 15 June 1973.

3. Captain "Crash" Abbotts to Mr Maxwell, 5 October 1969.

4. *Lancashire Evening Telegraph*, 15 January 1983.

5. *Midweek* programme, 12 June 1973.

6. *Wall Street Journal*, 19 May 1987.

7. *Financial Times*, 27 May 1987.

8. *Scotsman*, 20 June 1986.

9. *New Statesman*, 18 July 1986.

10. *Sunday Express*, 16 December 1984.

11. *The Mail on Sunday*, 16 December 1984.

12. *Financial Times*, 8 December 1984

13. *The Times*, 5 December 1984.

14. *The Observer*, 9 December 1984.

Chapter 2: Escape from Poverty

In describing Solotvino and Maxwell's early life there, I have made use of the contributions of his relatives and friends recorded in the "Birthday book". Information gathered by Mrs Maxwell in interviews with relatives and friends in the USA and Israel has also proved invaluable.

1. Rothkirchen, Livia. Deep-Rooted Yet Alien: Some Aspects of the History of the Jews in Subcarpathian Ruthenia, *Yad Vashem Studies*, Vol. XII (1977), p. 147.

2. Steward Smith, Lorna. *Hungary: Land and People*, Athenaeum, Budapest, 1933, p. 142.

3. Patric, John. Czechoslovaks, Yankees of Europe, *National Geographic Magazine*, Vol. LXXIV, July-December 1938, p. 212.

4. Wiesel, Elie. *One Generation After*, Schocken, New York, 1982, p. 14.

5. Dicker, Herman. *Piety and Perseverance, Jews from the Carpathian Mountains*, Sepher-Hermon, New York, 1981, p. 50.

6. Mills, John. *Famous Firsts*, Weidenfeld & Nicolson, London, 1984, p. 116.

7. Fermor, Pa.rick Leigh. *A Time of Gifts*, Penguin, London, 1977, pp. 231-2.

8. Shirer, William L. *The Rise and Fall of the Third Reich*, Secker & Warburg, London, 1960, p. 392.

9. Bauer, Lieutenant-Colonel E. *The History of World War 2*, Orbis, London, 1966, p. 9.

10. Shirer, William L. Op. cit., p. 377.

11. Ibid, p. 388.

12. Hilberg, Raul. *The Destruction of European Jews*, Holmes & Meier, New York, 1985, p. 894.

Chapter 3: From Private to Captain

I have gathered information about Maxwell's army career from a number of unpublished sources: from interviews with Maxwell, private family papers, "Birthday book" contributions and the recollections of his army colleagues at a reunion in Derby in September 1987. For the war action itself, I am also particularly indebted to regimental notes, especially Major D. J. Watson's account, *Surrey Troops in Grim Work on the Western Front*, written in February 1945, and *The Roer Offensive* by Major H. J. Dangle DSO.

1. Kulka, Erich. *Jews in the Czechoslovak Armed Forces Abroad During World War II, The Jews of Czechoslovakia*, Jewish Publication Society of America, Philadelphia, Vol. III (1984), p. 354.

2. Rhodes-Wood, Major E. H. *A War History of the Royal Pioneer Corps, 1939-45*, Gale & Polden, Aldershot, 1960, p. 65.

3. Wilmot, Chester. *The Struggle for Europe*, Collins, London, 1952, p. 353.

4. Maxwell, Elisabeth. *She*, May 1987.

5. Foster, Major R.C.G., MC. *History of the Queen's Royal Regiment*, Vol. VIII, Gale & Polden, Aldershot, 1953, p. 409.

6. Ibid, p. 411.

7. Ibid, p. 412.

8. Ibid, p. 485.

9. Ibid, p. 488.

10. Ibid, p. 491.

Chapter 4: Berlin, Barter and Books

Unpublished sources essential to the preparation of this chapter include a General Report by Springer-Verlag on co-operation with Maxwell, 1947-58, business documents relating to Simpkin Marshall, the "Birthday book" contributions of early business associates, personal and business correspondence for the period 1945-55.

1. Trevor-Roper, H.R. *The Last Days of Hitler*, Macmillan, London, 1956, pp. xxvii-xxviii.

2. Shirer, William L. *The Rise and Fall of the Third Reich*, Secker & Warburg, London, 1960, p. 1129.

3. Toland, John. *Adolf Hitler*, Doubleday & Co., New York, 1976, p. 885.

4. Foot, M.R.D. *SOE, 1940-1946*, BBC, London, 1984, pp. 130-4.

5. Piekalkiewicz, Janusz. *Secret Agents, Spies and Saboteurs*, David & Charles, Newton Abbot, 1974, p. 287.

6. Bullock, Alan. *Ernest Bevin, Foreign Secretary*, Heinemann, London, 1983, p. 309.

7. Jones, H. Kay. *Butterworths, History of a Publishing House*, Butterworth, London, 1980, p. 130.

8. Kramish, Arnold. *The Griffin*, Houghton Mifflin, Boston, 1986.

9. Jones, H. Kay. Op. cit., p. 132.

10. *Diamond Fields Advertiser*, 17 March 1964.

11. Baker, Captain Peter, MC. *My Testament*, John Calder, London, 1955, p. 240.

Chapter 5: Rise of Pergamon

In writing this chapter I have found the contributions of Pergamon's staff, editors and authors particularly valuable. They were written both for the 1983 "Birthday book" and for the 1988 *Festschrift*. I have also made extensive use of Maxwell's business documents and correspondence contained in the family archives.

1. *Late Night Line-Up* interview, 22 August 1972.

2. Development Means People, interview between Don Taylor and Robert Maxwell, 18 June 1963.

3. *Financial Times*, 9 July 1964.

4. Ibid, 9 September 1966.

5. *Daily Telegraph*, 2 May 1967.

6. *Campaign*, 1 November 1968.

7. *The Guardian*, 18 August 1967.

8. *King*, July 1967.

9. *Columbus Citizen Journal*, 1 September 1967.

10. Speech at a dinner of the Marketing Group of Interpublic, 18 September 1968.

11. *Hansard*, 12 March 1969.

Chapter 6 : Out and In

In writing Chapters 6 and 7 I found the family archives particularly useful in that they contained not only a wide range of press cuttings, but also much of Maxwell's election campaign material and documents relating to constituency politics. "Birthday book" contributions by Maxwell's political colleagues were also invaluable.

1. *Daily Mail*, 26 September 1959.

2. *Oxford Mail*, 15 September 1959.

3. *The Times*, 5 October 1960.

4. *The Guardian*, 5 October 1960.

5. *The Times*, 5 October 1960.

6. *Bucks Standard*, 22 October 1960.

7. Crossman, Richard. *The Backbench Diaries of a Cabinet Minister*, Hamish Hamilton and Jonathan Cape, London, 1981, p 1017.

8. *Nature*, 28 November 1964.

9. Benn, Tony. *Out of the Wilderness, Diaries 1963-67*, Hutchinson, London, 1987, p. 294.

10. Ibid, pp. 331-2.

11. Crossman, Richard. *The Diaries of a Cabinet Minister*, Vol. 2, Hamish Hamilton and Jonathan Cape, London, 1976, p. 661.

12. *Daily Mail*, 22 March 1965.

13. *Hansard*, 2 February 1965.

14. Ibid, 14 July 1965.

15. *The Illustrated News*, 12 June 1965.

16. *The Guardian*, 9 March 1965.

17. *The Observer*, 27 June 1965.

18. *Tribune*, 21 May 1965.

19. *The Times*, 5 October 1967.

20. *The People*, 6 August 1967.

21. *Oxford Mail*, 25 February 1966.

22. *Evening Standard*, 12 November 1966.

23. *Queen*, 4 January 1967.

Chapter 7: In and Out

1. *Bletchley Gazette*, 9 June 1967.

2. Crossman, Richard. *The Diaries of a Cabinet Minister*, Vol. 2, Hamish Hamilton and Jonathan Cape, London, 1976, pp. 267-8.

3. *Sunday Express*, 19 March 1967.

4. *Hansard*, 24 July 1967.

5. Ibid.

6. Ibid, 27 November 1967.

7. Ibid.

8. Ibid, 28 November 1967.

9. *Daily Express*, 15 March 1969.

10. Crossman, Richard. Op. cit., p. 731.

11. *The Guardian*, 8 July 1967.

12. Crossman, Richard. Op. cit., p. 597.

13. *The Sun*, 20 December 1967.

14. *The Observer*, 24 December 1967.

15. *Evening Standard*, 8 December 1967.

16. *Hansard*, 28 January 1969.

17. *Sunday Times*, 3 March 1968.

18. The "How to Help Britain and Yourself" Campaign, advertising campaign, 20 January 1968.

19. *Daily Mirror*, 8 February 1968.

20. Speech entitled "Whither Britain", Conservative CPC Conference, Lambeth Town Hall, 17 February 1968.

21. *Daily Mirror*, 1 February 1968.

22. *Financial Times*, 16 May 1968.

23. *Oxford Mail*, 29 March 1968.

24. *Today* programme, 4 June 1969.

25. *Wolverton Express*, 15 August 1969.

26. *Sunday Times*, 14 June 1970.

27. *The Guardian*, 14 June 1970.

28. Press release, 26 March 1971.

29. *The Guardian*, 13 February 1974.

30. *Daily Mail*, 28 February 1974.

31. *The Times*, 2 March 1974.

32. *Milton Keynes Express*, 8 March 1974.

Chapter 8: Pergamon Lost - Pergamon Regained

The legal documents which exist in the family archives were especially useful in the preparation of this chapter. In addition, I have made extensive use of material gathered in a series of interviews with some of Pergamon's leading editors and Maxwell's colleagues in the City by Anton Antonowicz, Feature Writer of the Daily Mirror and Robert Head, City Editor of the *Daily Mirror*.

1. *The Times*, 7 October 1969.

2. Ibid.

3. Ibid, 19 June 1969.

4. *The Observer*, 24 August 1969.

5. *The Times*, 27 August 1969.

6. *Financial Times*, 28 August 1969.

7. *Wall Street Journal*, 15 September 1969.

8. *Financial Times*, 16 September 1969.

9. Letter to Pergamon Press shareholders, 6 October 1969.

10. *Financial Times*, 14 July 1971.

11. *The Observer*, 3 October 1971.

12. *New Statesman*, 22 October 1971.

13. *Accountancy*, September 1973.

14. *Sunday Telegraph*, 23 August 1970.

15. *Evening News*, 18 September 1970.

16. Letter to Pergamon Press shareholders, 1 June 1973.

17. *Daily Mail*, 19 June 1973.

18. *Evening News*, 8 January 1974.

19. *Daily Mail*, 8 July 1976.

20. *The Sun*, 7 July 1976.

Chapter 9: Reflections in the Mirror

1. *Daily Mirror*, 14 July 1984.

2. *Sunday Citizen*, 18 June 1967.

3. King, Cecil. *The Cecil King Diary*, Jonathan Cape, London, 1972, 1975

4. Cudlipp, Hugh. *Walking on Water*, Bodley Head, London, 1976.

5. Davis, William. *Merger Mania*, Constable & Co, London, 1970.

6. Davis, William. Op. cit., pp. 195-6.

7. *Campaign*, 1 November 1968.

8. *Evening Standard*, 16 October 1968.

9. *Financial Times*, 19 October 1968.

10. *The Economist*, 19 October 1968.

11. *News of the World*, 20 October 1968.

12. *The Observer*, 20 October 1968.

13. *The Times*, 25 October 1968.

14. *Wall Street Journal*, 25 October 1968.

15. *Daily Mail*, 25 October 1968.

16. *New Statesman*, 1 November 1968.

17. *Financial Times*, 12 November 1968.

18. Regan, Simon. *Rupert Murdoch, A Business Biography*, Angus & Robertson, London, 1976, pp. 125-6.

19. Ibid., p. 24.

20. *Financial Times*, 3 January 1969.

21. *The Times*, 16 May 1969.

22. Cudlipp, Hugh. Op. cit., p. 252.

23. *The Times*, 3 September 1969.

24. Evans, Harold. *Good Times, Bad Times*, Weidenfeld & Nicolson, London, 1983, p. 158.

25. McKay, Ron and Barr, Brian. *The Story of the Scottish Daily News*, Canongate, Edinburgh, 1976.

26. Ibid., p. 29.

27. Ibid., p. 30.

28. *Financial Times*, 16 May 1974.

29. McKay, Ron and Barr, Brian. Op. cit., p. 6.

30. Ibid., p. 11.

31. Ibid., p. 62.

32. Ibid., p. 76.

33. *Scottish Daily News*, Special Press Conference, 27 September 1975.

34. McKay, Ron and Barr, Brian. Op. cit., p. 146.

35. Ibid., pp. 145-6.

36. Press statement, 22 October 1980.

37. *The Times*, 23 October 1980.

38. Ibid.

39. *Sunday Times*, 18 January 1981.

40. Unpublished interview with Robert Head, City Editor of the *Daily Mirror*, January 1988.

41. *Daily Mail*, 23 June 1984.

42. *Daily Mirror*, 5 July 1984.

43. *Daily Mail*, 5 July 1984.

Chapter 10: The Gravy Train

Unpublished sources essential to the writing of this chapter include a series of interviews conducted by Alan Law, Industrial Correspondent of the *Daily Mirror*, in January 1988.

1. *Sunday Times*, 15 July 1984.

2. *The Spectator*, 21 July 1984.

3. *Liverpool Echo*, 7 January 1985.

4. Mirror Group Newspapers, Maxwellgram, February 1985.

5. *Daily Mirror*, 26 April 1985.

6. *Financial Times*, 26 March 1983.

7. *The Times*, 2 April 1983.

8. *Sogat Journal*, March 1984.

9. *The Guardian*, 15 November 1983.

10. *Financial Times*, 24 August 1985.

11. *Sunday Times*, 1 September 1985.

12. *The Spectator*, 7 September 1985.

13. *Daily Telegraph*, 25 February 1986.

14. *Sunday Mail*, 2 March 1986.

15. *The Times*, 5 March 1985.

16. *Marketing Week*, 19 September 1986.

Chapter 11: The Family

1. *She*, May 1987.

2. *Woman*, 15 September 1984.

3. Herbert, Ivor. *The Way to the Top*, Robert Maxwell, London, 1969, p. 147.

4. *The World Tonight*, 27 July 1971.

5. *Evening News*, 1 September 1973.

6. *Daily Express*, 17 September 1984.

INDEX